PERSONNEL

THE MANAGEMENT OF PEOPLE AT WORK

DALE S. BEACH

Professor, School of Management
Rensselaer Polytechnic Institute

THE MACMILLAN COMPANY
COLLIER-MACMILLAN LIMITED · LONDON

PERSONNEL
THE MANAGEMENT OF PEOPLE AT WORK

SECOND EDITION

658.3008 BEA

The Macmillan Company
866 Third Avenue, New York, New York 10022

Collier-Macmillan Canada, Ltd., Toronto, Ontario

Library of Congress catalog card number: 77–92078

Fourth Printing, 1971

0023069708

To Shirley, Jeffrey, Eric,
and my mother, Octavia E. Beach

Preface

This book has been designed for use in courses in personnel management, organizational behavior, administration, and human relations in college and university programs in business administration, industrial management, industrial relations, and public administration. It is also suitable for use in management development programs and as a reference for executives, administrators, and supervisors in business, industrial, public, and other work organizations.

Personnel: The Management of People at Work seeks to provide a sound foundation in fundamentals, theory, principles, and practice for all those whose careers will require knowledge and skills in administration. Education in personnel management and human relations is essential not only for those in general management positions and those in personnel department activities but also for staff professionals and administrators (such as industrial engineers, systems analysts, executive assistants, and program planners).

This book draws extensively upon the point of view, theory, and experimental evidence provided by writers and investigators in the behavioral sciences. Personnel management is an applied, professional field of endeavor. As such it is built upon concepts, knowledge, and theory from the behavioral sciences and from economics and industrial engineering. In addition, over the years a substantial body of practices and techniques have evolved and been refined by practitioners in business, industry, and government. Much of this is sound and has survived the test of experience. Those methods and concepts which have demonstrated real worth have now become an essential part of personnel management and are therefore discussed in this book.

The management of people is an integral part of the process of management, not something that can be assigned solely to the personnel department. Getting out production and solving human relations problems are inseparable. In actuality there must be a partnership between the personnel specialist and the operating manager. The personnel officer performs policy, advice, service, and control functions and thereby enables the operating manager to do a more effective job of directing and developing his human resources. Traditionally, textbooks in personnel management have focused upon personnel policies, programs, and methodologies from the perspective of the personnel-industrial relations office. Such subject areas as personnel selection, training, performance appraisal, pay administration, and safety are essential elements in this treatment. More recently there has been growing sophistication of knowledge in organizational behavior (human relations) and a greater awareness of line management's responsibilities for personnel. Therefore, comprehensive coverage must be devoted to such topics as organization, motivation, group relationships, labor relations, leadership, participation, supervision, communication, discipline, and grievance handling. This textbook provides a balanced blending of the traditional personnel topics (including the latest thinking in these areas) with the newer organizational behavior concepts. Throughout, the author has attempted to provide a conceptual framework with which to analyze and solve problems involved in managing people.

Personnel management is not primarily a kit of tools to be used to control and direct employees. Rather it is a frame of reference, an understanding of why and how, and an application of theory, concepts, and principles so that the qualified manager can adapt his knowledge and skills to changing circumstances. The intention in writing this book has been to be realistic—to analyze and discuss the kinds of problem situations encountered by supervisors and administrators in going concerns. Not only are frequent examples given throughout the text material, but also meaningful discussion questions are included at the conclusion of each chapter. Realistic case problems are provided at the end of most chapters.

While retaining all that is of enduring value to the study of the management of people at work, this second edition includes significant new developments and research knowledge. The number of new and revised topics is too great to itemize in detail in this preface; however, it is worthwhile to call to the reader's attention a few of these subjects. Chapter 10, which deals with the pressing national problem of providing employment opportunities for America's culturally deprived peoples, is new to this edition. Chapter 3 has been revised to give recognition to the emergence of enlarged responsibilities of personnel departments in the areas of organization and manpower planning and personnel—behavioral research. The prominence of public policies in the field of fair employment practices and of federal manpower programs have been given systematic treatment in this second edition. Chapter 15 dealing with human behavior fundamentals and motivation has been entirely revised and updated. It contains an expanded discussion of theories of work motivation. Herzberg's motivation-hygiene theory is reviewed and analyzed. To Chapter 23 have been added a theoretical framework and rationale of financial compensation. In the area of leadership newer insights into the complex of situational factors are discussed. New or expanded treatment has been devoted to management training methods like sensitivity training and the managerial grid, to appraisal by results, and to the assessment center method of selecting managers. Other newer issues discussed are public employee collective bargaining, growth of leisure and its implications, and possible cultural bias in selection testing.

The author wishes to express his sincere appreciation to those whose constructive suggestions and cooperation have aided in the development and refinement of this work. Professor Delmar W. Karger, Dean, School of Management, Rensselaer Polytechnic Institute, has provided encouragement and substantial cooperation throughout the course of creating and revising this book. Professor Earl Brooks, Graduate School of Business and Public Administration, Cornell University, read the first edition manuscript and offered valuable constructive advice. Professor Roy V. Kirk, School of Management, Rensselaer Polytechnic Institute, and Dr. Edwin A. Fleishman of the American Institutes for Research read portions of the first edition manuscript and gave very useful counsel. Professor Orlando Behling of Ohio State University and Professor Raymond L. Hilgert of Washington University have reviewed the first edition and provided a great many valuable ideas that have aided in the writing of this second edition. In addition the author has gained from the feedback of many students who have used this book. I wish to thank Mrs. Beverly Folmsbee and Miss Barbara Whipple, who typed the manuscript for the first edition, and Miss Anita Cammuso, who typed the manuscript for this second edition.

Troy, N.Y.   Dale S. Beach

Contents

I Management, Employees, Unions, and Organization

Chapter 1   MANAGEMENT, WORK, AND WORKERS   3
Management/Industrialization/The Labor Force in
America/Evolution of Theory and Practice of Personnel
Management/General Observations/*Questions for Review
and Discussion/Suggestions for Further Reading*

2   PHILOSOPHY, PRINCIPLES, AND POLICIES   39
Organization Objectives/Managing People at Work/
Personnel Policies/*Questions for Review and Discussion/*
Case Problem/*Suggestions for Further Reading*

3   THE PERSONNEL FUNCTION   63
Terminology/Who Does Personnel Work?/Personnel and
Industrial Relations Functions/Organization for the
Personnel Function/*Questions for Review and Discussion/*
Case Problem/*Suggestions for Further Reading*

4   UNIONS AND MANAGEMENT   81
Motivation to Join Unions/Motivation to Reject Unions/
Union Membership and Growth/Union Organization and
Functions/Union Objectives and Behavior/Impact of the

Union Upon Management/Determinants of Labor Relations
Stability/*Questions for Review and Discussion/Suggestions
for Further Reading*

5   COLLECTIVE BARGAINING   114
The Nature of Collective Bargaining/The Legal Framework
of Collective Bargaining/Structure for Collective
Bargaining/Negotiating the Agreement/Subject Matter of
Collective Bargaining/Strikes and Dispute Settlement/
Questions for Review and Discussion/Case Problems/
Suggestions for Further Reading

6   ORGANIZATION   147
Growth of a Company—Organizational Phases/Grouping
Activities by Kind/Grouping Activities by Level/
Authority and Influence/Delegation/Decentralization/
Line and Staff/Span of Supervision/Bureaucracy/*Questions
for Review and Discussion*/Case Problem/*Suggestions for
Further Reading*

7   JOB ORGANIZATION AND INFORMATION   184
Job Information and Personnel Management/Analyzing
Jobs—Obtaining Job Information/Job Descriptions and
Specifications/Administration of the Job Analysis Program/
Questions for Review and Discussion/Problems/*Suggestions
for Further Reading*

II Employment and Development of People

Chapter 8   RECRUITMENT AND SELECTION   211
Planning for Manpower Needs/Recruitment and Selection
Policy Issues/Sources of Labor/The Selection Process/
Auditing the Recruitment and Selection Program/*Questions
for Review and Discussion/Suggestions for Further Reading*

9   SELECTION TESTING AND INTERVIEWING   248
SELECTION TESTING: Fundamental Guides to Testing/
Testing Concepts/Developing a Testing Program/Types
of Tests/Testing and Equal Employment Opportunity/
Selection Testing—A Final Comment

THE SELECTION INTERVIEW: Psychological
Foundations for Interviews/Knowledge and Skills of the

Interviewer/Types of Interviews/Preparing for the
Interview/Conducting the Interview/Common Pitfalls in
Interviewing/*Questions for Review and Discussion*/Case
Problems/*Suggestions for Further Reading*

10   EMPLOYING THE CULTURALLY DEPRIVED   286
Who Are the Culturally Deprived?/Government Action
for Hard-core Unemployed/Action by Private Business/
*Questions for Review and Discussion/Suggestions for
Further Reading*

11   PERFORMANCE APPRAISAL   308
Basic Considerations in Appraisal/Appraisal Methods/
Problems in Rating/Appraisal and Personal Development/
Appraisal by Results/Trends and Perspectives/*Questions
for Review and Discussion*/Case Problem/*Suggestions for
Further Reading*

12   PROMOTION, TRANSFER, LAYOFF, AND
DEMOTION   344
Promotions/Transfers/Layoff and Recall/Demotion
Discharge/*Questions for Review and Discussion*/Case
Problems/*Suggestions for Further Reading*

13   TRAINING   374
Training in the Organization/The Learning Process/
Training Methods/Training Programs/Evaluation of the
Training Effort/*Questions for Review and Discussion*/Case
Problem/*Suggestions for Further Reading*

14   MANAGEMENT DEVELOPMENT   405
Nature of Management Development/Planning and
Administering the Program/Development Through Work
Experience/Formal Training Courses/*Questions for
Review and Discussion*/Case Problem/*Suggestions for
Further Reading*

III   Understanding and Managing People

Chapter 15   UNDERSTANDING PEOPLE   441
Human Behavior Fundamentals/Motivation/Human
Adjustment/Dissatisfactions on the Job/Additional

Motivation Theories/Morale and Productivity/Applying
Motivational Concepts/*Questions for Review and
Discussion/Suggestions for Further Reading*

16   GROUP RELATIONS AND INFORMAL
      ORGANIZATION   472
      The Study of Group Behavior/Formation of Groups/
      Structure and Properties of Groups/Impact of Informal
      Group Relations upon the Formal Organization/Informal
      Vs. Formal Organization/The Supervisor and the Group/
      Status/*Questions for Review and Discussion*/Case Problem/
      Suggestions for Further Reading

17   LEADERSHIP   503
      Nature of Leadership/Foundations of Leadership/
      Informal, Elected, and Appointed Leaders/Authority and
      Power/Situational Factors in Leadership/Leadership—A
      Closing Word/*Questions for Review and Discussion*/Case
      Problem/*Suggestions for Further Reading*

18   SUPERVISION   526
      Nature of Supervisor's Job/Position and Problems of the
      Foreman/Pattern of Effective Supervision/Transmittal of
      Supervisory Style/Supervisor as a Counselor/Effective
      Supervision—Concluding Observations/*Questions for
      Review and Discussion*/Case Problem/*Suggestions for
      Further Reading*

19   MANAGING THROUGH THE USE OF
      PARTICIPATION   553
      Role of Participation in the Organization/Research into
      Participation/Participation Evaluated/Conditions for
      Effective Participation/Types of Participation/*Questions
      for Review and Discussion/Suggestions for Further Reading*

20   COMMUNICATION   580
      Communication Fundamentals/Communication in
      Organizations/Systems of Communication/The Grapevine/
      Questions for Review and Discussion/Case Problem/
      Suggestions for Further Reading

21   DISCIPLINE   603
      Approaches to Discipline/Administering the Disciplinary

Program/Rules and Penalties/*Questions for Review and Discussion*/Case Problems/*Suggestions for Further Reading*

22 GRIEVANCE HANDLING 623
Nature of Complaints and Grievances/Why Have a Grievance Procedure?/Need for a Judicial Body in Work Organizations/Grievance Settlement for Unionized Employees/Grievance Arbitration/Grievance Settlement for Nonunion Employees/*Questions for Review and Discussion*/Case Problems/*Suggestions for Further Reading*

IV Financial Compensation

Chapter 23 WAGE AND SALARY ADMINISTRATION 649
Rationale of Financial Compensation/Principal Compensation Issues/Wage Criteria/Wage Policy and Principles/Organization for Wage and Salary Administration/Job Evaluation/Job Evaluation Systems/ Establishing the Pay Structure/Administration of Pay Within Ranges/Union Considerations/Wage Surveys/ *Questions for Review and Discussion*/Problem/*Suggestions for Further Reading*

24 WAGE INCENTIVES 691
Work Measurement/Essential Requirements of a Sound Wage Incentive Program/Types of Incentive Pay Plans/ Human Relations and Incentives/Union Attitudes/ *Questions for Review and Discussion*/Case Problem/ *Suggestions for Further Reading*

25 INCENTIVES BASED UPON COOPERATION 718
Incentives and Labor-Management Cooperation/ Kaiser-United Steelworkers Plan/Profit Sharing/Some Comparisons and Conclusions/*Questions for Review and Discussion*/*Suggestions for Further Reading*

26 COMPENSATION FOR SALESMEN, MANAGERS, AND PROFESSIONALS 733
Compensation for Salesmen/Supervisory Compensation/ Executive Compensation/Compensation for Professionals/ *Questions for Review and Discussion*/*Suggestions for Further Reading*

V Security

Chapter 27   HEALTH AND SAFETY   755
Occupational Safety/Causes of Accidents/Establishing a
Safety Program/Environment Control—Industrial Hygiene/
Workmen's Compensation/Occupational Health/Mental
Health in Industry/*Questions for Review and Discussion/*
Case Problem/*Suggestions for Further Reading*

28   BENEFITS AND SERVICES   786
Types of Benefits and Services/Why Adopt Benefit and
Service Programs?/Some Significant Benefit and Service
Programs/*Questions for Review and Discussion/Suggestions
for Further Reading*

VI Perspectives

Chapter 29   PERSONNEL MANAGEMENT IN PERSPECTIVE   813
Personnel—Industrial Relations as a Career/Where Do
We Stand?/Continuing Problems and Needs/*Questions for
Review and Discussion/Suggestions for Further Reading*

Name Index   831

Subject Index   837

I

MANAGEMENT, EMPLOYEES, UNIONS, AND ORGANIZATION

Management, Work, and Workers

1

This book is about the management of people at work. Although man has for centuries collected into groups to form durable organizations for the purpose of accomplishing mutual goals, it is only in recent years that an organized body of knowledge has developed on the theory and practice of personnel management. This is partly because scientific and systematic inquiry into most branches of science has occurred primarily within the past hundred years. Work in the physical and life sciences occurred somewhat earlier and at a more rapid rate than in the social sciences. Personnel management, which is an applied, professional field of work as well as an academic discipline, derives much of its foundations from the social sciences, which have really emerged, in the main, since 1900.[1]

Now it is certainly true that men engage in many endeavors long before the scientists come along to provide the theoretical explanations. To a certain extent this has been so in the field of personnel management. Frederick W. Taylor and his disciples were designing and installing wage incentive plans long before the modern sociologists and social psychologists developed theories to explain the complex motivational and social factors involved. Workers have been hired and fired for centuries without benefit of formal theory to guide those in charge. Even today a great

[1] The basic and applied disciplines that have contributed to the development of the field of personnel management and industrial relations are institutional economics, labor economics, industrial psychology, industrial sociology, applied anthropology, organizational behavior, social psychology, political science, public administration, and industrial management. To these can be added the contributions made internally by those engaged in the practice of personnel management and industrial relations itself.

deal that comprises the field of personnel management is based upon the accumulated trial-and-error experiences of countless employers. But the research studies of scientific investigators are gradually adding to the fund of knowledge available to the management practitioner. He is entering firmer ground when he makes decisions in regard to organization, hiring, training, compensation, discipline, and supervision. The management of people at work is partly an art and partly a science. Undoubtedly for many generations to come the successful manager will still have to rely upon a good deal of judgment, intuition, and trial-and-error in directing his work force. But more and more he can come to decide on actions and predict consequences as a result of applying scientific knowledge.

So far we have related the recent emergence of personnel management as a distinct field of endeavor and as an academic discipline concurrent to the recent development of the social sciences. But there are other and quite different reasons as well. The farmer who manages his own family farm with the help of his wife and children has little need for the knowledge and skills of personnel management. The master craftsman who runs his own shop in town with the help of one or two men to make wagons, shoe horses, print newspapers, or make clothes has little need to employ sophisticated personnel management techniques. Until the latter part of the nineteenth century the economic activity of the United States was primarily centered upon agriculture and the handicrafts and trading of the country village. The financial tycoons were just beginning to put together their industrial empires in the late nineteenth century. The technology of mass production did not arrive until the early twentieth century. The point being made here is that personnel management problems did not really become pressing until we had large aggregations of people working together in one organization, and the American economy did not reach the point of widespread large-scale organizations until the twentieth century.

In the small establishments of yesteryear employee relations problems were handled largely on an informal basis between the owner and the individual employee. Elaborate organization structures did not exist. Personnel policies were rarely reduced to writing. Rather they evolved through practice and custom. Hiring arrangements were very simple. Psychological tests did not exist. The new employee learned by watching his fellow workers. Accident prevention programs and safety engineering were practically nonexistent. Because management was not recognized as a distinct field of endeavor or as a profession, management training was also nonexistent.

Terminology—Work Organization

Issues, problems, and principles involved in the management of people at work are common to all kinds of organizations: factories, offices, retail stores, hospitals, government agencies, and educational institutions. To emphasize this universality the term *work organization* will be used frequently throughout this book. It is a general term selected to apply to all kinds of establishments or organizations whether they be private business enterprises, governmental organizations, or nonprofit private bodies. It excludes social and religious bodies as well as trade unions. In order to provide for variety of language the terms *company, corporation, enterprise,* and *establishment* will be used from time to time.

MANAGEMENT

To a considerable extent the manager of today has achieved his position because of his knowledge, skill, and ability and not because the control of financial assets has entitled him to a seat in management. Although there are thousands of family-owned businesses in this country, these are predominantly small in size. The vast majority of medium and large-sized enterprises are directed by hired professional managers. The corporate form of business enterprise coupled with the diffusion of stock ownership, such that a single individual rarely has a controlling interest, has led to a separation of ownership from management. The board of directors then seeks to hire competent managers. Our industrial technology has become extremely complex. The managerial skills required to guide the modern corporation are likewise complex. These and other factors have resulted in the development of a professionalization of management. Although managers are actually hired employees, as a class they tend to identify their interests closely with those of the owners of the business. Top management considers the welfare of the corporation and its own welfare as identical on most issues.

In the field of public administration as a consequence of the merit or civil service system, the vast majority of the administrative personnel are selected on the basis of well-defined standards of competence. This system is most advanced at the federal level and least at the municipal level. In contrast to the private business system the policy-making positions at or near the top are filled by either popular election or by political appointment.

Thus far we have spoken of management as a group or class of people. Management also connotes a distinct kind of activity or process. *Management is the process of utilizing material and human resources to accomplish designated objectives. It involves the organization, direction, coordination, and evaluation of people to achieve these goals.*

In analyzing the work of management Newman and Summer state that the total task of management can be divided into organizing, planning, leading, and controlling.[2] Koontz and O'Donnell view the functions of

[2] William H. Newman and Charles E. Summer, Jr., *The Process of Management* (Englewood Cliffs, N.J.: Prentice-Hall, Inc., 1961, pp. 10-12.

management as planning, organizing, staffing, directing, and controlling.[3] Harbison and Myers have attempted to include the frames of reference of both economists and industrial management writers by listing the functions of management as (1) the undertaking of risk and the handling of uncertainty; (2) planning and innovation; (3) coordination, administration, and control; and (4) routine supervision.[4] Although in the very small firm all of these functions may be performed by the owner, in a company of any reasonable size these tasks are dispersed among various members of the entire management team.

If one studies the day-to-day activities of a manager, it will be found that he devotes a high percentage of his time to interacting with other people. In preparing plans he must consult his colleagues and subordinates. In organizing he must work closely with his subordinates to define and guide the relationships among them. The manager accomplishes results *through* and with others. He motivates, persuades, and influences. At times he conducts and at other times he participates as a member in decision-making conferences. The practicing manager must be skilled in the art of human relations. He spends a great deal of his time communicating with others mostly through face-to-face contact.

Management involves accomplishing results through other people. The skilled space technology manager does not design a space craft himself. The manufacturing executive does not build automobiles himself. The university president does no teaching. The role of the manager is to assemble the best work team he can obtain and then motivate and guide that team to accomplish agreed-upon objectives.

The essence of management is the activity of working with people to accomplish results. It involves organizing, motivating, leading, training, communicating with, and coordinating others. Lawrence A. Appley, President of the American Management Association since 1948, has written that management is the development of people and not the direction of things. He maintains that management and personnel administration are one and the same.[5]

Now the reader should not jump to the conclusion that the successful manager need only possess knowledge and skills in the fields of personnel management and human relations. He must also be trained in other fields, such as the technology of his particular industry, management science and administration, and personal communication skills. In addition, the modern-day executive must have knowledge of the economic, social and political environment in which he lives and works. The degree of competence a manager must have in these areas is determined primarily by the circumstances of his job, his company, level in the organization,

[3] Harold Koontz and Cyril O'Donnell, *Principles of Management* (3rd. ed.; New York: McGraw-Hill Book Company, Inc., 1964), pp. 38-41.

[4] Frederick Harbison and Charles A. Myers, *Management in the Industrial World: An International Analysis* (New York: McGraw-Hill Book Company, Inc., 1959), p.8.

[5] Lawrence A. Appley, "Management the Simple Way" *Personnel,* Vol. 19, No. 4, January, 1943, pp. 595-603.

and geographical location. Notwithstanding these other areas of competence demanded of the manager, his "world" is primarily one of human interaction.

Human Vs. Technical Problems

By and large the most vexing problems managers must face are human, not technical. In our civilization mankind is continually beset with human conflict, violence, war, political intrigue, riots, racial turmoil, and religious struggles. The technical problems of placing man upon the moon, great as they are, are more readily solved than the more pressing human problems of civilization.

Within the industrial world, management finds the situation to be similar. A man who has served as a management engineering consultant to several governments in Europe, the Near East, and Africa has stated that he has found the human relations and organizational problems to be far more difficult to resolve than the technical problems. The same situation is frequently true within a particular enterprise. On paper many designs, innovations, plant expansions, and methods changes are plausible. Yet the task of consummating these projects by working with people can be very difficult. The manager may encounter personal antagonisms, jealousies, political intrigue, resistance to change, absenteeism, or work stoppages.

Faced with such challenges the individual, who by aptitude and training feels more comfortable working with technical problems, often retreats deeper and deeper into his world of physical science and technology. But such human problems require leaders who have a sound understanding of the complex forces generated within and acting upon people. By reason of aptitude, training, and experience the skilled manager is able to gain the cooperation of those involved and resolve these challenging human problems.

INDUSTRIALIZATION

In order to gain perspective of the issues and problems involved in managing people in work organizations it is essential at this point to review briefly the main features of modern production and industry. Let us start with a concise review of early systems of work and production as they have evolved throughout the history of civilization.

Systems of Work and Production

At the outset it is important to note that sharp chronological boundaries do not exist to separate the period of slavery from that of serfdom or serfdom from the handicraft system. The changes from one system of work to another have been evolutionary—so gradual in fact that the participants hardly known they were occurring. Geographical differences have been great at any given point in modern history. Although the United States, Canada, Western Europe, Russia, and Japan are highly industrialized in the middle of the twentieth century, much of Africa is in the primitive tribal stage of development.

Ranged in chronological order for any one people and with due regard for the conditions noted above are the following systems of work and production:

Primitive tribes
Slavery
Serfdom
Handicraft
Putting-out, or Cottage
Factory
Modern industrial system

Primitive tribal society can be observed today in many parts of central Africa and on many islands in the South Pacific. The life of the American Indian at the time of the coming of the white man was of this type. The necessities of life are provided by hunting, fishing, and primitive agriculture. Tools are crudely fashioned from sticks, stones, bones, and animal hides. Authority is exercised by tribal chieftains, elders, and family heads. Property is generally communal. Division of labor is based upon tradition, sex, and age. There is little saving or accumulation of wealth. People live for the present only. Consumption equals production.

Slavery occurred throughout history as a result of the subjugation of one people by another. The slave was the personal property of his master. He could be bought and sold. The offspring of a slave also belonged to the master. Slaves received no wages other than room, board, and clothes provided by the owner. They were under the absolute authority of the master and generally had no recourse from his decisions. Slavery flourished most commonly in agrarian economies. Slavery still exists in parts of Africa, the Middle East, and the Far East. Saudi Arabia did not officially abolish slavery until 1962.

Under the feudal society of Europe during the middle ages the economy was essentially based upon agriculture, and the worker was a serf. The land was divided into large estates owned by princes, lords, and others who obtained their land by inheritance or royal grant. Although the serf was not considered the property of the lord, his lot in life was not much better than the slave. He worked a portion of the lord's land and was required to turn over to the lord a substantial share of his crops. The serf's children, by tradition, continued to reside on the same land and work under the same arrangement. The law and the king were clearly on the side of the feudal lords when it came to questions of rights and privileges of the serfs versus those of the lords.

The handicraft system of production existed over many centuries and is even in existence today in some trades and in some regions. Historically it occurred because of the growth of cities and towns, the increase of trade and commerce, the decline in power of the feudal lords, and the gradual escape of peasants from the soil. The craftsman was a skilled worker. He set up facilities for production in his own home. He owned his own tools as well as his materials. He sold his products directly to the customer. There was no middleman. He specialized by products. Thus there were separate craftsmen to make a suit of clothes, a pair of shoes, a loaf of bread, a wagon, and a bolt of cloth.

Sometimes an owner-craftsman would undertake to teach a boy the skills of his trade. The boy became an apprentice who was indentured to the craftsman (who was then called a master craftsman) for a period of years. The apprentice received no wages other than his room, board, and clothes. He did most of the menial work around the shop, helped the master at his work, and eventually learned the intricacies of the craft. Upon the completion of his apprenticeship, he received his working papers and was then a journeyman. A journeyman was a fully qualified craftsman who was free to work for wages for any master who would employ him. The typical journeyman hoped to save enough from his wages eventually to set up his own shop and become a master himself.

Throughout the middle ages and even later in Europe the craft guilds regulated economic and employment conditions in handicraft production. The guilds controlled entrance to a trade, regulated quality of materials and workmanship, set prices, and determined wages. Although the guilds were composed originally of masters and journeymen, the journeymen later formed their own guilds when they concluded that their interests conflicted with those of the masters over issues of wages and conditions of work. These guilds performed many of the functions of the modern craft union.

As the economic system developed, some individuals (often affluent masters) undertook to buy raw materials and farm out the work to craftsmen who worked in their own homes. If expensive equipment was involved, such as a hand loom, this was rented by the merchant-capitalist to the worker. Often the craftsman's whole family worked on the product. The craftsman was paid on a piecework basis for his labor. He was essentially a wage earner. Under this putting-out or cottage system of production, the craftsman did not buy his own materials, he often did not own his own tools, he no longer determined design, quality, or price, and he no longer dealt directly with the customer.

The transition from the putting-out to the factory system of production was relatively easy. The work was no longer done in the home; large aggregations of people were collected under one factory roof. This made it possible to supervise them and to regulate employees more closely. The flow of production through the various processes could be handled much more efficiently. The invention and manufacture of power-driven machinery in the late eighteenth and early nineteenth centuries was concurrent with and accelerated the development of the factory system. The rise of the factory system and the substitution of machine for human power has been called the industrial revolution. The vast majority employed in factory production have worked at jobs that can be learned in a few weeks. They have been primarily machine operators and bench assemblers.

Modern Industrial System

Modern industrialized society has greatly expanded and developed upon the original factory system of production. Science and technology have been applied to every phase of the production system, from the creation of new raw materials, to new products, to complex automated processes and to assistance in making managerial decisions. Let us now examine some of the more important features of the modern manufacturing system that have a bearing on personnel management.

Elimination of Heavy Physical Labor.   This is simply an extension of the process started with the advent of the industrial revolution. Most (but not all) of the heavy labor involved in moving materials and equipment has been taken over by mechanical handling equipment. This has made work less onerous and safer. At the same time it has reduced job opportunities for unskilled workers. For management the primary motivation has been economic. It is usually cheaper to use machine power, and in addition, far greater loads can be handled this way.

Key Role of Scientist and Engineer.   Modern industrial products and processes are extremely complex. Since World War I many of the achievements in industry have resulted from engineering developments. And especially since World War II the scientist has been employed in American industry in increasing numbers to add his talents to those of the engineer. Technological advances have been generated at a rapidly accelerating rate in recent decades.

The fusion of science and technology with industry has important implications. It has created a new class of professional employees in industry. These professionals are exerting a strong voice in the affairs of industry, education, and government. The engineer and scientist has interests and needs somewhat apart from those of both management and the workers.

The fruits of the labors of the scientists and engineers in industry have taken the form of such great technological advances that it is difficult for existing social institutions to cope with them. The problems of automation, technological obsolescence, elimination of occupations and industries, and the control of nuclear energy are but a few examples.

Many new occupations have been created. Computer programer is but one example. Many subprofessionals and technicians are needed to support the engineer or the scientist. By and large a general upgrading of the demands for education, training, and skill has been made upon the labor force.

Elaborate Control Mechanisms.   The modern corporation is big. To coordinate the efforts of the many hundreds and even thousands of individuals at work, companies have instituted elaborate managerial and organizational arrangements. In one sense this has meant the creation of whole departments and an array of jobs devoted to such things as production planning and control, methods engineering, systems and procedures, inventory control, scheduling, coordination, and expediting. Conferences, staff meetings, and briefing sessions must be held to keep all responsible personnel abreast of pertinent developments. Vast accounting and financial control procedures are employed to keep track of cash flow, customer billings, accounts payable, cost data, payroll, and many other accounts. The modern executive is acutely conscious of the need for good communication throughout the organization as an essential element in control and coordination. Whereas the factory of yesteryear employed mostly blue-collar production workers with only a bare minimum of front office "bosses" and clerical help, the contemporary industrial enterprise has reduced its direct labor force through mechanization and automation and expanded its white-collar and managerial groups to guide, regulate, and coordinate the production system.

Specialization of Function.   Two kinds of work specialization are basic elements of modern industrialization. One is technological or occupational specialization. Thus we have various kinds of mechanical engineers employed in a company. We may have research engineers, development engineers, production engineers, and product design engineers. Or we may have a number of personnel specialists, such as labor relations managers, wage analysts, training directors, safety engineers, and employment managers. Because of the great depth of knowledge and skill required of those who work in technical, professional, and subprofessional fields, one man could not hope to be fully qualified in all aspects of a broad field such as engineering or physics or accounting. Therefore, he must specialize. In most instances the individual gains expertise by specializing. At the same time his work is sufficiently deep and broad to challenge him and hold his interest. In fact, he must continually study and attend seminars to avoid falling behind and becoming obsolete.

The other kind of specialization is called division of labor. This is the kind of specialization that is so evident in the modern automobile assembly line. Much has been written and said about this type of specialization. The industrial engineer has analysed the components of work that are required to manufacture a given product. He has divided the process into operations and elements of operations. Sequential work elements that are simple, similar, and require relatively low-priced labor may be put together into one job. In making men's shirts, for example, it has been found much more economical to break up the entire process into many individual operations, such as cut front, cut back, cut sleeve, stitch sleeve to yoke, stitch cuff to sleeve, and stitch buttons to front, than it is to have one person make the entire shirt. Each worker becomes very proficient at a very specific (or narrowly defined) job. The principal demand upon the operator is manual dexterity, sustained attention, and speed of movement.

Mass Production.   Henry Ford really created the modern mass production system of manufacture. The "Detroit" system of assembly line production has spread to many other industries throughout the world. Although the mass production techniques of the automobile industry have not been adopted universally because they are not appropriate to all kinds of manufacture, they are sufficiently widespread for us to designate them as a feature of modern industrialization.

Mass production involves the continuous movement of the product and its components through the factory. All of the parts and materials are delivered to the workman, who remains at his fixed work station. All operations on the assembly line are carefully designed so that they require essentially the same length of time to perform. Thus the line is balanced and smooth running; continuous flow is achieved. In-process inventory is kept to an absolute minimum. The flow of subassemblies from feeder lines is carefully synchronized with the flow of product on the principal production line so that there is no interruption to product flow. In a mass production factory the worker has no control over his own work pace. This is determined by the industrial engineer and dictated by management. The work is highly repetitive and of very short cycle. The work demands close attention and rapid speed of movement. Most of the jobs can be learned within a few days or a few weeks.

Automation.   Whereas the industrial revolution substituted mechanical power for human power to produce goods (but with people being necessary to control the machines), automation has sought to eliminate the human operator from the production process entirely. With automation it is true that workers are necessary to maintain and service the production equipment, but by and large they are not needed to regulate the equipment when under production. Mechanical and electronic systems substitute for the man in controlling the production process.

Automation burst upon the scene in the 1950's. The key elements of automation are programing and feedback. Programing involves telling the machine the proper operations to perform in an orderly sequence of steps. Prior to automation the programing was done by the worker. With automation it is done mechanically or electronically, as, for example, with a punched tape. The second key element of automation, feedback, involves the obtaining of information from an ongoing process and then using this data to regulate the process. The operation of a home heating system thermostat is a simple example of feedback.

Because automation is such a recent innovation, its full consequences upon industrial relations are not known as yet. So far it has caused considerable displacement of the semiskilled machine tender type of labor. Considerable widespread unemployment has occurred in such industries as automobile, steel, and meat packing. Demand for new skills has been generated. This has been particularly true for technicians.

Industrialization—Benefits and Costs

There can be little doubt that industrialization has caused very substantial betterment to the general population. The very high standard of living enjoyed by the peoples of the United States, Canada, and much of Western Europe is a direct consequence of their advanced stage of industrialization. This had made it possible to support better education and better health services. The modern worker has much more leisure time than his ancestor of a century ago. This leisure has taken the form of more time away from the job each day, more holidays, and more vacation time. It is not an exaggeration to say that the modern worker in the United States lives as well as a prince or even a king did five hundred years ago.

However, the well-being enjoyed by peoples in advanced industrialized societies has not been achieved without some costs and problems. Let us examine some of these.

Hard Work and Saving. The only way that economic growth and industrialization can occur is through capital formation. Capital formation requires saving. Saving means an excess of production over consumption. In the United States, England, Germany, and certain other countries this was accomplished through the private enterprise, capitalistic system. Individual freedom and initiative have been emphasized. The prevailing religious, economic, and political beliefs that have been ingrained in the population have been responsible, to a considerable extent, for the advanced economic development. The "Protestant ethic," with its emphasis upon hard work, frugality, and self-denial, has been a major driving force among the people.[6] The prevailing economic, religious, and social attitudes have caused a strong drive for material progress and for the accumulation of money.

Although the sacrifices and the reduction of consumption below production have been largely self-imposed in these aforementioned countries, in recent years countries such as the U.S.S.R. and Communist China have struggled for economic progress by imposing a ruthless and pervasive governmental force upon the daily lives of the populace. This has been government-imposed saving. The fruits of a mans' labor have gone not

---

[6] See Max Weber, *The Protestant Ethic and the Spirit of Capitalism*, (*trans,* Talcott Parsons) (New York: Charles Scribners' Sons, 1930).

to him but rather to the state. Glorification of hard labor and high worker output has become a national "political religion" or cult. As of the early 1970's the U.S.S.R. has largely succeeded, whereas China has failed in the struggle for industrialization.

Strict Discipline. In addition to this hard work and denial of the immediate fruits of one's labor, industrialization imposes a very strict discipline upon the daily lives of workers. Kerr, Dunlop, Harbison, and Myers in surveying the process of industrialization throughout the world have made a strong point of the "web of rules" binding the industrial worker.[7] The factory worker lives by the clock. He must depart for work every day at the same time, struggle through a system of traffic signals, punch a time clock, work all day at a pace set by some time study engineer, eat lunch in precisely one half hour, take rest breaks at precisely 10 A.M. and 2:30 P.M., and then again punch the clock on his way out of the factory in late afternoon. He must not be tardy too often in arriving at work, or he will be disciplined by his foreman. He must not absent himself too often, or he will be punished. He must not refuse to obey an order from his boss, or again he will be punished. If a worker's conduct off the job should reflect unfavorably upon the employer, he may also be disciplined for his behavior. Attempts to introduce industrialization into more primitive societies often fail because the people simply will not submit to the very rigorous discipline that the system demands.

Monotony and Boredom. Monotony and boredom are consequences of the minute division of labor existent in the modern factory. Now it is true that workers had to perform many short-cycle, repetitive operations prior to mechanization in industry. Many agricultural tasks, such as sowing seed, cultivating, and harvesting, were quite repetitive. Many handicraft operations are quite repetitive as well. Consider, for example, weaving on a handloom. But there is a big difference between doing routine, simple tasks over and over again when one essentially works for himself, sets his own pace, and makes the final product and being an assembly line worker in the modern mass production factory.

The modern production worker on repetitive tasks cannot attach any interest or sentiment to his work. He cannot take pride in a completed product because he is not involved in the finished good. His job does not demand more than surface mental attention. His mind wanders because the job holds no real meaning for him. The union steward in the punch press department of a large factory once said, "We [operators] do our jobs mechanically and automatically. We do not have to think about what we are doing. Our thoughts are miles away from our work." This is daydreaming or reverie.

The worker in the modern factory often cannot set his own work pace. This is true not only in assembly line work but also in those factories hav-

---

[7] Clark Kerr, John T. Dunlop, Frederick H. Harbison, and Charles A. Myers, *Industrialism and Industrial Man* (Cambridge, Mass: Harvard University Press, 1960), pp. 198-200.

ing individual machine and bench jobs where management has installed a measured daywork system. Under measured daywork, workers are required to produce at a certain daily rate as determined by time study techniques.

In summary it can be said that the minute division of work has caused workers to be indifferent to their jobs and in many cases to even dislike them. The job is looked upon as simply a source of income. [8]

Job Displacement.   The rapid technological progress that has occurred in modern industrialized society has caused frequent upheavals and changes in the employment careers of working men. It has been observed that those in the labor force may have to change their basic trade or occupation one or more times during their working life span. For example, between 1940 and the mid-1950's the railroads shifted completely from steam to diesel-electric locomotives. This made the job of many thousands of firemen obsolete. The position of flight engineer was created in the late 1940's on the commercial airlines, yet by 1960 changes in aircraft design and the shift to jets have drastically reduced the need for these engineers. Up to the present time the brunt of the burden of job displacement due to technological change has been borne by the worker himself. He is laid off and must fend for himself. Perhaps in the future private industry will assume a greater responsibility for retraining its employees and for redesigning their whole personnel management programs to accommodate to technological change.

Interdependence.   The modern production system both within the individual enterprise and throughout the economy as a whole is designed in such a way that a shutdown in one sector will shut down large portions or all of the rest of the system. If certain key workers, say maintenance men, should go on strike, an entire factory may grind to a halt. If the steel industry is shut down due to a labor dispute, then within a few weeks the automobile industry and others dependent upon steel as a raw material will have to suspend operations.

The consequences of a breakdown in one sector of the economy upon the other sectors are magnified because there are so few companies in our key industries and because of the prevalance of industrywide collective bargaining. The net result has been the necessary intrusion of the Federal government into these disputes to protect the public interest.

THE LABOR FORCE IN AMERICA

How has the average American worker fared during the process of industrialization and economic growth that has occurred in the United States

---

[8] For a comprehensive analysis of the effects of the modern factory system upon workers see Georges Friedmann, *Industrial Society* (New York: The Free Press of Glencoe, 1955).

over the past several decades? What changes have occurred in the nature and composition of the labor force?

The labor force includes the noninstitutional population 16 years of age or over who are employed plus all those who are unemployed and are actually seeking work.

Rising Status of Labor

It has been said that the twentieth century is the age of the common man. In the United States the working man has risen to unprecedented heights in terms of his standard of living, educational attainment, freedom of opportunity, and voice in affairs affecting him. Let us briefly examine some of these elements in labor's advanced position.

Standard of Living. The best measure of the improvement in the level of living of working people is the change in "real wages" between two periods. "Real wages" show the relative purchasing power of wages in terms of a base period when changes in the price level have been canceled out. Gitlow has tabulated the real average hourly wage rates in manufacturing for every year from 1860 through 1957 in terms of 1957-1959 dollars. Excluding pay supplements (that is, fringe benefits) the average hourly real wage was $2.13 in 1957 compared with $.29 in 1860. This means that the worker of 1957 could buy approximately seven times as much goods and services as could the worker of 1860. For the entire period 1860-1957 the average annual rate of increase in average real wages was 2.2 per cent per year. Of course, the increase has not always been at a uniform rate. It was only 1.7 per cent per year during the period 1890-1914, whereas from 1930-1957 it averaged 4.0 per cent per year.[9]

Shorter Work Time. In 1850 the average work week for all industries was of 70 hours duration.[10] By 1960 it had declined to 40.8. The greatest reductions occurred between 1900 and 1930.

Prior to 1940 paid vacations for hourly paid workers were rather uncommon. Sometimes they received a week off in the summer but without pay. It was somewhat more common, however, for salaried employees to receive a paid vacation. Nowadays the typical hourly worker receives one week's paid vacation after one year of service with a company, two week's after two or three years of service, and three weeks after fifteen years of service. A goodly percentage of companies grant four weeks after 25 years of service. Salaried employees usually receive a full two weeks of vacation after the first year, with the longer time periods occurring as described for hourly workers. In 1963 the major steel producing companies and the United Steel Workers Union bargained a 13-week paid sabbatical leave for hourly workers every fifth year.

[9] Abraham L. Gitlow, *Labor and Industrial Society,* (Rev. Ed., Homewood, Ill.: Richard D. Irwin, Inc., 1963), pp. 325-330.

[10] *Monthly Labor Review,* Vol. 81, No. 1 (January, 1958), p. 24.

Previous to World War II major national holidays were frequently observed in private industry but without pay. As of the late 1960's the prevailing practice was to grant seven to eight paid holidays per year.[11]

Thus we can see that on the average the American worker devotes fewer hours per week and fewer days per year to his job. This does not necessarily mean that he sits idle during his remaining waking hours. He may consume it in a variety of ways, such as engaging in more recreational pursuits, working around his house, commuting longer distances to work, or holding an additional part-time job. But there can be no doubt that this added time off the job has given the American worker greater freedom in determining what he does with his life.

More Education.   There has been a long-term trend toward increased mass education in the United States. This trend seems to have accelerated in recent years. For those in the civilian labor force between the ages of 18 and 64, 32.0 per cent had completed four years of high school in 1940 while 54.9 per cent had done so in 1962. During this same time span of twenty-two years the percentage completing four or more years of college had risen from 5.7 to 11.1.[12] This higher educational attainment has resulted in better jobs and higher income for these individuals.

Expectations and Demands.   Aside from those changes that can be clearly documented with statistical data, it seems clear also that modern workers as a group or force in society have greater expectations and greater wants than did their forefathers of a few generations ago. They want better homes, cars, food, and clothing than could be obtained years ago. Many things considered luxuries years ago are now held to be necessities. They expect that their children shall finish high school and even obtain some college or technical institute education. They expect to spend more and more on services and recreation. This continual drive for more and more can be explained in terms of the psychological theories of motivation. As more basic needs for the necessities of life are satisfied, man strives to satisfy his higher social and egoistic drives. The fulfillment of these cannot be directly measured. Generally in these psychological and social areas man's wants are never satisfied. He always wants more.

Nowadays employees expect to have a greater voice in their own destiny at their place of employment. A considerable share of the labor force has found union membership to be an avenue for this expression. Through the collective bargaining process workers make greater demands upon management not only for such material things as higher wages and more fringe benefits but also for fair treatment, freedom from discrimination, and a say-so in matters affecting them. To a considerable extent the ideals of political democracy, which are so much a part of the American cul-

[11] James N. Houff, "Supplementary Wage Benefits in Metropolitan Areas" *Monthly Labor Review,* Vol. 91, No. 6 (June 1968), pp. 40-47.

[12] Denis F. Johnston, "Educational Attainment of Workers, March 1962," *Monthly Labor Review,* Vol. 86, No. 5 (May 1963), pp. 504-515.

ture, have seeped into the workplace. Management in recent years has come to be interested in and pay attention to the ideas of its employees. The techniques for providing for employee participation have been many. Among these are collective bargaining, consultative supervision, democratic leadership, labor-management cooperation, and suggestion systems.

Changing Composition of Labor Force

Over the years a great many changes have occurred in the way people make a living. In the mid-nineteenth century four out of five persons who worked for a living worked for themselves. That is to say, they were self-employed. Most were farmers, small shopkeepers, and craftsmen. By mid-twentieth century the situation had reversed. Self-employed workers constituted only about 15 per cent of those who worked, whereas 82 per cent of the employed labor force worked for someone else. (Unpaid family workers constituted the remaining 3 per cent.)[13] Thus we are a nation primarily made up of wage and salary earners. Whereas self-employed persons largely determine their own employment conditions, these are set by management for wage and salary workers.

Decline of Unskilled Workers. In 1900, 20 per cent of the nonfarm labor force was employed as laborers, whereas in 1950 only 8 per cent was so employed.[14] The demand for unskilled labor has shown this long-term decline because much of the heavy work in industry has been taken over by machines. Unskilled workers are undereducated workers. The unemployment statistics of the nation show a high correlation between low education and unemployment. In March 1967 white males, 18 years old and over, with eight years of schooling or less had an unemployment rate of 4.0 per cent, whereas those with four years of high school or more had a rate of only 1.8 per cent. Male Negroes with eight years of education or less had an unemployment rate of 6.8 per cent, whereas those with four years of high school or more had a rate of 4.7 per cent.[15]

More White-Collar Employees. There has been a long-term trend of increases in white-collar employment, both in absolute numbers and in percentage of the total labor force. This effect has been especially pronounced since World War II. In 1956 white-collar workers outnumbered blue-collar workers for the first time. The changes from 1946 to 1966 are graphically illustrated in Figure 1-1. In 1946 blue-collar workers constituted 40.9 per cent of all employed persons; twenty years later that number had declined to 36.7 per cent. On the other hand white-collar employment stood at 33.4 per cent in 1946 and had increased to 45.0 per cent by 1966.

[13] Gertrude Bancroft, *The American Labor Force: Its Growth and Changing Composition* (New York: John Wiley & Sons, Inc., 1958), pp. 4-5.

[14] Carol A. Barry, "White Collar Employment: I, Trends and Structure," *Monthly Labor Review,* Vol. 84, No. 1 (January 1961), p. 13.

[15] Harvey R. Hamel, "Educational Attainment of Workers," *Monthly Labor Review,* Vol. 91 (February 1968), p. 29.

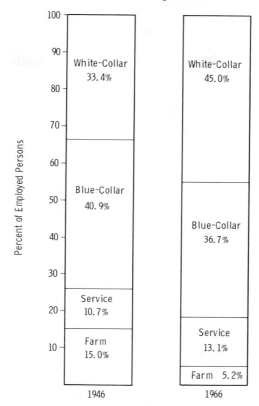

Figure 1-1. Employed Persons by Major Occupational Groups, 1946 and 1966, Expressed as a Percentage of Total. Data from Paul M. Ryscavage, "Changes in Occupational Employment Over the Past Decade", *Monthly Labor Review,* Vol. 90, No. 8, August 1967, pp. 27-30.

It is noteworthy also that the long-term trend away from the farm has continued.[16]

The occupations which have shown the most striking rate of growth have been those in the professional and technical category. In 1946 they constituted 6.6 per cent of total employment and twenty years later the figure had almost doubled to 12.6 per cent.[17] There has been an especially rapid increase in engineers, scientists, and technicians who are employed

[16] White-collar workers, according to government statistics, include professional, technical, and kindred personnel; managers, officials, and proprietors; clerical workers; and sales workers. Blue-collar classifications contain craftsmen, foremen, and kindred workers; operatives; and laborers. The service worker category includes private household workers and service workers (other than private household). Examples of service workers are policemen, firemen, and barbers. Farm workers include farmers, farm managers and farm laborers.

[17] Paul M. Ryscavage, "Changes in Occupational Employment Over the Past Decade," *Monthly Labor Review,* Vol. 90, No. 8 (August 1967), p. 28.

in industry as opposed to doctors and lawyers who are self-employed. The growth in these technical fields is related to accelerating technology in industry, a burgeoning defense industry, government encouragement of scientific research, and emphasis upon scientific and engineering education in the universities. There has also been a great growth in elementary and secondary school teachers and in university professors. This has been caused by accelerating population growth and the fact that an increasing proportion of high school graduates attend college.

Another category within the white collar group which has grown greatly in numbers and in percentage is the clerical group. Business and government have hired increasing numbers of secretaries, stenographers, clerks, and office machine operators. This is related to the increasing bureaucratization of our economic and public institutions.

Women in Labor Force.   There has been a long-term trend toward increasing participation by women in the labor force. In 1890 the total labor force consisted of 83 per cent males and 17 per cent females. By 1955 the female portion had increased to 29 per cent.[18] By 1960 it had reached 32.3 per cent.[19] Gertrude Bancroft has presented a very striking picture of the typical American women of 1900 contrasted with her counterpart in the 1950's.

> In the same period (1900-1950) the typical American woman had changed from a rural housewife to a city dweller. In 1900, she would be working for her living only if she had the misfortune to be unmarried or widowed, and provided she was young enough to find a job. She might be either a domestic servant or a textile or needle trades worker. Except for the very few educated and talented women, marriage was earnestly to be desired as the only possible escape from inevitable economic and social poverty.
>
> At the middle of the century, marriage was still the goal of the American woman, and was achieved by all but a few. But no longer was it also an escape route from dreary, ill-paid work as a servant or a factory hand. Typically, in the 1950's, American girls seek jobs on leaving school, marry shortly thereafter, and continue working until they start having children, when they retire for a period of years. While they are in the labor force at the beginning of their working lives, they are probably doing clerical or secretarial work in an office or selling in a retail store. It is probable that after they send their last child off to school they will return to the labor force, voluntarily and with enthusiasm, not to pursue a career for which they have been prepared by school and college but to supplement the family income at whatever kind of work is both available and agreeable.[20]

[18] Bancroft, *op. cit.,* p. 34.

[19] *Labor Force and Employment in 1961,* Special Labor Force Report No. 23 (Reprint No. 2395) (Washington, D.C.: U.S. Bureau of Labor Statistics, June, 1962).

[20] Gertrude Bancroft, *The American Labor Force: Its Growth and Changing Composition* (New York: John Wiley & Sons, Inc., 1958), p. 39. Reprinted by permission.

The Labor Force In Perspective

By whatever measures are used, objective or subjective, there has been a general upgrading of the American labor force. The gulf between those who "boss" and those who are "bossed" has narrowed. Not only are employees better educated and better trained, but the needs of our economy have shifted such that only the better qualified are able to find jobs. To a considerable extent American workers are becoming middle-class-oriented. The majority sit at desks where they can absorb the doctrines of management. Skilled blue-collar workers are generally so well paid that many of them can move to the suburbs, where they mingle with the junior executive and young professional groups. Having moved into the cultural milieu of the middle class, many employees have abandoned their working-class ideology. This means they are less prone to join unions. This is especially true for the younger workers who either have no family tradition of union membership behind them or have elevated themselves into the professional or managerial class by acquiring a college education.

EVOLUTION OF THEORY AND PRACTICE OF PERSONNEL MANAGEMENT

One of the best ways to understand the present is to examine the past. The past is our prologue. A brief examination of history helps us understand where we are today. We shall trace the various managerial theories and practices relating to the treatment and direction of employees from the early 1800's to the present. In studying these developments, it is important for the reader to keep in mind that at any one period there existed a variety of ideologies and practices. The various movements do not fit into a neat package of unified philosophies and practices commencing at one point in history and ending clearly at another.

The people contributing to the development of the personnel management field have had varied backgrounds and professions. An important group have been the university scholars, writers, and researchers who have pushed back the frontiers of knowledge. A large amount of soundly based experimentation and research has been conducted by these people in areas such as small group theory, organization theory, motivation, morale, productivity, leadership, personnel testing, fatigue, accidents, and personnel evaluation.

Another significant group of contributors have been the management practitioners themselves: industrial executives, personnel specialists, and consultants. These have been active in such fields as work measurement, wage incentives, job evaluation, organization design, industrial training, executive development, and union-management relations.

A third group have been government legislators and administrators who have shaped and administered public policy in the areas of wages, hours, collective bargaining, workmen's compensation, unemployment, and equal employment opportunity. These programs have had a decided impact upon the management of people at work in private business.

A fourth and final group of influential people have been the leaders of organized labor: Samuel Gompers, John L. Lewis, Philip Murray, Walter Reuther, George Meany, and their followers. In a large measure their influence in the personnel field has been felt through labor legislation advocated by organized labor and through management policies and programs adopted in response (and sometimes in opposition) to union initiative.

The principal themes and movements which have formed the developing stream of personnel management could be generally classified under (1) early philosophies; (2) drive for efficiency and productivity; and (3) recognition of human needs, satisfaction, and welfare. The scientific management movement and Taylorism quite clearly emphasized programs to increase output and reduce costs. The early emphasis in industrial psychology was oriented toward productive efficiency through the scientific selection, placement, and training of workers. On the other hand the welfare movement in the early 1900's and the human relations movement of the 1940's and 1950's leaned heavily in the direction of industrial humanism and employee satisfaction. The thrust of the American labor union movement has clearly been for employee welfare, security, and betterment.

However, the assumptions and point of view of such disciplines as employee training, management development, and modern organizational behavior tend to encompass both the concepts of productive efficiency and optimization of human satisfaction. Therefore, no simple classification correctly identifies all the major streams of thought and action in the field of personnel management. We shall now examine these streams in roughly the chronological order of their origin.

Early Philosophies

The United States followed somewhat after England in becoming an industrialized nation. It was not until 1880 that fewer than 50 per cent of the American labor force was engaged in agriculture. Being culturally close to the British, American entrepreneurs tended to adopt many of the British attitudes toward workers. Because the early American manufacturers and writers were less articulate on the subject than the English, we must look primarily to the latter for verbalization of the philosophies prevailing in the nineteenth century.

One of the pioneer industrialists was Robert Owen (1771-1858), a Scottish textile manufacturer, who in 1813 wrote a book entitled *A New View of Society*. If Owen were alive today he would be called a paternalistic employer. He built model worker villages by his cotton mills at New Lanark, Scotland. He built decent health and sanitation facilities in his factories and established schools for children and workers. Eventually he abolished child labor in his mills. Owen's views and practices contrasted sharply with those of the majority of employers in that period, for he took a genuine interest in the welfare of his people. He advised other manufacturers to devote as much attention to their "vital machines" (that is, workers) as they did to their inanimate machines. His goal was to maximize profits by so doing. Owen was similar to other owners, however, in that he considered workers somewhat like children who had to be continually trained and molded by a strict discipline. The authority of the employer was supreme. In his view, the workers, like children, had to be guided and protected.

John Stuart Mill, the eminent British economist, perhaps spoke for most employers when he stated in his *Principles of Political Economy* that in all things which affect them collectively the lot of the poor should be regulated for them and not by them. The rich should stand in relation to the poor as parents to children. The poor should do nothing but their day's work and be moral and religious.

Andrew Ure, in his *Philosophy of Manufacturers* published in London in 1835, praised the factory system over the coexisting cottage or putting-out system of home production. He defended the widespread use of child labor in the textile industry against the then current public criticism. He was a spokesman for the prevailing belief of members of the entrepreneural class that workers left to themselves were lazy and ignorant. But factory employment improved their morals and health and gave them higher wages than could be obtained in agriculture or cottage production. He denounced any combination of workers (that is, unionization) as a product of agitators who caused violence and crime.

Others whose works have a bearing on early managerial thought were Adam Smith, who wrote the *Wealth of Nations* in 1776 and Charles Babbage, who wrote *On the Economy of Machinery and Manufactures* in 1832. Smith emphasized that if each individual worked for his own economic self-interest, the greatest good would accrue to society. Babbage subscribed to Smith's ideas. In addition, he concentrated upon developing such principles of manufacturing as the division of labor. Babbage emphasized mutuality of interests between employer and workers. Hard work and high productivity were a source of good wages for the worker and high profits for the employer. In his book he advocated the adoption of such motivational techniques as wage incentives, profit sharing, and plans of employee participation in the establishment of shop rules. Babbage like Ure, however, was opposed to unions of working men.

Scientific Management

Frederick W. Taylor was the real father and driving force behind the scientific management movement.[21] He and his followers Frank and Lillian Gilbreth, Henry L. Gantt, Morris L. Cook, and Harrington Emerson exerted a profound effect upon management thought and practice not only in the United States but throughout the world.

Although Taylor created a number of important shop management techniques, such as time study, methods study, functional foremanship, standardization of tools, a differential piece-rate system, instruction cards for workmen, and a cost control system, he proclaimed that scientific management was primarily a mental revolution on the part of workingmen and management alike and not simply a set of efficiency devices.

He preached cooperation between labor and management but in a different way than that of most modern writers. He believed that by scientific measurement of work (that is, time study), specification of the best method, selection and placement of the right worker in right job, and establishment of an appropriate wage, the source of most of the conflict between management and labor would be removed. The increased output, higher wages through wage incentives, and higher profits for the employer would cause harmony to prevail.

Although Taylor claimed that he was not opposed to unions and collective bargaining as such, he really believed them unnecessary because the use of scientific methods in industry would satisfactorily settle disagreements between labor and management.

Just as he disliked employee soldiering on the job, so did he oppose the arbitrary exercise of authority by management. He felt that by applying his scientific methods, rules and procedures would be established that would be just as binding upon management as upon workers.

Implicit in Taylor's consulting activities and writings was a full acceptance of the "economic man" concept that dominated management thinking for such a long time, both before and after his time. This is the notion that man is primarily motivated to maximize his economic gain. This concept further holds that each person is individualistic in nature. It ignores the social and psychological drives of man.

In his book entitled the *Principles of Scientific Management,* Taylor asserted that no single element of his system constituted scientific management, but rather it was the entire program and philosophy that was its hallmark. He summarized this as (1) science, not rule of thumb; (2)

---

[21] A full explanation of Taylor's contributions and impact would be beyond the scope of this book. The interested reader may wish to consult the following works: Frederick W. Taylor, *Principles of Scientific Management* (New York: Harper & Row, 1919); Robert F. Hoxie, *Scientific Management and Labor* (New York: Appleton-Century-Crofts, 1915); George Filipetti, *Industrial Management in Transition,* (Rev. Ed., Homewood, Ill.: Richard D. Irwin, Inc., 1953), Chs. 2 and 3.

harmony, not discord; (3) cooperation, not individualism; and (4) maximum output, in place of restricted output. [22]

The scientific management movement has had a great impact upon management-employee relationships and upon management in general. It contributed greatly to the professionalization of management. It elevated management by plan, system, and design while causing management by hunch and intuition to decline. It brought the engineer (first the mechanical and later the industrial engineer) into a more active role in designing man-machine systems and even entire factory production systems. The work measurement and wage incentive systems introduced by the scientific management pioneers have become accepted practice (with improvements, of course) throughout a large segment of industry. Not only have these contributed to higher productivity, lower unit costs, and higher take-home pay, but they have "muddied the waters" of labor-management relations and caused innumerable disputes. The emphasis upon differences in worker abilities and a scientific selection of employees laid the groundwork for the widespread acceptance of the industrial psychologist and his selection testing programs.

Welfare Movement

In the early 1900's the welfare movement became fairly widespread in American industry. This movement aimed to uplift the physical, hygienic, social, and educational conditions of working class people for their own benefit and to make them better employees. More specifically, welfare work consisted of those programs instituted by the employer which sought to improve the employees' working and living conditions beyond the requirements of the law or the labor market.

Many factors contributed to the interest of employers in welfare programs. As corporations grew, top management became more distant from the workers and there occurred a decline in the tenor of relationships. Social reformers and writers had for some time awakened the general public to certain exploitive and sweatshop conditions of the factory system. Labor unions were knocking at the gates of many factories. Many towns which grew up around a single local industry lacked essential housing and decent community facilites. Thus corporate executives perceived a need and an opportunity to improve the well-being of their people as a positive value in itself and as a way of generating greater employee loyalty and possibly greater productivity.

These early welfare programs included health facilities; wash-up and locker facilities; lunch rooms; recreation facilities for employees and their families; libraries, schools and classes in English for immigrants; disability, group insurance and pension programs; and savings and legal aid programs.

[22] Taylor, *op. cit.,* p. 140.

Those who administered such programs were called welfare or social secretaries. They were looked upon as intermediaries between the top management and the workers. Having had prior experience in industrial welfare work, particularly with the railroads, the YMCA began training people for positions as welfare secretaries. The duties of one secretary were as follows:

> . . . the supervision and initiative of the traveling library of selected books, . . . weekly talks of fifteen minutes by the president, welfare manager, or invited guests; literature class during winter; question box; distribution of pamphlets, verses, etc., where most helpful; the free and careful use of the medicine chest; prescriptions and advice given to workers free; ice water during summer months; trips to various points of interest on Saturday afternoons; theater parties when possible; tickets for special occasions; mutual aid society for benefits in case of illness or death; Penny Provident for saving pennies; bringing odds and ends to give others less fortunate. [23]

By the 1920's welfare work in industry had declined and become somewhat discredited. Some companies operated their programs in a highly paternalistic manner and continued them only as long as the workers evidenced genuine appreciation. Other employers offered these benefits to their employees to placate them into accepting long hours, low wages, and bad working conditions. In short, opportunism and expediency were the motives of some businessmen. Executives became disillusioned when baseball and horseshoe-pitching leagues, company picnics, reading rooms, savings associations, and company housing did not increase productive efficiency. Employees became disillusioned when they sensed that employer interest in them was not always genuine.

Employment Management

Prior to the decade 1911-1920 the hiring of workers was performed principally by line supervision. In effect the foreman did his own hiring and firing. At about this time a number of forces began to operate that demonstrated to top management in American corporations the need for establishing a specialized department to handle employment management.

Frederick W. Taylor had emphasized the need for proper selection and placement of workers on jobs for which they could become superior producers. Indeed his incentive systems were most appropriate only for "first-class" workers. A number of researchers had demonstrated the very considerable costs associated with high labor turnover. World War

[23] Ling, Cyril C., *The Management of Personnel Relations: History and Origins* (Homewood, Ill.: Richard D. Irwin, Inc., 1965), p. 79, quoting William H. Tolman, *Social Engineering* (New York: McGraw-Hill Book Company, Inc., 1909), p. 57.

I created a demand for the hiring of many thousands for work in defense production factories. War production alone caused the creation of a great number of employment departments in industry. About this time a feeling developed among top managements that foremen were overburdened with problems of production, training, maintenance, and other supervisory duties and that they should be relieved of the responsibility for hiring and firing. There was considerable criticism in the management literature of that period of the "rough and ready" manner in which foremen had performed the employment function.

Thus employment management departments sprang up throughout industry around the time of World War I. In 1912, the first employment managers' association was formed in Boston. By 1917 there were ten such associations in the country with nearly one thousand member companies. In 1915 the Amos Tuck School of Dartmouth College offered the first training program for employment managers. The employment departments performed the functions of recruiting, selection, job placement, and record keeping. In some concerns their responsibilities also included training, grievance handling, welfare program administration, and final decision making on discharges for hourly workers. These early employment departments were the forerunners of the modern personnel or industrial relations department.[24]

Industrial Psychology

Industrial psychology had its beginnings in 1913 when Hugo Munsterberg (the father of industrial psychology) published his *Psychology and Industrial Efficiency.*[25] Major contributions to the professional practice of personnel have been made by industrial psychology in personnel testing, interviewing, attitude measurement, learning theory and training, fatigue and monotony studies, safety, job analysis, and human engineering (now commonly called human factors analysis). Of all these areas the major application of the knowledge and techniques of industrial psychology has been in testing for employment, job placement, promotion, and training. Psychologists have made a major contribution, over the years, by their adherence to careful experimentation, rigorous research designs, and use of sophisticated statistical methods.

As a rule, even today, only the very large corporations employ professionally trained psychologists on a full time basis. But the knowledge, findings, and skills of industrial psychology have been applied rather extensively through education, publication, and consultation services.

---

[24] A detailed explanation of the development of the employment management activity in industry is contained in Henry Eilbirt, "The Development of Personnel Management in the United States," *Business History Review,* Vol. 33, No. 3 (Autumn 1959), pp. 345-364.

[25] Boston: Houghton Mifflin Company, 1913.

Health and Safety

The passage of workmen's compensation laws by most of the states occurred in the period 1910-1920. These laws hold the employer financially responsible for all injuries occurring to workers while on the job. Employers since that time have been required to carry workmens' compensation insurance to compensate injured workers for medical expenses, loss of weekly earnings while off the job, and for loss of earning power due to permanent physical damage. Because premium rates are adjusted upward or downward to reflect the accident experience of a company, this has served as a powerful incentive for the employer to eliminate the causes of accidents in his plant.

The passage of these laws was a prime force causing employers to take positive steps to reduce and prevent work injuries and to organize company health programs. Thus we saw the creation of such positions as safety engineer, safety director, company physician, industrial nurse, and medical director. In more recent years the position of industrial hygienist has been added by many large companies.

In 1913 the most influential nationwide organization devoted to the promotion of occupational safety was formed. This is the National Safety Council, a nonprofit organization devoted to research, education, technical service, and publication in the field of safety. It is a membership organization composed largely of manufacturing, public utility, and transportation companies as well as insurance companies in the liability and workmen's compensation fields.

The fields of industrial hygiene and industrial medicine have matured during the same era as the accident prevention movement. The first major study of occupational diseases was made in 1902 by Dr. C. F. W. Doehring at the request of the first United States Commissioner of Labor. In 1918 Johns Hopkins' School of Hygiene and Public Health was established and it devoted considerable emphasis to industrial medicine. In the same year Harvard University pioneered in the launching of a degree program in industrial hygiene. In 1916 the American Association of Industrial Physicians and Surgeons was formed. Changing its name in 1951 to the Industrial Medical Association, this organization has been devoted to research, health service, and raising the standards of physicians engaged in industrial practice. The field of industrial medicine has made significant contributions to personnel management in regard to sanitation and environmental control, qualifications of personnel engaged in practice of industrial medicine and industrial nursing, physical examinations, medical records, health counseling for employees, and emergency health treatment.

Unionism and Management Reactions

Efforts by American workers to form trade unions to represent their interests in dealings with employers became very widespread and intense commencing in the mid-1880's. In this era, and indeed for many years thereafter, the principal efforts of the unions were directed toward getting the employers to recognize them and to bargain over wages, hours, and other employment conditions. After obtaining a foothold of membership in a company, the union would generally demand a closed shop (that is, employment of union members only) to secure its position.

All through the years, and even up to the present time, employers generally have not taken kindly to unionization of their workers. The "Declaration of Principles" of the National Association of Manufacturers in 1903 clearly expressed the opposition of the Association to the closed shop and, in substance, to any interference by unions with the employer's authority. For many years (up until the early 1930's) the National Metal Trades Association was active in marshaling the resources of member corporations to oppose unions.

Basically entrepreneurs and managers opposed unionism for their workers because such action constituted a serious challenge to their authority. With the enhanced bargaining power derived from unified action and the ever-present threat of a strike, a union was in a position to demand a voice in wage-rate determination; job assignments; promotion, transfer, and layoff policies; work schedules; working conditions, work loads, and many other vital factors. When a union entered the picture the authority of the employer was no longer supreme. In addition, union demands exerted a strong impact upon the cost of doing business.

During the 1920's managements in American industry, acting both individually and in concert through their various associations, launched a great ideological campaign against unions. This took the form of open-shop campaigns, company-established unions (called employee representation plans), and welfare capitalism (paternalism). The main features were education, training, indoctrination, and welfare programs. To a considerable extent management was successful in discouraging workers from joining unions during the 1920's, for union membership declined significantly during that decade.

Then came the Great Depression, the formation of the CIO, intensified union-organizing activity, and the passage of the National Labor Relations Act (Wagner Act) in 1935. The Wagner Act signified positive encouragement of collective bargaining as public policy. Peaceful means via National Labor Relations Board elections were instituted to settle the violence-fomenting issue of union recognition.

Not until the late 1930's and the 1940's did American management begin to develop a sophistication and maturity in the field of labor relations. Faced with the near inevitability of dealing with unions on a permanent basis, corporations established such positions as vice-president of labor relations, director of labor relations, and industrial relations director. Commencing in the 1940's, a number of major universities established industrial relations centers or schools that engaged in the triple functions of research, adult education extension activities, and on-campus undergraduate and graduate instruction. As people have become trained in the disciplines of labor economics, industrial relations, and human relations and have taken responsible positions in industry, the field has become professionalized to a large extent.

In the 1960's unionization of government employees at the federal, state, and local level spread rapidly. This was initially fostered by President Kennedy's Executive Order 10988 of 1962, which required Federal government agencies to recognize as exclusive bargaining agents unions that, by a secret ballot, have been shown to represent a majority of the unit.

Unionism has had a number of tangible influences upon the management of personnel. Among these have been the adoption of sound employee grievance handling systems, almost universal acceptance of arbitration to resolve conflicts of rights, due process discipline practices, expansion of employee benefit programs, liberalization of holiday and vacation time-off, clear definition of job duties, and job rights via seniority. Also union pressures have forced management to install rational, defensible wage structures. Decision-making in these and related areas has tended more and more to become a joint consultative process between management and union.

Labor Laws

Commencing with the passage of workmens' compensation laws in most of the states by 1920, government legislation has increasingly become an instrument for improving the conditions of labor in the United States. The National Labor Relations Act of 1935 (Wagner Act) as amended by the Taft-Hartley Act in 1947 guarantees to employees the right to form unions of their own choosing without interference by either the employer or another union. The Fair Labor Standards Act, originally passed in 1938 but amended many times, established a nationwide minimum wage and the requirement that rate and one half be paid for all hours worked over forty in one week. The Social Security Act, passed in 1935, has established a nationwide system of disability and old age benefits paid for by both employer and employee. In addition, this same Act established a joint state-federal unemployment compensation system financed by employers via a payroll tax. Title VII of the Civil Rights Act of 1964 prohibits discrimination because of race, color, religion, sex or national origin in hiring, upgrading, and all other conditions of employment.

How has labor legislation affected the practice of management-employee relationships? First, as said before, it has substantially improved the economic and the health and welfare conditions of working men and women. Second, it has sharply limited the freedom of choice that the employer formerly enjoyed. Sharp limits are set on his rights to make decisions in regard to wages, hours of work, health and sanitation, hiring, promoting, and discharge. The third major effect has been the impetus toward

the expansion and professionalization of staff personnel-industrial relations services in the firm. This effect is most striking in the position of
the labor relations officer who must possess a sound background in labor
economics, labor law, and collective bargaining expertise.

Rational Wage and Salary Administration

Years ago wages were set for individuals in a very haphazard manner.
A man's pay frequently depended upon the strength of his personal ties
to his boss, whether he had been hired during a period of business prosperity or recession, and a crude guess by management of the going rates
in the local area. Increases in pay after a man had worked for a period
of time were often based upon whim and expediency. Although this un-
tenable situation still exists in some companies, the trend for the past twenty-five years has been toward rational, systematic pay administration.

Two major driving forces behind this movement have been the pressures generated by unions and the War Labor Board of World War II.
Although the system of logics of unions and those of management are
often opposed in relation to wage determination, it has been clear that
union pressures both at the bargaining table and through the grievance
procedure have induced management to adopt a well-thought-out, defensible compensation program. In certain industries, such as steel, the union
and managements have cooperated jointly to administer a job evaluation
program. When it was called upon to resolve labor disputes and later when
it was called upon to administer the wage stabilization program, the War
Labor Board formulated a number of sound principles that were used
in arriving at wage decisions in companies. In many cases the Board directed that companies establish formal wage structures, job evaluation
programs, and reasonable pay administration policies.

Today industry has pretty well accepted the principles of basing internal wage differentials upon differences in job content, having a formal
job grade structure, and surveying the labor market area to ascertain going
rates for jobs of equivalent content.

Education

Employee Training. Although the apprenticeship system of training
workers has existed for centuries (it predates the factory system of production), it provided formalized training only for the small minority of
workers who were in the skilled trades. Widespread training of production workers, and to some extent of foremen, began during World War
II, with the Training Within Industry program. This program was designed
to develop employee skills in manufacturing industries for the war effort.
Many thousands received training in the three principal TWI programs
of Job Instructor Training (JIT), Job Methods Training (JMT), and Job

Relations Training (JRT). The principles and techniques developed in the Training Within Industry program have had a great impact upon industrial training in the years since. Industrial executives have learned that employees do not learn new jobs and new skills simply by watching others and by trial and error. The time required of the average man to reach acceptable performance can be shortened significantly by placing him in a proper training environment.

Management Development. Since 1950 American industry has devoted a great deal of time and money to formal management development programs. This has been due to several factors. There has been a growing recognition that management is an emerging profession that depends upon a distinctive body of knowledge and teachable skills. Years ago businessmen assumed that by working long years as an individual contributor, whether as a craftsman, clerk, or engineer, a man would develop the necessary abilities to function as a supervisor or executive. Such an assumption proved to be false. Prospective managers must be placed in the proper environment involving both on-the-job and classroom learning experiences if they are to develop managerial skills.

Management development activities have taken many forms. People have been sent to universities to attend special advanced management, nondegree programs of four to thirteen weeks duration. A few, such as a number of Bell Telephone Companies, have sent selected executives to liberal arts programs at the University of Pennsylvania, Dartmouth, Williams, and Northwestern. In the mid-1950's the General Electric Company established its own school, called the General Electric Management Research and Development Institute, at Crotonville on the Hudson River. This school has been for the development of higher level executives. The extension divisions of many state universities have offered a wide variety of short courses to management personnel both on company premises and at conference centers at the universities. The American Management Association, with headquarters in New York City and branches at Saranac Lake and Hamilton, New York, and in California, has been offering a very extensive program of publications, conferences, and seminars for management personnel.

Because much of the work of the executive demands knowledge and skills in human relations, an increasingly popular form of development has been in sensitivity training programs. Sensitivity training—also called T-group or laboratory training—aims to help participants improve self-understanding, interpersonal competence, interpersonal communication skills, and effectiveness in group situations. This type of training has been created and refined by the National Training Laboratories of Washington, D.C.,[26] which offers two week residential programs for executives at various centers throughout the country.

[26] In 1967 the name of this organization was changed to NTL Institute for Applied Behavioral Science.

Added to the programs above, which basically serve only a few from among the thousands of managers in business and industry, are the in-service training programs given on the premises and generally during regular working hours in companies. In recent years more and more attention has been given to development on the job via coaching, counseling, special job assignments, and cross-training (job rotation). Professional training specialists have also emphasized the importance of self-development.

Human Relations and Organizational Behavior

The term *human relations* has acquired several meanings that have relevance to the management of people at work. In its most basic sense, it refers to interpersonal dealings and relationships including person to person, person to group, and group to group. Some use the term from an ethical standpoint. Thus a manager may say that his management team practices "good" human relations in the plant. They respect the worth and dignity of the individual. Ethical and moral values and concepts of right and wrong that are respected in the society at large are adhered to in the factory.

A third meaning ascribed to the term *human relations* relates to interpersonal effectiveness such as "winning friends and incluencing people." Some companies give courses to their salesmen and to managerial personnel to help them be more effective in speaking before groups, to develop poise and self-confidence, and to increase their effectiveness in influencing others. These programs emphasize mannerisms, surface characteristics, and personality traits. Often a formula or cookbook approach is utilized rather than knowledge gained from research.

Because *human relations* also includes the meanings in the world at large of race, family, and community relations and because some have emphasized, quite unfortunately, the manipulative aspects of the term, a new designation has come into wide usage in the last ten years. This is the term *organizational behavior*. University courses in organizational behavior and administration have been introduced into nearly all graduate, and many undergraduate, programs in business administration throughout the country. Organizational behavior is concerned with such topics as individual and group behavior, motivation, learning, leadership, supervisory behavior, communication, social power, formal organization, status and role, and conflict resolution.

Causes of Management Interest. Management's interest in human relations in industry commenced, for the most part, in the 1940's, especially after World War II. Many factors operated to cause this development at that time. The rapid expansion of unionism in the late 1930's and early 1940's caused management everywhere to be more sensitive to the problems and needs of its work force. Management could not ignore festering human problems and employee complaints, because the union would not let these issues go unnoticed. Some managements saw the rise of unionism as a challenge to provide so sound a personnel program and so enlightened a leadership that their employees would find no need for a union.

Another factor causing management interest has been the rising educational attainment of the labor force in industry. This advance has occurred not only because the population of the United States in general is more educated than in previous years but also because of the changed occupational mix in industry. Industry, commencing especially in the 1940's, has been employing ever increasing numbers of technicians, engineers, and scientists and fewer unskilled laborers. Educated people demand better leadership. The social gulf separating managers and employees (at least in many industries) has narrowed. Educated employees can make substantial contributions to the company via the group decision-making process.

The great volume of research, writing, and lecturing that has been emanating from university researchers and scholars in the behavioral sciences has found a receptive audience among top business leaders.

As management has matured and become more professionalized, there has been a growing realization that human resources are the most valuable asset that any organization has. The way to build a thriving enterprise is by investing in capable people first. If this is done, the bricks and mortar and the technology will be taken care of in due course. But if the nurturing of human talent is neglected, no amount of attention to machinery and process will make the organization succeed.

Hawthorne Studies.   The research program conducted at the Hawthorne Works of the Western Electric Company in Chicago in the 1920's and early 1930's actually marked the beginning of what may be called the human relations movement. This research program consisted of a series of experiments and studies conducted jointly by Western Electric investigators and a team from the Harvard Graduate School of Business Administration, led by Elton Mayo. These studies sought to ascertain what relationship existed, if any, between productivity and such environmental factors as light intensity, length of work day and work week, and the introduction of rest pauses. After considerable analysis the researchers concluded that sociological and psychological phenomena often exerted even greater influence upon output than did physical, measurable conditions of work. As a result of the Hawthorne research, such concepts as social system, informal organization, group control of behavior, equilibrium, and logical and nonlogical behavior entered the language of human relations writers and personnel management specialists.[27]

---

[27] Portions of the Hawthorne research program are described in Chapter 16, "Group Relations and Informal Organization." The most complete account of this research is contained in F. J. Roethlisberger and W. J. Dickson, *Management and the Worker* (Cambridge, Mass.: Harvard University Press, 1939).

University Contributions. Commencing in the mid-1940's, a number of universities established centers or institutes to carry on research, teaching, publishing, and extension activities in human relations, industrial relations, personnel management, and organizational behavior. The Yale Labor and Management Center was set up in 1944. Cornell's School of Industrial and Labor Relations began operations in 1945. Very substantial research contributions have come from the Institute for Social Research of the University of Michigan headed by Rensis Likert. Significant research and writings have come from men such as Douglas McGregor at Massachusetts Institute of Technology; Chris Argyris, E. Wight Bakke, and Charles Walker at Yale; William Foote Whyte at Cornell; Herbert Simon and James March at Carnegie-Mellon University; Dorwin Cartwright and Alvin Zander at Michigan; George Homans and Robert Bales at Harvard; and Frederick Herzberg at Case-Western Reserve University, to name only a few. [28]

Recent Trends. In the past twenty-five years behavioral scientists have discovered that work organizations are a fertile area for research, experimentation, consulting, and writing. A major area of inquiry has dealt with employee motivation, morale, and productivity. A number of different, but relatively compatible, schools of thought have developed. [29]

Another major area of work has been in organization theory. The classical theories of the scientific management group—Frederick Taylor, Henri Fayol, James D. Mooney and Alan C. Reiley—emphasized fixed principles of organization, chain of command, span of control and line and staff. The human relations group led by Elton Mayo and others emphasized the informal organization, group pressures and norms, participation programs, and the need to modify the principles of formal organization due to the needs and complexities of people. The most modern school of organization theorists is best represented by March and Simon's *Organizations*[30] and Carzo and Yanouzas' *Formal Organization: A Sys-*

[28] Among the prominent works of these men are: Chris Argyris, *Interpersonal Competence and Organizational Effectiveness* (Homewood, Ill.: Richard D. Irwin, Inc., 1962); E. Wight Bakke, *Bonds of Organization* (New York: Harper and Brothers, 1950); Robert Bales, *Interaction Process Analysis: A Method for the Study of Small Groups* (Cambridge, Mass.: Addison-Wesley Press, 1950); Dorwin Cartwright and Alvin Zander, *Group Dynamics: Research and Theory,* (2nd Ed., Evanston, Ill.: Row, Peterson and Company, 1960); Frederick Herzberg, *Work and the Nature of Man* (Cleveland: World Publishing Company, 1966); George Hormans, *Social Behavior: Its Elementary Forms* (New York: Harcourt, Brace & World, 1961); Rensis Likert, *The Human Organization* (New York: McGraw-Hill Book Company, 1967); Douglas McGregor, *The Human Side of Enterprise* (New York: McGraw-Hill Book Company, 1960); James G. March and Herbert A. Simon, *Organizations* (New York: John Wiley & Sons, Inc., 1958); Charles R. Walker and Robert Guest, *The Man on the Assembly Line* (Cambridge: Harvard University Press, 1952); and William Foote Whyte, *Men at Work* (Homewood, Ill.: Richard D. Irwin, Inc., 1961).

[29] For a very readable discussion of the main channels of thought in motivation, morale, and employee productivity see Saul W. Gellerman, *Motivation and Productivity* (New York: American Management Association, 1963).

[30] Referenced in footnote 27.

tems Approach.[31] Basic to modern organization theory is the system concept that emphasizes the interdependence of all parts of the organization. Some of the recent work is heavily based in mathematics. Hallmarks of the new movement are its conceptual-analytic foundation, emphasis upon empirical research and a synthesizing approach. Cybernetics, which is the science of communication and control, is a part of modern organization theory.

GENERAL OBSERVATIONS

This chapter has explained the relatively recent emergence of personnel management as a distinct field of endeavor. We have examined the nature of management, both as a field of activity and as a group or class of people. It was shown that management involves working with and through others to accomplish organizational objectives. A manager himself does not operate a machine, design products, or wait on customers (except in an emergency). He creates the environment in which employees can work effectively to accomplish the goals of the enterprise and at the same time obtain substantial satisfaction of their needs.

Because the "management of people at work" is so much a product of the economic, social, and technological environment of the times, we have traced the evolution of production systems with major emphasis upon industrialization. The main features of our modern industrial system, namely, elimination of heavy labor, great impact of scientists and engineers, use of elaborate control mechanisms, specialization, mass production, and automation, have tended to exert a great influence upon personnel management policies and practices.

An analysis of the changes that have occurred in the American labor force over the past several decades gives us a better picture of the situation encountered by the modern executive who must establish realistic policies for managing his work force. Perhaps most notable of these developments have been the rising standard of living enjoyed by the American worker and his greater educational attainment. The modern work group is in a position both to expect more from the employer and to make substantially greater contributions to the running of the business than was his counterpart of two and three generations ago.

Finally we have traced the developments in theory and practice of managing people in work organizations. Management has gained, over the years, a more realistic appreciation of the great worth and potentialities of its work force both in terms of individuals and the group as a whole. Because people are truly the most precious resource of any company, management has developed rather elaborate programs for developing, maintaining, motivating, and caring for its work team.

[31] Rocco Carzo, Jr. and John N. Yanouzas, *Formal Organization: A Systems Approach* (Homewood, Ill.: Irwin-Dorsey, 1967).

Questions for Review and Discussion

1. Explain the reasons for the relatively recent emergence of personnel management as a specialized, professional area of management and as an academic discipline.

2. Define the term *management.* What are the functions of management?

3. Describe the role and activities of a manager. Does a manager personally make a product himself? Discuss technical versus human relations problems as they affect the manager.

4. Describe the principal features of our modern industrial system as they relate to the management of people at work.

5. Describe the benefits and costs (that is, problems) caused by industrialization. How has it affected the individual worker?

6. What effect has the higher educational attainment of the labor force had upon management—employee relationships?

7. Why has there been a long-term decline in the percentage of unskilled in the labor force, whereas the number of white-collar workers has increased greatly?

8. Describe prevailing philosophies of entrepreneurs and economists during the nineteenth century as they relate to management, work, and workers.

9. What was the "scientific management movement"? What has been its effect upon the field of personnel management?

10. Describe the relationship of the following to personnel management theory and practice:
   a. Workmens' Compensation legislation
   b. The growth of unions
   c. Human relations and organizational behavior
   d. Rational wage determination
   e. Industrial psychology

Suggestions for Further Reading

American Society of Mechanical Engineers, *Fifty Years Progress in Management,* New York: The Society, 1960.

Bendix, Reinhard, *Work and Authority in Industry,* New York: John Wiley & Sons, 1956, Ch. 5.

Eilbirt, Henry, "The Development of Personnel Management in the United States," *Business History Review,* Vol. 33, No. 3, Autumn 1959, pp. 345-364.

Eitington, Julius E., "Pioneers of Management," *Advanced Management-Office Executive,* Vol. 2, No. 1, January 1963, pp. 16-19.

Friedmann, Georges, *The Anatomy of Work,* New York: The Free Press of Glencoe, 1961.

Kerr, Clark, John T. Dunlop, Frederick Harbison, and Charles A. Myers, *Industrialism and Industrial Man,* Cambridge, Mass.: Harvard
University Press, 1960.

Knowles, William H., *Personnel Management: A Human Relations Approach,* New York: American Book Company, 1955, Chs. 1 - 5.

Ling, Cyril C., *The Management of Personnel Relations: History and Origins,* Homewood, Illinois: Richard D. Irwin, 1965.

Merrill, Harwood F. (ed.), *Classics in Management,* New York: American Management Association, 1960.

Spates, Thomas, *Human Values Where People Work,* New York: Harper & Row, 1960.

Walker, Charles R., *Modern Technology and Civilization,* New York:
McGraw-Hill Book Company, 1962.

Philosophy, Principles, and Policies

2

The pattern of beliefs, attitudes, and values of those who establish and manage an organization sets the tone for that enterprise in all of its relations with its customers, employees, shareholders, suppliers, and the public at large.

Executives, especially businessmen, sometimes hold that they are practical men who handle each problem on the basis of its merits and of the situation. If asked to express their philosophy of management, many would be hard pressed to articulate a unified, consistent set of guiding principles. Yet whether they express their philosophies or not and whether they are always fully aware of it or not, those who manage the work organizations of our society usually possess some fundamental beliefs about the nature of man and his behavior in an organizational context. To a considerable extent each enterprise possesses a distinctive personality or character. In many cases this business character is a reflection of the man who founded the firm, as is the case of Thomas Watson and the International Business Machines Corporation or of George Eastman and the Eastman Kodak Company. In other cases the corporate character seems to transcend the personality of any one man, as is the case with the Bell Telephone System (American Telephone and Telegraph Company). But in any case a particular image or character comes to one's mind at the mention of any of the above companies.

In this chapter we shall examine the role of philosophy and ethics in shaping the character of an organization, with particular reference to the management of people. The basic beliefs and assumptions that managers hold regarding the nature of man and the behavior of people in organized group activity determine the methods and procedures they employ to accomplish organizational objectives. We shall examine also the important issue of organizational objectives, especially with reference to a business enterprise. In guiding the affairs of a company, executives apply a certain philosophy or set of guiding principles to achieve the goals of the organization. If the goals are unclear or contradictory the business may founder. Likewise if the philosophy or creed of those in charge is confused or in conflict with prevailing standards of morality in the society of which it is a part, then again the enterprise is likely to fail.

Finally we shall examine the subject of personnel principles and policies. We shall discuss the necessity for creating a set of sound personnel policies and for communicating and applying these throughout the organization.

Ethics and Managerial Philosophy

Ethics, which are a set of moral principles, should play a very significant role in guiding the conduct of managers and employees in the operation of any enterprise. Although there are those who would say that any action that optimizes profit and that conforms to the established laws of the land is justified, such a standard clearly is insufficient.

Benjamin Selekman of Harvard has stated that in recent years businessmen have sought to interpret themselves in a manner that will make our industrial system consistent with American democracy and the Judeo-Christian tradition. He asserts that the recent interest in a moral philosophy is caused by two factors: (1) the hostility directed against business during the Great Depression of the 1930's, and (2) the rise of a professional management class.[1] It might be added that the price-fixing activities, brought to light in 1961, of many of our largest electrical equipment manufacturers in direct violation of federal antitrust laws awakened further interest in business ethics. The old-fashioned "ethics of the market place" are no longer sufficient in our society, if indeed they ever were.

Because the business community exercises such a pervasive influence upon the economic, political, and social life of the American society, the general public has a right to expect high standards of moral conduct not only from business executives as individuals but also from the corporation itself as an entity. A chief executive officer cannot absolve his corporation from accountability for the acts of major executives who behave in a grossly improper fashion simply by saying that they violated company policy.

---

[1] Benjamin M. Selekman, *A Moral Philosophy for Management* (New York: McGraw-Hill Book Company, Inc., 1959) pp. 4-5.

There are countless situations arising every day in the big corporation that put individuals to the test of ethical conduct. These are but a few:

1. Although management has a legal right to discharge a long service employee who violated a certain company rule, should it do so in the instant case?
2. Are the advertising claims for a particular consumer product likely to mislead the public?
3. Is it proper for a top executive of a corporation to own a controlling interest in a principal supplier?
4. Does a large corporation that is the principal source of employment in a town have any moral duty to consider carefully the impact of its planned factory shutdown upon the town's economy and the lives of the population?
5. Is it ethical to seek actively to destroy the local union with which the employees have cast their lot because it interferes with the unrestrained operation of the business?

From what source can executives derive a code of moral principles? It must be clear that these cannot be created in a vacuum. They must be derived from the generally accepted doctrines that mankind have evolved over the years since the beginning of recorded history. With these doctrines and codes as a foundation, management can develop specific ethical standards that may be applied to its particular business. Thomas G. Spates, in writing on this subject, has enumerated the principle milestones of civilization which lay down standards of conduct. He has written as follows:

> Some of the luminous milestones along the path of progress toward the civilization of man are:
> The Mosaic Ten Commandments.
> The Ethical Code of Confucianism.
> The Athenian Principles of Democracy and Individual Excellence.
> The Sermon on the Mount.
> The Roman Codes of Secular Law and Moral Equity.
> The British conception of individual justice under law and an incorrupt civil service to assure fair play to those within its jurisdiction.
> The Virginia Bill of Rights, with its Article XV, which reads: That no free Government, or the Blessing of Liberty, can be preserved to any People but by firm Adherence to Justice, Moderation, Temperance, Frugality, and Virtue, and by frequent Recurrence to fundamental Principles.
> The Declaration of Independence with its appeal to laws of nature and its Proclamation of inalienable Rights.
> The First Amendment to our Constitution, providing freedom of religion, speech, press, assembly and the right to petition for redress of grievances.

The General Principles of Social Justice embodied in Part XIII of the Treaty of Versailles, establishing the International Labour Organization.

The "Atlantic Charter" of August 1941, in which Great Britain and the United States announced Eight Principles upon which to base a better future for the world.

The United Nations Declaration of Universal Human Rights.[2]

ORGANIZATION OBJECTIVES

The objectives of an organization are the results it wants to achieve. In place of the term *objectives* executives sometimes speak of the terms *goals* or *purposes*. These three words are essentially synonymous when used in this context.

It is important that the leaders of an organization establish clearly its objectives and that the members of that organization agree upon these as desirable ends to be achieved. In democratically oriented organizations the members are expected to help shape the objectives.

Why is it important that the objectives of an organization be clearly established and agreed upon? There are many reasons for this.

1. Human beings are goal-directed. People must have a purpose. They must have something to work for. Announced organizational goals provide meaning to work.
2. Objectives serve as standards against which to measure performance.
3. If the participants in the organization have been sufficiently educated so that they believe in the objectives, then there is less need for close control of their behavior. Such education promotes voluntary cooperation and coordination. Self-regulated behavior is achieved.
4. Objectives stand out as guidelines for organizational performance. They help set the tone for action by participants. They also help establish the "character" of the organization.

Objectives of the Business Enterprise

In our discussion of organizational objectives, we shall concentrate upon the business enterprise because it stands as the cornerstone of productive activity in our society.

Fallacy of Profit as Sole Objective.   Oftentimes we will hear an employer or business executive assert that the only justification for the existence of his company is to make a profit. This is lauded as the noblest of business objectives and is held to be consistent with the statement of Adam Smith, who described capitalism as a system in which every individual must have freedom to pursue his own economic self-interest and

---

[2] Thomas G. Spates, *Human Values Where People Work* (New York: Harper & Row, 1960), pp. 204-205. Reprinted by permission.

that in so acting the natural forces of competition would take hold to achieve the best interests for society as a whole. In talking in this vein the businessman may concede that his company has certain responsibilities it must meet, but these are all viewed as distinctly subsidiary to the primary goal of profit.

If a man should start his own business concern and if he is the sole proprietor, his goal very likely may be to make as good a living for himself and his family as possible. In deciding whether he is making a good living he would undoubtedly lump together the salary he draws from the business with the profit. Our sole proprietor may have subsidiary motives, such as engaging in a kind of business he enjoys and achieving respect from his employees and from the general public, but all in all, economic gain is still probably his most important goal.

Now if a business becomes incorporated and a number of shareholders acquire interests in the firm, then there is a tendency for the executives in charge to assume that the primary objective of operating the corporation is to make profits for these owners. This condition often prevails when the members of one family are major stockholders and are also active in the management.

But when a corporation grows substantially in size, when the ownership becomes diffused among many stockholders, none of whom possesses a controlling interest, and when the direction of its affairs is entrusted to a group of hired professional managers, we can say that the situation has changed substantially, Especially is the situation changed when we are talking about a medium- or large-sized corporation that represents a concentration of great economic, social, and political power. Such a corporation may be the principal source of jobs, the major payer of property taxes, and, through its purchasing function, a major consumer in the area. As a group the managers may occupy positions of leadership in such organizations as the school boards of education, community chest, service clubs, charitable institutions, and religious bodies. Thus the corporation may directly and indirectly exert vast power in a community, a region, or even the nation. The national influence is especially apparent in the case of large corporations that have plants throughout the country and in the case of large corporations that do a substantial portion of their business with the Federal government.

Proper Role of Profits.   For the modern corporation profits are not an end in themselves. Profit is no more the sole goal of a corporation than is eating the sole goal of man. Profits, like food, are necessary for the continued existence of a business in a free enterprise economy. It must make profits to attract investment capital. Profit should be looked upon (1) as an incentive to produce goods or to perform services, and (2) as one important guide for measuring the success of a firm.

However, profit and related monetary measures, such as costs and sales, should not be used as the sole measures of performance in an organization. Rensis Likert has presented some convincing arguments for using other measures in addition to these. He maintains that management can show a very favorable record in the short run by using pressure-oriented supervision and close controls when measured by conventional performance figures of output, costs, and profits. But the good record may be achieved at the expense of a depletion of human resources so that in the long run the whole organization may suffer. In addition to employing the usual measures of profits, costs, product quality, and technical efficiency, Likert argues in favor of evaluating the performance of an organization in terms of such factors as extent of member loyalty, extent to which the organization's objectives are compatible with members' own goals, level of members' motivation, amount of anxiety felt by people in the organization, character of the decision-making process, and adequacy of the communication process.[3]

Goals of a Modern Publicly Owned Corporation

Whereas the tendency formerly was to view the objectives of the corporation solely from the standpoint of its owners, now scholars and business executives conceive of the matter in much broader terms. A business enterprise has multiple goals and multiple interest groups who are intimately involved and who have legitimate rights and interests. The stockholders want a good return on their investment, the employees want job security and adequate wages, the customers want a product or service of specified quality, delivered on time and at a fair price. Suppliers want the firm to treat them fairly and pay prices that permit them to exist, and the community expects the modern company to be a good corporate "citizen" and to use its power in a way that advances the interests of the general public. The professional managers who direct the affairs of the enterprise are expected to balance the interests of all parties to the best advantage of all.

It is pretty widely recognized that a business corporation really has multiple objectives. These may be viewed in the framework presented in the preceding paragraph, in which it is held that the corporation seeks to serve the wants and needs of the various interest groups that are vitally affected by it. Eells and Walton have expressed the objectives of the corporation as (1) profit making, (2) service, (3) social responsibility, and (4) survival.[4]

In *The New Industrial State* John K. Galbraith devotes his attention to the very large American corporations and their interaction with our economic system. He has coined the term "technostructure" to designate

---

[3] Rensis Likert, *New Patterns of Management* (New York: McGraw-Hill Book Company, Inc., 1961), Chs. 5 and 13.

[4] Richard Eells and Clarence Walton, *Conceptual Foundations of Business* (Homewood, Ill.: Richard D. Irwin, Inc., 1961), pp. 432-435.

that complex whole of managers, staff experts, professionals (engineers and scientists), and administrators who really make the key decisions and control the affairs of the corporation. From the standpoint of the technostructure the goals of the corporation in rank order priority are (1) survival and a secure level of earnings; (2) greatest possible rate of growth as measured in sales; (3) technological virtuosity that creates new products, jobs, and customers; and (4) social goals such as building a better community, schools, public health and the like.[5]

Figure 2-1 contains an illustration of one company's beliefs or creed and its objectives.

Social Responsibilities.   Increasingly in recent years spokesmen for business and for the public have emphasized that business firms must bear substantial social responsibilities. We live in a very interdependent world. Urban crises, racial riots, air and water pollution, strikes, plant shutdowns, and expansions of employment all have significant impacts upon both business and the general public. Few would now deny that private industry has a real stake in the welfare of the people and the nation. The enthusiasm with which big businessmen across the country contributed to the National Alliance of Businessmen, which was launched in 1968 to help solve the problem of the hard core unemployed, attests to this recognition of their real social responsibilities.

The social responsibilities of a corporation range all the way from concern for proper and just treatment of its employees, to concern for the consumers of its products (Are they safe and reliable?), to the community institutions (schools, government, and hospitals).

Nonbusiness Organizations

When we think of nonbusiness organizations we refer to such entities as government, the military, schools and colleges, hospitals, and charitable and philanthropic foundations. The profit motive does not exist in such institutions. Generally the motive of service to the organization's constituents is paramount. Other goals may be survival, growth, economy of operation, efficiency, and stability. But just as with the corporation, the goals are multiple, not unitary.

MANAGING PEOPLE AT WORK

The way that managers treat and deal with their subordinates in order to accomplish the multiple objectives of the organization is determined

[5] John Kenneth Galbraith, *The New Industrial State* (Boston: Houghton Mifflin Company, 1967). Galbraith asserts that profit maximization is not a goal of the technostructure because it does not benefit this group once a level of earnings has been achieved that is sufficient to placate the stockholders. For the technostructure growth is all important because it benefits this group with more jobs, more promotions, and more pay.

CROWN CORK & SEAL COMPANY, INC.

STATEMENT OF BELIEFS AND OBJECTIVES

Foreword

Individuals and organizations hold many beliefs. These beliefs provide the bases for the results we seek to achieve and guide our plans, policies, and procedures in seeking achievement.

Because beliefs can vary so, and can be misunderstood and misinterpreted, we all have a need to understand what we seek to achieve. To that end, we are publishing these statements of our beliefs and objectives.

STATEMENT OF BELIEFS

This We Believe:

That a business enterprise is a living, functioning institution, existing to perform a needed, satisfactory service.

That a business enterprise does not exist solely for the benefit of any one group, neither customers, nor stockholders, nor employees, nor public, but that the benefits for all groups must be in balance and that the resulting benefits are the products of a well-run business.

That the rights, interests, and obligations of these groups are inseparable.

That our opportunities in the Company carry with them great responsibilities, both economic and social.

That these obligations and responsibilities require from each of us a high degree of competence and performance in our jobs, and a high order of good citizenship.

That our individual and our Company relationships should be governed by the highest standards of conduct and ethics.

That within this Creed, we should devote our efforts toward achieving and maintaining a position of acknowledged leadership in industry.

That to meet our responsibilities and to reach a position of leadership, we must strive constantly to achieve these objectives:

STATEMENT OF OBJECTIVES

General:

1. Generate proper return on investment through profits adequate to provide security for employees, customers, stockholders, and suppliers.
2. Increase sales returns by greater efficiencies in manufacturing, distribution, and administration.
3. Produce a satisfactory and continuous volume of products for sale with minimum production cycles to assure maximum efficiency and equipment utilization; maintain inventories consistent with good customer service, sound economic practices and manufacturing procedures; and develop firm long-term commitments to cover the requirements of major customers so that a continuity of efficient plant operations and minimum labor turnover can be achieved.
4. Maintain plans for converting promptly and smoothly the Company's activities to meet emergency conditions in the event of mobilization or war.

Customers:

1. Offer products and services of unexcelled quality at the lowest possible prices consistent with an adequate return.
2. Strive to obtain the maximum possible share of available markets for our products.
3. Create new and enlarged markets by contributing and developing new and improved products and new uses for existing products.

Figure 2-1. The Statement of Beliefs and Objectives of the Crown Cork and Seal Company, Inc. taken from Stewart Thompson, *Management Creeds and Philosophies,* Research Study Number 32 (New York; American Management Association; © 1958), pp. 106-108. Reprinted

4. Foster the Company's reputation for fair dealing, prompt service, dependability, integrity, courtesy, quality of product, productive ability, and technical competence.
5. Provide a source of supply which will insure dependable service and security to those who choose our products.

With Suppliers:

1. Maintain adequate, reliable sources of supply at lowest costs consistent with necessary quality for materials and services.
2. Accord prompt, fair, and courteous treatment to suppliers' representatives.

In Research:

1. Conduct a vigorous program of technical research and development to improve costs of manufacture, quality of products, and to develop new products and new uses for existing products.
2. Conduct marketing research to assist in maintaining and increasing the Company's participation in the available markets, to determine the trends and growth factors in the market, and to make valid forecasts of present and future economic conditions.

With Employees:

1. Establish the view that our greatest assets are our human assets and these must be developed as a matter of moral obligation and material advantage.
2. Reward, encourage progress, fully inform, train and develop, and properly assign all employees in order that their lives and work be given meaning, dignity, satisfaction, and purpose both on and off the job.

With the Public:

1. Foster the Company's position as a good citizen in the communities where it is located and encourage employees to take an active part in making the community and nation a better place in which to live.
2. Cooperate lawfully with similar enterprises and industry generally for mutual betterment.

Crown's management will realize these objectives through the periodic preparation of specific short- and long-term programs, carried out through an effective organization, employing management techniques, methods, and procedures which are proven and based on the principle of decentralized operations governed by uniform policies.

By doing these things well, and in proper balance each with the other, Crown will serve the best interests of its employees, customers, stockholders, and suppliers, and will make a continuing contribution to the public welfare.

by permission of the American Management Association, Inc. and the Crown Cork and Seal Company, Inc.

primarily by management's system of beliefs about the nature of man and about the determinants of cooperation in an organized endeavor. The fundamental assumptions that leaders hold conditions their actions. How will they go about seeking performance from others? Will they trust people? exert tight control? centralize decision-making? Or will they create the conditions by which people can create, achieve, and assume responsibility?

We shall portray two dissimilar frames of reference. One will be called the "traditional" philosophy. Certain principal components of this philosophy have also been referred to as "Theory X," autocratic, and the pessimistic view of man. The other school of thought we shall designate as the "modern" viewpoint. This has also been given such appellations as "Theory Y," supportive management, management by integration and self-control, and the optimistic view of man. It should be clear upon reading these two descriptions that they represent wholly contrasting systems of belief. In actual practice the attitudes and behavior of business executives can be scaled along a continuum. Undoubtedly some clearly belong in the traditional camp, whereas others are entirely in the modern camp; but probably many managers also hold beliefs derived from both schools of thought. Some are also on the middle ground in their attitudes and day-to-day behavior.

Traditional Philosophy

An early and rather widespread view of man is that he is selfish, rebellious, and uncooperative. Left to his own devices he tends to act in a mean and base manner. Therefore, the leader must be ruthless and strict in the way he controls his men, even to the point of harshness. The classic spokesman for this type of reasoning was the Florentine nobleman and political philosopher, Niccolò Machiavelli. He stated that the "end justifies the means." A prince or ruler must put aside such questions as integrity, morality, and honor. He should follow any tactics that will maintain himself in power and preserve the state or the army. Machiavelli asserted that it was desirable for the ruler to *appear* to be straightforward, humane, clement, and trustworthy but that he should always be ready to follow the path of evil if the occasion should arise. He should have a spirit to adapt to the varying winds of fortune.[6]

Thomas Hobbes in his *Leviathan* (1651) asserted that men are acquisitive, and seek power and prestige. They want what their neighbor possesses. Therefore man must submit to the authority and law of a ruler and the state to regulate and constrain these avaricious and selfish tendencies.[7]

[6] Niccolò Machiavelli, *The Prince,* Thomas G. Bergin, trans. (New York: Appleton-Century-Crofts, Inc., 1947). Machiavelli wrote this work in the year 1513.

[7] Thomas Hobbes, *Leviathan* (Indianapolis: The Bobbs-Merrill Company, Inc., 1958).

Another underlying theme has been "social Darwinism" or survival of the fittest. During the nineteenth century Herbert Spencer, the British philosopher, derived social implications from Charles Darwin's biological theory. He preached the doctrines of individualism, liberty of action, and survival of the fittest. He claimed that the weak, the infirm, and the intemperate must fall by the wayside. Ultimately only superior human beings would survive. This process would evolve toward a superior type of society.

The ideas which Adam Smith propounded in his *Wealth of Nations* in 1776 have served for nearly two hundred years as the basis of our capitalistic system. He argued that the wealth of a nation was best served when everyone pursued his own self-interest in the utilization of his energy and capital. Government should not interfere in the economic system. Each man may seek as much private gain as possible, but the forces of competition in a free market will serve as a self-regulating mechanism. According to Adam Smith the "invisible hand" of the market place, that is supply and demand and the price mechanism, provided a just allocation of scarce resources. Like Spencer, Smith glorified individualism and the pursuit of one's self-interest. Unrestrained competition and profit maximization ultimately resulted in the public good even though the individual entrepreneur sought only his own private gain.

In the field of employment relationships there are many who maintain that the company is in business to make a profit. The strongest and best-run firms survive; the inefficient ones fail. Likewise, among employees, individualistic competition is emphasized. The rewards go to the best producers, who are retained and promoted; those who are less efficient are demoted, laid off, or discharged.

In a capitalistic society in the Western world, the basic moral values to be derived from hard work, self-denial, saving, and pursuit of monetary gain have been preached, directly or indirectly, over the years. Max Weber has written a classic study in tracing the blending of the ideas of capitalism and those of Protestantism. In certain regions of Europe and in the United States this synthesis has resulted in the practice of the aforementioned behavior. It has been considered a necessary virtue. This philosophy has been called the Protestant Ethic.[8]

During the late nineteenth and early twentieth centuries a great deal of both fiction and nonfiction was written publicizing the assertion that those who rose to the top in industry did so because of hard work, perseverance, superior innate abilities, and greater energy. It was felt that abundant opportunity existed in America for anyone to achieve personal and economic success if he tried hard enough. If a man did not succeed in the business world, if he forever remained a laborer or a clerk, it was because he was lazy, noncompetitive, and unimaginative.

[8] Max Weber, *The Protestant Ethic and the Spirit of Capitalism* (New York: Charles Scribner's Sons, 1930).

Man in the Organization.   According to Douglas McGregor the traditional managerial view regarding people in a work organization is that the average worker has an inherent dislike of work, avoids responsibility, lacks ambition, and wants to be closely directed. Faced with this fundamental "fact" the only course open to management is to exercise close control and to coerce and threaten workers in order to get them to exert sufficient effort to attain organizational objectives. McGregor has labeled this managerial philosophy, "Theory X."[9] In fact, if managers continually treat their subordinates as if these assumptions are actually true, this pattern of management can be self-validating. If one deals with his subordinates as if they are indolent shirkers who cannot be trusted to behave responsibly, then they will tend to act that way, especially in an authoritarian environment.

A basic tenet of the traditional point of view is that the authority of the employer is supreme, that authority is synonymous with power, and that authority comes from the top and is transmitted down through the organization structure. Authority and controls are the basic integrating force. Control is exercised through command. The power and right to make decisions must be centralized at the top.

In such a system the front-line supervisor is viewed as an agent of higher management. His job is to obtain obedience to orders received from his own boss. He tells his subordinates what to do and how to do it. He is expected to exercise close supervision over their activities. He tends to be highly production-centered, not people-oriented. The supervisor is expected to meet production goals, control costs, and maintain proper product quality.

Efficiency is enhanced when the organization is carefully defined and when job duties and responsibilities are clearly specified. Employees are expected to assume neither fewer nor more responsibilities than contained in their job descriptions. Maximum efficiency is achieved when policies, procedures, rules, and methods are clearly spelled out. The emphasis is upon fitting the man to the job rather than adapting the job to the man. Standardized, predictable performance is the goal. This is the essence of the bureaucratic model of organization.

The motives of man that are tapped are primarily the lower order needs: physical and economic security. In practice people are induced to produce through "the carrot and the stick." This means monetary incentives on the one hand and threats, fear, and the spector of discharge on the other hand. The response of the employees to such leadership can be either hostility or docile compliance. Actually those who rebel against authoritarian leadership tend to drift away from the organization; those who remain respond in a conforming sort of manner. They learn to accept it and gain certain economic and security satisfactions. They occupy

[9] Douglas McGregor, *The Human Side of Enterprise* (New York: McGraw-Hill Book Company, 1960), Ch. 3.

a dependency relationship to their superiors and to the employer generally.

Authoritarian or Theory X management is very widespread and pervasive. It is standard in all military forces and is very common in private business, industry, and in government bureaucracy. It often is effective in achieving performance up to a certain level. It frequently achieves satisfactory results especially in the short run. But it seldom elicits real enthusiastic response from the organization members. High achievement, creativity, and a feeling of self-responsibility are sacrificed in favor of a moderate level of predictable and regimented performance.

Paternalism. A fairly common variant of traditional, autocratic management is paternalism. This is basically benevolent autocracy. Management treats its employees well by providing job security, decent working conditions, and adequate pay. In return the employees are expected to be cooperative, loyal, and productive. A dependency relationship is created. The organization members are expected to be docile and do what they are told. As long as they stay in their place, they will be taken care of adequately. But the people are not expected to stand on their own two feet and make decisions for themselves. There is little delegation of authority and responsibility in a paternalistic enterprise. As in the bureaucratic autocracy, decision-making and influence are tightly held at the top. In the paternalistic enterprise people are taught to expect that the organization will take care of them in time of trouble, if they themselves have been loyal to the organization.

Role of the Union. Traditionalists in management generally do not accord a real place for a union in their thinking. They tend to feel that the authority of management should be supreme and that if a union represents the employees, it will try to restrict management's freedom of action. If a union has won bargaining rights and certification as a result of a National Labor Relations Board election, then management will certainly recognize the union and bargain over wages, hours, and other conditions of employment as required by law, but there will be no attempt by management to open up to bilateral determination any subjects that are not absolutely required by law. In effect the union will be confined to as small a role in the affairs of the business as possible.

Modern Philosophy

The modern philosophy of management is based upon an optimistic view of the nature of man. He is considered to be potentially creative, trustworthy, and cooperative. He is not inherently predatory. Man is not predisposed by inheritance or instinct to be either mean or good. Rather his behavior reflects the character of his life experiences as he matures. Man has potential for growth, achievement, and constructive action with others. It is the job of management to nurture and tap man's productive drives.

The writings of such behavioral scientists as Douglas McGregor,[10] Rensis Likert,[11] Chris Argyris,[12] Frederick Herzberg,[13] and Blake and Mouton[14] are richly illustrative of this modern school of management thought. This philosophy is somewhat ahead of actual practice in industry, although executives in the more progressive organizations are generally familiar with these ideas on the intellectual level and some have applied them in their day-to-day activities. As indicated previously this pattern of management has been variously called "Theory Y," supportive management, and management by integration and self-control. Rensis Likert calls it "System 4" management.

Advocates of this school of thought hold that people possess innate capacity for exercising initiative, accepting responsibility, and making worth-while contributions. They do not inherently dislike work. Work can be a meaningful, satisfying experience. Employees will actively work for the goals of the organization when such behavior is compatible with their own goals. This demands an integration of the goals of the organization with those of the individual. Commitment to organizational objectives is a function of the rewards associated with their accomplishment. Although external controls may be available, it is felt that the best control of employee behavior is self-control. Management should share information and objectives with subordinates. It is also advised to establish a climate where employees may contribute toward decisions affecting the business in those areas where they possess competence.

What is the role of the front-line supervisor under supportive, or Theory Y, type of leadership? He is expected to build a team which has a strong sense of responsibility for getting work done. He also is expected to represent his group to higher management as well as represent organizational needs to his men. He goes to bat for his people when warranted. He has trust in them and they trust him. He tries to understand their problems. He is both people- and production-centered.

Whereas traditional management depends primarily upon economic motivation and "the carrot and the stick," "Theory Y" holds that all motives—economic, social, and egoistic—must be activated. The employee is most highly motivated to work when the motivation is intrinsic—that

---

[10] *Ibid.*

[11] Likert, *op. cit.; The Human Organization: Its Management and Value* (New York: McGraw-Hill Book Company, 1967).

[12] Chris Argyris, *Personality and Organization* (New York: Harper & Row, 1957); and *Integrating the Individual and the Organization* (New York: John Wiley & Sons, Inc., 1964).

[13] Frederick Herzberg, *Work and the Nature of Man* (Cleveland: The World Publishing Company, 1966).

[14] Robert R. Blake and Jane Mouton, *The Managerial Grid: Key Orientations for Achieving Production Through People* (Houston: Gulf Publishing Company, 1964).

is the person derives satisfaction from doing the work itself. Emphasis is placed upon activating the higher motives of responsibility, recognition, achievement, and innovation. People are taught to accept responsibility and exercise self-control. External discipline and control is minimized when employees and supervisors control their own behavior. They evidence a high degree of commitment to the company and its programs.

Some critics have mistakenly asserted that the style of management we have been describing is soft or ineffective. They say that management relinquishes its responsibility to run the business. Manifestly this charge is not true. Modern supportive management seeks to enlist the full creative energies of all organization members. It is more of an open system. Information is widely not narrowly shared. Under authoritarian leadership the planning and controlling are done by top management and the doing is carried out by the employees. But the more modern approach involves a wider spectrum of members in the planning, doing and controlling processes. Nevertheless management still bears full and final responsibility for guiding the enterprise and achieving results.

How widely have the concepts we have been discussing become accepted by management practitioners? An interesting research project bearing on this subject has been conducted by Haire, Ghiselli, and Porter, all of the University of California. By means of a questionnaire they surveyed the attitudes of 3,000 managers in fourteen different countries throughout the world. They probed four areas of the manager's belief system: (1) belief in the individual's innate capacity of initiative, individual action, and leadership; (2) belief in the value of sharing information and objectives; (3) belief in participative management; and (4) the belief that internal control should be by self-control rather than control by supervisors. The results of their survey revealed a paradoxical condition. Rather generally the managers surveyed believed in shared objectives, participation, and individual control; yet they tended to have serious doubts about the capacity of people to demonstrate initiative, individual action, and leadership. The situation is paradoxical because the first premise above is a precondition for apply concepts 2, 3, and 4. The researchers conclude that their findings reveal a basic lack of confidence in the abilities of other people and that democratic leadership cannot succeed unless executives come to believe that lower level managers are capable of making worthwhile contributions at the decision-making level.[15]

Authority in the organization is viewed in a less absolute manner. The traditionalist maintains that authority is a fixed body of legitimate rights and powers that reside in the board of directors and the president of the organization. These are delegated down through the chain of command as required. The behavioral view is that authority and power become ef-

[15] Mason Haire, Edwin E. Ghiselli, and Lyman W. Porter, "An International Study of Management Attitudes and Democratic Leadership," Symposium Paper A9a, *International Management Congress,* CIOS XIII, 1963.

fective only when people accept it. A manager's influence and ability to get results is highly dependent upon the kind of relationships he builds up with his subordinates, peers, and superiors. Three managers may appear in the same level in the organization chart and yet each may effectively possess quite different amounts of authority and influence.

Management by Objectives.   Part and parcel of the modern philosophy of management is "management by objectives." This concept is a way of combining performance appraisal for managers with a pervasive process of developing and refining organization goals. Goals and specific objectives in terms of such things as profits, output, quality, share of market, and the like are established for the entire organization and for each divsion. These objectives are usually evolved and discussed in meetings of top level executives. At this point appraisal by results is brought into the picture. Each manager sits down in a private discussion with his immediate superior to set his own short term (one year or less) performance goals. This is really mutual goal setting between superior and subordinate. These goals or targets are set in the context of the objectives of the division or department in which the manager works. At the same time specific indicators or measurement criteria are spelled out and agreed upon. Typical objectives for a factory manager might be expressed in terms of such factors as actual production output for a given quarter, scrap losses, budget performance, development plans for his foremen, and safety performance of the plant. In addition the factory manager may plan to participate in an executive development seminar, himself.

By helping set his own performance targets the individual becomes committed to them. This is really management by integration and self-control. Periodically the manager and his superior get together to review progress toward the goals. The role of the boss is more that of a helper than of a judge. This approach is quite different from the traditional one, wherein the president unilaterally imposes his goals upon each of his vice-presidents, they do the same for the department heads, and so on down the line to the lowest level of management.[16]

Role of the Union.   Although not all writers of the modern school discuss unionism, a few do. The newer view accords a more significant role for the union than does the traditional philosophy of management. The union is not looked upon as the "enemy" or as a force that exists to make management's job more difficult. Rather it is recognized that for many sound reasons the union plays a very vital part in representing the interests of the employees. The process of managing the work force in an organization is probably the most important of all management functions. The holding of discussions with elected union leaders to make mutually satisfactory decisions on such issues as wage rates, work loads, trans-

[16] The concept of management by objectives was originally formulated by Peter Drucker in *The Practice of Management* (New York: Harper & Row, 1954), Ch. 11.

fers, safety, and employee suggestions is viewed as a legitimate way of managing the personnel.

In discussing relations between management and the union Benjamin Selekman has said:

> In truth, modern industry is a combined operation for management and labor. It is arrogant for either group to assume that it has a key to supervisor wisdom or morality. They represent adverse as well as common interests. They may differ as to the distribution of proceeds; they agree on the desirability of maximum productivity. And everyone is the greater gainer when both mutual and conflicting interests are recognized and the parties gather around the table to negotiate the best possible agreement in terms of efficiency as well as of social justice.[17]

Traditional Vs. Modern—Which Approach?

It is perhaps safe to say that the vast majority of executives in work organizations throughout the world lean closer to the traditional philosophy of management than to the modern view. This is evidenced by both their beliefs and their practices. Actually it is somewhat more true of their practices than their beliefs. Many profess to believe in self-discipline, self-control, participation, group methods of leadership, management by objectives, development of subordinates' abilities, and the like, yet they continue to deny their people true opportunities for assuming responsibilities and for growing in the organization. Philosophically they hold that they would like to trust people more and grant more discretion to their subordinates; yet they continue to hoard company information and centralize decision making.

It seems reasonable to assume, however, that as the level of education of people in work organizations continues to rise and as more highly talented people enter industry, executives will come to grant greater autonomy and discretion to their people. Also as younger generations of managers rise in the business world, they will gradually apply more of these concepts of modern management, which they absorbed while in college and from participation in management education programs.

PERSONNEL POLICIES

A policy is a plan of action. It is a statement of intention committing management to a general course of action. When management drafts a policy statement to cover some feature of its personnel program that statement may often contain an expression of philosophy and principle as well. Although it is perfectly legitimate for an organization to include phi-

[17] Benjamin M. Selekman, *A Moral Philosophy for Management* (New York: McGraw-Hill Book Company, Inc., 1959), p. 59. Reprinted by permission.

losophy, principles, and policy in one policy expression, it is well for the thoughtful student of personnel management to be able to separate the expression of principle from the policy statement.

The following is a statement of principle or objective in regard to the health and safety of company personnel:

> It is the intention of the company to provide a safe plant and a healthful working environment.

It can readily be seen that such a statement is quite general. A policy statement on the other hand is more specific. It commits management to a rather definite course of action, as shown in the following statement:

> Our policy is to institute every practical method for engineering safety into our processes and equipment, to provide protective clothing where necessary, to train employees in safe operating procedures, and to vigorously enforce established safety rules. Our policy is to provide a healthful plant by giving adequate attention to cleanliness, temperature, ventilation, light, and sanitation.

A policy does not spell out the detailed procedures by which it is to be implemented. That is the role of a *procedure*. A procedure is really a method for carrying out a policy. A policy should be stated in terms broad enough for it to be applicable to varying situations. Lower-level managers who apply policy must be allowed some discretion in carrying out the policy. The circumstances in Department A may differ from those in Department B; hence a rigid, excessively detailed, policy statement might cause an injustice if supervision is not granted some latitude.

Why Adopt Definite Policies?

Many organizations of all types have never created a set of personnel policies. Top management has never been sufficiently aware of the hazards of operating without them nor of the advantages to be gained from establishing a sound group of policies. Why should an organization have clearly established policies?

1. The work involved in formulating personnel policies requires that management give deep thought to the basic needs of both the organization and the employees. Management must examine its basic convictions as well as give full consideration to prevailing practice in other organizations.
2. Established policies assure consistent treatment of all personnel throughout the organization. Favoritism and discrimination are thereby minimized.
3. Continuity of action is assured even though top management personnel change. The president of a company may possess a very sound per-

sonnel management philosophy, he may carry the policies of the organization in his head, and he may apply them in an entirely fair manner. But what happens when he retires or resigns? The tenure of office of any manager is finite. But the organization continues. Policies promote stability.

4. Policies serve as a standard of performance. Actual results can be compared with the policy to determine how well the members of the organization are living up to professed intentions.

5. Sound policies help to build employee enthusiasm and loyalty. This is especially true where the policies reflect established principles of fair play and justice and where they help people grow within the organization.

Policies Should Be in Writing

Although this proposition may seem self-evident, countless companies have never bothered to reduce their practices, customs, and traditions to writing. In fact many executives actually are opposed to writing the personnel policies on paper and disseminating them to all concerned. They contend that such action would tie their hands and limit their freedom of action. Now if these executives mean that it would prevent the continued application of expediency and inequitable treatment, the answer is yes, it would. But if they reject management by expediency and intend to abide by reasonable principles, then the answer is no. Written policies do not so tie the hands of management that it cannot use some discretion and flexibility in handling particular cases. Policies are stated in broad terms. They are designed to aid the operation of the business, not impede it.

Written policies let everyone know just what kind of treatment he can expect to receive from management. It lets him know where he stands. Only when policies are reduced to writing can they be communicated to all employees.

In large organizations containing many dispersed plants, written policies are almost a necessity. They insure reasonably consistent treatment throughout the company on such matters as pay, promotion, transfer, layoff, pension rights, insurance benefits, training opportunities, and grievance handling.

Formulating Personnel Policies

If the chief executive officer of a company should decide that the time has come to prepare a comprehensive statement of personnel policies, what should the content be? How does management decide what its wage policy or its hiring policy should be? Policies are not created in a vacuum. There are five principal sources for determining the content and meaning of policies. These are (1) past practice in the organization, (2) prevailing practice among other companies in the community and throughout the nation in the same industry, (3) the attitudes and philosophy of the board of directors and top management, (4) the attitudes and philosophy of middle and lower management, and (5) the knowledge and experience gained from handling countless personnel problems on a day-to-day basis.

Because people are free to resign from their jobs and take employment elsewhere and because any company must make its employment opportunities attractive enough to recruit new people into the business, management must so design its personnel policies that they reflect current good practice. If all other companies grant two weeks of paid vacation after a year's employment, then it would be unsound for a firm to grant no paid vacation. Likewise if prevailing practice is to pay a 10 per cent premium to those who work the evening and midnight shifts, then a company that hopes to attract and retain qualified people must do something similar.

The actual work of formulating the written expressions of company personnel policy generally will be done by the personnel (or industrial relations) director. He will study existing documents, survey industry and community practices, and interview other executives within the organization to collect appropriate information. The actual and final decisions on the substantive content will, in most instances, be made by the president and the board of directors. Although the entire statement of personnel policy could be prepared by a very small group at the top of the structure or even by the president alone, there is considerable merit to the practice of bringing members of middle management (or even lower management in very small organizations) into the deliberations. These people can make particularly valuable contributions when it comes to evaluating the advantages and disadvantages of existing practices. And, of course, if these members of the management team are consulted, they will tend to support the fruits of their efforts when it comes to applying the policies.

Communicating Policies

The statement of the personnel policies does little good if it is locked in the company president's desk. It must be communicated throughout the organization.

All members of management, including shop foremen and office supervisors, are vitally concerned, because they must interpret and apply the policies. Not only must the policies be communicated to all management personnel, but also a real education program should be set up to teach them how to handle various personnel problems in the light of the newly enunciated policy. A policy is worth while only when it is carried out on a day-to-day basis.

The most common way of informing nonsupervisory employees is by means of the employee handbook. But to achieve real understanding this should be followed up with an oral explanation and interpretation generally by first-line supervision.

Questions for Review and Discussion

1. What role should ethics play in the management of a business corporation?
2. Discuss possible ethical implications of the following:
   a. Employment of friends and relatives in the company.
   b. Charging certain of the president's living costs to the company. (Assume he is a majority stockholder.)
   c. Management actions during a union-organizing campaign.
   d. Behavior of junior executives when all are actively competing for promotion in the company.
   e. Granting increases in pay to salaried employees.
3. Why is it desirable for management to establish clearly the objectives of the organization?
4. Discuss the role of profit in the context of corporation objectives.
5. How do the goals of the family-owned company typically differ from those of the large, professionally managed, publicly owned corporation?
6. How might top management of a corporation translate a concern for social problems in the community into action?
7. Describe the "traditional" concepts of the nature of man and the ways of managing people in a work organization.
8. Describe the "modern" philosophy of the management of people.
9. What is "management by objectives"?
10. Why should an organization establish a definite set of personnel policies? Why should they be in writing?
11. Do policy statements "tie the hands" of management?
12. From what sources may the content and meaning of policies be derived?

CASE PROBLEM

Miss Carson, having just finished her junior year in college, obtained a summer job as a teller in the branch office of the Central City Commercial Bank. She was majoring in social science in college. This was her second summer with the bank; however, she was new to this particular branch.

This branch office was located in a declining commercial-residential section of the city. Much of the housing was substandard and a substantial number of the residents were either retired and subsisting on their monthly Social Security checks, or else they were living on meager incomes or on welfare.

The first month on the job was uneventful as Miss Carson became adjusted to the routines of cashing checks, processing deposits, counting money, and reconciling the day's figures. Her relations with bank customers, fellow employees, and her supervisor were cordial.

One of the many services provided by this bank was that of a collection agent for the Mid-State Gas and Electric Company so that residents could conveniently pay their monthly bills. Miss Carson observed that invariably power company customers paid their bills about the second week of each month and that they were required to pay a 5 per cent penalty. The power company bills stipulated this penalty on all accounts paid after the first of the month. When she advised a number of individuals that they could save this penalty charge by paying before the first day of the month, they explained that they could not afford to pay their electric bills until they had received their welfare or Social Security checks. These usually arrived on the third or fourth day of each month. Miss Carson felt that these unfortunate people were not in a position to readily pay the 5 per cent penalty and that they were caught up in a huge impersonal system.

Having a social conscience and a desire to help these poor customers in some small way, Miss Carson decided to write a letter to the Mid-State Gas and Electric Company. She wrote the letter on her own time at home one evening and addressed it simply to the "President" of the power firm. In the letter she pointed out that a great many of the persons paying their bills at this particular bank were impoverished and were subsisting on either Social Security or welfare checks that arrived on the third or fourth day of the month. It would be very desirable if his company could change the date before which bills must be paid, without incurring a 5 per cent penalty, from the first to the tenth day of the month. Miss Carson closed her letter by saying that this slight adjustment in the due date would probably cause little difficulty to the Gas and Electric Company but that it could give company officials a real sense of satisfaction by knowing that they had helped many unfortunate people in the community.

Miss Carson never received a direct reply from the Mid-State Company. Instead, about ten days later, she was summoned to see Mr. Webster, the personnel director, at the main office of the Central City Commercial Bank. It was Mr. Webster who had hired her both last summer and this one and Miss Carson had always considered him a warm, friendly person. She was unprepared for the harshness of his manner at this time.

Mr. Webster told her that the bank president had just received a letter from the president of the Mid-State Company threatening to remove its bill collection business (and possibly all its accounts) from the bank and to place it with a competitor bank because of the improper letter one of the bank's employees (Miss Carson) had sent to him. The Mid-State president had considered it impertinent for one of the bank's employees to tell it to change its business practices for the convenience of certain customers whose cause Miss Carson chose to champion. Mr. Webster told Miss Carson that this was a very grave matter and that she must immediately write a letter of apology to the Mid-State president. Failure to do so would make it necessary for him to discharge her.

After recovering from her initial shock at the storm that had been raised over her simple letter, she countered by stating that she thought large companies ought to be socially conscious and responsive to the problems of people in the community. Mr. Webster replied that a private business was not a social welfare agency. He further stated that it was inappropriate to discuss social issues at this time. The problem at hand was the threat to the bank's relations with an important account. Would she or would she not write the letter?

Miss Carson complied with this order and drafted a letter in Mr. Webster's office. His secretary immediately typed it for Miss Carson's signature.

Miss Carson went back to her job as a teller at the branch office and finished out the summer. Nothing more was said of the incident.

Questions

1. Was it improper for Miss Carson to send the letter which she did to the president of the gas and electric company? Discuss.
2. Evaluate the reaction of the president of the gas and electric company to her letter. How would you have reacted?
3. Evaluate the response of the president of the Central City Commercial Bank and particularly that of Mr. Webster in this case.
4. Is a social conscience on the part of the management of a private business enterprise compatible with traditional business practices?

Suggestions for Further Reading

Baumhart, Raymond, *An Honest Profit,* New York: Holt, Rinehart and Winston, 1968.

Childs, Marquis W., and Douglas Cater, *Ethics in a Business Society,* New York: Harper & Row, 1954.

Eells, Richard, and Clarence Walton, *Conceptual Foundations of Business,* Homewood, Illinois: Richard D. Irwin, 1961.

Henderson, Hazel, "Should Business Tackle Society's Problems?," *Harvard Business Review,* Vol. 46, No. 4, July-August 1968, pp. 77-85.

Knowles, Henry P. and Borje O. Saxberg, "Human Relations and the Nature of Man," *Harvard Business Review,* Vol. 45, No. 2, March-April 1967, pp. 22-24 +.

Likert, Rensis, *The Human Organization: Its Management and Value,* New York: McGraw-Hill Book Company, 1967.

————, *New Patterns of Management,* New York: McGraw-Hill Book Company, 1961.

McConkey, Dale D., "Results-Oriented Personnel Management," *Personnel Administration,* Vol. 30, No. 3, May-June 1967, pp. 6-11.

McGregor, Douglas, *The Human Side of Enterprise,* New York: McGraw-Hill Book Company, 1960.

————, *The Professional Manager,* New York: McGraw-Hill Book Company, 1967.

Scott, William G., *Human Relations in Management: A Behavioral Science Approach,* Homewood, Illinois: Richard D. Irwin, 1962, Chapter 1.

Selekman, Benjamin, *A Moral Philosophy for Management,* New York: McGraw-Hill Book Company, 1959.

Seybold, Geneva, *Statements of Personnel Policy,* Studies in Personnel Policy, No. 169, New York: National Industrial Conference Board, 1959.

Thompson, Stewart, *Management Creeds and Philosophies,* Research Study Number 32. New York: American Management Association, 1958.

Wikstrom, Walter S., "Management by Objectives or Appraisal by Results," *The Conference Board Record,* Vol. 3, No. 7, July 1966, pp. 27-31.

The Personnel Function

3

The work of personnel management pervades the entire organization. Personnel work must be carried on in the company too small to justify a separate personnel department. In larger establishments that do contain personnel departments, personnel management activities are performed by both operating managers and by the staff personnel unit.

In this chapter we shall explore the terminology common to this field of endeavor, the personnel functions performed in organizations, the staff role of the personnel-industrial relations department, the division of authority and responsibility between line management and the staff personnel department in regard to the principal personnel functions, and organization of the personnel unit.

TERMINOLOGY

Over the years there has been some diversity in industrial practice in naming the function that is concerned with handling employment relationships. When specialized departments were first created in the 1920's and 1930's to handle the administration of the personnel program, they were usually called personnel departments. As a result of the rapid growth of unions in the 1930's and 1940's, many companies added the responsibilities of assisting at labor contract negotiations, contract administration, and grievance handling to the other activities of the personnel department.

When this labor relations activity was combined with the personnel management work, many companies adopted the term *industrial relations* to apply to the new, enlarged function. This practice became especially prevalent in manufacturing companies, where the word *industrial* implied the concept of manufacturing and hence was deemed appropriate. In government, in hospitals and schools, and in nonmanufacturing industries such as trade and finance the term personnel department is very commonly used. This term is employed even when the employees are represented by a union and the labor relations function is prominent.

Another frequently encountered term is *employee relations.* In current practice, then, the three terms—*personnel management, industrial relations,* and *employee relations*—are generally synonymous. If we wish to make fine distinctions, we can say that industrial relations is most often used in manufacturing firms especially where the employees are heavily unionized and labor-management relations represents a substantial portion of the total function. The term personnel department or personnel office is used more commonly in nonmanufacturing organizations and in organizations where either the workers are nonunion or only a moderate portion are unionized. Employee relations is often applied to both union and nonunion situations and to manufacturing and nonmanufacturing.

What is the content of this work? What functions are included under the designation industrial relations or personnel management? It encompasses the activities of employment, manpower planning, employee training and management development, organization planning, wage and salary administration, health and safety, benefits and services, labor-management relations, and personnel research.

Looking at the matter from the standpoint of a field of knowledge or an academic discipline, one finds that the terms *personnel management* or *personnel administration* have become widely accepted to designate that field concerned with personnel policies and programs; employee selection, training, and compensation; benefits and services; supervision of the workforce; motivation, leadership, and work group behavior; communication in the organization; and related human relations areas.

There are many departments, institutes, and schools of industrial relations (or industrial and labor relations) at colleges and universities throughout the country. These units carry on research, teaching, and extension programs in the whole broad areas of labor economics, human relations (often now called organizational behavior), collective bargaining, labor law, income security, personnel administration, and labor union history and administration.

In order to be most accurate in describing this function or field of work in the business organization, it would perhaps be best to use the combined term "personnel management-industrial relations." For the sake of conciseness we shall use the term "personnel management" (or just "personnel") and the term "industrial relations" interchangeably.

WHO DOES PERSONNEL WORK?

The very small company that employs say twenty-five or fifty people has no personnel department. Personnel policies and practices are generated by the president. Line management does the hiring, the training, the disciplining, and the firing. It establishes the rates of pay. Because the problems of production and sales usually seem more pressing to the employer, he generally does not develop a well-rounded, comprehensive personnel program. Decisions regarding employees are commonly made under the pressure of the situation without full regard for the long-run consequences.

In the larger organization it is not possible for the president and his line managers to handle adequately the many complex personnel management problems without specialized knowledge and help. Therefore, a personnel department must be established.

Now to the unsophisticated person it may seem that the creation of a separate staff personnel department is no different than the establishment of any other staff or service activity, such as engineering, purchasing, or advertising. If a company has grown to the point where functionalization becomes necessary, it can split off all product and equipment design work from line management and concentrate these duties in an engineering department. All relations with suppliers and the processing of purchase orders can be centralized in a purchasing department.

But personnel management is different from other staff specializations. Personnel management pervades the entire organization. Every individual who guides and directs the work of others from the shop foreman all the way up to the corporation president does personnel work. Now the nature of this work changes somewhat as one goes up the ladder of the organization structure. But regardless of level, every manager is truly a practicing personnel manager.

Consider for a moment the personnel management responsibilities of a first-line supervisor whether in factory or office. They are as follows:

Participate in the selection of new employees
Orient new employees to their environment, organizational requirements, and their rights and privileges
Train employees
Provide face-to-face leadership
Appraise performance
Coach and correct
Counsel
Recommend pay increases, promotions, transfers, layoffs, and discharges
Enforce rules and maintain discipline
Settle complaints and grievances

Interpret and communicate management policies and directives to employees

Interpret and communicate employee suggestions and criticisms to higher management

Motivate subordinates and provide rewards for good performance and behavior

Eliminate hazards and insure safe working practices

It is not truly possible to separate the human relations and personnel functions of operating management from day-to-day problems of getting out production, controlling costs, and meeting quality standards. Many personnel problems arise during the course of directing the work force and giving orders and instructions.

Staff Role of the Personnel Department

The personnel (or industrial relations) department operates in an auxiliary, advisory, or facilitative relationship to other departments in the organization. Any staff unit, whether it be personnel or otherwise, exists to help the line or operating departments do their work more effectively. It has been created in the first place to take advantage of specialized talent and knowledge.[1]

The personnel department generally performs the following functions:

1. Policy initiation and formulation.
2. Advice.
3. Service.
4. Control.

Let us examine each of these activities.

Policy Initiation and Formulation.   The executive in charge of the personnel department (he may be called the personnel director, the industrial relations director, or the vice-president in charge of personnel) is the one individual most actively involved in policy creation. It is his responsibility to propose and draft new policies or policy revisions to cover recurring problems or to prevent anticipated problems. Ordinarily he proposes these to the president of the company, and it is upon the latter's authority that the policy is actually issued. When proposing a new or revised policy the personnel director must analyze problems which have

---

[1] Line and staff concepts are discussed further in Chapter 6, "Organization." Line positions and departments are those without which the organization could not function even for a day. In a manufacturing company those who make the product and those who sell it are considered line. In a department store, buying and selling activities are considered line. In a college the faculty members are line, whereas such individuals as the dean of students, manager of purchasing, and the controller are staff.

occurred in the past, survey other companies to determine how they handle similar situations, discuss the matter with his colleagues and subordinates, and give due consideration to the prevailing philosophy in the organization. In effect he does all of the necessary research and staff work, but in most cases the new policy is actually authorized by the president and/or the board of directors. On small policy matters the personnel director ordinarily may determine and institute policies himself.

Advice.   A major portion of the activities of those engaged in staff personnel work is in the nature of counsel and advice to line managers. Countless examples can be given. A shop foreman may be confronted with a grievance over distribution of overtime. Another foreman may have a problem employee whom he feels should be disciplined or even suspended. How should he go about doing this? At the time of the annual review of all salaried personnel for possible pay increases, the personnel manager plays a key role in advising operating managers on the administration of the program. An apparent concerted slowdown may occur in the assembly department. It may have been instituted by the union in retaliation for the cutting of piece rates the week before. How should production supervision handle this situation?

In all of the foregoing examples the personnel director and his staff are expected to be fully familiar with personnel policy, the labor agreement, past practice, and the needs and welfare of both the company and the employees in order to develop a sound solution. The successful personnel specialist must be people-centered. He must be sensitive to the feelings, wants, and motives of other people. At the same time he must continually be cognizant of his obligation to preserve the structure and functioning of the organization. In fact this really is the essence of personnel management. Management must seek to so direct and coordinate the efforts of the people that the goals of the organization are achieved while at the same time providing need satisfactions for the members of that organization.

Service.   The service responsibilities of the personnel department are apparent when one examines such things as the employment, training, and benefits functions. The tasks of recruiting, interviewing, and testing job applicants are performed in the personnel office. Training programs are planned, organized, and often staffed through the personnel office. The personnel group must see that adequate instructional materials and facilities are available. Once pension and insurance programs have been set up, all claims must be processed through the personnel department. The maintenance of adequate employee records is a service function that permeates all functional specialties within the personnel field.

Control.   The personnel department carries out important control functions. It monitors the performance of line departments and other staff departments to insure that they conform to established personnel policy, procedures, and practices. The control function of the personnel department is quite comparable to the activities of a quality control group that measures product variables to insure conformance to engineering specifications or to the activities of the auditing staff that inspects accounting records to ascertain conformance with prescribed standards.

What are some examples of the control functions of the personnel-industrial relations department? There are many. Company policy may declare that all salaried employees shall be appraised as to performance and potential at least once per year. If certain supervisors fail to transmit their performance appraisal reports to the personnel office when required, then a follow-up is clearly required.

As part of a continuing program for bringing the safety message to production workers, foremen may be expected to conduct a brief weekly safety meeting for their men. If some foremen fail to do so, a member of the personnel department (usually the safety director) will certainly bring this matter to their attention. If discussion with the parties involved yields no direct improvement, then the safety director will generally bring the issue up with the foremen's immediate line superior.

A common form of staff control over line management personnel is *procedural control.* This means that managers and supervisors must follow established procedures in carrying out certain personnel management actions. For example, in order to discharge an employee who has allegedly committed a serious violation of a company rule, line supervision may have to follow a clearly defined procedure. Depending upon the particular circumstances this may involve submitting written evidence, obtaining testimony of witnesses, notifying the union, and granting the man a full hearing.

To raise an employee's salary the supervisor generally must abide by certain procedures. This may involve submitting a performance rating form at the time of the request, keeping the size of the increase and the man's total salary within prescribed limits, and doing this at certain designated times of the year.

Many times the personnel unit will conduct continuing audits of the line departments. Examples are measures of accidents, grievances, absenteeism, voluntary quits, and disciplinary actions. Quite often the control activities of a staff unit, such as the personnel department, require that it exert pressure upon line managers and supervisors. If the control work is not done with proper regard for the need to build a cooperative, healthy relationship with line personnel, serious dissension can occur. The personnel manager and his staff should exert their principal efforts toward counseling and educating line supervisors regarding the need for following established policies, procedures, and practices. The errant supervisor should be permitted to correct his ways first. If all attempts at persuasion fail, then, of course, the problem must be discussed with higher management.

PERSONNEL AND INDUSTRIAL RELATIONS FUNCTIONS

Just what is the content of personnel and industrial relations activities? As stated before, personnel management activities are carried on both by the staff personnel department and by operating management in the course of directing the activities of the work force. Let us now examine the principal personnel functions and note the more common division of responsibilities between the staff personnel unit and operating, or line, management. It should, however, be borne in mind that variation from the pattern described may occur in particular companies because of special circumstances.

Employment

This function includes recruitment, selection, and induction into the organization. The initial decision to add someone to the payroll is made by line management. It is also its responsibility to determine the content of the job to be performed and the employee qualifications necessary to perform the job satisfactorily. The personnel department must develop and maintain adequate sources of labor. It must also set up and operate the employee selection system, which may include interviews, selection tests, a medical examination, and reference checks. Quite commonly the role of the personnel group is one of screening with the final decision to hire or reject being made by the supervisor who requested the new employee. However, in the case of a large-scale hiring program of unskilled or semiskilled workers, the personnel department is commonly granted full and final authority to make the hiring decision.

The new employee's supervisor bears important responsibilities for introducing him to his new work environment. This is often called orientation or indoctrination.

Transfer, Promotion, Layoff

For these tasks the personnel department serves primarily in a coordinative capacity. When employees are moved from one department to another either because of the needs of the business or because of individual requests, the personnel records may be studied to ascertain that they possess the requisite skills. Layoffs typically are processed by the personnel department to insure that the proper order of preference is followed. This can become quite complicated if combinations of job, departmental, and plant-wide seniority rights must be observed. When a vacancy occurs in a position, it may be filled by promotion from within or by direct hiring from outside the company. This decision is often made jointly between the personnel director and the executive in charge of the department where the vacancy has occurred. Many companies have established policies to cover matters of this type. The actual final decision as to which candidate is chosen for the promotion is largely made by the executive in whose unit the vacancy has occurred.

Training and Development

On-the-job training and coaching is performed by the line supervisor or by a specially designated employee who acts in the role of an instructor. It is the responsibility of the personnel-industrial relations group to determine training needs in cooperation with line management. Once the needs are established the personnel training specialists must design a program to accomplish the desired results. If the program takes the form of in-service classroom courses, it usually is administered by the personnel unit.

Coaching, performance appraisal, and postappraisal counseling, job rotation, understudies, and special broadening assignments are largely executed by operating managers but coordinated by a central personnel staff.

Wage and Salary Administration

The work of designing and installing a job evaluation program is handled, for the most part, by the personnel department with some consultation with line managers. The decision to adopt a particular pay structure with pay grades and fixed minima and maxima for the grades is a top management responsibility.

The day-to-day work of analyzing jobs, evaluating their dollar worth according to a formal job evaluation plan, and maintaining suitable records is a staff personnel function.

Periodic wage and salary surveys of the labor market area are conducted by the personnel specialists, but any firm decision to raise or change the entire pay schedule is practically always reserved for the chief executive officer of the organization.

Health and Safety

Typical elements of an employee health program are preemployment medical examinations, periodic examinations for those in jobs containing health hazards, operation of a dispensary, treatment of first-aid cases, treatment of such minor ailments as colds and headaches, health education, and monitoring and alleviation of health hazards in the plant. Small companies typically hire physicians, nurses, and industrial hygienists only on a consulting or part-time basis. Large ones tend to be staffed with full-time personnel in these areas.

The safety program is directed toward the prevention of work injuries. The main elements are engineering, education, and enforcement. The safety director, who usually is a member of the personnel department, works closely with the plant engineering unit to have machines and equipment properly guarded. New production processes and machines must be so designed and constructed that the possibility of human injury is remote. Employee safety education is a cooperative program conducted by both the staff safety director and all foremen. The safety director must prepare safety displays, distribute safety leaflets, and develop safety instructional material. Every foreman must instruct his men to perform their jobs safely. He may also be called upon to run a weekly or monthly safety meeting. Enforcement of safety rules is primarily a responsibility of every foreman.

Discipline and Discharge

Discipline has two principal meanings. In the first sense it means "training which molds or corrects." This means the achieving and maintaining of orderly employee behavior because the people understand and believe in the established codes of conduct. The second meaning of the term *discipline* refers to punishment of wrongdoers.

The supervisor, whether in factory or office, must bear primary responsibility for training his people to abide by the rules of behavior and for initiating punishment for the few whose conduct deviates from the norm.

The personnel department commonly assumes the responsibility for formulating the list of necessary rules together with the range of penalties for each offense. Frequently this list of rules and penalties is discussed and cleared with high-level line management before it is issued and communicated throughout the organization.

In a survey of thirty-four companies in a variety of industries, Myers and Turnbull found that actual approval by the personnel department has to be obtained before a man may be discharged. The reason is that discharge is a very severe penalty and should only be used when a very clear case can be shown. In addition, it is especially vital to achieve companywide uniformity in the handling of such cases.[2]

Labor Relations

When a union has been certified by the National Labor Relations Board, as the result of an election, as the sole and exclusive bargaining agency for the employees, then management must bargain with it in regard to wages, rates of pay, hours of work, and other conditions of employment. The principal tasks involved in handling labor relations are contract ne-

[2] Charles A. Myers and John G. Turnbull, "Line and Staff in Industrial Relations," *Harvard Business Review,* Vol. 34, No. 4 (July-August 1956), pp. 113-124.

gotiation, contract interpretation and administration, and grievance handling.

The personnel-industrial relations staff plays a very significant role in labor-management relations. The director of industrial relations usually serves as a key member of the bargaining team, often acting as chief management spokesman. In operating on a day-to-day basis under the terms of the labor agreement, line supervision often finds frequent occasion to consult the personnel staff regarding such matters as allocation of overtime, handling of transfers and layoffs, and the application of contract work rules.

Although nearly all grievance procedures as spelled out in the labor contract specify that the foreman shall be the first to hear and act upon an employee grievance, in all but the most routine cases the foreman typically consults the personnel office before giving an answer. The personnel department is very commonly listed as either the second or third management step in the grievance procedure. In effect the personnel department representative is given line authority to make a binding settlement.

The personnel-industrial relations staff is granted such great authority in grievance handling in order to insure due regard for precedent and plantwide consistency of action. In addition, many grievances have plantwide or even companywide implications. Mishandling of a case could cause grave consequences.

Benefits and Services

Included under this category are pensions, group life insurance, hospital and medical insurance, sickness leave pay plans, supplemental unemployment compensation, loan funds, credit unions, social programs, recreational programs, and college tuition refund plans.

The actual decision to establish or to expand these programs is nearly always made by top line management upon the advice and consultation of the personnel staff. The actual design of pension and insurance programs requires a great deal of technical knowledge. These programs are generally worked out in conjunction with insurance companies or insurance consultants. After these plans are installed, the day-to-day processing of claims is handled by the personnel department.

Organization Planning

In the past ten years organization planning has emerged as a new and important function within personnel units at the corporate level of large enterprises. Organization planning requires the development of a concept of a company as a structure or system. It may require the delineation of the concepts of centralization or decentralization in terms of executive behavior and the locus of decision-making authority. The organization planning staff must prepare organization charts and position guides. It must counsel the chief executive officer and line management on organization theory and practice and with respect to company reorganization and expansion.

Originally this activity was carried on primarily in the office of the corporation president. And the president still has final responsibility in this area. But the growing complexity of large scale enterprises and the increasing sophistication of organization theory has caused organization planning to emerge as a specialty in itself. The personnel office gathers data, does research, prepares plans, and gives advice to the office of the president in this vital area.

Manpower Planning

Another new function that has emerged in very recent years is that of manpower planning. This work is most often performed at the company headquarters level. Occasionally a specific person or office has this as its primary responsibility; more commonly the responsibilities are shared by several staff specialists in the corporate personnel group. Manpower planning is the process by which a firm insures that it has the right number of people who possess the proper skills at the right time performing jobs which are useful to the organization. Principal activities involved in manpower planning are as follows: audit the present labor force in terms of skill mix, experience, and location; create a viable method for forecasting manpower needs giving consideration to present volume of production, anticipated company expansion, changing technology, and possible relocation; decide critical skills and establish plan for their allocation; analyze the labor market and trends in supply-demand relationships; and develop programs for meeting manpower shortages. In view of the long-term scarcity of high-caliber talent in the labor market (especially of technical, professional, and managerial personnel) the function of manpower planning takes on considerable importance.

Information and research data generated by manpower planning specialists are made available to personnel officers and operating executives in the divisions and plants of large multiplant corporations.

Personnel and Behavioral Research

Corporate research in the physical sciences for new products, processes, and technology has been going on for many years. It is only within the past ten years or so that business organizations have set up units to engage in full-time, systematic research into the human aspects of the organization. Leadership in this area has come from a few of the corporate giants: General Electric, International Business Machines, American Telephone and Telegraph, Procter and Gamble, and Texas Instruments

Company. Typical areas for current research are employee motivation, predicting success in management, performance appraisal, work group behavior, job design, and organization design. Application of the research findings and recommendations require close cooperation and participation by operating management, employees, and in some instances, union leaders.

ORGANIZATION FOR THE PERSONNEL FUNCTION

There was a time not many years ago when the personnel department was organizationally situated in the manufacturing division of industrial concerns. The personnel manager reported to the director of manufacturing. The reasoning behind this organizational arrangement was that the mass of people worked on production, and the majority of personnel problems occurred there. This practice has now passed into history.

The modern executive in charge of the personnel-industrial relations department must be an advisor to top management. He (with assistance from his subordinates) must set up executive development programs, recommend compensation plans for management personnel, recruit and help select managers and professionals, and develop a workable bargaining approach for union negotiations. Truly the personnel department serves the entire organization. The executive in charge must have sufficient stature in the organization to be an advisor to top management and to design and implement a really effective personnel program. In short, he should report to the president of the organization. A survey of 249 companies ranging in size from 1,000 employees to the over-25,000-plus category and spread across most industrial categories reveals that the executive who heads the corporate personnel staff reported to either the chairman of the board or the president in 161 of these companies. In 74 of the companies he reported to an executive vice president or a vice president. In only 14 companies did he report to someone of lower stature. In this same survey the corporate executive in charge of personnel-industrial relations held the title of vice president in about one half the firms. The three most common names for this unit were (1) industrial relations, (2) personnel, and (3) employee relations in that order.[3]

Unfortunately the presidents of some companies are ignorant of the proper role of a personnel department; hence they relegate it to a low level in the organization and staff it with unqualified people. Just because a supervisor gets along well with others and has accumulated many years of company experience, this does not mean that he is the ideal choice

---

[3] Allen R. Janger, *Personnel Administration: Changing Scope and Administration,* Studies in Personnel Policy, No. 202 (New York: National Industrial Conference Board), 1966, pp. 14-15.

for personnel manager. Some company presidents have the erroneous notion that personnel work is primarily one of record keeping, keeping the workers happy, running the employment office, and arranging the annual Christmas party. With such an attitude the company is bound to acquire a third-rate personnel program.

Personnel management and industrial relations is an emerging profession. A great many colleges and universities offer complete programs of study in this field. Some offer specialized degrees in industrial relations. The field contains a vast body of knowledge, much of which is derived from sound research and a considerable body of literature. There are a number of professional societies throughout the country representing practicing personnel managers and specialists. When looking for someone to head the personnel-industrial relations program, a company president would be well advised to seek an individual who possesses a proper professional background in terms of education and work experience.

Organization for a Medium-sized, Single-plant Company

For a company of, say, 3,000 employees, a typical organization structure for the personnel-industrial relations department is shown in Figure 3-1. The director of industrial relations is shown as reporting to the president. He is on the same level in the structure as the heads of finance, manufacturing, and marketing. Other common titles used in industry for the executive in charge of this department are personnel director, personnel manager, and industrial relations manager.

The six major groupings of personnel-industrial relations functions are shown in Figure 3-1. In this example it is assumed that the production and maintenance employees are represented by a union; hence we have included a labor relations section.

How large a personnel staff is necessary to service an organization of 3,000 employees as in this example? The answer to this depends to a considerable extent upon the attitude of top management, which really determines how comprehensive a personnel program is carried on. Some companies have no formal training for either their employees or their managers. They may have no job evaluation system and never conduct a real area wage survey. They may provide only marginal first-aid-facilities and have an inadequate safety program. With such an approach to personnel management, a company may get by with a very small personnel department and thereby save considerably on salaries. But it would certainly suffer in terms of lowered efficiency, more work injuries, lower morale, and more human relations problems.

Surveys have shown the average number of professional and technical staff members employed in the personnel department for various types of industries. These studies have shown the number of persons engaged in personnel work to range from about .60 to .90 per 100 total employees in the company. The ratio as it is called, tends to be closer to the .90 figure for smaller companies and closer to the .60 figure for the very large corporation.[4] Using .75 per 100 employees as an average, we would expect to find approximately 23 employees in the industrial relations de-

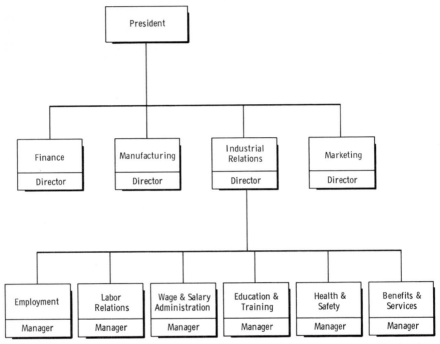

Figure 3-1. The Organization of the Industrial Relations Department in a Single-plant, Medium-sized Company.

partment shown in Figure 3-1, exclusive of clerical personnel. Thus such staff specialist positions as job analyst, interviewer, and safety engineer would be found in the various sections of this department.

Large Divisionalized Companies

Very large manufacturing concerns generally produce a number of products in many plants scattered throughout the United States and in foreign countries. Organizationally they typically contain three broad levels of management: (1) top corporate headquarters, (2) division man-

[4] Roberta J. Nelson, G. W. England, and Dale Yoder, "Personnel Ratios and Costs, 1962," *Personnel,* Vol. 40, No. 1 (January-February, 1963), pp. 17-26.

agement, and (3) plant management. They are often decentralized in the sense that each division and plant manager has profit-center account-ability. He possesses general authority and responsibility over his unit in order to obtain the results desired. He has nearly all the staff services such as personnel, purchasing, engineering, accounting, and so forth under his jurisdiction in order to realize the goals of his unit. Thus these large firms have a personnel-industrial relations group at corporate headquar-ters and at each of the manufacturing plants. They may also have units at the division level. In a study of 76 very large divisionalized companies the National Industrial Conference Board found that the staff functions of personnel administration along with legal, secretarial, and finance appear at the top corporate level in all or nearly all of these firms.[5]

The personnel director at the plant level typically reports to the plant manager. He receives policy direction and technical guidance from the headquarters group. He is responsible for administering the personnel program in the plant. This personnel director holds rank equivalent to other major executives in the plant, such as the chief engineer, control-ler, and the manager of manufacturing.

Questions for Review and Discussion

1. Explain the meaning of the following terms: personnel management, labor relations, industrial relations.
2. "The activities involved in personnel management pervade the entire organization. They are not performed solely by those in the person-nel department." Explain the foregoing.
3. Explain the following four functions performed by a personnel-indus-trial relations department:
   a. Policy initiation and formulation
   b. Advice
   c. Service
   d. Control
   Give examples for each of these.
4. Name and give the content of the principal personnel-industrial rela-tions functions.
5. Describe the staff role of the personnel department.
6. Explain the duties and responsibilities of the personnel department and of line supervision with respect to the following functions:
   a. employment
   b. training and development
   c. safety

[5] Harold Stieglitz and Allen R. Janger, *Top Management Organization in Divisionalized Companies,* Studies in Personnel Policy, No. 195 (New York: National Industrial Conference Board, 1965), pp. 13-15. Other staff functions—public relations, marketing, and research and development—were present at this level in only two-thirds of the companies.

7. Why does the personnel-industrial relations department often possess very great authority (at times full line authority) in handling labor relations problems?
8. At what level in the organization structure should the executive in charge of the personnel-industrial relations department be situated? Discuss.
9. In a multiplant company do you think it would be practical to have the personnel manager in each plant report directly to the corporate personnel vice-president? Discuss.

CASE PROBLEM

The Latham-Craft Company manufactures several lines of wood and metal products consisting of kitchen bowls, toys, croquet sets, and lawn furniture. The firm has been in business fifty years and is family-owned, the president being a major stockholder. Its branded items are well established in the market place. The company has earned a profit (though usually modest) for all but one of the past ten years. It employs a total of 350 people, of whom fifty are in the white-collar and managerial group. The production and maintenance employees are represented by a union.

The executive organization consists of the president, to whom report the sales vice-president, chief engineer, office manager, purchasing manager, director of product research and quality control, treasurer, and the plant superintendent. Sixteen factory foremen and two production control coordinators report to the plant superintendent.

The company is beset with a number of problems in regard to the management of its work force. The rate of employee turnover is high. This is caused by a high rate of voluntary quits and of discharges because of disciplinary problems and absenteeism. The Company pays its production and maintenance employees rates that are equal to the average for the wood products industry but considerably below the going rates in its community, which contains companies in the automobile, electrical, and steel industries.

The hiring of new workers is handled jointly by the purchasing manager, who does the initial screening, and the production superintendent, who makes the final hiring decision. Both complain frequently about the caliber of help they are able to obtain. Most are young men with little training and experience who had failed to finish high school. The probationary period as spelled out in the union agreement is sixty days. The purchasing manager does little or no checking into the background of the new hires. His reasoning is that the company invests little in them during their first few weeks on the job, and if they should prove unsatisfactory, they could be discharged easily.

The accident rate in the plant has been very high for several years. Most of the injuries occur when the employees get their fingers or hands caught while operating or servicing the machines. The Company president has become concerned about the mounting cost for workmen's compensation insurance, because the premium is based upon the actual loss experience in his plant. The foremen complain that whenever they try to suspend a worker for a serious infraction of a safety rule the company management usually backs down and rescinds the action in the face of pressure from the union business agent.

All of the present group of foremen have been promoted from the ranks of hourly paid employees. They have never received any formal training in supervision. They view their role as one of primarily pushing the workers to get out production. Very few exercise initiative or assume responsibility for seeing that housekeeping is improved, maintenance work is done on time, or that improved methods are instituted in their departments. The foremen are somewhat demoralized. They see few opportunities for advancement or even for salary increases. The Company has no system for evaluating the performance of any of its managerial or clerical employees. There is no formal salary structure. If a man has been doing a good job, if he has received no increase in pay for a long time, and if he complains firmly enough to his boss, he may receive a token pay increase.

The Company does have a hospital and medical insurance plan as well as a pension plan. Claims are handled by the office manager.

For many years the company made small interest-free loans to employees to help them purchase necessary household items, for extraordinary sickness expenses, and the like. This policy was finally abandoned because of the administrative burden and because of the ill will generated when management denied a loan which it felt was not justified. Recently there has been a rash of garnishments of employee's pay initiated by local small loan companies because employees have failed to repay their loans.

Questions

1. What appears to be the central problem in this company?
2. What organizational change or addition might be made to help solve the problem?
3. What personnel programs would you recommend be adopted?

Simulation Exercise

Zif, Jay J., *The Personnel Department* (Creative Studies Simulation) New York: The Macmillan Company, 1970.

Suggestions for Further Reading

American Management Association, *Manpower Planning: An Emerging Staff Function,* AMA Management Bulletin, New York: 1967.

_____, *A Look at Personnel Through the President's Eye,* AMA Management Bulletin 66, New York: 1965.

_____, *A Systems Approach to Personnel Management,* AMA Management Bulletin 62, New York, 1965

Fischer, Frank E., "The Personnel Function in Tomorrow's Company," *Personnel,* Vol. 45, No. 1, January - February 1968, pp. 64 - 71.

Fisher, Waldo E., "The Role and Functions of Industrial Relations in the Business Organization," Bulletin Number 34, Pasadena, Calif.: California Institute of Technology, 1961.

Henning, Dale and Wendell French, "The Mythical Personnel Manager," *California Management Review,* Vol. 3, No. 4, Summer 1961.

Herman, Stanley M., "The Personnel Field-Techniques and Trivia," *Personnel,* Vol. 39, No. 4, July - August 1962, pp. 17 - 24.

Janger, Allen R., *Personnel Administration: Changing Scope and Administration,* Studies in Personnel Policy, No. 202, New York: National Industrial Conference Board, 1966.

McFarland, Dalton E., *Company Officers Assess the Personnel Function,* AMA Research Study No. 79, New York: American Management Association, 1967.

_____, *Personnel Management: Theory and Practice,* New York: The Macmillan Company, 1968, Chs. 4 and 5.

Yoder, Dale and Roberta J. Nelson, *Jobs in Employee Relations,* Research Study Number 38, New York: American Management Association, 1959.

Unions and Management

4

Organized labor exerts a strong influence upon the individual company and upon the economic, social, and political climate in the United States. When the employees of a company are represented by a union, policies and practices affecting the employment relationship that were formerly decided by management alone are now subject to joint determination. Wages, hours, and other conditions of employment are bargained between union and management. The decisions reached in contract negotiations on economic items often have an effect upon the pricing of company products and services. This in turn may influence the competitive position of the firm in the product market. When management contemplates taking certain personnel actions it must give consideration to the attitude and position of the union on these matters. Many actions that had been conducted between management representatives and employees as individuals (before the entrance of the union) are now carried on through union stewards and other elected officers. This is particularily true in grievance handling. The attitudes of the union often shape the way in which such management techniques as job evaluation, time study, and wage incentive plans are applied.

In the broader social, economic, and political sphere, we find that organized labor plays a very significant role. Labor unions tend to adopt rather definite stands on social issues, such as racial discrimination, medical and hospital care for the general population, and public housing. They try to influence the decisions of state legislatures and the United States

Congress on unemployment insurance, workmen's compensation, and social security legislation (as do employer organizations, such as the National Association of Manufacturers also). Economically the wage (broadly defined to include fringe benefits) settlements reached in major industries through collective bargaining often affect the volume of employment and rate of introduction of technological improvements not only in individual companies but also in the whole industry.

Because of the very prominent role that unions play in many organizations and in our society as a whole, it is important to develop an adequate understanding of why employees join unions; why some persons reject unionization; union membership and rate of growth; union organization and objectives and behavior of unions; the effect of the union upon management; and factors contributing to harmonious labor-management relations. These topics and their ramifications will be covered in this chapter. Chapter 5, "Collective Bargaining," will be concerned with labor relations law, structure for bargaining, negotiating the agreement, principal bargaining issues, and dispute settlement procedures.

MOTIVATION TO JOIN UNIONS

Why do employees join a union? Since human behavior is goal-directed, what drives and wants can be fulfilled by membership in a union? Let us now examine the objectives that employees expect to satisfy through union membership.

Greater Bargaining Power

The individual worker possesses very little bargaining power in comparison with that of his employer. Very few employees are indispensable. A company can generally get along without a particular worker. The employer is in a position to say to the individual employee, "Take or leave the wage and conditions of work I offer you." A worker's bargaining strength lies in his ability to quit if he is not satisfied with his wage rate and other conditions of employment. However, he soon learns that he cannot continually resign from one job after another when he is dissatisfied. This imposes too great a financial and emotional burden upon him. Therefore, employees have found that although their bargaining power as individuals is very limited, they can frequently equal that of the employer by organizing a union and taking concerted action. The threat or actuality of a strike by the union represents the economic and social power that often causes the company to increase its wages to a point where they are acceptable to the union.

The only situation in which an individual employee possesses considerable bargaining power occurs when he has a rare and valuable skill or talent. Thus we find in artistic and athletic professions certain exceptionally gifted stars are able to bargain on equal terms with their employers. Likewise certain executive and professional people in industry are able to command very high salaries because they possess an exceptional talent. But the vast majority of the wage and salary earners are in no such fortunate position. They are replaceable and must take pretty much what is offered them.

Make Their Voices Heard

The desire for self-expression is a fundamental human drive for most people. They wish to communicate their aims, feelings, complaints, and ideas to others. Most employees wish to be more than cogs in a large machine. They want management to listen to them. The union provides a mechanism through which these feelings and thoughts can be transmitted to management.

The entry of a union into an organization brings with it the establishment of a formalized grievance procedure. This provides a means by which employee complaints and problems are brought to the attention of management. The union stewards and officers represent the interests of the employees in presenting these problems to supervision and to higher management.

Minimize Favoritism and Discrimination

Supervisors must make a great many decisions which affect the pay, status, position, and work of their subordinates. Many of these decisions are highly subjective in nature. They are influenced by the personal relationships existing between the supervisor and each of his employees. Sometimes when one man is granted a larger wage increase than others, they feel that favoritism may have had a part in the decision. Unions press for equality of treatment. For example, one of their maxims is "One job, one rate." This means that all persons doing the same kind of work should receive the same wage rate. As an alternative to this we may find that the union accepts the concept of a range of wages for each job, but that it insists that all in-grade wage increases be made strictly according to seniority. So it is with other personnel actions, such as promotions, transfers, layoffs, and vacation preference. Unions advocate that the major (but not necessarily the only) criterion for decision making be seniority. It may not always result in the best man getting the promotion or being retained during a layoff, but it is an objective way of making difficult decisions.

Social Factors

Man, being gregarious, friendly, and sociable in his outlook, is influenced in his actions by the behavior of his associates. Many employees are persuaded to join a union by their fellow workers. Often the individual is motivated to go along with the crowd—to be one of the gang. He seeks group acceptance and a feeling of belonging. The organizational strikes which were so common in the mass production industries in the 1930's were quite effective in inducing hesitant workers to join the union and help their friends on the picket line. Sometimes social motivation takes the form of group pressure. The individual who refuses to join the union often has a very difficult time of it at work. He may be ostracized, his machine may break down, or his lunch bucket may get "lost."

Cultural factors also play a part in the disposition of people to join a union. For those who have been raised in a working-class neighborhood where one's father and indeed all of the men in the community belong to the union, acceptance of the union as a normal part of the employment situation seems just natural. This condition in which union membership is simply accepted as a way of life is true in certain areas and certain industries in the United States (for example, in coal mining areas, and in the garment industry in New York City). However, this condition represents a minority of the situations when one looks at the union movement in general.

Most unions offer recreational and social activities that are attractive to their members. These consist of picnics, Christmas parties, bowling leagues, and the like. Some unions have dances after regular union meetings. When the union membership is well balanced between men and women, this brings out a large attendance at the meetings.

Outlet When Advancement Blocked

Many employees will have nothing to do with a union as long as they are doing well in their careers. If their expectations in terms of pay increases, better jobs as they gain more experience, promotions and greater status do actually materialize, then they may feel that there is no necessity to pay dues to a union. They may even feel that the union would impede their progress because of seniority rules and the fact that the individual member cannot get ahead faster than the entire group. However, we often find that when a person senses that his progress up the organizational ladder is blocked, when he can no longer get ahead on his own initiative, then he experiences a period of readjustment. Initially he may be frustrated. But often he turns to the union as an outlet for his wants. Through collective action the union may obtain the economic benefits from the employer that the individual could not get on his own. If the person has aspirations for a position of responsibility and leadership, he may even achieve an elective union office.

Compulsion via the Union Contract

Many agreements that are negotiated between employers and unions contain a "union shop" provision (or some variation of it) that requires that all employees must join the union and pay dues within a certain period of time after they have been hired. If they refuse to join they may be discharged. A "union shop" clause in a labor agreement is one form of union security. Other aspects of the union security issue will be discussed in Chapter 5.

MOTIVATION TO REJECT UNIONS

Since only one fourth of the labor force in the United States belongs to unions, it must be apparent that many workers either definitely oppose the prospect of unionization for themselves or at least are timid and reluctant to join. What influences operate to cause employees to reject the union?

Cultural Factors

Many people in American society distrust unions and what they stand for. They feel that unions stand for collectivism, socialism, and the welfare state. They feel that unions are somewhat un-American, that they stand in opposition to the traditional American concepts of free enterprise, individual freedom, and individual initiative. They feel that a man should stand on his own two feet and get ahead on his own merits. They read in the newspapers that a powerful union has shut down an essential service or industry and that the public must suffer. They resent the union, its method of action, and what it stands for. Sentiments such as the foregoing are much more common in certain segments of our society than others. Geographically they are common in the South, in rural areas, and in small towns. Small businessmen and farmers often hold such views. Likewise many in white-collar, professional, and executive occupations believe this way.

"Unions Are Beneath My Social Position"

Persons in the professions typically reject union affiliation for themselves. Instead they seek recognition as professionals and join professional associations, such as the American Medical Association, the American Association of University Professors, the American Society of Mechanical Engineers, and scores of similar organizations. Like unions, these associations seek to represent their members, to better their conditions, and to control entrance to that field of work. (While some unions restrict entrance to their trade by various devices, such as control of apprenticeship programs, closed unions, closed shop, and high initiation fees, many professional associations accomplish the same net result through rigorous entrance qualifications, examinations, and state licensing.) Basically professionals tend to look down upon unions as being beneath their status. They know that unions are predominantly composed of blue-collar workers. They feel that they, as professionals, should not become closely identified with the behavior and tactics of blue-collar workers (for example, picketing and strikes). They feel that they are above this. Professionals do not generally want to be restrained by a fixed and uniform wage for all who do a given class of work.

Professional associations as an alternative to unions tend to be the strongest and most effective in advancing the standing of their members when the members are essentially in business for themselves. This condition applies to physicians and attorneys. For them the wage (or price) bargain is between the person performing the service and his customer. Professional associations are somewhat less effective where the members are essentially employees and the wage bargain is between employee and employer.

Identification with Management

White-collar, technical, and professional employees tend to identify themselves with management. Since they work in close proximity to supervisors and executives, there is a tendency to acquire the management viewpoint toward unions. These groups also feel that they can advance into management. They are looking upward. They wish to impress favorably their immediate superiors in the organization. They often feel that membership in a union might even hinder their chances of promotion.

UNION MEMBERSHIP AND GROWTH

Unions in America first appeared on the scene during the 1790's and early 1800's. They were composed of such skilled craftsmen as shoemakers, tailors, carpenters, printers, and the like. They were formed initially as protective organizations to resist wage cuts and maintain acceptable conditions of employment. The rise of merchant capitalists as employers tended to accentuate the separate interests of employers and employees in the wage bargain. Price competition in the product market caused employers to cut wages or at least resist wage increases. In seeking to protect and improve their lot, unions of craftsmen posted their prices (wage scales) and refused to work for less. They also tended to resist any influx of lesser trained workers who would undercut their wage scale. Throughout most of the nineteenth century, unions in the United States were small and rather weak. To be sure the Knights of Labor created a flurry in the mid-

1880's when its membership reached 700,000, but the success of this union was short-lived, and it soon passed from the scene. The American Federation of Labor, officially organized in 1886 as actually a confederation of rather autonomous craft unions, proved to be an enduring and successful organization. However, its growth and impact during the closing years of the nineteenth century were rather limited. In 1890 total union membership in the United States was less than 400,000. By 1910 it stood at about 2 million. During the World War I era when employment levels were high, membership increased significantly. By 1920 it was slightly over 5 million. But from then until the depth of the Great Depression in 1933, the union movement lost membership. During the prosperous 1920's, when conditions would ordinarily have been favorable for union growth, employer organizations launched a massive offensive against unions. This took the form of "open shop" drives, antiunion publicity, resistance to unionization at the plant gate, employer-initiated welfare programs, and quasi unions in the form of employee representation plans. A lack of vigor in the leadership of the American Federation of Labor also contributed to the decline. Of course, mass layoffs and plant closings caused by the economic depression of the early 1930's caused people to lose the ability to pay their dues to maintain membership in their unions.

Rapid Growth—1935 Through 1947

The most spectacular rate of union growth occurred during the period from the mid-1930's through World War II until 1947. (See Figures 4-1 and 4-2 for graphs showing total union membership in the United States and membership as a percentage of the labor force and of nonagricultural employment for the period 1930 to 1966.) This growth had a number of causes. Perhaps foremost among these was the passage of the Wagner Act in 1935 (officially designated as the National Labor Relations Act). This law granted workers the right to form unions of their own choosing without fear of employer intimidation or coercion. Outlawed were blacklists, company-dominated unions, and discharges for worker participation in union activities. The Act provided a peaceful and democratic means for employees to express their wishes for or against union representation by means of elections conducted by the Federal government.

Another important cause for this rapid expansion of the organized labor movement was the formation of the Congress of Industrial Organizations in 1935-1936. Led by colorful and able men, such as John L. Lewis, as its first president, the CIO and its constituent national and international unions scored spectacular successes in organizing the mass production industries of the country, such as automobile, steel, rubber, electrical, and aircraft. The time was ripe for union organization in these industries. There was a powerful, pent-up demand.

Still another factor contributing to rapid union growth during this pe-

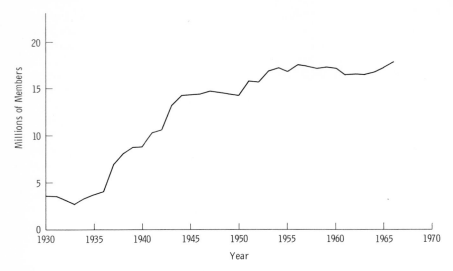

Figure 4-1. Membership of National and International Unions, 1930-1966, (Exclusive of Canadian Members). *Source: U.S. Department of Labor, Bureau of Labor Statistics, August 1968.*

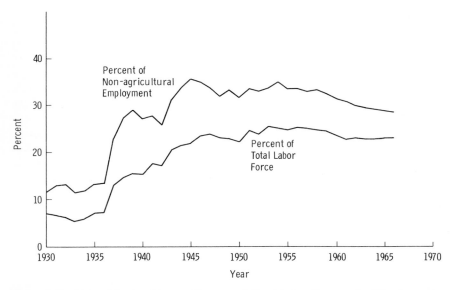

Figure 4-2. Union Membership as a Per cent of Total Labor Force and of Employees in Nonagricultural Establishments, 1930-1966, (Exclusive of Canadian Membership), *Source: U.S. Department of Labor, Bureau of Labor Statistics, August 1968.*

riod was the high level of employment and economic prosperity during World War II and for four years thereafter. During a period of booming business, companies are in a position to be conciliatory toward the demands of their workers and their unions. Wages can be increased and union security provisions bargained without serious immediate consequences to the employer.

An environmental factor that encouraged the growth and development of unions during this period was the generally sympathetic attitude toward unions and their aspirations held by the New Deal and Fair Deal administrations of Presidents Roosevelt and Truman. The favorable political climate did not mean, however, that the administration in Washington always approved of organized labor's tactics. On more than one occasion during World War II and immediately thereafter, strikes by Lewis' coal miners imperiled the security of the nation. He had to be toned down by presidential action. On these occasions the Federal government seized mines to keep them operating.

Leveling Off—1947 to the Present

In 1947 actual union membership stood at 14,787,000, whereas in 1966 it was 17,940,000.[1] When one takes into consideration the growth in the total labor force, we find that actually there has been little change in total union membership from 1947 through 1966 when expressed as a percentage of the civilian labor force. In 1947 union membership represented 23.9 per cent of the labor force, in 1953 it was 25.2 per cent, and in 1966 it was 22.7 per cent. So we can see that while membership has been increasing, it has barely kept pace with the expansion in the size of the labor force.

Why has the rate of growth slowed up so appreciably? There is no single factor responsible for this decline in rate of growth. Rather there are a multiplicity of causes. An important factor is that those groups which are still nonunion are difficult to organize. Many of these are concentrated in small companies of under 100 employees. It is very costly for unions to organize and administer contracts in these establishments. The South, because of cultural and other factors, remains a "tough nut to crack" for the union organizers. Organizing campaigns in the textile and wearing apparel industries in the South have been rather unsuccessful.

White-collar and professional employees (engineers, chemists, physicists, and so on) are reluctant to join unions. The fact that the rapid rate of technological innovation in American industry has increased the number of white-collar, technical, and professional people in the labor force in the last decade has made the unions' problem more difficult. The number of unskilled and semiskilled blue-collar workers has decreased. This

---

[1] Union Membership Tabulation, U.S. Department of Labor, Bureau of Labor Statistics, August 1968.

change in the composition of the work force has meant that those groups that have traditionally supported unionism (blue-collar workers) are decreasing in relative size, and those who resist unionization are increasing.

Public opinion, which was generally sympathetic to unions during the 1930's and early 1940's, has swung in the other direction to a certain extent. We live in a very interdependent society, and when essential goods and services are cut off during a strike, the public gets angry. Although it takes two to make a dispute, the newspaper headlines usually indicate that it is the unions who have broken the peace and become the aggressors in a breakdown of negotiations between management and labor. They are the ones who have gone on strike.

The exposure of racketeering and corruption in a few labor unions by the McClellan Committee[2] during hearings conducted from 1957-1959 has definitely added more tarnish to the public image of the labor movement. Although much of the public believed that the labor union movement was engaged in a righteous cause during the 1930's and 1940's in improving the lot of working men and women, it became apparent in the late 1950's that some union leaders were using their union offices primarily to feather their own nests.

Highlighting the decline in the rate of union growth during the 1950's is the fact that the unions have won a steadily declining percentage of the representation elections conducted by the National Labor Relations Board. These elections are conducted by the Board upon petition by workers, a union, or an employer to determine whether a majority of the employees in a company wish to be represented by a union for purposes of collective bargaining with the employer. In 1951, unions won 70 per cent of all new organizing elections, in 1955 the figure was 61 per cent, and by 1959 the percentage had declined to 58[3] To be sure, unions were winning more representation elections than they were losing, but their percentage of victories has declined significantly from the more than 80 per cent of the early 1940's.

Growth in Public Sector

Although the overall picture of union membership in the United States has been one of stagnation for a number of years, in one sector, that of government at all levels—local, state, and federal—there has been a rather rapid expansion of unionization since the early 1960's. Between 1960-61 and 1966-67 the American Federation of Government Employees increased its membership from 68,000 to 196,000. During the same time span the American Federation of State, County, and Municipal Employees went

---

[2] Officially called the Senate Select Committee on Improper Activities in the Labor or Management Field.

[3] Joseph Krislov, "New Organizing by Unions During the 1950's," *Monthly Labor Review* (September 1960), p. 923.

from 188,000 to 297,000 and the American Federation of Teachers grew from 57,000 to 125,000.[4] Overall membership of government employees in unions grew from 915,000 in 1956 to 1,717,000 in 1966.[5]

A major stimulus to the growth of collective bargaining in the public sector was the issuance by President John F. Kennedy on January 17, 1962, of Executive Order 10988 entitled "Employee Management Cooperation in the Federal Service." This order required Federal agencies to recognize as exclusive bargaining agents unions that represented a majority of the employees as determined by a vote of those in the bargaining unit. This represented a major advance for the aspirations of government employees. The National Labor Relations Act of 1935, which granted collective bargaining rights to employees in private industry, specifically excluded public employees from its coverage.

The Federal action encouraged many of the states to pass laws which granted to state and local employees the right to form unions, to have these recognized as bargaining agents by the appropriate governmental unit, and to negotiate contracts and process grievances. The New York State law, for example, evolved as a result of a study committee appointed by Governor Rockefeller and headed by Professor George Taylor of the University of Pennsylvania. New York's Public Employees' Fair Employment Act, popularly called the Taylor Law, became effective on September 1, 1967. It established a Public Employment Relations Board within the State Department of Civil Service to administer the Act. State agencies and local governments (municipalities, towns, villages, and school boards) are required to bargain with those unions which have been granted recognition.

Strikes by employees of government have generally been illegal under the common law. The Taft-Hartley Act (1947) added statute prohibition on strikes for federal employees. Although many states have recently passed legislation granting collective bargaining rights to their employees, they have also specifically banned strikes of public employees.

Commentary on Union Viability

The lesson of history tells us that unions in the United States thrive and grow only when supported positively by legislation or other governmental encouragement. The unionization of the mass production industries in the late 1930's and early 1940's was dependent, in large part, upon the material support given to collective bargaining by the Wagner Act. Certain AFL trade unions were able to demonstrate modest success prior to the passage of this law primarily because they represented craftsmen—notably in the building and printing trades and on the railroads—who

[4] *Report of the AFL-CIO Executive Council,* Seventh Convention in Bal Harbour, Florida, December 7, 1967, pp. 35-38.

[5] Everett M. Kassalow, "Canadian and U.S. White-Collar Union Increases," *Monthly Labor Review,* Vol. 91, No. 7 (July 1968), p. 41.

occupied strategic positions in their industries. They established a system of job control through union agreements that made their positions reasonably strong. But the laissez-faire economic and legal environment that predominated prior to the 1930's constituted a hostile climate for the collective bargaining aspirations of the masses of blue- and white-collar workers. In those days the employer could discharge union minded workers with impunity. The courts of that day viewed the business and property rights of employers much more sympathetically than the job rights of workers.

Although few still claim that the Taft-Hartley Act was the principal cause for the decline in the rate of union growth that set in about 1947, it is clear that the many restrictions upon union power contained in the Act have served to dampen the union advance to some extent.

Evidence in the field of public employment in the 1960's revealed that government employees have had a powerful desire to participate in decision making with respect to the terms and conditions of their employment. Following closely upon the issuance of Kennedy's Executive Order 10988

Union	Members	Union	Members
Teamsters	1,651,240	Letter Carriers	189,628
Automobile	1,402,700	Railroad Trainmen	185,000
Steel	1,068,000	Textile Workers (TWUA)	182,000
Electrical (IBEW)	875,000	Pulp	171,118
Machinists	836,163	Retail, Wholesale	170,500
Carpenters	800,000	Rubber	170,437
Retail Clerks	500,314	Electrical (UE)	167,000
Laborers	474,529	Oil, Chemical	165,329
Mine	Not Avail.	Iron Workers	162,006
Mine, District 50	232,000	Bricklayers	149,000
Garment, Ladies	455,164	Papermakers	144,300
Hotel	449,974	Postal Clerks	143,146
Clothing	382,000	Maintenance of Way	141,000
Meat Cutters	353,059	Boilermakers	140,000
Service	348,500	Transport Workers	135,000
Engineers, Operating	330,000	Packinghouse	135,000
Communications	321,117	Railway Carmen	125,615
Electrical (IUE)	320,000	Teachers	125,000
Plumbing	284,707	Fire Fighters	115,000
State, County and Municipal	281,277	Printing Pressmen	114,000
Railway and Steamship Clerks	270,000	Typographical	106,646
Musicians	252,487	Transit Union	103,000
Painters	200,569	Sheet Metal Workers	100,000
Government (AFGE)	199,823		

Figure 4-3. National and International Unions with 100,000 or More Members, 1966. *Source: United States Department of Labor, Bureau of Labor Statistics.*

and the passage of favorable legislation in many states, they joined up by the thousands. Without the pent-up demand this would not have occurred. Likewise without the sympathetic executive and legislative support this could not have occurred. The governmental support for unionization in the mid-1930's and again in the mid-1960's (for the public sector) was initiated to meet a pressing and wide-spread problem.

Membership of National and International Unions

The greatest concentration of union membership in the United States is in the manufacturing, construction, transportation, mining, and communication industries. Industries that have a low portion of the labor force organized by unions are agriculture, wholesale and retail trade, textiles, laundry and dry cleaning, beauty shops, crude petroleum and natural gas, fishing and dairy products. Likewise industries located in the South tend to have a low percentage of unionization. White-collar and professional workers have, for the most part, remained outside the union orbit. The largest unions tend to be those operating in the heavily unionized sectors of the economy. Figure 4-3 shows the 47 unions that had 100,000 or more members as of 1966.

UNION ORGANIZATION AND FUNCTIONS

There are about 186 national and international unions in this country (many unions call themselves "international" because they have members in Canada as well as the United States). Examples of such unions are the Automobile, Aerospace and Agricultural Implement Workers of America, the International Association of Machinists, the United Steelworkers of America, and the International Ladies' Garment Workers Union. Each of these types of unions is composed of a national headquarters organization, intermediate bodies primarily set up for administrative purposes, and many local unions. Commonly in manufacturing, for example, each organized plant or establishment will have its own separate local union. There are about 78,000 local unions in the United States.

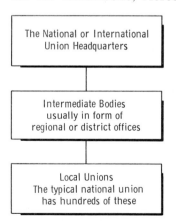

Figure 4-4. Schematic Organization Chart of a Union.

A simplified schematic organization chart of a union would look as shown in Figure 4-4.

Uniting the majority of national and international unions is the AFL-CIO, which was formed in 1955 through a merger of the American Federation of Labor and the Congress of Industrial Organizations. About 135 national and international unions belong to this loosely knit federation.

The Local Union

The local union is the basic, and a very important, unit of organization of a union. If it is a craft union, such as the carpenters', then a local may consist of all unionized carpenters in a particular town or city even though they may work for different employers; if it is an industrial union, then the local may consist of all union members in a particular factory.

Local unions are generally operated in a democratic fashion, with officers elected usually for a term of one year by the dues-paying members. Each member has one vote, and election rules ordinarily require advance notice of impending elections, open nominations, and secret ballots. The elected officials usually consist of a president, secretary-treasurer, and an executive board. Some unions also have a business agent, trustees, a negotiating committee, and a grievance committee. Every local union also has a number of shop stewards who are elected by the employees in each department of the company.

The president of a local is most commonly a worker who has been elected by the membership to be its principal leader but who devotes only part time to his union duties. It is only very large locals (consisting of several thousand members) that can afford to have a full-time, salaried president. In most instances the president has a regular job, is paid a wage by the employer, and attends to his union responsibilities during the work day (for which the company grants him time off) and on his own time evenings and on weekends. Many unions pay these part-time union presidents a few hundred dollars a year in salary plus their necessary expenses for attending international union conventions and for other items. The local president is typically the chief union spokesman in contract negotiations with company representatives. He becomes involved in major union grievances, leads the members in time of a strike, and in general tries to create and maintain teamwork and solidarity among the group. His job has many political overtones to it. He often is placed in the position where he must "deliver the goods" in dealings with the company or risk being defeated for re-election. The political nature of his job is emphasized when the union is divided into factional groups.

Certain unions, especially those in the construction, clothing, and metalworking industries, have a business agent. He is a full-time, salaried union official who is usually elected by the membership. He exercises a great deal of power and in many instances overshadows the local president in authority, influence, and prestige. His duties and responsibilities are manyfold. He plays a key role in contract negotiations with the employer, is alert to see that the employer and his management representatives abide by the contract, helps settle grievances, and leads the union members when there is a strike. In addition, he may also have to administer the operation of the local's headquarters, direct clerical help, handle union publicity, and make arrangements for business meetings.

A shop steward is another important person in a local union organization. Although the term *steward* is the one most commonly used, in some unions he is called a departmental representative, a committeeman, or a grievance man. The shop steward appears at the same level in the union organization structure as does a foreman in the company structure. However, he does not have the authority over the workers that a foreman has. Technically speaking, he is not considered to be an "official" of the local, although his position is vital to union operations. He is usually elected for a term of one year to represent the employees in that department in the processing of their grievances to management. He represents the interests of the employees and goes to bat for them when he feels they have a justifiable grievance. He is on guard to insure that supervision lives up to the letter and spirit of the labor-management agreement. If there is no "union shop" provision in the labor agreement, which requires employees to join the union, then he takes steps to increase the membership by persuading people to join. If there is no payroll checkoff of union dues, then he must also collect dues from the members.

The locals are the heart of any union. Although there is a trend in the direction of more and more contract negotiations being conducted at the national level of the union, what with multiemployer bargaining becoming more prevalent, it can be said accurately that the majority of all negotiations are still conducted at the local level. Even in those situations where the top management of a multiplant company bargains a labor-management agreement with national union officials, it is common practice for each local to bargain a supplementary agreement with local plant management over local issues, such as work standards, time study, rest periods, seniority rules, and so on. In addition to carrying on contract negotiations, other functions of the local are to obtain new members, handle grievances, administer the agreement with management, and conduct strikes when other choices fail to resolve disagreements. In addition, many locals carry on an active program of social activities for their members.

Intermediate Organizational Units

For purposes of coordinating the activities of a number of local unions in a given area and to act as an intermediate unit of union government, most national unions have established intermediate organizational bodies. Usually these are set up on a geographical basis. In the Amalgamated Clothing Workers Union (men's and boy's clothing) all of the locals in a city in several crafts will be grouped together in a joint board. Ordinarily the joint board will have an office or building of its own that will serve as headquarters for all of the locals in that joint board. The chairman of the joint board will assist the business agents in contract negotiations, and in many instances he will actually conduct them. Other unions, such as the United Automobile Workers, are divided into regions, with each one being supervised by a director. The United Mine Workers and the United Steel Workers call their regions districts. In the railroad industry all of the locals of a single railroad company are grouped into a system federation.

National and International Unions

The top organizational entity of a union is called the national or international (if it contains branches and locals in Canada). For brevity the term *national* will be used here. A great deal of power, authority, and responsibility resides in the national. Let us look at the functions performed by the national.

First of all the national officers establish basic policies. They determine in what direction the efforts of the union will go. For basic guidance in setting policy, the officers are bound by the constitution of the union. The national frequently sets the wage policy that locals must seek to accomplish. Uniformity of practice among all of the organized enterprises in a given area or industry not only on wage matters but also on seniority rules, group insurance practices, and others, is often a union goal. The national union provides a host of services to the locals. It may send out specialists to help the locals negotiate their contracts with management. It provides data to the locals on such matters as cost of living, comparable wages, and details of the contract settlements in other companies. Because the turnover of local union officers is rather high, many nationals find that they must continually train key personnel of the locals in such subjects as parliamentary procedure, grievance handling, labor law, and the administration of a local. National unions also build up strike funds in their treasuries with which to pay benefits to members when on strike and to take care of the many extra costs required during a strike. In fact, because a strike is the equivalent of going to war for a nation, most nationals keep tight control on the right of a local strike. The local must get permission from the national first, and generally it must support its position with sound reasons.

Most nationals are continuously involved in efforts to expand their unions. This means that they are attempting to organize the unorganized or nonunion employees of certain industries. It also means that they may try to persuade the workers in a company who already belong to another union to give up their allegiance and switch membership to their own union. This activity is called "raiding" and is officially discouraged by the AFL-CIO. However, it still goes on to a considerable extent.

Elected officials of the national consist of a president, secretary-treasurer, and several vice-presidents, who usually represent regions and who constitute the executive board. This executive board is theoretically the top policy-making body in the interval between conventions.

In addition to the elective positions, there exist at the national level a considerable number of appointed staff specialists. These include lawyers, economists, statisticians, and public relations personnel. Most unions have a research director, who, along with his staff, is responsible for collecting, analyzing, and disseminating economic and other information which can be of great value to the union and its locals in collective bargaining. Another key appointive position is that of educational director. His job is to set up training programs for local union officers and stewards so that they can conduct the affairs of the union more effectively.

International representatives are a key group of appointive personnel. Their main responsibility is to aid the local unions both at contract negotiation time and in the day-to-day administration of the union. It is not uncommon to find the international representative acting in the role of chief union spokesman during contract bargaining. He may also have to show local officials how to set up and keep financial records, educate them as to their rights and responsibilities under the law, and perform a multitude of other services. Another prime duty of an international representative is to organize unorganized plants and establishments in his assigned jurisdiction.

Trend Toward Centralization of Power

During the past twenty years there has been a noticeable shift in power from the locals to the nationals. This has occurred, in most instances, without any significant changes in the union constitutions. A number of factors have caused this shift. An important one is the growing trend toward multiemployer, regionwide, and industrywide bargaining. In order to marshal enough economic power to deal effectively with giant corporations and large numbers of companies allied in an employers' association, unions have found it necessary to concentrate much of their power at the top. Another cause is the one party system of government practiced in so many unions. Manifestations of this are the appointment of the nominating committee by the incumbent president, the solid slate of incumbents for re-election, and the infrequent ceremonial conventions. Because of their ability to build a strong political machine, appoint their supporters to jobs as international representatives and others, and to control the channels of union communication, top officials are often able to squelch grass roots opposition. Incumbent officials often claim that those in the locals who challenge their decisions may seriously weaken the union by their tactics of dividing it into factions.

The AFL-CIO

The American Fderation of Labor (often referred to simply as the AFL) was formed in 1886 as a loose federation of rather autonomous national craft unions. The goals of the AFL and its member unions through the years have been typical of what is called business or market union-ism. This means that primary emphasis has been placed upon achieving higher wages, shorter hours, and better working conditions through col-lective bargaining. The member AFL unions tended to organize work-ers according to craft or occupational lines. This means that all union-ized employees in the same trade (such as laborers or carpenters) would belong to the same union regardless of the company or industry in which they were employed.

The Congress of Industrial Organizations (CIO) was formed in 1935, when a number of unions under the leadership of John L. Lewis broke away from the AFL. This group originally was called the Committee for Industrial Organization. The reason for the schism in the AFL is that Lewis and his supporters wanted to organize actively the nonunion workers in the mass production industries. Lewis believed that the craft union method of organization was totally inappropriate and ineffective for factory work-ers. He advocated the industrial or factory union system of organization, in which all workers in a single factory would belong to the same local union, regardless of their occupation. The leaders of the AFL gave only lukewarm support to the idea of organizing factory workers and strong-ly opposed the concept of industrial organization. So the CIO separated from the AFL and was spectacularly successful in organizing the auto-mobile, steel, rubber, oil, textile, and electrical industries within a few years.

Whereas the AFL typified business unionism, the CIO advocated not only business unionism but also "welfare" and "social" unionism. Through the years they emphasized (in addition to high wages, shorter hours, and better working conditions) social legislation in such areas as old-age se-curity, improved unemployment insurance, antidiscrimination, public housing, and government-sponsored medical insurance.

In 1955 the AFL and the CIO merged into a federation known simply as the AFL-CIO. The old animosities that had existed in the 1930's had subsided, and under new presidents (George Meany of the AFL and Walter Reuther of the CIO) the two groups found it advantageous to reconcile their differences and form a joint federation. At the time of the merger, the AFL had 108 national unions and about 50,000 locals, whereas the CIO had 32 nationals, with about 11,000 locals.

The activities of the AFL-CIO are manyfold. Two of its principal func-tions are the organization of unorganized employees and the securing of federal, state, and local legislation that is favorable to the organized labor movement and, more generally, of benefit to working men and women throughout the country. It carries on an active research program and publishes a great volume of information in the fields of economics, em-ployment, collective bargaining, labor statistics, labor law, and so on. Through its many publications the AFL-CIO seeks to get its message to the general public, its own union constituents, and to such special interest groups as businessmen, farmers, consumers, and elected government leaders. The AFL-CIO has many special staff groups and committees that function in such fields as civil rights, international affairs, economic policy, safety and health, education, and social security. The Federation has, as another of its important functions, the settling of jurisdictional disputes between its member unions. Its constitution contains a "code of ethical practices" that outlaws any corruption, racketeering, communism, or fascism in member unions. It is up to the Executive Council and the president to implement this code.

Organization Structure of AFL-CIO. Figure 4-5 shows the organization structure of the AFL-CIO. It should be emphasized that this is a loose federation of independent national and international unions. The president of the AFL-CIO does not have the power to compel a member union to follow his directives. Most of the leadership of the president and the Executive Council is exercised through persuasion, influence, and appeals to the good sense of leaders of member unions. Appeals to public opinion also play a part. The only really significant sanction that can be applied is that of suspension or expulsion from membership in the organization. This action must be approved by the Convention.

The Convention is the legislative body of the organization. It meets once every two years. The delegates are composed primarily of officials of affiliated unions. The number of persons that each union is allowed to send is determined by its total membership.

The president supervises the affairs of the organization, appoints study committees that make recommendations to the Convention, presides at conventions, calls meetings of the Executive Council, appoints staff department heads and union organizers, and serves as the official spokesman for organized labor in the United States.

The Executive Council serves as a policy-making group. It roughly corresponds to the board of directors in a corporation. It is composed of the president, secretary-treasurer, and twenty-seven vice-presidents (who in turn are presidents of their own national unions). It has the authority to direct the activities of the Federation and to make such decisions as are necessary to promote the best interests of the AFL-CIO. It keeps informed of legislative affairs affecting the labor force, makes rules that are consistent with its constitution, and can conduct investigations into the affairs of member unions that it suspects are under corrupt or totalitarian influences. The Council has the authority, upon a two-thirds vote of its members, to suspend a member union found guilty of internal corruption, racketeering, or communist or fascist influences. The Council also has the responsibility to oversee the extension of union organization and to charter new national unions.

The Departments that appear on the organization chart are a carryover from the former structure of the AFL. When the two federations merged, the Industrial Union Department was added to those already

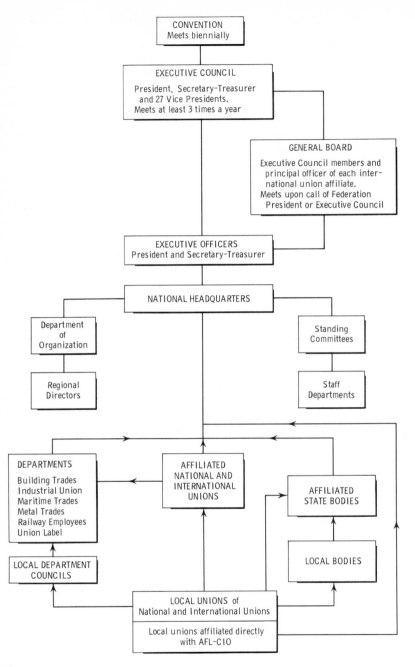

Figure 4-5. Structure of the AFL-CIO. Source: United States Department of Labor, Bureau of Labor Statistics, *Directory of National and International Labor Unions in The United States,* 1967. Bulletin No. 1596, Washington, D.C., p. 52.

existing in the AFL. Most of the former CIO unions and many of the former AFL ones belong to this department. It is designed to promote and coordinate the affairs of the industrial type of unions. All nationals that decide to affiliate with a department pay dues to that department on a per capita basis.

The Union Label Department promotes the sale of union-made goods by having manufacturers attach "union-made" labels on items such as clothing, magazines, calendars, and books.

The other Departments help coordinate collective bargaining activities among member unions and try to settle work jurisdictional disputes. When several craft unions are represented on a construction project, for example, it is inevitable that there be disagreements as to which union has the right to have its members perform certain jobs.

UNION OBJECTIVES AND BEHAVIOR

Unions basically seek to advance the interests of their members. In this sense they are no different from any other voluntary organization, such as the United States Chamber of Commerce, the Farm Bureau, or the American Legion. Unions work to achieve a better life for their membership. This means an ever increasing standard of living, more leisure time, and financial protection against many of the risks of life—namely unemployment, injury on the job, sickness, and insufficient income in old age. Another, and a more specific, set of goals of unions are job security, job rights, and opportunity for advancement. Practically all unions have the foregoing as their goals. In addition to these, some segments of the labor movement have broader social goals. They advocate government legislation to affect improvements in educational opportunities, obtain better housing, and insure equal opportunities in employment, education, and housing regardless of race, color, or national origin. They are continually pushing for improvements in protective labor laws. Many have sought some form of federal government participation in health and medical insurance.

There exist two principal means by which unions seek to fulfill their goals. First and foremost is collective bargaining. This involves the union serving as a representative of the employees in the negotiating of a formal written agreement with management, which in turn represents the employer. Collective bargaining also includes within its compass the day-to-day administration of the agreement, the enforcement of the agreement, and the resort to collective action (such as a strike and picketing). The second principal way in which unions advance their aims is through efforts to influence government legislation. This takes the form of grass roots campaigns to elect the friends of labor to political office, lobbying, and the dissemination of mass information to mold public opinion.

We have talked so far about the objectives of unionism to advance the economic and social position of its constituents. This is its principal goal. But in addition, most unions have social and fraternal goals. They provide a feeling of belonging for the members. This gives members a sense of identification and purpose. Union meetings, picnics, banquets, and the feeling of solidarity evidenced on a picket line emphasize the social and fraternal aspects of unionism. For some persons unionism is almost a way of life in the same sense that top executives in industry tend to integrate their lives wholly with the corporation. To be sure, this way-of-life attitude holds true for only a small proportion of union members—most of these are officials and stewards.

Although we have been discussing union goals in general, it should be pointed out that there exist some important differences in the specific objectives and behavior of craft unions as distinct from industrial unions.

Craft Union Objectives and Behavior[6]

Craft unions, as illustrated by those in the building trades (carpenters, bricklayers, electricians, ironworkers, and so on), the printing industry, or the artistic professions tend to be the epitome of business unionism. They concentrate on goals related to the employment relationship. Primarily they seek control over jobs and job rights. They have an underlying belief that job opportunities are scarce in both the short and long run. They seek to protect in every way possible not only the job rights of their members but also their skill rights. Primarily representing, as they do, skilled craftsmen, the unions tend to oppose the technological advances that will reduce or water down the level of skill needed. They fear that a reduction in pay might follow.

By restricting the supply of labor, craft unions hope to keep the price (that is, wage) for that labor high. There is little doubt that many of them have been eminently successful. There are many devices by which these unions restrict the supply of labor. One is to control the number of apprentices in training at any one time. Another is to obtain licensing regulations in cities and towns so that only a licensed plumber or electrician will be permitted to do certain work. The closed shop is still a further means of keeping people out of a trade. Although outlawed by the Taft-Hartley Act, the closed shop flourishes in the building, maritime, and longshoring trades. The closed union (refusal to admit outsiders into union membership), high initiation fees, and the union hiring hall are other devices for restricting and controlling the supply of labor. It should be pointed out that the majority of craft unions do not have closed shops, they are not closed unions, and a great many do not operate hiring halls; however,

[6] For a detailed analysis of craft union and industrial union objectives, strategy, and tactics see Edwin F. Beal and Edward D. Wickersham, *The Practice of Collective Bargaining* (3rd Ed., Homewood, Ill.: Richard D. Irwin, Inc., 1967), pp. 9-14 and Ch. 3.

a significant minority do attempt to limit entrance to the trade through one or more of these devices.

In additon to controlling the supply of labor, craft unions establish what they consider to be a fair work pace. The example of bricklayers being permitted to lay only so many bricks per day is well known. Whereas in factories, management generally has the upper hand in establishing and enforcing work standards, in construction the union tends to be dominant. In part, this is a consequence of relative bargaining power. In many of the industries where craft unions predominate, employers are small and the union is big.

Most craft unions are fortunate because of the fact that their membership is composed largely of skilled workers who are in short supply in the labor market and who are difficult to replace. Thus when many craft unions call a strike, as, for example, in the building trades, they need post only token pickets who carry signs explaining the strike. The strike becomes a waiting game—a contest of economic holding power. The employer usually would be unable to hire any significant number of replacements because of the usual shortage of skilled workers. Added to this situation is the fact that any other unions that have been accustomed to dealing with the company will now refuse to cross a picket line. Thus the company is completely shut down until an agreement is reached with the union. Strikes by most craft unions tend to be peaceful, because employers know that it would be extremely difficult to hire replacements to keep operating.

Industrial Union Objectives and Behavior

Whereas craft unions gain their strength by artificially restricting the number of workers in a trade—that is by keeping people out—industrial unions acquire power by doing just the opposite. An industrial union which has been recognized by a company as the bargaining agent for the employees seeks to encourage all of the workers—unskilled, semiskilled, skilled, and sometimes even white-collar—to join the union. The union hopes to develop a feeling of solidarity among all who work in that company and in that industry. The United Automobile Workers is an example of an industrial union. In contrast to craft unions, the initiation fees and monthly dues of an industrial union are modest. A typical initiation fee is $10, with monthly dues being about $5.

The strike behavior of an industrial union is usually quite different from that of a craft union. The factory union seeks total and simultaneous action by all of the workers. Because semiskilled workers predominate in most factories, replacements can rather easily be recruited by management if it decides to keep the plant in operation during the strike. To bring the union to terms during a strike, a company can follow either of two tactics. It may simply elect to shut down the plant and wait out the union. In this case it counts upon the fact that its economic holding power is greater than that of the workers and the union. (Workers' savings are usually exhausted after a few weeks.) On the other hand, management may try aggressively to break the strike by hiring nonunion replacements and launching a back-to-work movement. Because a permanently replaced economic striker loses all claim to his former job, his situation and that of the union becomes desperate at this point. The union usually resorts to mass picketing at the plant gate to prevent scabs and strike-breakers from going to work. This usually leads to picket line violence. But mass picketing has been held to be illegal under the Taft-Hartley Act, and the local police usually prevent such picketing when they see it occurring. Thus an industrial union often is faced with a dilemma. If the company hires nonunion workers to keep operating, the union can either resort to mass picketing in violation of the law, or it can risk losing the strike by posting only token pickets and allowing nonunion workers to walk through the picket line. This description of the strike behavior of an industrial union shows why it must have the support of the vast majority of the workers in order to win a strike. A concerted refusal to work must be, for all practical purposes, a 100 per-cent refusal.

The principal bargaining issues in a factory, in addition to the usual wages and hours, are union security, management security, job security, and control of work pace. The union seeks some form of compulsory unionism, such as the union shop, in order to maintain a secure position. By requiring all employees in the bargaining unit to belong after they have been employed at least thirty days (the union shop) the union is assured of financial security and 100 per cent membership. Because the turnover in many factories is rather high, the unions feel that they would be continually faced with the problem of persuading new workers to join if they did not have a union shop provision in the contract.

Whereas workers in craft unions obtain their security and rights to a job primarily through the union, factory workers seek their security from their company. This explains why the union places such great emphasis upon handling job changes—promotions, transfers, layoffs—on the basis of seniority. This eliminates the possibility of any favoritism or discrimination. It is an objective method, and most workers tend to accept it as fair.

The amount of work that a worker must do in a day—the pace at which he must work—constitutes a frequent point of clash between workers and the union on the one hand and management on the other. To operate its plant efficiently and to control labor costs, management feels that it must have full control over the amount of work turned out by each man. It may use time and motion studies and other industrial engineering techniques to set work standards. But unions often cry "Speed-up" or "Stretch-out." The speed of assembly lines and the amount of relief time is a perennial bargaining issue in the automobile industry. Industrial unions push grievances over work standards, and this often becomes a hotly contested issue.

IMPACT OF THE UNION UPON MANAGEMENT

After a union has won bargaining rights for the employees in an organization, management finds that the way in which it handles employment relationships and its manner of dealing with employees is considerably altered. Let us now examine the effects of the union upon the management of people in the company.

Restriction upon Management's Freedom of Action

Unilateral action and individual dealings with workers over wage adjustments, hours, and the conditions of work are no longer possible. The first-line supervisor must be sure he does not violate the labor agreement in handling his employees. He is continuously aware of the presence of a shop steward who will go to bat for the workers in presenting their complaints and grievances. Basically the greatest change that occurs with the advent of the union on the scene is the restriction upon management's freedom of action. Its flexibility becomes limited. Management is closely bound by the conditions set forth in the union-management agreement. At times, this loss of managerial freedom to act may impair plant efficiency. It may not be able to shift workers from one job to another as easily as before. If a man is asked to perform certain tasks that are of a higher skill than he has been accustomed to previously, both he and the union will usually demand a higher job classification. If sales decline and management finds it necessary to reduce the size of the work force, it cannot lay off the least competent employees. Instead it must lay off those having the least seniority. If management wishes to install a profit-sharing or pension plan, it cannot do so without consulting the union and obtaining its consent. Thus we see that management has considerably less freedom to operate the business as it sees fit than before the union entered the picture.

Union Pressure for Uniformity of Treatment

Another effect of the union upon management is its insistence upon uniformity of treatment of all employees. For example, unions usually advocate that all employees who are assigned to the same job should receive exactly the same rate of pay or, at least, that in-grade increases in pay be based solely upon seniority. Management officials often claim that unions introduce a leveling effect upon the employees, so that individual initiative is discouraged. The psychology of individual differences tells us that among people there is great variation in aptitudes and capabilities. To be sure, those on the payroll of a given company will have a much smaller range of abilities than the general population, because the employee selection process has eliminated those of inferior abilities. One of the principal reasons unions press for uniformity of treatment of all employees and for the rule of seniority to be applied to most job changes is that they do not want to introduce cliques, factionalism, and "fair-haired" boys among the union membership. Because everyone pays the same dues, he is entitled to the same benefits.

Improved Personnel Policies and Practices

On the other hand it is fair to state that the presence of the union encourages management to become fully conscious of employee wants and needs. Any omissions or faults in a company's labor policy and its manner of carrying out the policy will tend to be quickly noted by the local union officials. Thus we find that many organizations have found it advantageous to institute supervisory and executive training programs that contain a strong emphasis upon sound personnel policies, labor relations, and human relations. Good leadership on the job tends to reduce the number and severity of problems about which the employees and union stewards may submit grievances. In fact, some companies have deliberately gone "all out" to provide for their employees' needs and wants, to exercise good leadership, to foster social groupings around company-sponsored recreational activities, and to maintain high morale. This is intended to blunt the union's "sword," so that the employees will feel little need for the union. Local union leadership may thereby be rendered impotent, because the employees are content and the company takes care of them.

One Spokesman for the Employees

In a sense the presence of the union simplifies management's problems in dealing with employees, because it can look to the elected union leaders as spokesmen for the employees. How will the workers react to rotating instead of fixed shifts when the plant must operate around the clock? When business is slack, would the workers prefer a reduced work week (work sharing) to layoffs for a certain percentage of the work force? For these and other employee relations questions the local union leaders are generally in a good position to feel the pulse of the work force and fairly represent their attitudes to management. In those relationships that have developed to a stage of mutual respect and maturity, management often finds that it has much to gain by engaging in joint consultation with union officers on such subjects as working conditions, plant safety, suggestion system operation, and similar topics. Such action need not infringe upon management prerogatives, and many actually result in improved plant efficiency.

Centralization of Labor Relations' Decision Making

Because of the critical importance of many labor relations decisions, top executives have a tendency to take authority in labor matters away from lower ranks of supervision and centralize this in the industrial relations department. This is quite noticeable in grievance handling. Although in theory the first-level supervisor occupies the first step in the grievance procedure in all organizations, in actual practice he is often required to go to the industrial relations manager before he can give a definite answer. He then becomes a messenger boy. The power to discipline is sometimes taken away from the supervisor when there is a union. The reason for this state of affairs is that a union often does not accept the word of lower management if a decision does not meet with its approval. It goes directly to the top of the organization in many cases.

In the long run a company will develop better labor-management relations and better day-to-day leadership on the job by thoroughly training its supervisors in labor policy, personnel relations, and the elements of supervision. Top management should help foremen to do a better job instead of acquiescing or encouraging their being bypassed.

Another, perhaps inescapable, aspect of the tendency for top management to centralize labor relations authority when it is dealing with a union is found in multiplant companies. Largely as a reaction to the union that demands uniformity of practice throughout all of the bargaining units in the organization, the corporate industrial relations officers (rather than the plant industrial relations directors) negotiate the labor agreement with the union. These industrial relations officers also formulate corporate labor policy to a large extent as well as play a key role in applying and administering the labor contract.

DETERMINANTS OF LABOR RELATIONS STABILITY

American labor history prior to the 1950's was turbulent. It was filled with such elements of strife as violent battles on the picket line, blacklisting of union sympathizers, sit-down and sympathy strikes, calling out of the state militia to maintain order, mass picketing, and importation of hired strike-breakers. The symbols of the struggle between management and labor stand out vividly on the pages of American labor history—the Homestead and Pullman strikes of the 1890's, textile strikes in Lawrence and Lowell, Massachusetts in 1912, the great steel strike of 1919, the open-shop drives in the 1920's launched by employers, the sit-down strikes in the automobile industry, and the strikes against "Little Steel" during the 1930's—these and others are highlighted as one reviews the background to present-day labor relations. But to a considerable extent the relations between employers and unions have substantially improved in recent years. There is growing evidence that the managements of our business firms have come to accept the fact that unions are here to stay. Management has learned to live with unions. Unions have achieved a measure of security, for the most part they are respectable, and they have accepted the fact that higher wages and benefits for their members depend upon healthy businesses and increasing productivity.[7]

When the management of an organization is faced with the prospect of dealing with a union as the bargaining agent for its employees, it basically has two choices: (1) opposition, or (2) acceptance.[8] Within each of these choices are a variety of approaches. Opposition may take the form of forceful action to weaken the union and to break off the bargaining relationship (as occurred in the Kohler Company in Wisconsin in 1954-55), or it may involve subtle attempts to discredit the union in the eyes of the workers and to build up respect, loyalty, and pride in the company and complete trust in management. Patterns of acceptance vary along a continuum, from grudging acceptance with strong attempts at controlling the power of the union to accommodation, to labor-management cooperation, and occasionally even to collusion and the making of special deals between the top leaders of the union and those of management.

The majority of the relationships in the United States, as far as management's approach is concerned, can be classified into one or the other of two forms of acceptance. It may take the form either of reluctant acceptance of the union coupled with positive management action to contain the union within certain limits or else accommodation. In the former the employer zealously seeks to preserve the traditional management prerogatives and to use a wide range of strategies and tactics to keep the union from gaining the upper hand. It implies an acceptance of the union as a legitimate institution that possesses certain rights under the laws of the land. However, management feels that it must continuously press to keep the union from encroaching upon management's freedom to operate the business in a profitable manner. Accommodation as a characterization of a type of bargaining relationship is becoming increasingly common. It implies a rather complete acceptance of the union by management, and both union and management have considerable respect for one another. Collective bargaining is confined to the traditional areas of wages, hours, and other (well-accepted) conditions of employment. There are no excursions into labor-management consultation and cooperation on such topics as safety, cost reduction, productive efficiency, and employee suggestions. These latter joint activities are found in those bargaining relationships properly classified as labor-management cooperation. Under this setup both the union and the management are work-

[7] For an informative discussion of changes in the labor-management relations climate since the 1920's see Douglass V. Brown and Charles A. Myers, "The Changing Industrial Relations Philosophy of American Management," *Proceedings of the Ninth Annual Meeting of the Industrial Relations Research Association,* (Madison, Wisc.: The Association, 1957), pp. 84-99.

[8] For a well-known classification system of bargaining relationships see Benjamin M. Selekman, Stephen H. Fuller, Thomas Kennedy and John M. Baitsell, *Problems in Labor Relations,* (3rd Ed., New York: McGraw-Hill Book Co., Inc., 1964), pp. 2-8.

ing for the same goals. There is a maximum of joint dealings on ways to increase productivity, cut costs, eliminate waste, and improve working conditions. However, labor-management cooperation represents a very advanced stage of relationship and of working harmony and is not particularly common in the United States.

The negotiation of special deals and of collusive arrangements by management and union officials is not common, but it does occur. Sometimes employers and unions work together to keep other companies out of a particular product market.[9] The McCellan Committee hearings of 1957-59 uncovered situations in which employers signed "sweetheart" contracts with union leaders at substandard wages. The union leaders sometimes took a direct money pay-off in exchange for granting a low wage contract to the company.

Causes of Harmonious Labor Relations

A number of years ago an eminent labor relations practitioner, Cyrus Ching, who later became the first director of the Federal Mediation and Conciliation Service, said:

> You can't write any ticket or any procedure on how to handle it, except this: In our company—I am going to try to impress this on the industrialists here—we are going to get about the type of labor leadership that we develop by our own actions. If, in dealing with labor organizations, we are ethical, are entitled to the confidence of people, use fair tactics and use friendly attitudes, we will get that in return; if we are going to be militant, use underhanded tactics, and fight all the time, that is the type of organized labor leader we will get. So I think we all must realize that, where we are dealing with organized labor, we are going to get about the type of leadership that we are ourselves.[10]

It seems that Mr. Ching's statement is particularly true in an industrial situation where the management oftentimes represents a large company that is in a strong position and that initiates most actions. It exercises a position of leadership. The union reacts to management's leadership. Perhaps in those bargaining situations characterized by many very small shops dealing with one powerful union, his description might not be quite so accurate. Here the union is in a strong position to be dominant, and the companies react to the union's leadership but cannot strongly influence the behavior of these union officials.

[9] For an enlightening account of collusion between a powerful financier-employer and a powerful labor leader to achieve some substantial benefits to the union and the employer but with certain harmful consequences to other firms and some union members see Nat Caldwell and Gene S. Graham, "The Strange Romance Between John L. Lewis and Cyrus Eaton," *Harper's Magazine,* Vol. 223, No. 1339 (December 1961), pp. 25-32.

[10] Cyrus S. Ching, "Problems in Collective Bargaining," *The Journal of Business of the University of Chicago,* p. 40, Vol. XI, No. 1, Part II, copyright January 1938 by The University of Chicago. Quotation by permission.

In a significant and pioneering research effort conducted during the years 1948 through 1953, the National Planning Association, a nonpartisan and nonprofit research organization, sought to discover those factors which contribute to successful and peaceful labor-management relations. It conducted its research by making a number of detailed case studies of many companies and unions who had developed stable and harmonious relations.[11]

The conclusions of this research support the position that the basic attitudes of management and of the union toward each other are major determinants of the state of relations. The researchers found that positive acceptance by management of the union as an institution and of collective bargaining as a desirable way of handling employment relationships are necessary to labor peace. If management is philosophically opposed to unionism, as such, then the chances for stable, sound relations developing are practically nil. Management must also appreciate the fact that unions are, to a considerable extent, political in nature. An elected union president cannot always make agreements with managements solely on the surface merits of the issue. He cannot always act, as management would like him to, in a purely "businesslike manner." He must sometimes "play politics" in order to maintain his support among the membership and in order to be elected. Union officials act pretty much as elected public officials do. Sometimes they must dramatize an issue, go along with a powerful faction (at least for a while), and sometimes advocate issues they themselves are not fully in accord with.

Another important management attitude is one of genuine concern for the needs and wants of the employees. Management must have a sound human relations philosophy. It must not look upon the workers simply as tools to get the work out—as instruments of production.

For the union's part the researchers found that it must show a full acceptance of management and an understanding of its responsibilities to operate the business in a profitable and efficient manner. The union must accept the concepts of private ownership and free enterprise. It must have a concern for the economic welfare of the organization.

For labor peace another important ingredient is mutual confidence and trust. Each side must believe in the sincerity and fair play of the other party. There must be no serious ideological conflicts.

In addition to essential elements of management and union philosophy and beliefs, the National Planning Association researchers found that certain procedures and methods bore a significant relationship to labor peace. These may be summarized as follows:

1. Joint union-management consultation on matters beyond those strictly required by law. An example would be a discussion of the impact of technological improvements on the number of jobs.

[11] Clinton S. Golden and V. D. Parker (eds.), *Causes of Industrial Peace Under Collective Bargaining* (New York: Harper & Row, 1955).

2. Joint information sharing. Both management and the union had their channels of communications to the employees. Instead of competing with one another, they looked upon the other's channel as an aid and supplement.
3. An effective grievance machinery. In addition to using grievances as a means of solving problems arising out of the interpretation and application of the contract, the parties used the grievance process as a means of preventing future problems from arising. They looked upon it as a way of improving understanding.
4. In contract negotiations the chief spokesmen for each side had great authority to make commitments. They were not just go-betweens for the real decision makers, who may have stayed in the background.
5. The unions involved were strong, operated in a democratic manner, were responsive to their members' needs, and acted responsibly toward management.[12]

Questions for Review and Discussion

1. Why is it important for students and practitioners in management to have a sound understanding of labor union philosophy, objectives, and organization?
2. How does personnel management in a unionized organization differ from that in a nonunion establishment?
3. What motivates employees to form and to join a union?
4. Why have unions succeeded in organizing only about one fourth of the total labor force?
5. Compare the status, position, and rights of an individual factory worker before and after the entry of a union into the plant.
6. Compare the objectives, practices, and tactics of a craft union (such as the carpenters or electricians) with those of a professional society like the American Medical Association.
7. Why has the American labor movement failed to increase its total membership significantly since the late 1940's?
8. Identify and give the functions of the following union positions:
   a. Business agent
   b. Research director
   c. Education director
   d. International Representative
   e. Shop steward

[12] For an updating of the situations occurring at the various companies since the original National Planning Association researches and for a recent re-evaluation of the conclusions of this pioneering study into causes of industrial peace under collective bargaining see Herbert R. Northrup and Harvey A. Young, "The Causes of Industrial Peace Revisited," *Industrial and Labor Relations Review,* Vol. 22, No. 1 (October 1968), pp. 31-47. Northrup and Young assert that economic conditions in a company and an industry play a larger role in determining labor relations peace than was recognized by the original National Planning Association researchers.

9. "Prior to the 1940's, at a time when the typical industrial worker had few basic job rights and little defense against arbitrary treatment, unions were certainly necessary. However, in this day and age of enlightened management, which fully recognizes its social responsibilities, there is little real need for unions. Unions no longer have a vital role to play in employee-management relations." Defend or refute the foregoing statement.

10. There are many local independent unions that are not affiliated with any national union or with the AFL-CIO. They are simply composed of the employees at a single company. What advantages do such unions enjoy over those that are part of a national union? What benefits and services would independent unions obtain by becoming part of a national union?

11. A national union for scientists and engineers is engaging in an active campaign to organize the engineers in a medium-sized electronics company (total of 4,000 employees; 500 engineers and scientific personnel). As an engineer in this company, what would be your attitude toward joining the union? As the president of the company, what would be your attitude? Would you as the president take any action in regard to the organizing campaign?

12. What attitudes and behavior on the part of management tend to build harmonious, constructive union-management relations? What union attitudes and behavior?

13. Contrast the objectives, organization, and authority system of a local union with that of a business concern.

14. In recent years field organizers and office employees of several national unions have sought to organize their own unions to obtain bargaining rights with their employers (that is, the national unions). Their efforts have usually been opposed by the top union leadership. What would motivate these top officials to oppose unionization of their own employees?

Suggestions for Further Reading

Barbash, Jack, *Structure, Government, and Politics of American Unions,* New York: Random House, Alfred A. Knopf, 1967.

———, Labor's Grass Roots: *A Study of the Local Union,* New York: Harper & Row, 1961.

Beal, Edwin F., and Edward D. Wickersham, *The Practice of Collective Bargaining,* 3rd Edition, Homewood, Illinois: Richard D. Irwin, 1967.

Chamberlain, Neil W., *The Labor Sector,* New York: McGraw-Hill Book Company, 1965.

Cohen, Sanford, *Labor in the United States,* (2nd ed.) Columbus, Ohio: Charles E. Merrill Books, 1966.

Dunlop, John T., *Industrial Relations Systems,* New York: Holt, Rinehart and Winston, 1958.

Lombardi, Vincent and Andrew J. Grimes, "A Primer for a Theory of White Color Unionization," *Monthly Labor Review,* Vol. 90, No. 5, May 1967, pp. 46-49.

McCart, J. A., Richard J. Murphy and F. A. Nigro, "Labor Management Relations; Where Do We Stand?," *Civil Service Journal,* Vol. 8, No. 1, July-Sept. 1967, pp. 2-8.

Perlman, Mark, *Labor Union Theories in America: Background and Development,* Evanston, Ill.: Row, Peterson and Company, 1958.

Sayles, Leonard R., and George Strauss, *The Local Union,* (Rev. Ed.), New York: Harcourt, Brace & World, 1967.

Sloane, Arthur A. and Fred Witney, *Labor Relations,* Englewood Cliffs, N.J.: Prentice-Hall, 1967.

Sturmthal, Adolf (ed.), *White Collar Trade Unions,* Urbana: University of Illinois Press, 1966.

Collective Bargaining

5

Collective bargaining is concerned with the relations between employers, acting through their management representatives, and organized labor. It is concerned not only with the negotiation of a formal labor agreement but also with the day-to-day dealings between management and the union. The nature and course of collective bargaining is heavily influenced by labor law. Especially in recent years the structure for bargaining, the manner of dealing, and the content of collective bargaining have become closely regulated by Federal (and to some extent State) labor law. Because the direction of people in so many organizations is so closely intertwined with union-employer relationships, it is essential that the student and the practitioner of management develop a sound knowledge of collective bargaining. This chapter will delve into the nature and characteristics of the collective bargaining process. It will explore (necessarily briefly) the legal framework for bargaining, with particular emphasis upon the Taft-Hartley and Landrum-Griffin acts. The structure for bargaining, negotiating the agreement, the content of collective agreements, substantive issues, and dispute settlement methods are covered in this chapter.

THE NATURE OF COLLECTIVE BARGAINING

Collective bargaining has existed in the United States since the early 1800's. However, it did not develop into its present form until comparatively re-

114

cently. In the very early days the general practice was for either the employer or the union, depending upon their relative economic strengths, to notify the other party of the wage rates and other conditions of employment which it intended to put into effect. There was very little negotiation and discussion between the parties. If one party refused to accept the terms imposed by the other, then either a strike or a lockout ensued.

In 1885 Samuel Gompers was called to testify at hearings into labor relations conducted by the Commissioner of Labor Statistics of the State of New York. In reporting to the state legislature on this investigation the Commissioner used the term *arbitration* to designate the process by which employers and unions would negotiate with one another to settle their differences. In the hearings themselves Gompers used both the words *arbitration* and *conciliation* to cover the process by which unions and management bargained with one another. The modern term *collective bargaining* was actually first used by Sidney and Beatrice Webb, the well-known historians of the British labor movement, just prior to 1900.[1]

The nature, scope, and methodology of collective bargaining is continuing to evolve even today. Collective bargaining is dynamic. But in order that the reader obtain a concrete understanding of what is involved in modern-day collective bargaining, the following definition is given:

Collective bargaining is concerned with the relations between unions representing employees and employers (or their management representatives). It involves the process of union organization of employees; negotiation, administration, and interpretation of collective agreements covering wages, hours of work, and other conditions of employment; engaging in concerted economic action; and dispute settlement procedures.

The bargaining is collective in the sense that the chosen representative of the employees (that is, a union) acts as the bargaining agent for all the employees in carrying out negotiations and dealings with management. The process may also be considered collective in the case of the corporation where the paid professional managers represent the interests of the stockholders and the board of directors in bargaining with union leaders. On the employer side it is also collective in those common situations where the companies have joined together in an employer association for purposes of bargaining with a union.

Characteristics of Collective Bargaining

Collective bargaining has been characterized as a form of industrial democracy and industrial government. The management and union representatives sit down at the bargaining table, where they deliberate, persuade, try to influence, argue, and haggle. Eventually they reach an agree-

---

[1] For the evolution of concepts and terminology in this field see Vernon H. Jensen, "Notes on the Beginnings of Collective Bargaining," *Industrial and Labor Relations Review,* Vol. 9, No. 2 (January 1956), pp. 225-234.

ment, which they record in the form of a labor-management contract. This is the legislative phase, in which the two parties set up a type of company-wide set of laws and regulations. This "industrial law" sets forth the rights and responsibilities of the company, the union, and the employees. Ordinarily management takes on the authority and responsibility to administer and operate the agreement. Management initiates actions in conformance with the agreed-upon provisions. This corresponds to the executive function of government. When employees or the union feel that they are being denied their rights under the contract they may submit a grievance to management. This may, if conditions warrant, be eventually taken to an impartial arbitrator for a final decision. This is analogous to the judicial function of government.

Some who are not thoroughly familiar with the collective bargaining process have asserted that there is no essential difference between the negotiating of a commercial contract (for, say, the buying or selling of a commodity) and the bargaining of a labor agreement. But this point of view is somewhat naive. The employment of human beings cannot be handled in the same manner as the purchase of physical goods. If one businessman contracts with another for the purchase of a load of lumber and the seller delivers inferior merchandise, the buyer can terminate the relationship at that point. But this cannot be done in the relations between management and labor. Generally speaking the union and the management must learn to live with one another whether they like it or not. They must accommodate to each other. Under the labor law of the land, once bargaining relationships have been commenced, both sides must honestly seek an agreement. They must bargain in good faith. Dealings cannot arbitrarily be broken off.

Further, the negotiation of a labor agreement is quite different from the handling of a commercial contract because of the human relations and political aspects of labor-management relationships. A union is a political-economic organization. Union leaders, being elected, must represent the interests of their constituents. They are often placed in a position where they must cater to the pressures of a strong faction within the union. Union leaders are interested in being re-elected. They have to contend with dissident groups within the ranks. They cannot always negotiate a contract with management according to the cold logics of an issue. In short, the social aspects of collective bargaining set it apart from the negotiation of an ordinary business contract.

THE LEGAL FRAMEWORK OF COLLECTIVE BARGAINING

Labor-management relationships are heavily regulated by both Federal and state labor laws at the present time. This state of affairs commenced in the 1930's with the passage of the Norris-LaGuardia and Wagner acts. Prior to this time the policy of the federal government was to leave the two parties—unions and employers—alone and to exert a minimum of legislative interference. Although prior to the 1930's there existed only a minimum of statute law that dealt directly with collective bargaining, there was an abundance of court decisions which did, in effect, create a common law that provided a form of regulation for labor-management relations. Thus we find that common law and the court interpretations played a major part in expressing government labor policy from 1800 through the early 1930's, whereas since then statute law has played the dominant role. Each of the major labor relations laws has been enacted in response to pressing needs of society in general as well as needs of the direct parties involved—employees, unions, and employers. An intelligent understanding of the management of people at work and of labor-management relations is not possible without a brief study of the law of collective bargaining.

Pre-Wagner Act Era—Labor and the Courts[2]

Prior to the passage of the Wagner Act in 1935 the basic struggle of unions was for existence and recognition. They sought to exist in an environment where the economic and political power of the business organization was dominant. Employers were strongly antiunion in their sentiments and actions. Unions, if they successfully met the struggle to survive, then had to win recognition from the employer as the bargaining agent for his employees.

Employers, for their part, did not take the rise of unions complacently. They looked upon unions as a challenge to their basic rights to operate their businesses as they saw fit. They considered that unions threatened the property rights of ownership. It was felt that unions interfered with the relations between management and the workers.

During this era Federal and state courts tended to be sympathetic to the views of employers. As rational bases for their rulings, jurists used three principal common-law concepts: (1) the necessity for preserving free competition with a minimum of interference in the affairs of business organizations; (2) the sanctity of private property rights; and (3) the right to freedom of individual contract.

When unions sought to improve the conditions of employment for their members during the early part of the nineteenth century by calling strikes, they found their efforts frustrated by court orders that held strikes to be criminal conspiracies. It was not until 1842 that the legality of strikes per se was established. This arose as a result of a Massachusetts court decision. Henceforth judges examined union motives and methods in strike actions to decide whether the strike should be ruled illegal or not.

In 1890 Congress passed the Sherman Act to outlaw business combina-

[2] A comprehensive analysis of common and statute labor law and court opinions can be found in Charles O. Gregory, *Labor and the Law* (2nd rev. ed.; New York: W. W. Norton & Co., Inc., 1958).

tions and conspiracies in restraint of trade. Although there is some doubt as to whether Congress ever intended to include union activities within the coverage of this law, nevertheless for many years employers were successful in obtaining court orders to break union strikes under the guise that they constituted combinations and conspiracies in restraint of commerce among the states. It was not until the Apex Hosiery Company and the Hutcheson cases of 1940 and 1941 that the United States Supreme Court ruled that labor unions are not subject to antitrust prosecution under the Sherman Act.

For many years employers were quite successful in impeding union activities by obtaining court injunctions whenever unions called an organizational strike or a strike to improve economic conditions. An injunction is a legal device derived from English common law. It is a court order prohibiting a certain activity in order to prevent property damage where there is no other remedy at law. Courts in the United States went beyond the original English concept, because they granted injunctions to employers if there was impending or actual interference with their business even though there had been no damage to physical property. During the late nineteenth and during the first three decades of the twentieth century, the repeated and widespread use of the labor injunction served effectively to render unions impotent.

In 1932 Congress passed the Norris-LaGuardia Anti-Injunction Act, which effectively rendered the Federal judiciary neutral in labor disputes. It defined permissible union activities in very broad terms and placed such tight restrictions upon the issuance of an injunction that for all practical purposes the private injunction has ceased to be used as a device to defeat strikes.

The Wagner Act—1935

Labor unrest was rampant during the 1930's. The Great Depression, which began in 1929 with the stock market crash, had caused approximately one fourth of the labor force to be unemployed by 1933. Wage cuts were widespread. Industrial workers in the mass production industries were ripe for unionism. Management during this era had not been sufficiently alert nor enlightened to adopt sound industrial relations policies in keeping with the needs of their employees.

In June, 1935, the National Labor Relations Act—popularly known as the Wagner Act after its author and sponsor, Senator Robert Wagner of New York—became law. With the adoption of this far-reaching law, public policy became one of encouragement for collective bargaining as preferable to individual bargaining. The act, in effect, encouraged the unionization of employees and provided the mechanism of secret ballot elections to ascertain the free choice of workers. If the employees voted for union representation, employers were compelled to bargain with that union over wages, rates of pay, hours of work, and other conditions of employment.

The heart of the Wagner Act was contained in Section 7, which stated that "employees shall have the right to self-organization, to form, join, or assist labor organizations, to bargain collectively through representatives of their own choosing, and to engage in concerted activities for the purpose of collective bargaining or other mutual aid or protection."

Unfair Labor Practices of Employers. To insure that employees could actually engage in collective bargaining activities without retaliation by their employers, Section 8 of the Act listed five practices that employers were forbidden to undertake. The law stated that it shall be an unfair labor practice for an employer: (1) "To interfere with, restrain, or coerce employees in the exercise of the rights guaranteed in Section 7." Examples of employer conduct prohibited by this provision are: (a) threatening employees with loss of jobs or benefits if they should join a union, (b) threatening to close down the plant if a union should be organized in it, and (c) spying on union gatherings.

The second unfair labor practice made it illegal "to dominate or interfere with the formation or administration of any labor organization or contribute financial support to it." This provision of the law put an end to the company-dominated unions (generally called "employee representation plans") which flourished in the 1920's and early 1930's. The third unfair labor practice of employers made it illegal to discriminate in regard to hiring or tenure of employment or any term or condition of employment in order to encourage or discourage membership in a union. This provision prevented a company from demoting or discharging a worker because he was active in forming the union. It also made it illegal to refuse to hire a qualified job applicant because he belonged to a union. The fourth unfair labor practice prevented discharging or discriminating against an employee who filed charges or testified before the National Labor Relations Board, the agency charged with the administration of the law. The final unfair labor practice was refusal to bargain in good faith. Thus if management put into effect a unilateral wage increase without discussing it with the union, this constituted a violation of the law.

National Labor Relations Board. In order to provide machinery for operating the Wagner Act, the National Labor Relations Board was established. The Board had (and still does have) two major functions. The first is to conduct representation elections to determine if the employees in a company wish to be represented by a union. An important part of this responsibility is the task of deciding which employees should be in the bargaining unit and which should be excluded. If a union wins a bargaining election, then the board certifies that it shall be the "sole and exclusive bargaining agent" for all of the employees in that unit. The second major function is that of adjudicating charges of employer unfair labor practices. If the Board decided that an unfair labor practice has occurred it is empowered to order a cease and desist order, to order the reinstatement of a wrongfully discharged employee, or to order the payment of back wages.

Experience Under the Wagner Act.   This law played a significant part in fostering the growth of organized labor. In 1935 total union membership stood at about 3.9 million, whereas in 1947, when the Taft-Hartley Act was passed, it had reached 15 million. Other factors, of course, contributed to this rapid expansion as well.

Representatives of American management expressed vigorous objection to the Wagner Act on the grounds that it was very one-sided and that it tied the hands of management while giving the unions free rein. It is true that the Act sought to encourage unionization and collective bargaining while imposing no restraints whatever on union behavior. There was great unrest, and many bitter struggles occurred between labor and management during the 1935-1947 period. Much of this could be attributed to the fact that unions and management were going through the difficult process of learning to live with one another. A record number of strikes occurred in 1946. The general public and Congress tended to blame unions for the wave of strikes that occurred during this period. A reaction set in against unions, and this culminated in the passage of the Taft-Hartley Act in June, 1947, over President Truman's veto.

Taft-Hartley Act—1947

Officially titled the Labor-Management Relations Act, this law amended the Wagner Act to a considerable extent. In addition, it initiated a number of new provisions completely beyond the scope of the Wagner Act. The primary purposes of this new law were to regulate and restrict the activities of unions, to protect individual employees and employers against the power of unions, and to attempt to restore a balance of power in labor relations. The Taft-Hartley Act is a very complicated law; therefore we can cover only the highlights here.

The law basically retains all of the provisions of the original Wagner Act that were designed to guarantee to employees the right to form and join unions and to engage in collective bargaining free of any restraint or coercion by the employer. Section 7, dealing with rights of employees, contains the original wording of the Wagner Act plus the statement that employees shall also have the right to *refrain* from any or all of such activities related to union organization and collective bargaining.

The five unfair labor practices of employers contained in Section 8 were retained. However, Congress added six unfair labor practices of unions.

Unfair Labor Practices of Unions.   The first unfair union practice consists of restraining or coercing employees in the exercise of rights guaranteed in Section 7 of the Act. The National Labor Relations Board and the courts have interpreted this to outlaw mass picketing, which bars non-striking employees from entering the plant. Also outlawed are violence on the picket line in connection with strikes and threats to do bodily injury to nonstrikers.

The second unfair labor practice of unions involves causing or, attempting to cause the employer to discriminate against an employee in order to encourage and discourage union membership. When the second unfair union practice is combined with the original third unfair employer practice as revised by the Taft-Hartley Act, the net result is to outlaw the closed shop. (The union shop which requires union membership on or after the thirtieth day of employment is legal under the Act.)

The third practice consists of a union refusal to bargain in good faith. Examples of such union conduct are the insistence upon the inclusion of illegal provisions, such as a closed shop or a discriminatory hiring hall, in a contract and adamant refusal to make a written contract of reasonable duration.

The fourth unfair union practice in reality consists of four separate activities as follows:

1. Requiring an employer or self-employed person to join a union.
2. Forcing an employer to cease handling the products or doing business with any other person. This is the ban on secondary boycotts. What is a secondary boycott? Let us assume that a union has a dispute with Company A (the primary employer). The union is unsuccessful in taking direct action against Company A, so it pickets or otherwise takes action against Company B (a secondary employer) to induce B to cease buying from or selling goods to A. This action is one type of secondary boycott.

   Of the 100 secondary boycott cases that went to a formal hearing and decision by the National Labor Relations Board during the period from 1947 through 1958, the largest single type (42) occurred in connection with a union's attempt to organize nonunion companies. The union most frequently involved in all secondary boycott cases (regardless of type of issue) was the International Brotherhood of Teamsters, Chauffeurs, and Warehousemen of America. This union was involved in 45 of the 100 cases.[3]
3. Forcing an employer to bargain with one union when another union is already the certified bargaining agent.
4. Forcing the employer to assign particular work to employees in one union rather than to employees in another union. This provision outlaws the jurisdictional strike. Jurisdictional disputes are prevalent where a number of craft unions struggle for control of the same jobs.

[3] Paul A. Brinker and W. E. Cullison, "Secondary Boycotts in the United States Since 1947," *Labor Law Journal,* Vol. 12, No. 5 (May 1961), pp. 398-399.

Each of the competing unions hopes to obtain employment for their own members.

The fifth unfair labor practice is that of charging excessive or discriminatory initiation fees. In judging whether a particular fee is excessive the Board considers the practices and customs of other unions in the same industry and the wages currently paid to the employees affected.

The sixth unfair practice is that of causing or attempting to cause an employer to pay money or other thing of value for services which are not performed or not to be performed. This outlaws featherbedding. Unions tend to engage in this practice when employment opportunities for their members are declining. It is a common reaction to prevent displacement of workers due to technological advances.

As with unfair employer practices, the National Labor Relations Board has the power to issue cease and desist orders in connection with union unfair labor practices. It can order a union to reimburse an employee for any wages he may have lost as a result of union discrimination or coercion, and it can require the refund of dues and fees illegally collected. Charges of unfair employer or union practices can be filed at any of the Board's regional offices by employers, unions, or individual employees.

Supervisors and Professionals. The Taft-Hartley Act contains provisions that have an important effect upon certain groups of employees. Whereas foremen and supervisors had received some protection by the National Labor Relations Board if they sought to unionize during the years when the Wagner Act was in effect, the Taft-Hartley Act excluded supervisors from the definition of employees. They are now considered to be members of management and receive no protection under the Act if they choose to form a union. Professional personnel, such as engineers and scientists, are considered to be employees and do receive the full protection of the law in regard to self-organization. However, the Board is not allowed to include them in the same bargaining unit as all other (nonprofessional) employees, unless a majority of them vote for inclusion in the larger unit. This provision gives recognition to the fact that professional employees feel their problems and interests are quite distinct from those of production and maintenance workers.

Free Speech. Under the Wagner Act management complained vigorously that it was not allowed to speak freely in connection with unions and their activities. To meet this situation the law states in Section 8c that "the expressing of any views, argument, or the dissemination thereof, whether in written, printed, graphic, or visual form, shall not constitute or be evidence of an unfair labor practice under any of the provisions of this Act, if such expression contains no threat of reprisal or force or promise of benefit." Employers now have considerable latitude to make antiunion speeches to their employees as long as they do not threaten workers or promise benefits. Unions also have the right of free speech.

National Emergency Disputes. In order to provide a means of settling labor-management disputes and strikes that imperil the national health and safety, a systematic procedure has been established to deal with this serious problem. Whenever, in the opinion of the President of the United States, a threatened or actual strike or lockout will affect an entire industry or substantial part thereof such that the health and safety of the nation will be endangered, he is empowered to appoint a board of inquiry that will investigate the facts in the dispute and report back to the President. Upon receiving this report, the President may direct the Attorney General to petition a federal district court for an injunction to prevent or terminate the strike or lockout. Upon the issuance of this injunction the strike must terminate, and the two parties must make every effort to settle their differences with the help of the Federal Mediation and Conciliation Service. If the strike is not settled, then at the end of 60 days the board of inquiry must make a public report on the status of the dispute and the current position of the two sides. Within 15 more days the National Labor Relations Board must conduct a secret ballot of the employees to ascertain whether they wish to accept the employer's last offer to the union. The results must be certified to the Attorney General within 5 days. The injunction must be discharged at the end of 80 days if the strike is still not settled. The President must make a full report to Congress, together with any recommendations he wishes to make. The union has a right to strike after the 80-day injunction is lifted if no agreement has been reached.

Between 1947 and 1968 the national emergency provisions of the Act were utilized 28 times. The industries most frequently involved have been maritime, ship loading and unloading (stevedoring), atomic energy, and basic steel. In the vast majority of those cases where the dispute continued to the point of a last offer vote by the striking employees, they have voted to reject the employer's offer. Generally they feel that they have more to gain by supporting the position taken by their elected union leaders than by supporting the position of the employer.

Appraisal of the Act. The Taft-Hartley Act was passed primarily to control and restrain union activities. It has been partially successful in this respect. There has been a noticeable decline in secondary boycott and jurisdictional strikes. However, the ban on featherbedding has not been effective. The law has been a factor in retarding the organization of non-union sectors in the South. Employers acquired a potent new device to weaken union organizing campaigns by use of the "free speech" provision. In addition they can delay a representation election by charging the union with an unfair labor practice if any hint of coercion occurs during the campaign. The inclusion of union unfair labor practices has required unions to exercise the same degree of responsibility in collective bargaining as has been required of employers (via employer unfair labor practices) ever since the Wagner Act became law in 1935.

The Landrum-Griffin Act—1959

During the late 1950's dramatic exposes were made of racketeering, violence, lack of democratic procedures in unions, and collusion between unions and employers. A large share of these malpractices occurred in the Teamster's Union. The basic work of uncovering and publicizing these abuses was done by the Senate Select Committee on Improper Activities in the Labor or Management Field, which conducted investigations and public hearings from 1957 through 1959. This Senate committee was popularly known as the McClellan Committee, after its chairman, Senator McClellan of Arkansas. The law which was passed as a result of the work of this committee is known as The Labor-Management Reporting and Disclosure Act of 1959, commonly called the Landrum-Griffin Act (after its sponsors). This law does far more than merely require the reporting of certain information by unions and management as its name implies. It establishes very detailed Federal regulation of the internal affairs of unions, regulates the conduct of union officers, and drastically curtails recognition and organizational picketing. In addition it has made certain amendments to the Taft-Hartley Act, including prohibitions against hot-cargo agreements and other types of secondary boycotts. Because the Landrum-Griffin Act is very lengthy and complicated it will be possible to mention only the highlights here.

The Act contains seven titles, each dealing with a major subject area. We shall discuss briefly all titles except title VI which deals with miscellaneous provisions.

Bill of Rights of Union Members. A considerable number of the provisions of the Landrum-Griffin Act are designed to insure that unions are run democratically with full protection for the rights of individual members. Title I of the law, entitled "Bill of Rights," contains some of these provisions. This title stipulates that members shall have the right (1) to attend, participate in, and vote at union meetings and elections, (2) to meet, assemble, and express views at union meetings, (3) to vote on increases in dues and fees, (4) to testify and bring suit when unions infringe the rights of members, and (5) to receive notice and a fair hearing before any union disciplinary action can be taken except for nonpayment of dues. Enforcement of these five "Bill of Rights" provisions is accomplished by employees themselves, who must bring a civil action in a federal district court.

Reporting Requirements. Title II specifies those reports that unions, union officers, employers, and labor consultants must file with the Secretary of Labor. They become public information when they are filed. Congress felt that reports pertaining to union administration and finances are necessary because union members are the real owners of the money and property of the organization and are entitled to a full accounting thereof.

Unions must file a copy of their constitutions and bylaws with the Secretary of Labor as well as a complete explanation of their administrative practices. They must also file a detailed financial report annually.

Union officers and employees must report on any financial interests or income from a company whose employees the union represents or actively seeks to represent. This is designed to uncover or eliminate "conflict of interest" transactions in which union leaders and appointive officials take loans, gifts, and under-the-table payments from management in return for special concessions. Bona fide wages for services as an employee and investments in securities that are traded on an exchange under the Securities Exchange Act are exempted from the reporting requirements. Employers must report any payment or loan to a union or union officer, except the wages paid to a union officer who is at the same time a regular employee. Employers must report payments to employees or a group of employees designed to get them to persuade other employees to exercise or not exercise their self-organizational rights. Labor relations consultants must also report on any payments or arrangements they have made with an employer where the objective is to interfere with the self-organizational and union rights of employees.

All of the reports by union, union officials, employers, and consultants are designed to remedy abuses uncovered by the McClellan Committee. Typical of these are payments to consultants who would then organize "no-union committees" or bring in a union with which the employer would rather have dealings in preference to the one the employees were organizing. These provisions are aimed at all sorts of shady and collusive arrangements among union leaders, employers, and consultants to the detriment of union members.

Trusteeships.   When a national or international union takes over control of the operation of a local union, including control or seizure of its property and funds, this action is called a trusteeship. In effect, the national ejects the local officers, appoints new local leaders, and closely supervises the running of that union. The McClellan Committee found that while many trusteeships were established to eliminate dishonesty and corruption and to insure democratic processes in local unions, a great many were set up to strengthen the power of corrupt national union officials, to plunder the treasuries of the seized locals, and to thwart the growth of competing political factions.

Under the Act a national union must file a report with the Secretary of Labor for each trusteed local every six months. The report must contain a detailed explanation of why the trusteeship was established or why it has been continued. It is unlawful to count votes of national convention delegates from a trusteed local unless they were elected by secret ballot in an election where all members in good standing could vote. It is also illegal for the national to take any funds from the local except for normal per capita taxes and assessments that are paid also by other locals.

A trusteeship will be presumed valid only for eighteen months and will be considered invalid after that period unless clear and convincing proof to the contrary is given.

Election of Union Officers.   Because union officers, acting in conjunction with management, have the power to fix wages, hours, and other conditions of employment, Congress felt that government regulation of the election of union officers is necessary to insure that these leaders be responsive to the wishes of the members. Title IV of the Landrum-Griffin Act requires that elections of union officers in local unions be conducted at least once every three years; once every four years in intermediate bodies; and once every five years in a national or international union. At the local level the elections must be by secret ballot of members in good standing. For intermediate bodies and nationals it must be either a secret ballot of all members in good standing or by representatives who were chosen by a secret ballot.

To insure that democratic procedures are followed the Act stipulates that campaign literature must be distributed on equal terms for all candidates at their expense. Lists of members under union security agreements must be made available for inspection without discrimination, and any candidate has the right to have an observer at the polls and at the counting of the ballots. It is illegal for the union to use union dues and assessment funds to promote the candidacy of any person.

Fiduciary Responsibilities.   Title V restates the common law applicable to trust relations by declaring that union officers, agents, and shop stewards occupy positions of trust and that they must hold and use the funds and property of the organization solely for the benefit of the members and in accordance with the constitution and bylaws of the organization. The Act makes it a Federal crime for an officer or union employee to embezzle, steal, or willfully misappropriate union assets. Violation of this provision carries with it a penalty of a fine of up to $10,000 and imprisonment up to five years.

Amendments to the Taft-Hartley Act.   The Landrum-Griffin Act makes a number of important changes and additions to the Taft-Hartley Act. These are as follows:

1. Tight restrictions are placed upon organizational and recognition picketing. Such picketing is prohibited if another union has been lawfully recognized by the employer, a valid NLRB election has been conducted within the preceding 12 months, or if the picketing union has not filed an election petition within a reasonable time (not to exceed 30 days).
2. Economic strikers whose jobs have been taken by other workers are granted the right to vote in any new NLRB representation election up to 12 months after the strike has begun. This provision was added to prevent an antiunion employer from deliberately getting rid of a union by hiring new workers and then obtaining a new election.

3. It is an unfair labor practice for employers and unions to enter into "hot-cargo" agreements. During the period 1947-1959 the Teamsters Union, in particular, used such contracts as a way of getting around the ban on secondary boycotts contained in the original Taft-Hartley Act. Under a hot-cargo contract an employer agrees to refrain from handling or dealing in the products of any other company or to cease doing business with any other person with whom the union has a dispute.

General Observations of the Act.   The Landrum-Griffin Act imposes quite detailed and sweeping controls upon the conduct of union affairs. It requires that they be operated in a democratic fashion. Although most of the general public will applaud this objective, the question may be asked whether it is right to single out only one type of organization in our own society and require that it be run democratically. Should the same principle be applied by law to farm organizations, corporations, and nonprofit institutions? A major objective of the law is to eliminate racketeering, corruption, and collusion between employers and union leaders wherever it exists. It will require a number of years of experience with the Act to determine accurately whether this goal is being met. A major premise of Congress in passing the law was that union members, if given adequate control over their officers through democratic procedures, would see that their unions are run honestly and with due respect for the rights of the membership. This seems to be a sound generalization; however, there have been instances in the past where democratic unions were nevertheless corrupt.[4]

Practically all of the provisions of the Act were put in for the purpose of correcting some specific abuse or evil in the labor-management field. Taken as a whole the Act appears to be sound, although there may be some who would quarrel with the extremely close regulation it demands of internal union affairs.

STRUCTURE FOR COLLECTIVE BARGAINING

The listing below shows the various structures for conducting contract negotiations that exist in the United States.

A. *Single-Employer Bargaining*
   1.   Single-Plant
   2.   Multiple Plants
B. *Multiple-Employer Bargaining*
   1.   Local Area (City or Labor Market)

---

[4] See Philip Taft, *Corruption and Racketeering in the Labor Movement,* New York State School of Industrial and Labor Relations, Cornell University, Ithaca, New York, Bulletin 38 (February 1958), pp. 26-28.

2. Region-wide
3. Industry-wide

The majority of agreements throughout the country are bargained by a single company dealing with a single union. However, there has been a very pronounced trend for many years toward multiemployer bargaining. Usually when companies band together to bargain with one or more unions, they set up a formal organization with a paid, professional staff. This is called an employer association. On the other hand, sometimes companies cooperate with one another during contract negotiations in order to present a united front to the union, but they do not go so far as to set up a formal or enduring association. In the 1958 and 1961 negotiations with the United Automobile Workers Union, General Motors, Ford, and Chrysler cooperated in this fashion to reduce the possibility of the union "whipsawing" one firm against another in this very competitive business field.

In single-employer bargaining in the field of manufacturing, a company may have contracts with more than one union, but negotiations are usually conducted separately with each union. Many large multiplant companies, such as General Motors and United States Steel, have practically all of their plants organized by a single union. Each local union of the United Auto Workers from each plant of General Motors, for example, elects representatives to what is known as a conference board, which meets to prepare bargaining demands and bargaining strategy. The actual negotiations are handled by the General Motors Department of the union, which is a permanent organizational branch of the union located at national headquarters in Detroit. Quite often the president of the national union takes part in negotiations, particularly when the going gets tough. A master agreement is signed to apply to all plants. Then each plant negotiates a supplementary agreement with its local union to cover issues that apply specifically to that unit.

Multiemployer Bargaining

This type of bargaining originated with craft unions at the city level for bargaining with a number of employers under a single contract. Thus a local of the carpenters union may sign an agreement with a number of construction firms in an area. The most common practice in the construction industry at present is for all of the unions (for example, carpenters, electricians, operating engineers, laborers, and bricklayers) to bargain jointly through their building trades council with an employer association composed of all unionized contractors in the area. The negotiation process is centralized and simultaneous for all crafts. When agreement is reached separate contracts are signed between each local of each union and each employer.

Multiemployer bargaining is extremely common in the local area in construction, hotels and restaurants, laundries, dry cleaning, retail stores, dairy products, book and job printing, and local delivery trucking.

Regional multiemployer bargaining is common in the following industries: pulp and paper, lumbering, nonferrous metal mining, maritime and longshoring, trucking, and textile manufacturing.

Industry-wide bargaining is a term used to designate that type of bargaining that covers many companies in an industry that are distributed widely throughout the nation. Although there is much talk about it, with charges that it is monopolistic, true industry-wide bargaining occurs in only a very few industries. It has been going on in the railroad and bituminous coal industries for a number of years. In very recent years the basic steel industry has shifted from pattern bargaining to industry-wide bargaining. Under pattern bargaining, which persisted until the late 1950's, the United Steel Workers of America bargained a contract initially with "Big Steel," that is, the United States Steel Company. This settlement then became the pattern for agreement with all the other major steel producers. Commencing in the late 1950's, all of the large steel companies have participated jointly in negotiations with the union.

Reasons for Multiemployer Bargaining

The basic reason for the development and spread of multiemployer bargaining is to take wages out of competition. From the viewpoint of businessmen this means that other companies who are competing in the same product market cannot obtain a price and cost advantage by paying lower wage rates for the same classes of labor. One firm may indeed obtain a lower cost advantage over its competitors, but it will be achieved by better management, greater efficiency, and technological improvements and not by paying lower wage rates.

Unions have frequently been the initiators of the demand for multiemployer bargaining. They have long realized that they could not force wages up in one firm if that firm was faced with low wage competition from other companies. Therefore unions tend to press for uniformity of wages and conditions of employment among all unionized companies in an industry within the area of market competition.

In those industries where there are many small employers, unions find that contract negotiations and contract enforcement are simplified and less costly when bargaining is carried on with an employer association.

Just as individual workmen organized unions many years ago to increase their bargaining power, so have companies found it advantageous to pool their resources when confronted with a strong union at the bargaining table. By presenting a united front, they can often obtain a more favorable settlement than they could by acting individually.

Disadvantages of Multiemployer Bargaining

The general public and the consumer often suffer as a result of this type of bargaining. A generous wage increase may be granted by the employers, and this may then be followed by a price increase by all the firms. The consumer is then given no choice. He cannot patronize one company that bargained more vigorously with the union to obtain a more favorable settlement, because all companies are covered by the same agreement.

When a strike occurs, the entire industry may be shut down. This can cause great inconvenience to the buying public.

The marginal employer who cannot afford to pay the wages nor meet the working conditions agreed upon in association bargaining is often placed at a serious disadvantage.

NEGOTIATING THE AGREEMENT

Years ago union-employer labor agreements were generally for one year's duration. During the inflationary period just after World War II, many of these contracts could be reopened for wage negotiations at the end of only six months. This meant that both parties were involved in the ferment of preparation for and the actual conduct of contract negotiations nearly continuously. Since the early 1950's there has been a pronounced trend toward contracts of two and three years' duration. This provides greater security for both sides. It is evidence of greater faith in the grievance process and in day-to-day discussions to solve problems as they arise. It demonstrates increased maturity on the part of labor and management in their bargaining relationship.

Preparations for contract bargaining commence long before the actual negotiating sessions open. For the company the principal spade work is done by the industrial relations director. He and his staff must gather data on prevailing rates of pay and fringe benefit practices in the labor market area and in the industry. The company's financial situation must be analyzed carefully to determine what wage and fringe benefit improvements can be offered, if any. The experience of living with the present union agreement will undoubtedly have demonstrated a number of contract provisions that could be altered to management's benefit. The industrial relations director may hold discussions with plant supervision to collect views on troublesome problems that arose when administering the current agreement. Before entering the negotiations, management will have pretty well decided what its position will be regarding expected union demands. It will have formulated its proposals and possible demands upon the union.

Assuming that the bargaining is being conducted by a local union, the union will normally elect a bargaining committee that includes the principal elective officials plus some shop stewards. The rank and file often participate in expressing their thoughts regarding bargaining demands at a general membership meeting. Many of these stem from unresolved worker complaints and grievances. The leaders cannot simply echo the often varied and conflicting wishes of the membership; but rather they must carefully weigh the merits of each issue and consider the hard realities of what is possible. Quite frequently the international union will help guide the preparatory process. It may insist upon certain uniform union-wide demands and a standard wording of contract clauses.

At the actual negotiating sessions the company may be represented by the chief executive officer, the industrial relations director, the treasurer or the controller, and the manager of manufacturing. The ranking company executive generally serves as chief spokesman. The chief spokesman for the union is usually either the international representative or the local union business agent. Other members of the team may include the local union president, secretary-treasurer, members of the executive board, and perhaps a few shop stewards.

Because the union demands practically always involve increased costs and sometimes restrictions on management's freedom of action, the company spokesmen generally resist or refuse to accede to these proposals. Management typically offers far less than the union demands. The union always asks for more than it really expects to get. A great many sessions may be required to reach agreement upon the issues and upon the specific contract language. The pressure on management is the threat of a strike with consequent loss of business. The union leadership will not call a strike lightly, because a lost strike can mean loss of jobs, a depleted union treasury, and a weakened union. Yet the elected union leaders are under considerable pressure from their constituents to show some gains, that is, to extract concessions from management.

Although strikes make exciting newspaper headlines, the vast majority of contracts are negotiated without a strike year after year. A strike usually occurs when one side (or both) miscalculates the other's limit.

Joint Union-Managment Committees

When a current labor agreement is about to expire and talks are underway to agree upon the terms of a new one, great pressure is on both parties. They are working against a deadline. Quite generally the union threatens to strike at the expiration date of the old contract if agreement has not been reached on the new one. In a sense this is crisis bargaining.

Over the years since 1945 this country has witnessed repeated strikes in the basic steel industry. The 116-day strike in 1959 proved climactic for both sides. It was very costly, required federal government intervention at the highest level, and brought on considerable public criticism.

Both industry and union leaders recognized that many of their common problems were too complicated to be solved in the crisis atmosphere of contract negotiations. In 1960 a joint human relations committee was set up to explore continuously issues during the life of the agreement. Although its original purpose was rather limited in scope, its efforts have been so successful that its "charter" has been broadened. The agreements hammered out in this committee were the basis for peaceful contract settlements in 1962 and 1963.

In 1960 a committee consisting of three company, three union, and three neutral (public) members was set up by the Kaiser Steel Company and the United Steelworkers Union to figure out a way of handling the problems of technological advances and employment. It evolved a long-range sharing plan that provides employment security to those displaced by machines and methods improvements, a plan for sharing the benefits from savings in production costs, and a means for gradual elimination of direct wage incentives.

A joint labor-management-public committee set up by Armour and Company and the two unions in the meat-packing industry has worked for several years to alleviate the problems of unemployment caused by automation.

In 1963 the American Arbitration Association launched a new program to help management and labor to explore their problems by using informed neutral parties to guide and shape free discussion and study through industry and labor conferences and joint committees. The American Arbitration Association has long been active in arranging voluntary arbitration of labor disputes through its Voluntary Labor Arbitration Tribunal.

The joint committee, which works day-to-day during the life of an agreement to solve basic labor-management problems, promises to be a successful feature in the ever-evolving institution of collective bargaining. Many of the issues encountered are much too complex to be solved successfully in the crisis atmosphere that prevails at contract negotiation time.

SUBJECT MATTER OF COLLECTIVE BARGAINING

What are the subjects about which management and labor negotiate when they meet at the bargaining table? What topics commonly appear in a union contract? It is appropriate at this point to examine the subject matter of collective bargaining and to discuss the union and management views on the major bargaining issues. Below is a listing of topics commonly appearing in union-management agreements. This is a general list; any individual agreement would necessarily contain special items particular to that situation. The order of topics necessarily varies from one agreement to another.

SUBJECT MATTER OF UNION-EMPLOYER AGREEMENTS

I   Union Recognition and Scope of Bargaining Unit
II   Management Rights (Management Security)
III   Union Security
IV   Strikes and Lockouts
V   Union Activities and Responsibilities
    Check-off of dues
    Union officers and stewards
    Union bulletin boards
    Wildcat strikes and slowdowns
VI   Wages
    General wage adjustments
    Wage structure
    Job evaluation
    Wage incentives and time study
    Reporting and call-in pay
    Shift differentials
    Bonuses
VII   Working Time and Time-Off Policies
    Regular hours of work
    Holidays
    Vacations
    Overtime regulations
    Leaves of absence
    Rest periods
    Meal periods
VIII   Job Rights and Seniority
    Seniority regulations
    Transfers
    Promotions
    Layoffs and recalls
    Job posting and bidding
IX   Discipline, Suspension, and Discharge
X   Grievance Handling and Arbitration
XI   Health and Safety
XII   Insurance and Benefit Programs
    Group life insurance
    Medical insurance
    Pension program
    Supplemental unemployment benefits

Substantive Issues

We shall now examine some of the principal substantive issues and note how union and management views tend to differ.

Union Security.   The term *union security* refers to both the right of a union to exist as an organization and its right to continued existence in a particular company. The first right is guaranteed by the labor laws of the nation. It is the second right that has caused so much controversy between labor and management. It has been primarily because of long-standing employer opposition to unions that unions have pressed hard to get incorporated into the labor contract some provision that formally insures the union's continued presence in the company. Union security provisions may take any of the following forms:

Union Shop. All present employees are required to join the union. Newly hired employees must join within a specified number of days after being hired. (The Taft-Hartley Act says this period cannot be less than 30 days, except for the construction industry, where 7 days is stipulated.)

Modified Union Shop. At the time the agreement is signed, present employees who do not belong to the union are not required to join. Those who already belong must continue their membership as a condition of employment, and all new hires must join within a specified number of days. This type of provision is common in the steel industry. In a survey of 1931 labor contracts each covering 1,000 or more workers in 1958-59, the Bureau of Labor Statistics found that 74 per cent of the workers were employed under contracts having some form of the "union shop."[5]

Maintenance of Membership. Popular during World War II, this type of union security has declined steadily since that time. Workers who do not belong to the union are not required to join; however, those who do join are required to stay in the union until a brief "escape period" (usually of 10 to 15 days) just prior to the contract termination date. In 1958-59, 7 per cent of major contracts provided for maintenance of membership.[6]

Agency Shop. Employees are not required to join the union but must pay a fee to the union for the bargaining services and benefits that the union provides for all in the bargaining unit.

As indicated above, unions nearly always demand contractual protection for their existence as the bargaining agent in a company. They usually seek the maximum form allowed by law, namely, the union shop. They feel that they need protection against management efforts to oust the union from the shop. Unions feel that all employees within a bargaining

---

[5] "Union Security Provisions in Major Union Contracts," *Monthly Labor Review* (December, 1959), pp. 1348-1356.

[6] *Ibid.*

unit should pay to support the union, which, under the Taft-Hartley Act, bargains rates of pay and other conditions of employment for all workers regardless of whether they are union members or not. Unions are opposed to nonunion workers becoming "free riders" and enjoying benefits of union membership without supporting it financially. In an open shop the problem of maintaining union membership is extremely difficult in those organizations where employee turnover is high.

Management views on union security (management tends to refer to it as compulsory unionism) are divided. Some companies encourage employee membership in the union because they do not want factional struggles between union and nonunion groups within the plant. Also they want all employees to belong and to participate in union affairs so that the union will faithfully represent the will of the majority of employees.

It is probably accurate to state, however, that the majority of employers oppose any form of compulsory unionism. Employer groups, such as the National Association of Manufacturers, have advocated state "right-to-work" laws that outlaw the closed shop, union shop, maintenance of membership, and all other forms of union security. As of 1969, 19 states have enacted such legislation. These are mostly Southern and Midwestern states, where antiunion sentiment is strong. The popular argument against compulsory unionism is that no man should have to join a union in order to obtain a job. Such a practice violates the allegedly inalienable right of citizens of the United States to obtain work free of such hampering restrictions. However the primary reason why many employers and associations of employers oppose union security provisions is that they feel that the union shop grants the union too much economic power. They seek to blunt the power of unions and to discourage union growth by obtaining legislative bans at the state and federal level on all forms of compulsory unionism. Thus this is primarily a power struggle and not a matter of principle.

Management Rights.   Since the entry of unions into the mass production industries in the 1930's, professional business managers as a group and as a class have viewed with some alarm the extension of union influence into subject areas that had been traditionally considered to be exclusive management prerogatives. Management has argued that it has a right and even an obligation to make its own business decisions free from union interference. This concept stems from the property rights of ownership and management as the representative of the stockholders in the corporation. In collective bargaining relationships, management often seeks to obtain union agreement that certain specified subject areas, such as determination of products to be made, pricing the product, deciding production methods and processes, setting up accounting methods, direction of the work force, determination of job content, and so on, are sole and exclusive management rights. Basically the management rights issue is the counterpart of the union security problem. The former grants management security and a certain management sphere of influence. The latter provides security to the union as an institution.

Unions, in the United States, have not sought to share with management the authority and responsibility to operate the business. But they generally take the position that a fence should not be built around management prerogatives. They tend to believe that labor should have a voice in all those things that affect employees and employee relationships. They tend to adopt a pragmatic view. Although certain topics may not be of concern to the union today, conditions in the future may change in such a way that then the union may become interested in negotiating over a particular subject. There are many subject areas over which management and unions differ sharply over the relative amount of union and management control. Examples are the setting of production standards, imposition of disciplinary penalities, assignment of duties to jobs, subcontracting of work outside the plant, scheduling of work, and the discontinuance of a kind of work.

Here are two examples of management rights clauses from union contracts.

Management

The control of all matters relative to the management and operation of the plants and the operation of the Company's business is vested exclusively in the Company, except as these matters may be expressly limited by the terms of this Agreement.[7]

Management Responsibilities

The union agrees that the Company shall continue to exercise its responsibilities for the Management of the Plant and the selection and direction of the working force except as specifically restricted or otherwise provided in this Contract. These responsibilities include, but shall not be limited to, the following: determining the methods and means of production; planning and scheduling production; assigning employees to job, to shifts, and to working schedules; hiring, transferring, promoting, disciplining, suspending, or discharging employees for cause; laying off employees and the right to make and enforce rules and regulations not in conflict with the provisions of the contract.[8]

Wages.   The topics that appear in the typical union contract under the heading of wages are many and varied. Among these are the general across-the-board wage adjustment, the labor grade structure, in-grade rate progression, special rates for learners and apprentices, job evaluation, time study, wage incentives, premium pay practice, reporting and call-in pay, cost of living or escalator clause, and productivity increments.

---

[7] Agreement between SKF Industries, Inc., and the United Steelworkers of America, AFL-CIO, on behalf of itself and the members of the Local Union No. 2898, October 12, 1959.

[8] A recent contract between a large manufacturing concern at Niagara Falls, New York, and a local affiliated with a large international union.

Space does not permit an explanation and analysis of each of these items.[9]

When negotiating, management looks upon wages primarily as a labor cost. Fringe benefits are likewise translated into labor costs. A given union demand for x cents per hour increase in wages is expressed by management as a certain dollar increase in payroll for a month and a year. This affects the cost of goods sold.

In determining what its wage rates should be, management seeks (sometimes in only a general way) to pay rates equal to the average prevailing in its own labor market for each job classification. In deciding upon a wage policy, management also gives consideration to its own ability to pay (that is, profitability), future business expectations, productivity, and the relative supply of labor available in the local labor market.

Unions, for their part, seek to eliminate wages as a factor in competition among employers whom they have organized. They press for wage uniformity throughout an industry for the same class of work. Although this is the long-range union goal, unions frequently have to settle for something less. But certainly within each company they demand "equal pay for equal work." All employees on the same job should receive the same pay. Unions often demand a single rate for each job. Employers usually want a rate range for each job or for each labor grade in order to pay different wages to people according to variations in ability and contribution.

In making its wage bargaining demands upon management, a union typically gives consideration to the company's profit picture, the pattern of settlements in other companies in the same and allied industries, changes in the cost of living, and prevailing wage levels in the area and in the industry. It also keeps careful watch of the wage settlements obtained by rival unions to insure that it does as well.

Job Rights. Unions try to furnish as much job security to their members as possible. In a craft union, in those common situations where workers frequently change employers (for example, construction), the union members primarily look to their union for security. By maintaining their membership in the union they can usually obtain a job via the union hiring hall.

However, in the industrial union situation workers look to their employer for job security. This is why unions seek to have all job changes decided on the basis of company seniority. Unions feel that this is a fair and objective criterion for making transfers, promotions, and layoffs. They feel that it eliminates any likelihood of favoritism and discrimination influencing decisions on personnel changes of status.

Management typically desires the freedom to move people from one job to another and to lay off workers when business gets slack, unham-

---

[9] For a discussion of these wage problems in collective bargaining see, C. Wilson Randle and Max S. Wortman, *Collective Bargaining* (2nd Ed., Boston: Houghton Mifflin Company, 1966), Ch. 13, 14; also Gordon E. Bloom and Herbert R. Northrup, *Economics of Labor Relations* (6th Ed., Homewood, Ill.: Richard D. Irwin, Inc., 1969), Ch. 5.

pered by union imposed restrictions. Management feels that the application of rigid seniority rules reduces efficiency and often causes unqualified men to be assigned to jobs. There is no close correlation between ability and length of service.

The net result of these two opposing points of view is usually a compromise. In the vast majority of companies today, layoffs are handled on the basis of seniority. This means that the most recent workers hired are the first to go in the event of a layoff. Management always retains full authority to promote a man out of the bargaining unit to an administrative or supervisory position. Criteria for promotion within the bargaining unit are frequently a combination of seniority and ability. Some contracts specify that when choosing from among several employees for a better job, seniority will be the deciding factor only when two or more candidates have equal qualifications. Other contracts state that the most senior man will receive the job, provided he has the minimum qualifications to do the work.

Grievance Handling.   The subject of grievances is dealt with extensively in Chapter 22, "Grievance Handling." However, there are certain collective bargaining aspects of grievance handling that must be mentioned at this point. Nonunion organizations usually do not have formal grievance procedures, although it is generally understood that employees have a right to discuss their dissatisfactions and problems with their immediate supervisors. But the entry of a union into an organization nearly always brings about the establishment of a grievance procedure. Ordinarily an employee who wishes to obtain satisfaction and settlement of a grievance will present it to his supervisor or to his shop steward, who will represent him in discussions with the supervisor. The supervisor as a representative of management will give an answer to the employee and the steward. If they are not satisfied with this action, they may appeal the decision to successively higher levels of management until a mutual agreement is reached. In processing the grievance up through the management hierarchy, higher officials in the union structure enter the picture at each step. Generally officials of the union at each step occupy positions in the union hierarchy that roughly correspond to those in the management organization with whom the grievance is discussed.

Basically, in presenting grievances to management, the union is asserting that the company has not faithfully and properly administered the terms of the labor agreement. The contract establishes the *rights* of the company, the union, and the employees. The grievance procedure provides the means for adjudicating and interpreting the way in which the labor agreement is applied in practice.

Over 90 per cent of the agreements in force in the United States provide for arbitration as the final step in the grievance procedure. Most agreements provide that the union, if not satisfied with top management's answer to a grievance, can appeal it to an impartial arbitrator who will hold a hearing, listen to testimony from both sides, and examine briefs and documents that may be submitted by the parties. After hearing all of the facts he will render a decision (usually within 30 days) and submit a written statement of his award together with his reasons. In submitting an unresolved grievance to arbitration both parties usually agree that the arbitrator's decision will be final and binding.

STRIKES AND DISPUTE SETTLEMENT

A *strike* is a concerted withholding of labor supply in order to bring economic pressure to bear upon the employer to cause him to grant the employee's and/or the union's demands. It is a test of economic strength and a contest of staying power. Generally in free societies (as contrasted with totalitarian regimes) the right to strike is considered a fundamental right of working men. This does not mean, however, that workers have an unrestricted right to strike under all circumstances. Under our labor law secondary boycott, jurisdictional, and sympathy strikes are illegal.

A *lockout* consists of a shutdown of a plant or place of business by management in the course of a labor dispute with his employees and their union for the purpose of forcing acceptance of his terms. Management ordinarily desires to keep a business in full operation, because work stoppages are costly; they stop production, interrupt sales, and may cause a company to lose its customers. Unions are usually initiators of work stoppages if progress at the bargaining table breaks down. However, we do find that management sometimes resorts to a lockout of the employees after a strike has begun. This is a way of retaliating against the union and is designed to bring the union to its knees. It has become increasingly common in recent years, where companies are organized into an employer association, for all to lock out their workers if the union should strike just one of the member companies.

Dispute Settlement Methods

When there are disagreements between labor and management, they ordinarily meet with one another to negotiate a settlement that will be acceptable to both parties over matters of *interest* (that is, the interests of the two sides in negotiating a new agreement) and over matters of *right* (that is, interpretation of the agreement as in grievance handling). However, there are times when an impasse is reached. The parties are at loggerheads, and resort to economic force sometimes ensues. At this point one of several dispute settlement methods may be brought into the picture.

Voluntary Arbitration. This procedure is most commonly used as the terminal step in a grievance procedure as previously described. Generally either side to the dispute may initiate action to take the unresolved grievance to arbitration. In disputes over matters of interest, as when labor and management are at odds over wages for a new contract, voluntary arbitration is only infrequently employed. This is because it is difficult for an outsider to perform a legislative function and impose a set of conditions upon the two disputants. The union and management are most intimately aware of all ramifications of the problem. The stronger party is rarely willing to let an outsider impose conditions upon it which its adversary could not win by resort to economic force (that is, a strike or lockout).

Compulsory Arbitration.   This requires the submission of the dispute to a third party or to a board for settlement. Ordinarily compulsory arbitration has been used when the government has felt it necessary to protect the public from the harmful consequences of strikes in certain essential industries. A number of state laws provide for compulsory arbitration in lieu of strikes for such industries as electric light and power, gas, water, urban transit, and telephone. Compulsory arbitration usually requires not only compulsory submission of the dispute to arbitration but also compulsory acceptance of the award. Compulsory arbitration is unpopular with both labor and management, because it opens the way for a struggle at a higher level, namely at the political and governmental level. The responsibility for working out common problems is transferred to a government-appointed agency.

Conciliation and Mediation.   These terms are synonymous. They refer to the activity of a third party, often a government official, to help the disputants reach an agreement. The concilator or mediator helps to keep the parties talking; he makes suggestions; and he tries to persuade and influence them to reach an agreement. He has no final power of decision making, however. The Federal Mediation and Conciliation Service has the authority to offer its services in cases of labor-management disputes. Also, a union or a company may request help from this agency. Many of the industrialized states, such as California, Connecticut, Massachusetts, New Jersey, New York, and Pennsylvania, have a state mediation agency whose staff mediators perform services in a manner similar to their federal counterparts.

Fact-Finding Boards.   A fact-finding board is generally appointed by either the Federal or a state government to conduct a complete investigation into the facts, issues, and opposing positions in a labor dispute. Frequently it has the power to recommend a particular settlement. An exception is the Taft-Hartley Act's National Emergency Provisions, whereby the Board of Inquiry does not have the power to make definite recommendations to the parties. The statement of the complete facts and recommendations (if called for) are almost always made available to the general public. The theory is that public opinion will force the parties to reach an agreement once the issues and positions of the two sides, and any board recommendations, are made public. Presumably if one side has been holding to a position that is unreasonable, it will be forced to become more conciliatory when exposed to the glare of public view.

Questions for Review and Discussion

1. What is meant by the term *collective bargaining?* What are its characteristics?
2. How does bargaining a labor agreement differ from negotiating an ordinary commercial contract?
3. In what way were labor union activities subject to antitrust prosecution prior to 1941?
4. Do you think that labor unions should, at present, be subject to the Sherman Act, as are business firms? Explain your reasoning.
5. What role did the court injunction play in labor-management relations during the early decades of the twentieth century?
6. In what ways did the National Labor Relations Act (Wagner Act) aid the expansion of unions?
7. A union and management are unable to agree upon terms for a new labor agreement; therefore, the union calls the employees out on strike. In order to meet customers' orders management subcontracts much of its production to other manufacturing concerns in the area. The union then proceeds to place picket lines around these subcontractors. Is this action legal or illegal? Do you think it *should* be legal or illegal?
8. Explain how the Taft-Hartley Act tries to cope with the problem of national emergency strikes. Can you think of ways by which the procedure might be improved?
9. In what way does the Landrum-Griffin Act seek to provide democratic rights for union members?
10. Define the following terms:
    a. *"Unfair labor practice"*
    b. *Jurisdictional strike*
    c. *Union trusteeship*
11. What factors have contributed to the growth of multiemployer bargaining in recent years?
12. As the president of your own company (that is, you are a principal stockholder), would you favor or oppose the granting of a union shop provision to the union with which you have been dealing for several years? Explain your position.
13. In what ways does the entry of a union into an organization restrict management's freedom of action?
14. Distinguish between disputes over matters of *interest* and those over matters of *right.*

CASE PROBLEMS

Note: Case problems for Chapter 4, "Unions and Management," and Chapter 5, "Collective Bargaining," are placed here because these two chapters deal essentially with the single subject area of labor-management relations.

Problem 1: A Talk by a Personnel Manager

The personnel manager of a local manufacturing company was invited to speak before a class of college seniors taking a course in Industrial Relations at the University. He was a man of about forty-five and had arrived at his present position via the financial and accounting departments of his company. He had been personnel manager for three years at the time of his talk. As the subject of his lecture he chose to concentrate upon the relations between his company and the local union, with particular emphasis devoted to the political nature of the union. His talk, in abbreviated form, was as follows.

"Our company prides itself on having recognized unions early in the game and on having sound labor-management relations. We granted recognition to our union over forty years ago without there being a strike. I am proud to say that we have never had a single work stoppage due to a labor dispute in all the years since.

"The management of our company believes in dealing honestly and in a straightforward manner with the employees and the union. We believe that common sense, logic, and sound business judgment should be all that are necessary to arrive at satisfactory agreements between union and management.

"I am continually annoyed, however, by the fact that political expediency seems to be the guidepost for the behavior of union leaders. Now, the elected officials of our local union consist of the president, vicepresident, secretary-treasurer, chairman of the shop committee, and fifteen departmental stewards. All of these fellows are regular company employees who take on these union jobs as extra assignments. The union pays their president about five hundred dollars a year extra for his services. Stewards get no pay from the union. I think those people seek union jobs to be important; to be big shots in front of the men. Getting elected to a union office is nothing but a personality contest. When union election time is getting near, the incumbent officers and stewards become the biggest bunch of back-slappers and hand-shakers that can be found anywhere. They want to get re-elected. They try to show the boys that they are going to bat for them. If problems don't exist, they deliberately create them. They try to give the impression that they aren't letting the company get away with anything. At union meetings you rarely find good solid citizens in attendance. It is always the troublemakers and malcontents who go.

"It is difficult for me to understand, sometimes, why the union officers are so politically oriented. Why don't they act more responsible? Even when the company institutes some new fringe benefit or service for the employees, like new coffee machines or better washroom facilities, the union bigwigs try to claim that they had to work hard to extract these benefits from management.

"Let's take the case of the increase in pay for a special setup man's job on which two men were employed. The skill requirements of the job had increased. We offered the union eight cents more per hour, and they accepted. However, when the chairman of the shop committee informed the workers of their eight-cent raise, they complained that they should have gotten twelve cents per hour. The committeeman lacked the courage to tell them the increase was proper and just. Instead he returned the complaint to management and asked for a higher rate.

"Before closing I will give you students one other illustration of the political way our union officers act. Joe has been employed as a laborer for three years. He works on the evening shift, which starts at 4 P.M. At 8 P.M. he was reported to be under the influence of liquor. I was called into the case, as I was working late that evening. The evening superintendent and I talked to Joe in the presence of two shop stewards. Joe reeked of alcohol. He could not stand straight even while hanging on to a chair. He became belligerent toward the superintendent and myself. One of the stewards agreed that Joe was very drunk. We told Joe to report to my office at 10 A.M. the next day. He came in accompanied by the chairman of the shop committee and one of the stewards from the previous evening. They claimed that he had been taking antihistamine pills for a cold and that he was doctoring with brandy to ease his cough. They even claimed that a friend of Joe's had passed away and this upset him. They clearly lied to save his job. They wanted to build themselves up in the eyes of the other workers to show how much they did for them. I recommended immediate discharge for Joe, but upon appeal by the union, top management overruled me. He was suspended for two weeks without pay then returned to his job."

Questions

1. Do you agree that all that is required for successful labor-management dealings is "common sense, logic, and sound business judgment"?
2. Why do you feel the union officers and stewards acted in such a "political" fashion?
3. What conditions are necessary in order for union leaders to act in a truly responsible manner?
4. Do you think that politics can or should be divorced from the affairs of a local union?
5. Based upon his talk, what do you surmise regarding the experience and knowledge of labor relations possessed by the personnel manager?

Problem 2

The S. O. Nolsco Company, established in 1955, manufactures a line of women's accessories and certain clothing items. It is located in eastern New Jersey, within the Greater New York area, about twenty miles from downtown Manhattan. Employment totals about 150 persons, most of whom are women stitchers and semiskilled machine operators. The company is nonunion. The manufacturing facilities are located in a rented loft on the third floor of an old building, the other floors of which are leased to other small manufacturing firms. The owner of the firm has always prided himself on maintaining good relations with his workers. He has always provided a Christmas bonus, which has tended to be equal to one week's pay; has continued to pay workers' wages for up to a month if they have been out due to sickness; and has tried to maintain a clean, orderly shop. He has always felt that he would like to be close to his workers so that they could discuss their dissatisfactions and complaints with him. In point of fact, however, he seldom received much feedback from the employees.

About one month ago the company on the first floor became organized by the Warehousemen's Union. The owner of S. O. Nolsco Company heard rumors from one of his foreladies that both the Warehousemen's and the Garment Worker's union have been quietly trying to organize his employees. Because his financial position is not as strong as he would like, the owner feels that he would be placed in a very precarious position if the workers should become organized. He feels that he compensates his people for the slightly lower wages they receive (lower than the union scale) by liberal day-to-day treatment plus a Christmas bonus. Frankly he is quite fearful of a union-organizing drive, especially at this time. He wonders just what sentiments his employees hold regarding unionization.

Questions

1. If you were the head of this company, what would be your attitude toward union organization of your employees?
2. What course of action would you follow?
3. Would you poll your employees to determine their sentiments toward unionization?

Problem 3

The Everlasting Shoe Company, located in an Eastern city, manufactures a full line of men's footwear. It employs 1,700 persons. Its wage rates are slightly higher than the leather goods industry as a whole but are lower than those paid for similar jobs in other manufacturing firms in its labor market. Working conditions are generally good. Top management prides itself upon having a clean plant.

Both financial control and top executive management has been concentrated, over the years, in the hands of three families.

The factory was organized in 1940 when the Leather Workers Union won a National Labor Relations Board election by obtaining a favorable vote from 61 per cent of those voting. The only strike in the company's entire history occurred in 1942, when the union struck over the closed-shop issue. The company was adamant in its refusal to grant the closed shop. After sixteen weeks the workers returned to the plant, and the Union gave up its demand. Although the Union has repeatedly demanded the union shop over the years in its bargaining sessions with management, the company has still avoided, successfully, any form of compulsory unionism.

The company makes every effort to practice good human relations in its dealings with employees as individuals. All of the production foremen have received extensive training in supervision. The president tries to develop and maintain a friendly relationship between the executives and the workers. Every executive is required to go through the shops at least once a week to chat with the workers.

Top management makes no secret of its antipathy toward the union. When new employees are hired, they are advised against joining the union. Union stewards and officials are not permitted to solicit new members on company property at any time. The time allowed union stewards to process grievances is restricted to one hour per week by contract. The company has established a separate grievance procedure for nonunion employees in the bargaining unit. Nonunion workers file their complaints and grievances under Procedure A, which goes up through the various levels of management, starting with the foreman. Procedure B is for union members who may have the shop steward there to present their grievances if they wish. The goal of the company is to have the employees look to management for leadership and not to the union.

Unlike many other unionized firms the company does not provide any union bulletin boards where the union can post its notices.

Prior to bargaining a new labor agreement the company makes a careful study of its financial position and of prevailing wage rates in the leather goods industry. It then calculates exactly what it will offer to the union (if anything) and makes it a practice never to deviate from this figure. It will take a strike rather than give more to the union.

By treating the employees well and by continuously rebuffing the union leadership, the company has succeeded in reducing union membership to 37 per cent of the total employees in the bargaining unit. It has not actively sought to have the union ousted through a National Labor Relations Board decertification election, because it does not wish to arouse the employees. It feels that overt action might cause sentiment to swing toward the union. In addition, the top management feels that the size of the union membership is a useful barometer. If the membership increases, it feels that somehow management must be falling down in the way it treats the employees. Conversely, if the membership declines, it feels it is doing a good job of managing the people.

Question

1. Analyze and evaluate the philosophy and practices of the Everlasting Shoe Company toward the union. Consider business efficiency as well as economic, social, moral, and legal aspects.

Simulation Exercise

Zif, Jay J., *Contract Negotiations* (Creative Studies Simulation), New York: The Macmillan Company, 1970.

Suggestions for Further Reading

Chamberlain, Neil W., "Strikes in Contemporary Context," *Industrial and Labor Relations Review,* Vol. 20, No. 4, July 1967, pp. 602-616.

Chamberlain, Neil W. and J. W. Kuhn, *Collective Bargaining,* 2nd Ed., New York: McGraw-Hill Book Company, 1965.

Cohen, Sanford, *Labor Law,* Columbus, Ohio: Charles E. Merrill Books, 1964.

Gregory, Charles O., *Labor and the Law,* 2nd Rev. Ed., New York: W. W. Norton & Co., 1958.

Healy, James J. (ed.), Henderson, James A., *et. al., Creative Collective Bargaining,* Englewood Cliffs, N.J.: Prentice-Hall, 1965.

Macdonald, Robert M., "Collective Bargaining in the Postwar Period," *Industrial and Labor Relations Review,* Vol. 20, No. 4, July 1967, pp. 553-577.

Randle, C. Wilson, and Max S. Wortman, Jr., *Collective Bargaining,* 2nd Ed., Boston: Houghton Mifflin Company, 1966.

Slichter, Sumner H., James J. Healy, and E. Robert Livernash, *The Impact of Collective Bargaining on Management,* Washington, D.C.: Brookings Institution, 1960.

Walton, Richard E., and Robert B. McKersie, *A Behavioral Theory of Labor Negotiations,* New York: McGraw-Hill Book Company, 1965.

Organization

6

Organization and the management of people at work are intimately related. The genesis of organization occurs when two or more people unite to achieve a common goal. If, for example, four friends decide to build a camp in the mountains to be used as a base for hunting and fishing trips, they must organize into a smoothly functioning team. The foremost organizational steps that these four friends must take are as follows: (1) decide their specific objectives for a camp in terms of location, cost, size, and design; (2) allocate different tasks to the individual persons according to their interests and abilities; and (3) develop the pattern of relations among the four individuals. This will involve designation of the person who will be in charge of the project, communication, coordination of efforts, and group and individual decision making. If the people in this group know each other well and are compatible, the problem of creating a smooth working team that successfully gets the camp built may not be particularly difficult. However, if one switches his thinking to the level of the large-scale organizations that have tended to become increasingly dominant in our society, he may appreciate that more careful planning and more complex organizational arrangements are required to make them function properly. To initiate, operate, and regulate entities having thousands of members is no simple managerial problem. Consider the organizational problems involved in managing the military forces of the United States with its millions of men and women in uniform; the United States government itself, with its countless departments, bureaus, agencies, and services; or the great business corporations, such as the American Telephone and Telegraph Company, General Motors, or Standard Oil of New Jersey.

In order to function effectively a large organization must formalize its ways of doing things into policies, plans, procedures, rules, specific jobs, departments, and so on. A definite chain of command must be established. The great flexibility and informality characteristic of the small organization does not exist in large systems. On the other hand the large organization exhibits greater stability than does the small one.

A large organization, whether it be a company, church, or government, takes on the features of a *bureaucracy,* a term coined by Max Weber, the German social scientist. According to Weber the main features of a bureaucracy are emphasis upon form, hierarchy of levels, specialization of labor, established rules and standards of conduct, records and data keeping, and professionalization of administration.

The working together and interacting of people in an organization give rise to numerous human relations problems. For example, the authority structure and the relations between supervisor and subordinate often develop tensions, conflicts, and morale difficulties. There is often a basic incompatibility between the needs and motives of individuals and the requirements of the organization. Vast communication networks may not function as planned. The intended messages may be altered, stopped, and distorted. The receivers of the communication may misinterpret the messages. Excessive specialization of activities can increase the problems of coordination and communication. At the worker level, too much specialization may result in boredom and monotony. Staff specialists, who are usually technicians and professionals, have different work orientations than do line supervisors. Problems of the relations between staff and line personnel are sometimes difficult to resolve.

In this chapter we shall be concerned with formal organizations that are specifically established to produce a product or perform a service. Small informal groupings of people that are often fluid in composition and that are sometimes called "informal organization" are discussed in Chapter 16 "Group Relations and Informal Organization."

Organization Defined

A formal organization is a system, having an established structure, in which people work and deal with one another in a coordinated and cooperative manner for the accomplishment of recognized goals.

Organizing involves dividing all the work that has to be accomplished and assigning it to individuals, groups, and departments. This includes division of activities by level of authority and responsibility and also division of work across the establishment into different kinds or types. It further entails the utilization of procedures for coordinating the efforts of individuals and groups. The relationships among members must evolve and become productive. Authority, responsibility, delegation, consultation, and decision making are part and parcel of organization.

Examining the definition of organization and its amplifying ideas, one will conclude that it has wide application to all fields of endeavor. It includes not only business enterprises, but also government, the military, colleges and schools, churches, and such community service organizations as the Boy Scouts, Rotary, Kiwanis, YMCA.

GROWTH OF A COMPANY—ORGANIZATIONAL PHASES

A vivid understanding of organization can be acquired by examining the development of a business enterprise as it grows from a one-man operation into a moderate size manufacturing concern employing, say, 600 persons. Let us assume that the Arrowsharp Company starts, as so many businesses have, with an idea for a marketable product that can be made rather readily in the entrepreneur's basement. Initially no organization is required, because the owner works alone and personally performs all the work of financing, designing, manufacturing, and selling his product. As the business prospers and grows. Mr. Arrowsharp finds that he needs assistance. Therefore he obtains the services of his wife, to whom he assigns all of the record keeping, bookkeeping, and clerical work. As the volume of orders increases he hires a man to physically operate the machines and do the assembly work. Mr. Arrowsharp concentrates his own efforts upon raising capital to finance a move into larger quarters, marketing, overall planning, and direction of the business. Although the enterprise requires the services of only three persons up to this point, we can see that already it has become necessary to subdivide the work into three separate jobs and to establish a manager (Mr. Arrowsharp) and a worker level. A simple superior-subordinate relationship has been created.

Later, after moving into a leased factory building, Mr. Arrowsharp hires several production workers and appoints one person to the position of shop foreman. Since his own talents lie primarily in the areas of promotion, public contact work, and general management, he continues to reserve this work for himself but hires an expert engineer to modify the original product and to design new ones. This engineer also creates improvements in the manufacturing facilities. To relieve his wife of the burden of the heavy office work responsibility, he engages the services of a fulltime private secretary and an experienced accountant. We can now see that staff specialist positions have been created in the case of the engineer and the accountant. As is common with most small businesses, the exact authority, responsibility, and duties of these new positions will evolve and stabilize after some amount of trial and error. But sooner or later the relationship between Arrowsharp and the incumbents of these two positions must be rather definitely determined. This involves the problem of delegation and the question of line and staff relations.

As the firm continues to grow, employment of production workers reaches twenty-five men. Because the single production foreman can no longer effectively cope with the myriad problems of supervising this many men, Arrowsharp selects another foreman from the ranks. The productive work is then split up into machine and assembly work, with a foreman in charge of each. Later, when a foreman of inspection and one for maintenance are added, the owner finds it necessary to create the post of general foreman to supervise the activities of the four shop foremen. A chain of command exists from Arrowsharp down to the general foreman, to the foreman, and to the workers.

Figure 6-1 shows an organization chart of this company at this stage of its growth.

During the course of the next few years, the company has become incorporated, and shares of stock have been sold. New organization features have been the creation of a board of directors whose function is to set basic policies, review the operations of the business, and in general insure that the enterprise is well managed. New functional staff departments that have been created are sales, industrial relations, and purchasing and traffic. An executive planning and control committee has been

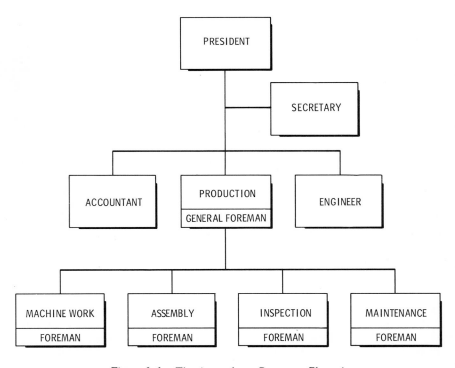

Figure 6-1. The Arrowsharp Company, Phase 1.

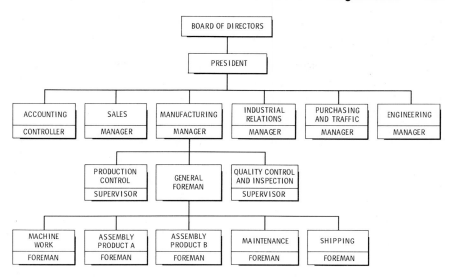

Figure 6-2. The Arrowsharp Company, Phase 2.

created. It is composed of the president as chairman, and the managers of manufacturing, sales, accounting, industrial relations, and purchasing, and traffic. In review it can be seen that a certain amount of group decision making has been developed at the board of directors level and at the executive committee level. Mr. Arrowsharp, over the years, has found it necessary to change his role in the company. Originally a manager and worker combined into one person, he has had to delegate more and more authority and tasks to subordinates. He now concentrates more on planning, handling of unusual situations, and seeing that the work gets done properly (control). He also handles contacts with public and governmental organizations. He has found it necessary to consult others on many diverse and specialized problems for which he lacks knowledge and experience. The human relationships among individuals, groups, and levels in the hierarchy have become quite complex and often very difficult.

Figure 6-2 illustrates the organization structure after the company has been in operation for several years.

GROUPING ACTIVITIES BY KIND

If a company is in the business of manufacturing bicycles, it would be possible for every worker to perform all of the operations required to make the complete bicycle. He could collect the materials at one point, form the frame and wheels on the proper machines, weld the parts of the frame together, machine the parts for the axle and sprocket assemblies, assemble the bicycle, paint it, and pack it in a shipping container. However, such a method for making bicycles would be very costly. Considerable machinery would stand idle much of the time while the worker was performing other types of operations. He would waste much time trotting from one place to another to collect materials and supplies. The worker would be a Jack-of-all-trades and a master of none. From this simple example it can be seen that a more efficient manner of arranging the work would be to assign different portions of the job to separate individuals who could then specialize at, say, machining or welding or assembling. On a larger scale, by looking at the factory as a whole, it can be seen that whole departments might be set up to specialize on the different steps in the process of manufacturing bicycles. Indeed the grouping of activities by kind, which is the heading for this section, is often called departmentalization.

The grouping of similar activities together provides a number of benefits. It permits employees (and managers, too) to become expert at one type of work. At the worker level this often means that semiskilled workers can do the tasks formerly performed by more highly paid skilled craftsmen. If a job requires the setting up, operating, and adjusting of several machine tools, such as a lathe, boring mill, milling machine, and a shaper, then this requires a highly paid skilled machinist. But if the work can be subdivided so that one man simply operates a lathe all day long and someone else sets it up and adjusts it, then the company need hire only a semiskilled worker to operate the lathe. Specialization of activity also avoids the duplication of costly production equipment that would otherwise stand idle much of the time. Specialized, high production machines can be utilized, whereas universal equipment must be used where there is no specialization of activity.

Patterns for Grouping

There are five basic ways of grouping work activities. These are as follows:

1. Location or geographic area.
2. Product.
3. Customer.
4. Function or type of work or knowledge.
5. Numbers of persons.

Sales forces are typically organized according to *location or geographic area.* Thus a particular company may have a sales office in San Francisco to cover the Western part of the country, one in St. Louis to cover the Midwest, and one in New York City to take care of the East.

Organization according to *product* lines is very common in the manufacturing field. The General Electric Company, for example, has over 100 separate operating departments, each of which makes a different line of products. Examples are the Clock and Timer Department, Power Transformer Department, Large Lamp Department, and the Silicone Products Department.

In the selling field it is quite common to find organizational units set up according to type of *customer*. Thus the sales force may be divided into those calling on government agencies, industry, and private individuals.

To subdivide according to *function* means that all work that is similar in nature is grouped together. This is true whether it be predominantly "brainwork," such as engineering, research, and legal, or whether it is predominantly manual work, such as punch press, pipe fitting, welding, heat treating, or assembly. Some authorities have tended to apply the designation *function* to mental and office type of activities and use the term *process* to apply to productive operations. This separation appears unnecessary.

Often there are large numbers of employees who are doing the same thing, working in the same location on the same products and for the same customers; yet it is necessary to set up units, sections, or departments for administrative control purposes. Thus in the army privates are grouped together into squads and supervised by sergeants. In a large office 100 clerks who are doing identical work would have to be grouped into sections for direction and control reasons. This criterion for grouping activities relates very closely to the span of control concept that will be discussed later.

Dangers of Overspecialization

Although there are substantial benefits to be derived from specialization of work activities according to type and although the proponents of the scientific management movement and of modern mass production methods have demonstrated positive gains for specialization, it can be and often has been carried too far. The costs (human and financial) often outweigh the profits. As a result of research conducted in recent years the pendulum has been swinging away from specialization toward integration and generalization.

At both the worker and management levels, it becomes much more difficult to synchronize and coordinate activities when several specialized persons or departments are required to produce the end result. As an illustration let us consider the case of teaching a college course in accounting. The course can be planned and taught entirely by one professor or segmentalized as follows: The professor in charge can plan the course, select the text and problem material, and deliver two lectures per week. The computing sessions can be given by a graduate assistant. Quizzes, examinations, and written problems may be graded by another graduate assistant. Attendance in the lecture hall can be recorded by the departmental stenographer, who comes in at the beginning of each lecture specially for that purpose. When movies are required they may be supplied by an audio-visual department, which acts in a service capacity to all academic departments. Thus to give one course in accounting the part-time services of five persons may be employed. If anyone fails to do his part due to lack of information, training, illness, or other reason, the classes may be delayed, impeded, or canceled. Considerable time and effort must be expended by the professor in charge to coordinate the activities of four other people.

Numerous other examples could be given in other fields of endeavor. Many factories employ whole corps of expediters, dispatchers, coordinators, and follow-up men to aid in the dovetailing and synchronization of a multitude of specialized departments. To make such systems work management must establish elaborate controls, exert close supervision, and apply frequent pressure on people. Research conducted at Sears, Roebuck and Company has shown that less specialization in the make-up of organizational units and the combining of tasks into broader, more challenging jobs achieve higher *esprit de corps,* greater morale, and higher production.[1]

Employees on repetitive routine jobs often experience a high degree of boredom, monotony, and even frustration. They lose interest in their work. One who has actually worked on an automobile assembly line stated that the production line workers acted like "zombies" at work. It was only after they walked out the plant gate at the end of the shift that they became alive, vibrant, and enthusiastic. They became awakened at the prospect of engaging in need-satisfying off-the-job activities.

Extensive experience at the International Business Machines Corporation has resulted in substantial benefits from the combining of a number of specialized jobs into larger, more inclusive ones. This process is called job enlargement. Improvements were noted in quality, lower costs, job satisfaction, and morale.[2]

Specialization evidences itself in conflicting work orientations by practitioner's in different fields of work. Narrow perspectives and overemphasis on one's own background and interests often obstruct solutions to problems. If production is low in the factory, the mechanical engineer sees it as a need for better machinery and conveyors, the industrial engineer feels that the major problem is lack of production standards and wage incentives, and the training director sees this as a problem to be solved by better employee training.

[1] James C. Worthy, "Organization Structure and Employee Morale," *American Sociological Review,* Vol. 15, No. 2 (April 1950), pp. 169-179.

[2] Charles R. Walker, "The Problem of the Repetitive Job," *Harvard Business Review,* Vol. 28, No. 3 (May 1950), pp. 54-58.

GROUPING ACTIVITIES BY LEVEL

The grouping of work into different levels in the organization is another form of specialization. All manual work may constitute the bottom level in the organizational hierarchy, supervision of this manual work makes up the foreman level, coordination and control of departmental operating and staff functions represents middle management, and policy making and overall direction of the business makes up the top management level. Figure 6-3 shows a partial organization chart of a large manufacturing corporation. This chart shows typical functions; levels of management, and formal channels of authority. Including the board of directors, there are seven levels of management.

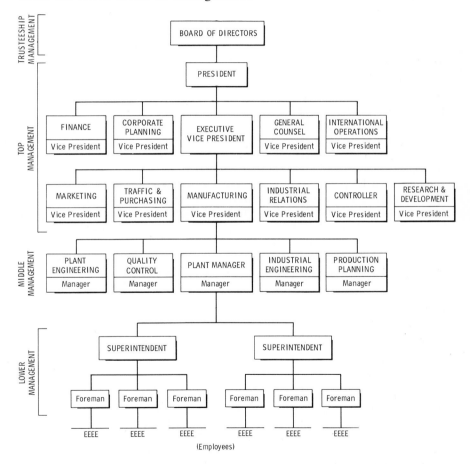

Figure 6-3. Partial Organization Chart of a Large Manufacturing Corporation Showing Levels of Management and Formal Channels of Authority.

A generally sound principle of organization that has been promulgated by both theorists and practical men over the years is that of *unity of command.* This means that each employee, whether he be a manager or a worker, should have only one boss. There should be a definite channel of authority from the top executive down through the intermediate levels of management to each worker. Sometimes officials hire persons to carry out a specific assignment but fail to clarify to whom the new employee reports. If an employee is under the impression that he has several bosses whom he must please, there tends to be confusion in his mind. If in fact he does have more than one superior he may be faced with conflicting orders.

An important (but by no means the only) channel for downward and upward communication is through the chain of command. Orders, information, instructions, and requests for data flow down through the levels in the hierarchy. Information about work in progress, suggestions, questions, complaints, and grievances flow up through the chain of command. An important reason for not skipping intermediate supervisors when communicating is that they must know what is going on in their units. Their position, value, and status is strengthened if they serve as vital and essential links in the vertical channel of communication.

For an organization to work effectively there must be a great deal of lateral communication as well as vertical. If a worker has completed making certain items that are now ready for inspection, generally he need only notify the floor inspector that the work is complete. It would waste much time if he had to notify his foreman who would in turn pass the request up the chain of command until a single manager over both production and inspection was reached. This manager would then tell the supervisor of inspection to have an inspector examine the product. Such a procedure is, of course, too cumbersome. Indeed in many organizations lateral communications and discussion are encouraged. The settlement of many problems at subordinate levels reduces the burden on higher executives.

Levels of Management

If a very capable and promising first-line supervisor were promoted rather rapidly up the organization ladder, he would find that the nature of his activities would change. Although he would be a manager both as a first-line supervisor and later as a member of middle or top management, the emphasis given to the different segments of the management function would be materially altered. To be successful as he rises in the hierarchy he must adjust his behavior, outlook, and general orientation. Frontline supervisors devote a high proportion of their time to immediate direction and interaction with their subordinates. Top management, on the other hand, spends a high percentage of its time on planning, policy development, forecasting, and participating in meetings. All levels perform the five management functions of planning, organizing, staffing, leading, and controlling; however, the emphasis given to each and the nature of the specific tasks within each major function are different.

If we look at a large manufacturing corporation, what generalizations can we make to describe the work and behavior of the principal levels?

Lower Management.   The term *lower management* includes assistant foremen, foremen, general foremen, and office supervisors. The word *supervisor* is the generic term meaning a member of lower management. They instruct employees in the methods of performing their jobs, assign and reassign employees to specific jobs and tasks, and take prompt action to overcome delays and breakdowns in the production process. Definite production schedules of a short-term nature (daily and weekly) are assigned to them from higher authority. Their authority to make expenditures for capital improvements (tools, equipment, and so on) is extremely limited. As far as personnel actions are concerned they have some limited say in selection of their subordinates; can assign minor disciplinary penalties; have great authority in evaluating employees and obtaining in-grade wage increases for their people. They generally have full authority to take whatever steps are necessary to get production out on time. They can requisition materials and supplies, authorize overtime work, obtain maintenance and inspection services, and request technical assistance where necessary. Communication down to employees and up to higher management is usually funneled through the supervisors.

Middle Management.   In the multiplant corporation the term *middle management* includes supervisory and executive personnel in production, sales, engineering, accounting, and other functional fields both within the plants and at corporate headquarters. Titles such as manager of industrial engineering, plant controller, assistant plant manager, and district sales manager are typical. No sharp lines of demarcation exist between lower and middle management. The terms are relative. Middle managers transmit and sharpen up information and orders from top management. They serve to help solve major difficulties when lower supervisors experience trouble. They operate within the policies and programs set by higher officials but shape them to fit the particular needs of their departments. They evaluate performance results in accordance with the program and standards established for them. They do not question, generally, the adequacy of the program itself. Considerable time tends to be spent in meetings with colleagues of similar rank.

Authority over such personnel matters as the selection, training, changes of status and position, and settlement of grievance and disciplinary problems is considerable.

Top Management.   In the business corporation this includes the president, vice-presidents and major division executives. In the large organization it covers the top two levels and sometimes the third level below the board of directors. Top executives are concerned with corporate strategy and the formulation of both long- and intermediate-range plans and programs. The chief executive officer provides an integrating function for the entire organization. He gives it direction and purpose. He must balance the internal interests of the firm with its external environment. The top executive team must concern itself with the survival and growth of the organization. Group decision making through committees and meetings is common. Considerable time is devoted to deliberation and reading of reports. The world of the top manager involves a lot of contact with the public and outside groups, such as government officials, trade association personnel, and other business executives. Business travel tends to be rather frequent. Authority and responsibility in monetary and personnel matters are very great and actions are only checked by higher authority (for example, the board of directors) at relatively long intervals. There is a tendency to be insulated from the problems, needs, and views of rank-and-file employees and even of first-line supervisors.

A rather recent development in the affairs of some of our huge corporations is the establishment of a "president's office." Essentially this means that a committee of senior executives directs the business. Commonly the president's office or a group president consists of the chairman of the board, the president, and two or three executive vice-presidents. They act as a close knit team that guides the affairs of the business. One of these, usually the board chairman, serves as the chief executive. The reason for the popularity of a president's office is that the responsibilities at this level are so complex that one man cannot possibly have enough time, knowledge and diverse skills to handle these awesome burdens. Among the companies which have an office of group president are General Electric; Armco Steel; Pet, Inc.; and Mead Corporation.

Trusteeship Management.   The Board of Directors of an organization carries out a number of very important functions. For a business corporation the board serves a trusteeship function by overseeing the direction of the business for the benefit of the stockholders, who are the owners. It decides upon the proper distribution of profits: for dividends, for retention in the business for expansion, and for paying off indebtedness. In both business and nonbusiness organizations the board of directors also bears important trusteeship responsibilities for the employees, clients or customers, and the public. It must be remembered that it is at the discretion and indulgence of the public, operating through government, that private organizations exist.

Other vital functions of a board are the establishment of objectives, selection of the president and other top executives, approval of overall budgets, and auditing of results. The board must continuously review the operations of the organization and insure that it is viable and being run properly. If necessary it can replace the top executive team.

Boards of directors typically are composed of both insiders and outsiders. Insiders are major executives such as the president and key vice-presidents who have day to day operating responsibilities. Outside members do not work for the corporation. They may be major stockholders or people such as bankers, lawyers, and professionals who have an expertize that can be valuable to the firm. Although many boards are composed predominantly of insiders, management authorities generally hold that it is most desirable to have a substantial portion of outsiders on any board. They can act as an independent review of the performance of the management group.

AUTHORITY AND INFLUENCE

Authority can be defined as the legitimate right to direct or influence the performance of others. It is a right to expect performance or action. In the formal organization the legitimacy is ordinarily conferred by the organization upon an office or person through its customs, rules, charter, and operating policies. Some writers in the field of management have defined authority as the power to command performance. However, it is very important to distinguish between the legitimate right and the actual power or capacity to get something done. Let us take the case of a voluntary student organization in a college, such as a radio club, debating society, or social organization. These organizations will have duly elected officers and will engage in activities where the members have certain duties to perform. But if some individuals fail to attend meetings or carry out their responsibilities, the officers have very few sanctions they can apply to compel performance. They must rely upon personal persuasion and influence. To take another illustration in a different field, we find sometimes that a government leader such as a president or a premier has the legitimate and vested power to order citizens to do something, but in actual practice they may flout his authority. The rebellion of the Algerian nationalists against the legal authority of the French government during most of the 1950's is a case in point. So we see that there is a distinction between authority (right to expect performance) and power (capacity to obtain performance and results). In normal circumstances in most organizations (companies, hospitals, army, government, and so on), the persons possessing authority also possess the power to achieve reasonable obedience to their wishes. They have at their disposal a whole host of rewards and penalties with which to control the actions of subordinates.

Source of Authority

What is the source of authority and power in an organization? Organization writers and theorists have had differing opinions on this question. In the business corporation an appealing explanation is that it comes from the owners (stockholders) to the board of directors, the president, and down through the chain of command. Certainly to the individual employee, he sees that the authority and orders come from above. In business enterprises the belief that authority comes from the top derives to a considerable extent from the concept of private property rights. It is claimed that the owners of the physical property (land, buildings, and equipment) have a right to use these resources as they see fit. Authority also derives from the state and society as a whole, which permits business and other organizations to exist and operate.

Yet in looking at the question in another light, we can see that the authority and power of a leader are dependent upon the willingness of his subordinates to accept and support him. "You can lead a horse to water, but you can't make him drink." This proverb applies to leadership in this situation. The willingness of people to follow does influence the effectiveness of a leader or executive. Chester Barnard was one of the foremost writers (and a successful industrialist as well) to challenge the old idea that authority always comes from the top down.[3]

Of course, if one studies democratic organizations, it is clear that the authority and power stems largely from the members and citizens. This is true for a labor union, a political democracy at the local, state, and federal level, a social club, and a professional association. The members elect their officials, and these are responsive to the will of the majority. Politicians generally cater to the powerful factions among their constituency in order to be re-elected. For the employees of these democratic organizations (for example, the government bureaucracies and civil service personnel), the flow of authority and power is very similar to that in a business corporation.

Influence and Politics

In order to maintain their positions and to get things done effectively through others, leaders and managers may employ any of several methods. They may simply issue orders and expect to have them obeyed because of the traditional authority that attaches to their position. However, if this is the only way in which a manager tries to get things done, he will be ineffective in the long run. Another way is to pass out rewards (pay increases, promotions, status symbols) and penalties (demontion, discharge, and so on). Another leadership device is personal persuasion, communication, and the development of strong personal ties with subordinates. The use of influence and politics is still a further means by which one can achieve his goals. This involves the dispensing of rewards and penalties and personal persuasion as building blocks, but influence and politics go much further. The government leader or business executive who is

[3] Chester I. Barnard, *The Functions of the Executive* (Cambridge, Mass.: Harvard University Press, 1938).

desirous of consolidating his position and getting results for his program will build alliances among other important people and groups. He will do favors for others and expect favors in return. He may actually get others quite indebted to him. He may promote those who support him and ease out potential opponents. If the chips are down he may threaten and cajole. The pay, title, status symbols, personal bearing, and manner all have an effect upon a leader's ability to achieve his goals. Influence maneuvering and political pressure are not confined to government. This activity goes on behind the scenes in private industry to a considerable extent. A careful sense of timing, pressing hard when one has the advantage, backing off when power is weak, knowing when to change horses, building upon friendship and alliances, judiciously dispensing rewards; these and many others are in the kit of tools of many a succesful leader.

DELEGATION

Because the single individual at the top of a pyramidal structure cannot do all the work of the organization himself, he delegates work to his immediate subordinates; they in turn redelegate part or all of this work to their subordinates and so on down to the nonsupervisory employees. There are three primary aspects to the delegation of authority.

1. Assignment of duties and functions to be performed.
2. Giving of authority to the subordinate sufficient to accomplish the results expected. Illustrations of the granting of authority are the right to purchase materials, right to engage the services of an outside consultant, right to hire employees, right to speak for the company in public, and so on.
3. Holding the subordinate accountable or responsible for his actions. The superior expects the subordinate to carry out conscientiously the work assigned to him.

In every organization that has multiple levels of management, successive delegations must take place. The question is not whether it shall occur, rather it is to what degree it should occur. By and large the successful manager is one who leans toward more delegation rather than less. Delegation has these advantages: (1) It unburdens the executive or supervisor from the details of his subordinates' jobs. This means that the superior has more time for planning and overall direction of his department and that his subordinates are encouraged to exercise broader decision making responsibilities for their own work. (2) Because the subordinates exercise their own judgment and handle their activities on their own they tend to generate greater commitment, enthusiasm, and pride in their work. They are less dependent upon the boss. (3) Delegation is a way of training and developing subordinates to take on varied and larger projects and responsibilities. They learn to plan more effectively and evaluate their own work when they know that their immediate superior trusts them and is not going to make every decision for them.

In delegating work to those below him in the organization, the executive himself does not evade his own responsibility for the work. If the captain of a ship delegates the job of guiding the vessel through intricate waterways to a pilot and if that pilot runs it aground, the owners of the ship will hold the captain responsible. If the cashier of a commercial bank embezzles $100,000 from the bank, the bank president and board of directors are ultimately held accountable for this action. The fact that a superior is held accountable (within reason, of course) for the behavior of his employees is necessary for the orderly operation of the organization.

Authority Relative to Responsibility

Broadly speaking, when a manager assigns work to a person and holds him responsible for accomplishing results, he should at the same time grant him enough authority and power to achieve those results. It is sometimes a human failing of executives to want to hang on to their powers tightly and not share them with subordinates. If the head of a department in a store is told that he must make a complete inventory accounting of his merchandise over the weekend, he must be granted the authority to bring in employees to work overtime and to borrow persons from other departments if this is necessary to achieve results. Thus we can see that authority should be sufficient to match the level of results expected.

There are many situations in which the superior does not himself possess the means and power to guarantee that the goal can be reached. The president of a company may delegate to his industrial relations director the job of negotiating a new contract with the labor union, which represents the employees. But the president cannot assign him the power to achieve a particular settlement or to prevent a strike. The attitude and strength of the union are not controlled by the president or the industrial relations director. Or to take another example, the general foreman in a factory may delegate to a foreman the full job of running the machine shop. But the general foreman can't assign to the foreman the authority and power to *make* the employees produce.

Dynamics of Delegation

One of the most frequent problems in connection with delegation is that executives are reluctant to delegate adequately to their subordinates. Delegation requires giving freedom to the employee to exercise some of his own initiative to get the job done. The superior must place confidence in his men. He must recognize that they will not carry out each and every assignment precisely as he, the boss, would. In delegating, the boss should not then stand over his subordinates to control their every action.

At the time the delegation is initially made to the employee, the outline of the task to be done, the limits of authority, and the requirements as to completion date, depth of effort, quality, and the like, should be made clear. There should be a full meeting of the minds on the nature and scope of the project. In many cases the manager and his employees have worked together so long that the limits of authority and responsibility are not spelled out each time. The employee knows that he is to operate in accordance with past practice and established company policies and procedures. For unusual or new projects or for new employees, the superior should define rather specifically the limits of authority and responsibility. Many companies have developed policy and organization manuals in which these matters are recorded for the major management positions.

One obstacle to effective delegation is the fear on the part of an executive of developing and building up the abilities and prestige of his subordinates so that they can eventually overtake or unseat him. Management development and proper delegation go hand in hand. If an executive believes that his own position is insecure, he may hesitate to build up his subordinates to the point where they have as much know-how and outside recognition as he himself has.

DECENTRALIZATION

Since the late 1940's decentralization has been a very popular concept in American management circles. This has been especially true in large corporations. *Decentralization means placing the authority and decision-making power as close as possible to the level at which the work is done.* As many functional specialties as are necessary to accomplish results are placed under the manager in charge of that organizational unit. Decentralization is really delegation on an organizationwide basis. Delegation involves superior to subordinate relations on a man to man basis; decentralization relates top management to lower level organizational units. If an enterprise is centralized, most decisions, both major and minor, are made by the president and top management. On the other hand, in a decentralized approach division and departmental managers are granted considerable authority to run their own units as they see fit as long as they achieve the desired results.

A secondary meaning of the term decentralization relates to the physical or geographical dispersion of the units and facilities of a company. Thus a company may have manufacturing plants and offices scattered throughout the country. The management control for a physically decentralized company could be either centralized or decentralized. When the term is used in the literature without qualification the context is usually decision-making decentralization. This is its most important current usage and this is what we are here concerned with.

What are the advantages of decentralization (relative to centralization)?

1. It permits quicker decision making. The managers who are closer to the work have the authority to take action.
2. Problems of coordination, communication, and red tape are reduced. If a product design problem comes up, it is not necessary to delay making a decision in order to contact a centralized engineering department.
3. Autonomy of subordinate units permits greater experimentation and flexibility to meet new conditions.
4. It encourages subordinates at every level in the structure to exercise greater initiative and ingenuity. Ideas do not have to be sold to top management before they can be tried.
5. It insures the development of more capable managers. They have had ample opportunity to "sink their teeth" into problems. Middle and lower managers are not messenger boys in the chain of command. They have learned to stand or fall on their own decisions and actions.

Decentralization is not an unmixed blessing. Local units may fail to utilize the expert services that staff units at headquarters have to offer. There is a danger of duplication of effort by local units. For example, a marketing or personnel problem may be tackled from scratch in one plant, whereas another plant has just spent thousands of dollars to successfully solve the same problem. The problem of control is made more difficult under decentralization. Very competent managers are an absolute must for decentralization to succeed.

Factors Governing Decentralization or Centralization

Whether a particular enterprise should be managed on a centralized or a decentralized basis depends upon a number of factors. The absolute size of the firm in terms of dollar volume of sales, number of plants, and number of employees is an important factor. It is very difficult to coordinate day-to-day decision making in a huge corporation. Efficiency may be enhanced by making the subordinate units semiautonomous. Another important factor is the nature and history of the firm. If it has only one product line and has grown primarily from within, then the company is more likely to remain centralized. This has certainly been true of the Ford Motor Company and of the International Harvester Company. The author is familiar with a grocery supermarket corporation that operates about thirty nearly identical stores in a section of upper New York State. Buying and selling decisions are highly centralized. Store managers do not make decisions on pricing or what items to stock. They do not even hire their own people. Their primary function is to supervise the employees, to keep attractive displays, and to give courteous, prompt customer service. This firm is profitable and successful operating in a highly centralized fashion. On the other hand, where a firm is engaged in the making of diverse and unrelated products and where it has grown by acquisitions and mergers, it is much more likely to be decentralized. If a large corporation purchases a smaller firm, most generally the management of the latter is allowed to operate semi-independently as long as its profits, sales, and general performance are satisfactory. It appears then that speed and adequacy of decision making, flexibility, and efficiency are enhanced through decentralized operations for very large, multiproduct, diverse and complex businesses.

Another consideration is the philosophy and personalities of the top management. Henry Ford, prided himself on making all major decisions in the Ford Motor Company, which he founded. Historically we note that owner-managed corporations have tended to be more centralized, whereas professionally managed firms have had more diffused responsibility and authority. If the president of a corporation is autocratic and tolerates no challenge to his views and if he also has substantial ownership in the firm, we can be fairly sure that a centralized pattern of control will be adopted throughout the entire organization.

It is very difficult to maintain centralized authority and control in a business that has branches and units scattered throughout the country and the world. This is particularly true if these units must deal directly with customers and the general public and must take prompt action on complex problems.

If a company is dealing with a strong national union that has won bargaining rights for all production employees in all plants, there tend to be strong demands for centralization and uniformity in wage structure, hours, grievance procedures, arbitration procedures, seniority standards and the like. This makes central control of labor policy and contract negotiation almost a necessity. Some management functions are more amenable to decentralization than others. In the large multiplant company such functions as purchasing, traffic, cost accounting, quality control, plant engineering, and personnel tend to be decentralized. Yet financial planning and resource allocation is reserved for the very highest level of decision-making and control. Marketing may or may not be decentralized depending upon the nature of the markets and the variety of products. A company manufacturing steam turbines, electric generators, transformers, and switch gear in decentralized divisions may run into trouble in selling to electric light and power companies if it does provide for well synchronized selling effort. This almost demands a measure of control from the top.

Human relations factors also are important. Talented division and departmental executives often are unwilling to accept close domination from their organizational superiors. They desire independence. They want to run their own show and to be rewarded for what they are able to accomplish in their own units. Innovation and adaptability are encouraged by decentralization. If every contemplated action must first be approved by the front office, frustration and hostility tend to be by-products. Decentralization can only succeed with competent well trained managers. A company that is thin in talent below the top level would do well to hire and develop a strong management corps before launching into decentralization.

Case Example—General Motors

Under the leadership of Alfred Sloan, the General Motors Corporation pioneered in decentralized management beginning in the 1920's. G.M. has a number of semiautonomous product divisions such as Chevrolet, Buick, and Frigidaire. Each division designs, develops, manufactures, and sells its own products. It buys its materials and components from other divisions of General Motors or from outside suppliers—whichever is to its own advantage in price and quality. Each division employs and trains its own employees and managers. Although the divisions are free to adopt either centralized or decentralized management internally, the philosophy of decentralization has tended to infuse the corporation for many years, and managers are brought up to believe in its values. It is a fact, however, that certain operating divisions are more centralized internally than is the company as a whole.

General Motors does have strong centralized top policy planning. This is achieved by means of four policy-making committees that report to the board of directors. These committees are: executive, finance, auditing, and salary and bonus. Reporting to the executive committee are several policy subcommittees for such functions as overseas business, engineering, personnel, public relations, research, and household appliances. G.M. at the highest corporate level exerts strong financial control of its multitude of divisions. Auditing controls are independent of lower level management authority. Budgets and major capital expenditures are coordinated at a very high level.[4]

LINE AND STAFF

In very small organizations all the employees and supervisors are *line* personnel. But as organizations grow it becomes necessary to employ specialists who give technical advice and provide services to line person-

[4] Further information on decentralization at General Motors can be found in Peter F. Drucker, *Concept of the Corporation* (New York: The John Day Company, Inc., 1946); Ernest Dale, *Planning and Developing the Company Organization Structure,* Research Report No. 20 (New York: American Management Association, 1952), pp. 98-106; and Alfred P. Sloan, Jr., *My Years With General Motors* (New York: Doubleday & Company, Inc., 1964).

nel. Thus a personnel director can help a superintendent with his training, safety, and grievance-handling problems. A production engineer may design a fixture for a machine. In this case the factory supervisor might have neither the time nor the knowledge to design this item himself.

In organizations the following kinds of positions may exist. These are

A. Line
B. Staff
    1. Specialized staff and service staff
    2. "Assistant-to" staff
    3. General staff

Line positions and personnel are involved directly in doing the work for which the organization was created. Generally the enterprise could not function, even for a day, without these activities. In a manufacturing concern, manufacturing and selling are considered line functions. Line personnel would be workers, foremen, superintendents, plant managers, and the president. In a department store both buying and selling are line functions. In a university devoted to the discovery and dissemination of knowledge, the faculty is line.

Specialized staff and service staff are closely related in their roles and responsibilities. They are also the most widespread of the various staff types. Specialized staff departments provide planning, advice, and control functions for the entire organization. Industrial relations and personnel, engineering, research and development, legal counsel, and auditing are examples of specialized staff groups. Such units are usually composed of people who are technical experts in their fields. They frequently are professionals and technicians. In addition to providing advice and control functions for all departments of a company, specialized staff units located at the level of top management also bear heavy responsibilities for policy formulation. Thus the office of the vice-president of personnel would formulate policies in regard to executive compensation, recruitment, training, labor relations, organization development, manpower, and benefit programs.

Service staff aids the organization predominantly in a physical sense. Examples of service staff are purchasing, maintenance, inspection, a real estate department for property acquisition and a stenographic pool. Like specialized staff, service staffs serve the organization as a whole.

Now in actuality a sharp distinction between specialized and service staffs is not possible nor really necessary. Many of the sections within a personnel department are engaged more in rendering services than they are in policy planning, advice, and control. This is true for the employment office and for the unit that administers pension and insurance benefits. Some service staff units give technical counsel and perform control functions. This is true for quality control and purchasing. In Figure 6-4 the personnel department is shown having a dotted-line staff relationship with other line and staff departments within the company.

"Assistant-to" staff is depicted in Figure 6-4 in the position of executive assistant to the president. The "assistant-to" position is created to relieve an executive of some of his burdens. It can be found at any level in the organization and there may be more than one reporting to an executive. The President of the United States has several staff assistants: a press secretary, a military aide, assistant for Congressional relations, economic advisor, speech writers and many others. The assistant to the president is apparently a growing phenomenon in American business. Assistants-to serve in the capacity that their bosses desire. Some are special purpose (for example, speech writers or public relations), but many are broad gauge. The broad gauge ones often perform such assorted tasks as reviewing and commenting upon staff reports before they go to the chief, handling a multitude of administrative details, making special investigations, serving as a sounding board for the chief's ideas, and in general serving as one whom the executive can confide in.

It should be clear that an assistant-to is really a personal assistant. He performs as an extension of his superior. Of necessity there must exist a close personal relationship between this assistant and his boss.

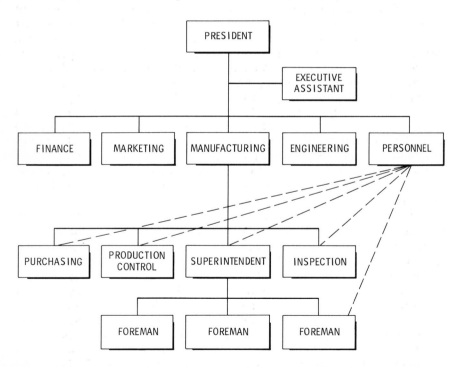

Figure 6-4 A Partial Organization Chart to Show Line and Staff Positions and their Relationships. The dotted lines from the personnel office to the various departments in the manufacting division and to the foreman show the flow of specialized advice, aid, service, and communication. The personnel office does not give direct orders to these individuals.

There are certain dangers to the usage of this position. Some staff assistants may usurp their position and start to issue orders to those below their bosses' in the structure. Generally speaking they have no authority to issue orders because such orders can cause dual lines of authority with attendant confusion. While assistants-to have little formal hierarchical authority, they often exert tremendous informal influence. When a subordinate wishes to see his boss, he may find an assistant-to blocking his path. This screening out of subordinates' problems, although it may relieve the line executive of worry, can be frustrating to the subordinate.

General staff, although seldom used in private business, is widely employed in military forces throughout the world. It is also fairly common in government. It is similar to assistant-to staff in its organizational position. However, instead of providing help to one man, general staff consists of a group of experts who operate an *office*. It is used primarily for planning. Historically, Gustavus Adolphus in seventeenth century Sweden is credited with first setting up a top staff of experts. The Prussian general staff, organized by Scharnhorst in the early nineteenth century, was a complete advisory service coordinated under a single head, the chief of staff. As a result of inefficiencies during the Spanish-American War in 1898, Elihu Root, the Secretary of the Army under President Theodore Roosevelt, created the general staff device for the United States Army.

Relations Between Line and Staff

The relationship between line and staff personnel is often quite vexing. (It should be pointed out here that in every staff department there exists a line chain of authority and responsibility from manager down to employee. Therefore, if people in another staff department interact with subordinates in this department, this is properly a line and staff contact; for example, industrial relations with engineering.) Set up to advise and service the line, staff personnel often find that their ideas are not wanted. Their personal presence on the production floor is sometimes resented by the line supervisor as a form of intervention.

The following are some typical examples of frictions between line and staff:

The foreman of the foundry department suspended a molder for two days without pay for insubordination. The industrial relations director then canceled the suspension on the grounds of insufficient cause.

The process engineer in a chemical plant has just instructed the process operator to increase the temperature on the reactor 30° F. The operator is confused, because this represents a departure from standing instructions from his foreman.

After weeks of intensive analysis and study, a team of two young systems and procedures engineers submitted their comprehensive report, which revealed serious weaknesses in the handling of orders in the purchasing department. Their report was on the desk of the purchasing director for months. Then it was finally returned to them with the written comment "Deemed inadvisable to make changes in system at present time. Present system has been getting results. Installation of proposed plan is too costly." The two engineers felt that their efforts had been wasted.

Dual Authority.   Overeager staff men often give orders to line personnel. This violates the principle of unity of command. When one considers that the typical business may have a whole host of functional staff people each of whom has some contacts with line employees, it is apparent that direct order giving is unworkable.

Staff Initiates Change.   The author has heard many factory foremen say that one thing they enjoy about working on the night shift is the freedom from the annoyance by white-collar experts that exists on the day shift. By background and because of the requirements of their jobs, staff specialists are innovators, creators, cost reducers, and initiators of change. This constant pressure from staff is upsetting to the line personnel. When an industrial engineer tells a general foreman that he can cut costs 10 per cent by changing existing work methods, the general foreman considers this a personal criticism of his ways. He feels he must defend himself. His defense is often interpreted as lack of cooperation by the industrial engineer.

Pipeline to the Top.   The chain of command for staff usually has fewer levels from bottom to top than does the chain for the line. The staff specialists can therefore reach the chief executive officer quicker with his proposals and pleas than can the line supervisor in many organizations. Besides, staff officers are often physically located closer to the chief executive than are those of production supervisors. A line supervisor often learns from experience that he must cooperate with staff, because if he doesn't, the staff officer will go to the top executive to have pressure put on the line supervisor to conform.

Different Perspective.   A line manager is a generalist, whereas a staff man is a specialist. When he calls upon the staff for help he will often obtain expert technical help, but it will be provided in compartmentalized fashion. If the accident record in the plant is poor, the engineer will see this as a need for better guarding of machines and the elimination of physical hazards, whereas the personnel specialist will tend to recommend more intensified safety training and indoctrination. The line manager is well situated to integrate the proposals of various staff groups. Since it is he who is held responsible for what happens in his operating department he must not abdicate his authority for decision making to staff.

Instrument for Control.   Staff is charged with the responsibility of checking up on the performance of operating units. This is carried out by comparing results with standards that have been established (presumably with line participation). What is the variance with respect to budget? Is quality up to standard? Do deliveries of completed product conform to schedule? What is the accident frequency of this plant compared to other plants in the company? These and many others are the ways in which control is exerted by staff. To hire new people a line supervisor must go through staff personnel. To increase someone's salary the request must be processed by the personnel department.

Improving Line-Staff Relations

Harmonious and cooperative relations can be achieved by a better understanding of each other's mission and orientation. Adequate communication and education in this respect is vital.

Staff should look upon itself as a helper to line and not as an instrument for clubbing line into obedience. If a staff specialist is called upon to enter a line department to solve a problem, he should work closely with the supervisor in charge from the outset. The supervisor should be closely involved in the project. His ideas should be solicited. He should have a part in decision making. Any recommendations that are developed should be with the consent and approval of the line supervisor. In this fashion the line man does not look upon the staff specialist as a threat to his security but rather as one he can call upon for assistance when he needs it. So often we find that the staff expert is aloof from the line supervisor. He prepares a critical report of his findings and submits this for approval through the staff hierarchy to top management. In this way the staff man feels he will get credit for his contributions. A better way is for the staff man to work out his written recommendations with the line supervisor. If higher authority is required to put into effect the changes proposed, then they are both recommending it. It should not be a contest to see who gets credit for the improvements. If profits, costs, efficiency, and morale are improved, *both* will receive credit in the eyes of top management.

In exercising its control function over line, staff can foster improved relations by discussing the performance with the line supervisors concerned, before a written report goes to higher management. If the variance is negative, if performance is below standard, this gives line some advance warning and an opportunity to take corrective action.

Staff, as a general rule, should not issue orders to line. Staff will be respected for its technical competence and its prestige, but except for special circumstances, it should not have the power to issue orders to line. Staff nevertheless does have great influence. If a physician tells his patient he must lose weight, the latter will pay great attention to the doctor's advice even though the doctor has no formal authority over his actions. This analogy fits the relations between staff and line rather well.

To be accepted by line, staff groups need the full support of top line management. This means that the president must approve of the work and costs required for particular staff groups to be effective. They need his moral support and influence. If a line manager senses that the president or another high line executive does not approve of the efforts of a personnel manager to launch a morale-building program or improve relations with local union leadership, for example, then the staff officer's cause is lost. Top management support for staff efforts is essential.

SPAN OF SUPERVISION

How many subordinates can one supervisor effectively control? Three, five, ten, twenty? This question has plagued organization theorists for decades. Older and traditional writers and practitioners have generally stated that the optimum number of persons reporting to one supervisor should be six. Some have stated that the maximum should be no more than five or at the most six where the work of the subordinates interlocks.[5] V. A. Graicunas, the French management consultant, proposed in the early 1930's a mathematical means for analyzing the interrelationships between subordinates and superiors. He noted that any supervisor must be involved in direct single relationships with each of his men, direct group relations with the various pairings and groupings of subordinates, and with the cross relationships between various pairs of employees. Graicunas concluded that five is the maximum number of subordinates one man could effectively handle.[6]

Modern writers, particularly behavioral scientists, have challenged the belief that a particular, rigid span of control must be adhered to. They contend that it can vary within wide limits, depending upon such factors as the personality of the executive, complexity of the work, level of competence of the subordinates, geographical dispersion of the employees, closeness of control exercised, and related factors. In actual practice the figure of six as a maximum is often exceeded. In the Sears, Roebuck and Company retail store, managers often have as many as thirty to forty immediate subordinates. Morale and efficiency have been reported high in these stores.

A narrow span of control (three to five subordinates) means that the resultant structure must be "tall." A wide span of control (over seven or eight) means that the structure is "flat." This can be visualized by con-

[5] Lyndall F. Urwick, *Notes on the Theory of Organization* (New York: American Management Association, 1952), p. 53.

[6] V. A. Graicunas, "Relationship in Organization," *Bulletin of the International Management Institute* (Geneva: International Labour Office, 1933).

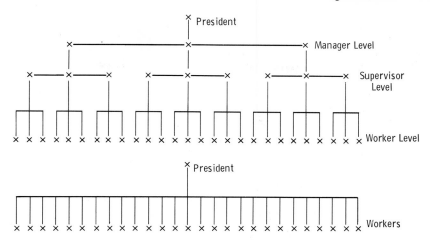

Figure 6-5. A Tall Organization Structure (top) and a Flat Organization Structure (bottom).

sidering a simple example. Assume there are twenty-seven employees in a company. If it has a narrow span of control, with three subordinates reporting to each supervisor, there will then be three management levels. On the other hand if there is a very wide span of control, twenty-seven, we find only one management level. See Figure 6-5.

A narrow span of control permits the manager to exercise very close control over his people. He can make most of their decisions for them. Those who favor rigid control tend to utilize a narrow span. On the other hand a wide span of supervision requires that the employees make more of their own decisions. They are given more freedom and latitude. A wide span of control encourages general supervision. As we shall see in Chapter 18, "Supervision," empirical research has shown considerable benefits to be gained with general supervision. Employee morale, interest in work, job satisfaction, and often productivity are higher when general supervision is practiced. For the flat structure to succeed employees must be well trained and competent to perform more on their own.[7]

BUREAUCRACY

The term bureaucracy is derived from the French word *bureau* meaning writing table, desk, or office; hence an organization composed of large numbers of clerical and administrative people. More precisely, a bureau-

[7] For a good analysis of tall versus flat structures see Burleigh B. Gardner and D. G. Moore, *Human Relations in Industry* (3rd ed.; Homewood, Ill.: Richard D. Irwin, Inc., 1955), pp. 237-243.

cracy is a large scale organization in which there exist well defined departments and jobs, specialization of work and competence, clear standards of performance, a hierarchy of authority and routinized procedures. The authority is legitimate and resides in the office, not the person of the incumbent.

Now in everyday usage the term bureaucracy has acquired a different meaning. Almost daily in the newspapers and slick paper magazines we read of the inefficiency, red-tape, delay, evasion of responsibility, cumbersomeness and waste in government bureaucracy. Bureaucracy has become an epithet—a synonym for inefficient large-scale organization, especially government.

In all serious books on organization theory and management, however, the term bureaucracy is used in its original and neutral meaning. Actually, the phenomenon of bureaucracy is not peculiar to government. Rather most medium- and large-size corporations, labor unions, large churches and hospitals, and universities exhibit the essential features of a bureaucracy. Bureaucracy is an inescapable component of modern, large scale organizational society. The study of bureaucracy is really an analysis of how large complex organizations operate and of the impact of this form of organization upon employees, managers, clients, and the public at large. Bureaucracy is both a concept and model of administration and an instrument of power and influence.

The concept of bureaucracy as a model of formal organization was originally created by the great German sociologist Max Weber, who was most productive during the period 1900 - 1920. In looking at the development of civilization through the broad sweep of history, Weber viewed the world, especially industrialized societies, as becoming progressively more rational and secular. In constructing and operating the institutions upon which man was dependent for the necessities of life, mankind tended to base its actions more and more upon knowledge, rational decision making, and technology and less and less upon mysticism and the occult. Man, in the modern advanced nations of the world, spends a large amount of time and effort on the job and trying to advance himself economically and socially. In short, he is practical and materialistic. In more underdeveloped areas of the world, man tends to devote more attention to contemplation and religious affairs.

Figure 6-6 gives the principal identifying features of a bureaucracy. Anyone who has ever worked in a large corporation or in government or any student of administration knows that these factors fairly accurately describe the way in which these organizations are structured. More and more in the large organization the activities are professionalized. People obtain their jobs because of their ability to perform and not because they are personal friends of the appointing official. They undergo formalized education and training to qualify for employment. Management sets objective standards of performance and selection criteria.

Work activities within the enterprise are grouped into departments,

1. <u>Formal authority</u>: Authority to command is formally assigned and regulated.

2. <u>Autocratic authority</u>: Authority and the office hierarchy are essentially autocratic.

3. <u>Positional authority</u>: It resides in the office, not the person.

4. <u>Chain of command</u>: Orders, communications, and appeals flow through a clear chain of offices.

5. <u>Job duties</u>: These are clearly defined.

6. <u>Employee qualifications</u>: These are clearly defined.

7. <u>Employee selection</u>: Based upon qualifications, not personal friendship or nepotism.

8. <u>Specialization of work</u>: Activities logically grouped.

9. <u>Education and training</u>: Occupations require substantial specialized study and training.

10. <u>Professionalization of management</u>: Administration handled by trained experts.

11. <u>Appointed office holders</u>: Officials and employees are appointed, not elected.

12. <u>Records</u>: Extensive use of records, documents, and files.

13. <u>Rules</u>: Extensive use of rules impersonally administered.

14. <u>Job security</u>: Long job tenure.

15. <u>Promotion from within</u>: Based upon qualifications and seniority.

16. <u>Decision and planning aids</u>: Mathematical models, electronic computers, sophisticated accounting and financial techniques.

Figure 6-6. Characteristics of Bureaucracy.

sections, subsections, and jobs according to objective criteria. This is simply an application of the familiar organization principal of specialization of work.

A hierarchy of authority, a chain of command, and authority and power flowing from the top downward through the echelons of the organization— these are the classical concepts of authority.

Rules, regulations, and discipline help insure that the employees and administrators perform consistently, predictably, and in accordance with policies and plans. When people are well trained and know the rules, there is less need for supervision to exercise close, personal coordination.

To free men's minds from anxiety and insecurity so that they can devote full attention to their jobs, the modern large establishment provides a considerable measure of job security, seniority rights, and insurance protection for retirement and illness. Morale is further enhanced by well-established promotion-from-within practices. Higher level positions are rarely filled from outside the company. Pay increases within a particular job grade are often related, directly or indirectly, to length of service. This is especially true of government bureaus and in the lower levels of private industry.

The decision-making process in many areas of management has been made more rational because of the use of applied mathematics, operations research, and modern high-speed electronic computers. These techniques have been applied extensively to the marketing, production, and procurement functions as well as to product and process design. Other modern extensions of the principles of bureaucracy have been the development of much more refined accounting and financial control techniques through accurate costing, cost centers, budget accountability, and profit responsibility for organizational components. Still other modern features are statistical quality control, job evaluation, employee selection via standardized psychological tests, and performance appraisal techniques.

Organizations Along a Continuum

If one were to classify work organizations along a continuum according to the degree to which they are institutionalized, we could start on the left-hand side of the scale with the family, which historically was the basic unit for producing the necessities of life in primitive and agricultural societies as well as in cottage production, the precursor of the factory system. A slightly more complex form of organization is the tribe or clan in which the activities of a larger number of people must be coordinated and in which different people perform somewhat specialized roles based more upon tradition than conscious design. It is only after we progress beyond the tribal society that we enter the arena of truly formal work organizations. In a formal work organization the participants work for money wages, and the assignment of work, grouping of functions, and flow of orders, and communications is, at the very least, somewhat structured and formalized. The least institutionalized of formal organizations is the highly personalized entity typified by the princely state of earlier days and of the small family owned company of today. In these organizations people obtain their jobs because of who they are and their relationship to the leader. Personal loyalty is the prime requisite for office. An individual may be assigned a variety of jobs, not because he possesses special knowledge and training but because his superior knows him to be loyal and devoted. A given individual in a personalized organization may be called upon to perform quite different types of work from time to time. Generalized knowledge and various skills are required, although competence in any one endeavor can be only of a modest order. For example, a king's aide may lead an ambassadorial party to a foreign power one month and be expected to redecorate his ruler's palace the next month. Jobs and subunit objectives are not programmed.

As one moves further across the spectrum he encounters organizations of all sizes which possess only a moderate degree of those features which epitomize the so called "ideal-type" bureaucracy. This can be due to a lack of knowledge of modern management techniques on the part of the top executives in some instances, and it can be due to a deliberate attempt to foster informality, freedom, and creativity in other cases.

A number of very modern organizations are deliberately structured to be somewhat intermediate between the highly personalized informal establishment and the highly regimented bureaucracy. These are typified by the small research and development companies which make no products but employ scientists and engineers to create and design military defense systems and aerospace components and by organizations in biological, medical, and social sciences. Hallmarks of these project and team-oriented organizations are group leadership and decision making, fluid structures, informal hierarchy, colleagueship rather than man-boss relationships, a permissive atmosphere, and a high degree of personal commitment to the work and goals of the firm.

At the far right end of the scale one finds the modern corporation, military establishment, and government. By design the participants are highly regimented. Organization goals and suborganizational goals and procedures are specified in detail down to the lowliest job. People operate by the book. Procedural manuals for engineering, personnel, finance, accounting, operations, and marketing are the order of the day.

From the foregoing discussion it must be apparent that bureaucracy constitutes but one model, albeit a very common one, of organization. Many organizations do, however, function on a more personalized, informal basis. Often these less formalized establishments are smaller in size. In terms of their distinct objectives, clientele, and environment these less institutionalized organizations may be as effective as the large bureaucracy.

Advantages of Bureaucracy

Permanence.   An acquaintance once remarked, "I traded at that corner grocery store once a week for years and years. I liked the man who owned it, his merchandise, and his service. All of a sudden when I went there last week I found a sign on the door stating that the store had gone out of business. I had no warning." The transient character of small businesses is quite apparent to the interested observer in any community. In sharp contrast the bureaucracy goes on and on. The customer, the employee, and the public at large can be reasonably certain that General Motors, General Electric, the American Telephone and Telegraph Company, and other organizations of their kind will always be there. In fact the welfare of the modern bureaucracy is so intertwined with the welfare of the community that the public generally will not permit the large organization to be destroyed.

Dependability.   The large, stable institution tends to build a reputation for consistency of action. The emblem of one of our largest insurance companies is a picture of the Rock of Gibralter, which people associate with integrity, stability and permanence. Because of written policies and procedures and emphasis upon extensive employee training, the client can expect to receive uniform, consistent treatment. A meal in a Howard Johnson restaurant in Boston is essentially the same as a meal in a Howard Johnson restaurant in Buffalo. The Internal Revenue Service will treat both its employees and the tax payer essentially the same in Portland, Maine, as in Portland, Oregon. And this bureaucratic behavior will be relatively unchanged from year to year. So predictability is the watchword. The client may not always like the treatment he receives from the bureaucracy, but he certainly knows what to expect.

Efficiency.   The great rise in productivity and living standards of industrialized societies since the mid-nineteenth century has been due not only to the industrial revolution and capital formation but also to advances in administration that have enabled man to marshall his human and material resources effectively. Thus rationalization of administration has enabled man to fully exploit his inventions and technology.

For the production of a standardized quality product (or service) on time, day in and day out, throughout the year, the bureaucratic form of organization cannot be surpassed. It gets the job done.

Disadvantages of Bureaucracy

Excessive Sanctification of Procedures and Rules.   Employees are taught to carry out their work in conformity with detailed procedures, rules, and regulations that are issued from higher authority. The purpose is to insure automaticity in accomplishing the goals of the company or establishment. Indeed this automatic, obedient performance is just what happens in most cases. However, the intermediate and lower level bureaucrats (and indeed some of the top-ranking ones too) tend to look upon rule compliance as a goal in itself. Thus, they lose sight of the original and true objectives of their enterprise and feel that they must uphold their rules at all costs. They forget that the rules are procedural in nature. They were set up as means to an end not as ends in themselves. This process of transforming means into ends has been called *displacement of goals* and is a prevalent phenomenon in bureaucracies. When santification of the rules becomes excessive to the point where it interfers with efficient goal accomplishment of the organization, then we have the familiar case of "red tape."

Goal displacement and red tape become most dysfunctional when a client or employee has an unusual problem not covered by the rules or when he feels an exception to the rules should be made in his case. The petty bureaucrat generally does not bend. He does not use his judgment. He upholds the rules blindly even if it means an outlandish conclusion.

Regimentation and Monotony.   In his novel *The Civil Service* the French author Honoré de Balzac made this statement many years ago: "The clerks of departments find themselves sooner or later in the condition of a wheel screwed on to a machine; the only variation of their lot is to be more or less oiled." These conditions hold true today, perhaps even more so than in earlier times.

Over the past twenty years industrial psychologists and sociologists have devoted a great deal of research and scholarly attention to the monotony, boredom, and fatigue experienced by blue-collar workers. The frustrations of workers in mass production industry have been rather extensively investigated. This monotony and regimentation is caused by the factory system, mass production techniques, modern technology, extreme job specialization, and lack of individual autonomy and control. In a broad sense we can say that it is caused by the bureaucratization of factory work.

But regimentation and monotony are not confined to blue collar factory workers. File clerks file only correspondence for certain customers; buyers purchase only certain classes of items and deal with certain vendors; and an engineer spends his career designing steering mechanisms for automobiles.

Client Frustration.   Compared to the haphazardly administered enterprise, a bureaucracy clearly better serves the needs of most of its clients most of the time. But client frustration does arise for those who feel their cases justify an exception to the rules. This problem was alluded to previously in our discussion of sanctification of the rules and goal displacement. The frustrated client calls this "red tape." Red tape is the label applied to the routing of a client's case through excessively slow and tedious channels because his problem is a little different from that covered by the rules and when, in fact, the first bureaucratic official refuses to make clearly warranted exceptions to the rules.

In the smaller, more personalized organization such as the service station, small private employment agency, plumbing and heating company, or small home building contractor, the client may also experience rejections and dissatisfactions. But here he can immediately go to the owner or top manager—the man who holds the power—and get a prompt decision and action. He is not dealing with a huge depersonalized machine.

Resistance to Change.   Behavioral scientists have often observed that bureaucracy is quite efficient in the production of a standardized product or service but quite inefficient in creative capacity. This observation is probably true in the majority of cases but it is not inevitably so and under certain conditions the bureaucracy can innovate.

The American public is familiar with the 1925 court martial of General Billy Mitchell, who was an outspoken advocate of a separate Air Force and a severe critic of the War and Navy Departments in the realm of military aviation. He was vindicated to a considerable extent years later when his ideas regarding air power were applied in World War II.

The American public is also familiar with the battles that Admiral Hyman Rickover, father of the nuclear submarine, had during the 1950's with the entrenched Navy establishment. Because of his controversial stance he was passed over for promotion more than once. It was due primarily to Congressional concern and Presidential action that the conservative Navy power structure was overruled, Rickover was promoted and the nuclear submarine fleet was built.

What forces within a bureaucracy cause it to suppress new ideas and change? Those forces which maximize routine efficiency often mitigate against new methods and ideas. Foremost among these is the autocratic (or monocratic) authority structure. Functionaries are rewarded for doing what they are told, not for suggesting changes in programs developed by their own bosses. The latter action is looked upon as threatening by many superiors, especially if they possess any feelings of insecurity in their positions or abilities. Most policies, programs, and plans are developed from "on high," and lower-level personnel are indoctrinated to comply. Responsibility tends to be shifted upward; work is shifted downward. Problems that fall outside the narrow limits of one's jurisdiction are referred upward until they come to a manager with sufficient authority to render a decision. Participation programs such as consultative supervision, democratic supervision, and labor-management cooperation are a recent development in the realm of management and are still none too widely used.

The regimentation, discipline, and rules all operate to induce employees to follow the path of least resistance. That path is simply to do as one is told.

Questions for Review and Discussion

1. In what ways is a thorough understanding of organization essential to the practice of personnel management?
2. Give five bases or methods of grouping activities into departments.
3. What is meant by the term *delegation?* What problems do managers sometimes have in delegating effectively?
4. For each of the following positions indicate whether it is line, specialized or service staff, or assistant-to staff:
   a. A college professor who teaches economics full time
   b. An outside salesman for a soap company
   c. An assistant plant manager
   d. A job analyst in the personnel department of a factory
   e. A buyer in a department store
5. What is meant by the term *decentralization?* Under what circumstances would you recommend that it be used? Not used?

6. Describe the nature of the problems that often are encountered when staff and line personnel deal with one another. How can these be resolved?
7. Identify the principal levels of management. Explain their characteristics and functions.
8. What factors determine the number of subordinates one individual can properly supervise?
9. What is a bureaucracy? What are its identifying features? What are its virtues and shortcomings?

CASE PROBLEM

Management Associates, Inc.

Management Associates, Inc., is a management consulting firm that provides consultation services to business and industry on a wide variety of management problems. It deals in organization studies, attitude surveys, job evaluation, management development, efficiency studies, systems and procedures, selection testing, and management audits.

The organization consists of a president, an administrative assistant to the president, two senior staff consultants, five staff consultants, and a number of secretaries and clerks. Offices are located in New York City.

The position of administrative assistant to the president was created one year ago to relieve him of some of the administrative details of his job. The position is occupied by an ambitious man of thirty-four years of age who started as a staff consultant four years ago. He possesses a bachelor of business administration from an Eastern college. His position involves answering correspondence from prospective clients, scheduling of work assignments, supervising the office clerks, screening visitors to see the president, and digesting reports and accounts of new developments for the president. When the president is pressed for time he often delegates to this assistant the responsibility of analyzing and reviewing the reports that the staff consultants have prepared for clients. This is prior to their submission to the clients.

The staff consultants have noticed that, in the year since the administrative assistant has assumed his position, his influence and power in the organization have been on the rise. He has established a warm personal friendship with the president. The two frequently play golf together on Saturdays. They have noticed that he has developed the tendency of saying with increasing frequency phrases such as "The president would like you to fly to a new assignment in Chicago on Monday," or, "The president is too busy to see you now. I'll handle your problem," or, "Your report for this client needs complete revamping, I will not approve it this way."

In effect they have observed that he tends to "throw his weight around" and assume authority over their work which they do not think he possesses. This situation has been particularly disturbing to the five staff consultants, who are mostly in their late twenties and thirties and who have had experience with the firm ranging from three to ten years. The two senior consultants have a great deal of stature in their professional fields of competence, are older, and have generally had full and ready access to the president. They are rarely in the office and have tended to be aloof from the interpersonal office difficulties.

The tension between the administrative assistant to the president and the five staff consultants has recently come to a head as a result of the very sharp criticism that two of them have received from the assistant in connection with their expense accounts. The president has a reputation for fair treatment of his subordinates; however, it is somewhat difficult to see him, because he is out of town frequently. When he is in the office his time is monopolized by visitors and the administrative assistant. The men know that the president's judgment on salary increases for them is influenced by the administrative assistant's attitude to a considerable extent.

Questions

1. What course of action, if any, should the staff consultants take? Should they act individually or as a group?
2. Would it be sound for the staff consultants to do nothing at the present time and wait to see how the situation develops?
3. What is the responsibility of the president in this problem?
4. Is a problem such as this inherent in the structural position of an "assistant-to"?

Simulation Exercise

Zif, Jay J., *Reorganization* (Creative Studies Simulation), New York: The Macmillan Company, 1970.

Suggestions for Further Reading

Blau, Peter M., *The Dynamics of Bureaucracy,* Rev. Ed., Chicago: University of Chicago Press, 1963.

Brech, E. F. L., *Organization: The Framework of Management* (2nd Ed.), London: Longmans, Green, 1965.

Brown, David S., "Shaping the Organization to Fit People," *Management of Personnel Quarterly,* Vol. 5, No. 2, Summer 1966, pp. 12-16.

Carzo, Rocco, Jr., and John N. Yanouzas, *Formal Organization: A Systems Approach,* Homewood, Ill.: Richard D. Irwin, 1967.

Dale, Ernest, *Management: Theory and Practice,* New York: McGraw-Hill Book Company, 1965.

Etzioni, Amitai, *Modern Organizations,* Englewood Cliffs, N.J.: Prentice-Hall, 1964.

Fayol, Henri, *General and Industrial Management,* London: Sir Isaac Pitman & Sons, 1949.

Litterer, Joseph A., *The Analysis of Organizations,* New York: John Wiley & Sons, 1965.

March, James G. (ed.), *Handbook of Organizations,* Chicago: Rand McNally & Company, 1965.

March, James G. and Herbert A. Simon, *Organizations,* New York: John Wiley & Sons, 1958.

Rubenstein, Albert H. and Chadwick J. Haberstroh (eds.), *Some Theories of Organization,* Rev. Ed., Homewood, Ill.: Richard D. Irwin, 1966.

Scott, William G., *Organization Theory: A Behavioral Analysis for Management,* Homewood, Ill.: Richard D. Irwin, 1967.

Thompson, Victor A., *Modern Organization,* New York: Alfred A. Knopf, 1961.

————, "Bureaucracy and Innovation," *Administrative Science Quarterly,* Vol. 10, June 1965, pp. 1-20.

Job Organization and Information

7

Current information about the content and nature of the jobs in the organization is vital to effective management. All organizations that exist to accomplish both long- and short-term goals fulfill these objectives by means of the united work efforts of those employed in them. The total work to be done must, of necessity, be divided and grouped into packages that we call jobs. The complexity and depth of tasks that are collected together into one job are determined both by the availability of manpower that can fulfill these particular job requirements and by the particular needs of the organization. In a sense, people and jobs are the building blocks of any organization.

Job analysis, which is simply a detailed and systematic study of jobs, furnishes information of great value to a personnel program. It plays a role in manpower and organization planning; employee recruitment, selection, and placement; determination of equitable employee rates of pay; work methods improvement; the development of training programs; performance appraisal; and accident prevention programs.

JOB INFORMATION AND PERSONNEL MANAGEMENT

Accurate and up-to-date job information is essential to the operation of a sound personnel program. An organization is composed of people who are grouped together into teams (designated as sections, departments, divisions, and so on) to do work in order to achieve agreed-upon goals. These basic elements, people and their assigned jobs, are organized into small units, which in turn are combined into larger units, such as divisions and plants, and these are finally related one to the other into companies, institutions or governmental units. These relationships may perhaps be more easily visualized by referring to Figure 7-1.

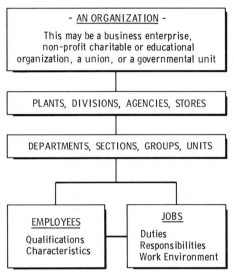

Figure 7-1. Diagram of Relationships of Units in an Organization.

Sound management practice requires that each of the entities above be defined and specified. The purpose and objectives of each organizational unit from the top on down to individual jobs should be determined, recorded, and communicated to appropriate parties involved. Likewise the functions of each organizational unit and the relationship of one to the other must be established and agreed upon. This work is all part and parcel of good organization planning. The determination and recording of the specific content of each job and of the necessary employee skills and abilities to fill the jobs is likewise vital to successful administration. The method and procedure employed to determine the duties, responsibilities, working conditions, and working relationships of and between jobs and the human qualifications of employees is called job analysis.

What Is Job Analysis?

An excellent definition of job analysis is that developed by the United States Department of Labor. It is as follows: "*Job Analysis* is defined as the process of determining, by observation and study, and reporting pertinent information relating to the nature of a specific job. It is the determination of the tasks that comprise the job and of the skills, knowledges, abilities, and responsibilities required of the worker for successful performance and which differentiate the job from all others."[1]

Modern-day usage of the term *job analysis* has tended to restrict it to the type of job study associated with various personnel programs, such

[1] Department of Labor, United States Employment Service, Occupational Analysis and Industrial Services Division, *Training and Reference Manual for Job Analysis,* June, 1944, p. 1.

as employee selection, job evaluation, wage surveys, training, accident prevention, and the like. However, the term is also sometimes applied to a detailed and quantitative study of jobs and job operations by industrial engineers in connection with time and motion study, methods improvement, and work measurement programs. The industrial engineering approach usually breaks down each job into detailed tasks and often specifies each hand and arm motion to be utilized by the worker. In other words the work is subdivided into elements, and times are determined for each one. The goal is usually to establish a standard time for each type of operation performed by each worker. Work simplification and methods improvement are generally part and parcel of every analysis.

When used in connection with personnel programs (selection, job evaluation, training, and the like) as opposed to engineering the job, the objective is not to redesign the job. To be sure a realignment of jobs may be a by-product of a searching job study program. However, the personnel department representatives ordinarily analyze a job after it has been previously designed and established by industrial engineers, production engineers, and by managers in the particular departments involved. Job analysis for personnel program purposes rarely goes into such great detail as describing individual body motions and their sequence. Likewise time standards for operations are ordinarily not sought. Rather the emphasis is upon determining the principal duties of a job, the nature and level of aptitudes and skills required to perform these activities, the relation of the job to others in the organization, responsibilities involved, and working conditions. Often a purpose is to be able to describe and define the distinctions among various jobs. Considerable emphasis is placed upon an accurate detailing of the human characteristics—physical and mental skills, personality traits, and so on—needed to adequately perform the job.

Because industrial engineering techniques, such as work simplification, methods engineering, time and motion study, and work measurement, are outside the scope of this book, our explanations in this chapter will be confined to job analysis from the personnel management viewpoint.[2]

Simply stated, job analysis is a procedure for obtaining pertinent job information. This information is recorded, basically on two forms or pieces of paper, to make a permanent record. One is called a job description and the other is called a job specification. The relationship between these is shown in Figure 7-2.

The actual content and format of job descriptions and specifications varies greatly from one organization to another. Indeed there is even some

[2] For further information on these industrial engineering techniques the interested reader may consult: Krick, Edward V., *Methods Engineering* (New York: John Wiley & Sons, Inc., 1962); Maynard, Harold B. (Ed.) *Industrial Engineering Handbook* (2nd Ed., New York, McGraw-Hill Book Company, 1963); Niebel, Benjamin W., *Motion and Time Study* (4th Ed., Homewood, Ill.: Richard D. Irwin, Inc., 1967.)

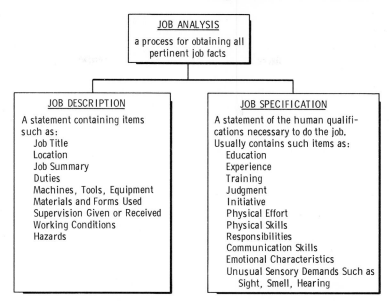

JOB ANALYSIS
a process for obtaining all pertinent job facts

JOB DESCRIPTION
A statement containing items such as:
   Job Title
   Location
   Job Summary
   Duties
   Machines, Tools, Equipment
   Materials and Forms Used
   Supervision Given or Received
   Working Conditions
   Hazards

JOB SPECIFICATION
A statement of the human qualifications necessary to do the job.
Usually contains such items as:
   Education
   Experience
   Training
   Judgment
   Initiative
   Physical Effort
   Physical Skills
   Responsibilities
   Communication Skills
   Emotional Characteristics
   Unusual Sensory Demands Such as
      Sight, Smell, Hearing

Figure 7-2.   Job Description and Job Specification in Job Analysis.

confusion between the two terms in some circles. Some practitioners make no distinction between a job description and a specification. They use them interchangeably. However, the more common practice is to designate the objective listing of job title, summary, and duties as the description and to call the enumeration of employee qualifications the job specification. This latter term was originated by the United States Employment Service, and it seems very useful to distinguish between two quite different kinds of information. The determination of the human characteristics needed to fill a job calls for value judgments. The specification is actually derived from the description by translating the job activities and requirements into particular skills and abilities. But to a certain extent the level of ability demanded is dependent upon management policy and standards. For example, some organizations require that their secretaries have a post-high-school business education (one to two years), whereas others accept simply a high school diploma and concentrate upon training from within.

Uses for Job Analysis and Job Information

A comprehensive job analysis program is an essential ingredient of sound personnel management. Job information derived from such a program has many important applications. These are as follows:

Organization and Manpower Planning.   When it is determined that certain types and amounts of work must be done, this work must be divided into specific jobs at all levels in the organization, from unskilled laborer up through the chief executive officer. In establishing the organization structure it is necessary to "package" the work to be done into meaningful units. Job analysis aids in determining the number and kinds of jobs and the qualifications needed to fill these jobs. Thus it is an essential element of effective manpower planning. At managerial levels, accurate job descriptions and specifications are intimately related to the preparation of inventories of executive talent.

Recruitment, Selection, and Placement.   To carry out an employment program, it is necessary to have clear statements of the work to be performed and of the skills and knowledge that must be possessed by the employees who will fill these jobs. Basically the goal is to match, as closely as possible, the job requirements with the worker aptitudes, abilities, and interests. It is not possible to staff accurately varied jobs in an organization by having available job title data only. Full job information is necessary.

Establishment of Proper Rates of Employee Compensation.   This involves a determination of the relative worth of jobs within the organization by means of the technique called job evaluation and a comparison of wages paid inside the organization with those paid for comparable jobs in other companies via a wage survey. The purpose of job evaluation is to insure internal pay equity of one job to another, whereas the purpose of surveying the going wages in a labor market is to insure that the level of wages within an organization is correct in relation to the community or the industry. For job evaluation purposes, job descriptions must be very complete; for conducting a wage survey, condensed descriptions are generally sufficient.

Engineering Design of the Operation and the Job.   Job analysis for this application basically takes two forms. One is the present-day industrial engineering activity, which is an outgrowth of the original work of Frederick W. Taylor and Lillian and Frank Gilbreth. This concerns operation analysis, motion study, work simplification, methods and workplace improvement, and work measurement. The objective is usually to improve efficiency, reduce unit labor costs, and establish a production standard that the employee is expected to meet. A second and more recently developed type of engineering job analysis is called human engineering (or often human factor analysis). This type of job study originated in World War II, when the design of weapons systems took into consideration human capabilities, both physiological and psychological. This type of work combines the disciplines of industrial engineering and industrial psychology. It has come into prominence in recent years in connection with the design of man-machine systems for aircraft, submarines, rocket ships, space capsules, and the like, as well as for industrial applications. As indicated previously, the engineering approach to job analysis is outside the scope of this book.[3]

Employee Training and Management Development. Many firms provide new employees with copies of the descriptions and specifications for the jobs to which they have been assigned. This practice aids in orienting them and acquainting them with what they are expected to do. Job information is also very helpful to those who administer training and development programs. It helps them determine the content and subject matter needed in training courses. Selection of trainees is also facilitated by studying job information.

Performance Appraisal. Job analysis data can be adapted to help establish clear-cut standards of performance for every job. Standards of performance are mostly qualitative (they may also contain some quantitative information) statements of what management expects of the employees assigned to each job. In evaluating the performance of each employee (for pay adjustments, employee development, and so on) the supervisor can compare the actual contribution of each man with the written standard. Performance appraisals can never become fully objective and impartial; but the usage of written standards helps make them more objective.

Safety and Health. The process of conducting a detailed job analysis provides an excellent opportunity to uncover and identify hazardous conditions and unhealthy environmental factors (such as heat, noise, fumes, and dust), so that corrective measures can be taken to minimize and avoid the possibility of human injury.

Variation in Practice

It should be pointed out that all organizations do not have such far-reaching personnel management programs that they actually develop and utilize job information for all of the foregoing purposes. If job analysis is performed solely for organization planning purposes, the amount of data collected and the format for writing the descriptions and specifications will be different than if the end use of the data is job evaluation. In short, the use for which the job study is made determines the depth, scope, and emphasis given. Most companies are unwilling to spend the money that would be necessary to conduct such an exhaustive and thorough job analysis program that the resultant information could be applied to all seven of the aforementioned applications. In industry one of the most common uses for job descriptions and specifications is as a part of a job evaluation program. Indeed the accuracy of such a wage

---

[3] Those interested in delving into the subject of human engineering may consult Ernest J. McCormick, *Human Factors Engineering* (2nd Ed., New York: McGraw-Hill Book Company, Inc., 1964).

rationalization program depends mainly upon the possession of accurate and complete job facts.

Definitions of Terms

It is important that both the student and the practitioner acquire a clear understanding of the terminology involved in job analysis. Because this work is analytical in nature it is perhaps especially important that clear-cut distinctions be made among the various job and occupational designations.

A *task* is the same as a duty. It is a component of a job. Every job consists of many tasks or duties.

A *position* is a collection of tasks and responsibilities regularly assigned to one person. A *job* is a group of positions which involve essentially the same duties, skills, knowledge, and responsibilities. Thus we can see that a position consists of the particular, and often unique, set of duties assigned to an individual. There may be ten people, all of whom are classified under the same job title, and yet each may perform slightly different work. Therefore each would have a distinct position. An illustration of this would be the job of a secretary. All the secretaries in a business organization may have that as their job title. Yet the secretary to the treasurer may be a distinctly different position than the secretary to the plant manager, because the detailed requirements of the work may be different. In actual practice some people use the terms *job* and *position* interchangeably, and there probably is no great harm in doing so.

The term *position* also has acquired a status or prestige connotation. When a person uses the word *position,* it is supposed to signify a higher rank in the organization than the word *job*. Business firms generally designate their job evaluation plans for executive and professional jobs as position evaluation.

An *occupation* is a composite of many very closely related jobs found in many establishments. Basically when we are within the four walls of an organization, we use the term *job*. But when we refer to that job as it may be set up in a number of companies, the variation is great enough that a more generalized description must be used to designate the work. We would call this an occupation description. *The Dictionary of Occupational Titles*[4] is the standard reference work in the occupational information field. It consists primarily of two volumes. Volume I contains the definitions of over 22,000 separate occupations, together with code numbers for each. Volume II gives the classification structure of the dictionary. The occupations are classified into seven major groups. Professional and managerial occupations constitute one group, clerical and sales occupations are another, and so forth.

The terms *unskilled, semiskilled,* and *skilled* are commonly used to

[4] Published by the Department of Labor, available from the Superintendent of Documents, U.S. Government Printing Office, Washington, D.C.

distinguish between skill levels among blue-collar or hourly paid workers. The lines of demarcation are not always sharp and distinct. Indeed the management of one plant may consider that certain of its jobs are skilled, whereas in another plant the same work may be relegated to the semiskilled category. Typically the crafts or trades are considered to be skilled occupations. Although even here technological advances over the years may reduce the level of training and experience required. A skilled job or occupation is one that requires comprehensive knowledge of work processes, independent judgment, and often considerable manual dexterity. Generally an apprenticeship or the equivalent is required to enter a skilled trade. Periods of apprenticeship in the United States vary in length from two to six years, with four years being the most common training period.

Semiskilled work constitutes the great bulk of jobs in our manufacturing industries. These jobs are often characterized by considerable manipulative ability confined to a definite work routine, alertness to avoid damage to products or equipment, and the exercise of judgment in the work situation. This judgment does not generally depend upon a wide or deep knowledge of the field of work, however. The learning period for semiskilled jobs commonly varies from several weeks to several months. A milling machine operator is an example of a semiskilled job. Whereas a machinist, who is a skilled worker, must be able to plan his work, set up, adjust, and operate not only a milling machine but all other machine tools as well, a person who can set up and operate only a single machine tool is considered to be semiskilled.

An unskilled job is one that requires an extremely short training period—generally from a few hours to one or two weeks. Common laboring work which involves heavy physical effort to dig holes and ditches, carry materials and supplies, load and unload trucks, and so on, is an example of unskilled work. The percentage of unskilled labor in the labor force of the country has steadily declined over the years because machinery has been replacing human muscle power.

A technician is one who possesses some formal education and training beyond the high school level, generally in a field of science and technology. A technician is a semiskilled professional or a subprofessional. Examples of technician type of occupations are electronic technician, layout draftsman, laboratory technician, and dental technician.

Swinging over to the white-collar occupations we encounter the terms *executive, administrative,* and *professional.* In business and industry the term *executive* is often used rather loosely to designate anyone who holds a high-ranking management position, whether it be line or staff. Some would include only very high-ranking positions, such as president, vice-president, and general manager, and others include middle management personnel within the scope of this term. Thus in common parlance the word *executive* has status connotations in addition to designating a kind of work. A more precise definition of an executive is that developed by the United States Department of Labor, Wage and Hour Division, for establishing overtime exemptions in connection with the Fair Labor Standards Act. In essence the Department states that an *executive* is one whose primary duty consists of the management of an enterprise or a recognized department thereof. To be classified as an executive, a person must direct the work of two or more employees, have the authority to hire or fire or to effectively recommend hiring or firing of employees, and must customarily and regularly exercise discretionary powers. In addition he must not devote more than 20 per cent of his time to activities of a nonsupervisory nature, and he must be paid a designated minimum salary per week to be exempt from the overtime requirements of the law. In effect these regulations include within the meaning of the term *executive* all those who exercise bona fide supervision from a foreman all the way up to a corporation president.[5]

An *administrative* employee is one whose primary duty consists of office or nonmanual work directly related to management policies or general business operations. He exercises discretion and independent judgment. He directly assists a proprietor or a bona fide executive, or he performs under only general supervision work along specialized or technical lines requiring special training, or he executes under only general supervision special assignments. He must be paid a designated minimum weekly salary and not devote more than 20 per cent of his time to work other than that described above.[6] The term *executive* and *administrative* both connote authority and status within the organization. However, an executive supervises other employees, whereas an administrative employee does not. He establishes, affects, or carries out policies but does not "boss" other people.

A *professional* employee is one whose work requires knowledge of an advanced type in a field of science or learning that is acquired by a prolonged course of specialized instruction and study. The work requires consistent exercise of discretion and judgment, and it is predominantly intellectual and varied in character. The output of professionals cannot be standardized in relation to a given time period. Like executives and administrative employees, they must be paid a designated minimum weekly salary and cannot spend more than 20 percent of their time on nonexempt work.[7] Examples of professional employees are engineers, chemists, physicists, lawyers, and physicians.

ANALYZING JOBS—OBTAINING JOB INFORMATION

Methods of Analyzing Jobs

There exist seven ways by which job information can be gathered: (1)

---

[5] Wage and Hour Division Regulations, Part 541, Section 541.1.
[6] *Ibid.*, Section 541.2.
[7] *Ibid.*, Section 541.3.

observation, (2) questionnaire, (3) interview, (4) check list, (5) daily diary, (6) conference of experts, and (7) a combination of two or more of these.

It is generally not possible to use the observation method alone to gather enough information to prepare a job description and a specification It is true that industrial engineers rely principally upon observation to conduct motion and time studies. However, they deal primarily with repetitive, short-cycle, unskilled, and semiskilled jobs. They do not have to develop a job specification that calls for value judgments on worker qualifications (best obtained by interviewing the supervisor). Actual observation is very desirable to acquaint the job analyst with the materials and equipment used, the working conditions and hazards, and to obtain a sharp visual impression of just what is involved in the work.

The questionnaire method is popular with management engineering consultants who are hired to install a job evaluation plan and who feel they must accomplish a lot in a minimum of time. Usually the procedure involves the preparation of a detailed questionnaire, which is then distributed to all employees, who fill it out on company time and who return it to their supervisors for verification. The supervisor is supposed to discuss any errors in the employee's response with him, make corrections, and then transmit it to the group responsible for conducting the job analysis program (generally the personnel department). Figure 7-3 shows an example of a questionnaire for collecting job analysis data directly from the employees themselves.

The questionnaire method requires somewhat less staff time than does the interview method. In other words the cost of collecting the job data is lower with this technique. All of the employees participate and answer questions about their jobs. With the interview method commonly only one or perhaps two individuals on a job are interviewed. However, the questionnaire approach has serious disadvantages. The accuracy of the information leaves much to be desired. Job analysis work requires specialized knowledge and training. The average employee, although he knows best just what his duties are, is not trained to identify the essential aspects of his work and often cannot express the information in a meaningful and clear fashion. Any questionnaire is open to varying interpretations. To depend exclusively upon questionnaires as the source of job information is bound to introduce some errors into the program.

Many organizations employ job analysts (other titles may be used) who interview the employee and/or his supervisor to obtain all of the pertinent information. When the interview of both the supervisor and the employee is combined with a short observation at the job by a trained analyst, this procedure constitutes a very thorough and sound approach. It is the one most widely used. The analyst essentially asks the same kinds of questions that appear in Figure 7-3, Employee Job Analysis Questionnaire. However, the analyst knows how to differentiate between essential and nonessential information. He has a consistency of viewpoint and judgment. He can ask probing questions to uncover facts that might be

INDIVIDUAL JOB ANALYSIS QUESTIONNAIRE

Name_____ Department _____

Payroll Title_____ Name, Immediate Supervisor_____

Instructions: Please read the entire form before making any entries. Answer each question as accurately and carefully as possible. When completed return this form to your supervisor. If you have any questions ask your supervisor.

Your Duties

What duties and tasks do you personally perform daily?

What duties do you perform only at stated intervals such as semi weekly, weekly or monthly? Indicate which period applies to each duty.

What duties do you perform only at irregular intervals?

Supervision of Others

How many employees are directly under your supervision? (List job titles and number of people assigned to each job.)

Do you have full discretionary authority to assign work; correct and discipline; recommend pay increases, transfers, promotions and discharge; and to answer grievances?

Do you only assign work, instruct, and coordinate the activities of your subordinates?

Materials, Tools, and Equipment

What are the principal materials and products that you handle?

List the names of the machines and equipment used in your work.

List the names of the principal hand tools and instruments used in your work.

What is the Source of Your Instructions? (e. g. oral, written, blue prints, specifications, etc.)

What Contacts Are You Required to Make with Persons Other Than Your Immediate Supervisor and Departmental Associates?

a) Give the job titles and the department or organization of those with whom you deal.

b) Describe the nature of these contacts.

Decisions

What decisions do you have to make without consulting your supervisor?

Responsibility

a) Describe the nature of your responsibility for money, machinery, equipment, and reports.

b) What monetary loss can occur through an honest error?

Figure 7-3. Employee Job Analysis Questionnaire.

Records and Reports

    a) What records and reports do you personally prepare?

    b) What is the source of the data?

Checking of Your Work

    a) How is your work inspected, checked or verified?

    b) Who does this?

Physical Requirements

    a) What percentage of the time do you spend in the following working positions?

        Standing _____ %,   Sitting _____ %,   Walking about _____ %?

    b) What weight in pounds must you personally lift and carry?____pounds

    c) What percentage of the working day do you actually spend lifting and carrying this weight?_____ %

    d) Are any special physical skills, eye-hand coordination, and manual dexterity skills required on your job?

Working Conditions

Describe any conditions present in the location and nature of your work, such as noise, heat, dust, fumes, etc., which you consider unfavorable or disagreeable.

Hazards

Describe the dangers or accident hazards present in your job.

THIS PORTION IS TO BE FILLED OUT BY YOUR SUPERVISOR.

Education Requirements

What is the lowest grade of grammar school, high school, or college required of a person starting in this job?

Previous Experience

    a) What kind of previous work experience is necessary for minimum satisfactory performance for a new employee on this job?

    b) Give the length of experience required.

Training

Assuming that a new employee on this job has the necessary education and experience to qualify for the work, what training is necessary after the employee is on the job to achieve an acceptable performance level? (Specify training needed and period of time to acquire it.)

Date	Signature of Supervisor

Figure 7-3. (Cont'd.)

overlooked if employees simply filled out a questionnaire. Because the analyst must compose and write the job description, he is in the best position to do so if he has actually seen the job being performed and if he has talked to the employee and his immediate superior. The principal disadvantage of the interview-observation method is that it is time consuming and costly. To analyze an unskilled job and then write a job description and specification would require perhaps one to two hours. But to do the same thing for skilled jobs, professional jobs, and other highly complicated work often consumes four to eight hours.

An important by-product of a job analysis program is that it often creates greater understanding and common agreement between the job holder and his boss on the precise requirements of his job. So often, in actual practice, the analyst runs into cases where the worker has stated that he performs a certain task, whereas the supervisor states that that task is really not a part of his job and belongs to someone else. The opposite of this situation is common also.

The check list method can be used in large organizations that have a large number of people assigned to the same or similar jobs. The staff group that prepares a check list for each of the various jobs in the enterprise or agency must first collect enough information to prepare a meaningful check list. Such information can be obtained by asking supervisors, methods engineers, and others familiar with the work to record the tasks comprising each job. When a check list has been prepared for a job, say a supply clerk in an Army depot, then it is sent to all supply clerks in all depots. The job holders are asked to check all listed tasks that they perform and to indicate by check mark the amount of time spent on each task as well as the training and experience required to be proficient on each task. They may also be asked to write in additional required tasks not contained on the prepared list. A typical job may contain 200 or 300 task statements. This technique is amenable to tabulation and recording on electronic data processing equipment. The check list method is rather costly and somewhat impractical for small organizations, however, because of the set-up costs involved in developing checklists for every job.[8]

The daily diary method requires the job holders to record in detail their activities throughout each day. If done faithfully this technique is accurate and eliminates the error of memory recall of the questionnaire and check list devices. However, it adds considerably to the workload of each production employee and for this reason is seldom used in practice.

The conference of experts technique of collecting job information is quite useful for obtaining various viewpoints and an overall perspective of the jobs. However supervisors, staff specialists, and technicians may

---

[8] A description of the check list method as applied by the United States Air Force is contained in Joseph E. Morsh, "Job Analysis in the United States Air Force," *Personnel Psychology,* Vol. 37 (1962), pp. 7-17.

be enough removed from the work itself that they lack intimate familiarity with its details and complexities. Thus accuracy suffers.

Content of Information Collected

As indicated previously, the nature of the information collected when analyzing jobs is determined by the use that will be made of the data. If a company simply wishes to prepare brief descriptions so that it can conduct a labor market wage survey, then the analyst will obtain only that information necessary to describe the significant duties and requirements of jobs with special emphasis upon those features that differentiate it from related jobs. Because the most common practice in business and industry is to prepare job descriptions and specifications for purposes of hiring, job evaluation, and for acquainting new people with the exact nature of their jobs and with what management expects of them, the content of information collected will be explained from this standpoint.

The items given next are the principal ones covered in a job analysis program. After each item a few brief comments are given to indicate why this data is important and what is included in the item.

Job Title and Location: These properly designate and identify the job. Some standardization and consistency of job titling is considered advantageous.

Job Summary: This is included in most job descriptions to give the reader a quick capsule explanation of content of job. Usually one or two sentences in length.

Job Duties: Usually a comprehensive listing of the duties is included together with some indication of the frequency of occurrence or percentage of time devoted to each major duty. Always include what the job holder does as well as some indication of how he performs the tasks.

Relation to Other Jobs: This item helps to locate the job in the organization by indicating the job or jobs immediately below the one being analyzed and the one immediately above it in the hierarchy.

Supervision Given: For those jobs possessing a supervisory responsibility, an explanation of the number of persons directly supervised and their job titles is given.

Mental Complexity: This and similar terms, such as *initiative, ingenuity, judgment, resourcefulness,* and *analytical requirements,* are used to cover the degree of mental difficulty and skill required by the job.

Mental Attention: This factor relates to the degree of mental concentration and alertness required.

Physical Demand: Commonly included under this heading is an enumeration of the types of physical activity and effort required. It may involve such actions as walking, lifting, bending, climbing, and sitting.

Physical Skills: Examples are manual dexterity, eye-hand-foot coordination, motor coordination, and color discrimination.

Responsibilities: There are many kinds of responsibility that may be assigned to a job holder. Examples of these are responsibility for the supervision of others, responsibility for product, process, and equipment, responsibility for safety of others, responsibility for confidence and trust, and responsibility for preventing monetary loss to the company. For certain jobs, such as high-level management ones, the responsibility factors weigh heavily in establishing the pay and status of the work.

Personal Characteristics: For certain jobs such personality attributes as personal appearance, emotional stability, maturity, initiative and drive, and skill in dealing with others are important.

Working Conditions: This item pertains to the environment in which the job holder must work.

Hazards: The conditions of work may be such that the job holder faces certain hazards to life and limb. The nature of the hazards and their probability of occurrence must be considered.

United States Employment Service Job Specifications

As an aid to employers who wish to specify accurately and concisely the worker traits that job candidates should possess in order to qualify adequately for certain jobs, the United States Employment Service has prepared a manual that gives worker trait requirements for 4,000 jobs as defined in the *Dictionary of Occupational Titles.*[9] Basically this publication serves as an aid to employers who wish to recruit, select, and place people in jobs, whether from the outside labor market or by promotion from within the organization. It helps match men and jobs.

As a result of their research program to develop these estimates, the United States Employment Service established six rating scales. Certain of these major scales are broken down into subscales or components. Thus the human requirements for each of the 4,000 jobs are expressed in terms of scores or levels for each scale. In effect a standard profile has been developed for each job. In selecting employees to fill a job an attempt can be made to find those who come closest to fitting the profile.

The major scales or factors used are as follows:

1. Training time
2. Aptitudes
3. Temperaments
4. Interests
5. Physical capacities
6. Working conditions

[9] Department of Labor, *Estimates of Worker Trait Requirements for 4,000 Jobs as Defined in the Dictionary of Occupational Titles,* U.S. Government Printing Office, Washington, D.C.

In preparing job specifications with the aid of the estimates, an analyst may compare the actual job duties and the worker requirements for a job in his company with the description contained in the *Dictionary of Occupational Titles (D.O.T.)* and with the rating given in the *Estimates*. Any variation of the actual job from the standard one can be taken into account by altering the ratings on the rating scales listed above. Thus if a particular job in one's plant appears to call for greater color discrimination or eye-hand-foot coordination than the standard job listed in the *D.O.T.*, an appropriate adjustment can be made. The *Estimates* provide a convenient, standard, shorthand technique for expressing worker quaifications. Figure 7-4 gives trait requirements for five jobs.

The *Estimates* manual contains definitions of each factor, explanations for rating jobs, and illustrative bench mark jobs for the various levels of each factor. It should be noted that for the temperaments and interests factors in Figure 7-4 only the two factors judged to be most significant in each instance are recorded. The relative amounts of every temperament and interest factor have not been determined.

JOB DESCRIPTIONS AND SPECIFICATIONS

Job descriptions and job specifications are the forms upon which the data obtained through the job analysis process are recorded. A job description contains the objective facts that explain *what* the job is, *what* the specific duties and responsibilities are, and *what* general conditions and situational factors are involved. *Where* the job is performed is usually revealed on the description. Some brief indication of *how* the duties are performed may be shown particularly for manipulative and repetitive jobs.

The information recorded on a job specification describes the amounts of various qualification factors that job holders must possess in order to perform their work adequately. Although the data recorded on the description can be rather objectively determined, that shown on the specification is rather subjective. It depends upon the value judgments of a number of people, such as the job analyst, job holder, and members of supervision.

Figure 7-2 shows the most common items of information recorded on a job description and a job specification. There is some variation, however, from one organization to another in terms of what is actually recorded. Figure 7-5 is a job description and specification for a secretary. The information shown in the specification is written in the form of substantiations for factor ratings used for a point plan of job evaluation. Job evaluation is a procedure for establishing relative pay differentials within an organization and is explained in Chapter 23 "Wage and Salary Administration." If the specification were written for employee selection and placement purposes, the explanations for each factor would be similar in general but different in detail. The working conditions and hazards

Figure 7-4. A Portion of One Page from *Estimates of Worker Requirements for 4,000 Jobs* as Defined in the *Dictionary of Occupational Titles*, U.S. Department of Labor, G.P.O., Washington, D.C.

Line No.	D.O.T. Job Title	Vol. II Code	Part IV Code	Train. Time GED	Train. Time SVP	Aptitudes GVN	Aptitudes SPQ	Aptitudes KFM	Aptitudes EC	Temperaments (4)(5)	Interests	Phys. Cap. Strength	Phys. Cap. Talking-Hearing (5) / Seeing (6)	Working Cond. Inside-Outside (1)	Industry Code	OAP No.	OOH page	Line No.
1	Manager, Operations --	0-98.83	0-X8.49	7	8	112	344	444	55	4 5	5 7	S	5 5	I	023		107	1
2	Manager, Personnel I--	0-39.83	0-X8.10	7	8	113	444	444	55	4 5	4 5 8	S	5 5	I	138			2
3	Manager, Production -	0-97.51	0-X8.41	7	8	112	344	444	55	4 5	5	S	5 5	I	138			3
4	Manager, Retail Food-	0-72.21	0-X8.10	5	7	333	433	444	54	4 5	5 6	L	5 5	I	747			4
5	Manager, Sales - - -	0-97.61	0-X8.10	6	8	212	443	444	55	4 5	6	S	5 5	I	138			5

TRAINING TIME

GED (See Appendix A)

SVP
9 - Over 10 years
8 - 4-10 years
7 - 2-4 years
6 - 1-2 years
5 - 6 months - 1 year
4 - 3-6 months
3 - 30 days - 3 months
2 - Short demonstration - 30 days
1 - Short demonstration only

Levels
1 - Upper 10%
2 - Upper 1/3 less 1
3 - Middle 1/3
4 - Lower 1/3 less 5
5 - Lowest 10%

APTITUDES

GVN — INTELLIGENCE, VERBAL, NUMERICAL
SPQ — SPATIAL, FORM, CLERICAL
KFM — MOTOR COORDINATION, FINGER DEXTERITY, MANUAL DEXTERITY
EC — EYE-HAND-FOOT COORDINATION, COLOR DISCRIMINATION

1 - Upper 10%
2 - Upper 1/3 less 1
3 - Middle 1/3
4 - Lower 1/3 less 5
5 - Lowest 10%

TEMPERAMENTS

1 - VARIETY AND CHANGE
2 - REPETITIVE SHORT CYCLE
3 - UNDER SPECIFIC INSTRUCTIONS
4 - DIRECTION, CONTROL, PLANNING
5 - DEALING WITH PEOPLE
6 - ISOLATION
7 - INFLUENCING PEOPLE
8 - PERFORMING UNDER STRESS
9 - SENSORY OR JUDGMENTAL CRITERIA
0 - MEASURABLE OR VERIFIABLE CRITERIA
X - FEELINGS, IDEAS, FACTS
Y - SET LIMITS, TOLERANCES OR STANDARDS

INTERESTS

1 - THINGS AND OBJECTS
2 - BUSINESS CONTACT
3 - ROUTINE CONCRETE
4 - SOCIAL WELFARE
5 - PRESTIGE
6 - PEOPLE, IDEAS
7 - SCIENTIFIC, TECHNICAL
8 - ABSTRACT, CREATIVE
9 - NONSOCIAL
0 - TANGIBLE, PRODUCTIVE SATISFACTION

PHYSICAL CAPACITIES

STRENGTH
1 - CLIMBING-BALANCING
2 - STOOPING-KNEELING
3 - REACHING-HANDLING
5 - TALKING-HEARING
6 - SEEING

S - Sedentary
L - Light
M - Medium
H - Heavy
V - Very Heavy

WORKING CONDITIONS

1 - INSIDE-OUTSIDE
2 - COLD
3 - HEAT
4 - WET-HUMID
5 - NOISE-VIBRATION
6 - HAZARDS
7 - FUMES, ODORS, ETC.

I - Inside
O - Outside
B - Both

200

are included under the specification; however, they might also have been contained as part of the description.

Detailed Vs. General Job Descriptions

Just how much detail to include in a description is determined by management's intent and the end use of the description. If it were to be used to help teach workers how to do their jobs, a considerable amount of explanation of the *how* and *why* of the job would, of necessity, have to be included. When prepared for job evaluation purposes the practice in many firms is to write rather general descriptions with little or no details explaining how the work is done. Although this approach saves time and money it does make it very difficult to gauge the required amount of skill and knowledge just by reading the description. Some companies deliberately write general (and often vague descriptions) so that management can have a free hand in assigning additional tasks without incurring objections from workers and the union. Actually the issue of job flexibility (or its counterpart, narrow craft jurisdictions) is a policy and a collective bargaining problem. The author feels that the usefulness of job descriptions should not be impaired by deliberately making them so vague as to be meaningless.

Another problem arises when an organization has several job levels represented within the same occupation as Mechanic A, B, and C or Junior Engineer and Senior Engineer. In theory the duties and responsibilities of a senior engineer should be of a higher level and more complex than those of a junior engineer. The actual difference between these jobs should be readily discernible upon reading the job descriptions and specifications. But in actual practice management often has not set up definite distinctions between these different levels within an occupation. A young man will be hired as a junior engineer, and at some point in his career, his boss will decide that his achievements have been such that he can be reclassified into a senior engineer title with accompanying higher pay. But his duties may still be the same. Thus what management really wants here is a wide range in pay to reward people according to differences in merit. But different job titles and descriptions should be set up only if there is truly a difference in duties and responsibilities. Or to state the matter another way, if it is not possible to describe clearly the difference between two jobs in words, then there is considerable justification for calling them one and the same job.

"As Is or as Ought to Be Performed"

Very frequently one finds that jobs are not being performed as management wants. This may be caused by any of several factors. It might be that the process, equipment, or methods are not quite what they should be, and it may take some time to get them in order. It may be that cer-

---

JOB DESCRIPTION
Office Type Jobs

Job Title ___Secretary_____ Job Number ____A66____

Date Effective ___August 21, 1962_____ Grade ___5_____

Job Function: Perform secretarial duties involving taking dictation, typing, preparing routine correspondence and reports, maintaining records, distributing incoming mail, scheduling appointments, and related clerical duties.
Handle information of a confidential nature.

Job Duties: Take dictation in shorthand, or from dictation machine, transcribe and type letters, memoranda, and reports.

Take shorthand notes in meetings, transcribe and type into final form.

Compose and type routine letters and memoranda.

Open, read, sort, distribute, and follow-up incoming mail.

Set up and maintain files of such items as letters, reports, catalogs, and manuals.

Obtain data and information by telephone or personal contact for supervisor.

Answer telephone and take messages. When supervisor is busy, determine importance of call and whether to relay immediately to supervisor or have call postponed.

Compile routine departmental reports.

Compile and maintain records dealing with such subjects as safety, output, employee time, and expenses.

Receive, disburse, and keep records of petty cash funds.

Receive visitors; schedule appointments.

Requisition and maintain inventory of office supplies.

Arrange hotel and travel reservations.

May be required to take technical dictation involving engineering and chemical terminology.

Frequently deal with information of a confidential nature.

Equipment, Instruments or Machines: Typewriter, dictation machine.

---

* This job description contains the facts necessary to evaluate and distinguish it adequately from other jobs. It is not intended to be a detailed description of every duty and responsibility.

Figure 7-5. Job Description: Secretary.

	JOB SPECIFICATION
	Job Rating and Substantiation

Points	Factor and Substantiation	
30	Mental Development:	Compile routine correspondence and departmental reports.

	Previous Experience:		Months
		Stenographer	24
50	Special Course:	12 months Stenographic	12
	Training Period:		3
			39

	Dexterity:	Precise movement of hands and fingers required to operate typewriter rapidly by touch system.
20	Adaptability:	Resourcefulness required to adapt to frequent changes in tasks such as typing, filing, composing letters, and receiving visitors.

	Analysis and Judgment:	Break down simple conditions in sorting and distributing mail, tracing down information for supervisor, and classifying information for filing. Procedures are established. Decide course of action from complex facts to determine whether to interrupt supervisor when in meeting, to compose routine letters, to establish a filing system, and to deal with executives, supervisors, and visitors.
35		

	Mental and Visual Demand:	Confining vision over 50% of time to take dictation, read incoming mail, keep records, type letters. Over 50% mental application to receive visitors, take dictation, obtain data for supervisor, and take messages.
20		

5	Physical Demand:	Under 1 lb. 11-50% of time to operate typewriter. Normal work position is seated.

15	Responsibility for Loss to Company:	Low probability of $100-149 loss through error in compiling routine letters and reports.

5	Responsibility for Work:	General directions provided. Details of keeping records, maintaining inventory of office supplies, and scheduling work are left to employee. No responsibility for work of others.

20	Contacts with Others:	Exchange of information with customers, visitors vendors, salesmen, and other persons from outside the company.

	Job Conditions:	
0	Working Conditions:	Normal office conditions
	Hazards:	No probable injury

200	Total	Score Range ___185-214___	Grade__5__
	Analysis by _____		
	Approved by _____		
		Dept. Head	Ind. Relations Director

Figure 7-5. (Cont'd)

tain individuals possess talents not really called for by the job assignment. Nevertheless they have shaped their jobs to fit their abilities. Or it may be that an employee must, temporarily, perform a highly skilled task that his boss states rightly belongs to another job. The question then arises, should the job be described as it is being performed, or should it be described the way it should be performed? The answer is that it depends upon the use for which the description will be applied.

If the description and specification are used for determining the proper rate of pay according to a system of job evaluation, then, most assuredly, the job must be written up precisely as it is being performed at present. If any changes occur in job content in the future, then the job can be reanalyzed. This might result in an adjustment in the rate of pay if a significant change occurs in the skill, effort, responsibility, or job conditions. On the other hand if the description is used for selection and placement of personnel, for training, and for organization planning, it seems logical that it should be written to include precisely those duties and responsibilities that it is supposed to contain. The desired content is a goal to shoot for.

Managerial and Professional Descriptions

Figure 7-6 is a position guide for *supervisor of statistical procedures* at General Mills, Inc. Descriptions of professional and managerial jobs are similar to those for production and nonsupervisory jobs; however, they generally do not explain the mechanics of how the tasks are carried out. Because high-level work tends to be complex and variable from day to day and week to week, the duties and responsibilities are usually written in more general terms. The descriptions tend to highlight relationships with others (both within and outside the organization) and show how the position fits into the organization structure. The specifications de-emphasize such factors as physical skill, effort, working conditions, and hazards. Instead, they emphasize education, experience, knowledge, decisions, authority, responsibilities, outside contacts, standards of performance, and creative work.

ADMINISTRATION OF THE JOB ANALYSIS PROGRAM

Organizationally the responsibility for analyzing jobs and preparing descriptions and specifications is usually assigned to the industrial relations (or personnel) department. If the organization is very large, undoubtedly, there will be a section within this department that does this work. This may be called the wage and salary section, employee compensation section, or the job analysis group. The reason for placing responsibility for job analysis within the personnel department is that it is inti-

EXEMPT POSITION GUIDE   GENERAL MILLS, INC.

POSITION TITLE			POSITION NUMBER	
Supervisor - Statistical Procedures			APPROVAL	
DIVISION OR STAFF DEPT. Quality Control	LOCATION Minneapolis	CODE	EFFECTIVE DATE January 1962	
DEPARTMENT OR ACTIVITY	SECTION	DISTRIBUTION	REVISES	

I.   FUNCTION

     To develop and provide statistical techniques for use in the evaluation and control of quality factors involving ingredients and products.

II.   SCOPE

     Act as statistical consultant to all Quality Control supervisors and technicians in the application and implementation of statistical principles and techniques as used in the evaluation and control of quality factors.

III. RESPONSIBILITIES

    A. Operating

    He will:

    1. Provide the necessary training for all Quality Control supervisors and technicians in the use of statistical principles and techniques for evaluation and control of quality factors.

    2. Develop measures of quality costs to aid in determining the effectiveness of each quality control group.

    3. Analyze problems and recommend sampling plans or other quality control devices for use in the evaluation of ingredient and product quality.

    4. Aid in the planning of special tests and in the analysis of resulting data.

    5. Aid in the design of more efficient laboratory-scale and plant-scale experiments for use in evaluating quality factors.

    6. Conduct special assignments as directed.

IV. RELATIONSHIPS

    A. Assistant Director of quality Control

     He reports to the Assistant.

    B. Others in the Company

     His contact with Division Quality Control Directors is for the purpose of providing consultation on matters within his province.

    C. Outside the Company

     He maintains professional affiliations to keep abreast of developments in his field.

Figure 7-6. Position Description for Supervisor—Statistical Procedures. *Reproduced through the courtesy of General Mills, Inc., Minneapolis, Minnesota.*

mately concerned with utilizing job information for so many of its other programs—that is, manpower planning, recruitment, selection, placement, training, job evaluation, area wage surveys, and safety.

Sometimes the industrial engineering department prepares the job descriptions and specifications, especially for production and maintenance type of jobs. Many feel this is logical because it is a natural outgrowth of the industrial engineer's activities in methods study and work measurement. Many practitioners feel that this work requires engineering talent, because it is analytical, precise, and detailed in nature.

Procedurally it is advisable for those charged with the job analysis function to obtain full cooperation and participation from operating supervision. Many companies follow the practice of submitting the completed description and specification to the supervisor of the job involved for his approval. This is to insure that the job as described is accurately represented and that he agrees with the way it has been written up. Some firms also follow the practice of showing the job write-up to the job holder himself for his approval. This is particularly true for professional, executive, and administrative positions. The policy of obtaining approval from operating management reduces the possibility of later complaints and obstruction of the program.

If there is anything certain in our modern complex industrial system, it is the constancy of change. This certainly applies well to jobs and positions. There are many circumstances that can cause changes in the nature, content, and worker requirements of jobs. New machinery and equipment may be introduced. Operating procedures may change. The company may be reorganized. If the firm grows and employment expands, jobs may become more specialized. Changing technology may add new skill requirements to some jobs and take them away from others. Therefore, a job analysis program must be kept up to date. Descriptions cannot be filed away and then forgotten. There are two ways of insuring that the information on file is an accurate representation of current conditions in the organization. One method places major reliance upon the operating supervisors. They must be trained to report any significant changes in the make-up of the jobs in their units. This responsibility is likely to rank quite low in their system of priorities, because their superiors will generally emphasize production, costs, quality, and efficiency. The second approach is more positive, more thorough, and also more costly. It requires the job analysis group to conduct periodic audits (usually annually) of the jobs in every department in order to pick up and evaluate any noteworthy changes in the composition and nature of the jobs.

Questions for Review and Discussion

1. Some organizations have never established a job analysis program Consequently they have neither job descriptions nor specifications.

What difficulties and problems do you feel organizations such as these are likely to encounter?

2. Distinguish between a job, a position, and an occupation.

3. How does job analysis for industrial engineering purposes differ from job analysis for such personnel programs as organization planning, employee selection, and employee compensation?

4. Explain the meaning of the following occupational designations:
   a. Semiskilled labor
   b. Skilled labor
   c. Executive position
   d. Administrative position
   e. Professional position

5. What are the principal methods that might be utilized to analyze jobs and positions? What method or combination of methods is the soundest? Explain.

6. What items of information are collected when analyzing a job?

7. Distinguish between a job description and a job specification. What items of information commonly appear on each?

8. Assume that top management is planning to inaugurate a brand new job analysis program in its organization (500 employees). Explain how you would recommend the program be launched. Give consideration to announcing the program, gaining support in the organization, selection of personnel to do the work, and so on.

9. Assume that in the process of analyzing a job the analyst learns that the employee and his supervisor disagree over the content and requirements expected of the employee. What course of action should the analyst follow?

10. Some companies are reluctant to prepare descriptions of the jobs in their organizations, because they feel this will make the job duties and requirements too rigid. They feel this will give workers and their union representatives grounds for insisting that no employee should perform any work that is not contained in his job description. Do you feel that this is a valid argument against the adoption of a job description program? Explain.

11. What questions and doubts are likely to arise in the minds of the following personnel if the personnel department were immediately to start analyzing jobs without "paving the way" first?
    a. Supervisors
    b. Workers
    c. Local union leaders

PROBLEMS

1. Using the job descriptions in Figures 7-5 and 7-6 as examples, prepare a job description and a specification for some job that you have held in the past or now hold.

2. Make a thorough analysis of a job as it is currently being performed by interviewing an employee of your college or university (or in some other organization where you can obtain good cooperation). Concentrate upon interviewing the employee to obtain the information you desire. You may wish to supplement this with an interview with the person who supervises this employee plus a brief observation of the job and its work environment. Use the job analysis questionnaire in Figure 7-3 as your guide to the questions to ask. (This questionnaire can serve not only as a form for every employee himself to fill out but also as a schedule or guide to assist the job analyst in covering all the necessary points when interviewing an employee.)

   After you have collected the necessary data, prepare a job description and a specification. Show these to the employee and/or his supervisor to determine whether they feel your write-up accurately describes the job and the human qualifications.

Suggestions for Further Reading

Bennet, C. L., *Defining the Manager's Job,* New York: American Management Association, 1958.

Berenson, C. and H. O. Ruhnke, *Job Descriptions: How to Write and Use Them,* Swarthmore, Penna: The Personnel Journal, 1967.

Brennan, Charles W., *Wage Administration: Plans, Practices, and Principles,* (Rev. Ed.) Homewood, Illinois: Richard D. Irwin, 1963, Ch. 7.

Howard, Daniel D., "Let's Put the Job on the Couch!", *Commerce,* July 1967.

Langsner, Adolph and Herbert G. Zollitsch, *Wage and Salary Administration,* Cincinnati, Ohio: South-Western Publishing Co., 1961, Chs. 11 and 12.

Lanham, Elizabeth, *Administration of Wages and Salaries,* New York: Harper & Row, Publishers, 1963, pp. 125-154.

Patton, John A., C. L. Littlefield, and Stanley A. Self, *Job Evaluation: Text and Cases* (3rd Ed.) Homewood, Illinois: Richard D. Irwin, 1964, Chs. 4-5.

United States Department of Labor, *Training and Reference Manual for Job Analysis,* Washington, D.C.: Government Printing Office, 1944.

Wiley, Llewellyn N., "Does Industry Need Task Qualifications Analysis?", *Personnel Administration,* Vol. 24, No. 2, March 1961, pp. 23-30 *ff.*

II

**EMPLOYMENT
AND DEVELOPMENT
OF PEOPLE**

Recruitment and Selection   8

The human resources of any organization constitute one of its most important assets. Its successes and failures are largely determined by the caliber of its work force (including managers) and the efforts it exerts. Therefore, the policies and methods an organization adopts to meet its manpower needs are of vital significance. This chapter explores the recruitment and selection process—the problem areas, policy issues, and procedures involved. The major subject areas covered in this chapter are planning for manpower needs, recruitment and selection policy issues, sources of labor, the selection process and methods utilized, and auditing the recruitment and selection program.

PLANNING FOR MANPOWER NEEDS

The number and type of employees who must be hired by a company are determined by several factors. Assuming that we have a going concern (that is, it is not just starting up as a new company), then the needs for additional manpower are influenced by (1) employee turnover, (2) nature of present work force, and (3) rate of growth of the organization.

A high rate of turnover, involving voluntary quits, discharges, and retirements, means that the personnel department must constantly seek out new employees. For example, telephone companies typically employ a high proportion of young women as telephone operators and clerks.

Because of early marriage and motherhood these women typically work only a very few years before quitting. Therefore, companies such as these must engage in a continual recruitment and selection campaign even if the total work force does not increase. Layoffs may also affect the employment problem. Although companies generally recall laid-off workers when the volume of production picks up after a business decline, they often find that many of their former employees have taken other jobs and will not return. This is particularly true if the layoff has extended for a period of several months.

The nature of the present work force of a company in relation to its changing needs also affects the requirements for new manpower. If the technology of the firm is changing, if new product lines are being substituted for old, it may be that the present work force must either be retrained, or else new blood must be brought in from the outside to fill certain positions. In addition, vacancies may occur in key positions (executive, technical, and professional) for which there are no qualified persons within the organization. This situation then requires hiring from the outside.

The third major factor affecting the need for new employees is the rate of growth of the organization. This in itself is influenced by management policy, extent of competition in the product market, state of the national economy, and many other considerations. The mere fact that a company's sales and volume of production are increasing does not automatically mean that employment must expand, however. During the 1950's, for example, many manufacturing firms in such industries as automobile manufacture, basic steel, and electrical apparatus increased production while actually reducing the volume of employment. This was caused by mechanization, automation, and other technological advances.

Estimating Quantity and Type of Employees Needed

An organization has two alternatives in handling its requirements for new employees. It can either systematically forecast and plan for the future, or it can wait until specific openings occur or are imminent and then seek replacements or additions. This latter approach is more common. It is perhaps acceptable for small- and modest-sized organizations and for those organizations where there is only one or at most a very few persons assigned to each job and turnover is extremely low. The objective of these organizations should be to maintain an attractive company reputation as a good place to work so that they can recruit good talent when it is actually needed.

On the other hand large organizations, those that are expanding, those that are dynamic in character, and those that have high turnover, must systematically plan for their short- and long-term manpower needs. Because our economy is so strongly characterized by constant change, this means that the manpower estimates of an individual company must be under frequent review and adjustments made as conditions dictate.

For estimating direct labor quantities in an organization that has established time standards for each type of work, the problem is straightforward. Basically the procedure involves forecasting the volume of business expected (in suitable units of measure), translating this into a master production schedule for the whole organization, breaking this into department production schedules, and then applying the established time standards to ascertain the number of man-hours and man-days of each class of labor required. This is compared with the present volume of labor available to find out if acquisitions (or reductions) are necessary. Indirect labor, clerical help, and supervisory needs cannot be established so easily, because time standards for these types of labor are difficult to obtain. This means that carefully prepared estimates based upon past experience must be relied upon in this area.

The number and types of professional and managerial employees needed is not closely related to production volume. Therefore, judgment and past experience serve as major guides here. Top management policy and intent really is an important direct determinant of the volume of employment in these higher level positions. Some companies are research conscious; therefore, they deliberately create a research laboratory with consequent need for scientists. Yet the volume of sales may be exactly equal to that of another firm in the same industry which does no research. The first company, of course, has invested in a research activity with the reasonable expectation that it will pay off in future increased volume of business.

At the same time that estimates are being made of the quantity of people required to perform the work in the organization, this data must be integrated with job analysis information in order to establish definite jobs composed of specific duties and responsibilities.

Job specifications must be developed so that it will be possible to know just what qualifications those selected to fill the jobs must possess. If brand-new jobs are being created for operations, projects, and programs which never previously existed, then the initial outlines of the jobs may have to be somewhat tentative. The content and boundaries may not become stabilized until after the jobs have been staffed and performed for several months. The subject of job and employee requirements has been covered in detail in Chapter 7, "Job Organization and Information."

Labor Market Considerations

Many employers have adopted a policy of filling as many job vacancies as practical from within the organization. This is commonly referred to as a policy of "promotion from within." It means that the better jobs are staffed by upgrading and advancing present employees. This then causes vacancies at the lowest levels of blue-collar (that is, production worker) and white-collar jobs. The employer must then recruit and select unskilled and semiskilled workers. On the other hand, some employers do not rigorously follow a program of promotion from within. Instead they fill a high proportion of their job vacancies directly from the outside at whatever level they occur. But whichever policy is followed, an employer must go to the labor market in order to make net additions to his labor force.

A labor market is a geographical area within which employers recruit workers and workers seek employment. It is the place where the forces of supply and demand interact. It is usually thought to consist of a central city or cities and the surrounding territory in which persons can change their place of employment without changing their place of residence. When management decides to go into the labor market to obtain additional employees, it finds that it operates vastly differently from product or financial markets. A labor market tends to be unstructured for the most part; it is unorganized. The procedures by which a company recruits workers and the methods by which workers go about obtaining jobs are highly variable. The process is not necessarily channeled through a public or a private employment agency. Laws and regulations governing the process are of a very minimal nature. In fact, if one looks at the process from the standpoint of workers seeking jobs, the whole procedure seems rather haphazard and catch-as-catch-can. Some job seekers obtain employment through friends and relatives, others through direct visits to the plant gate, others through their unions, and still others through employment agencies. Pure chance plays a large part in determining whether John Smith gets a job in plant A or in plant B.

A labor market is characterized by a great diversity of wage rates for the same occupations. If one were to examine occupational wage survey statistics compiled by the Bureau of Labor Statistics of the United States Department of Labor for any of a number of major cities in the country, he would find the highest wage paid for an occupation being in the nature of two to two and one half times that of the lowest. This variation in wages for the same kind of work is caused by many factors. Principal ones are differences among the employers in ability to pay, productivity, and management attitude toward wage levels. Certain nonwage factors, such as greater job security, may mean that a firm that pays only modest wages may still attract and hold the labor it requires. Variation in the quality or caliber of labor employed in the same occupation in different firms is also a factor relating to wage differences. However, this is usually a consequence of wage differences rather than a cause. For in the labor market (except for very high-level talent) it is the buyer (employer) and not the seller (worker) who establishes the wage level.

Lack of labor mobility is still another characteristic of a labor market. An employee will not resign his job simply to take a job in another part of town because it pays 5 cents more per hour. Labor can be said to be "sticky." It tends to stick in one place. There are many reasons for this. One important reason is that the average working man possesses quite incomplete and inaccurate knowledge of job opportunities in his labor market. Wage rate data is not generally made public. If a job opening occurs in a company, it is often filled through informal contacts (you must know somebody to get the job) rather than being announced in the newspapers or listed with an employment agency. Besides a man can rarely determine in advance whether he would be really happy in another job just from the information he can gather in an interview. He must actually work on it a while to find out whether the supervisor treats him fairly, whether the other employees are congenial, and whether the opportunities for advancement reflect what he was told in the employment interview. From this it can be seen that many a worker is unlikely to quit his present job simply because the grass appears to be greener on the other side of the street. There are too many unknowns involved. An additional obstacle to labor mobility derives from the existence of seniority systems and added fringe benefits that accrue to long service employees in a company. An employee who has built up a sizable pension fund in his account, gets four weeks vacation per year, and has acquired considerable job seniority will be quite reluctant to give up all these advantages to take a job with another company for only slightly more pay.

All of the foregoing hindrances to labor mobility do not mean that people will not, at times, actively search for other employment. But they do serve to emphasize the point that the labor market and the process by which labor supply is allocated is quite disorganized and sluggish.

Labor Supply to the Company

From the standpoint of an individual company, the considerations that determine the quantity and quality of labor which it can recruit are quite complex. The supply is influenced by the population in the labor market, the attractiveness of the jobs and the company (for example, wage rate, benefits and services, reputation of company for job security), amount of unemployment in the labor market, commuting patterns (location of the employer with respect to transportation lines), and the particular skills needed in relation to their availability in the local community. First to come to the attention of an organization seeking additional employees, quite logically, would be those who are presently unemployed. Those who are currently drawing state unemployment insurance benefits are registered with the local state employment service office. It has been the author's experience in working with unemployment statistics in industrial cities that those registered for unemployment benefits at any one time represent only 60 to 70 per cent of the total number who are out of work. Many persons may have already exhausted their maximum number of weeks of benefits. Many people do not register if they are unemployed for only a very brief period. Professional, executive, and technical persons are sometimes too proud to register for benefits.

The labor force is not fixed and unchanging in size. It expands and contracts according to the intensity of the demand for labor. During times of war and accelerated national defense preparations, many people who would not ordinarily seek work are enticed to enter the labor force. Women, particularly housewives, represent the largest segment of the population that will take jobs if conditions are attractive. Older men and women who are past normal retirement age, youths who would ordinarily be in school or college, and marginal workers who are employable only during periods of peak demand also enter the work force when job opportunities are very attractive. Experience with labor market statistics reveals that as demand declines, these people initially join the ranks of the unemployed and are so classified by the United States Department of Commerce enumerators. But gradually, if demand remains low, these housewives and others withdraw from active interest in obtaining new jobs.

The personnel policies of an individual employer are a major determinant of his ability to obtain the labor that he requires. What kind of a reputation as a place to work has the organization created for itself by its actions and treatment of present employees? Does the company arbitrarily cut itself off from such labor sources as particular racial or religious groups, persons over forty years of age, and the handicapped? Has the company fully explored the possibility of utilizing women for jobs on which it has had trouble obtaining sufficient men?

The experience of companies that have built new plants or facilities in towns or small cities where one would ordinarily expect they would find difficulty in obtaining sufficient labor has often revealed that a good reputation as a place to work (that is, good wages, steady employment, and so on) can exercise a powerful pull to draw people off the farms and from great distances to obtain employment. In-plant training programs for previously untrained people can frequently adequately supply the requirements for necessary skills.

RECRUITMENT AND SELECTION POLICY ISSUES

It almost goes without saying that the caliber of the work force of an organization largely determines its strength and its success as an enterprise. The employment policies of many companies are not formalized. They have just evolved as practices over the course of many years. They are changed and canceled as the immediate situation dictates. However, there is much to be gained from the adoption of carefully worked out, stable policies in the employment area.

Policies, being statements of intention and guides to action, can be positive instruments to shape the entire recruitment and selection program. They serve as necessary guides to the personnel department representatives and operating managers who must administer the hiring and placement program. They insure consistency of action throughout the entire organization. They let everyone know where he stands and what he can expect in terms of treatment.

Economic Utility or Social Responsibility

It must be obvious that people are hired by a firm to do a job. That is to say, management will not hire a man unless it feels that that man's productive contribution will exceed, or at least equal, the value of the wage paid to him. In classical economic terms rational employers will hire workers (units of labor) up to the point at which their wage rate equals the marginal revenue product (the added sales revenue obtained from the output of an additional unit of labor). Likewise, corporations tend to lay off workers whose services are no longer needed due to a decline in production requirements or other factors.

However, in very recent times many employers have felt a growing sense of obligation to hire and train the hard-core unemployed. The National Alliance of Businessmen established by the administration of President Johnson in 1968 and first headed by Henry Ford II, Chairman of the Ford Motor Company set a goal of 500,000 jobs for the hard core by July 1971. This expanded social consciousness of many managements has developed out of a realization that they have a real stake in the welfare of the communities in which they operate. The frustration and hopelessness of the culturally deprived, centered in the ghettos of the big cities, has been such a pressing national problem that the full cooperation of private business, government, and labor has been essential as a condition for working out a solution.

Although many private businessmen have launched programs to employ the hard-core unemployed in their firms—it must be remembered that these people do not meet normal hiring standards—they expect that with adequate orientation and training the new workers will be able to perform at an acceptable level. Thus the risk-taking in the interest of advancing the human welfare of these people is confined to the first few weeks and months on the payroll. Employers can be expected to terminate those workers who do not eventually make a reasonable economic contribution.

Fill Vacancies from Within or from Outside?

If an opening occurs for a bookkeeping-machine operator or a buyer, should people be hired from the outside and assigned directly to these jobs? Most companies announce to their employees that they follow a policy of promotion from within as far as possible. There are several advantages to such a policy:

1. Most people expect to advance to positions of higher pay and status during their work careers. Therefore, this policy fosters high morale. One opening in a higher-level position may cause a succession of individual advancements as people each in turn move up.
2. Management can more accurately appraise the skills, knowledge, and personality characteristics of its present employees than it can job applicants who are interviewed in the employment office. Therefore, there is less risk of error in selection and placement.
3. The recruitment and selection problem is simplified because there are only a few entry jobs, and the formal education, skill, and knowledge requirements for these are relatively modest.

Although there are manifestly beneficial effects from following a policy of filling vacancies from within as much as possible, there are inherent problems and limitations also. In order for a company to fill its job openings from within, it must have in operation training programs by which people on lower-level jobs can learn new skills in order to qualify for upgrading to more demanding work. In a sense this is a strength and an advantage of the "fill vacancies from within" policy. However, small organizations often feel that they cannot afford the expense of comprehensive employee training programs. A policy of upgrading from within requires that the persons hired have aptitudes and potential for moving ahead. In some cases they may be overqualified for the entry jobs. If promotions do not actually materialize, these overqualified persons will be disappointed and frustrated at their lack of progress. An exclusive promotion-from-within policy prevents the infusion of new ideas and knowledge at the upper levels. This in effect might be called organizational inbreeding. Subordinates, having been taught and molded by their bosses, often know no other ways of doing things. When promoted to positions of power and influence they tend to perpetuate outdated practices.

As a generalization, the most fruitful policy is probably that of filling the majority of vacancies from within but going to the outside when fully qualified talent is not available inside the organization. It is also probably wise to fill a moderate percentage of the higher level managerial and professional positions by going to the outside labor market to inject new ideas into the organization.

Public Policy—Fair Employment Practices

Concentrated attention, in both private and public circles, has been focused for a number of years upon the desirability and even the necessity of making employment opportunities available to all qualified persons regardless of their race, creed, color, or national origin. Added to this has been the more recent concern at the state and Federal level to prevent job discrimination based upon sex and age barriers.

Of the various categories of discrimination, racial bias has drawn the greatest national attention. Such discrimination can take many forms. An employer may have had a long standing policy of hiring only white Americans or he may have hired some Negroes but denied them promotional opportunities. Thus the Negroes could not advance beyond the level of unskilled jobs. Or the employer may have paid Negroes a lower rate of pay than whites for the same work. Or the employer may have always laid off Negroes during slack periods before whites. Some labor unions, particularly in the construction field, where entry into the trade is heavily controlled by the local union, have also denied employment opportunities to Negroes.

National concern for rooting out discriminatory practices in employment derives from several causes. One of these is a broadly based American sense of justice and fair play. Americans have recognized rather generally that from the days of slavery the Negro has been exploited and relegated to the ranks of second-class citizenship. Constituting by far the largest minority ethnic group in the United States, black Americans have recently acquired a stronger sense of racial identity. They have become better organized through such groups as the National Association for the Advancement of Colored People, the Urban League, and the Southern Christian Leadership Conference. Through mass meetings, civil rights marches, and lobbying for legislation, they have succeeded in getting public support for programs and laws to reduce, and one hopes, eliminate discrimination in employment (and also in housing, public accommodations, voting, and judicial proceedings). There has also been increasing recognition of the fact that unemployment rates are much higher for Negroes than whites, and annual incomes and educational attainment are much lower. Although discriminatory practices are not the sole cause of these disparities, they are a real part of the problem and are amenable to correction.

Legislation and Executive Orders. In 1941 by executive order President Franklin D. Roosevelt established a Fair Employment Practices Committee, which was active throughout World War II. The executive order stated that employers and unions had a duty "to provide for the full and equitable participation of all workers in defense industries, without discrimination because of race, creed, color, or national origin." The Committee lacked statutory authority to require compliance with its orders, but it did settle thousands of cases by conciliation and negotiation. Since 1945 every President has had a similar committee whose jurisdiction was confined to establishments doing business with the Federal government. Under President Kennedy the Committee was given the power to apply sanctions and to cancel government contracts.

In the field of legislation, the states preceeded the Federal government by nearly twenty years. New York State pioneered by adopting a general antidiscrimination law in 1945. By 1960 sixteen states had laws with positive enforcement powers. As of 1967 the number had grown to thirty-two states. This includes practically all of the states outside the South. To this day, however, the New York law has been probably the most effective because its human rights commission is much more adequately staffed and financed than those in most other states.

Culminating many years of struggle in the halls of Congress, the Civil Rights Act of 1964 was passed on July 2 of that year. Title VII of this Act "Equal Employment Opportunity" makes it an unlawful employment practice for an employer to "fail or refuse to hire or to discharge any individual, or otherwise to discriminate against any individual with respect to his compensation, terms, conditions, or privileges of employment, because of such individual's race, color, religion, sex, or national origin."[1]

This ban on discriminatory practices applies also to employment agencies and labor unions. It became effective on July 2, 1965. It covers employers having 25 or more employees. Administration of Title VII is handled by a five-member independent agency, the Equal Employment Opportunity Commission, appointed by the President.

In those states having laws with positive enforcement powers the Federal Commission has authority to enter into a cooperative agreement with the state agency whereby the Commission relinquishes part or all of its enforcement function to that agency. Even if no such agreement has been made, the aggrieved individual may not appeal to the Federal Commission until 60 days after the commencement of action under the state law. If, on the other hand, the state has no such law, the aggrieved person files a charge directly with the area office of the Equal Employment Opportunity Commission. The Commission investigates, and if the charge is substantiated, the Commission is required to attempt a settlement by conference and conciliation. If voluntary compliance cannot be arranged, the aggrieved person can file a civil action against the employer (or employment agency or union) in a Federal district court. The Commission, itself, does not have the power to issue cease and desist orders, to order remedies, or to take a case to court as do many other Federal and state regulatory agencies.

Discrimination Based Upon Sex. The days of females obtaining employment only as domestics, seamstresses, teachers, and nurses have long since passed. They now work in practically every occupational category. Upon entering the man's world, they initially faced many barriers such as rejection at the employment office, lower rates of pay and other arbitrary rules. For many years, for example, certain firms enforced a policy of employing only single women. Once a girl married she was discharged.

---

[1] Sec. 703 (a) (1) of the Act.

Title VII outlaws discrimination due to sex. In addition thirteen states and the District of Columbia have laws with positive enforcement powers in this area.[2]

To protect women in pay treatment, Congress enacted the Equal Pay Act of 1963 as an amendment to the Fair Labor Standards Act. The Equal Pay Act forbids employers from discriminating between male and female employees by paying lower wage rates to employees of one sex than those of another for equal work performed under similar working conditions. This law is administered by the Wage and Hour and Public Contracts Division of the U.S. Department of Labor.

Age Bias. Corporations tend to prefer hiring young people. This preference applies to most occupational categories from unskilled through executive. Want ads in newspapers typically have specified such openings as "route salesmen, 21-35; salesladies, 18-40; and mechanic, 21-40." If a person becomes unemployed after the age of 40 to 45, even if he is an executive, he generally experiences some difficulty in obtaining a satisfactory position.

Corporate policy makers tend to prefer younger employees because they are easier to mold. The "right" attitudes and work habits can be inculcated more readily in young than older people. Also there is a prevailing notion that younger employees work faster than old ones. Yet older workers must work, live, and eat too. And there is evidence to demonstrate that absenteeism, turnover, and work injury rates for older employees are lower than for younger people.

To meet this problem, the United States Congress enacted the Age Discrimination in Employment Act of 1967. Congress declared that the purpose of the Act was to promote the employment of older persons based upon ability rather than age and to prohibit arbitrary age discrimination. The law affords protection only to individuals who are between 40 and 65 years of age. The Secretary of Labor is charged with administration of the law under guidelines drawn by the Fair Labor Standards Act. At the time this law was enacted twenty-four states also had adopted age discrimination laws.

Bona Fide Occupational Qualifications. Congress recognized that some situations occur where a justifiable exception can be made to the bans on discrimination in regard to race, creed, color, religion, national origin, sex, and age. Thus a religious institution may restrict employment to persons of a particular religion for jobs expressly related to that organization's religious functions. Physical fitness requirements may in some cases constitute a basis for legitimate age restrictions.

Overview. The broad objective of all the fair employment practice laws, both Federal and state, is to ensure equal employment opportunity to all qualified persons unfettered by artificial restrictions. The enforce-

---

[2] These states are Colorado, Connecticut, Hawaii, Maryland, Massachusetts, Michigan, Missouri, Nebraska, Nevada, New York, Utah, Wisconsin, and Wyoming.

ment agencies tend to rely most heavily upon education, conciliation, and mild but continuing pressure to secure compliance. Court action and the police powers of the state are only occasionally brought into play, and then only as a last resort. It is recognized that changes in the customs, values, and mores of the people occur slowly.[3]

Applicants Having Influence Within Organization

What course of action should be taken with those applicants who allegedly or actually have personal contacts and friends in management positions within the organization? Although the top management of most companies would not want to admit that it gives special preference to those having pull within the organization, in actual practice for certain types of jobs this element plays an important part in the operation of some employment programs. This means that ability alone is not the prime criterion for selection. It may result in a dilution or weakening of selection standards.

Closely related to the foregoing problem is the policy question of whether to hire relatives of present employees. For a large organization this practice of hiring the sons and daughters of present employees (wives, and so on) generally does not cause difficulty if care is taken to insure that one person is not placed in a position of authority over a relative or family member in such a way as to show favoritism or partiality. In the large organization morale is generally enhanced if a father, because he thinks very highly of his company and is loyal, finds that his son or daughter can also obtain employment there. Care must be exercised in job placement, however, so that nepotism does not occur.

In the small organization a general practice of hiring relatives of present managers and employees has serious implications that top management must weigh carefully. This might result in excessive inbreeding and a decline in performance standards if carried too far.

Realistic Selection Standards

Oftentimes companies adopt qualification requirements that lack a proven relationship to success or failure on the job. Unrealistic hiring standards can be of two types: (1) credentials barriers based upon education, certification, or licensing and (2) idiosyncrasies based upon whim, prejudice, or outdated criteria.

Credentials Barriers. Educational attainment is a principal selection hurdle used by most organizations. Thus some companies specify that a high school education is necessary for employment in unskilled and semiskilled factory jobs such as materials handler, laborer, and machine

---

[3] Authoritative information, including text of laws, interpretative rulings, recent developments and discussion, on the various federal and state fair employment laws can be found in the *Employment Practices Guide* published by Commerce Clearing House. This is a loose leaf labor law service. New developments are included as they occur.

operator. A college degree is usually a prerequisite for admission into administrative and managerial positions. Certain craftsmen and certain engineers are required to be licensed in order to perform certain tasks. As a screening device education possesses a considerable measure of merit. The process of going through elementary and high school and college is in itself a selection screen. By and large those who possess the greatest perseverence and demonstrated ability to learn under the specified conditions of the educational system are the ones who successfully complete school. These are presumed to have the right talents and acquired skills, both technical and social. But heavy reliance upon a diploma or a college degree as a condition of employment yields some clear disadvantages.

It automatically eliminates from consideration those who have dropped out of school. By and large these are the poor, the underprivileged, and those who are poorly adapted to the discipline of the school system. Those who have not gone through the formal credentializing process are not necessarily unqualified. Sometimes the barriers are erected by a small elite group who are already in an occupation or profession and who want to maintain their choice economic and social position by sharply restricting entrance to the field of work. Some craft unions, for example, achieve just such an end by artificially long periods of apprenticeship, high initiation fees, and contractual limits on the number of apprentices who can enter the trade. Certain professional associations act similarly by licensing rules and control of educational and internship programs. "Credentialitis" is another manifestition of the trend toward bureaucratization of modern organizational life. But this not only denies job opportunities to those who might do well if given a chance but it also artificially shrinks the pool of talent available to an industry, firm, or occupation. A number of brilliant men did poorly in school—Albert Einstein and Winston Churchill are two outstanding examples. The educational establishment tends to homogenize its students. The nonconformist is rejected or rejects himself.

If one grants the line of argument above to be true, what course of action should a personnel executive adopt for an employment policy? Clearly he should not ignore educational attainment as a selection guide. It does correlate with probability of occupational success in a generalized way when one is speaking of large numbers of persons. A realistic policy would be to set general educational qualifications for the various jobs in a company based upon a sound job analysis program. But deliberate emphasis can be given to hiring some people, say 5 to 15 per cent of the total in a given category, who lack the formal education desired but who give promise of reasonable success by virtue of appropriate work experience, interest, motivation, and recommendation by qualified observers. Additional training can be obtained after hiring through participation in evening school and in-service corporate training programs. Such an approach is quite analagous to the "high risk" student admission policies instituted by several major universities in recent years. These universities have deliberately admitted some students who fall below cutting scores on the college board tests and rank decidedly lower in their high school graduating classes than the average student who is admitted. In some instances special tutoring and remedial course work has been provided. The distribution of grades in college and the percentage who ultimately graduate is not much different for these "high risk" groups than for the college population generally.

Idiosyncrasies.   The author knows of one firm that will not hire left-handed men or men over thirty years of age or men who have faulty color discrimination of vision. Another company will not hire anyone who had or had had asthma. In each of these instances the selection standard used had been justifiable at one time in the past when it had been found that those who were left-handed, and so on, failed on the job. However, as the organizations and technology changed and new employees were assigned to a wide variety of jobs, it has been found that these artificial grounds for rejection are totally without merit except for a very few entry jobs. Inertia and resistance to change, in these cases, prevented a reexamination and updating of selection standards.

Basically the general principle can be stated that only those screening criteria should be used that have been shown—on the basis of research within one's own organization—to have a definite relationship to success on the job. The notion prevails in the selling field that big men make better salesmen than small men. But it would be dangerous and wasteful of money and talent to adopt such a selection requirement unless there existed a significant statistical correlation between success on the job and height. Many employment and personnel managers are not research oriented. They are willing to adopt a particular hiring rule just because it seems logical to them. An eminent market researcher working in the field of package styling and design made the statement that whenever he tried to guess consumer preferences on the basis of his own *a priori* reasoning he was usually wrong. He found, from experience, that the only sound way to attack the problem was on the basis of market surveys of consumer tastes and preferences. So it is with the selection process. Although judgment and intuition will always be an important part of the process of management (because it is partly an art and partly a science), it behooves managers to utilize the scientific method wherever appropriate. It is certainly necessary in the field of employee selection.

The Lie Detector

Certain organizations experience serious problems of employee dishonesty and disloyalty. Theft and embezzlement of company property occur. Certain technical and marketing personnel in highly sensitive spots may sell trade secrets to competitors. Although the dishonest or illegal behavior may be exhibited by less than 1 per cent of the employees in a firm, the damage may nevertheless be very great. To screen out dishonest people and to keep present employees honest, a fairly substantial number of corporations and government agencies have resorted to the lie detector (polygraph) in recent years. It has been estimated that 200,000 to 300,000 lie-detector tests are conducted annually for business and government employment situations.

Originally developed in the 1920's, the polygraph has had its greatest use by the police to aid in crime detection. This instrument is attached at various points on the subject's body. It measures rate of breathing, heartbeat rate, relative (not absolute) blood pressure, and skin current (galvanic skin response, associated with sweating of the palms). The theory behind the polygraph technique is that lying causes distinctive physiological reactions in a person who knows he is not telling the truth.

Although the idea of a "truth machine" to classify people is appealing to many executives, the simple truth of the matter is that they would be well advised categorically to avoid the use of the polygraph for employment purposes. Although the machine measures physiological states or changes fairly accurately, there is no simple correlation between these conditions and the truthfulness of the subject. Scientific researchers have found great individual differences in the reaction of people to various kinds of stress. An apparent response of guilt can be caused by other factors such as the physical and emotional state of the subject. Polygraph interpretations are essentially invalid when subjects show extreme nervousness; have high or very low blood pressure, heart disease, and respiratory disorders; have pronounced neuroses or psychoses or are pathological liars; and when they suffer from emotional and physical fatigue. The polygraph technique plainly lacks scientific validity.

In addition many people contend that its use constitutes an invasion of privacy and forced self-incrimination. It is an assault upon individual rights and human dignity.

By 1967 eleven states had enacted statutes banning the use of the polygraph as a condition of employment or of continued employment.[4] When arbitrators have been called upon to rule on the use of the lie detector in disputes between union and management, the overwhelming majority of them have rejected its use. Most arbitrators have refused to admit the test results as evidence of "just cause" for a discharge. They have likewise upheld the right of workers to refuse to take such a test.[5]

Thus we can see that personnel directors and other executives would

[4] These states are Massachusetts (1950), Oregon (1963), California (1963), Rhode Island (1964), Alaska (1964), Washington (1965), Hawaii (1965), Delaware (1966), Maryland (1966), New Jersey (1966), and Connecticut (1967).

[5] Further information on the lie detector can be found in Burk M. Smith, "The Polygraph," *Scientific American,* Vol. 216, No. 1 (January 1967), pp. 25-31; Lee M. Burkey, "Lie Detectors in Labor Relations," *Arbitration Journal,* Vol. 19, No. 4 (1964), pp. 193-205; U.S. Congress, House Committee on Government Operations, *Use of Polygraphs as "Lie Detectors" by the Federal Government* (89th Congress, 1st session, House Report No. 198, March 22, 1965, Washington: Government Printing Office, 1965), p. 45.

be ill advised to order the use of the polygraph in screening job candidates or for ascertaining the innocence or guilt of employees in specific cases.

SOURCES OF LABOR

Recruitment is the development and maintenance of adequate manpower sources. It involves the creation of a pool of available labor upon whom the organization can draw when it needs additional employees. Since the selection process involves a screening out or elimination of those not considered suitable for hiring, it is clear that any company must have on tap a larger supply of people than it will actually hire.

One convenient way of classifying the sources of supply is to divide the sources into the two categories: (1) inside sources and (2) outside sources. Thus if a particular job vacancy occurs, it can be filled by transferring or promoting another employee from within the company to that post. If there is to be a net addition to the size of the work then, of course, someone will have to be employed from the outside as well. In filling vacancies from within, it is still necessary to match job requirements with worker qualifications. The selection process must still be employed. But it means that present employees are given first chance for any better or more attractive jobs before outsiders are considered.

Inside Sources

The process of filling job openings by selecting from among the pool of present employees can be implemented by either of two methods. One involves a review of the personnel records and appraisal forms by the personnel director and members of operating management to find qualified candidates. Very frequently fresh performance ratings are prepared, a meeting of interested parties is convened, and a decision is made to give the job to one of the persons under review. With this procedure it is very common for the employees under consideration to be totally in the dark about the goings-on until the selection is formally announced. There is also the possibility that fully qualified potential candidates will be overlooked due to an oversight. Despite this weakness, this procedure is the one most generally followed in business and industry. Some organizations have formalized and systematized the process to the point where job vacancies are announced in writing to all appropriate members of supervision and management. They are requested to review all of their subordinates and submit nominations to the personnel office, which then coordinates the process of selection and placement.

Job Posting and Bidding.   With the advent of industrial unions in the late 1930's, the practice of announcing all job vacancies on plant bulletin boards and inviting employee bids or applications became quite widespread. This is, in effect, a means of advertising for job applicants within the plant. It is granting employees just as much right to apply for a job as the employer would grant to outsiders who answered an advertisement in the newspaper. Normally in a unionized plant the job posting and bidding procedure is spelled out in the labor agreement. It typically applies only to jobs within the bargaining unit. The bulletin board notice specifies the job title, rate of pay, and qualifications that the employee must possess. Unions, in negotiating this contract provision, often seek to have the employee selection based primarily upon seniority. Employers, quite logically, seek to have the job assignment go to the most qualified person as decided by management. Often a compromise must be made. The principal virtue of the job post and bid system is that it grants every qualified employee within the bargaining unit a fair opportunity to obtain a better job. It reduces the likelihood of special deals and favoritism from entering into the selection process. If the selection is based solely upon seniority, then, of course, management may find itself saddled with mediocre workers in key jobs.

Outside Sources and Recruitment Methods

The particular sources and means by which workers are recruited varies greatly. It depends upon management policy, the type of jobs involved, the supply of labor relative to demand, and the nature of the existent labor market institutions, such as employment agencies, unions, and the like. Let us now examine the principal sources and methods for obtaining manpower.

Public Employment Agencies. Every state in the United States has a state employment service, which operates branch offices in most cities of about ten thousand population or more throughout each state. The initiating force behind the establishment of these employment services was the Wagner-Peyser Act of 1933, which created the United States Employment Service and established a program of Federal-state cooperation. Federal funds are made available to the states on a matching basis for the support and administration of these state programs. In return for this Federal money the states must conform to standards and procedures prescribed by the United States government. Upon the passage of the Social Security Act in 1935 the state employment services were assigned the added responsibility of administering the unemployment compensation program. In order for an unemployed worker to be eligible for unemployment insurance benefits, he must register for employment and be ready and able to take a job if a suitable one is available. There has been a tendency over the years for the placements made by public employment offices to be concentrated heavily in certain occupational groups, such as domestic service, farm and construction labor, unskilled and semiskilled factory work, and retail store sales clerks. Professional, managerial, and white-color groups tend to utilize other job-seeking methods.

Private Employment Agencies.   Privately operated employment companies are quite widespread throughout the United States. For a fee collected usually from the employee (after he is hired) but sometimes from the employer, they help to meet employer requests for people from their files of job seekers who have registered with them. In many jurisdictions the fees charged and the operations of these employment "brokers" are regulated by state law. Many agencies do a careful job of interviewing, testing, counseling, and screening to match the employer specifications and demands with the abilities and needs of the job applicant. A great many of these agencies concentrate upon white-collar office and retail sales personnel, because demand is generally high, and turnover is great. Thus there is a continuous flow of business in these occupations.

Labor Unions.   It is primarily in those occupations in which the employees are represented by craft unions that much of the hiring process is carried on through union hiring halls. Industries and occupations in which companies tend to obtain all or most of their labor force through union-controlled hiring halls are construction, longshoring, maritime, clothing, popular dance bands, and the like. Generally those union members who have been unemployed the longest are given the first opportunity to fill the job opening. The hiring hall system flourishes where there are many small employers and where employment is intermittent or casual. The union lends a degree of stability to the labor market situation and guarantees that unemployed workers will get jobs in their rightful turn.

Unsolicited Applicants at the Employment Office.   For jobs requiring only routine abilities and skill, many employers are able to fill their labor needs largely by means of direct hiring at the gate. In a survey of 284 employers in the San Francisco Bay Area labor markets, it was found that for manual workers direct hiring at the gate was the second most commonly used source of workers. (Recruiting through labor unions was first.) For obtaining sales personnel, retail stores very commonly used this method also.[6] One of the most influential factors affecting the desirability of this method as a source is the image and reputation of the organization in the community. If a company, by its actions, has demonstrated that it treats its employees well, pays adequate wages, and has enlightened personnel practices, then those seeking work will gravitate to that enterprise. Another important variable is the state of the labor market. In times of high unemployment even firms with a less glittering reputation will find a large volume of unsolicited applicants at the employment office.

Employee Recruiting.   Some organizations announce to their own employees that they wish to hire additional people possessing such and such type of skills. The employees will then pass the word to their friends and relatives who may be seeking work. There are essentially two approaches to this type of employee recruiting. One is quite informal. In one

[6] F. T. Malm, "Recruiting Patterns and the Functioning of Labor Markets," *Industrial and Labor Relations Review,* Vol. 7, No. 4 (July 1954), pp. 507-525.

steel company the personnel manager, working through production supervision and word of mouth, transmits the message that the company will start hiring production workers the next day. Generally speaking, this grapevine approach to recruitment produces a waiting line of applicants for unskilled and semiskilled jobs the next morning.

A more organized approach is that taken by some telephone companies in the Bell System. Because of high turnover of young women telephone operators and clerks due to early marriage and child rearing these companies must constantly recruit new employees. One way in which they solve this problem is by means of employee recruiting. Bulletin board announcements inform employees of the specific qualifications which candidates must possess to fill job openings. Periodic meetings are held with selected employee groups to discuss with them the opportunities and needs for additional personnel. Special explanatory booklets are prepared for distribution to employees. It is important, when conducting an employee recruitment program, that the sponsoring employee be apprised of the action taken on his candidate (that is, hired or rejected and why) and be given due credit when a person he recommended has been hired. The principal advantage of employee recruiting is that it is selective. Grossly unqualified persons will not be recommended by an employee, because he feels this would reflect adversely upon his own reputation.

Advertising. Advertising in newspapers, trade magazines, and professional society journals is a widely used method of recruiting. Although there are some justifiable exceptions, the author feels that employers who advertise for applicants should reveal their own identity rather than use a blind ad, in which the person must send a resume to a box number at the newspaper or magazine. Sound ethics suggests that the employer reveal his identity if he expects candidates to supply detailed autobiographical information. Likewise, this prevents the possibility of the employer's own employees (those who are dissatisfied and seeking to make a change) unknowingly applying for a job at their own company.

Schools and Colleges. At the secondary school level alert employment managers make it a practice to get acquainted with school principals and guidance counselors to inform them of job opportunities and employment practices in their companies. Even if a company is not hiring people for the present it often is sound to develop these channels and contacts in case of future needs.

At colleges and universities the recruitment of graduating seniors has been a large-scale operation for many years now. Nearly every institution of higher learning has a placement office containing rooms where employers can conduct interviews and give selection tests. The greatest activity is in engineering and scientific fields—areas in which the demand is great and the supply of graduating students is short. This recruitment practice tends to be utilized primarily by the larger companies, which can afford to send teams of interviewers throughout the country and can afford to pay the travel expenses to the most promising students for visits to the plant where the final employment decision is usually made.

Special Problem of Professional and Managerial Personnel.   As a general rule business firms rarely have difficulty in finding adequate employees for manual, clerical, sales and general run type of work. But in this age of rapidly advancing technology and more complex civilization, there is an ever-increasing need for persons possessing advanced education and specialized talent. Examples of such occupations for which there is is an insufficient supply of good talent are nurses, physicians, teachers, engineers, chemists, physicists, mathematicians, and capable high-level executives and administrators.

The long-range solution to the shortage of personnel in these fields is for private organizations, the government, and society in general to initiate programs that will channel more young men and women into these fields and to give financial and other support not only to individual students but also to educational institutions. Private business organizations can contribute to such a program by providing scholarships, fellowships, and direct grants to colleges and universities. Another method is to establish programs by which promising individuals can gain practical experience through industrial "internships" and applied research opportunities in industry.

In the short run the individual firm faced with a shortage of qualified high-level talent must resort to an aggressive recruiting effort. Among the more prominent recruitment techniques employed by some companies for professional and managerial talent are the following:

1. Advertising in prominent newspapers and college papers
2. Indoctrination seminars for college professors
3. Management consulting firms
4. Executive recruiters
5. Professional association meetings

In the field of advertising for scientists and engineers, A. R. Deutsch has provided some advice on the content of the written copy based upon his own research and that of others. He recommends that the ad provide specific information on the job requirements and opportunities for growth, adequate data about the company and its overall projects and plans, and benefits of working for the company. The ad should emphasize the job dignity and professional aspects of the situation as well as point out that the individual will be rewarded and recognized for his work. Frilly ads containing exaggerated claims and gimmicky appeals are to be avoided.[7]

In the last few years a number of industrial concerns have adopted a rather subtle, soft-sell approach to the recruitment of new college graduates, particularly engineers and scientists. They invite professors from a number of colleges in a particular region to attend seminars on the com-

[7] Arnold R. Deutsch, "Where Recruiting Ads Go Wrong," *Management Review,* Vol. 50, No. 10 (October 1961), pp. 26-35.

pany premises. Typically the programs are one to two days in length and include a banquet, speeches by company officials, discussion groups, and a tour of the company's production, engineering, and research facilities. Ostensibly the program is for the purpose of getting acquainted and discussing mutual problems and needs. The companies (which pay for the transportation and living expenses of the professors) hope that the faculty members will be sufficiently impressed so that they will speak favorably of the sponsoring company in their contacts with students. Because students often do ask professors for advice in selecting a future employer, this indirect approach to recruitment in all probability does direct some young college graduates to these firms.

Since management consulting firms (often called management engineering consultants) become intimately acquainted with the personnel of numerous client companies, they often are in a position to recommend an individual as a likely candidate for, say, a controller's or a marketing manager's position. It should be pointed out that the employment agency aspect of this business is distinctly a sideline for most management consultants. On the other hand, there are some specialized kinds of consultants whose principal business is that of executive recruitment. They maintain extensive files on the qualifications and interests of large numbers of executives who are employed at present. They are not employment agencies in the typical sense of the word, because they work for and owe allegiance to the company that has engaged their services. They do not take a fee from the employee. Because the most desirable prospects are often already employed in an executive position, the recruiting firm or "talent scout" seeks to entice these persons away from their employers.

The annual conferences or meetings that all professional associations hold in the major cities throughout the country almost always serve as a market place where employers and job seeking members of the association can meet and discuss job opportunities. In some cases this is done informally over a cocktail at the bar. In others a formal system is established whereby employers can place their written job requirements on file and job seekers can submit their resumes and applications.

Because high talent manpower is in short supply and will likely continue to be so for many years to come, company personnel executives must recognize that a substantial part of their efforts have to be devoted to selling the job prospects upon the desirability and benefits of taking a position with their organization. Instead of having a pool of, say twenty or thirty mathematicians from whom to pick, the employer may have a choice of only one or two persons. Thus it behooves the personnel director to appraise carefully his entire recruiting and employment program to insure that it accurately represents the company and that it does not inadvertently offend or repel promising job candidates.[8]

[8] For a discussion of this issue from the standpoint of hiring new college graduates see Orlando Behling, George Labovitz, and Marion Gainer, "College Recruiting: A Theoretical Base," *Personnel Journal,* Vol. 47, No. 1 (January 1968), pp. 13-19.

THE SELECTION PROCESS

Whereas the goal of recruitment is to create a large pool of persons who are available and willing to work for a particular company, the selection process has as its objective the sorting out or elimination of those judged unqualified to meet job and organization requirements. Thus, in a sense, recruitment tends to be positive in that it seeks to persuade people to apply for work at the company, whereas selection tends to be somewhat negative because it rejects a goodly portion of those who apply.

The most common approach to the selection problem is to choose individuals who possess the necessary skills, abilities, and personality to successfully fill specific jobs in the organization. Thus the employment manager typically has in his possession an employment requisition initiated by some operating manager requesting, say, one design draftsman with five years drafting experience to start work on April 15 at a certain wage rate. This is essentially a problem of matching a man to the job. But what course of action should the employment manager follow when a bright young man, fresh out of technical school but with no practical experience, applies? The question being raised here is as follows. Does the employment policy of the company permit the hiring of a good candidate because he will be a valuable asset to the organization even if he does not meet the specific requirements of the present job opening? Let us now go one step further. What action should be taken if the company is not hiring anyone at present, but one or more very promising individuals apply for a job, and the employment manager has every reason to believe that hiring will be resumed within a few weeks or months? Should the good candidates be rejected, or should they be hired and placed in a reserve pool or training program in expectation of future needs? As implied earlier, the prevailing practice in industry is to reject all applicants in these hypothetical situations unless there is a specific job vacancy and the applicant meets the stated qualifications.

But there is another approach to selection that admittedly is more feasible for a large than for a small organization. Under this system certain basic entrance standards are established, such as a minimum amount of education, minimum age, physical requirements, minimum score on a mental ability test, and so on. All those who meet or exceed these requirements of the organization are considered further for specific aptitudes, abilities, and vocational preferences that would fit them for one of a number of possible jobs. The military services, in effect, follow this policy of selecting first for the organization and then differentially placing men where they are best fitted.

Fundamentally, then, there can be certain very positive aspects to the selection process. Instead of concentrating simply upon the rejection of applicants, the employment manager can transform his thinking into the task of deciding where in the organization the man would best fit.

Considerations in Making the Selection Decision

There are a number of important factors that must be taken into account when attempting to make a decision regarding an applicant or applicants.

Organizational and Social Environment. The selection process necessitates the matching of a person with the job in a particular organizational and social environment. Those charged with operating the hiring program must have available a complete set of job descriptions and specifications for all jobs in the organization so that they can have detailed knowledge of the duties and human qualifications necessary to fill these jobs. A prime objective of the selection process is to find out enough about the applicant's background, training, personality, aptitudes, skills, and interests so that this matching process can be done accurately. But there is more to it than this. Even if a person is eminently qualified to perform the work of, say, a bookkeeping machine operator or a quality control laboratory technician, he may fail because of the particular organizational and social environment in that company.

For example, in one company a very attractive and well-qualified young lady, age 21, was hired as a stenographer in an office containing several men engineers and two middle-aged, long-service women secretaries. Although the young lady performed her work well and the men liked her work, she was eventually frozen out and forced to resign because of the antagonism of the two older women, who were very jealous of her charms.

Many factors affect the success or failure of an employee besides his basic ability to do the job. Miller and Form have developed a rating scale method (analogous to a point rating plan of job evaluation) for evaluating the social skills required in the performance of jobs. They give consideration to seven social factors: scope of social contacts, status range of contacts, social demands off the job, social leadership, skill intensity, social participation, and direct and indirect personal responsibility for others.[9] In addition to these, many other environmental factors must be taken into account. Among these are social cliques, degree of receptiveness of work group to newcomers, personality and idiosyncrasies of the boss, group standards and norms, and organizational pressures. In general, it is not possible actually to measure all of these organizational and social influences. The best that can be done is for the employment manager to be perceptive and aware of these environmental factors so that he can judge whether a particular applicant will adapt himself successfully to the situation.[10]

[9] Delbert C. Miller and W. H. Form, *Industrial Sociology* (New York: Harper & Row, 1951), pp. 430-436.

[10] For additional thoughts on the subject of social and organizational environment see Milton M. Mandell, "The Effect of Organizational Environment" in M. J. Dooher and E. Marting, *Selection of Management Personnel* (New York: American Management Association, 1957), pp. 336-341.

Successive Hurdles or Multiple Correlation? The vast majority of employee selection programs are based upon the successive-hurdles technique. This means that to be hired, applicants must successfully pass each and every screening device (that is, application blank, interviews, tests, medical examination, and background check). Some candidates are rejected at each step or hurdle. For a person to go successfully from one hurdle to the next, he must meet or exceed the requirements for each hurdle. For example, the job seeker may be rejected as early as the application blank stage because the education and previous work experience that he has recorded may be insufficient to meet the established hiring standard. In designing a selection procedure according to the successive-hurdles method, the selection device that has the highest correlation with job success (validity) is placed first in the sequence, the one with the next highest relationship with on-the-job performance is placed second, and so forth. Those applicants who have little chance of succeeding on the job are eliminated at the first hurdle. Both the candidates' time and the company's time and expense are saved by not having to put grossly unqualified persons through the entire procedure before a decision is made.

The multiple-correlation approach, which is less commonly used, is based upon the assumption that a deficiency in one factor can be counterbalanced by an excess amount of another. For example the education of one candidate as shown on the application form may be below the job requirements, yet the interviewer may decide to carry the man further along in the selection sequence because of his superior related work experience and apparent high motivation (as revealed during the interview). Also, if a battery of selection tests are used, the procedure may entail the compiling of a composite test score index. A low score on one test can then be counterbalanced by a high score on another. In the multiple-correlation technique a person is routed through all the selection stops before a decision is made. The decision criteria may be all reduced to numbers. Thus a scored application blank may be used, the interviewer may assign a numerical rating to the candidates, and of course all tests may be numerically graded. If the combined score on all selection criteria exceeds the level needed to qualify, then the job seeker is hired. If not, he is rejected.

Which selection method should be adopted? If an applicant is grossly unqualified to pass even the preliminary interview because he lacks essential abilities, there is no point in sending him through all of the remaining hurdles. On the other hand, if a man looks reasonably good on the early hurdles, and is mediocre in one minor factor, there is some logic in giving him the full treatment before making the final decision.

Certain chance factors may cause a person to fail one hurdle (for example, the interviewer may dislike his looks, or the conditions under which a test is administered may be nonstandard); therefore, for borderline cases it makes sense to judge the *whole* man before rejecting anyone.

Avoid Gimmicks. Sometimes busy executives with pressing production problems seek easy gimmicks to evaluate human beings. Over the years there have been a host of pseudoscientific shortcuts to human appraisal. Some have claimed that it is possible to predict ability and personality according to the shape of one's head (physiognomy); according to body build (some types: mesomorphic, endomorphic, and ectomorphic); and a host of other oversimplified devices. The simple fact of the matter is that human beings are just too complex for simple gauges as these to be effective and accurate.

Selection Procedure

Selection procedures are most properly tailor-made to meet the particular needs of the employing organization. The thoroughness of the procedure depends upon a number of factors. First, the consequences of faulty selection must be weighed. This is influenced by the length of the training period, money invested in the new employee, level and complexity of the job, and possible damage to the organization if incumbent job holder fails.

A second factor influencing the thoroughness of the selection sequence is company policy and top management attitude. Some organizations deliberately overhire and count upon weeding out poor performers after a few months on the payroll. This simply defers the selection decision until management has had a chance to observe the new employees' behavior closely. However, this procedure is costly for both the organization and the individuals involved. It wastes their time, because they might more profitably be employed elsewhere, where the employer does not overhire.

A third consideration governing the thoroughness of the hiring procedure is the length of the probationary period. A probationary period is a length of time after a new employee has been on the payroll, during which he has absolutely no job security rights. It is essentially a trial period, which usually varies in length from one employer to another from a minimum of thirty days to a maximum of one year. Where the employees are represented by a union, the union usually seeks in negotiations to have a very short probationary period, whereas employers generally press for a long one. If the period is of short duration, then the selection process must be quite accurate in its predictions, because a supervisor is hard pressed to be confident of his decision at the end of the period on whether to retain or discharge the new man. This problem is especially acute if the learning period on the job is much longer than the probationary period.

A Proposed Selection Procedure. Although it is true that the steps in the selection procedure should be varied to meet the special needs of the organization, the following is a model program that will work well in most cases. Adaptations can be made to suit individual situations. For example, the medical examination can be placed quite early in the procedure if physical stamina, agility, strength, and so on, are critical to the work and if only a small portion of the general population can be expected to pass the examination.

Steps in Selection Procedure
1. Reception in employment office
2. Preliminary interview
3. Application blank
4. Selection tests
5. Main employment office interview
6. Investigation of applicant's background
7. Final selection interview by manager or supervisor
8. Medical examination
9. Induction

The decision to add persons to the payroll in particular departments of an organization is not made in the personnel department. This is a function of operating or line management, which then initiates an employment requisition that is sent to the personnel department.

In a large company processing a heavy stream of applicants at all times, the preliminary interview would be conducted by a special interviewer located in the employment office. But in most moderate or smaller-scale operations the preliminary interview and the main employment office interview would be conducted by one and the same person. Thus all candidates might be given a ten-minute screening interview, at which time the interviewer would inform applicants of the nature of the current job openings. He might then elicit data from the candidates pertaining to their education, experience, skills, job interests, and data of availability for accepting employment. If the requirements of the company and the interests and qualifications of the job seeker seem to match in this rough initial screening, then the individual would be given a much more detailed and comprehensive interview.

Selection tests (often called psychological or personnel tests) should be administered prior to the main employment office interview so that the interviewer can have the test results before him when he evaluates the candidate.

It is now appropriate to examine in some detail each of the major selection devices.

Application Blank

The application blank is used to obtain information, in the applicant's own handwriting, sufficient to identify him properly (name, address, telephone number, sex, age, height, weight) and to make tentative inferences regarding his suitability for employment. Primarily the choice of questions put on the blank should be such that they are valid predictors of employment success or failure. Superfluous questions should not appear. The application form should be complete enough to relieve the interviewer of the burden of recording considerable factual data that could better be written on the application by the job seeker. In addition, the questions must not by their wording or nature encourage dishonest answers, as do the following questions:

> How often do you drink intoxicating beverages? Never _____, Seldom _____, Occasionally _____, Excessively _____.
> Do you have marital difficulties?
> Have you ever broken the law?

There are two fundamental methods of evaluating a filled-in application form. One is the clinical method, and the other is the weighted or statistical method.

Clinical Evaluation. In the clinical method the interviewer carefully studies the answers to the questions to find meaningful patterns that can reveal important information regarding the individual's personality and make-up. Advocates of this method claim that a properly designed blank can provide clues to a person's leadership ability, how he gets along with others, his industriousness, emotional stability, assertiveness, speaking ability, attitude toward his boss, and so on. It should be pointed out that the conclusions derived can be considered only tentative. They must be verified by further checking. Likewise an untrained and inexperienced interviewer would make some serious errors with this method. To be done properly the evaluator should have a sound grounding in psychological and personnel management theory.

In explaining how to detect whether the applicant possesses energy and enthusiasm (necessary in selling work), G. J. Spencer has suggested the following as indicators: an unusual number and variety of activities, such as sports, extracurricular activities, types of jobs held, hobbies, and interests; past work experience in active type jobs; dislike of a previous job because it was too detailed and routine. Evidence of narcissism (love of oneself) can be found in the way the applicant writes his name, extracurricular school activities, hobbies, and plans for his future. Thus if the applicant spells out his name in full as John Jonathan Jones and if he played the lead in two class plays, he is likely to have narcissistic tendencies.[11] William H. Whyte, Jr., has made a sharp criticism of this method of psychologically analyzing a job applicant in his book *The Organization Man.* Whyte's point of view is that in making these psychological predictions the analyst is projecting his own world, value judgments, and standards too heavily into the picture. He claims that even if interviewers and analysts are able to diagnose accurately an applicant's personality,

[11]Gilmore J. Spencer, "The Application Form Revisited," *Personnel,* Vol. 36, No. 5 (September-October 1959), pp. 20-30.

personnel specialists are still not at all certain nor in agreement upon what characteristics are essential for, say, a successful salesman or an executive.[12]

In perspective it seems safe to say that a well-trained interviewer is on solid ground if he makes only tentative inferences based upon a clinical study of the application blank and waits for much more conclusive evidence in interviews, tests, and background investigation.

Statistical Evaluation.   A second major way of analyzing the application form is by statistics. Over the years a great deal of statistical correlation work has been done with the weighted application blank.[13] In order to use a weighted application form in selection, it is necessary to have a different form for each occupational group. Points are assigned to the various answers which the applicant gives. A certain critical or passing score is necessary for the applicant to pass this hurdle.

In developing a weighted blank, it is necessary to identify those items of personal history of present employees that differentiate between groups of successful and unsuccessful employees. Thus if it is found that an insurance company's successful life insurance salesmen tend to be married, have high living expenses, and belong to a large number of clubs and organizations, whereas their unsuccessful ones are single, have low living expenses, and belong to few organizations, then these factors can be given a definite statistical scoring when evaluating a person's application. For picking store management trainees a large retailing chain has found definite correlations with job performance and the following: location of last permanent residence, marital status, father's occupation, health, previous experience in retailing, rank in high school or college class, and compensation of last previous job compared to starting salary of this job.

Reliance upon the statistical formula of a weighted application can result in false predictions in individual cases. However it improves predictive probabilities. Or stated another way, it increases the employment office's batting average in the long run when hiring and rejecting large numbers of people.

Selection Tests

In recent years selection tests, which are usually constructed by industrial psychologists, have become a well-accepted part of the selection procedure for the majority of medium- and large-sized companies.

---

[12]William H. Whyte, Jr., *The Organization Man* (New York: Simon & Schuster, Inc., 1956), Ch. 15.

[13] Marion A. Bills, "Selection of Casualty and Life Insurance Agents," *Journal of Applied Psychology,* Vol. 25, No. 1, (1941); Morris S. Viteles, *Industrial Psychology* (New York: W. W. Norton & Company, Inc., 1932), pp. 182-185; Joseph Tiffin, B. T. Parker, and R. W. Haberstat, "The Analysis of Personnel Data in Relation to Turnover on a Factory Job" *Journal of Applied Psychology,* Vol. 31, No. 6 (1947), pp. 615-616; Edwin A. Fleishman and Joseph Berniger, "Using the Application Blank to Reduce Office Turnover," *Personnel*, Vol. 37 (1960), pp. 63-69.

They may not utilize them for all of the jobs for which they hire, but certainly for some. Widespread use of tests commenced with World War I, when the Army Alpha Test was used to aid in the selection and placement of soldiers. The testing movement picked up momentum between the two wars, and has certainly come into its own since the 1940's.

The installation of a sound testing program in an organization is time consuming and costly. Just because a test has been found useful for selecting clerks in company A is no reason to assert that it will be useful for picking clerks in company B. Each test adopted must be proven out (validated) in one's own organization before reliance can be placed upon it. The proper way to look at tests is to ask this question. To what extent will a given test or test battery improve the accuracy of selection predictions over that obtained without tests? Will the organization obtain a higher percentage of successful employees through the use of tests? The theory and application of selection testing, because it is such a complex and important topic, will be treated at length in Chapter 9, "Selection Testing and Interviewing."

Interview

Despite the impressive development of the testing process as an aid to selection, the interview remains the single most important tool in the hiring program. The interviewer is in the unique position of being able to evaluate information obtained from the application blank, a preceeding interview (such as the preliminary employment office interview), tests, and background investigation. He can integrate this data with his own impressions and observations to reach a decision regarding the suitability of the applicant for employment.

Interviewing is primarily an art, not a science. It is subjective. Untrained interviewers will make many erroneous judgments. They will often decide to accept or reject a man upon totally insufficient evidence. However, research studies have shown that adequately trained interviewers using sound procedures can and do achieve good results.

As with the subject of selection testing, interviewing will be comprehensively treated in Chapter 9.

Medical Examination

The pre-employment medical (or physical) examination plays an important part in the screening process. It serves four major purposes:

1. To reject those whose physical qualifications are insufficient to meet the requirements of the work they are being considered for.
2. To obtain a record of the physical condition at the time of hiring in the event of a workmen's compensation claim for an injury that occurs later.

3. To prevent the employment of those with contagious diseases.
4. To place properly those who are otherwise employable but whose physically handicapped condition requires assignment to specified jobs only.

The first three purposes of the medical examination are generally well understood. The fourth is not. The examination should be used as a positive aid to selective placement and not as a device to eliminate all but the perfect physical specimen. Those with physical handicaps must live and seek to support themselves by gainful employment if at all possible. There is no need for their plight to be intensified by an arbitrary denial of employment opportunities. Fundamentally, physical standards should be geared to job requirements. They must be realistic and justified. The physical demands of all jobs are clearly not the same. Some require great physical stamina, others demand accurate color perception, and still others call for manual dexterity. The job analysis program should identify and record the specific physical demands of the various jobs and job families. Thus it can be determined to what jobs persons with specified physical handicaps may be safely assigned.

Large companies typically employ a staff physician or medical director. He is generally in charge of the entire medical program including the operation of a dispensary or infirmary. Organizationally he is usually a member of the personnel department. Small organizations, not requiring the full-time services of a physician, generally make arrangements with a panel of practicing doctors who will conduct pre-employment medical examinations on an individual fee or an annual retainer basis.

Stone and Kendall have outlined the content of the normal or most common physical examination as follows:[14]

1. The applicant's medical history is obtained. Practice varies. In some companies the applicant is required to complete as much of the medical history blank as he can. In other companies, the medical history is obtained by interview between the applicant and a nurse or medical technician. In some cases the physician prefers to obtain the medical history as a first step in his physical examination, since it provides an opportunity for observing the applicant.
2. Physical measurements such as height, weight, and chest and abdominal circumferences.
3. General examination, including skin musculature, and joints.
4. Examination of special senses of the applicant. Visual and auditory acuity, being most important, should be checked closely.
5. Clinical examination of eyes, ears, nose, throat, and teeth.
6. Examination of the chest and lungs.

[14] Harold C. Stone and W. E. Kendall, *Effective Personnel Selection Procedures* (Englewood Cliffs, N.J.: Prentice-Hall, Inc., 1956), p. 198. Quotation by permission.

7. Check of blood pressure and heart, and where indicated, electrocardiographic examination.
8. Laboratory tests of urine, of the blood, and such other tests as may be indicated.
9. X-ray examinations of chest and other areas indicated.
10. Special tests, if indicated, such as basal metabolic rate or consultation by specialists.
11. Neuro-psychiatric examination when medical history or physician's observation indicates an adjustment problem.

Background Investigation

An investigation into a promising candidate's background is too often overlooked by the employing organization. It requires a little time and money, but the trouble is generally well worth the effort. Previous employers and school officials can often provide valuable insights into the applicant's personality and behavior. Because—as stated previously—the best guide to what a person will do in the future is what he has done in the past, it behooves the careful employment manager to examine this past.

What are the sources for obtaining this background information? There exist four categories of sources. These are (1) school and college officials, (2) previous employers, (3) character references supplied by the applicant, and (4) other sources, such as neighbors of the applicant, the retail credit bureau, police records, and so on.

Category (3)—character references supplied by the applicant—is generally unreliable and can be eliminated for all practical purposes. It is a rare person who will list on his application persons who would supply anything but a most favorable recommendation. In addition, personal friends of the applicant have usually not been in a position where they can actually observe the work habits of the individual. They know him as a "nice guy" not necessarily as a worker in the work environment.

Previous employers are in a position to supply information regarding quantity and quality of work produced, cooperativeness, dependability, initiative, and relations with associates and supervisor. This is a good opportunity to verify the accuracy of information the applicant has given, such as jobs held, wage rate, wage increases, and reason for leaving. Previous employers can be asked if they would be willing to rehire the man and why.

If the person has graduated from high school within the last five to six years, it is advisable to contact the school principal or guidance counselor to obtain information on attendance record, grade point average, rank in graduating class, extracurricular activities, level of aspiration, motivation, emotional adjustment, and other impressions. Similar data can be elicited from college professors and department chairmen.

If the employment manager himself is doing the checking, his most fruitful approach is to do it by telephone or actual personal visit to the source of information. Previous employers and school officials will seldom be as frank and specific if they are called upon to write a formal reference letter. Conversation over the phone or in person permits a much deeper probing than can be obtained by letter.

Because other employers, supervisors, personnel men, and school officials have their biases, just like anyone else, it is very important to evaluate the source of each piece of information. Is a particularly negative appraisal due primarily to a clash of personalities between a former boss and the applicant? How well do the informants know the person?

Responsibilities of Line Management

Line or operating management plays a key role in an employee hiring program. Not only does the line manager or supervisor make the initial decision to add someone to the payroll, but he also conducts the final selection interview, at which point he can either accept or reject the candidate who has been sent to him from the personnel department.

Because personnel departments in industry were originally established many years ago to relieve operating managers of certain personnel responsibilities and to take advantage of specialized competence by means of centralization, the question may reasonably be asked as to why the line manager should be involved in the selection process. Could he not trust the personnel department to do a competent job? The answer is that organizationally the line or operating department manager is being held responsible for the successful and efficient operation of his unit. Accordingly he must be given a say-so in the selection and placement of workers in his department. The caliber of his work force vitally affects the success of his efforts. The personnel department performs very valuable services for line management by recruiting, testing, and interviewing job applicants. Normally it will choose the individual whom it feels is best qualified to fit the particular work situation. He will then be sent to the departmental manager or supervisor for a final selection interview and decision. In most cases the line manager will concur with the choice of the personnel department. However, he should be granted the right of rejection.

There is still another reason for involving the prospective supervisor in this hiring process. Employment is a two-way street. Not only does the company have a right to reject the applicant, but also the candidate has the right to interview his future boss to decide whether he would like to work for that person.

In certain situations it is practical to endow the personnel department with final authority to hire new people. Typical situations are those in which common laborers and unskilled workers are being hired for laboring and routine work or where other types of employees are being hired into a training program or pool, and the department to which these people will ultimately be assigned is unknown at the time of hiring.

Rejecting Applicants

Interviewers, being no different from most other people in this respect, frequently find it awkward to inform an applicant, directly to his face, that he does not measure up to the company's standards—that he is unsuitable. There is thus an urge to let the rejected applicant off lightly with such statements as "Perhaps at another time we will be able to hire you," or, "We will keep your application on file and call you if we need you."

If those responsible for making the employment decision are sure in their own minds that the applicant should not be hired, there is no justification for holding out vague hopes to him. If, indeed, he is a well-qualified individual but there are no openings at present for one of his talents but it is expected that there will be openings in the near future, then it makes sense to so inform him. But if he is definitely not suitable he should not be kept dangling.

The interviewer has the threefold objectives of maintaining the person's ego and self-concept, maintaining goodwill toward the organization, and definitely letting the applicant know that he is rejected. There are a number of ways of communicating to the person the fact that he is being rejected. If the applicant can clearly see that his vocational interests and aptitudes or his wage level needs are totally incompatible with the situation, he may reject himself by gracefully withdrawing. If the individual possesses certain skills and abilities that might be very appropriate in another job situation (other than that which is open in the company), he may be informed that while the pattern of his skills, interests, and abilities is good, they do not match the particular job for which the company is now hiring.

If the person possesses all the required technical abilities but is being rejected because of his personality, this presents a difficult challenge to the interviewer. Since personality traits cannot be measured objectively, there is danger of creating the feeling that he is being rejected capriciously or discriminated against if he is told that his personality is unsuitable. This situation demands real skill on the part of the interviewer so that he can diplomatically convey the impression that the interviewee is being rejected. At times it is best to just imply that the company is going to pick just one or a very few out of a number of good candidates. The competitive situation will cause just the top few to be hired.

AUDITING THE RECRUITMENT AND SELECTION PROGRAM

In order to insure that the employment program is effective—that it accomplishes the results expected—and that it is carried on in the soundest way, it is desirable that a comprehensive periodic audit be made. To insure objectivity, it is advisable to have this audit performed by persons independent (organizationally) of the personnel department. Below is an outline which highlights the areas and questions to be covered in a systematic evaluation.

Audit of the Recruitment and Selection Program

I. Analysis of the Program

    A. Is the recruitment and selection program consistent with sound personnel management theory and practice?

        1. Have well-defined recruitment policies and procedures been developed?

        2. Have well-defined selection policies and procedures been developed?

        3. Are the employment policies consistent with public policy?

        4. Do the wage levels, fringe benefits, and level of employee satisfaction within the organization have a beneficial effect upon the ability to attract and retain good employees?

II. How adequately is the program and its procedures communicated to all those involved in and affected by it?

III. How well is the program implemented?

    1. Have those charged with carrying out the employment program been adequately trained?

    2. Does performance of the program match stated goals?

    3. Are policy and procedure manuals utilized?

IV. Feedback

    1. What image has been created in the minds of school officials, college placement officers, and public and private employment agencies by the actions of the company in conducting its hiring program?

    2. Have recently hired employees and rejected applicants been surveyed to gauge the type of treatment they have received in the selection process?

    3. How many persons have rejected the company as a poor place to work because of low wages, a poor reputation, and so on?

V. Analysis of Results

    A. Recruitment Program

        1. Is there a sufficient pool of applicants available from which to draw? How many persons apply for each job vacancy?

2. Do those who apply possess the necessary skills? Is the recruitment effort selective?

B. Selection Program

1. How well do those hired perform on the job?
2. What percentage of those who apply are hired?
3. Of those hired what percentage are discharged during the probationary period? What percentage resign because the job and employment conditions were misrepresented to them?
4. What portion of employee turnover can be attributed to faulty selection?
5. What contribution does each of the selection tools (that is, tests, interview, medical examination, and so on) make to the program? How well do the predictions from each of the selection tools correlate with job success? Have these selection devices been properly validated?

The questions above can serve as a broad guide to a very thorough and intensive analysis and evaluation of the employment program.

Questions for Review and Discussion

1. What procedure can a commercial bank follow to forecast and plan for its employment needs? Would the procedure be the same for a building construction firm? The army? What factors would affect manpower needs in each organization?
2. What is a labor market? How does it differ from a product market?
3. What factors tend to encourage labor mobility? To inhibit labor mobility?
4. If you were president of your own company, what considerations would guide your judgment on the following employment practices:
   a. Hiring relatives of employees.
   b. Promotion from within as opposed to finding the best man available for a job, regardless of whether he is now a company employee or must be recruited from the outside
   c. Hiring physically handicapped persons
   d. Hiring college students for the summer
5. In what ways may Federal and state fair employment practice laws cause companies to alter their existing employment policies and practices?
6. Do you feel that the use of a lie detector in employment situations, for either selection purposes or for monitoring present personnel, is advisable?
7. What procedure can an organization adopt to implement a promo-

tion-from-within policy to insure that no qualified and interested employee is overlooked?

8. Compare the process by which students are admitted or selected for college with the typical selection procedure for industrial employment. Are the differences that exist fully justified by the circumstances?

9. In what ways may the social and organizational environment affect the performance and adjustment of an otherwise fully qualified new employee?

10. Give examples of employment situations where it would be advisable to alter the selection sequence given on page 236. Justify the changes.

11. Distinguish between a clinical and a statistical evaluation of an application form.

12. Contrast the successive-hurdles approach to making a hiring decision with the multiple-correlation approach.

13. If a previous employer, who has been contacted by telephone as part of a background check on a promising applicant for an engineering position, indicates that the man was too individualistic and had negative attitudes toward the organization, what course of action would you as the employment manager follow?

14. An employment interviewer has decided that the applicant he is talking with is not suitable for hiring. Accordingly he informs the job seeker that he has nothing available at the present time but will keep his application on file and contact him if anything turns up. Evaluate this method of rejecting a job seeker.

15. Explain in some detail how you would go about analyzing and evaluating the effectiveness and efficiency of an employee selection program.

Suggestions for Further Reading

Alfred, T. M., "Checkers or Choice in Manpower Management," *Harvard Business Review,* Vol. 45, January-February 1967, pp. 157 - 169.

Davis, James V., "Trainee Problems That Managers Ignore," *Management of Personnel Quarterly,* Vol. 6, No. 4, Winter 1968, pp. 18 - 22.

Dellman, E. G., "A Behavioral Science Approach to Personnel Selection," *Academy of Management Journal,* Vol. 10, June 1967, pp. 185 - 198.

Dunnette, Marvin, *Personnel Selection and Placement,* Belmont, California: Wadsworth Publishing Company, 1966.

Habbe, Stephen, *Company Experience With Negro Employment,* Studies in Personnel Policy, No. 201, New York: National Industrial Conference Board, 1966.

Hawk, R. H., *The Recruitment Function,* New York: American Management Association, 1967.

Kaumeyer, R. A., "Automated Skills Retrieval," *Personnel,* Vol. 44, January-February 1967, pp. 16-18.

Mandell, Milton M., *The Selection Process: Choosing the Right Man for the Job,* New York: American Management Association, 1964.

Marting, Elizabeth (ed.), *AMA Book of Employment Forms,* New York: American Management Association, 1967.

Mayfield, Harold, "Equal Employment Opportunity: Should Hiring Standards Be Relaxed?," *Personnel,* Vol. 44, No. 5, September-October 1964, pp. 8-17.

Myers, J. G., "Hiring Costs: Some Survey Findings," *Conference Board Record,* Vol. 4, January 1967, pp. 33-42.

Odiorne, George S., and Arthur S. Hann, *Effective College Recruiting,* Ann Arbor: Bureau of Industrial Relations, University of Michigan, 1964.

Uris, Auren, *The Executive Job Market,* New York: McGraw-Hill Book Company, 1965.

Selection Testing and Interviewing

9

The preceding chapter was concerned with recruitment and selection policies and procedures. The two employment techniques upon which greatest reliance is usually placed when making hiring decisions are selection testing and interviewing. The interview is the primary selection tool in nearly all employment programs. Testing programs have, in the past thirty years, achieved ever-increasing significance in employee selection. In order to do full justice to these important hiring methods, this entire chapter is being devoted to the theory and application of testing and interviewing for selection.

SELECTION TESTING

In our society psychological tests are used for a variety of purposes. They are used in public and private schools and colleges for guidance and counseling students, for vocational guidance for adults seeking help in their careers, for assessment and counseling of patients in mental hospitals, for research into human behavior and personality, for choosing students for college admission, and for selection of employees in business and other organizations. We are interested, in our discussion, in the value and usage of tests in the employment process.

Not only are tests used as an aid for selecting new employees for the organization (their most common purpose in industry), but they are also used for differential placement or assignment to the most suitable job after a person has been hired. They are frequently used to select employees for promotion and transfer within the organization, to select candidates for assignment to a company training program, and to act as an aid for diagnosis when counseling individual problem employees.

A test (the term *psychological test* is commonly used because psychologists have done the most work in developing tests, and the field has tended to become their special province) has been defined in a number of ways. A very broad definition is that given by Cronbach, who states that a test is a systematic procedure for comparing the behavior of two or more persons.[1] Blum states that a test is a sample of an aspect of an individual's behavior, performance, or attitude.[2] We may define a *psychological test as a systematic procedure for sampling human behavior*. Usually in employment situations a test is given under standardized and controlled conditions.

Acceptance of Testing

Tests are used quite widely in industry at present. According to the National Industrial Conference Board, nearly all of the giant corporations and more than half of the large companies have testing programs. However, only one out of four companies having 250 employees or fewer use tests. A survey by the Bureau of National Affairs of 170 companies in 1963 showed that practically all large companies of 1,000 or more employees and 80 per cent of smaller companies give pre-employment tests to job seekers.[3] Over 1,000 tests are on the market.[4] The vast majority of tests are distributed and sold by a very few firms that specialize in psychological testing and test development.

In 1960 over 1,800 executives responded to a survey conducted by the Harvard Business Review on the subject of selection testing for management personnel. More than half of the executive respondents reported that their companies use tests for personnel selection. Tabulation of the returns from this study revealed also that a higher percentage of large companies use tests than small ones. For salaried personnel selection 60 per cent of executives in companies employing over 10,000 employees reported that their companies used tests frequently, whereas, only 34 per cent of those respondents in companies under 100 employees used tests frequently. This Harvard study found that the majority of execu-

[1] Lee J. Cronbach, *Essentials of Psychological Testing* (2nd Ed., New York: Harper & Row, 1960), p. 21.

[2] Milton L. Blum, *Industrial Psychology and Its Social Foundations* (Rev. Ed., New York: Harper & Row, 1956), p. 267.

[3] Bureau of National Affairs, Inc., Personnel Policies Forum, *Employee Selection Procedures,* Survey No. 70, Washington D.C., 1963.

[4] Stephen Habbe, "Developments in Psychological Testing," *Management Record,* Vol. 21, No. 4 (April 1959), p. 124.

tives are favorably disposed to taking tests themselves and to testing in general. They felt, however, that it was vital that test results be used with discretion and not be substituted for thoughtful judgment.[5]

In another study of executive attitudes toward employment testing Ware and Kerr surveyed 116 executives (mostly presidents and vice-presidents) in a variety of industries. Two thirds of the respondents considered dexterity, interest, vocational achievement, and personality tests to be definitely valuable. Four fifths of them believed intelligence tests also to be valuable for selection. Of those surveyed 86 per cent felt tests to be beneficial to both the company and the worker. Less than one in ten thought they were solely for the benefit of the employer.[6]

Contributions of Tests to Selection

Most tests are objective. The score received by the person taking the test is not influenced by the opinions of those evaluating the test results. If tests are looked upon as a part of the total selection process (not as a substitute for other devices), they can add significantly to the accuracy of prediction of job success for applicants. In other words the utilization of valid tests can result in the hiring of better qualified employees. This in turn may mean less turnover of newly hired employees, lower training costs, and higher output and quality of work. It may also mean better adjustment to the job and working environment. Insofar as tests aid in the evaluation of people, fewer errors will be made in placement of employees on particular jobs. If a costly and lengthy training course is necessary for certain types of work, more accurate appraisal of candidates through testing would reduce the number of failures in the course.

FUNDAMENTAL GUIDES TO TESTING

Because the field of selection testing is an involved subject, it is important, at the outset, to examine some of the necessary requirements and conditions surrounding their usage.

1. Tests should be used only as a supplement to other selection devices, not as a substitute for them. Even a full battery of tests will provide only a small sample of a person's total pattern of behavior. Therefore, it is necessary to give credence to information derived from other procedures, such as interviews, application form, and background check to obtain a reasonably complete picture of the candidate.
2. Tests are more accurate at predicting failures than success. If we

[5] Lewis B. Ward, "Putting Executives to the Test," *Harvard Business Review,* Vol. 38, No. 4 (July-August 1960), pp. 6-12, 165-179.
[6] F. L. Ware and W. A. Kerr, "Management Attitudes Toward Employment Tests," *Personnel Psychology,* Vol. 10, No. 3 (Autumn 1957), pp. 311-318.

divide the characteristics that make for success on the job into the "can do" factors (skills, knowledge, general abilities) and the "will do" factors (personality and interest), we find that tests in their present stage of development are more accurate at measuring the "can do" characteristics. Therefore, if a man fails tests of capacity and ability, we can reasonably conclude that he is unable to perform the work satisfactorily. However, if he does pass these tests, he may still fail because of poor adjustment to his supervisor and work associates, lack of motivation, lack of interest in his work, family difficulties, and many other factors that are very difficult to predict at the time a person is hired.

3. Tests are most useful in picking a select group of people who are most likely to succeed on the job from among a much larger group. It is difficult for a testing program to reveal with certainty that a particular individual will succeed on the job. But such a program can predict rather well that a particular group, from among a much larger group who took the tests, will succeed on the job. Thus tests can raise the batting average but will make errors on an individual case. By analogy a certain major league baseball player may have been a consistent .300 hitter for many seasons. However, for any particular game he may very well get no hits at all. Indeed he may strike out all four times at bat.

4. A test must be validated in one's own organization to be of any value. It is always necessary to test the test itself before any degree of confidence can be placed in its ability to predict successful performance on the job. This practice is a vital necessity, but it is often not done because of ignorance and the expense involved. A valid test is one that measures what it is supposed to measure. It will, with reasonable accuracy, predict success or failure on the job. The only way to validate a test properly (or a battery of tests) is to conduct a research study within the organization where it is to be used. Just because a certain aptitude test has been useful for picking assembly workers in company A, that is no reason to conclude that it will also be useful in company B. The job requirements and organizational environment in company B may be quite different from those in company A; therefore, different characteristics may be demanded of the workers.

5. Tests can make their greatest contribution in those situations where it has been difficult to obtain satisfactory employees by using other selection methods. Conversely if it has been relatively easy to find good employees by other selection devices, there may be no need to resort to the expense of testing. Thus an employer picking common laborers probably has no need to test them, because there are many in the labor force who can do this work, and it requires few special abilities that cannot be identified by a physical examination and an interview.

Taylor and Russell have constructed statistical tables by means of which an employment manager can determine the amount of improvement that can be obtained from using a test above the level or percentage of satisfactory employees hired without using a test. These tables will tell one the proportion of employees who will be satisfactory among all those hired for a given value of the proportion of present employees considered satisfactory (without using tests), the selection ratio (number hired compared to number tested), and a given value for validity of the test.[7]

6. Those who administer tests in an employment situation and then make decisions whether to hire or reject are cautioned not to consider the numerical score from the test to be a precise or exact measure of the characteristic being tested. If we are measuring the weight of all applicants, we can have confidence in the fact that if the scale shows one man to weigh 180 and another 178, then in fact there is a difference of two pounds between the candidates. But this is not so with test scores. Psychological tests are not so accurate that we can say that one man with a score of 92 is emphatically better qualified than another with a score of 90. Likewise it is possible for an applicant to score a number of points below the passing score on a test and still be a successful employee.

7. If several applicants pass a selection test, those with the very highest test scores are not necessarily a better choice than those scoring lower. This is because the relationship between test score and job success is not always linear. For certain kinds of work it may be necessary to establish a maximum as well as a minimum score. For example, for certain types of routine repetitive work people with too high an intelligence may fail on the job due to lack of interest, boredom, and monotony.

TESTING CONCEPTS

It is pertinent at this point in our discussion of selection testing to examine those significant testing concepts and methods that are essential to a sound understanding of how to use tests in a practical situation.

Reliability

The reliability of a test is the consistency with which it yields the same score throughout a series of measurements. If a test is to be of any value, the person being tested should receive the same score (or nearly the same)

---

[7] H. C. Taylor and J. T. Russell, "The Relationship of Validity Coefficients to the Practical Effectiveness of Tests in Selection: Discussion and Tables," *Journal of Applied Psychology,* Vol. 23 (1939), pp. 565-578.

or his relative standing in the group should show little change if he takes the test on April 15 or on May 12.

A considerable number of factors can cause a test to have low reliability. If the test is not administered under standardized conditions, then the reliability will tend to be low. Thus in a shorthand test for stenographers if the material is not dictated with the same degree of clarity and at the same speed every time, we cannot expect the test to be reliable. In addition people vary from time to time in their emotional state, their degree of attention, attitude, health, fatigue and so on. If a particular test has few test questions and is short, chance factors may determine whether an individual does or does not know a particular fact. Also luck in the selection of answers by guessing may introduce variance into the scores.

There exist four different ways in which the reliability of a test can be determined. More precisely there are four distinct types of test reliability. These are (1) equivalent- (alternate-) form, (2) test-retest, (3) split-half, and (4) odd-even item split.

The equivalent- or alternate-form type of reliability requires the creation of two essentially equivalent forms of the same test. These should be made up by a systematic selection of test items from the same universe or population of possible questions. The scores of a group of people on Form A of the test can then be compared statistically with their scores on Form B.

The test-retest method involves administering the test to a group of persons today and then having them take the same test at a later date. This is generally a good way of measuring reliability. However, the individuals may remember some of their answers from the first time and score slightly higher the second time, especially if it is a speed test.

The split-half form of reliability is found by dividing a test in half and relating scores obtained on the first half to scores on the second half of the same test.

The odd-even item split is simply another way of cutting a test in half. The scores on odd numbered test items and those on the even numbered items are correlated. Both the split-half and the odd-even methods are used to ascertain the internal consistency of a test.

The reliability can readily be determined by the test designer and is commonly reported in the manual that accompanies a test. Reliability is expressed by a coefficient of correlation, which will be explained on page 255. Generally the reliability coefficient should exceed .85.

Validity

The validity of a test is the degree to which it measures what it is intended to measure. Or expressed slightly differently, it shows the extent to which a test does the job for which it is used. In an employment situation a valid test is one that accurately predicts the criterion of job success.

A criterion is a measurement of how satisfactory an employee is on the job or in the total employment situation. Actually there are five distinct kinds of validity:

1. Concurrent validity (present-employee method)
2. Predictive validity (follow-up method)
3. Content validity
4. Construct validity
5. Face validity

Concurrent and predictive validities are of primary importance to the personnel testing practitioner in industry. Content and construct validities are of principal concern only to those psychologists who design tests and do research in this area. Face validity is not a scientific concept but is used sometimes to refer to the way a test appears to the user or test subject.

Concurrent validity refers to the degree to which test scores relate to the performance of employees presently on the payroll. This is often referred to as the present employee method of validating a test. The procedure involves giving the test to a group of present employees who are working on the job for which the selection test is to be used. Then the scores that they receive are correlated with some measure of their performance on the job. Commonly used gauges of job performance are quantity and quality of work, attendance, accident frequency, dollar volume of sales (for sales personnel), and supervisors' ratings. If those who receive high scores on the test are also the best workers, then the test is valid.

Predictive validity (follow-up method) is determined by giving the test in question to all who apply for the job. Since we are testing the test to see whether it is valid, acceptances or rejections are not made on the basis of test scores at this time. Rather the hiring decision is made on the basis of the other selection instruments such as the application form and the interview. After those who have been hired have been on the job for a long enough time to obtain a true measure of their work performance (several months to a year or more) a statistical correlation is computed between the criterion of performance and test scores for the group of people involved. If those who made the highest scores at the time of hiring later turned out to be the most proficient workers and those who made the lowest scores turned out to be the poorest, then the test is valid.

In comparing the concurrent with the predictive method we find that the concurrent approach permits an immediate determination of the usefulness of a test. The predictive technique requires a long wait before one knows whether the test is going to be useful. Hence the concurrent validation is most commonly used in business and industry. However, this present employee method possesses inherent weaknesses. With it we are dealing with a group of very select people, namely, those who have remained on the job for a period of time. They have passed their probationary period, and presumably most of the unsatisfactory employees either have been already discharged or have quit. Few supervisors will endure incompetent workers for an extended period of time. Thus present employees are not a representative sample of future job applicants. If one is trying to validate an aptitude test he will find that the experience that present workers have had in that type of activity will cause them to score higher than untrained applicants. In addition, the validity coefficient obtained by using the narrow range of test scores and performance scores for this select group of people will tend to be lower than if the range of performance were very wide.

Content validity shows how well the content of the test questions relates to the subject matter being measured. It is used primarily for achievement tests. Thus a test of blueprint reading ability should contain commonly used mechanical drawing symbols, drawings, sketches, and terminology. Content validity cannot be expressed in statistical terms. Rather it is judged by experts such as a panel of judges, an instructor, or a textbook author. Examinations in schools and colleges would be evaluated on content validity. The personnel test user in industry finds very little application or need for content validity.

Construct validity is a concept employed by psychologists to explain just what a particular test is measuring. Does the test measure and correlate with the theoretical construct or hypothesis? Thus the concept of anxiety may be hypothesized to be measured by certain test items derived from the meaning and description of anxiety in its technical or scientific sense. Construct validity is most commonly used in clinical psychology, projective-personality techniques, and counseling with personality inventories. It is important in test development and research. Personnel practitioners in industry generally need not be concerned with it.

Face validity simply refers to whether the kind of test questions seem to relate to the job or subject in question. People are more willing to accept tests that seem logically valid. A test for hiring mechanics should, many people feel, contain questions relating to tools, gears, levers, cams, machinery, and so forth. However, face validity cannot be measured statistically. Also a test may appear logically valid on the surface, but a careful validation study may yield a very poor statistical correlation with the criterion.

In summary then, the really important types of validity for personnel management purposes are concurrent and predictive.

Coefficient of Correlation

Correlation is a statistical concept that indicates the degree of closeness of relationship between two series of numbers. In selection testing it is applied to both reliability and to validity. However, it should be noted that a high degree of correlation between one factor and another does not necessarily mean that the first causes the second. All it means is that the first measure relates closely to the second. It may actually be that the first factor causes the second, or it may be that both factors are influenced by some other common factor that has not been determined.

A correlation coefficient can range from zero up to $+1.00$. A zero coefficient indicates absolutely no relationship between the two series of numbers, whereas a coefficient of $+1.00$ indicates a perfect positive relationship. Negative correlation is also possible. Thus a coefficient of -1.00 indicates a perfect inverse relationship between the two measures. For validation work it is impossible to obtain a correlation coefficient of $+1.00$. Commonly the validity coefficient for a single test ranges between .25 and .40. By using a number of tests and entering into a rather involved statistical process called multiple regression analysis, it is possible to develop a combined predictive equation from those several tests that often give a significantly higher validity coefficient.

If the correlation between test scores and job performance scores is .50, this means that the test is measuring or accounting for $(.50)^2 = .25$, or 25 per cent of the variability. Other factors that are often unknown or at least not measurable account for the rest of the variation. Thus tests generally cannot account for future problems that an employee may encounter, such as financial, health, or domestic difficulties, changes in the demands of the job, or unusual and unexpected job pressures.

There are a number of procedures for computing the coefficient of correlation. If there are only a few numbers involved, the rank-difference method can be effectively used. For a large number of individual cases the Pearsonian product-moment method is most appropriate. This technique requires that both test scores and criterion scores be quantitative and continuously distributed.

If it is not possible to obtain continuous data for job performance, as in certain cases where supervisory ratings are employed, then the biserial correlation method may be appropriate. This is true if the data are divided into two groups, such as acceptable and unacceptable performance.[8]

DEVELOPING A TESTING PROGRAM

There are over one thousand tests on the market and literally scores of tests that purport to measure such similar attributes as intelligence or clerical aptitude. For a particular application one test is certainly not as good as another. It requires a great deal of planning, analysis, and exper-

---

[8] Those interested in the techniques of statistical correlation can consult F. E. Croxton and D. J. Cowden, *Applied General Statistics* (2nd. Ed., Englewood Cliffs, N.J.: Prentice-Hall, Inc., 1955); Robert L. Thorndike, *Personnel Selection* (New York: John Wiley & Sons, Inc., 1949).

imenting to develop a useful battery of tests for a particular selection situation.

Because a great deal of technical knowledge is necessary to establish a new testing program, the services of a qualified person are required to guide the effort. Who is qualified to do this work? The individual in charge should be either a fully qualified industrial psychologist or else a personnel management specialist who has taken a number of college level courses in psychology, psychometrics, and statistics. For the administration of the ordinary testing program, the services of a professional psychologist are not required; however, the individual in charge must have had adequate training and experience in the theory and practice of testing and in statistics. If, on the other hand, a company wishes to conduct a full-scale testing program, including projective tests of personality, then only a professionally qualified psychologist who has had intensive graduate training in the psychology of personality can properly interpret such tests.

Steps to Install a Program

The steps that must be carried out to create a new testing program are as follows:

1. Decide objectives of testing program.
2. Analyze jobs to identify those characteristics that appear necessary for job success.
3. Make a tentative choice of tests for a tryout.
4. Administer these tests to an experimental group of people.
5. Establish criteria of job success.
6. Analyze results and make decisions regarding test application.

Decide Program Objective.   A wide range of choices are available as far as testing objectives and policy are concerned. Shall tests be utilized only for hiring new employees, or shall they also be used for picking present employees for upgrading, transfer, and promotion? Shall all the present employees be tested (executives as well) in order to make a comprehensive assessment of present manpower capabilities? If the testing program is to be developed only for the selection of new employees, shall it be for all types of work in the organization or only for certain jobs? Initially should the testing effort be directed only toward improving the accuracy of selection for a particular group of jobs? If this last approach is adopted, it is logical to start with those jobs for which it has been difficult to find satisfactory employees in the past. Let us assume, in the discussion which follows, that a testing program is being set up for certain jobs. From this initial installation, it may be reasonable, then, to expand the program to cover all types of work in the organization.

Analyze Jobs.   Although a great many companies have on file job descriptions and specifications that were prepared for job evaluation and recruitment and selection purposes, it is unlikely that the jobs were analyzed from the standpoint of identifying detailed human characteristics that may be revealed in selection tests. Job analysis of this type must be very specific and detailed. Generalities will not do, because they cover too wide a range of skills and aptitudes. Among the items the analyst will seek to uncover are the need for such things as motor habits, eye-hand coordination, finger and arm dexterity, perceptual and sensory abilities, and specific personality characteristics. One useful frame of reference for making this job analysis is to seek those attributes that differentiate good from poor workers.

Choose Tests for Tryout.   Once the list of attributes deemed essential for success on the job has been uncovered, it is then possible to choose tests to measure these characteristics. Usually the test program designer will choose from among commercially available tests rather than undergo the time an expense of creating his own test to apply to this one job. This latter approach, though necessary at times, is quite costly. Generally the program designer will select an individual test to measure each of the essential job characteristics. Therefore he will, in essence, be constructing a trial test battery. In picking commercially available tests he will give weight to such factors as reliability, content or face validity, proper level of difficulty, ease of administration, and cost.

Administer Tests to an Experimental Group.   It is now necessary to try out these tests by administering them to an experimental group. The best group upon whom to try out the tests consists of, as was discussed previously under the topic of *validity,* applicants for the job under consideration. It is absolutely essential that none of these applicants be rejected on the basis of his test score during this trial period because it is not known as yet whether there is any relationship between test scores and future work performance. We are testing the test at this point. Because this follow-up method of ascertaining test validity is a very lengthy process, many organizations will find it advisable to administer the test battery to those presently on the job as well. There is no reason why concurrent and predictive (follow-up) validity cannot be computed in the same test tryout.

Establish Criteria of Employee Success.   Establishing criteria of success is one of the more difficult parts of the test installation program. It is difficult, not because of a lack of criteria, but because it is extremely hard to find criteria that accurately, fully, and fairly measure job success. Most of the criteria available measure only one small aspect of the job. The one that is all inclusive—supervisor's ratings—is often inaccurate because it is so terribly personal and subjective. Where possible, it is most fruitful to obtain several measures of work behavior and performance and correlate test scores with each of these. The following is a listing of commonly used criteria:

1. Quantity of output

2. Quality of output
3. Grades in training courses
4. Accident frequency
5. Attendance
6. Rate of promotion in the organization
7. Professional achievements, such as patents, published writings, and formal awards
8. Performance ratings made by supervisor

Analysis and Decision Making.   Let us assume, for the present, that we are concerned with only one test and that we are relating scores on this test to a measure of job performance that is continuously distributed, such as units produced or dollar volume of sales. The most useful way of working with this data is to plot a graph of the criterion scores for the ordinate and the test scores for the abscissa. Figure 9-1 represents a hypothetical case of monthly dollar sales for twenty-five salesmen plotted against their test scores at the time of hiring. The product-moment coefficient of cor-

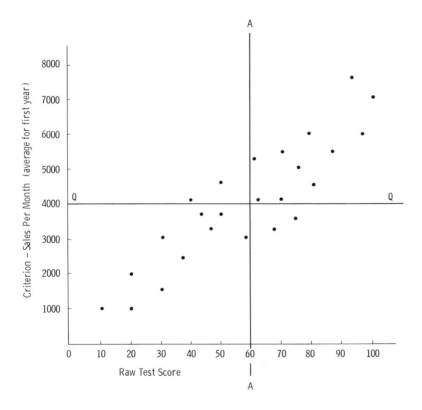

Figure 9-1.   Scatter Diagram of Average Monthly Sales vs. Test Scores.

relation between the criterion and test scores can be computed to find the validity coefficient.

Assuming that we have obtained a representative sample of the population of applicants in this validation study, it appears by inspection that this test will be a useful instrument for selecting salesmen. The dispersion of scores from the trend line is not great. Those who scored high on the test turned out to be good salesmen and vice versa.

The next question is where shall we place the passing or cutting score on the test? Before this can be done intelligently, it is necessary to establish the level of acceptable sales performance. Line Q-Q has been set as $4,000. Now we can evaluate the alternatives related to placing the passing score far to the right (high) against placing it far to the left (low). The *selection ratio* is the number placed on the job or hired divided by the total number tested. If the cutting score (line A-A) is moved to the right, say to 80 or 90, we are almost certain not to have any failures. However, the supply of labor available to a particular organization may not permit it to be so "choosy." If the cutting score, line A-A, is placed at 60, it is clear that some employees who passed the test sold less then $4,000 per month. Likewise some who scored below 60 were successful, because they sold over $4,000, so a few future applicants scoring under 60 would be successful if they were not rejected at that figure. This is the risk inherent in all selection instruments that have a validity coefficient less than 1.00. They will always reject some potential successes and accept some future failures. If the line A-A were to be placed very low, say at 20 or 30, it is evident by inspection of the scatter diagram that a great number of failures would be hired.

The decision of where to place the cutting score is determined by the level of acceptable performance expected, the supply of labor to the organization in relation to its needs for labor, the cost involved in screening many applicants just to hire a few, and the seriousness of hiring a failure (cost of training, and so on). Over a period of time some companies find it necessary to lower their standards if they cannot obtain people of the caliber they desire. We know that during World War II the Army had to relax its standards on physical examinations in order to obtain sufficient manpower.

Combining Several Tests into a Battery.   Because no single test can be expected to measure all of the capacities and abilities necessary to perform a job satisfactorily, personnel specialists often find it advantageous to use a number of tests. A series of tests developed for a particular purpose is called a *battery*.

If, for example, a particular test has a validity coefficient with job performance of .29, it is often possible to utilize additional tests that measure different characteristics and thereby obtain a higher combined validity coefficient. The statistical procedure by which tests can be selected and combined in this fashion is called multiple correlation. Initially it is necessary to have a number of tests for which the validity coefficients are known. Presumably each test measures a different aptitude or ability. Those tests are used that have a high correlation with the criterion and a low correlation with each other. If they had a high correlation with each other, they would be measuring the same characteristic. The multiple correlation technique, which is explained in most standard statistics textbooks, selects the most appropriate tests and develops weighting factors so that a prediction equation is constructed. With this prediction equation it is possible for a particular candidate to overcome a low score on one test with a high score on another and still obtain a passing composite score.

When a battery of tests is used, it is possible, instead of computing a composite score, to simply plot a profile of the scores that an applicant has obtained on the various tests, as shown in Figure 9-2. By means of this approach the profile can be compared with a normal or standard profile typical of successful workers in that occupation in the organization.

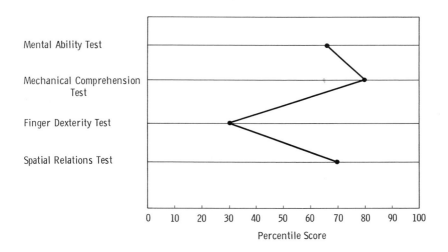

Figure 9-2. A Profile for Expressing Scores on a Number of Tests.

TYPES OF TESTS

Tests can be classified according to the type of human behavior measured as follows:

1. Aptitude
   a. General mental ability or intelligence
   b. Special aptitudes, such as mechanical aptitude, dexterity, manipulative capacity, clerical, sales, vision, and perception.
2. Achievement
3. Vocational interest
4. Situation
5. Personality

Aptitude tests measure the latent or potential ability to do something, provided the individual is given proper training. Achievement tests, which are also called proficiency tests, measure an acquired skill or acquired knowledge. Ordinarily this acquired skill is obtained as a result of a training program and on-the-job experience. With both aptitude and achievement tests, measures of maximum performance are ordinarily obtained, because it is expected that those being tested will exert their utmost while taking the test.

If a company trains most of its employees for the work they have to do and if it hires inexperienced help and develops it within the organization, then aptitude tests are most necessary to measure what new employees will ultimately be able to do. On the other hand if a company, as a matter of employment policy, hires only experienced stenographers and machinists, then achievement tests are most appropriate for measuring the level of skills and abilities they already possess.

In addition to basic capacity to do a given kind of work, the success or failure of people at work is strongly determined by their personalities and how they interact with other people. Personality tests seek to evaluate such characteristics as emotional maturity, sociability, ascendancy, responsibility, conformity, nervous symptoms, and objectivity.

Situational tests are really combination tests representing elements of achievement or performance and elements of personality. Because they are quite different from standard objective, pencil and paper, tests they are properly classified as a distinct type of test.

General Mental-Ability Tests

Psychological testing really began with mental-ability (also called intelligence) testing around 1900. More work has been done in creating, developing, experimenting, and refining general mental-ability tests than any other major type of test. The original work on mental-ability testing was done by Alfred Binet, a French physician, who created a test to classify school children according to their ability to learn and succeed at schoolwork.

Just what is meant by the term *intelligence?* Although a variety of sometimes conflicting definitions have been proposed, and thus there is no general agreement as to a precise definition, Thurstone has isolated the specific types of mental abilities that most of these tests measure. These are verbal comprehension, word fluency, memory, inductive reasoning, number facility, speed of perception, and spatial visualization.[9]

In reporting on the work of a great many investigators, Tiffin and Mc-Cormick state that significant positive correlations have been found between scores on general mental-ability tests and job success in a variety of clerical occupations, supervisory occupations, machine skills, utility plant work, and teletype work.[10]

Some of the more widely used tests for employee selection are the Otis Employment Tests,[11] Wesman Personnel Classification Tests,[12] Wonderlic Personnel Test,[13] and Adaptability Test.[14] Many of these brands of tests actually consist of two or more tests designed for people of different educational attainments. Also some tests, such as the Wonderlic have several forms that are intended to be equivalent to one another in difficulty level. This is to minimize the likelihood of a person obtaining a higher score than he normally would simply because he had recently taken the exact same test elsewhere.

Special Aptitude Tests

A great number and variety of tests have been created to measure capacity to learn a particular kind of work.

Mechanical aptitude tests, for example, measure the capacities of spatial visualization, perceptual speed, and knowledge of mechanical matter. They do not measure manual dexterity and manipulative skill. Mechanical aptitude tests have been found useful for selecting apprentices and other employees for the skilled mechanical trades as well as for certain technician jobs. Typical occupations for which such tests have proved useful are machinists, mechanics, maintenance workers, and mechanical technicians. Some widely used tests of this general type are the Bennett Test of Mechanical Comprehension, Revised Minnesota Paper Form Board Test,[15] Purdue Mechanical Adaptability Test,[16] and the Science Research Associates Mechanical Aptitudes Test. Figure 9-3 contains two sample items from Form BB of the Test of Mechanical Comprehension by Bennett and Fry.

[9] L. L. Thurstone, *Primary Mental Abilities,* The Psychometric Laboratory, the University of Chicago, No. 50 (September 1948).

[10] Joseph Tiffin and Ernest J. McCormick, *Industrial Psychology* (4th Ed., Englewood Cliffs, N.J.: Prentice-Hall, Inc., 1958), pp. 116-122.

[11] Published by the World Book Company, also distributed by the Psychological Corporation.

[12] Published by the Psychological Corporation.

[13] Published by E. F. Wonderlic, also distributed by the Psychological Corporation.

[14] Published by Science Research Associates.

[15] Both the Bennett Test of Mechanical Comprehension and the Revised Minnesota Paper Form Board Test are published by the Psychological Corporation.

[16] Published by Occupational Research Center, Purdue University.

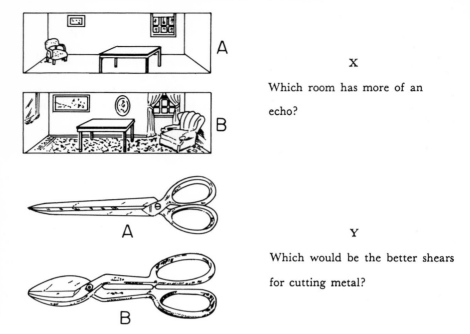

X

Which room has more of an echo?

Y

Which would be the better shears for cutting metal?

Figure 9-3. Two Sample Questions from the Test for Mechanical Comprehension, Form BB, by George K. Bennett and D. E. Fry. Reproduced by permission. Copyright 1941 by the Psychological Corporation, New York, N.Y., renewed 1969. All rights reserved.

Psychomotor tests are those that measure such abilities as manual dexterity, motor ability, and eye-hand coordination. Tests of this type are primarily important for selecting workers to do semiskilled, repetitive operations, such as bench assembly work, packing, certain testing and inspection, watch assembly, and the like. Research has shown that rapid manipulative skill is relatively unimportant for the skilled mechanical and electrical trades. Understanding of the techniques and processes involved is more important for these occupations than is manual dexterity. Commonly used psychomotor tests are the Purdue Pegboard,[17] Minnesota Rate of Manipulation Test,[18] Mac Quarrie Test for Mechanical Ability,[19] and the O'Connor Finger Dexterity Test.[20]

Clerical aptitude tests have been created to measure specific capacities involved in office work. These typically have test items on spelling, computation, comparisons, copying, word meaning, and the like. Three examples of clerical tests are the SRA Clerical Aptitudes, the Minneso-

[17] This test and the SRA Clerical Aptitudes Tests listed below are published by Science Research Associates.
[18] Published by Educational Test Bureau.
[19] Published by the California Test Bureau.
[20] Published by Stevens Institute of Technology and C. H. Stoelting Company.

DIRECTIONS

In this test you are to find the CREDIT RATING for each of a list of names. The CREDIT RATING is a letter which shows how large the AVERAGE BALANCE is. Look at the column headed CREDIT RATING further down the page. Look at the name numbered 1. It is "Barnes, M. V." Now look for the same name in the alphabetical list at the left headed AVERAGE BALANCE. This name has an AVERAGE BALANCE of $5004.18. To find the code letter for this balance, look in the box just below the words CREDIT RATING. If the balance is $999.99 or less, the code letter is R; from $1000.00 to $1999.99, the code is S; for $2000.00 or more, the code is T. Since "Barnes, M. V." has an AVERAGE BALANCE of more than $2000.00, the code letter T has been written in the space after the name "Barnes, M.V." in the CREDIT RATING column. Now take the second name, "Bosworthy, A. G." and look for it in the AVERAGE BALANCE list. There is no "Bosworthy, A. G." although there is a "Bosworthy, A. P." Since "A. G. Bosworthy" cannot be found, an O has been written after the name.

CREDIT RATING

Balance	Code
$ 999.99 or less	R
1,000.00 to 1,999.99	S
2,000.00 or more	T
Name Missing	O

AVERAGE BALANCE

Adams, D.B.	$2375.81	Carey, R.E.	$6144.14	
Adamson, B.D.	1942.89	Clark, C.U.	318.89	
Allen, J.F.	267.45	Clark, C.V.	1731.43	
Anderson, H.G.	1712.50	Cooper, B.L.	1135.58	
Andrews, G.L.	2130.26	Corbin, G.P.	395.23	
Armstrong, C.P.	1543.37	Corwin, G.P.	1074.77	
Atwell, C.R.	724.16	Cosgrove, J.J.	2597.16	
Barnes, M.V.	5004.18	Coughlin, M.H.	1374.04	
Baxter, A.N.	384.62	Cowan, F.L.	3418.21	
Bloomfield, H.T.	637.42	Crane, N.D.	954.16	
Bosworthy, A.P.	1822.77	Dale, A.M.	8914.67	
Botts, K.L.	187.16	Daly, L.E.	2354.36	
Bronson, D.H.	4768.33	Daniels, R.T.	1317.85	
Brown, J.R.	967.26	Dearborn, F.F.	895.22	
Browne, J.R.	1542.87	Decker, M.H.	527.59	

TAKE NAMES IN ORDER.
BEGIN HERE.

1. Barnes, M.V.   _T_
2. Bosworthy, A.G.   _O_
3. Clark, C.V.   _____
4. Botts, K.L.   _____
5. Andrews, L.G.   _____
6. Daly, L.E.   _____
7. Cosgrove, J.J.   _____
8. Allen, J.F.   _____
9. Decken, M.H.   _____
10. Cooper, B.L.   _____
11. Baxter, A.N.   _____
12. Dale, A.M.   _____

Figure 9-4. Sample Question from Test CA-2 of the Short Employment Tests Used to Measure Clerical Aptitude. Copyright 1951 by the Psychological Corporation; New York, N.Y. All rights reserved. Reprinted by permission.

ta Clerical Test, and the Short Employment Tests (SET).[21] Figure 9-4 shows sample items from the CA-2 portion of the Short Employment Tests. This subtest is designed to measure the quantity of numerical and clerical production in fixed periods of time.

Achievement Tests

If a company wishes to hire experienced employees who should already possess the requisite skills and knowledge, it would do well to investigate

[21] The Minnesota Clerical Test and the Short Employment Tests (SET) are both published by the Psychological Corporation.

the value of specific achievement or proficiency tests to evaluate these candidates. Achievement tests can be classified into two categories. One measures job knowledge and may be either of the oral or the written type. The other category is a *work sample,* in which a typical portion of the actual job is administered as a test. Thus a stenograher may have to listen to a recording, take down the words in shorthand, transcribe these, and type them.

Quite logically many companies have developed their own achievement tests to select people for specific jobs. Because the work carried on in many organizations is peculiar to these businesses only, it is understandable that these tests are not distributed commercially. Many work sample tests have content validity only. Personnel specialists and operating supervisors have taken portions of real jobs and asked job candidates to do the work. If a man claims to have had experience as a truck driver or a milling-machine operator, there is probably no better way to find out if he can do the work than to try him out on it.

Vocational Interest Tests

Vocational interest tests are inventories of the likes and dislikes of people in relation to occupations, hobbies, and recreational activities. The basic assumption behind these tests is that there exists a definite pattern of interests for those who are successful in an occupation and that if one likes the same kind of things that practitioners in an occupation like, then the person being examined will like that kind of work.

One of the most widely used interest tests is the Strong Vocational Interest Blank, which was first published in 1927.[22] It contains 400 questions of the "like-indifferent-dislike" variety. The blank for men is scored for 47 occupations while the one for women is scored for 27 occupations. Strong developed the scoring system for his test by administering it to successful members of each of the various occupations. If an examinee answers the 400 items in a pattern similar to the way in which successful personnel managers have answered it, he is given a high score opposite personnel manager on the report form.

The Kuder Preference Record is another commonly used interest test.[23] It scores for ten broad interest areas or clusters. These are outdoor, mechanical, computational, scientific, persuasive, artistic, literary, musical, social service, and clerical. Profiles for a considerable number of occupations have been developed empirically in terms of these ten interest areas.

Because it is possible for a job-seeking person definitely to fake or slant his answers in a certain direction in order to be hired, interest tests are much more useful for individual vocational guidance than they are for employee selection.

[22] Published by The Stanford University Press.
[23] Published by Science Research Associates.

Situational Tests

A situational test evaluates individuals in a real life-like situation by asking them to cope with or solve critical elements of a real job. An illustration of this type of test is the group oral performance test. In this test a group of candidates for a job (usually of a supervisory or executive type) are placed in a room, given a practical problem to discuss and solve, and observed by others. The observers note how they interact with one another. Who had the most useful ideas? Who emerged as a leader? Who conciliated opposing views? Who was most convincing in oral expression? These and many other qualities are noted by the observers. The group oral performance test makes it possible to evaluate effectiveness and skill in interpersonal relations.

Another type of situational test is the "in-basket" test. This simulates key aspects of the job of an administrator. It consists of realistic letters, telephone messages, memoranda, and reports which have supposedly collected in the "in-basket" on the desk of a manager. Each person taking this test is provided with adequate background information about the particular organization and its line of business. He is told that he is a new incumbent in his position and must take action on the various items in his in-basket. He must actually write letters and memos and prepare brief reports; he must not simply say what he would do in these matters. Thus the in-basket exercise is a realistic sample of a manager's job. Scoring of the subjects' performance is carried out by a group of raters who consider both content and style of responses and who grade the responses on a rating sheet. The in-basket technique has been extensively employed by the American Telephone and Telegraph Company and General Electric for picking managers, especially by promotion from within.[24]

Personality Tests

There are two types of personality tests:

1. Objective, pencil and paper, tests (personality inventories)
2. Projective tests

Because they are suitable for group testing and can be scored objectively, most personality tests are of the objective type. One well-known personality test is the Bernreuter Personality Inventory, which measures neurotic tendency, self-sufficiency, introversion-extroversion, dominance-submission, self-confidence, and sociability. Some other tests are the

[24] Further information on the in-basket test is contained in Norman Frederiksen, "Factors in In-Basket Performance," *Psychological Monographs: General and Applied,* Vol. 76 (1962), pp. 1 - 6; and Felix M. Lopex, Jr., *Evaluating Executive Decision Making: The In-Basket Technique,* American Management Association, Research Study No. 75 (1966).

Humm-Wadsworth Temperament Scale, the Guilford-Martin Personnel Inventory, and the Minnesota Multiphasic Personality Inventory.

Personality tests of this type have the disadvantages of interest inventories. They can be faked by sophisticated candidates. There is a strong motivation always to give socially acceptable answers. In addition, self-report devices such as these reveal how a person thinks he would behave in a certain situation. This does not necessarily mean he would actually act that way in a real-life problem. In other words many persons do not really know themselves. Cronbach reports that personality inventories have had rather limited success in predicting employee performance on the job.[25] They are more useful for individual counseling.

A projective personality test is one in which the subject is asked to project his own interpretation into certain standard stimulus situations. The meaning which the individual attaches to the stimulus depends upon his own values, motives, and personality. Theoretically the number of responses which various people can give to a single stimulus is infinite. Two well-known projective tests are the Rorschach and the Thematic Apperception Test.

The Rorschach test, developed in 1921 by Hermann Rorschach, consists of ten cards, each containing a different ink blot. These ink blots are of various colors. The person is asked to explain what he sees in each blot. His explanations provide clues to his personality. A full evaluation can be made only when the analyst knows about the subject's family background, education, past experiences, and has evaluations obtained from others who know the individual.

The Thematic Apperception Test, developed in 1938, consists of a series of twenty pictures, there being a different set for men and women. The person tested must interpret each picture by telling a story about it in terms of what he believes is happening and what will be the outcome.

All projective tests must be administered individually. Interpretation of the results is a job only for a qualified clinical psychologist or a psychiatrist. The interpretation is highly subjective and unstandardized. In a sense it is impressionistic. Quantiative scores are not developed.

Personality Testing in Perspective. If one were to ask a representative sample of personnel managers the most common reason for employee failure on the job, they would undoubtedly say that temperament, personality, and adjustment to the job environment, not ability, are the main causes. Yet the measuring instruments now available—objective and projective tests—are not sufficiently advanced in their stage of development to obtain really accurate predictions of employee performance. In reviewing a number of validation studies in connection with employee selection in the British Civil Service, the Veterans Administration, the Air Force, and others, Cronbach concluded that evaluations made by those having psychological training were not necessarily superior to

[25] Lee J. Cronbach, *Essentials of Psychological Testing* (2nd Ed., New York: Harper & Row, 1960), p. 485.

those obtained from peer ratings, that structured, group-performance, work-sample tests have good validity for jobs requiring group acceptance, and that the evaluators must have a clear knowledge of the psychological requirements of the tasks involved. In general Cronbach was critical of the value of impressionistic interpretations derived in much personality testing.[26]

Two psychologists, Guion and Gottier, have made a comprehensive analysis of published validation studies of both personality inventories and projective tests used for employee selection. The record is disappointing. Guion and Gottier state that it cannot be said that any of the conventional personality measures have demonstrated really general usefulness as selection tools in employment practice. In the conclusion of their study they assert:

> In brief, it is difficult in the face of this summary to advocate, with a clear conscience, the use of personality measures in most situations as a basis for making employment decisions about people.[27]

Richard S. Barrett, another esteemed psychologist, has stated that a dismal history has been recorded by personality tests. The typical personality questionnaire, test, or inventory has not proved to be useful. Of the Rorschach inkblot test Dr. Barrett states that it has been studied very thoroughly but that it has accumulated a long record of failure as a selection device.[28]

A very scathing denunciation of personality testing has been made by William H. Whyte, Jr., in his book *The Organization Man*.[29] His criticisms are made in connection with the use of these tests for selecting and promoting executives in industry. Whyte claims that personality tests are being used to select only those who are conformists and hence "good" organization men. The testing process is not scientific, because the value judgments of the test designers determine the interpretations of an individual's personality to a large extent. Especially in interpreting a projective test, he claims that the analysis of a person is often more revealing of the personality of the psychologist than it is of the subject. Who can say that the values and standards of the test makers and interpreters are right? Whyte further claims that the process by which personality tests are validated within an organization is erroneous and unscientific. It involves circular reasoning. In order to be hired the candidate must match the average profile of present company executives in terms of a pattern of traits. But how could different types of individuals ever be hired so

[26] *Ibid.,* pp. 589-590.

[27] Robert M. Guion and Richard F. Gottier, "Validity of Personality Measures in Personnel Selection," *Personnel Psychology,* Vol. 18, No. 2 (Summer 1965), pp. 135-164, The authors investigated 95 different validation studies on 15 leading personality inventories, 11 validation studies on 6 projective tests, and 11 validation studies on 3 special inventories.

[28] Richard S. Barrett, "Guide to Using Psychological Tests," *Harvard Business Review,* Vol. 41, No. 5 (September-October 1963) pp. 138-146.

[29] William H. Whyte, Jr., *The Organization Man* (New York: Simon & Schuster, 1956), Ch. 15.

that they themselves are included in a criterion group for a validation study if they had the wrong pattern of traits in the first place?

A number of thoughtful writers have pointed out that personality testing probes very deep into the individual's inner self, into his own private world. It is of utmost importance that the personnel specialists and psychologists not divulge this information to other organizations and persons in such a way as to injure the individual and damage his career. Gellerman has warned that the most potent danger to the privacy of the person is the fact that his test data is preserved but it is not under his control. He advocates that the highest ethical and professional standards be followed in handling test results.[30]

TESTING AND EQUAL EMPLOYMENT OPPORTUNITY

The personnel profession was rocked (at least temporarily) in 1963 by the famous Myart vs. Motorola case. The Motorola Company had rejected a Negro job applicant who had failed a preemployment ability test. Mr. Myart took his case to the Illinois Fair Employment Practices Commission charging discrimination. A hearing examiner for the Commission ordered the company to cease using that particular test on the grounds that it discriminated against culturally deprived groups. The full Commission decided in favor of the aggrieved person but did not rule directly on the question of possible racial or ethnic bias on the part of tests. It did say however that tests may be inherently discriminatory against persons who are alien to the predominant middle-class white culture. Although the ruling of the Commission was eventually overturned by the Illinois State Supreme Court, personnel specialists were seriously concerned lest fair employment practice commissions elsewhere might begin to outlaw selection testing programs because of possible racial or ethnic discrimination.

Title VII, Equal Employment Opportunity, of the Civil Rights Act of 1964 does provide that an employer may give and act upon the results of any professionally developed ability test provided that such test is not designed, intended or used to discriminate because of race, color, religion, sex, or national origin.[31] In order to provide guidance to employers the Equal Employment Opportunity Commission convened a panel of psychological consultants who issued a report that served as a basis for testing guidelines issued by the Commission in 1966. The Commission advocates a total personnel assessment system that includes (1) job analysis to define skill requirements, (2) special efforts to recruit minorities, (3) screening and interviewing related to job requirements, (4) tests selected on the basis of specific job related criteria, (5) comparison of test performance with job performance, (6) retesting of rejected job can-

---

[30] Saul W. Gellerman, "The Ethics of Personality Testing," *Personnel,* Vol. 35, No. 3 (November-December 1958), pp. 30-35.

[31] Selection 703 of the Act.

didates to ensure maximum opportunity to qualify for jobs, and (7) inclusion of representative numbers of minority groups in the sample of people used for test validation studies.

Although psychologists have made some efforts to create culture-free tests, the problem is very complex and progress is slow. Employers should endeavor to conduct special validation studies on the particular minority group they may be concerned with in the community, for example, Negroes, Puerto-Ricans, Mexican-Americans. The key question is how they perform on the job; not how they score on a test having a cutting score based upon a white middle class American criterion group.[32]

SELECTION TESTING—A FINAL COMMENT

It was pointed out very early in our discussion of testing that tests can be a valuable aid in improving the accuracy of personnel assessment. It was further explained that tests, before they are finally adopted for making employment decisions, must be validated in one's own organization. Selection tests are very appealing to managers who want to get the facts and make a definite assessment of people. In their eagerness some executives abandon their realism and sense to depend exclusively upon this crutch.

Ross Stagner has described an experiment in which a group of personnel managers themselves answered the questions on a published personality inventory. To determine whether they were gullible, all participants were given identical fake reports which contained statements taken from dream books and astrology charts. The person's name was written in red pencil at the top of each sheet. Thus each personnel manager thought he was receiving his own personality score card. One half of the group of 68 managers considered their descriptions to be amazingly accurate, whereas an additional 40 per cent felt them to be rather good![33] The point being made is that selection testing is a powerful tool. But it must be used only by those who have an adequate background in psychological theory and in personnel selection work.

THE SELECTION INTERVIEW

The interview is the most universally used selection method. Although many employers do not use tests to aid in reaching an employment de-

---

[32] Further information on testing and possible job discrimination can be found in John H. Kirkwood, "Selection Techniques and the Law: To Test or Not to Test?," *Personnel,* Vol. 44, No. 6 (November-December 1967), pp. 18-26; Gerald A. McLain, "Personnel Testing and the EEOC," *Personnel Journal,* Vol. 46, No. 7 (July-August 1967), pp. 448-452; and Robert M. Guion, "Employment Tests and Discriminatory Hiring," *Industrial Relations,* Vol. 5, No. 2 (February 1966), pp. 20-37.

[33] Ross Stagner, "The Gullibility of Personnel Managers," *Personnel Psychology,* Vol. 11, No. 3 (Autumn 1958), pp. 347-352.

cision, there are hardly any who do not interview the applicant in order to help make a definite assessment. In fact, multiple interviews are commonly employed. In the proposed selection procedure outlined in Chapter 8, provision is made for three: the preliminary, the main employment office interview, and the final decision-making interview by the prospective supervisor. For high-level positions in many organizations, several operating executives interview the candidate and compare impressions before a definite decision is made.

The interviewer is in the unique position of being able to integrate all of the information and impressions obtained about the applicant from all sources: application form, preliminary interviews, test scores, and background checks. The interviewer can assess the applicant on such attributes as personal appearance, mannerisms, emotional stability, maturity, attitudes, motivation, and interests. He can gauge how well the candidate will adjust to the social situation in the organization. The interview permits deep probing into the person's home and family background, education, previous work experience, avocations, and other pertinent areas.

Interview Defined.   An interview is a conversation or verbal interaction, normally between two people, for a particular purpose. The intention is to explore certain subject areas. Extraneous topics are ordinarily minimized. There are a great many types of interviews that occur in an organization, such as appraisal interview between supervisor and subordinate, a salesman dealing with a purchasing agent, a counseling interview, a grievance interview, a data-gathering interview in connection with a research project, and a job analysis interview. The basic principles of interviewing apply alike to all of these; however, the specific techniques employed will differ.

Objectives of the Selection Interview.   The goals of a selection interview can be grouped into three broad categories. First, the interviewer seeks to obtain enough knowledge about the candidate to determine whether he is suitable for employment in the organization and for the particular job under consideration. Many will believe that this is the only purpose of an employment interview. But this is not so. Employment is a two-way proposition. Not only is the employer choosing an employee, but also the job seeker is choosing an employer. He may reject many as being unsuitable for his needs. Therefore, the interview has as a second purpose the giving of sufficient information about the organization, the job, and the people such that the applicant is able to make an intelligent decision on acceptance or rejection of the job if it should be offered to him. The third goal of an interviewing situation is to deal with the candidate in such a manner as to maintain and create good will toward the company and its management.

Limitations of the Interview.   The author once met an industrial executive who claimed he could determine five minutes after a job seeker entered the office door whether he was suitable for hiring. Nonsense! Anyone planning to engage in employment interviewing must understand the inherent weaknesses of this technique. Fundamentally, the major defect of the interview is its subjectivity. The decisions made by the interviewer are based upon his opinion, and that opinion is subject to bias and prejudice. Two interviewers may interview the same candidate and come up with different evaluations.

The applicant, trying to create a favorable impression of himself in the eyes of the interviewer, may behave in an unnatural fashion. The behavior and responses of the applicant are considerably affected by the interviewer's own personality. Interviews are not standardized, and it is difficult to quantify the results.

Many attributes cannot be measured by an interview. Intelligence, motor abilities, manual skills, creativity, strength, health, and many other factors can be measured more appropriately by other devices.

However, numerous research studies have shown that when combined with other selection techniques, interviews that are conducted by properly trained personnel under the proper conditions do have a very positive and significant predictive value.

Some Research Findings.   In a comprehensive review of published research on the employment interview, starting with Walter D. Scott's pioneering investigations in 1915 through to the work of recent researchers, Eugene C. Mayfield has uncovered a number of important findings: (1) Interviewers are quite consistent in the way they rate the same interviewee. When re-interviewing the same person or listening to a tape recording of the original interview at a later date, they make about the same ratings as originally; (2) If different interviewers conduct an unstructured interview and have no prior information on the condidates, they generally come up with quite different ratings of the same interviewees. In other words, the interrater reliability is low; (3) Structured interviews, for instance, the patterned interview, yield fairly consistent ratings of the same persons by different interviewers. The interrater reliability tends to be high. However, if the interviewers used quite different structured forms, then their ratings of the same candidates differed substantially; (4) Many investigators report rather low validity (predictions of job success) with the interview. However, very encouraging results are obtained when a team approach is used. The team method can be applied through the "board" technique where three or four interviewers sit as a panel to interview applicants. The team method can also be used when applicants are interviewed separately by a number of persons who then compare judgments to arrive at a final group decision; (5) The attitudes and biases of interviewers heavily influence their ratings; (6) Interviewers tend to be influenced in their judgments more by unfavorable than by favorable information. They tend to search for negative data. Experiments have shown that it is easier to induce shifts in ratings toward rejection than toward acceptance; (7) Interviewers tend to arrive at their decisions to accept or reject fairly early in the course of an unstructured interview.[34]

Edwin E. Ghiselli, a psychologist, has reported on personal involvement in a situation where a moderate interviewer validity (coefficient of correlation of .35) was obtained for a group of 275 men hired as stock brokers over a seventeen year period. The interviewer had no prior information about the applicants. Each interview lasted about an hour.[35]

PSYCHOLOGICAL FOUNDATIONS FOR INTERVIEWS

A working knowledge of the psychological basis for interviewing is desirable for those who engage in this activity.[36]

Motivation of Interviewee

The desire of the interviewee to explain himself fully and to reveal freely his experiences, goals, and attitudes is strongly influenced by the personality and behavior of the interviewer. The applicant is most likely to speak freely and honestly if he perceives that the interviewer understands him and accepts what he has to say. The interviewer must be empathic. He must understand the applicant's point of view and refrain from criticizing, directly or by implication, what he has said. The job seeker is most likely to be motivated to communicate freely and fully when he receives satisfaction from the interviewing process and when the personal relationship between himself and the interviewer is healthy and need satisfying.

It is important to recognize that people are often unaware of the reasons for their own actions and attitudes. If called upon to explain why they behaved in a certain way, they may honestly not know their own motives.

Human beings exhibit both rational and nonrational or emotional behavior. An engineer may pride himself on being coldly objective and analytical in his work at the office, yet he may be guided almost entirely by his feelings and emotions in choosing a political party, buying a new suit, or choosing his friends. There is a great tendency for people to "think

[34] Eugene C. Mayfield, "The Selection Interview: A Re-evaluation of Published Research," *Personnel Psychology,* Vol. 17 (1964), pp. 239-260.

[35] Edwin E. Ghiselli, "The Validity of the Personnel Interview," *Personnel Psychology,* Vol. 19, No. 4 (Winter 1966), pp. 389-394. Other research studies on the employment interview are contained in W. V. Bingham, B. V. Moore, and J. W. Gustad, *How to Interview* (4th Ed., New York: Harper & Row, 1959), Ch. 1; Newell C. Kephart, *The Employment Interview in Industry* (New York: McGraw-Hill Company, Inc., 1952); Robert N. McMurry, "Validating the Patterned Interview," *Personnel,* Vol. 23, No. 4 (January 1947), pp. 263-272.

[36] Certain of the ideas presented here are derived from Robert L. Kahn, and Charles F. Cannell, *The Dynamics of Interviewing* (New York: John Wiley & Sons, Inc., 1957).

with their hearts" and not their minds. In an interviewing situation the interviewer should be perceptive when he seems to receive a very emotional response to such questions as "How did you get along with your boss?" or, "Tell me about your childhood."

Barriers to Communication

If the person being interviewed feels there is a basic clash between his values and goals and those of the interviewer, he will tend to be inhibited. If he feels that the interviewer is not "with him," that he will reject, as being socially unacceptable, certain of his statements, then he will present only that information which will reveal himself favorably. Should the candidate feel that his statements and opinions might at any time be used in a way as to harm him, then he will also be reluctant to speak freely. A vast gulf between the interviewer and the applicant in social status, language, and education can cause a breakdown in communication if the interviewer gives evidence of being snobbish, aloof, or indifferent toward the candidate.

Interviewer Bias

Countless research experiments have demonstrated that the opinions and biases of the interviewer have a powerful influence upon the decisions reached. An early and classic experiment in this field was conducted in 1914, when the New York Commissioner of Public Charities organized a study of the physical, mental, and social characteristics of 2,000 destitute men. Twelve men did the interviewing. One of the areas under investigation was the cause of the men's poverty. One of the interviewers, who happened to be a prohibitionist, attributed the men's destitution primarily to the excessive use of liquor, whereas another interviewer, who was a socialist, reported that their difficulty was due mainly to depressed economic conditions and factory layoffs. A more recent study by Ferber and Wales, in connection with the public's attitude toward prefabricated housing, showed that the responses were definitely influenced by the interviewer's own bias toward such housing.[37]

In view of the foregoing, it is vital that each interviewer be made aware of the effects of bias upon evaluations. Each interviewer must seek to know fully himself and his own prejudices so that he can discount these biases when appraising people in the interview.

Past Is Clue to Future

The most accurate guide to how a person will perform in the future can be obtained by reviewing what he has done in the past. Most people's

[37] Robert Ferber and Hugh Wales, "Detection and Correction of Interview Bias," *Public Opinion Quarterly*, Vol. 16 (1952), p. 107-127.

fundamental personalities, attitudes, and ways of behaving are developed early in life. In analyzing a person's background, it is necessary to explore his childhood environment, school and college experiences, previous job experience, social life and recreations, present family life, health, and financial picture. It is unsound for the interviewer to draw categorical and dogmatic conclusions from a single incident. If the applicant failed on one job, it does not necessarily follow that he will fail on all future jobs. If his grades in high school were only mediocre, it does not prove that the person has only a mediocre mentality. It is the whole pattern that counts. The interviewer must make tentative inferences from certain disclosures and then look for evidence in other facets of the person's life to substantiate the impression. If the inference cannot be verified by other facts, then it should be rejected.

KNOWLEDGE AND SKILLS OF THE INTERVIEWER

The mere fact that a man has served in a supervisory or executive position in business for many years does not mean that he automatically possesses the skills and knowledge demanded of a successful interviewer. Competence as an interviewer comes from systematic, sound training and actual experience in conducting interviews. Let us now examine the skills, knowledge, and abilities which an interviewer must possess.

He must have a thorough understanding of the organization, relationships among departments and jobs, objectives of organizational units, job content, and worker requirements. An interviewer must have available comprehensive job descriptions and job specifications for the jobs he seeks to fill. He should have a good understanding of the company's employment policies and procedures.

Since an interviewer must render critically important judgments on human beings, he should possess a background, derived from formal course work, in personnel psychology. He must have a working knowledge of such topics as individual differences, personality dynamics, motivation, frustration, attitudes, abilities, aptitudes, and human traits.

Objectivity in sizing up people is a desirable quality. The interviewer must walk a thin line here. In order to elicit unrestrained response from the interviewee, he must have an appreciative understanding of the other person's point of view. In short, as stated previously, he must have empathy. Yet he must be sufficiently detached so that he is not carried away by the candidate's emotions and problems.

A major fault of the novice interviewer is the tendency to do too much talking. In his enthusiasm about the organization and himself, the novice is likely to recount his personal experiences and events in the company to such an extent that there is inadequate time to obtain enough information about the candidate. In fact some interviewers are subtly flattered when they have such a captive audience, and they make a favorable evaluation of the job seeker who listens to their stories in a willing and interested fashion.

The interviewer must be perceptive and sensitive to the way his behavior affects others. He must be alert to detect any nuances of voice, expression, emotion, hesitation, and the like. He must note whether certain things cause the respondent to alter his manner or expression during the course of the interview.

Interviewing is an art applied in an organized fashion. A training course for interviewers should contain initial lectures and readings to develop the necessary background in the learners. This can profitably be followed by observation of actual employment interviews conducted by a skilled interviewer. If a group of persons is being taught the theory and practice of interviewing, then actual role-playing sessions have much to offer. They provide for learning by doing. Some of the trainees may take the parts of job applicants, whereas others may play the role of company interviewers. Mistakes may be noted by the instructor and the rest of the class. When trainees reach the stage of conducting actual decision-making selection interviews, they may do it initially in the presence of an instructor or a more skilled interviewer. Tape recordings can also be made of these learning interviews. Later they can be dissected to note errors and strengths.

TYPES OF INTERVIEWS

Interviews can be classified according to the techniques and structure utilized. Such a method of categorizing interviews would be (1) Planned; (2) Patterned; (3) Stress.

The *planned* interview has also been referred to as the depth interview and as the action interview. Basically, in this approach, the interviewer has outlined in advance the subject areas he wishes to explore. For the beginning interviewer this would be recorded in writing, although it would be unwise for him to refer to his notes frequently, because of the unfavorable impression created in the interviewee. The practiced interviewer knows from experience all the areas that must be explored. Subjects to be probed include home life, present domestic situation, education, previous work experience, social adjustment, attitudes, and recreational interests. The object is to get the individual to talk freely and expansively on these topics. The interviewer probes in depth for clues that would indicate potential success or failure on the job. In this interview it is also necessary to provide information about the organization, nature of the work, pay, opportunities for advancement, and demands made on the employee. The applicant must be given sufficient information to decide whether he would find the employment opportunity suitable to his needs and interests.

The *patterned* interview, which is sometimes called the standardized interview, uses as its basis an extremely comprehensive questionnaire used by the interviewer in asking his questions. It is therefore highly structured. Two of the best-known patterned interview procedures are the McMurray Patterned Interview Form[38] and the Diagnostic Interviewer's Guide developed by E. F. Wonderlic. McMurray has prepared different interview forms for office and factory jobs, for sales positions, and for executive positions. Since patterned interview forms ask so many detailed questions, literally no stone is left unturned in exploring the background, knowledge, attitudes, and motivation of the job seeker. In a survey of the interviewing practices of 273 companies Mandell found that 72 (26 per cent) used a patterned interview form.[39] Validation studies have revealed good results with this method. These favorable results are probably due as much to careful training of interviewers and sound selection procedures as they are to the form itself. Experienced interviewers generally do not like to be constrained by adherence to a rigid schedule of questions.

The *stress* interview was devised during World War II by the United States Government for selecting undercover agents for the Office of Strategic Services. In this type of interview the interviewer assumes a role of hostility toward the subject. He becomes an interrogator. He puts the man on the defensive and deliberately seeks to annoy, embarrass, and frustrate him. He seeks to cause the candidate to lose control of his emotions. Sometimes the candidate is assigned a problem of unusual difficulty and with considerable annoyances thrown into the situation. The object of the stress interview is to find those persons who are able to maintain control over their behavior when they are highly aroused internally. They must be able to act poised and well adjusted. They must be resourceful and have their wits about them in this situation.

The stress interview should be used only by a very well-trained person and only for those types of occupations where action under stress is an essential ingredient of the job, for example, police work, spying, or secret agents. For the typical industrial or business situation this technique is generally inappropriate. It tends to inhibit open and complete response. When an interviewer deliberately adopts a hostile attitude toward the applicant, he finds that the latter, being on the defensive, will tend to guard his every response and give only socially acceptable answers.

PREPARING FOR THE INTERVIEW

A number of actions should be taken prior to the actual interview itself. Privacy is of utmost importance. The conversation between the interviewer and the interviewee must not be overheard by other ears. This is to insure unrestrained responses from the applicant. Closely related to privacy is freedom from interruptions.

---

[38] Published by the Dartnell Corporation, Chicago.

[39] Milton M. Mandell, *The Employment Interview,* Research Study 47 (New York: American Management Association, 1961), p. 23.

The technical employment manager of one large company was repeatedly interrupted with telephone calls while he was talking to Bill Johnson. Whenever the phone rang, the manager asked Bill to leave the office until the call was completed.

Not only was this rude to Bill Johnson, but it also interrupted the channel of thought, so that it took several minutes to realign their thinking each time the interview was recommenced. Freedom from interruptions creates the impression in the individual that the interviewer considers him and what he has to say so important that he will devote undivided attention to the interview.

Enough time should be allowed in the interview schedule to permit a complete exposition of all the facts necessary for a fair assessment of the job seeker. For a main employment office selection interview (not a preliminary interview), this would mean a time period of 25 to 30 minutes for candidates for unskilled and semiskilled work. On the other hand for higher-level jobs, such as technical, managerial, and sales, where personality and motivation are critically important, an allowance of one hour per interview is not excessive.

Immediately prior to the actual interview, the interviewer should study all available data pertaining to the applicant. This may include the application form, preliminary interviewer's comments, test scores, and so on. Certain facts may thus stand out and indicate the need for intensive investigation. Also, from past experience, the employment interviewer will know those areas that are critical to job success.

In order to insure that all of the vital areas have been explored, a guide sheet may be utilized. This is especially useful for beginning interviewers. The topics and items in Figure 9-5 can serve as a guide or checklist.

CONDUCTING THE INTERVIEW

In commencing the interview, the employer representative must take the lead. His immediate objective is to establish a feeling of confidence and trust. He must develop a favorable emotional feeling or a feeling of harmony between the job seeker and himself. This is called rapport. Generally this can be accomplished by showing that one is interested and that one is going to be helpful and supportive in manner. The conversation should be opened with items that do not have sharp emotional overtones. Because the job seeker is almost always under tension and apprehension, at least initially, the interviewer must create a relaxed atmosphere so that the individual will be able to express himself spontaneously.

Because a prime objective is to learn as much about the candidate as is necessary to make a reliable assessment, the interviewer must make skillful use of questions. He should use broad questions in order to encourage a thorough response. Thus it is sound to say "Tell me about the

INTERVIEWER'S GUIDE

A. APPEARANCE AND MANNERISMS

Dress
Poise and bearing
Speech and voice
Facial expression
Neatness and cleanliness
Nervousness

B. EARLY HOME AND FAMILY BACKGROUND

Father's occupation
Did parents live together or were they separated?
Number of brothers and sisters
Attitude toward father, mother, and siblings
Economic situation of family
Activities, hobbies, and interests when young
Social contacts, friends

C. EDUCATION

Did he actually graduate from high school, college?
Courses taken, major area of concentration
Reasons for choice of major course area
Rank in class
Courses liked best and least and reasons
Extra curricular activities
Method of financing higher education
Special recognition and honors achieved

D. WORK HISTORY

Reasons for choice of jobs
Relations and attitude toward superiors on previous jobs
Reasons for changing jobs
Career goals
Type of work liked best
Method of obtaining previous jobs
Progress (salary increases, promotions, etc.) made

E. PERSONALITY AND SOCIAL ADJUSTMENT

Marital status
Present interests and spare time activities
Wife's interests and outlook
Financial responsibility
Emotional stability
Emotional maturity
His personal goals in life; level of aspiration
Attitudes toward work associates, toward authority
Sincerity
Initiative
Perserverance

F. HEALTH

Past and present health problems
Observe physical limitations

Figure 9-5. Interviewer's Guide.

duties, responsibilities and relationships of your last job." This is better than "Did you have to write reports? Did you take readings of the meters on the chemical equipment? How did you coordinate with other departments?" By opening up a general area for discussion in an interested but very broadly structured fashion, the interviewer will elicit those ideas that are most important in the applicant's mind. He will tend to speak about those things that are most critical to him. This will provide clues to his values and personality. If he wanders off the subject and wastes time, the interviewer can gently channel the conversation by another question.

For the person who seems reluctant to speak, often a deliberate pause on the part of the interviewer can be stimulating. By looking at the individual in a warm but expectant manner, the interviewer can convey the idea that he is receptive and would like the man to amplify more fully.

Leading questions—those which signal a desired response—should be avoided because the applicant may then refrain from expressing his true feelings. Examples of leading questions are "Did you get along well with your supervisor?" "You would not object to shift work, would you?" Instead of these it would be better to say "Tell me about your last supervisor," or, "How do you feel about shift work?"

By refraining from criticizing or acting shocked at the individual's responses, one thereby encourages him to reveal his true self. He will tend to talk about his failures as well as his successes if the interviewer does not show he is upset (by facial expression, voice, or nature of comments) by his revelations. The interviewer might indicate that others have had somewhat similar difficulties.

Immediately after the interview is completed and the candidate has left the room, the interviewer should record his impressions on a rating form. If several other interviews have intervened, then much will have been forgotten. On the other hand it is generally unwise to engage in extensive note taking and impression recording during the course of the interview. Not knowing what is being recorded, in such a situation, the interviewee may become apprehensive. He may speak in a more guarded fashion henceforth. Occasional note taking of objective data is acceptable. However, recording of the subjective conclusions of the interviewer during the conversation should be avoided.

COMMON PITFALLS IN INTERVIEWING

It is pertinent at this time to discuss some of the frequent errors made in selection interviewing. By being aware of these problems, a practicing interviewer can seek to minimize their occurrence in his work.

In judging people, probably all of us are, initially at least, prone to the condition called the halo effect. The halo effect is a situation in which a single prominent characteristic of the individual may dominate one's judgment of all his other traits. This can work in both a positive and a negative fashion. Thus if a person is neat, clean-cut, and alert, the interviewer might jump to the conclusion that he is also intelligent, ambitious, and dependable. Conversely if a person is sloppy and slovenly, the interviewer might conclude that he is also ignorant and lacking in essential skills and job knowledge. But these conclusions are not necessarily so. In rating an individual on each of a number of traits, the interviewer should have definite substantive evidence. If this has not been obtained, he must note that he cannot fairly judge certain attributes.

Previously, in discussing the psychological foundations of interviewing, the subject of interviewer bias was explained. Because man is not entirely a rational being, emotion, bias, and subjectivity cannot be eliminated. But it is essential that the interviewer be fully aware of his own attitudes and prejudices so that he can seek to discount them. Certain mannerisms or expressions of the applicant may evoke strong emotional overtones for the interviewer. These may be either positive or negative. But the key question is whether the matter has any real bearing on future job performance. Some interviewers subconsciously conclude that those who have interests and values similar to their own are therefore good men. In fact many organizations acquire a distinct "personality" because the employer tends to think that those who are just like himself are good men and those who have opposing attitudes, motivations, and values are poor men.

Failure to listen is a common weakness, especially for untrained interviewers, who in their enthusiasm might tend to do most of the talking. But a talking interviewer can learn but little of the other fellow while he is vocalizing.

The district manager of the public utility company visited a college campus to recruit engineering seniors. When talking with one college senior, he devoted nearly all of the interview to reminiscing about his experiences in the company. The student listened attentively and sympathetically. At the end the interviewer stated that he had to fill out a rating form and that he had evaluated the individual as being interested 50 per cent in economic affairs, 35 per cent in people, and 15 per cent in scientific and theoretical matters. How in the world could he have concluded that?

Questions for Review and Discussion

1. What is a selection test? What contribution can tests make to the employee selection process?
2. Because tests are objective and factual, could they be used in place of interviews for selection?
3. Explain why tests are most useful for selecting, from a large group of people, a particular group who will have a good probability of job success.
4. A personnel manager has stated that a certain test battery has been very accurate in predicting success for salesmen in his company. What reliance could we place in this same test battery for picking salesmen in another company?
5. What is test reliability? How can it be measured?
6. Distinguish among the following kinds of validity:
   a. Content
   b. Concurrent
   c. Predictive
7. A company uses a simple mathematical test as one of its selection hurdles for technicians. If an applicant fails the test but appears, on the basis of the interview, to show considerable promise, he is told to go home to study his algebra and mathematics books and come back at a later date to retake the same test. What do you think of this procedure?
8. If you were designing a test battery to select employees for each of the following jobs, what criteria of job performance would you use for validation purposes?
   a. Stenographer
   b. Foreman
   c. Project engineer
   d. Job analyst
   e. Salesman
9. Distinguish between an aptitude and an achievement test.
10. Discuss the issue of possible discrimination against culturally deprived groups by selection tests.

11. Discuss the serious problems involved in the use of personality tests for selection purposes. Give and evaluate the various techniques that can be used to obtain information about a job applicant's personality and temperament.
12. What kind of knowledge and background should an interviewer possess?
13. Is there any way that the effect of interviewer bias can be minimized?
14. What is a stress interview? Is it useful for industrial selection purposes?
15. How can an interviewer obtain willing and full responses from an interviewee?
16. Of what value is a probing into the applicant's early home and family life?
17. Do you feel that there is a moral limit to how far a company should delve into a person's life by means of tests and interviews? Discuss.

CASE PROBLEMS

Problem I

The ABC Company, which employs 280 people, manufactures a variety of small electrical items, such as switches, wall receptacles, plugs, and fuses. The office manager serves also as the personnel manager. In this capacity he handles employment, benefits and services, safety, and employee records.

Possessing neither the background nor the time to install a selection testing program, the office-personnel manager relies heavily upon the results of tests administered to applicants by the State Employment Service. A uniform series of tests is given to job seekers at all offices throughout the state. For applicants for production and maintenance jobs, the State administers mental ability, mechanical aptitude, manual dexterity, and vocational interest tests. For applicants for office and clerical jobs it gives mental ability, clerical aptitude, typing, and vocational interest tests.

The ABC Company obtains nearly all its applicants through the State Employment Service. When an applicant has been referred to the Company, he is given an interview by the office-personnel manager and his test scores are examined. In order to be considered for hiring, his scores must exceed the norm on each test. The final decision to hire or reject is made by the office-personnel manager for all office and clerical candidates. Applicants for shop jobs are further sent to the manufacturing superintendent, who makes the final decision in these cases. Promising candidates for all jobs are sent to a local physician for a routine physical examination. Character references listed by each candidate on his application form are contacted by a form letter before a final decision to hire is made.

Questions

1. Evaluate the employee selection program used in this company.
2. Recommend a proposed program that would be an improvement over the present one.

Problem 2

The XYZ Company manufactures a wide diversity of industrial and consumer products. Each year it hires approximately twenty-five college graduates (engineering, business administration, and liberal arts graduates) by sending its college-relations manager to about fifteen college campuses to recruit graduating seniors. In a conversation with a college professor, the college relations manager made the following statement:

"I have been doing nearly all of the college recruiting for my company for the past ten years. I have full authority to hire these new graduates. My company does not think it is necessary to invite the best prospects to the home plant for further interviews by other managers (as many other companies do). I allow one half hour for each interview. In that length of time I am able to make a pretty accurate evaluation of the prospect. Although I have full authority to hire on the spot, I generally wait until I return to my office. At that time I review my written notes on all of the better persons whom I interviewed and then send out letters containing offers of employment. I have been quite happy with this method of hiring. My company has found it to be an economical and practical procedure."

Question

1. Evaluate this approach to the hiring of college graduates.

Suggestions for Further Reading

Barnett, W. Leslie Jr., *Readings in Psychological Tests and Measurements,* Homewood, Illinois: The Dorsey Press, 1964.

Barrett, Richard S., "Gray Areas in Black and White Testing," *Harvard Business Review,* Vol. 46, No. 1, 1968, pp. 92-95.

Bassett, Glenn A., *Practical Interviewing, A Handbook for Managers,* New York: American Management Association, 1965.

Bingham, W. V., B. V. Moore, and J. W. Gustad, *How to Interview,* 4th Ed., New York: Harper & Row, 1959.

Carlson, R. E., "Selection Interview Decisions: The Relative Influence of Appearance and Factual Written Information on an Interviewer's

Final Rating," *Journal of Applied Psychology,* Vol. 51, No. 6, 1967, pp. 461-468.

Ghiselli, Edwin E., *The Validity of Occupational Aptitude Tests,* New York: John Wiley & Sons, Inc., 1966.

Guion, Robert M., *Personnel Testing,* New York: McGraw-Hill Book Company, 1965.

Kahn, Robert L., and Charles F. Cannell, *The Dynamics of Interviewing,* New York: John Wiley & Sons, 1957.

Lawshe, C. H. and Michael J. Balma, *Principles of Personnel Testing,* 2nd Ed., New York: McGraw-Hill Book Company, 1966.

Lovell, V. R., "Human Use of Personality Tests", *American Psychologist,* Vol. 22, May 1967, pp. 383-393.

Mandell, Milton M., *The Employment Interview,* Research Study 47, New York: American Management Association, 1961.

_____ *The Selection Process,* New York: American Management Association, 1964.

Mayfield, Eugene C., "The Selection Interview—A Re-evaluation of Published Research," *Personnel Psychology,* Vol. 17, No. 3, Autumn 1964, pp. 239-260.

Tiffin, Joseph and Ernest J. McCormick, *Industrial Psychology,* Fifth Edition, Englewood Cliffs, N.J.: Prentice-Hall, 1965, Chs. 2, 5, 6, 7, and 8.

Employing the Culturally Deprived

10

The plight of the poor people of America was brought dramatically to the attention of the general public in the decade of the 1960's. In 1968 thirty million persons in the United States lived in poverty, that is, they were members of families having less than $3,130 annual income. Although we have always had a substantial poor population, these persons have been largely ignored by the predominant middle-class majority. Prior to this decade the poor were quiescent, unorganized, and politically weak. Now the great majority of Americans can no longer conceal from themselves the fact that there exists a large "underclass" of impoverished peoples who are essentially cut off from the life and aspirations of our nation.

Powerful forces acting in the 1960's dispelled the complacency and compelled governmental and business leaders as well as the general public to recognize the gravity of the problem and to institute corrective measures. The civil rights movement and the militancy of many Negro organizations such as the Congress of Racial Equality and Martin Luther King's Southern Christian Leadership Conference served to awaken the nation. The Negro rioting in the slums of our large cities not only frightened white Americans but also inspired a host of public and private programs to provide housing, education, and jobs for the underprivileged. The War on Poverty created by the administration of President Lyndon Johnson contained a variety of broad scale programs, some of which provided for close cooperation between government and business. In addition to emphasis upon programs for the poor in the areas of housing, education, family service, health, and racial equality, a primary goal has been the providing of jobs. It is in this field of job opportunities that individual employers are able to make perhaps their greatest contribution.

Reasons for Involvement of Private Employers

Why has the issue of providing jobs to the culturally deprived become so important to both large corporations and small companies? After all, as we have just said, the poor people have been generally ignored for generations, and historically this hard fact has had no real impact upon private business.

Shortage of Labor.   The booming economy of the 1960's, fed by the demands of the Vietnam war, created a high demand for labor of all kinds, even for unskilled labor. To get factory help, employers generally were forced to lower their educational, physical, and intellectual standards. They innovated all sorts of strategies to induce the unemployed to seek jobs.

Negro Militancy.   Although in terms of absolute numbers there are more white people who exist in the throes of poverty, the whites have not been organized and they have not suffered under the added burden of racial discrimination. In addition to the long established moderate Negro organizations, the National Association for the Advancement of Colored People and the Urban League, militant Negro groups such as the Congress of Racial Equality and the Students Nonviolent Coordinating Committee became active in demanding better conditions for Negroes. "Black power" became the battle cry of many Negro activists. The nonviolent crusades of Martin Luther King increased the Negroes' sense of identity and the importance of their struggle. In 1966-67 a very aggressive Negro organization called FIGHT, operating in the city of Rochester, New York, demanded that the Eastman Kodak Company hire 600 Negroes. The insistent demands of the American Negro could not be ignored.

Negro Rioting.   Mob violence, killing, looting, and arson in the slums of scores of cities have stimulated private businessmen to realize that conditions are desperate and that they have a stake in the preservation and revitalization of our cities. Many of the rioters were Negro youth. Among these, unemployment has averaged 20 to 25 per cent.

Government Encouragement.   The National Alliance of Businessmen established by President Johnson in the winter of 1968 and first headed by Henry Ford II set for itself the goal of 500,000 jobs for the hard-core unemployed by 1971. The Federal government under the Manpower Development and Training Act of 1962 provides substantial payments to employers for the costs of on-the-job training programs. The public employment agencies of all the states and the human rights (antidiscrimination) commissions of those states having fair employment practice laws work actively with private business to aid employment opportunities for the underprivileged.

Enlightened Self-Interest. Some corporations, particularly the large ones that are in the public eye, have established programs to make jobs available to the hard-core unemployed because they feel it enhances their public image. They are helping the community. This, they feel, aids recruitment of upper level employees, promotes the sale of their products, and makes the community fathers more responsive to the special needs of the corporation.

Social Responsibility. Some top corporate executives are motivated by a genuine sense of humanitarianism in that they feel they have a responsibility to help people who exist in unfortunate circumstances. This may be based upon Judaeo-Christian values fundamental to the American ethos.

Management Commitment

A program to launch a program of employment of the culturally deprived can only succeed if top management is totally committed to the endeavor. If the president believes that it might be good to introduce a token program for public relations goals only, then the likelihood of success is indeed quite dim. Too much is at stake to adopt a casual, opportunistic attitude. The well-being of the company, of its present employees, and certainly of the newly hired disadvantaged people would all be threatened by such an approach.

A real investment in money, time, and qualified talent is necessary to insure a reasonably rewarding program. Substantial changes in traditional recruitment, selection, training, and employee utilization may have to be made. Steps must be taken to develop a cooperative attitude on the part of supervision and the entire work force.

Will the caliber of the work force be so seriously diluted as to impair the ability of the firm to produce and compete in the market place? This is a justifiable worry for the small firm particularly. Clearly a machine shop employing thirty skilled craftsmen could destroy itself if it brought in twenty unskilled, semiliterate workers and promptly assigned them to operate machines and turn out a product. Nor could a small business office load itself down with a high percentage of school dropouts to do typing, filing, payroll, customer billings, and so forth. However, experience with programs of this type has demonstrated that companies can effectively bring into their work forces a modest percentage of the disadvantaged for training. As these trainees become productive, new groups can be recruited. This must properly be looked upon as a long-term, carefully planned program rather than a one-shot injection.

WHO ARE THE CULTURALLY DEPRIVED?

The culturally deprived are the poor people of America. The poor are those who have an inadequate level of consumption. That is, they have an insufficient money income for subsistence according to current standards of living. In 1966 the U.S. Social Security Administration established $3,130 at 1964 prices as the annual income line for four-person urban families. For single persons living alone the figure is $1,540. Below these levels people are living in poverty. On the basis of these guidelines, the Council of Economic Advisors estimated that in 1964 there were 34.1 million poor people in the United States.[1] This represented about 18 per cent of the entire population.

Actually poverty is a worldwide problem. The vast majority in Asia, Africa, and South America are very poor. Chronic hunger is a widespread problem. In the United States the problem of starvation has been all but eradicated, but there are millions who have improper diets, insufficient clothing, and substandard housing. Actually the percentage of Americans with incomes below the poverty line has decreased from 32 per cent in 1947 to 18 per cent in 1964 (in terms of 1962 purchasing power). Although conditions are improving for many, the barriers to a decent, more abundant life are almost insurmountable to many others. As the standard of living rises in the United States over the years, the aspirations of people go up. The gap between what poor people have and what they might have becomes more and more a source of gnawing discontent.

In terms of race and ethnic composition, the poor are composed of whites, Negroes, American Indians, Puerto Ricans living in the United States, and Mexican-Americans. Because of the civil rights issue and the struggle of well organized Negro groups for social and economic equality, national attention has tended to focus upon the Negro. Although the phenomena are not confined to Negroes, researchers, writers, the news media, and public spokesmen have identified insufficient education, hardcore unemployment, inadequate medical care, and bad housing as primarily Negro problems. Statistics reveal that, relatively, a nonwhite family is more than two and one half times as likely to be poor as a white family. In 1963, 44 per cent of all nonwhite families were poor as compared with only 16 per cent of white families.[2]

Persons living in poverty include the aged, children under 16, those who are physically or mentally incapacitated, fully employed persons earning substandard wages, mothers caring for young children, and able bodied unemployed persons. In this land of affluence, it is rather paradoxical to note that several million people employed the year round are

[1] 89th Congress, 2nd session, *Economic Report of the President* (Washington, D.C.: Government Printing Office, January 1966).
[2] Burton A. Weisbrod, ed., *The Economics of Poverty: An American Paradox* (Englewood Cliffs, N.J.: Prentice Hall, Inc., 1965), p. 18.

paid wages insufficient to provide a decent standard of living for their families.[3]

In this textbook we are concerned primarily with the "management of people at work," hence we shall concentrate our attention upon problems, issues, and programs for the able bodied unemployed. These are often labeled, the hard-core unemployed. These people tend to be handicapped by reason of poor education, marginal language and literacy skills, no job skills, welfare dependency, low income, and often racial discrimination.

Negroes and the Heritage of Discrimination

The century-long struggle of the American Negro for equality of treatment and opportunity is well known. In the South up until very recent years, the Negro was required by law to attend a segregated public school, to eat in lunch rooms for colored only, and to ride in the colored section of busses and trains. Jobs reserved for Negroes were primarily in the unskilled category: farm hand and factory laborer for men and household domestic for women.

Commencing with World War II, Negroes began migrating by the scores of thousands every year from the rural South to the big cities of the North: Chicago, Detroit, Cleveland, New York. Lacking the education and skills necessary to qualify for good jobs in an industrialized economy, they obtained only laboring jobs in the mass production industries or else filled the ranks of the unemployed. The public assistance rolls swelled. Even though many northern states had passed antidiscrimination laws in the late 1940's and early 1950's, the Negro in the North encountered pervasive discrimination in the job and housing market. Even if qualified, he was often denied a decent job. Even if financially able, he was denied housing in the white suburbs. His home and life pattern was more and more confined to the big city slums.

Some quantitative evidence which shows the negative effects of discrimination upon annual income of selected ethnic groups is provided by Walter Fogel. Using 1960 census data he compared education and annual income for the male population age 25 and over for the following ethnic groups living in the United States: Japanese, Chinese, White, Puerto Rican, Indian, Negro, Filipino, and those with a Spanish surname. In the state of California, for example, Negro incomes for 1959 were only 72 per cent of white income, Indian 65 per cent, Chinese 78 per cent, and Japanese 81 per cent. This was after adjustment for differences in educational attainment. Fogel stated that differences in educational attainment

---

[3] Although we are concerned here primarily with programs to employ the able-bodied unemployed, it is important to note that in 1963, 8.5 million wage earners worked throughout the year at full-time jobs, yet earned less than $3,000 for their efforts. See Laurie D. Cummings, "The Employed Poor: Their Characteristics and Occupations," *Monthly Labor Review*, Vol. 88 (July 1965), p. 828-829.

between whites and the various nonwhite groups accounted for less than half the difference between the 1959 median income of each group and that of whites. The causes of the differences after adjusting for education were not determined, but he felt that variation in education quality and especially discrimination appeared to be most important as causal factors.[4]

Low Education, High Unemployment

In recent times a great deal of national attention has focused upon the school dropout problem. Actually the percentage of school-age children quitting school before graduation has declined rather steadily for many decades. Or stated differently, 61 per cent of American workers had a high school diploma or better in 1967, whereas only half this number were high school graduates in 1940.

Nevertheless, the school dropout problem is very serious today because undereducated workers cannot get jobs. The rapid advance of industrialization and technology has increased the demand for skilled workers—white collar, technical, and professional personnel—but drastically reduced the need for the unskilled. Machines have largely supplanted the unskilled.

An inverse correlation exists between amount of education and unemployment. As Figure 10-1 shows, white males with an elementary education or less had a 4.0 per cent rate of unemployment, whereas those with one year of college or more had only 1.3 per cent unemployment

	MALE			FEMALE		
Years of school completed	White	Non-white	Ratio*	White	Non-white	Ratio*
TOTAL	2.7	6.5	2.4	4.0	8.4	2.1
Less than 4 years of high school	4.0	7.5	1.9	5.4	9.7	1.8
Elementary: 8 years or less	4.0	6.8	1.7	5.0	7.0	1.4
High school: 1 to 3 years	4.0	8.8	2.2	5.8	13.0	2.2
4 years of high school or more	1.8	4.7	2.6	3.2	6.9	2.2
High school: 4 years	2.3	5.4	2.3	3.7	7.7	2.1
College: 1 year or more	1.3	3.2	2.5	2.4	5.0	2.1

*Nonwhite unemployment rate divided by white unemployment rate.

Figure 10-1   Unemployment Rates and Education of Persons 18 Years Old and Over, March 1967. Source: Harvey R. Hamel, "Educational Attainment of Workers," *Monthly Labor Review*, Vol. 91 (February 1968), p. 29.

[4] Walter Fogel, "The Effect of Low Educational Attainment on Incomes: A Comparative Study of Selected Ethnic Groups," *The Journal of Human Resources*, Vol. 1, No. 2 (Fall 1966), pp. 22-40.

as of March 1967. It should also be noted from an examination of this figure that the unemployment rate for nonwhites (primarily Negroes) averages more than twice that of whites for all educational classes.

The burden of unemployment has fallen very heavily upon Negroes, particularly young Negroes. These persons find it more difficult to locate a job than do older persons with the same education because they have not yet acquired the occupational skills that employers require of potential workers. The unemployment rate in March 1967 of 18- to 24-year-old Negroes who had completed 1 to 3 years of high school was 18 per cent for men and 29 per cent for women.[5]

Culture of the Poor

In order to understand adequately the problems of the hard-core unemployed and to be able to plan programs to help these people, one needs to gain knowledge of the outlook, values, customs, and habits of the poor. When we speak about the culture of the poor, we include both white and nonwhite residents of the United States. At certain points in our discussion, we will specifically make reference to the Negro poor and unemployed where we wish to emphasize their situation as it may be distinct from that of whites.

A review and analysis of available research evidence about the life style of the American lower-class family has been made by Suzanne Keller.[6] She has pointed out that the influence which the family holds for the development of children is pre-eminent, particularly for the teaching of basic social skills, formation of moral character, and the establishment of deep-rooted emotional bonds. The foundations of personality, character, and behavior are laid down in the family. Adults reflect rather strongly the home influence of their formative years.

Here follows some important generalizations on the lower class as reported in the Keller study.

a. Short time perspective—they are oriented to the present rather than the future and do not plan ahead.
b. Preoccupation with the need for money is pervasive.
c. They feel insecure much of the time.
d. They often are reluctant to meet new people and to initiate interaction with strangers. They lack confidence in their ability to say and do the right things with strangers, are uncomfortable in such relationships, and therefore seek security in a small circle of old friends and relatives.
e. They believe that authoritarianism is essential, that leaders should be strict, that children should be respectful to parents, and that vio-

---

[5] *Ibid.,* p. 28
[6] Suzanne Keller, *The American Lower Class Family,* (Albany, N.Y.: New York State Division for Youth, 1966).

lators should be harshly punished. Men feel that they should make the important family decisions.

f. In their attitudes toward homes and possessions, lower-class individuals value appliances more than their houses, which they tend to neglect. Keller speculates that this attitude may be because their housing is unpleasant and inadequate and because they move from residence to residence rather frequently. They generally do not own their homes.

g. Life in the lowest social class is often violent and is highly unstable as people move about seeking jobs, adventure, escape from the law, and more living space.

h. Juvenile delinquency, school failures, and functional psychoses are more prevalent in the lower classes than in the higher ones.

i. They are inactive in community affairs, belong to few formal organizations, and make little use of community facilities.

j. For Negroes the relations between men and women are pertinent. Negro men wander restlessly from one place to another seeking jobs and women. The women hold the steady jobs or get welfare checks and thus are dominant in all family matters except sex. The women take love on male terms and the men try to trade in love for a source of economic support. The Negro man tends to be uneducated, unskilled, poor, and highly dependent upon his wife who earns more than he does. This is a reversal of the prevailing husband and wife roles in middle-class society.

k. The rate of school failure is very high for the lower class. A high percentage of the children quit school before graduation. Their parents tend to show little interest in their school work.

Further insight into the culture of the hard-core unemployed is revealed in a research project described by Patten and Clark. In Detroit in the summer of 1965 an eight-week literacy training program was provided for 53 hard-core unemployed fathers of families receiving public assistance under the Aid to Families with Dependent Children program. Of the 48 men who completed the program eight were white, four were Spanish-American, and 36 were Negro. Approximately six months after the completion of the course of instruction a follow-up study was made. Twelve of the 48 men now held jobs. At that time automobile production was high and jobs were plentiful. Of those who were still unemployed the authors pointed out that they used a hit-and-miss approach to seeking a job. Many talked about failing tests when they applied for work, but this usually meant inability to fill out an application blank. Many of the interviewees stated that unless there was a substantial differential between welfare payments and factory wages, they preferred to stay on welfare. Some of the men indicated that they stayed at home to care for the children while their wives went out to work. Patten and Clark concluded that the hard-core unemployed person in Detroit, especially if he was a Negro, could squeak by on welfare payments and spend his time on minor household chores. Notwithstanding the general view that long-term unemployment is demoralizing, most of the respondents accepted welfare, unemployment, and household chores as a compatible and meaningful way of life.[7]

Attitudes Toward Work and Achievement

By and large those values which are so important to the middle class—success, achievement, a good job, a good education, acceptance in the community—do not exist for the culturally deprived. They are conditioned by failure in school, in employment, and in life. Parents do not impart achievement motivation in their children.

Harvard psychologist, David McClelland, has studied extensively the role of motivation in economic behavior. He has pointed out that the conditions of slavery influenced the nature of Negro adjustment toward obedience and away from achievement and self-betterment. Interestingly, those few Negroes who reach middle- or upper-class status reveal conspicuously high levels of achievement motivation on McClelland's projective tests.[8]

Many will not accept the discipline of the industrial system. Such behavior as coming to work every day on time, staying at the machine until 4:30 P.M., and accepting orders from a foreman are foreign to these people. Absenteeism and tardiness are a way of life. Most of the jobs which they may have had—laborer, janitor, dishwasher, porter—are lost through poor attitudes rather than lack of ability to do the work. Basically they are as maladapted to the life and discipline of the factory system as would be peasants in the backward nations of the world.

GOVERNMENT ACTION FOR HARD-CORE UNEMPLOYED

It is not the nature of Americans to allow serious and widespread economic and social problems to fester and remain unsolved. In addition to the humanitarian spirit of the public, there has been the insistent demand of the poor, especially the Negro poor, for a larger share of the abundance of America. The Federal government under the Kennedy and Johnson administrations took the lead in getting legislative programs through Congress to outlaw racial discrimination, to educate and train the poor, and to provide them with economic opportunities. Many of these programs require full cooperation from private business for their implementation and success. The Federal government recognized that this partnership approach was vital. We shall now review three programs instituted by the Federal government in the 1960's.

[7] Thomas H. Patten, Jr, and Gerald E. Clark, Jr., "Literacy Training and Job Placement of Hard-Core Unemployed Negroes in Detroit," *The Journal of Human Resources*, Vol. 3, No. 1 (Winter 1968), pp. 25-46.

[8] David McClelland, *The Achieving Society* (Princeton: Van Nostrand, 1961), p. 377.

Civil Rights Act of 1964

An essential precondition for the fulfillment of economic opportunity is the removal of discriminatory practices by employers, labor unions, and employment agencies. It does little good to launch comprehensive and varied education programs for disadvantaged Negroes if they encounter a stone wall of resistance in the employment offices of the country.

Title VII of the Civil Rights Act of 1964 is called the Equal Employment Opportunity title. It became effective on July 2, 1965. It bans discrimination in employment because of race, color, religion, sex, and national origin. It applies to employers, private employment agencies, the United States Employment Service, state employment services utilizing Federal funds, and labor unions. Under this statute it is unlawful for an employer to refuse to hire, or to discharge or otherwise to discriminate against any individual with respect to compensation, terms, conditions, or privileges of employment because of such individual's race, color, religion, sex, or national origin. It is unlawful for a labor union to exclude from membership or segregate its members on the above criteria.

Prior to the enactment of Title VII, there had been considerable experience with efforts by government to eliminate discrimination in employment. During World War II, President Franklin D. Roosevelt, by executive order, established a Fair Employment Practice Committee to combat discrimination particularly by government contractors. President Kennedy established a committee under the chairmanship of Vice-President Lyndon Johnson to secure compliance from corporations doing business with the government. Nearly all of the states in the North and West had already enacted fair employment practice laws by the time the Civil Rights Act of 1964 was adopted.[9]

Manpower Development and Training Act—1962

The Manpower Development and Training Act (MDTA) became law in March 1962. Amendments to expand and liberalize the program were passed by Congress in 1963 and 1965. Its purpose has been to provide education and training in both vocational schools and on-the-job for those who are unemployed and underemployed. MDTA courses last up to two years for people who need basic literacy and arithmetic education as well as occupational skills training. Trainees receive a living allowance equal to state unemployment compensation plus, in cases of special need, an extra 10 dollars per week. Workers enrolled in on-the-job training programs that are set up under the Act, receive smaller allowances because they also receive wages from their employers.

The preponderance of training activity under MDTA has been institutional training, that is, programs of training which take place in regular vocational education facilities (both public and private) for eligible

[9] In 1945, New York and New Jersey were the first states in the nation to enact antidiscrimination laws.

unemployed and underemployed individuals. From September 1962 through December 1966, 9,800 different projects were approved for about half a million trainees.

Occupations for which vocational training has been provided include such ones as automobile mechanic, baker apprentice, tractor operator, grocery checker, practical nurses, sheet metal worker, electrical appliance service man, secretary, and typist.

In order for a community to obtain a federal grant to establish an institutional training program, it must organize and obtain full cooperation from the local public employment service, employers, vocational education system, labor unions, and city officials. If any of these groups is unwilling to cooperate, the likelihood of preparing an application for Federal funds and getting it approved is slim.

The proof of the pudding is in the eating. Have those who completed their courses of instruction been successful in obtaining employment? In 1965, a year of high economic activity and high levels of employment, 71.3 per cent of those completing their programs obtained jobs. Those who had a high school education or more did better than those with fewer years of schooling. Whites were more successful in obtaining jobs than nonwhites. Those trained in subprofessional and technical fields (practical nurse and draftsman) were more successful in obtaining jobs than those in semiskilled and clerical fields.[10]

Evaluation.   Although the original goal of MDTA was to retain experienced adult family heads who had been displaced by economic and technological change, by 1965 the emphasis had clearly shifted to the disadvantaged. Enrollment in vocational school programs since 1965 has been more heavily in the direction of the nonwhite, young, public assistance recipient and those with less than a high school education. The majority of enrollees have family incomes of less than $3000 per year.

On-the-job programs have enrolled far fewer persons than the institutional programs, and the proportion of true disadvantaged people has been quite low. The primary reason for this is that employers who do the recruiting, selection, and training have aimed for higher quality inputs in order to maximize performance.

In summarizing experience under MDTA, Garth Magnum has stated that the cost-benefit experience has been favorable. Those completing courses have more stable employment and higher earnings after training when compared with their own pretraining experience and with control groups. Disadvantaged persons have a difficult time getting admitted to on-the-job training programs, but once accepted their retention rates are not much different from those of the nondisadvantaged.[11]

[10] Seymour L. Wolfbein, *Education and Training for Full Employment* (New York: Columbia University Press, 1967), pp. 155-158.

[11] Garth L. Magnum, "Evaluating Federal Manpower Programs" in *The Development and Use of Manpower,* Proceedings of the Twentieth Annual Winter Meeting, Industrial Relations Research Association (Madison, Wisc.: The Association, 1967).

Economic Opportunity Act of 1964

The Johnson Administration's War on Poverty had as its core the Economic Opportunity Act of 1964. This act contains seven Titles:

TITLE I: *Youth Programs*

Part A: The Job Corps. This established rural conservation camps for young men and urban residential centers for young men and women. The purpose is to provide education and training for youth from impoverished homes who have failed in school and who have no salable job skills.

Part B: Neighborhood Youth Corps. Provides work experience and training for school dropouts and for those continuing in school. Ages are sixteen to twenty-one. Administered by the U.S. Department of Labor.

Part C: Work Study Program. The Office of Economic Opportunity makes agreements with colleges and universities to pay part of the wages of students from low-income families who are employed part-time by the educational institution.

TITLE II: *Community Action Programs*

Part A: General Community Action Program. The Federal government pays up to 90 per cent of the costs of antipoverty programs planned and carried out at the community level. Such programs include employment, job training, counseling, health, vocational rehabilitation, housing, home management, welfare, and special remedial educational programs.

Part B: Adult Basic Education Programs. A program of literacy training for adults over eighteen years of age.

Part C: Voluntary Assistance for Needy Children. This is designed to enlist the voluntary involvement of parents to take on the financial support of needy children.

TITLE III: *Programs to Combat Poverty in Rural Areas*

Part A: Loans to very low-income rural families for farm operations and nonagricultural, income producing enterprises. Administered by the Department of Agriculture.

Part B: Assistance for Migrant and Seasonal Workers. Government aid to establish and operate housing, sanitation, education, and child day-care programs.

TITLE IV: *Employment and Investment Incentives*

This part of the Act authorizes loans and guarantees to small businesses on more liberal terms than regular loans granted by the Small Business Administration.

TITLE V: *Work Experience and Training*

These are experimental, pilot, and demonstration projects to provide constructive work experience and training for unemployed fathers and needy persons.

TITLE VI: *Administration and Coordination*

This title established the Office of Economic Opportunity to administer the Act. It also authorized the establishment of the VISTA (Volunteers in Service to America) program. These persons serve in various antipoverty work.

TITLE VII: *Treatment of Public Assistance*

An individual's opportunity to participate in programs under this Act shall neither jeopardize, nor be jeopardized by receipt of public assistance.

The Office of Economic Opportunity (OEO) is attached to the Executive Office of the President. Within this Office separate staffs operate the Job Corps, VISTA, Community Action Programs, and special programs for migrant workers. The Office also distributes funds to existing agencies to operate certain programs under the Act such as the work-study and adult basic education programs through the Department of Health, Education, and Welfare.

Evaluation.   The war on poverty has attacked poverty on a number of fronts and by a number of approaches. Some of these have been, quite frankly, experimental. The primary emphasis has been upon the rehabilitation of people through education and training. Just how effective have been the various manpower programs of the Economic Opportunity Act?

Job Corps.   An enrollee who has spent nine months in a job corps center improves his reading ability by one and a half grades and his arithmetic skills by two grades. Experience has shown that the longer youths remain in the program the greater the likelihood that they will obtain employment. However, only one out of three persons completes his specified training course. Another problem has been that the annual cost of over $8,000 per enrollee has been judged to be high.[12]

Neighborhood Youth Corps.   As of the end of 1967 the Neighborhood Youth Corps program had provided income for about one million youths. Although Congress assigned the dual objectives of part-time employment to in-school youths from poor families and of helping school drop-outs develop their maximum occupational potential, the net result has been one of income support with very little useful vocational skill training being accomplished. The evidence has shown that the in-school program has been effective in keeping young people from quitting school. However, the out-of-school program has emphasized "make-work" activities in governmental units and in nonprofit private organizations. It has provided necessary income support to youths in very poor families. In addition

---

[12] Primarily as an economy move, a large number of Job Corps centers were closed in 1969 during the early months of President Nixon's administration. The program was continued on a much reduced scale.

it has been credited by some authorities with keeping youth out of trouble with the law and with preventing them from rioting.

Work Experience and Training.   The goal of the Work Experience and Training program has been to help needy adults become self-supporting. The major benefit has been that the government has put people to work on special projects and thereby saved them from terrible deprivation. But 50 per cent of those in this program who were on relief at the start of their work experience continued to remain on it at the termination of the program. A major source of the difficulty is that these people can command only slightly more in the job market than they can obtain on welfare. The incentive to work is lacking.

Community Action Programs.   Sar Levitan has reported that the training provided for those employed in community agencies has been sporadic or nonexistent. These programs offer jobs with low-income and limited-career prospects.[13]

ACTION BY PRIVATE BUSINESS

As stated before, action to combat poverty and hard-core unemployment demands substantial effort on the part of private industry. Business, particularly big business, has shown that it is ready and willing to help. At the request of President Lyndon Johnson, the National Alliance of Businessmen was formed early in 1968. Henry Ford II, board chairman of the Ford Motor Company became chairman of this group. He and his associates quickly enlisted the enthusiastic cooperation of major corporation executives throughout the country. The goal of this group was to secure 100,000 jobs for the hard-core unemployed by July 1969 and a total of 500,000 jobs by July 1971. It also set for itself the goal of providing thousands of temporary summer jobs for urban youths.

The technique employed by the Alliance is similar to the "Community Chest" idea. Community chairmen get pledges from individual company presidents to provide an agreed upon number of jobs by a specified date.

The basic premise is different than that of most of the other Federally designed programs. Here the emphasis is upon jobs *first* and training *later.* The belief is that this materially aids employee motivation. In fiscal 1968 the U.S. government allocated $106 million to reimburse companies for extraordinary costs incurred in hiring and training disadvantaged persons with low productivity. A company is eligible to receive up to $3,500 per trainee.

[13] This observation and the evaluative information on the other manpower programs of the Economic Opportunity Act are based upon Sar Levitan's "Manpower Aspects of the Economic Opportunity Act", in *The Development and Use of Manpower,* Proceedings of the Twentieth Annual Winter Meeting, Industrial Relations Research Association, (Madison, Wisc.: The Association, 1967).

Programs for the Individual Company

Company programs basically represent investment in human capital. The potential for return on this investment is great, both for the employer and for the disadvantaged who are hired.

The employer contemplating the installation of a full-blown program to employ the culturally deprived must recognize that the road is not easy. Jobs in American business exist within the cultural framework of the predominant group in our society, not that of the big city slum nor that of the rural South. People from these backgrounds are truly handicapped in competing for and holding jobs in modern industry. But we need not accept their deficient reading and writing ability, their deficient know-how, and their deficient motivation as a fixed condition. Under proper conditions they can learn to adapt to the prevailing system of industrial behavior.

Let us now examine the essential elements of a program to employ and utilize the deprived.

Set Plans and Objectives.   Management must have clearly in mind why it is launching a program and what it hopes to accomplish. In some cases, quite frankly, the program may be a defensive one. The NAACP or a state or federal antidiscrimination agency may be pressuring the company to hire more Negroes. More positively though, the management on its own initiative may have decided to launch a program because it wants to help alleviate hardship, it recognizes a pressing national problem, it knows that poor people are not good customers, or simply because it needs the manpower.

Responsibility within the organization for operating the program must be pinpointed. In most instances the personnel-industrial relations office will handle the program planning responsibilities guided by a steering committee of the major corporate executives. The program will certainly require a budget and authorization to spend money. Company personnel must do enough research to become knowledgeable about state and Federal antipoverty programs, consultation services available, community agencies, and the experiences of other firms in this field. Those in charge must become familiar with the local labor market, composition of the labor force, type and duration of unemployment, and the like. It must also learn about community values and certainly the culture of the people it seeks to employ.

Recruitment.   By and large disadvantaged people will not respond to a routine help-wanted advertisement in the newspaper. Many of the hard-core unemployed are functionally illiterate. They don't read newspapers. They won't come knocking at the employment office door. They have been so conditioned by rejection that they feel they don't have a chance. Contact can be made with organizations which are experienced in getting jobs for the underprivileged and the Negro. The Urban League with offices in most of the major cities has had a long and creditable record in this domain. The Opportunities Industrialization Centers, a Negro-led group, started by Reverend Leon H. Sullivan of Philadelphia has offices in sixty-five cities. Churches and settlement houses in minority group areas are usually able to help find applicants.

Under prodding by the U.S. Department of Labor, the various state divisions of employment have established programs to go directly into the slums to talk to the unemployed and encourage them to register for job counseling and referral.

Working through local public employment offices, personnel managers associations, and chambers of commerce, many companies have set up "job fairs" in a large convention hall to recruit and interview people enmasse.

Selection.   Classically and traditionally selection has been a negative process. People are rejected at each successive hurdle, and only the very best qualified get hired. Quite naturally an employer wants the best people he can obtain. But if the usual standards are applied, the hard-core unemployed just won't be hired.

According to a McGraw-Hill Special Report, Warner Swasey eliminated its usual hiring yardsticks, including testing. Pacific Telephone and Telegraph, along with other companies, has hired people with police records. Lockheed Missiles went looking for high school dropouts for its Vocational Improvement Program. [14]

Realistically employers should re-examine their hiring standards and modify those that are purely arbitrary and without justification. You don't need a high school education for a machine tender's job. If promotion-from-within programs require higher skills at a later date, these can be acquired through evening school attendance and in-service training activities.

The interview should seek to uncover applicants who can grow, who have some potential, and who hold promise of developing sound work attitudes. The interviewer can explore such things as the way a man spends his spare time, his relationship with his family, previous efforts to get a permanent job, and his concepts of fruitful behavior on the job. How aware is the candidate of the kind of behavior which is considered socially acceptable in an industrial situation?

Considerable controversy has arisen over the charge that intelligence, aptitude, and achievement selection tests may be culture bound and thereby discriminate against poor whites and Negroes. In 1967 the Ford Motor Company abandoned the use of tests for hourly jobs for this reason. There is considerable evidence that tests do have a cultural bias. Efforts to devise truly culture free tests have not been notably successful. Nevertheless, Title VII of the Civil Rights Act of 1964 does clearly establish that employers do have the right to use tests in the selection process as long as

---

[14] *Business and the Urban Crisis,* A McGraw-Hill Special Report (1968), p. 7.

they have been developed by professionally qualified personnel. In 1966 the Equal Employment Opportunity Commission issued procedural guidelines for the administration of testing programs.[15]

Restructure Jobs.   In some instances it may be desirable to simplify jobs by taking away the easily learned parts of a more complex job and creating a new routine job which can be mastered by an undereducated employee. This is essentially what was done in World War II in defense plants to make it possible for women to perform many of the operations.

Simplifying and specializing jobs to make them very elementary in content runs counter to much of modern behavioral science research evidence which has advocated job enlargement and job enrichment because these practices often (but not always) enhance morale and productivity. However, this research has been based upon experienced employees with normal qualifications. Some experimentation to meet individual situations is needed in this area.

Training and Indoctrination.   Most assuredly training and indoctrination are the most difficult and most important part of the entire program. In the ordinary training program the trainer can concentrate upon imparting job knowledge and skills. But with the disadvantaged this is only part of the story. Many of them are seriously deficient in reading, writing, and arithmetic. One Los Angeles bus company that had recruited in a slum area found very few people who could make change for a dollar. In another company trainees could not measure with a ruler.

In addition to basic literacy training and training in job skills, the third and perhaps most challenging area for learning has to do with attitudes, motivation, and discipline. It is very important to build self-confidence and self-esteem. Actually most jobs are lost by bad attitudes rather than the inability to master the basic job skills. People must be taught to come to work every day and on time. They must be taught not to sleep on the job, not to bring guns and liquor into the plant, to give a fair day's work, and to accept the orders of a foreman. For people who have been idle for years and who have loitered on street corners and in bars as a way of life, the discipline of the factory is difficult to adjust to. Leo Beebe, who was executive vice-chairman of the National Alliance of Businessmen has said, "In many cases, creating the desire to work is a company's first and most difficult task with hard-core unemployed persons. They have lived in an atmosphere of hopelessness or frustration or insecurity for so long that the value of being employed full time has little meaning."[16]

---

[15] For a further discussion of selection standards and testing see Harold Mayfield, "Equal Employment Opportunity: Should Hiring Standards Be Relaxed?," *Personnel.* Vol. 41, No. 5 (September-October 1964), pp. 8-17; Gerald A. McLain, "Personnel Testing and the EEOC," *Personnel Journal,* Vol. 46, No. 7 (July-August 1967); and Robert M. Guion, "Employment Test and Discriminatory Hiring," *Industrial Relations,* Vol. 5, No. 2 (February 1966). pp. 20-37.

[16] As quoted in Kent McKamy, "Putting the Jobless to Work: Toughest Part Still Ahead," *Business Management* (June 1968), p. 26.

Counseling.   People who have been considered unemployable tend to become easily discouraged and to give up. They have problems with transportation, finance companies, getting gas and electricity turned back on, the police, drinking, the family, and a host of others. They can profit from supportive advice and friendly interest on the part of their immediate supervisors and from experienced coworkers. Some companies have found the buddy system to be effective.

Union Cooperation.   Most union leaders, having risen from the ranks, are closely attuned to the patterns of thinking and feeling of their constituents—the rank and file. Their cooperation and counsel on plans and programs can prove valuable. They often can perceive impending trouble with a projected action and suggest meaningful modifications.

If lower rates of pay are contemplated for the new recruits until they can meet the regular company standards, then of course concurrence must be obtained from the union.

Some Case Examples

Eastman Kodak Company.   In the mid-1960's the Eastman Kodak Company launched a program in basic education for those lacking the education to qualify for entry-level jobs or traditional entry-level training programs. Each person was assigned to one of five training programs: (1) trade trainee—a program to qualify for skilled trades as apprentices, (2) trade handyman trainee—to prepare people for work as handyman in the skilled trades, (3) production handyman trainee—for production or service type jobs, (4) laboratory trainee—to work as assistants in a laboratory, and (5) construction trainee—for work in the construction trades.

The trainees devoted six hours a day to on-the-job work under the guidance of a highly qualified instructor. Two hours each day, five days per week, were devoted to reading, writing, and arithmetic in the classroom. The educational level of entrants was established by an achievement test. Level I of the classroom education was designed to bring the people who required this phase up to the fifth grade in reading and arithmetic. Level II, starting where Level I left off, went up to 8th grade and beyond. It expanded the usable vocabulary to 7,000 words; taught fractions, percentages, and graphs; and covered principles of good citizenship and family economics.

The program utilized the services of an outside educational consultant, The Board for Fundamental Education, which is a nonprofit organization skilled in creating and implementing innovative programs. This particular program eliminated the traditional competitive classroom atmosphere, which causes learners such as these, already conditioned by failure, to doubt their competence. The classroom was arranged symposium-style so that everyone could see everyone else's face and expression when conversing. The learning emphasized a success every day, no matter how small or insignificant it may have seemed to someone else. The instructors continually reassured the learners that they were progressing.

During the first year of operation, 71 persons completed the program. The new trainees showed an average reading level improvement of 1.4 years, and in arithmetic they gained 3.0 years (school grade levels). Certain regular company employees (hired before the start of this program) who suffered from lack of education or who had a language difficulty because of foreign birth were also enrolled. These persons showed an average reading-level improvement of 2.7 years and an arithmetic improvement of 4.0 years.

Foremen who supervised the new trainees noticed a marked improvement in attitude and performance on the job.[17]

Pontiac Division of General Motors.   The Pontiac Division of General Motors located in Pontiac, Michigan started hiring the hard-core unemployed in September 1967. The primary motivation was to meet a serious labor shortage. In addition to the usual recruiting sources the Division called upon the Pontiac Urban League for help in locating workers. Selection hurdles were deliberately set very low. A short interview was used to gauge whether the candidate was *willing* to work. A medical examination was used to decide if the man was physically *able* to do the work available.

A total of 281 former "unemployables" were hired over a two-month period. Practically all were Negroes. These were selected from a pool that included men with poor education, physical handicaps, little or no previous work experience, with drinking problems, and criminal records. Some were unable to read or write. The Urban League sent representatives into the bars, barber shops, pool halls, street corners, and churches to recruit the men.

The Division assigned the vast majority to entry-level factory jobs such as assembler, core cleaner, sweeper, and press operator. They were scattered throughout the entire plant and mixed in with older workers. The Company gave them no special indoctrination or training although it did appoint a coordinator to handle special problems.

The newcomers generally lacked orientation. Many were confused. They could not endure the discipline of working at a task for eight hours a day. Nevertheless, the management considered the record of these men as about average based upon past experience with regular employees. Of the 281 hired, 150 (53 per cent) still were on the job after six months and were considered satisfactory. Absenteeism, tardiness, intoxication, and medical problems were more common for this group than regular new employees, and these were major reasons for terminations.

Although the Pontiac Division made no special effort to educate and train these disadvantaged people, this project did demonstrate that a pro-

[17] This account of the Eastman Kodak program is derived from Lee S. Gassler, "How Companies Are Helping the Undereducated Worker," *Personnel,* Vol. 44, No. 4 (July - August 19 1967), pp. 47 - 55.

gram of very extraordinary recruiting effort and lower selection standards can yield a body of workers who can perform simple jobs with moderate success and an average rate of failure.[18]

Lockheed Aircraft Corporation.   In 1967 the Lockheed Aircraft Corporation conducted two experimental programs to train and employ the hard-core unemployed. These programs were quite successful.

One program at the Marietta, Georgia, plant commenced with 98 persons who were recruited for a twelve-week sheet-metal worker course. The trainees were not on Lockheed's payroll, but they did receive modest government stipends under the Manpower Development and Training Act. About three fourths of the trainees were Negroes, 60 per cent came from families on welfare, 63 per cent had police records, and two-thirds were school dropouts. To get into the program applicants had to demonstrate reading proficiency of at least the fifth-grade level. Such job skills as drilling and riveting were taught. Related classroom instruction in blueprint reading and shop mathematics was also provided. Of the 98 persons who entered the program, 70 completed it. Dropouts were mainly due to loss of interest and bad attendance. The first 43 to complete the program were hired at Lockheed. Because of a personnel reduction at the company, the remainder had to be placed at other companies. Of those taken on at Lockheed none resigned and only four had to be dismissed.

The other program was conducted at the company's Sunnyvale, California plant. The 111 trainees (men and women) had an average age of 26. Racially they were composed almost equally of Negroes, Mexican-Americans, and Caucasians. More than 80 per cent were heads of households; 76 per cent came from families on welfare, and 40 per cent had police records. Median years of schooling was ten. The trainees were divided into three groups and given four weeks of classroom and vestibule school instruction. One group was given instruction in general helper-factory, another in electrical assembly, and the third in keypunch operation. The majority of the trainees were on the company payroll at the regular rates for the jobs for which they were being trained. These averaged about $100 per week. Some of the trainees, mostly women, were not on the payroll during training but did receive welfare payments. Of the 111 who entered the program early in 1967, 108 completed it and then became regular employees. By the end of 1967 only 10 of these 108 had left the employ of the company.

In both the Georgia and California programs, work performance on the job was satisfactory and essentially no different from other employees who met traditional hiring standards.

One of the keys to success of these programs was the careful attention to training. The people were trained for specific jobs and they were given somewhat more training than strictly required for these jobs. Most of the

---

[18] Information on the Pontiac Division of General Motors program has been derived from Stephen Habbe, "Hiring the Hardcore Unemployed," *The Conference Board Record,* Vol. 5, No. 6 (June 1968), pp. 18-22.

instruction was by demonstration, by doing, and by repetition. Small units of accomplishment were used and recognition was frequent.

A great deal of personal counseling and help was given. Lockheed program directors found that the trainees required an enormous amount of help with financial, family, and vocational problems. The trainees generally acted withdrawn and lacked self-confidence in the early stages of their programs.

As a consequence of favorable experience with these initial programs, Lockheed greatly expanded the size and scope of its activities with the culturally deprived.[19]

Questions for Review and Discussion

1. What groups in the population of the United States comprise the culturally deprived?
2. What is meant by the term *hard-core unemployed?*
3. What motivates companies to launch programs to hire and train the hard-core unemployed? Can these programs be justified economically?
4. Give some principal cultural and sociological characteristics of the culturally deprived poor people of America. How do they differ from the middle class?
5. Describe the special problems of the Negro poor.
6. Relate educational achievement, age, race, and unemployment rates.
7. What are the objectives of the Manpower Development and Training Act of 1962? Has this Act been successful?
8. Give and explain the principal programs of the Economic Opportunity Act of 1964. How effective have the manpower programs of the Act been?
9. Outline the principal features of a program to employ the hard-core unemployed for a private business firm.
10. Describe the problem of attitude, motivation, and adaptation to the industrial system for the typical culturally deprived person.

Suggestions for Further Reading

Becker, Joseph M. (ed.), *In Aid of the Unemployed,* Baltimore: The Johns Hopkins Press, 1965.

Gassler, Lee S., "How Companies Are Helping the Undereducated Worker," *Personnel,* Vol. 44, No. 4, July-August 1967, pp. 47-55.

[19] Information on the Lockheed program was obtained from James D. Hodgson and Marshall H. Brenner, "Successful Experience: Training Hard-Core Unemployed," *Harvard Business Review,* Vol. 46, No. 5 (September-October 1968), pp. 148-156.

Ginsburg, Eli, *Manpower Agenda for America,* New York: McGraw-Hill Book Company, 1968.

Habbe, Stephen, "Hiring the Hardcore Unemployed," *The Conference Board Record,* Vol. 5, No. 6, June 1968, pp. 18-22.

Harrington, Michael, *The Other America: Poverty in the United States,* New York: The Macmillan Company, 1962.

Hoos, Ida R., *Retraining the Work Force: An Analysis of Current Experience,* Berkeley and Los Angeles: University of California Press, 1967.

Magnum, Garth L. (ed.), *The Manpower Revolution: Its Policy Consequences,* Garden City, N.Y.: Doubleday & Company, 1965.

Ornati, Oscar, *Poverty Amid Affluence,* New York: The Twentieth Century Fund, 1966.

Patten, Thomas H., Jr., and Gerald E. Clark, Jr., "Literacy Training and Job Placement of Hard-Core Unemployed Negroes in Detroit," *The Journal of Human Resources,* Vol. 3, No. 1, Winter 1968, pp. 25-46.

Research Institute of America, *What You Can Do About the Hard-Core Unemployed,* New York, 1968.

Seligman, Ben B., *Poverty as a Public Issue,* New York: The Free Press, 1965.

Wolfbein, Seymour L., *Education and Training for Full Employment,* New York: Columbia University Press, 1967.

Performance Appraisal

11

In our daily lives we continually size up and form opinions of the people with whom we come in contact. In social relations this is done quite casually, often subconsciously, and rarely systematically. If one wishes to select a barber, dentist, physician, or a home builder, he may be somewhat more thorough in the manner in which he forms judgments. When we move into the area of cooperative group endeavors—in short, organizations—we find that supervisors must continually judge the contributions and abilities of their subordinates. Certain individuals are more adept at doing one type of work than another, certain ones cannot be depended upon to carry through an assignment to completion, others show great initiative and reliability and can take on projects with a minimum of supervision. The supervisor must frequently make decisions pertaining to the pay treatment of his employees, as well as employee placement, transfer, promotion, and individual development. Shall these personnel actions be based upon spur-of-the-moment decisions, or shall they be based upon carefully thought-out judgments made by a supervisor in collaboration with others and formulated in a systematic manner?

Because managers must make judgments of their employees almost constantly and for many reasons, the question naturally arises as to whether this should be formalized into a systematic performance appraisal program or whether it should be a haphazard, disorganized affair. Because evaluation goes on all of the time, the question is not whether to appraise employees. Rather it is *how* to evaluate people. The overwhelming weight of argument is in favor of the formalized performance appraisal approach.

Under a formalized appraisal system supervisors and managers are encouraged to observe the behavior of their people. They tend to be interested in their training and development. Judgments, often from many raters, are recorded on paper and placed in the individual's personnel folder. Decisions on personnel changes of status are not left to the vagaries of recollections of busy supervisors. Human memory is often unreliable. Hidden talents are sometimes uncovered, especially if a number of raters appraise the same individual. A formal rating procedure minimizes the likelihood of capable people being overlooked for training opportunities, pay raises, promotions, and new assignments. It is difficult to operate a large organization without some form of written appraisal plan. When comparing candidates for promotion from different organizational units, management must have written records of ratings so that sound decisions can be made. Sometimes the ultimate decision maker is high in the organizational hierarchy, and he does not personally know the individuals being considered for the post. He must rely heavily upon ratings, records, and written recommendations.

How widespread is the use of formal employee appraisal programs? In a survey of 400 companies, the National Industrial Conference Board found that about one half of these had an employee rating program.[1] A survey of 567 firms, known to have progressive personnel programs revealed that 60.5 per cent had performance appraisal programs for supervisors, and 45.3 per cent had plans for executives.[2] These were companies selected because of well-developed personnel programs; hence, it is very likely that among the general population of business organizations the prevalence of rating programs is somewhat less.

Evolution of Performance Appraisal

Systematic employee appraisal techniques came into prominence at and immediately after the World War I era. During this war, Walter Dill Scott succeeded in persuading the United States Army to adopt his "man-to-man" rating system for evaluating military officers. During the 1920's and 1930's, industrial concerns began installing rational wage structures for their hourly employees. They established the policy that in-grade wage increases would be based upon merit. The early employee appraisal plans were called merit-rating programs. Indeed, the term *merit rating* was by far the most widely accepted designation right up until the mid-1950's.

Most of the merit rating plans from 1920 to the mid-1940's were of the

---

[1] "Personnel Practices in Factory and Office," *Studies in Personnel Policy,* No. 145 (New York: National Industrial Conference Board, 1954).

[2] W. R. Spriegel and Edwin W. Mumma, *Merit Rating of Supervisors and Executives* (Austin: Bureau of Business Research, The University of Texas, 1961).

rating-scale type with factors, degrees, and points. Indeed, the analogy between a point plan of job evaluation and a rating-scale plan of merit rating is very close.

Commencing in the early 1950's, great interest developed in the performance appraisal of technical, professional, and managerial personnel. This was tied in closely with the wave of interest in formal management development programs. It was recognized that appraisal, on a systematic basis, was an integral part of a well-designed development program.

At the same time that action in the area of performance evaluation of upper-level personnel has grown and intensified, interest in the rating of hourly paid workers has somewhat declined. A major reason for this is that in so many companies their pay and advancement is regulated by seniority. Management can still merit-rate the workers, but there is less opportunity to make use of these ratings.

Accompanying this change in emphasis has been a change in terminology. The older term, *merit rating,* has tended to be restricted to the rating of hourly paid employees. It has also been used more frequently where the object is to develop criteria for pay adjustments, transfers, and promotions. The newer terms *employee appraisal* and *performance appraisal* have the connotation of emphasis upon development of the individual. They are used more commonly to designate plans for white-collar, managerial, and professional personnel. They are broader in scope, because an appraisal interview with the ratee is almost always included in the appraisal program.

However, it should be pointed out that terminology in the personnel field is neither fixed nor rigid. Many other terms are commonly utilized in addition to the aforementioned. Among these are *personnel appraisal, personnel review, progress report, service rating, performance evaluation,* and *fitness report.*

Appraisal Defined

Performance appraisal is the systematic evaluation of the individual with respect to his performance on the job and his potential for development. Ordinarily the evaluation is made by the individual's immediate superior in the organization, and this is reviewed in turn by his superior. Thus everyone in the organization who rates others is also rated by his superior. This is true for all except nonsupervisory employees. As we shall see later there are some variations of this boss-rates-subordinate practice, but it is by far the most common arrangement.

Appraisal by results, which is a newer appraisal system, emphasizes the setting of performance goals on a mutually agreeable basis by discussion between subordinate and his immediate superior. The superior plays more of a supportive and coaching role rather than a judgmental one.

This appraisal system is most commonly applied to managerial, professional, and sales personnel.

Applications of Appraisals

Employee appraisal is an essential part of effective personnel management. Its purpose and uses are as follows:

Employee Performance. Appraisals are an aid to creating and maintaining a satisfactory level of performance from employees on their present jobs. When the actual evaluation process is followed up with an appraisal interview with each employee, it may contribute toward more effective or improved performance on the part of many individuals.

Employee Development. The appraisal may highlight needs and opportunities for growth and development of the person. Growth may be accomplished by self-study, formal training courses, or job-related activities, such as special broadening assignments and job rotation. It should be clear that training and development of employees and managers strengthens the organization as well as aids the individuals.

Supervisory Understanding. A formal and periodic appraisal encourages supervisors to observe the behavior of their subordinates. Encouraged by the proper top management attitude, they can be motivated to take an interest in each person and to help him. If carried out properly the entire appraisal process can facilitate mutual understanding between the supervisor and his subordinates.

Guide to Job Changes. An appraisal aids decision making for promotions, transfers, layoffs (where seniority may not be the controlling factor), and discharges (for inadequate performance). Systematic assessments of an individual by a number of raters, made over a period of time and recorded in writing, help to make this process reasonable and sound. It should give due consideration to the needs of both the organization and the individual.

Wage and Salary Treatment. Many organizations relate the size and frequency of pay increases to the rating assigned to the employee in the performance appraisal.

Validate Personnel Programs. The accuracy of predictions made in the employee selection process is often determined by comparing or correlating performance ratings with test scores, interviewers' evaluations, and so on. An indication of the worth of a training program can sometimes be determined by an analysis of employee performance after completion of a particular course of instruction.

BASIC CONSIDERATIONS IN APPRAISAL

When a rater evaluates someone, he tends to think in terms of what kind of a person he is and what he has done. Thus appraisal plans require the

rater to rate or score the employee on his personal traits and characteristics and on his contributions. Determination of the former is rather subjective, since different raters may appraise the same individual differently. Bill Smith's attitude toward the company may seem acceptable to one
supervisor, but another boss may feel that Smith is a little too critical of
company policies and score him lower on that account. Employee contributions—what a man actually accomplishes on the job—can be more
objectively ascertained. For many jobs the quantity of work produced
is readily measurable, and it serves as an excellent gauge of the employee's performance. Such measures are available for a high proportion of
direct labor jobs in industry. On the other hand, it is very difficult to measure the output of a receptionist, an engineer, a maintenance man, or
a public relations director.

It might be readily conceded that an employer is primarily interested
in assessing his employees' performance (that is, contributions), and therefore these factors should be counted most heavily. However, it is also
apparent that such personal traits as cooperativeness, dependability, attitude, initiative, and ability to get along with others also have a bearing
upon the employee's value to the organization. These characteristics affect
a person's relations with his boss and with his co-workers, and they influence his effectiveness on the job.

In recent years management has tended to place the greatest weight
in appraisal upon the actual results people achieve on their jobs. It is recognized that two people can have quite different personalities and yet
be equally effective in their work. This can be true even on the same job
or occupation.

Standards of Performance

In order to evaluate employees, it is necessary to have something against
which to compare them. Thus it is possible simply to compare one man
with another. This in essence is the ranking method of rating. However,
an approach that is likely to be more fruitful is to establish, in writing,
definite standards of accomplishment employees can reasonably be expected to meet. Such a method makes it possible for both the supervisor and
his subordinate to reach agreement on just what is expected in terms of
performance.

A useful starting point for developing written standards is the job description. For professional and managerial personnel much can be gained
by having the individual and his boss jointly develop the standard. For
lower-level employees, whose jobs tend to be very precisely defined and
limited, the supervisor quite generally will inform his subordinate of his
expectations in terms of quantity and quality of work, attendance, punctuality, job knowledge, and thoroughness.

The following are some examples of performance standards for management personnel. It will be noted that they are of necessity expressed

in somewhat general terms. Judgment on the part of the rater is required to determine how well the individual meets these expectations.

For a controller: effectiveness of and improvement in accounting procedures; promptness with which management is informed of operating and financial results; soundness of policies and procedures recommended; quality, quantity, and timeliness of suggestions given to corporate office executives; quality, quantity, timeliness of suggestions and guidance given to plant management.

For a manufacturing manager: production schedules for his division are met; product meets established quality standards; accident frequency is less than 10.0 per million man-hours; manufacturing overhead maintained within expense budget limits for level of operations; equipment down-time does not exceed 8 per cent; efficiency of direct labor utilization is at least 90 per cent of established standards; manager creates and maintains satisfactory level of morale within his division; manager provides adequate cross-training assignments for his personnel.

It should be pointed out that performance standards are relative to the group and to the organization. Not only are the needs of each organization different, but from one company to another the caliber of the manpower will vary. The expectations of management are higher in some companies than others.

Performance and Potential

Depending upon the purposes of the employee appraisal program, the evaluation may be directed toward the actual performance of the individual on his present job or toward his potential for promotion to a higher-level position. Quite often the rater(s) is asked to make judgments in both areas.

To determine a man's potential for taking on enlarged job responsibilities and for advancement requires a great deal of knowledge and skill on the part of the appraiser. The demands of the individual's present job may not give him an opportunity to demonstrate his full abilities. The question of a man's potential for growth can be answered fairly only when one considers "growth for what?" If an engineer is being considered for promotion to a supervisory position in the engineering department, he must possess a certain cluster of aptitudes and abilities. On the other hand, if he is being considered for a high-level staff position, he will need quite different qualifications. Thus it would be folly to design an appraisal-rating form that simply asked the question "Potential for Promotion?"

Quite generally a supervisor can more accurately appraise the potential of a subordinate if he deliberately plans new and varied job assignments that will confront the person with a variety of problems and require him to demonstrate a number of his abilities.

Of couse, the issue of employees' performance on their present jobs is often more urgent than that of advancement to higher-level ones. In this case the appraisal program will give major emphasis to contributions in comparison with established standards, to quantity and quality of work, to attendance, dependability, job knowledge, and to cooperation with others. Where present day-to-day job performance is more vital than the potential for future advancement, the appraisal program is more likely to be geared to improving performance on one's present job, wage and salary treatment, and training needs for the individual.

Who Does the Appraising?

The prevailing practice in nearly all private and public organizations is to have the supervisors and managers of each department evaluate the performance of each of their subordinates. Most commonly these ratings are reviewed by their immediate superiors. The presumption for such a procedure is that the person charged with responsibility for managing a department has the proper understanding of organizational objectives, needs, and influences. Being held accountable for the successful operation of his department or unit, he must, presumably, have control over personnel-administration decisions affecting his people.

However, there is another aspect to this picture. The view that a supervisor receives of his subordinates is not complete. Certain features of their behavior are unknown or only partially known to him. If given the opportunity, a person's work associates could supply considerable information and insight into his make-up. The military services of the United States have done considerable work with peer ratings (often called "buddy ratings"). Much of the work in this connection has been carried on in officer candidate schools in all branches of the armed forces. Peer ratings do not supplant ratings by superior officers; rather they supplement the customary types of rating in order to make decisions on promotions, job assignments, and selection for special training schools. In reviewing the many research studies conducted in connection with peer ratings in the military services, Hollander found that in some of the studies peer ratings were a more valid predictor of leadership performance than were ratings by superior officers. In summary he found that peer ratings yielded good reliability and validity and were a very useful appraisal method.[3]

The group appraisal method, wherein each supervisor evaluates not only his own subordinates but also those working for other supervisors, holds considerable promise. The rating process is actually done in a group meeting of the supervisors. This meeting is presided over by a coordinator, who may be a personnel administrator or the immediate superior

[3] E. P. Hollander, "Buddy Ratings: Military Research and Industrial Implications," *Personnel Psychology,* Vol. 7, No. 3 (Autumn 1954), pp. 385-393.

of these supervisors. The group appraisal process yields multiple judgments and can often modify biased ratings that would be made by the single supervisor under the traditional rating method.

Characteristics of Good Raters

What kind of people make the best judges of the abilities, traits, and motives of others? Do some raters possess a greater skill in this area than others? After making an intensive study of the available research in this area Ronald Taft, found that there is a positive correlation between the ability to judge others and high intelligence and academic ability, esthetic interests, emotional stability, high social skill, and social detachment. Strangely enough those with psychological training and even clinical psychologists were not as successful in judging others as were physical scientists. He found no correlation between ability to judge and age (for adults) or sex or training in psychology.[4]

There is some evidence that supervisors who are highly rated by their superiors in terms of overall performance do a better (or at least a different) job of performance rating than those who are considered poor supervisors. In a research investigation Kirchner and Reisberg found that: (1) Better supervisors are more discriminating in rating their subordinates. There is more spread between high and low producers. Less effective supervisors tend to rate down the middle. (2) Better supervisors identify and place greater importance upon achievement oriented behavior such as initiative, persistence, and planning ahead. Less effective supervisors consider group conformity and follower-type actions to be most important as "strengths" in their subordinates.[5]

APPRAISAL METHODS

Over the years a considerable number of appraisal systems have been developed. There has been a continuing effort to make them more objective, more valid, and less dependent upon unsupported whims of the raters. The following are the major types of rating systems:

1. Rating scales
2. Employee comparison
   a. Ranking
   b. Forced distribution
3. Check list

[4] Ronald Taft, "The Ability to Judge People," *Psychological Bulletin,* Vol. 52, No. 1 (January 1955), pp. 1-23.

[5] Wayne K. Kirchner and Donald J. Reisberg, "Differences Between Better and Less-Effective Supervisors in Appraisal of Subordinates, *"Personnel Psychology,"* Vol. 15, No. 3 (Autumn 1962), pp. 295-302.

   a. Weighted check list
   b. Forced-choice
4. Critical incident
5. Field review
6. Free-form essay
7. Group appraisal
8. Appraisal by results

Rating Scales

Being the oldest and most widely used type of rating procedure, the scaling technique has appeared in various forms. Most commonly the rater is supplied with a printed form, one for each person to be rated, that contains a number of qualities and characteristics to be rated. For hourly paid workers typical qualities rated are quantity and quality of work, job knowledge, cooperativeness, dependability, initiative, industriousness, and attitude. For management personnel, typical factors are analytical ability, decisiveness, creative ability, leadership, initiative, job performance, coordination, and emotional stability.

One form of scale is the continuous scale wherein the rater places a mark somewhere along a continuum. Figure 11-1 is an illustration of one factor having a continuous scale.

Another form of rating scale is the discontinuous type. This is sometimes called the multiple step form of scale. Figure 11-2 is an illustration of one factor using a discontinuous scale. The rater simply checks the box most descriptive of the employee.

In both the continuous and the discontinuous forms, the points assigned to each degree may be actually shown on the rating form, or they may be omitted from the form and then tabulated after the completed forms have been returned to the personnel office.

One means of insuring that the rater has based his scoring upon substantial evidence is to leave space on the form after each factor and require that he explain the reason for his rating. In effect he is asked to give examples of the subject's behavior that justifies the assigned rating.

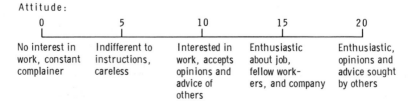

Figure 11-1.   Continuous Rating Scale.

Job Knowledge:

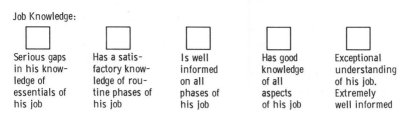

| Serious gaps in his knowledge of essentials of his job | Has a satisfactory knowledge of routine phases of his job | Is well informed on all phases of his job | Has good knowledge of all aspects of his job | Exceptional understanding of his job. Extremely well informed |

Figure 11-2. Discontinuous Rating Scale.

An interesting research study that bears upon the wisdom of subdividing human performance into factors as is done in the rating scale system is that conducted by Seashore, Indik, and Georgopoulos.[6] They investigated a delivery service firm having 27 offices in different parts of the country and employing a total of 975 nonsupervisory employees. They studied the extent to which five different measures of job performance correlated with one another. These measures of performance were overall effectiveness as judged by the station managers, productivity, chargeable accidents, unexcused absences, and errors. The latter four items were objective measures of performance and were obtained from records maintained at the offices. In substance the researchers wanted to find out if one overall measure or rating of work performance would be just as effective in evaluating an individual as several measures on separate factors.

The results of the experiment, in which statistical intercorrelations were calculated, showed a low degree of relationship among these measures of job performance. The size and direction of the relationships were to a large degree unique to each group and situation. The researchers concluded that their data contradicts any proposition that "overall job performance as a unidimensional construct has validity." Their data shows that the use of a single job-performance variable as a "sample" of a set of job performances is not justified unless there as been previous research pertaining to the interrelations of the various factors of work performance.

The rating-scale method is easy to understand and easy to use. It permits the statistical tabulation of scores in terms of measures of central tendency, skewness, and dispersion. It is relatively easy to construct a rating scale. It permits a ready comparison of scores among employees. These scores presumably reveal the merit or value of every individual.

However, rating scales have serious disadvantages. Does a total score of 77 for Bill and 80 for Henry really mean much? There is an illusion of precision when definite numbers are assigned to a supervisor's opinions. There is also an implication that a high score on one factor can compensate for a low score on another. If a man scores low for quantity of work produced, can this really be counterbalanced by high scores for attend-

[6] Stanley E. Seashore, B. P. Indik, and B. S. Georgopoulos, "Relationships Among Criteria of Job Performance," *Journal of Applied Psychology,* Vol. 44, No. 3 (June, 1960), pp. 195-202.

ance, attitude, and cooperativeness. Frequently, in practice, ratings tend to cluster on the high side with this system. Supervisors tend to rate their men high because they want their men to receive their fair share of pay raises in some cases. In other situations they honestly believe all of their men are above average. In others they want to demonstrate improvement since the preceeding rating. Sometimes the competitive position between supervisors causes them to rate their men higher and higher.

Employee Comparison Methods

To overcome certain of the disadvantages of the rating-scale method, the rank-order and forced-distribution methods have been devised.

The ranking method requires the rater, who is usually the supervisor, to rank his subordinates on an overall basis according to their job performance and value to the organization. Thus someone must end up low man on the totem pole, and someone must be the high man. One aid to this ranking process is to have the rater choose the best and poorest men first. Then he can select the best and poorest of the remaining persons and so on until he has rated all of his group.

In other ranking plans the rater is simply expected to place his ratees in groups like the lowest third (below average), middle third (average), and top third (above average).

The paired-comparison technique is basically a way of achieving a rank order listing of employees in a very organized manner. It necessitates the comparison of each employee with all other persons in the group, one at a time. Thus the kind of judgment involved is easier and simpler than with the ordinary ranking method. The number of times each individual is preferred over another is tallied on a sheet of paper. These numbers yield the rank order for the entire group. If there are N employees to be rated, then $N(N-1)/2$ separate judgments must be made. If the group is large, the number of judgments becomes excessively tedious. This is a prime weakness of the paired-comparison technique.

A major weakness of the ranking method is that it does not reveal the difference between persons in adjacent ranks. Ranks are ordinal numbers. They tell how a person stands relative to others in the group, but they do not indicate how much better or poorer one person is than another. Also the method does not consider specific aspects of behavior. Only the whole man is considered.

Forced Distribution Method. The forced-distribution procedure has been designed to prevent supervisors from clustering their men at the high end of the scale or at some other point on the scale. It requires the rater to distribute his ratings in a pattern to conform to a normal frequency distribution. The supervisor must allocate 10 per cent of his employees to the top end of the scale, 20 per cent in the next highest category, 40 per cent in the middle bracket, 20 per cent in the next lower category, and 10 per cent in the bottom grouping.

The objective of this technique to spread out the ratings is commendable, because in any work group it is quite unlikely that all employees make equal contributions. One time the author asked a group of four industrial supervisors to assign each of their men to one of three categories—below average, average, and above average. They refused to place any in the lowest category. They considered the vast majority of their men to be above average.

However, the forced distribution technique is based upon rather fallacious reasoning. Although it is true that most abilities in the general population are distributed according to a normal curve, in any organization we are dealing with a select group of persons. They have been selected by the personnel department and by line management. Misfits have been weeded out or reassigned during the probationary period. Therefore, the distribution of abilities and performance in a working group should be decidedly skewed. It is unlikely that the employees in any small group will conform to a normal curve.

This procedure brings to mind the college professor who was teaching a graduate course in statistics to a class of four students. At the beginning of the semester he announced that there would be one A granted, two C's, and one F, and this is exactly how he assigned the grades at the completion of the course!

Check List

There are two kinds of check-list methods. One is the weighted check list, and the other is the forced-choice method. Both require a considerable amount of preliminary research in the company involved to develop the plans.

Weighted Check List. The weighted-check-list form of rating consists of a large number of statements that describe various types and levels of behavior for a particular job or family of jobs. Every statement has a weight or scale value attached to it. When rating an employee the supervisor checks all those statements which most closely describe the behavior of the individual. The rating sheet is then scored by averaging the weights of all the descriptive statements checked by the rater.

The weighted check list is constructed by having persons who are quite familiar with the job or job group under consideration write a great many statements describing actual behavior on that type of work. After being reviewed and edited, these are placed on separate cards. Then judges, who have actually observed the work being performed, are selected. They sort the cards into categories according to whether the statements define certain levels of performance, ranging from poor to excellent. Weights are then assigned to the statements in accordance with the way they were ranked by the judges.

The weighted check list makes the supervisor think in terms of very specific kinds of behavior. Vague impressions do not form the basis for scoring. However, this system is very costly (in terms of staff developmental time) to install where there are a large number of diverse jobs involved. It will be remembered that a separate check list must be established for each different job or job family.

Forced-Choice.   The forced-choice method of rating was developed at the close of World War II by a group of industrial psychologists to evaluate the performance of officers in the United States Army. Since that time a number of industrial concerns have adopted the technique.

The rating form, which must be constructed specifically for a general type or group of jobs, consists of a large number of tetrads, or groups of four statements each. In some cases groups of five statements are used. For each tetrad the rater must check the one statement that is most descriptive of the performance of the person and the statement that is least descriptive. The tetrads are so designed that each contains two statements that appear favorable and two that appear unfavorable. The actual value or weighting of the statements is kept secret from the supervisors. This is supposed to prevent deliberate bias on their part. They cannot slant the rating to make the final score come out the way they want it to. They are essentially reporters in that they check statements to report behavior as accurately as they can. Of the two favorable-sounding statements only one actually discriminates between high and low performance employees. Likewise, of the two unfavorable-sounding statements only one actually distinguishes between good and poor performers. By reading the statements it is not apparent which actually count for or against the rated individual. The scoring is done in the personnel department. If large numbers of persons are involved, machine scoring can be employed.

Here is a group of statements used to rate the performance of foremen in an oil refinery.[7]

Most	Least	
A	A	Seldom makes mistakes
B	B	Respected by subordinates
C	C	Fails to follow through assignments completely
D	D	Feels his job is more important than other jobs
E	E	Does not express own views with any degree of self-reliance

While both A and B sound favorable, only statement B actually differentiates high from low performance foremen. Item C is actually descriptive of low performance foremen, although item E also appears to be unfavorable. Item D is neutral.

Experiments with the forced-choice technique in comparison with the rating-scale procedure have shown that there is less bias in the forced-

---

[7] Industrial Relations Counselors, Inc., "The Measuring of Supervisory Ability—A Case Study, [Part] I. Performance Rating Program," Industrial Relations Memo No. 119 (September 22, 1950). Quotation by permission.

choice method. When it was used for making administrative decisions regarding personnel, there was less piling up of scores on the high side of the distribution than for the rating-scale method.[8] When validated with other measures of job performance, the forced-choice method has shown good correlations. It also seems to have greater objectivity than most other methods.[9]

The principle disadvantages of this method are the fact that it is very expensive to install and that it is difficult for a supervisor to discuss ratings with his subordinates because he himself does not know how the items are scored. This latter is, of course, a very serious limitation.

Critical Incidents

Having been developed relatively recently, the critical-incidents method requires every supervisor to adopt a practice of recording in a notebook all of those significant incidents in each employee's behavior that indicate effective or successful action and those that are indicative of ineffective or poor behavior. These are recorded in a specifically designed notebook which contains categories or characteristics under which the various behaviors can be recorded. Examples of such categories or types of job requirements for workers are judgment, learning ability, productivity, dependability, accuracy of work, responsibility, and initiative. For engineers, examples of job requirements are planning ability, decision-making ability, report writing, coordination with other groups, creativeness, technical knowledge, cost of errors, and the like. Daily recording of these items seems to be most effective. Otherwise, supervisors soon forget the incidents of their men.

This method provides an objective basis for conducting a discussion of the individual's work performance. There is little likelihood of vague impressions and generalities dominating the discussion, since the supervisor has been trained to record actual incidents from the daily activities of the employee. The supervisor is supposed to refrain from making overall judgments and concentrate upon discussing facts as he sees them. Theoretically this should provide a sound basis for employee development and improvement. Strictly speaking, the critical-incidents technique is not a rating method. It does require the supervisor to pay close attention to what his men are doing.

The danger of this method is the very real possibility that it will lead to overly close supervision, with the boss breathing down the necks of his subordinates. It may give the people the impression that everything they do will be written down in the boss's "little black book."

---

[8] Erwin K. Taylor and Robert J. Wherry, "A Study of Leniency in Two Rating Systems," *Personnel Psychology,* Vol. 4, No. 1 (Spring 1951), pp. 39-47.

[9] Lee W. Cozan, "Forced Choice: Better Than Other Rating Methods?" *Personnel,* Vol. 36, No. 3 (May-June 1955), pp. 80-83.

Field Review[10]

The essential feature of the field-review appraisal method is that the departmental supervisors fill out no forms. Rather they are interviewed by a representative of the personnel department, who questions the supervisor to obtain all of the pertinent information on each employee. This personnel man then writes up his notes later, and these are sent to the supervisor for his approval or suggested modifications. There is no rating form with factors and degrees. Rather overall ratings are obtained. Usually a three-way classification scheme, such as outstanding, satisfactory, and unsatisfactory, is used. The interviewer questions the supervisor about the requirements of each job in his unit and about the performance of the man in the job. He probes to find out not only how a man is performing but why he performs that way and what can be done to improve him (if improvement is clearly in order) or to advance and develop him.

The field-review method relieves the supervisor of the paper work of filling out appraisal forms. It also insures a greater likelihood that the supervisors will give adequate attention to the appraisals, because the personnel department largely controls the process. Superficial judgments can be eliminated if the personnel representative probes deeply. The principal limitation is the fact that it ties up the services of two management representatives to carry out the appraisals.

Free-Form Essay

The free-form essay evaluation does not use scales, check lists, or any other devices. It simply requires the supervisor or other rater to write down his impressions of the individual on a sheet of paper. The comments can, if desired by the organization, be grouped under headings such as nature of job performance, reasons for this behavior, employee characteristics, and developmental needs for future.

To do a sound job with this method, the supervisor must devote considerable time and thought to the procedure. This is both a virtue and a defect. On the one hand it makes it necessary for the supervisor to be observant and analytical. On the other hand it demands more time than the average supervisor can spend (or is willing to spend). It is also true that the resultant appraisals often depend more upon the skill and effort of the writer-rater than upon the real performance of the people. Some supervisors are just poor writers. But this does not necessarily mean that their subordinates are poor employees, although a personnel officer reviewing the records might get this impression.

[10] Experience with this method of appraisal is described in Guy W. Wadsworth, "The Field Review Method of Employee Evaluation and Internal Placement," *Personnel Journal,* Vol. 27 (June through December 1948); and Stephen Habbe, "Merit Rating—Plus," *Management Record,* Vol. 15, No. 9 (September 1953), pp. 323-324.

Group Appraisal

The group-appraisal method, as usually carried out in industry, emphasizes the training, growth, and development of the individual. Decisions pertaining to pay increases and job changes are most commonly made by the employees' immediate supervisor in discussion with his boss. The appraisal group usually consists of the supervisor of the employees being judged plus three or four other supervisors who have knowledge of the employees' work performance. The other supervisors are picked because they have had numerous contacts with the people being rated and can presumably contribute something to the discussion. This method, like all the other appraisal procedures previously discussed, is suitable for rating all levels of nonsupervisory and managerial personnel.

All appraisal groups have a chairman or coordinator who leads the discussions. He is often the manager who is directly superior, in the organization, to the three or four supervisors involved. In some companies this role is carried out by a trained conference leader from the personnel department.

In the appraisal meeting the immediate supervisor of the person to be evaluated must explain the nature of his job duties, because he, of all the persons present, is in the best position to do this. Then the group discusses the standards of performance for that job, the actual performance of the job incumbent, the causes for such a level of performance, ideas for improving performance where required, and a specific action plan for the development of the individual. Practice varies as to whether the group agrees upon a specific rating for the ratees, such as outstanding, good, satisfactory, poor, and so on. In some organizations the actual assignment of a rating to each employee is left to the immediate supervisor and his boss. Presumably this rating should be consistent with the tenor of the group discussion. The group appraisal method is widely employed in the Bell Telephone System Companies.

The great virtue of this method is that it is thorough, and multiple judges can modify or cancel out a bias by the immediate supervisor (who makes the sole determination in most appraisal systems). Research experiments conducted by the Personnel Research Branch of the Department of the Army in 1950 have demonstrated that the average ratings of a number of raters for each employee were more valid than a single rating for each man.[11] Multiple judges can often think up better and more comprehensive development plans than one supervisor can. There is less likelihood of a promising individual being overlooked for promotion. The one serious limitation of the procedure is that it is very time consuming.

[11] A. G. Bayroff, H. R. Haggerty, and E. A. Rundquist, "Validity of Ratings as Related to Rating Techniques and Conditions," *Personnel Psychology,* Vol. 7, No. 1 (Spring 1954), pp. 93-103.

PROBLEMS IN RATING

Being conducted by humans, performance appraisal is frequently subject to a number of errors and weaknesses. Certain of these errors are more common in some appraisal methods than others, as will be revealed by the discussion to follow.

Halo Effect

The halo effect is the tendency of most raters to let the rating they assign to one characteristic excessively influence their rating on all subsequent traits. Many supervisors tend to give an employee approximately the same rating on all factors. (This halo error also occurs when an interviewer is sizing up a candidate for employment.) The rating-scale technique is particularly susceptible to the halo effect. One way of minimizing its influence is to have the supervisor judge all of his subordinates on a single factor or trait before going on to the next factor. In this way he can consider all of the men relative to a standard or to each other on each trait.

Leniency or Strictness

Some supervisors have a tendency to be liberal in their ratings, that is, they assign consistently high values or scores to their people. This is a very common error in rating programs. Somewhat less common, but equally damaging to the usefulness of appraisals, is the tendency of some supervisors to give consistently low ratings. Both of these trends can arise from varying standards of performance among supervisors and from different interpretations of what they observe in employee performance. It is due to the subjectiveness of man. It can be partially overcome by holding meetings or training sessions for the raters so that they can reach common agreement on just what they expect of their men. Of course, if the employees in Department A are consistently judged higher than those in Department B, it is difficult to determine whether this reflects true differences in their abilities and contributions or whether it simply reveals leniency on the part of one manager and strictness on the part of another.

Central Tendency

Some raters are reluctant to rate people at the outer ends of the scale. Quite frequently this central tendency is caused by lack of knowledge of the behavior of the persons he is rating. He knows that management policy dictates that he must appraise his employees at periodic intervals. But if he should be unfamiliar with some of the individuals, he may play it safe by neither condemning nor praising. He would be hard pressed to substantiate such judgments. As we shall see shortly, under the heading "Organizational Influences," the way in which the appraisal information is handled by higher management sometimes induces supervisors to rate down the middle.

Interpersonal Relations—Bias

The way a supervisor feels about each of the individuals working for him—whether he personally likes or dislikes them—has a tremendous effect upon his ratings of their performance. This is especially operative in those situations where objective measures of performance are either not available or difficult to develop.

> In one working group consisting of professional employees in the government, there was a change of directors in charge of the force. A new director was brought in from a distant location when the previous head was promoted to another branch. Within the space of a few months, the new man had completely inverted the ratings of his people. Those who had been rated high by the previous director were rated unsatisfactory by the new man, and vice versa. One man who had been classified lowest in the group because the previous head had considered him unsatisfactory, was promoted to be second in command within the space of eighteen months. Although all of the men were sincere, conscientious people, there was a difference in point of view and of personalities between the new director and most of them.

Experimental evidence to demonstrate the powerful force of interpersonal relations has been developed by Kallejian, Brown, and Weschler.[12] In this experiment, which concerned a research and development laboratory, a clinically skilled interviewer interviewed 32 employees regarding their relations with their co-workers and superiors. On the basis of these interviews, he formulated an evaluation of the personality of the superiors who rated each group of employees. The interviewer then predicted how the superiors actually had rated these people. He did it on the basis of his knowledge of interpersonal relations because he was not familiar with the technical work of the laboratory. When his ratings were correlated with the supervisors' ratings on overall effectiveness the results were accurate at the 3-per-cent level of significance. When correlated for 17 specific characteristics of performance, his ratings were accurate at the 5-per-cent level of significance.

Organizational Influences

Nowhere is the subjectivity of performance evaluation more glaring than when ratings change according to the way they are going to be used

[12] Verne Kallejian, Paula Brown, and I. R. Weschler, "The Impact of Interpersonal Relations on Ratings of Performance," *Public Personnel Review* (October 1953), pp. 166-170.

by management. Fundamentally raters tend to take into consideration the end use of the appraisal data when they rate their subordinates. Perhaps this is only natural.

If they know that promotions and pay increases hinge on the ratings, they tend to rate on the high side (they are lenient). Effective supervisors tend to go to bat for their men. Besides it would look bad for a boss (and his relations with his subordinates would suffer) if other departments received higher pay increases than his group.

On the other hand, when appraisals are made principally for the development of the employees, supervisors tend to emphasize weaknesses. The whole focus is upon what is wrong with these people and what they have to do to improve.

Actual experience with rating plans has demonstrated that supervisors will rate their people near the middle of the spectrum (average) if their bosses put pressure on them to correct the subpar performers (or get rid of them) and if they are called upon to really justify a rating of outstanding. In other words they will follow the path of least resistance, because they know that the "big boss" will be demanding of them in relation to those rated low or very high.

Experience has also shown that ratings tend to be higher when supervisors and managers know that they must explain their judgments to their subordinates.

APPRAISAL AND PERSONAL DEVELOPMENT

The appraisal process is quite properly viewed as an integral part of the development of people in the organization. Such development leads to improved job performance and the acquiring of new skills and knowledge by the individual. This qualifies him for broader responsibilities, more rewarding assignments, and promotion. A development plan should be tailor-made for each employee (whether he be an hourly worker, an engineer, or a manager).

A development program generally includes the following action steps by the supervisor or manager:

1. Analyze job duties and responsibilities. Discuss with employee to reach agreement upon these requirements.
2. Establish standards of job performance. Supervisor discusses these with employees so that there is common understanding and agreement.
3. Observe employee performance.
4. Appraise the employee. Judge potential for growth and advancement. Supervisor prepares appraisal report.
5. Supervisor conducts discussion of performance with the employee. May discuss the rating he received. Coaching and counseling may be done after filling out of periodic appraisal report (commonly an-

nually). Often coaching is carried out informally on day-to-day basis as supervisor and subordinate interact on the job.

6. Establish a plan of action for employee development. Supervisor may initiate special assignments and projects, may send to formal training courses, may delegate more decision-making responsibilities and authority. Much of employee development must be self-initiated in a proper organizational and managerial atmosphere. Supervisor can stimulate growth by providing appropriate financial and nonfinancial incentives. Development plans should emphasize strengths upon which the person can build rather than trying to overcome weaknesses of character and temperament.

7. Periodically review progress with employee. Grant proper recognition for his accomplishments. Set new goals.

Although the details will vary from one organization to another, the foregoing steps outline the principal features of a sound program.

A keystone of this developmental program for each employee is communication between the supervisor and the individual regarding his performance and behavior—in short, a discussion of the appraisal. Nearly all staff personnel men insist that every supervisor and manager must hold a postappraisal interview with each person to communicate the evaluation to him and to discuss plans and ideas for the future (especially improvement where such is needed). Yet most operating supervisors are very reluctant to conduct these postappraisal discussions. If company policy compels them to do it, they tend to do it sometimes informally so that the employee is not fully aware that it is an appraisal interview. Or some supervisors do it perfunctorily. Some do it only as long as the initial enthusiasm emanates from top management. Later they give only lip service to the discussions with their subordinates. Why does this reluctance exist?

Problems with Postappraisal Interviews

Operating supervisors and managers tend to resist postappraisal interviews because of the experiences they have had with them, both with their subordinates and with their superiors when they themselves have been appraised. Let us now look at the typical interview conducted according to the rules laid down in many company manuals and in textbooks.

Usually on an annual basis the boss calls his employees into his office one at a time for the appraisal interview. Both parties tend to build up emotionally for this. The boss plans what he is going to say, and the subordinate tends to be apprehensive about what he is going to hear. When the actual interview commences, the supervisor tries to put the man at ease by talking about the weather, the latest big league ball game, his golf play, or his family. The employee knows that this is just an interlude before getting down to serious business. Then the supervisor explains his overall evaluation in broad terms. He initially mentions some good aspects of the employee's performance. He may then give the employee a chance to express his views. Next the supervisor tells him his weaknesses and past failures. He allows the man to explain himself. Then the supervisor explains what steps he must take to improve his performance. He may, at this point, ask for the employee's ideas on improvement. One variation of the procedure above provides an opportunity, before the boss announces his evaluation, for the man to tell how he would rate himself.

Let us now examine the sources of trouble with this approach. In the first place the employee is put on the defensive. He is on the "hotseat" and he knows it. When the boss, who is in a position of authority over the man, criticizes him, it is a threat to the employee's self-esteem and his integrity. His personal security may even be threatened by the process.

According to Douglas McGregor this conventional approach to the appraisal interview comes very close to a violation of the integrity of the individual. The boss is placed in the position of playing God. He is judging and at times criticizing the personal worth of the man.[13]

There is a tendency for the supervisor to slip into the practice of criticizing those personality traits that annoy him. There is the case of the well-qualified and competent engineer whose boss picked on him in the interview because he did not smile more often. This trait did not affect his work performance, and being forty years old he would find it difficult to change anyway. The question may be further explored by asking what right the supervisor had to try to remake this engineer's personality. It is possible that in a few months' time a new supervisor might have been put in charge of this man, and he would be perfectly content with his mannerisms.

The subordinate may disagree with his boss's rating and may fight back at the criticism leveled at him. But knowing the power his superior has over his job tenure, he will be at a disadvantage in doing so. In any case the interview will become unpleasant for both parties. If the employee is submissive, he may simply take the criticism with little visible reaction. The boss may misinterpret this passive behavior and assume the man fully agrees with him.

Employees and managers alike often say that they want to know where they stand in the eyes of their superiors. But what they really want is reassurance, approval, and support.

That a postappraisal interview is an emotionally charged experience and even a traumatic one for some is revealed by the following example:

> John, a man of 48, was clearly exhausted emotionally when we met at the restaurant. He had taught at this junior college for two years and had just, this morning, gone through his second appraisal interview with

[13] Douglas McGregor, "An Uneasy Look at Performance Appraisal," *Harvard Business Review,* Vol. 35, No. 3 (May-June 1957), pp. 89-94.

the director. John had been called on the carpet the previous year for the way he organized his courses. This time to prepare himself for the experience he had gone to his minister for words of advice on how to stand up to the criticism. Despite this encouragement and help John was clearly "beat" when I talked with him. His whole conversation was devoted to the way he had again been raked over the coals by the director.

Most personnel specialists would agree that the purposes of postappraisal interviews are to let a subordinate know where he stands in the eyes of his boss, to point out weaknesses so that the man can correct them, to point out strengths, and to show the man how to improve his performance. But research evidence shows that things often do not work out as planned. Based upon an investigation in a large industrial corporation that had prided itself for having a sound traditional performance appraisal system, Meyer, Kay, and French found that criticism has a negative effect on achievement of goals and that defensiveness on the part of the subordinate in the face of criticism causes deteriorated performance. In comparing actual interviews containing many criticisms with those having few criticisms it was found that goal achievement was poorer 10 to 12 weeks hence for those receiving an above average number of criticisms. High criticism constitutes a threat to one's self-esteem and it prevents a meaningful, constructive relationship between superior and subordinate from emerging.[14]

Approaches and Solutions to Appraisal Interview Problems

Nearly everyone agrees that there should be feedback from the supervisor to his employees. One of the very important responsibilities of a supervisor is to coach and counsel his subordinates. The most fruitful approach to the interview is dependent upon the situation, the job, the person, and the goals to be accomplished.

For the New Employee. If an employee is new to the company and if he is relatively inexperienced and untrained, he expects to have to learn a great deal before he is fully qualified and is accepted. Most organizations designate the initial learning time as a probationary period. The person knows he is on trial and so does his supervisor. If the probationary term is six months in length, the supervisor does not wait until the very end to talk to the man about his performance. On the contrary, from the very start he has made a concerted effort to orient the person to his new environment and to train him properly. In his day-to-day contacts the supervisor will coach the employee. He will give help on methods, techniques, and the details of the job. He will guide and mold his behavior to conform to the standards of the organization. If all of the foregoing is carried out with proper regard for the rights and feelings of the newcomer, he will readily accept the guidance and correction. He will be

[14] H. H. Meyer, E. Kay, and J. R. P. French, Jr., "Split Roles in Performance Appraisal," *Harvard Business Review,* Vol. 43, No. 1 (January-February 1965), pp. 123-129.

eager to be accepted. So this type of appraisal discussion should in ordinary circumstances pose no great obstacles.

For Other Employees. For trained and experienced employees, for those who have worked for the organization for some time at whatever level they may be (worker or manager), certain general principles can be followed.

The success of the appraisal discussion depends to a large extent upon the climate that management in general and the supervisor in particular have established ahead of time. There must be an atmosphere of confidence and trust. The subordinate must know that his boss is *for* him, that he approves of him and supports him. In this kind of atmosphere, the man knows that criticism and suggestions for improvement are meant to assist rather than damage him.

Prior to the discussion the supervisor must have done a very thorough job of evaluating the man's performance, so that he feels confident of his position.

The supervisor must concentrate upon results rather than personality traits. People can readily accept discussion of the objective facts of work schedules, outputs, accomplishments, reports completed, sales made, scrap losses, budgets, profits, and the like. Criticism and discussion of personality traits, mannerisms, and so on, are seldom fruitful. This usually causes resentment. Managers must recognize that a number of employees, each having different personalities, can all achieve satisfactory results. Suggestions for improvement should be directed toward the objective facts of the job. Develop with the individual joint plans for the future. Do not criticize the individual as a person.

The supervisor should try to capitalize upon a man's strengths. This may mean giving full range to a man's assets and skills. If a person is poor at doing detail work but good at assignments where breadth and vision is demanded, then it makes little sense to try to force him to be effective at detail work.

The subordinate is most likely to understand and accept ideas for improvement if he has thought of these ideas himself. This means that the principles of nondirective interviewing and counseling, which are discussed in Chapter 18, "Supervision," are particulary appropriate here.

Finally the supervisor must recognize that he himself may have biases, idiosyncracies, and faulty impressions. His concepts of how people and things shape up is just one view. His concept is not the only one possible. There may be a number of ways of performing work and of reaching job and unit goals.

Frequent Coaching and Guidance. The alert and effective supervisor does not wait until the end of the year to talk to his employees about their work and progress. As the needs of the situation dictate, he makes it a practice to praise Bill, who has done a fine job on his assigned project, to find out what help Henry needs because he has fallen behind, and to redirect Joe's seemingly scatter-shot types of efforts. On these occasions, if he deems it desirable, the supervisor may expand the discussion somewhat into other areas of the man's work and his interests and aspirations. Although not labeled as formal appraisal interviews, these conversations serve to regulate the work, motivate the individual, let him know where he stands, and provide an opportunity for the boss to coach his team members.

APPRAISAL BY RESULTS

In recent years a new approach to performance appraisal has emerged and has been found fruitful in a number of companies. Appraisal by results has been designed to overcome certain of the inherent problems of traditional appraisal systems. It really constitutes a new way of managing. A major goal is to enhance the superior-subordinate relationship and improve the motivational climate.

The key features of appraisal by results are as follows:

1. Superior and subordinate get together and jointly agree upon and list the principal duties and areas of responsibility of the individual's job.
2. The person sets his own short-term performance goals or targets in cooperation with his superior. The superior guides the goal setting process to insure that it relates to the realities and needs of the organization.
3. They agree upon criteria for measuring and evaluating performance.
4. From time to time, more often than once per year, the superior and subordinate get together to evaluate progress toward the agreed-upon goals. At these meetings new or modified goals are set for the ensuing period.
5. The superior plays a supportive role. He tries, on a day-to-day basis, to help the man reach the agreed-upon goals. He counsels and coaches.
6. In the appraisal process the superior plays less the role of a judge and more the role of one who helps the person attain the goals or targets.
7. The process focuses upon results accomplished and not upon personal traits.

As appraisal by results is applied in practice, certain variations from the method, here described, occur. The procedure given here is closest to that formulated by Douglas McGregor.[15] It is also very similar to the work-planning-and-review method developed by a team of behavioral researchers at the General Electric Company.[16] The method recommend-

[15] McGregor, *op. cit.,* pp. 89-94. See also Douglas McGregor, *The Human Side of Enterprise* (New York: McGraw Hill Book Company, 1960), Ch. 5.
[16] Meyer, Kay, and French, *op. cit.,* pp. 127-129.

ed by the well-known management consultant Arch Patton is also similar, but it deviates in one important respect. Under Patton's formulation the superior does serve in the role of a judge. He rates his subordinate on how well he did in meeting the assigned targets and he tells him his rating.[17] Some writers emphasize that top executives meet with their immediate subordinates in groups to set goals for the company and for the major divisions. This process is carried on down the various echelons of the organization. Also the executives meet privately with their subordinates to establish individual goals.

Targets set can be both quantitative and qualitative. Thus for a manager of manufacturing, for the ensuing year he might set targets for himself (and his division) of a reduction in direct costs of 4 per cent, reduction of spoiled product by 2 per cent, and increase of return on investment to 14 per cent. Qualitative goals may be to improve work flow and housekeeping and to institute better on-the-job training.

Appraisal by results that involves mutual goal setting is most appropriate for technical, professional, supervisory, and executive personnel. In these positions there is generally enough latitude and room for discretion to make it possible for the person to participate in setting his work goals, tackle new projects, and invent new ways to solve problems. This method is generally not applicable for hourly workers because their jobs are usually too restricted in scope. There is little discretionary opportunity for them to shape their jobs. Their duties, responsibilities, and performance targets are imposed upon them by industrial engineers and supervision.

Appraisal by results possesses a number of advantages. By participating in the setting of the goals, the man acquires a stake or a vested interest in trying to meet them. The General Electric Company research (referred to earlier) revealed definitely greater accomplishment for those persons who set definite goals than for those who did not.[18] Both the superior and subordinate are on the same team working for a better functioning group. A person is not rated against a fixed rating scale. His targets and responsibilities are set and evaluated in terms of his particular situation and abilities. Defensive feelings are minimized because the superior is not a judge but a helper. Emphasis is on performance and not personality traits. The emphasis is also upon the present and the future, which can be controlled. In conventional appraisal the focus is upon the past, which cannot be altered.

A basic requirement for success with this method is that the subordinate must be interested in his work and in the organization. He must have ideas and ambition.

However, it must be made clear that appraisal by results is not a pana-

---

[17] Arch Patton, "How to Appraise Executive Performance," *Harvard Business Review,* Vol. 38, No. 1 (January-February 1960), pp. 63-70.

[18] Meyer, Kay, and French, *op. cit.,* p. 127.

cea. A highly directive, authoritarian manager may find it difficult if not impossible to lead his people in this participative, human-being-centered, supportive style. The subordinate may try to set easily attainable goals in order to look good when he meets with his superior to review progress. If too much weight is placed upon quantifiable goals such as profits, costs, and efficiency, qualitative goals such as investment in human resources (training, health, and morale builders) may be downgraded. Because emphasis is given primarily to objective items of performance in the present job, the superior may not devote adequate attention to uncovering capabilities required for promotion to a new and different position.

All in all, however, the appraisal-by-results method shows rather reasonable evidence of being superior to traditional appraisal systems.

An interesting experiment with this goals method as contrasted with the typical supervisor-rates-his-man-and-tells-him-results approach was conducted by Morton, Rothaus, and Hanson.[19] In the standard rating method of appraisal the supervisors rated their subordinates on a trait-rating scale. Both the subordinates and the supervisors reported their feelings and experiences on a behavior-rating scale. For the "goals method" the supervisors and subordinates participated jointly in goal-setting appraisals. Both groups also reported their feelings and experiences on a behavior-rating scale. Results of this experiment were distinctly favorable to the goal approach. There was greater agreement between the supervisor and the subordinate, less resistance to suggestions, a more friendly attitude, greater sense of responsibility by the subordinate, a greater understanding by subordinates of the areas in which change was needed, a clearer view of the routes to improvement, and greater eagerness to change.

In the General Electric study referred to previously, the weight of superiority was on the side of the "work planning and review method" (appraisal by results). It proved to be far more effective in improving job performance than the traditional rating system. Attitudes and actions improved significantly. Subordinates stated that their managers gave them more help, were more receptive to new ideas and suggestions, and made greater use of their abilities and experience.[20]

TRENDS AND PERSPECTIVES

It was stated at the outset of this chapter that appraisal is an integral and inevitable part of the process of management. Since the early efforts to systematize the rating process in the military and in private industry in

---

[19] Robert B. Morton, Paul Rothaus, and Philip C. Hanson, "An Experiment in Performance Appraisal and Review", *Journal of the American Society of Training Directors,* Vol. 15, No. 5 (May 1961), pp. 19-27.

[20] Meyer, Kay, and French, *op. cit.,* pp. 126-127.

the 1915-1920 era, a great deal of study, experimentation, and work has been done. Progress has been made. Some former notions have lost popularity. On the whole the present emphasis and trend seems to be healthy and fruitful. Figure 11-3 summarizes changes in performance appraisal that have developed over the years.

In interpreting the chart, it should be made clear that the activities listed under the heading "Former Emphasis" have not disappeared from the scene. Many of these practices are still much in evidence. For example, rating scales are still fairly commonly employed. But when viewed as a whole picture, organizations throughout the country are devoting increased attention to the items on the right side of the chart and less attention to those on the left.

Let us discuss some of the trends stated in the chart. Although it is certainly true that people are still being appraised and rated to determine who deserves a pay increase, promotion, transfer, and a layoff, there has been increasing recognition that these personnel actions are determined

TRENDS IN PERFORMANCE APPRAISAL

ITEM	FORMER EMPHASIS	PRESENT EMPHASIS
Terminology	Merit Rating	Employee Appraisal Performance Appraisal
Purpose	Determine qualification for wage increase, transfer, promotion, layoff	Development of the individual; improved performance on the job
Application	For hourly paid workers	For technical, professional, and managerial employees
Factors Rated	Heavy emphasis upon personal traits	Results, accomplishments, performance
Techniques	Rating scales with emphasis upon scores. Statistical manipulation of data for comparison purposes	Appraisal by results, mutual goal setting, critical incidents, group appraisal, performance standards, less quantitative
Post-Appraisal Interview	Supervisor communicates his rating to employee and tries to sell his evaluation, seeks to have employee conform to his views	Supervisor stimulates employee to analyze himself and set own objectives in line with job requirements, supervisor is helper and counselor

Figure 11-3. Chart Summarizing Changing Emphasis in Performance Appraisal over the Years.

by many factors other than a man's merit. Let us examine the situation with respect to pay increases.

Over the years some employers have announced to their employees that their progress in terms of their wage or salary was based primarily upon individual merit. Some managers have even gone so far as to state that for those who really produce there would be no limit to how far they could go in terms of higher pay! Now as a matter of fact it is somewhat of a deception to create the impression that pay treatment and merit are correlated that closely. Many of the factors that determine the size and frequency of pay adjustments have nothing to do with individual ability. General economic conditions, extent of competition in both the product and the labor market, and profitability of the firm and its ability to pay higher wages are prime factors. If a company has a "good year" and prospects for the future look bright, then it will tend to grant liberal increases in pay. Conversely, even though a man may work extra hard throughout the year, if business has been bad, he may receive no pay increase. If labor is in short supply and the demand is high, there may have to be a general upward adjustment in the wage structure of a company. The position of an employee within his pay grade has an effect upon his pay treatment. If he is at the top of his bracket he may receive no further raises unless he is promoted to a higher-paying job. If there has been a general upward adjustment in wage rates in the labor market, then management may decide that it is advisable to raise its wage level. A union may negotiate an across-the-board wage increase for all employees in a bargaining unit. In times of a severe business recession a company may be forced to slash all wages. Thus it should be evident that merit alone plays only a small part in determining how much money a man is paid. Merit certainly counts, but it must be given its proper place along with all the other wage determinants.

The shift in emphasis from the rating of hourly workers to the appraisal of higher-level employees has been brought about by a number of factors. The job of an hourly paid worker tends to be quite restricted in scope. If he works in a factory, it is quite likely that his job has been engineered in every detail by an industrial engineer. There is only limited opportunity for him to display initiative or to try new ways of doing his tasks. He has little chance to demonstrate leadership skills or to reveal special talents. For organized workers, unions press for single rates of pay for each job classification and upgrading on the basis of seniority. They usually oppose merit rating because it differentiates among people in the group and can be highly subjective. Added to these factors is the fact that automation has decreased the number of unskilled and semiskilled workers in our production system. People are being displaced by machines. For all of these reasons, performance appraisal plans when applied to hourly rated workers in many industries are up against an unfavorable environment.

The picture for the appraisal of white-collar, technical, professional, and managerial personnel, on the other hand, is very bright. The increasing technological complexity of industry and the rapid rate of innovation has increased the demand for larger numbers of these personnel. By and large these groups are not unionized, and where they are (engineers' unions, for example), there is little or no resistance to performance appraisal. The jobs of professionals and managers are not engineered. They are not narrowly defined. These people are encouraged to exercise initiative and ingenuity. Indeed, they are appraised on such factors as creativeness, initiative, judgment, leadership ability, and the like. There is considerable opportunity (in some organizations) for growth and development. Indeed, many companies will pay a substantial portion of the tuition for their engineers, scientists, and executives who are enrolled in evening courses in colleges and universities. Top management tends to place heavy emphasis upon thorough appraisal of this type of human resource. It feels that there is a great likelihood of gain for both the organization and the individual.

The decline in emphasis upon personal traits has been caused by a recognition that it is very difficult for a supervisor to change the personality of his men anyway. It certainly must be agreed that personal traits and characteristics are important, especially for certain types of jobs. Yet it is results that really count; and if Joe Johnson gets good results as a supervisor even though he does not have the temperament, attitude, and conformity to be an "organization man," then he should be adequately recognized for his good work. The decline in emphasis upon personality traits is also due to a recognition that there are no standards against which to compare the individual's personality. Raters certainly have their opinions as to what kind of personalities they favor, but most of them would not qualify as experts to grade others in this respect. Even clinical psychologists and psychiatrists do not always agree upon their evaluation of a man.

Salary Increase Vs. Personal Development

Current thinking indicates that appraisal discussions between the manager and his subordinate that are focused upon the man's performance, growth, development, and career goals should be conducted at entirely different times during the year from the discussion concerned with the man's salary treatment during the ensuing time period. The purposes of these two appraisal interviews are quite different. For salary administration a manager is normally provided a budgeted amount of money that can be allocated among the people in his department. He may rate his people by himself and have it reviewed by his own superior, or he may participate in a group rating process. In rating for salary adjustments, he must do some comparing of achievement among all his people. When he then invites each of his subordinates to meet with him privately, his goal is to tell the man how much of an increase he will receive for the coming year (if anything) and then hope that the individual accepts the amount as just and proper. If there is disagreement, the manager often feels he must sell the subordinate on the amount. Remember the manager has already committed himself. To raise the amount, the manager would have to admit that he may have made a mistake, and then he would have to go to his boss to seek approval for an upward adjustment.

Another reason for separating the two interviews by at least several weeks is that the subordinate himself ordinarily finds it difficult to concentrate upon plans for his personal development at the same time he learns how much money he will be paid for the forthcoming year.

The developmental interview on the other hand should be very supportive. There should be a free interchange of plans, suggestions, and targets. There should be full opportunity to review past accomplishments and future prospects. Neither party should be put on the defensive. Nor should bargaining for salary occur in a developmental interview.

Questions for Review and Discussion

1. What arguments can you give for the adoption of a formal employee-appraisal program in a business organization? Is such a program practical or necessary for a small organization of, say, 100 employees?
2. What objective measures can be used to evaluate performance in the following occupations: salesman of electronic computers, development engineer, foreman in a factory, machine operator in a factory, the president of a department store, stenographer?
3. How can a supervisor judge or evaluate whether a production-line worker would be suitable for promotion to the position of a foreman? How can an engineer be judged for promotion to a supervisory engineer?
4. When appraising people, is it better to compare one person's performance with another's or compare his performance with a written standard?
5. Develop a written standard of performance for a college professor. For a job that you now hold or have held.
6. Compare appraisal by a supervisor in the organization to appraisal by one's peers.
7. Explain the meaning of the following:
   a. Halo effect
   b. Central tendency
   c. Leniency or strictness
   How can these problems be overcome?
8. In some organizations the initial wave of enthusiasm upon the installation of a new appraisal program soon subsides. Appraisal forms are filled out by supervisors, filed in personnel folders, and then for-

gotten. Supervisors rarely conduct postappraisal interviews unless a man is doing very poor work. Supervisors look upon appraisal as an extra chore done somehow to satisfy the personnel department. What actions can you suggest to solve these problems?

9. What can be done to minimize the impact of favoritism and bias upon appraisals?
10. Do you feel that every employee should be shown the appraisal sheet that has been made out for him? What are the advantages and disadvantages?
11. What are the problems involved in postappraisal interviews between superior and subordinate? How can these difficulties be alleviated?
12. Describe appraisal by results. How does it differ from traditional appraisal methods? What are its advantages and possible limitations?
13. Describe the changes in emphasis that have occurred in employee appraisal in recent years.
14. Why does current thinking indicate that appraisal for salary increases should be conducted entirely separately from appraisal for development of the person?

CASE PROBLEM

The Case of Mary Jones

The Cadman Manufacturing Company employs about 2,500 people and produces electrical apparatus and electronic equipment. The shop employees are unionized, but the office employees are not. Although the white-collar personnel are not represented by a union, the Company has made it a policy to give careful consideration to seniority as well as ability in all promotions, transfers, downgradings, and layoffs. Because of fluctuations in sales and production, as well as ups and downs in the business cycle, the Company has experienced many changes in the size of the work force in recent years. This has occasioned frequent hiring followed by layoffs some months later.

All initiations of action by supervisors for the downgrading, layoff, or discharge of white-collar employees are reviewed by a placement committee. The objective of this committee is to see that the needs of the business are adequately taken care of while at the same time insuring fair treatment for the employees. This committee is chaired by the Personnel Manager. Other members are the heads of the production, engineering, and accounting departments.

On June 5, 1962, the placement committee met to consider the case of Mary Jones, whose supervisor, Mr. Williams, the Head of the Product Engineering Section, had recommended that she be removed from his section and either put in a lower-level job elsewhere in the company or else be discharged. As far as he was concerned, her work performance was quite unsatisfactory. In addition to the four regular members, the committee meeting was attended by Mr. White, Safety Supervisor; Mr. Williams, Head of Product Engineering; Mr. Kline of Merchandise Billing; Mr. Lilga, Office Manager; and Mr. Hanover, Specification Engineer.

In opening the meeting, the Personnel Manager outlined Mary's educational and experience record. (See Figure 11-4.)

The personnel manager explained to the Committee that Mary was hired on May 3, 1957, as a salary-grade 3 stenographer. On April 4, 1958, she was upgraded to a grade 4 secretarial-stenographer assigned to the head of the Payroll Department. During the business recession that occurred in 1958 it was necessary for the Company to reduce its entire work force, including supervisory as well as nonsupervisory personnel. Accordingly when Mr. Larson, a supervisor in the engineering service section, was transferred to the production department as a temporary demotion, it was necessary to find a position for June Smith, who had been Mr. Larson's secretary (grade 5). (Mr. Larson's position as well as that of his secretary's had been combined with another position within the engineering department.) Because June Smith had the qualifications and the length of service to displace Mary Jones, Mary was downgraded to a grade 2 stenographer and transferred to the office services department. Later she was transferred to the merchandise billing section.

On August 15, 1959, she was promoted to a grade 3 job as employment service clerk in the safety section of the personnel department.

In continuing his description of her Company career the Personnel Manager said that several months after Mary was raised to a grade 3 job, an opening arose that permitted June Smith to return to a grade 5 secretary's job with the Manager of Manufacturing. Mary then expected that she would be returned to her old job as secretarial-stenographer (grade 4) to the head of the payroll department. At that time, however, Helen Black, a grade 4 secretarial-stenographer, also was available for reassignment, because she had just finished her work of typing the notes of the recent union-management contract negotiations. From a company viewpoint it was considered advisable to retain Helen as a grade 4 secretarial-stenographer. Even though she had less service than Mary, she was selected for the Payroll Department job, much to Mary's disappointment. In fact, Mary had even gone to see the head of the payroll department to request reassignment to her old job.

On March 27, 1960, she was upgraded to a grade 4 secretarial-stenographer in the product engineering department, headed by Mr. Williams.

After his review of her career the meeting was opened up for discussion. Mr. White, Safety Supervisor, said that he had informed Mr. Williams, Head of Product Engineering, of her poor work habits but that he accepted her anyway. Mr. Lilga, Office Manager, stated that he told Williams that Mary was not capable of assuming all the duties of a grade 4

Name:	Mary Jones
Date of Birth:	January 15, 1932
Education:	Williamsport High School - graduated
	Williamsport Business School - Secretarial Course - one year - graduated
Marital Status:	Married, no children
Service Date:	May 3, 1957
Department:	Engineering
Present Job Title:	Secretarial-Stenographer
Salary Grade:	4

Previous Work Experience

Company	Occupation	Pay	From	To
Upstate Power Company	Clerk	$40/wk.	6-51	1-53
State Employment Service	Stenographer	$48/wk.	2-53	5-54
Edwards Department Store	Stenographer	$52/wk.	5-54	4-57

Cadman Company Experience

Department	Grade	Job Title	From	To	Last Rate
Payroll	3	Stenographer	5-3-57	4-3-58	$58/wk.
Payroll	4	Secretarial-Stenographer	4-4-58	9-26-58	$63/wk.
Office Service	2	Stenographer	9-27-58	11-14-58	$55/wk.
Merchandise Billing	2	Stenographer	11-15-58	8-14-59	$55/wk.
Personnel	3	Employment Service Clerk	8-15-59	3-26-60	$64/wk.
Engineering	4	Secretarial-Stenographer	3-27-60	Present	$70/wk.

Figure 11-4. Employee's Educational and Experience Record.

secretarial-stenographer. Mr. Williams denied that he was so informed and said that no one would have accepted her for this job if he had been so advised.

Mr. Williams told the committee that she was unable to take dictation properly. Her transcription revealed her shorthand to be so poor that her typed reports and letters often grossly distorted the original thoughts. As a consequence his engineers have resorted to writing everything out in longhand. Even on straight copy work from typed manuscript, she made mistakes and appeared unable to proofread adequately to achieve satisfactory typed work. He said that he had interviewed her formally on several occasions to discuss her shortcomings. He appealed to her to improve her performance, but no change resulted.

Contrary to the tenor of Williams' remarks were those of Mr. Hanover, Specification Engineer, who said that she had done a good job of typing reports for him while she was on loan to his unit for the past four weeks pending a decision by the placement committee. Mr. Kline of merchandise billing said that when she worked for him she did acceptable work as long as he kept prodding her. She had the basic capability to do good work, but her motivation and job interest seemed deficient. The Safety Supervisor supported this view. He had never considered Mary outstanding, but by close supervision he had been able to obtain acceptable work.

The Manager of the Accounting Department then pointed out that she attempted to retain her job by "crying on the shoulders" of various managers. She had actually pleaded her case before the plant manager on two separate occasions. She claimed that she was being unjustly treated in the engineering department.

In summation the Personnel Manager stated that the evidence showed that she had been doing wholly unsatisfactory work for Mr. Williams and that she probably was not really qualified to do grade 4 secretarial-stenographer work. However, she apparently had performed at least adequately on a grade 3 level job.

The consensus of the nine persons present was that the Company should try to place Mary Jones on some job at the level of salary grade 3. They considered and voted upon the following two alternatives:

1. Transfer her back to the last previous grade-3 job on which her work had been considered satisfactory

or

2. Have her displace the shortest-service grade-3 girl whose job Mary could fill.

The nine men present voted 7 to 2 in favor of choice number 1. This meant that she would be downgraded to Employment Service Clerk in the safety section of the personnel department.

Questions

1. Why do you think management devoted so much consideration to this one case?
2. Do you think that Mr.Williams, Head of the Product Engineering Department, should have accepted Mary Jones as his secretary-stenographer? Should he have investigated more thoroughly?
3. Does the fact that Mary had worked for Williams for over two years have any bearing on the proposed downgrading?
4. What can be done in the future in this company to facilitate the making of decisions of this kind? Why was there so much disagreement over her performance?
5. What do you think of the two alternative solutions posed to the committee? Can you suggest other choices?
6. What do you think of the solution decided upon by the committee?

Suggestions for Further Reading

Barrett, Richard S., *Performance Rating,* Chicago: Science Research Associates, 1966.

Coleman, Charles J., "Avoiding the Pitfalls in Results-Oriented Appraisals," *Personnel,* Vol. 42, No. 6, November-December 1965, pp. 24-33.

Hughes, Charles L., "Assessing the Performance of Key Managers," *Personnel,* Vol. 45, No. 1, January-February 1968, pp. 38-43.

Huse, Edgar F., "Performance Appraisal—A New Look," *Personnel Administration,* Vol. 30, No. 2, March-April 1967, pp. 3-5, 16-18.

Kellogg, Marion S., *Closing the Performance Gap,* New York: American Management Association, 1967.

————, *What to Do About Performance Appraisal,* New York: American Management Association, 1965.

Kindall, Alva F. and James Gatza, "Positive Program for Performance Appraisal," *Harvard Business Review,* Vol. 41, No. 6, November-December 1963, pp. 153-159, 162*ff.*

Lopez, Felix M., *Evaluating Employee Performance,* Chicago: Public Personnel Association, 1968.

Maier, Norman R. F., *The Appraisal Interview: Objectives, Methods, Skills,* New York: John Wiley & Sons, 1958.

Mayfield, Harold, "In Defense of Performance Appraisal," *Harvard Business Review,* Vol. 38, No. 2, March-April 1960, pp. 81-87.

McConkey, Dale D., *How to Manage by Results,* New York: American Management Association, 1965.

McGregor, Douglas, "An Uneasy Look at Performance Appraisal," *Harvard Business Review,* Vol. 35, No. 3, May-June 1957, pp. 89-94.

Meyer, H. H., E. Kay and J. R. P. French, Jr., "Split Roles in Performance Appraisal," *Harvard Business Review,* Vol. 43, No. 1, January-February 1965, pp. 123-129.

Sloan, Stanley and Alton C. Johnson, "New Context of Personnel Appraisal," *Harvard Business Review,* Vol. 46, No. 6, November-December 1968, pp. 14-20, 29-30, 194.

Stolz, Robert K., "Can Appraisal Interviews Be Made Effective?," *Personnel,* Vol. 38, No. 2, March-April 1961, pp. 32-37.

Whistler, Thomas L., and Shirley F. Harper (eds.), *Performance Appraisal: Research and Practice,* New York: Holt, Rinehart and Winston, 1962.

Promotion, Transfer, Layoff, and Demotion

12

In the modern organization, whether it be a business or a charitable or governmental entity, there is frequent (and at times almost constant) shifting of people from job to job both laterally and vertically in the structure. There is also considerable movement of people into and out of the organization as the volume of employment fluctuates. We shall be concerned in this chapter with the nature of these movements, management policies and procedures, criteria for decision making, and the effects upon the people involved. Specifically we shall study issues connected with promotion, transfer, layoff and recall, demotion and discharge. Discharge will be referred to only briefly in this chapter because it is covered more fully in Chapter 21, "Discipline."

The frequent shifting of employees, which necessitates changes in jobs and employees' status, is caused by many factors. Top management may decide that the business can be conducted more effectively by making certain changes in the organization structure. This may involve regrouping jobs, changes in departmental boundaries, elevation or lowering of jobs and functions, and physical relocation of people, jobs, and departments.

If there is an expansion in the volume of production and employment, this usually necessitates creation of new jobs and the promotion of some employees to positions of greater scope and responsibility. Often jobs are made more specialized as the volume of work and employment expands. Take the case of a personnel department as an illustration. In a very small company the personnel manager himself must handle employment, wage administration, training, benefits and services, labor relations, and safety. If the volume of employment should grow greatly, the personnel manager would have to choose someone to devote nearly full time to interviewing and selecting new employees. Likewise he would need the help of a training specialist to launch and coordinate training programs for the new employees. Conversely, as the size of the work force declines, there often is not enough work to keep a specialist busy all day at his specialty. Therefore, his job would be enlarged, and a number of functions may be assigned to him. This may be readily appreciated by examining the maintenance activity in a factory. A large plant would be able to utilize effectively the services of a number of specialized maintenance personnel, such as electricians, plumbers, carpenters, painters, millwrights, and the like. But if the volume of production should decline greatly, then each of these types of employees would not be busy enough to make a full work load, and their jobs would have to be combined. The excess personnel might be transferred to other jobs or laid off.

Another cause for changes of jobs and status is the introduction of new products, services, processes, and methods of operation. Reductions in force are occasioned by abandonment of product lines or services and by plant closings. General business conditions and the business cycle have a powerful effect upon the movement of employees in organizations. Those companies that are heavily involved in government defense contracts, experience frequent extreme fluctuations in employment.

In addition to all of the foregoing, shifting of people is caused by retirements, quits, and discharges. When a top official of an organization retires or resigns, this may trigger a whole series of promotions if the organization has a policy of promotion from within the company.

PROMOTIONS

A promotion is a reassignment of the individual to a job of higher rank. Ordinarily this higher-level job will entail more demands upon the individual. The scope of responsibility will be greater. Usually, but not always, the person's pay is raised at the time he is promoted. Quite frequently attached to the new position are symbols of higher status, such as a more important job title, more authority, a bigger desk, greater freedom of movement around the plant, and less close supervision of one's activities.

In our society promotions are much coveted. Most employees (but not all) have a desire to get ahead. They want the higher pay that accompanies a promotion in order to achieve a better standard of living. Their wives and children want more material possessions and conveniences around the home. The concept of starting at the bottom of the ladder when one is young and rising in status and income as one grows older is part of our culture. One's status in the neighborhood and the community is often gauged by his income level and the importance of his job. Some individuals who have a high level of aspiration set goals for themselves to reach certain positions in their companies at selected ages. If they do not achieve their objective, they may become severely frustrated. Because of the way advancement is looked upon by the majority in our society, it is important that companies and other work organizations adopt and follow sound promotion policies.

Promotions and Job Distinctions

It was previously stated that a promotion involves assigning an employee to a higher-ranking job. According to prevailing personnel management practice, this means that upon being promoted the individual's duties and responsibilities are of a higher level and are usually different from those of his previous job. In effect, the person leaves one job and assumes a more responsible one. Although this is the most generally accepted meaning of a promotion, many organizations make an exception to this strict definition.

Many organizations have set up rather arbitrary and nebulous job distinctions in order to be able to achieve a promotion sequence.Some examples might serve to make this point clear. In colleges and universities the academic ranks begin at the instructor level and progress through assistant professor, associate professor, and professor. Yet there commonly is no real distinction in regard to the job duties and responsibility among the job titles. Presumably the full professors are more experienced and have made demonstrated contributions to their college and to their field of work. But persons at all the levels may do identical work in terms of teaching, research, writing, counseling students and administrative tasks.

In industry, in engineering work, the titles assistant engineer, engineer, and senior engineer are common. Yet in actual practice management would often be hard pressed to explain in writing the real differences in the duties and responsibilities among these job titles. Most commonly management would state that those having the higher title would handle more complex projects and would be given less guidance from their supervisors. They would have to exercise more independent judgment. There would be fewer guidelines and precedents for their work.

Similar gradations of job levels are commonly found for chemists, biologists, mathematicians, and even secretaries and craftsmen. For example, most crafts have several different levels or grades, such as Toolmaker A and Toolmaker B. When we get into skilled clerical and manual work, it is somewhat easier to pinpoint and define the real distinctions between the jobs. But in professional, technical, and administrative jobs, the distinctions are often vague. They are often hard to justify.

Really what management is doing when it creates these rather vague and arbitrary job sequences is to make a great range of pay and status from the bottom of the lowest job title to the top of the highest job within the job family. This makes it possible to reward individuals with more pay and higher-sounding job titles as they become more experienced and demonstrate superior performance. This also means that arbitrary ceilings are placed on the pay and status of certain employees whom management feels do not merit reclassifying to a higher title. Some organizations even establish rigid tables of organization which specify that there can be only so many assistant chemists and senior chemists, irrespective of the ability of the job incumbents. This is done for salary control purposes primarily.

All of the foregoing discussion serves to emphasize that management possesses considerable discretion in the establishment of job titles and promotion sequences. It can create the illusion of granting many and frequent promotions by having a proliferation of job titles and levels with minute pay differences. Or it may follow the opposite course of having very few pay and title levels. The strict job evaluation principle of having differences in job title and pay reflect actual distinctions in work content is often ignored, especially for higher-level positions.

Filling Vacancies—From Within or from Outside?

Most business firms tend to fill most of their jobs openings by promoting their present employees. This has a number of distinct advantages to both the company and the employees. Because the nature of the processes and technology is unique in many companies, present employees already have a good background and can step into higher-graded positions with a minimum of orientation and training. Because management has had ample time to observe their behavior, there is less risk in selecting a present employee than in taking in an outsider who is largely an unknown quantity. The prospect of future reward in the form of a promotion serves as an incentive for employees to excel in their present jobs. Morale is higher when employees know they can progress within their own organization. Those who have stayed in the company for a long period of time tend to be socially compatible. Those who did not "fit in" will have left. Therefore, there is greater likelihood of harmonious interpersonal relations. Outsiders will not upset the established social groupings.

One of the most serious weaknesses of exclusive reliance upon promotion from within to fill all vacancies is in-breeding. Any incompetence and mediocrity will be perpetuated and even intensified. Excessive self-satisfaction may set in. The infusion of new ideas and methods that competent outsiders could supply will be prevented. Quite often a company just has no qualified employees to fill certain jobs. It must hire in the open labor market. This happens often in jobs requiring advanced and specialized education and training.

Promotion of Management and Professional Personnel

This section deals with the promotion of professional and administrative personnel, of nonsupervisory persons into the ranks of management, and of managers to higher level positions.

Promotion Planning.   Many companies make no advance plans for administering promotions. When a vacancy occurs, they start searching for someone who is qualified to fill the post. This process is haphazard and often results in a hasty, poorly considered decision.

A carefully conceived promotion program consists of the following elements: (1) policy, (2) identification of promotion channels, (3) selection and appraisal, (4) training and development, (5) communication, and (6) centralized records and coordination.

Among the policy issues that must be decided are whether to fill vacancies primarily from within the organization or to hire directly in the open labor market. Shall promotion opportunities be confined to a selected "elite" corps within the company? Many companies give special preference to those college graduates whom they have hired directly out of college and who have gone through a special training program. These people are variously called the "crown princes" or the "fair-haired" boys. Is it sound to give special preference to a few and deny promotional opportunities to other qualified personnel? Another policy question is whether to grant an increase in pay at the time of promotion, and if so how much? The author considers it sound to grant a significant increase in pay at the time a man is actually promoted. Otherwise, the promotion is hollow, and the individual resents management for being "cheap." If promotions are to be an incentive for improved performance on present assignments, then there must be some financial reward to deserving individuals.

Promotion channels, stepping-stone jobs, and logical job sequences should be identified and recorded on paper. This process is intimately related to job analysis and to organization planning. Ordinarily these paper plans are to serve only as general guides. There will always arise special circumstances in which nonstandard routes up the organizational ladder are perfectly reasonable.

The selction of individuals for promotion is closely related to performance appraisal and to centralized records maintenance. The education, experience, skills, abilities, and evaluations of all employees should be recorded and maintained in central files in the personnel office. The actual procedure for selecting one man from among several prospects will vary from organization to organization. Ordinarily labels are not placed upon each employee in the sense that he is tagged for a certain higher position far in advance. Rather a committee of superiors in the organization in consultation with a personnel officer will commonly review the qualifications of a number of candidates. In some instances management personnel are invited to nominate, from among their subordinates, people whom they consider qualified for the vacancy.

The job post-and-bid system of filling vacancies, although usually confined to unionized groups, has worked successfully in filling positions for upper-level personnel in some companies. Fundamentally, this is a technique for recruiting job candidates from within the establishment. Job vacancies, giving job title, duties, pay, and qualifications, are posted on company bulletin boards. Interested employees make application at the personnel office, where they are initially screened. Final decision to take the person is normally made by the manager of the department that has the vacancy. In contrast to the ordinary method of selecting a person for promotion, the job post-and-bid system prevents the possibility of overlooking a deserving man.[1]

Training and development of people is an investment in human resources that can yield dividends when people are moved into higher-level positions. By planning and selecting job assignments and formal classroom courses with an eye to the future, employees and supervisors can be pretrained and fully qualified to step into more challenging positions.

Official Selection Criteria.   For nonunion personnel nearly all organizations state that promotions are decided upon the basis of merit in one's present position and ability and potential to assume the responsibilities of higher-level positions. Sometimes other factors are considered, such as length of service,[2] education, training courses completed, previous work history, and the like. The rating that a person receives from his supervisor under a formal appraisal plan plays a significant part in the decision. But there are other, unofficial selection criteria that are often employed. However, top management rarely talks about these factors.

Unofficial Selection Criteria.   One of the best sources for gaining an insight into the sociological and interpersonal factors that so strongly determine who is promoted and when he is promoted is the field research of Melville Dalton, a sociologist.[3] Dalton conducted field studies into the behavior of managers in a number of companies. He studied organizational, sociological, and interpersonal influences. His work emphasizes the conflicts among people and groups in the frequent informal compromises with principle and policy that managers made to achieve their goals.

In the chapter entitled "The Management Career Ladder" (in his book

---

[1] For a case example of how an electronics plant filled a large number of key jobs when it received a large government defense contract see E. S. Barber, "How to Plug Key Job Gaps —With Your Own Employees," *Management Methods,* Vol. 19, No. 5 (February 1961).

[2] In some civil service systems a person must have served a minimum length of time at his present grade level before he can be considered for promotion. In the military services length of service is weighed along with other factors such as merit and ability.

[3] Melville Dalton, *Men Who Manage: Fusions of Feeling and Theory in Administration* (New York: John Wiley & Sons, Inc., 1959).

Men Who Manage) Dalton examines the factors that influenced the promotion and careers of management personnel at the Milo Company, a factory of about 8,000 employees. He also used additional data gathered from other companies.

Although high officials and company manuals at Milo emphasized that people were promoted on the basis of ability, hard work, honesty, cooperativeness, and merit, he found that many unofficial and informal influences were powerful determinants as well. There was a high correlation between being a Mason (hence a non-Catholic) and being a member of the management ranks. Likewise, managers (from foreman on up) were mostly of Anglo-Saxon or Germanic ancestry. All higher-level managers were Republican in politics or else pretended to be because they considered it essential to their success. Membership in the local yacht club was also deemed essential for progress in the management ranks. Family connections and personal friendships also had an influence upon who was chosen to fill certain management positions.

There was a high correlation between years of schooling and rank in the company. Yet there was very little relationship between the individual's courses of study at college and his type of work at the company. Dalton theorized that the social and political skills that students acquire through participation in campus activities serve as a good background for later membership in management. Many successful college students become adept at analyzing their professors, identifying their pet theories, and trying to win their favor. In short, the man who was successful as an "operator" on the campus, Dalton feels, has acquired some of those very skills that are essential for success as a manager.

In picking persons for promotion into responsible management posts, there is a tendency for the top executive to choose those who think and feel just as he does. He often values loyalty to himself and to the organization as being as important (or more important) than ability. He tends to select those who have social, political, economic, and religious interests that are similar to his own. In short, top executives tend to choose those who are carbon copies of themselves. Often this is done subconsciously. One of the reasons for the great emphasis upon these factors is the absence of clear-cut, objective measures of performance for most managerial positions.

All of the foregoing places the ambitious subordinate in the position where he feels he must ape the boss in order to be appraised favorably and be recommended for promotion. Organizations acquire a personality of their own, and the personality of the top executive sets the pattern for the whole group of management personnel. Those who do not match the attitudes, beliefs, and culture of the organization tend to leave. They will look elsewhere until they find an organization and a niche where they fit in well.

Assessment Centers.   Because thoughtful managers and personnel experts have long recognized that the traditional methods of selecting managers are highly subjective and fraught with error, some corporations have inaugurated large-scale programs to solve the problem. They have adopted the assessment center method of evaluating people. An assessment center is a place where candidates are put through a series of interviews, tests, and exercises. They are observed and rated by specially trained managers. Predictions of possible success or failure in management are based upon the combined judgments of this group of observers. In reaching their decisions, they are guided by scores obtained on the various tests and exercises.

The assessment center technique was first used by the German Army prior to World War II. The British used the procedure for selecting officers during that war. At that time also the United States Office of Strategic Services used assessment centers to pick undercover agents. The first application in American industry has been by the American Telephone and Telegraph Company, which launched its Management Progress Study in 1956.

Bell System's Management Progress Study, which is still in progress, is a longitudinal research investigation into selection techniques and the careers of managers. The purpose of the project is to determine whether measurements and ratings made in the early phases of a man's career at an assessment center are predictive of his subsequent accomplishments five, ten and twenty years later. In this study small groups of young men were brought to the center for three and a half days of intensive measurement, observation, and evaluation. A total of 422 men were assessed. Two thirds of these were college graduates who were assessed soon after being hired. The other third were former hourly paid craftsmen who had advanced to the lowest (foreman) level of management. They were not college graduates except for a handful who had earned them via evening school.

The techniques used for collecting information on the people included: (1) a two-hour interview; (2) an in-basket exercise; (3) a business game involving a manufacturing problem; (4) a leaderless group situational exercise that involved the evaluation of foremen for promotion; (5) projective personality tests such as the Thematic Apperception Test; (6) pencil and paper intelligence, aptitude, and personality tests; (7) a personal history questionnaire and an autobiographical essay. In addition it should be pointed out that trained staff members observed each group problem and recorded impressions of each individual. In 1965 correlations were made between predictions made at the assessment center and criteria of performance in subsequent years. Specifically these criteria were management level achieved and current salary. In two of the groups who had the longest service in management from the date of original assessment, the assessors made accurate assessments of management level to be achieved in 78 per cent of the cases. Of those men whom the raters judged would not reach middle management within nine to ten years, the raters were correct in their predictions in 95 per cent of the cases.

Of the specific techniques used, the situational exercises and the aptitude tests exhibited the highest correlations with subsequent job performance. Among the aptitude tests the intelligence test, particularly the verbal portion, showed the highest correlation. The personality questionnaires showed the lowest correlations with performance.

It should be pointed out that the Management Progress Study has been strictly a research endeavor. The information collected on each person and the predictions made were kept under strict control. They were not made available to line managers because this might influence their judgments on promotion of the people who had been assessed. The results of the Management Progress Study were so favorable that the Bell System established in the mid-1960's over fifty assessment centers throughout the country. The measurement techniques are essentially the same as those employed in the research project. But since the method has been proven, the results of the ratings and measurements *are* transmitted to operating management for actual use in making personnel decisions regarding those who have gone through the centers. The staffs of these centers are experienced Bell System managers of proven competence. They are assigned to a center for a six-month tour of duty.

Another corporation to adopt the assessment center method is the Standard Oil Company of New Jersey. Their project is called Early Identification of Management Potential. It has included all ranks of management from the first-line supervisor up to the chairman of the board. Measuring instruments have included both published and custom-made pencil-and-paper tests, a personal interview, and a biographical questionnaire. Situational exercises were not employed. The best predictors in the Jersey Standard project have turned out to be the biographical data and the mental ability data.

Sears, Roebuck and Company has also instituted the assessment center technique for identifying managerial talent. Their approach differs from that of AT&T and Jersey Standard in that Sears uses it for selection of young college graduates before they are hired.

Because the assessment center method is costly and requires a fairly advanced degree of sophistication of personnel and psychological knowledge, so far it has been used primarily by large companies. But those now using it have clearly indicated satisfaction with the results. And if one considers the cost of faulty selection of managers with its consequent effect upon performance, turnover, and morale, the cost benefit effectiveness becomes evident.[4]

---

[4] Further information on the Bell System Management Progress Study and Assessment Center is contained in Douglas W. Bray and Donald L. Grant, "The Assessment Center in the Measurement of Potential for Business Management," *Psychological Monographs: General and Applied,* No. 625, Vol. 80, No. 17 (1966). See also Walter S. Wikstrom, "Assessing Managerial Talent," *The Conference Board Record* (March 1967). On assessment centers in general and their use by various companies, see "How to Spot Executives Early," *Fortune* (July 1968), pp. 106 - 111; Saul W. Gellerman, *Management by Motivation* (New York: American Management Association 1968), Ch. 7; and D. L. Hardesty and W. S. Jones, "Charac-

Promotion of Organized Employees

Prior to the 1940's most unions tended to take little interest in company promotion policies and practices. This was largely because they had the much more pressing problems of fighting for their survival, negotiating general wage increases, and handling charges of unfair treatment and discrimination. But in recent years most unions, particularly the industrial type of unions, have taken an active interest in representing their constituents in regard to promotion practices. Among the things they have done is press for seniority as a major criterion for selection for a better job, insist that present employees be upgraded before hiring on the outside, adopt job-posting procedures, and make the choice of the individual to be promoted subject to the grievance procedure. As a result of their comprehensive survey of the effect of union policies and collective bargaining upon management Slichter, Healy, and Livernash have stated:

> Although management once felt that promotion decisions were one of its most important prerogatives, it is now coming to realize that proper use of the seniority criterion in these decisions is not necessarily incompatible with efficiency and employee morale.[5]

This statement does not mean that merit and ability have been cast aside or that seniority is the only criterion for selection. But in recent years labor agreements and actual practice have given seniority an ever-increasing role in the selection of people for promotion.

Promotion Methods. Generally speaking the employer administers the promotion system, and the union may submit a grievance if it is dissatisfied with the action management has taken. The right of the union to challenge an employer's decision is, of course, guided by the wording of the labor agreement. In some companies the employer may privately follow pretty much whatever selection scheme he wishes. It is only when he makes the formal announcement of an appointment that the union may step in. In other companies the job post-and-bid system is used, and this is spelled out quite specifically in the union agreement. Many employers have refused to accept a job-bid system because they feel they will be forced into a position where they must always assign the most senior employee to the new job. However, job bidding and ironbound seniority do not necessarily go hand in hand. In plenty of companies management has maintained its right to give primary weight to merit and ability.

A fairly common practice is for management (sometimes in consultation with the local union) to establish, on paper, definite channels of promotion. These charts look like the typical company organization chart

---

teristics of Judged High Potential Management Personnel—The Operations of an Industrial Assessment Center," *Personnel Psychology,* Vol. 21, No. 1 (Spring 1968), pp. 85-98.

[5] Sumner H. Slichter, James J. Healy, and E. Robert Livernash, *The Impact of Collective Bargaining on Management* (Washington, D.C.: The Brookings Institution, 1960), p. 181.

upside down. Often these promotional lines of progression are set up on a departmental basis. A man may start out as a laborer in a steel mill, for example. As time passes and vacancies occur he may move up any one of various channels, such as crane operation, furnace operation, rolling mill operation, materials handling, and the like. Each step in the various branches of these promotion "trees" serves as a learning post for the next higher job.

Seniority as a Factor in Promotions.   Many union-employer agreements specify that some weight must be given to seniority when selecting candidates for promotion. Simply defined *seniority is length of service.* When the term is used, it usually has the added connotation of certain rights or benefits attained on the basis of length of service. Some rights and benefits are based upon competitive seniority among the employees. Rights to promotion, transfer, order of layoff, and recall are examples of competitive seniority. Other benefits tied to seniority have nothing to do with one man relative to another. Thus a man may be entitled to three weeks' vacation after ten years of service, a pension after thirty years, and a certain amount of sick leave after six months of service.

What are the arguments in favor of using seniority as a factor in selecting people for promotion? Unions typically want it to be the only criterion for selection.[6] Although an impartial observer would probably not wish to go that far, he could find some very solid arguments in favor of using seniority as a major consideration.

Seniority is impartial. It eliminates any possibility of favoritism influencing the choice. Because special favoritism to a few would soon disrupt the group, it helps maintain group solidarity. If promotion decisions are left solely to the discretion of management, there is a greater tendency for ambitious employees to apple polish and try to seek the favor of their superiors. Not only does this create dissension within the work group, but union leaders feel it weakens loyalty to the union.

Seniority fits in with the cultural expectations of mankind. From primitive tribal society through modern civilization, greater benefits, status, respect, and privileges have accrued to older people. We speak of elders in a tribe as being the leaders and decision makers. Likewise some present-day churches are governed by those called elders. Committee chairmanships in the United States Congress are assigned on the basis of length of service. Promotions in the lower grades of military ranks are based heavily upon seniority.

Up to a certain point, employees increase their proficiency at work as their length of service increases. Of course, this does not go on indefinitely. But it would be fair to say that there is a very rough correlation between length of service and performance.

---

[6] Unions of engineers and scientists are usually in favor of promotion based upon merit and ability rather than seniority. They do not emphasize group solidarity as much as do unions of blue-collar workers.

A final argument in favor of the seniority criterion is that it rewards loyalty. As many people work for an organization, they tend to build up a proprietary interest in their jobs, workplaces, and their departments. They tend to feel that the rewards of promotions should go to those who have been there the longest rather than to raw newcomers.

A principle argument against using seniority as a basis for promotion is that it may cause unqualified people to occupy important positions. If this occurs extensively throughout an organization, it can eventually lead to the organization's deterioration. In other words, efficiency may be seriously impaired.

The incentive to excel on one's present job is weakened if he knows it will not count toward advancement. Ambitious short-service employees are discouraged if they know they must wait many years before being promoted. Further, if grossly unqualified individuals are assigned to positions of influence, this can undermine the morale of the group.

Even if a man with long years of service exhibits superior performance on his present job, this is no guarantee that he has the skills, knowledge, and ability to perform some other higher-level job.

In balancing the equities, it is frequently the wisest choice to give consideration to both ability *and* seniority when choosing individuals for promotion.

Union Agreement Provisions.   The two most common union-employer contract provisions pertaining to promotion are (1) the most senior employee in the particular seniority unit will receive the promotion if he is qualified for the job; and (2) where ability, skill, and competence are relatively equal (as between two employees) then seniority shall govern in the applicable unit.[7] Clause number 1 above means that the most senior employee in the appropriate seniority unit (occupation, department, or plant) will get the promotion if he can meet the minimum performance expected on the job. Clause number 2 above means that management has the right to select the best man for the vacancy if one is clearly well above the other possible candidates in ability. But if there is little difference in the skill and ability of persons in a group of two or more employees, then management must select the most senior man for the job. This second clause is generally considered to grant greater flexibility to management in picking the most qualified individual. However, with either type of provision there is the likelihood that either the union or an aggrieved employee may submit a grievance, if it is felt that the promotion went to the wrong man or did not give the right weight to seniority.

Problems with Promotions

A great many administrative and human relations problems tend to arise through the application of a promotion program.

[7] Slichter, Healy, and Livernash, *op. cit.,* pp. 198-199.

Disappointed Candidates.   There once was a man in his middle thirties who was a graduate of a prestige men's college and who held a staff position in the personnel department of a large company. His post was roughly equivalent in rank to that of a shop general foreman. In other words, he was in lower management. The company was expanding rapidly, and most of this man's colleagues, who had been hired at about the same time he had been employed, had been promoted to positions of much higher status and authority. Coming from a socially prominent family, this man had high aspirations. Initially he had simply been overlooked for promotion. He had not been in the right spot at the right time under the right boss. He felt that he was losing out. He continually pressed his boss for a promotion. He eventually became embittered. Then his boss refused to recommend him for promotion because of his "bad" attitude.

This little story has a number of important lessons. First, top management must establish a clear-cut promotion program, and controls must be built into the system to insure that deserving candidates are not overlooked. Second, continual bypassing of an aspiring person can undermine his morale and his performance. The whole process may become circular. He may develop a "bad" attitude because he was not promoted when he thought he deserved it, and this attitude may be the very thing that prevents his advancement.

There is one further ramification. Most of us do not see ourselves as others see us. If a man has not been performing up to par, his supervisor should apprise him of the fact. On the other hand, If a man is clearly doing well on his present job but is not qualified to move up to the next higher position, his superior should discuss with him ways in which he can obtain the necessary qualifications. If he is in a blind alley, his supervisor should inform him of his chances and eventually try to move him into a department where opportunities are more favorable. This assumes that the man wants and is capable of moving ahead.

Some Refuse Promotion.   Not everyone seeks advancement. Many people know their limitations and know that they would probably fail on a more difficult job assignment. As a man gets older and after his children have been raised to adulthood, he might value other things in life ahead of climbing the executive ladder at his company. A man may value his leisure more than material rewards associated with a higher-paying job.

Quite frequently blue-collar workers will refuse promotion to foremen because they are unwilling to give up the security of belonging to a union and being in a bargaining unit. If production cutbacks occur, workers will be laid off in inverse order of seniority. But having left the work group, foremen often have no seniority rights to displace other workers. To remove this impediment to promotion, management often insists, when negotiating a labor agreement, that a man promoted to foreman shall retain the seniority rights he had at the time he was advanced. Sometimes workers are reluctant to take a foreman's job because they will lose the protection which a union affords them against capricious or arbitrary treatment by management. There are very few formal grievance procedures for nonunion personnel in industry.

Supervisor Will Not Release the Employee. Sometimes a supervisor adopts the view that his subordinates are indispensable to his operation, and he cannot possibly release anyone to take a better job in another department. This viewpoint may arise simply because the supervisor is selfish. It may come about also because some supervisors are good at training their subordinates, but as soon as a few superior employees are developed, they are transferred or promoted out of the unit. The supervisor may feel that the efficiency of his department may suffer if he loses his most capable people.

The solution to this problem rests with higher management. By giving credit to subordinate managers and supervisors for developing promotable employees, it can prevent the feeling that it is necessary to hoard good men to meet top management's expectations. If there is a balanced emphasis among all departments, then there will be little need for certain departments to hoard their best employees.

Promotion Opportunities Not Equitable. Often a company will drift into a situation where it is favoring people from certain departments for promotion into the ranks of management. Over the years one large company has tended to give rapid promotion to college graduates who work in the production and sales departments while relegating those in the engineering department to positions of individual contributors. In fact quite often in industry the man with specialized technical training, such as an engineer, mathematician, or chemist, is not given equal promotion opportunities with the generalist who may rise through administrative posts at a rapid rate. The facts of life in many industrial corporations are such that the generalist may take on administrative and executive assignments in a large number of different fields, whereas the engineer or scientist tends to be considered for supervisory and executive positions only within his own technical department.

To correct this inequity and to provide incentives for engineers and scientists, some companies have established what they call "parallel paths to success." They have set up a number of high-level salary grades for functional individual contributors. These carry salaries equivalent to those paid lower- and middle-level managers.

Another impediment to balanced promotion opportunities is the fact that some managers are very conservative about upgrading their people, whereas others are quite liberal. Thus employees are placed in the position where pure chance plays a large part in their careers. When an applicant interviews for a job, he cannot tell with any degree of accuracy whether his prospective supervisor will be liberal or conservative regarding recommending his employees for promotion.

TRANSFERS

A *transfer consists of a reassignment of an employee to another job of similar pay, status, and responsibility.* A transfer is a horizontal move from one job to another. It is to be distinguished from a promotion, which is a vertical move in rank and responsibility. A transfer may involve a slight change in level of responsibility and status, because ranks and grade levels in many organizations are defined very broadly.

Causes of Transfers

People may be transferred either because of the needs of the business or at their own request, because they feel they would be happier in a different job. The term *needs of the business* covers a multitude of reasons. Most shifts of personnel are occasioned by changes in volume of output, changes in organization, introduction or dropping of product lines, and similar adjustments in business operations. Absences of key employees from work make it necessary to reassign others to fill their shoes.

Quite often management will make a remedial transfer because an individual is not performing adequately on his present assignment, and an analysis of his qualifications causes management to feel that he would be more suitable in a different spot. It is this author's belief that managers as a rule are not alert often enough to the fact that an employee who is a failure under one supervisor and on one kind of work might be very successful if he were to be transferred to a type of work suited to his aptitudes and interests. Too often managers will not take a second look at the person who is unsuccessful in his initial job assignment.

Sometimes employees request a transfer because they do not like their present work situation or because they feel that opportunity for advancement is better in some other department. The typical procedure for handling these requests makes it necessary for the man to discuss his desires with his present supervisor first. The personnel department coordinates such internal transfers. The employee, in effect, must apply for a job in another department. When an opening occurs, he must be interviewed by the manager of the department concerned.

Administration of Transfers

Transfers are classified as temporary or permanent. Those caused by changes in volume of production and by absence of key employees are often of the temporary variety. Those caused by fundamental changes in the nature of a company's business, by reorganization, at the individual's own request, and in an effort to salvage a person who has been misassigned, are often of a more permanent nature.

If the employees are represented by a union, management may find that its freedom to shift people around as it sees fit is restricted. If the union contract specifies that job vacancies must be posted on the bulletin board so that interested employees may bid for them, this process may slow up the work of reassigning people. It may also prevent management from reassigning those it wishes to move. To overcome this problem many union-employer agreements provide that temporary transfers of, say, one or two weeks' duration can be made without posting the job on the bulletin board. Sometimes rigid seniority regulations can interfere with management's freedom to make transfers at its own discretion.

Unions over the years have sought to insure that their constituents are properly paid for the level of skill and effort they must exert in their jobs. They have pressed for a close matching of duties and responsibilities with pay. If management then wishes to shift certain people to somewhat different types of work, the union will be zealous to see that they are not then required to work harder or at a higher level of skill and effort for the same pay. Management sometimes feels that this hampers its efficiency, but in reality if a well-developed job evaluation system is maintained, a proper matching of job titles, pay, and duties poses no serious administrative burden.

Relocation of Personnel

The modern multiplant and multibranch corporation finds it necessary to transfer personnel from one unit to another on frequent occasions. Sometimes the transfers are in fact promotions, and the individuals are willing to pull up stakes and move to a new town because of the greater pay and other rewards they will receive on their new jobs. In many cases the transfers are strictly horizontal moves dictated by the needs of the business. In a few instances a man is moved from job to job and city to city as part of a planned program of training and development.

It is almost a universal practice for business and governmental organizations to pay the actual costs of moving household furniture and of transportation for those transferred to a new location. It is nearly always managerial and professional personnel who are transferred and whose expenses are absorbed by the employer. Except for very special skilled workers it is rare for a company to transfer blue-collar workers. Most employers are able to obtain locally whatever needs they have for semiskilled and unskilled workers.

Another type of relocation is that caused by the closing down of one plant and the opening of a new one in a distant location. This is plant migration. For years now many companies operating plants in the high-wage, heavily unionized Northeast and Great Lakes regions have been abandoning these in favor of new plants in the South, where wage levels are lower and unions are generally quite weak. Employers are often enticed by the tax concessions and favorable leases that many industry-starved communities have been offering.

Most commonly in such relocations the company moves only its executives and a few other key personnel. Hourly paid workers and clerical personnel are left behind without jobs. However, there have been recent precedent-setting court decisions that will change the job-rights situation for those employees covered by union contracts that contain seniority provisions. In one major court case a food-processing division of a large company closed down its plant in New York State and moved much of its equipment and production operations to a new plant in Pennsylvania. It timed its move to coincide with the termination of its collective bargaining agreement. Five of the employees who were discharged when the plant shut down brought action in court to recover their jobs at the new plant.

In handing down its decision in March, 1961, the United States Court of Appeals ruled that seniority rights in a contract "vest" in the employees, and an employer cannot disregard these rights by discharging employees when a contract expires. It further ruled that when a company moves its plant, the seniority and employment rights that workers acquired at the original plant survive the move, because the location shown in the contract is merely descriptive, and it does not limit the employees' rights to that location only.[8]

A similar decision was made in United States District Court in June, 1961, in regard to a move by a factory from Detroit, Michigan, to Lebanon, Tennessee. Affirming the fact that workers' seniority rights become vested through the union agreement, the court ruled that the company must rehire present Detroit plant employees at its new location in Tennessee.[9]

LAYOFF AND RECALL

One of the disadvantages of our free enterprise economy is the fact that mass layoffs and unemployment occur frequently throughout the country. To be sure, we feel that the benefits of our free economy far outweigh its limitations. Nevertheless, the frequent ups and downs of product and financial markets, changes in the business cycles, and uncoordinated decisions of thousands of business firms often result in large-scale layoffs and rehirings of workers.

A layoff is an indefinite separation from the payroll due to factors beyond the employee's control. It is caused by such factors as loss of sales, shortage of materials, seasonal fluctuation in markets, production delays, and technological displacement. At the time a worker is laid off, the employer often does not really know how long it will be before he can recall the individual. Some temporary layoff's actually turn into permanent sepa-

[8] *Olga Zdanok* vs. *The Glidden Company, Durkee Famous Foods Division.* U.S. Court of Appeals, 2 Cir., No. 26542, March 25, 1961, 288 F. (2nd) 99. Reported in *American Labor Cases,* 1392, Prentice-Hall, 1961.

[9] *James Oddie* vs. *Gear and Tool Company.* U.S. District Court, Eastern District of Michigan, Southern Division, Civil No. 21350, June 16, 1961. Reported in *American Labor Cases,* 1398, Prentice-Hall, 1961.

rations because the volume of production never picks up sufficiently to warrant rehiring laid-off workers. A layoff should be clearly distinguished from a discharge. When someone is discharged he is permanently separated from his job because of poor performance or violation of company rules of conduct.

Depending upon company policy and union-employer contract provisions, laid-off workers retain certain rights with their employer. In some instances they continue to accumulate seniority for a certain period of time, they may have certain recall rights, and time spent on layoff may count toward vacation, pension, and sickness benefits. Depending upon the circumstances, the employer often hopes that the laid-off workers will remain attached to his company rather than permanently sever the relationship. This will save the company the cost of training green help if all laid-off employees return to work when they are asked. Of course, the longer the duration of the layoff, the less likely it is that the separated workers will ever return.

Layoff of Unorganized Employees

When employees are not represented by a union, management is free to use whatever criteria it wishes in deciding whom to let go and whom to retain. Some companies see a layoff as a golden opportunity to weed out undesirable employees. But this should be the exception, because management that is enlightened and efficient should have continuously done a careful job of selection, training, placement, appraisal, and separation from the payroll where necessary, so that it does not need the excuse of a layoff to get rid of incompetent people. It must be agreed, however, that the performance of employees on any type of work will range along a continuum, and any organization will want to retain its top performers and drop those who contribute the least.

In actual practice in nonunion situations, management usually selects people for retention (or its counterpart layoff) on the basis of many factors. Among these are ability, age, length of service, number of dependents, financial obligations, and health. Job performance and ability are usually given the greatest weight, followed next by length of service. The other factors reflect management's concern with what might be hardship cases if the individual is laid off.

Layoff of Organized Employees

Layoff procedures have always been of utmost concern to unions. The goals of the union in regard to layoffs are to preserve the union as an institution, to maintain its organization structure, to protect the union members' jobs insofar as possible, to insure equitable and impartial treatment as among individuals, to prevent dividing influences within the group, and to maintain certain re-employment rights for those who are laid off.

Most union agreements contain provisions designed to forestall or min-imize layoffs. Quite frequently the contract will specify that all tempo-rary and probationary employees shall be laid off first. Sometimes the contract will prevent subcontracting of work while people are on layoff. This is quite common in the wearing apparel industries. The scheduling of overtime may also be banned while workers are on layoff.

Work-Sharing. In actual practice there are two kinds of work-shar-ing provisions. In the first and less drastic case the agreement specifies that there shall be a temporary reduction of scheduled weekly hours for all workers to forestall or minimize layoffs. In the second type, which is true work sharing, there shall be an equal division of work in lieu of layoffs. According to an extensive analysis of virtually all labor agreements in this country covering 1,000 or more workers made by the Bureau of Labor Statistics of the United States Department of Labor in 1954 and 1955, 20 per cent of the 1,743 agreements studied required the employer to reduce hours of work before regular employees were laid off. Ac-tually only 4 per cent of the 1,743 agreements provided for true equal division of work in place of layoff. These were mostly in the apparel industries.[10]

This method is popular in these industries because the work is seasonal, and if low seniority employees were always laid off each slack season, it would work an undue hardship upon them. Most work-sharing agree-ments specify a minimum number of hours below which the work week cannot be reduced. At this point layoffs would commence. Below, say, 30 hours per week, it would be uneconomical for management to run the plant in many cases, and workers might do better to collect unemploy-ment compensation or obtain jobs elsewhere.

Seniority in Layoffs. When layoffs actually take place, seniority is by far the most common criterion for determining the order in which peo-ple will be separated. Figure 12-1 shows the relative percentages of major union agreements that handle layoffs by straight seniiority, qualified se-niority, and work sharing and those that have no provisions affecting order of layoff.

One third of the agreements specified that layoffs were to take place on the basis of straight seniority. This means that no other factor was to be considered in making the order of layoff determination. More than half of the agreements provided for layoffs on the basis of qualified se-niority. With qualified seniority, ability, physical fitness, and other factors are taken into account in addition to length of service.

The most common type of qualifed seniority provision, which was found in nearly half of the 749 contracts having qualified seniority clauses, stated that length of service was the primary consideration and other factors were secondary. A typical contract provision is as follows:

[10] Rose Theodore, "Layoff, Recall, and Work-Sharing Procedures: IV—Recall Procedures; Work-Sharing," *Monthly Labor Review,* Vol. 80, No. 3 (March 1957), pp. 334 and 335.

It is agreed that whenever the company either reduces or increases its working forces within any of the departments . . . the principle of seniority shall prevail, provided the employee retained or recalled is capable of doing the work.[11]

Another common type of provision states that ability to do the work, physical fitness, and length of service are all considered, but that it is only when ability and physical fitness are equal (when choosing among several employees) that length of service will count as the determining factor.

Seniority Units and Measurement.   The seniority provisions of a contract and their application in layoff, bumping, and recall often are exceed-

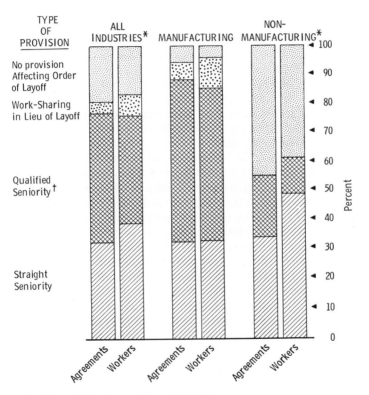

× Exclusive of railroad and airline agreements.
† Includes small number of agreements classified as "other."

Figure 12-1.   Order of Layoff Provided in 1,743 Major Collective Bargaining Agreements, 1954-55. Source: *Monthly Labor Review.* Vol. 80, No. 2, February, 1957, p. 178.

[11] Joseph W. Bloch and Robert Platt, "Layoff, Recall, and Work-Sharing Procedures: III—Seniority and Bumping Practices," *Monthly Labor Review,* Vol. 80, No. 2 (February 1957), p. 180.

ingly complex. When layoffs occur, employees may be able to exercise their seniority rights to protect their jobs according to job family boundaries, departmental boundaries, or on a plantwide basis. Seniority rights for bumping and layoffs on a companywide basis for multiplant companies are rather infrequent.[12]

If there are fifteen welders in a company and the lowest three in seniority are laid off when a plant reduction in force occurs, then this is considered job or job-family seniority. It might be that the three welders possess much higher seniority than employees who are retained in other departments, but if the contract has set up seniority units on the basis of job-classification boundaries, then these three must be laid off. The same principle applies to a departmental seniority unit. With plantwide seniority the shortest service employees are let go regardless of their jobs or departments.

Management usually favors narrow seniority units and as little bumping as possible in the interests of maintaining plant efficiency. Unions press for as wide a seniority unit as they can get in order to provide as much job protection as possible.

With departmental or job-classification seniority the actual calculation of a man's seniority may be made in either of two ways. His seniority for layoff purposes may date only from the time he entered that job or that department, or it may date from the time he was first hired by the company regardless of department.

As a useful compromise between a narrow seniority unit that management wishes and a wide unit that many employees and their union desire is one in which job or departmental seniority shall initially apply. But then an employee could exercise plantwide seniority rights to displace (bump) a shorter service employee on a low-level or unskilled type of job.

Bumping on Layoffs. Exigencies of business operations may cause the elimination of the jobs of some very senior workers. Shall these people then be separated from the payroll? Most commonly the answer is no, because these employees are allowed to bump or displace the shortest-service employees in their seniority unit. These short-service workers may actually hold quite different jobs, but if the long-service people are capable of doing this work, then they can displace the newer men. Heavy layoffs that extend over a period of weeks or months usually cause a chain reaction of displacements in which those who bump others are in turn bumped themselves a short time later. This process can disrupt plant efficiency to a considerable extent. It is for this reason that management tries to set up narrow seniority units.

There are a number of other restrictions on bumping that appear in some collective bargaining agreements. Bumping may be made inoperative for temporary layoffs of less than two weeks duration. Certain em-

---

[12] *Bumping* is the term commonly used in unionized establishments to denote the displacement of one employee by another who has more seniority. The "bumped" worker may in turn displace another of lower seniority or be laid off.

ployees (usually 2 to 5 per cent of the labor force) may be declared by management to be "essential" and thus exempt from bumping. A man may be permitted to bump only into a job on which he has had previous experience. Or a man must possess a specified amount of seniority in excess of the person he seeks to displace. All of these limitations serve to maintain plant efficiency while at the same time decreasing the job security of the senior employees as a group.

Recall from Layoff. When the work force expands after a layoff, the general principle applies that workers will be recalled to work in inverse order of layoff or according to seniority. However, the process is not as simple as this implies. Certain operations and certain departments will expand their activities before others. The activities of those low-seniority workers who were first laid off may be the first to be resumed. So in practice recalled workers may be assigned to jobs different from those they had previously held. In view of this fact, the majority of labor agreements specify that ability, skill, and physical fitness will be given consideration in addition to seniority. The United States Department of Labor study referred to previously states that of the 1,347 agreements having layoff procedures, 58 per cent provided for recall on the basis of qualified seniority and 28 per cent on the basis of straight seniority.[13]

DEMOTION

A demotion is the reassignment of an employee to a job of lower status and pay. Usually the level of difficulty and responsibility is lower on the new job.

Demotions may be caused by factors beyond the employee's control. This is the typical case when a reduction in force occurs. Although some employees may be laid off, often those who remain must take lower-level positions because departments may be combined and jobs may be eliminated. This can affect both managerial and hourly paid personnel. When large-scale layoffs occur and the bumping process is set into motion, workers pretty much expect that they will be forced to take lower-level jobs, at least until the level of plant activity picks up in the future.

The other major type of demotion is caused by some inadequacy (or alleged inadequacy) on the part of the individual in terms of job performance, attitude, and capability. He may have recently been promoted but failed to meet the standards of performance for the higher position. It often happens that technology, methods, and practices change but that old timers are unable to adjust to the new ways. In other words, management has raised the requirements of their jobs substantially, and they cannot meet the new expectations. Should these long-service employees be demoted to less demanding jobs? People age at different rates. Occasional-

[13] Theodore, *op. cit.,* p. 330.

ly the health and vigor of certain individuals have deteriorated before the customary retirement age, so that they can no longer do their work adequately. What action should be taken with these individuals?

A man's work career is often one of the most important things to him in his whole life. His hopes, pride, and joy may be wrapped up in his company and his job. His job title, pay, and level of responsibility determine his social status and his living standard. A good job is a symbol entitling one to certain rewards and respect both within the organization and in the community. Thus, for some people, it can be a devastating blow to suffer a demotion. This feeling is not so likely to arise when the demotion is caused by a reduction in force, because this action is often taken impartially and objectively. It is not a black mark against the man. Furthermore there is the expectation that business will pick up again in the future, and one's old position can be regained.

For the long-service employee, for the ones who have performed effectively in the past, the most satisfactory solution is generally to make no demotion. Rather it is to keep the person in his present job but to take away some of his duties and responsibilities and assign these to someone else. Another solution is to create a position for the person at the same pay and status but with lowered job demands. Both of these solutions permit the man to retain his dignity and the respect of others as well as his accustomed level of income.

Do Not Demote for Discipline

It is unwise for management to use a demotion as a penalty for violation of company rules of conduct. If a man has a poor record of attendance, has been insubordinate, or has come to work drunk, a demotion will not change his behavior. He may simply retain his old habits on the lower-level job. Discipline is a form of training and correction. If a person were to be demoted as a form of discipline, not only would he have to learn his new job, but he would have to learn to overcome his previous unsatisfactory behavior. In addition, he would have to make the psychological adjustment occasioned by the loss of pay and status.

Demotion in a work situation would be akin to putting a fourth-grade school boy back to third grade because of bad deportment in the fourth grade. The punishment is simply inappropriate for the offense.

DISCHARGE

A discharge is a permanent separation from the payroll, usually because of some inadequacy or offense by the individual. At executive levels people are sometimes discharged or forced to resign because of clashes over basic philosophy and policy. At any level in the organization employees are subject to discharge for grossly inadequate work performance and for violation of company rules of conduct.

Discharges for poor work most often occur during the employee's probationary period. This is a period varying in length from one month to one year during which the individual is on trial. If the employees are represented by a union, it is relatively difficult for a company to discharge a man after he has passed the probationary period. Most labor agreements provide that discharge must be for "just cause," and unions tend to challenge discharges of employees who have been on the payroll for a considerable length of time. Whether a union is present or not, most progressive managements pride themselves on the job security and freedom from arbitrary firing that they provide their employees. Therefore, they are very cautious about discharging employees, and they make sure that their cases are well proven and documented before actually separating a man from the payroll.

Discharge, invoked as a penalty for violation of company rules, will be discussed in Chapter 21, "Discipline."

Questions for Review and Discussion

1. What are the forces and factors in organizations that cause such job changes as promotions, transfers, and layoffs to occur?
2. The point has been made that a promotion involves the reassignment of a person to a new job having higher level duties, responsibilities, and job requirements. Do you think there is justification for having a great many job titles and pay grades so that it is possible to reward a good employee with a higher title even though there has been no change in his job duties and responsibilities?
3. Describe the purposes and operation of an "assessment center." What are the advantages of an assessment center over traditional methods of choosing persons for promotion? Disadvantages?
4. What factors should top management consider when establishing a policy for the filling of vacancies with respect to promotion from within or going to the outside labor market?
5. Explain the principal features of a sound promotion program.
6. The job post-and-bid system of filling job openings is most commonly instituted at the request of a union. Do you feel that such a system can be useful to an organization for filling jobs for nonunion groups?
7. Why is it that top management will announce that the official criteria for promotion are such factors as merit, initiative, and ability but fail to give open recognition to the unofficial and informal factors, such as interpersonal and sociological influences? How important do you think these unofficial criteria are in the average company?
8. What are the relative merits of giving weight to length of service when

selecting employees for promotion? Is seniority more appropriate at the worker level than at the manager level?

9. What policy and procedure would you adopt regarding the handling of employee requests for transfer to a different job? Why do employees make such requests? How can these affect efficiency and morale?

10. If a man is promoted or transferred on the initiative of management and he clearly fails to perform adequately on the new job, should he be returned to his old job? demoted? discharged? What if someone else has been promoted into his old job?

11. If a plant closes down and resumes operations in a new plant in a different section of the country, what rights to jobs in the new plant should rank-and-file employees have? What job rights should professional or technical employees have? Should job rights be accorded status similar to property rights? Discuss.

12. What part does seniority play in layoff of unionized employees?

13. In balancing the equities, does layoff according to seniority help or hinder management? The union? Individual employees? Employees as a group?

14. Under what conditions would a layoff be preferable to work sharing for a company? For the employees?

15. Explain how a chain reaction of bumpings could occur with mass layoffs.

CASE PROBLEMS

Problem 1

Harold has been the sales manager of a subdistrict office for an automobile manufacturer in an Eastern city for four years. His work involves close liaison with automobile dealers in marketing relationships with the factory. He is also responsible for selecting and starting up new dealers in towns where none are presently franchised.

In April, Harold, at the age of 37, had a heart attack which kept him in the hospital for six weeks and at home for seven more weeks. During his absence his position was filled by a man who was promoted to the job and transferred from a neighboring district. After about three months Harold returned to the office to work half days for a period of a month. He gradually got into the swing of things, and four months after his attack, he was able to resume a full work schedule. He assumed that he would return to his regular position at this time. Much to his chagrin his superior, the area director, who made a trip to his office from area headquarters in New York City, told him that he was being demoted to assistant sales manager in order to relieve some of the work pressures from his shoulders. There would be a slight reduction in his salary (amounting to 4 per cent) to bring his pay into line with the assistant manager classification.

Questions

1. Evaluate the handling of this personnel situation by the area director.
2. Should the man who had been transferred and promoted to fill this temporary vacancy when Harold was ill be demoted and reassigned to his old location?
3. What type of policy would you recommend be adopted on a company-wide basis to take care of similar problems in the future?

Problem 2

The ABC Company, a public utility, has an engineering department composed of two hundred employees. The major share of the work involves cost estimation, specification writing, and equipment planning and ordering. Some of the work also involves basic engineering analysis and design. Over two thirds of the engineering force is composed of employees who possess only a high school education and who have served a number of years as mechanics, electricians, and other types of craftsmen before being promoted into the engineering department. Quite frequently foremen who had been inept at supervising people but who had good technical knowledge were transferred to the engineering department and classified as engineers. The one third of the engineering force that does possess college degrees in engineering are assigned to the more complex technical phases of the work, involving the application of engineering principles. Most of the supervisory positions in the engineering department are held by graduate engineers.

Over the years the company has placed major emphasis upon the operating phases of the business. Those recruited directly upon graduation from college are placed in a management training program of twelve months' duration. They are rotated through a number of assignments in various departments of the company including the engineering department. Only a small percentage of these "college hires" are assigned permanently to the engineering department, however. Of the total number of college graduates hired by the company each year, about one half hold engineering degrees, and the other half are composed mostly of liberal arts and business administration graduates. Many of the engineers eventually attain mangerial positions in the nontechnical phases of the business.

As technology has advanced, the top management of the ABC Company has experienced a real need for more graduate engineers in the engineering department. It feels that in the past it diluted the manpower in this department too thin by assigning too many nonengineers and nondegree holders to this type of work. In many instances the engineering department had become the dumping ground for misfits from operating departments. For these interdepartmental transfers the engineering department had had no practical selection methods. It had pretty much taken whoever was offered.

In recent years there has been a problem of low morale, particularly among those engineering personnel who have had an engineering education. They have noticed that promotions for engineers were few and far between, whereas those college graduates who had gone into other departments rose in the organization quite rapidly. The general attitude has evolved in the minds of higher management that engineers were best utilized as technical specialists—as functional individual contributors. There was also the feeling that engineers as a group are poor at dealing with people, and therefore they would make poor supervisors.

Recently the personnel department made an analysis of the salaries and rate of progress of all those college graduates hired fresh from college during the years 1960-1965. During these years engineers and nonengineers had been hired in about equal proportions. It was found that those persons who were now working in nonengineering departments (regardless of their college preparation) were receiving higher salaries and had attained higher-ranking positions than those who are doing engineering work.

Salary levels for engineering personnel are considered adequate in comparison with rates paid by other companies for the same occupations. The company conducts an annual salary survey and makes a sincere effort to keep its salaries competitive.

Questions

1. Assuming that you have been given the task of recommending a program of action to solve the problems contained in this case study, what would be your proposals for the following critical areas?
   a. Selection policies and procedures for transfers of employees to engineering jobs
   b. Low morale of graduate engineers within engineering department
   c. Inequitable promotion opportunities
   d. Using former craftsmen and foremen on engineering jobs
2. Should engineers look to their advancement primarily by going into administrative and executive work or by achieving status and economic advancement within the engineering profession itself?

Problem 3

Ralph V., age 39, mill manager for The Pulp and Paper Company, arrived at his office on Friday morning as usual. Shortly after his arrival he received a telephone call from Mr. Jenkins, the executive vice-president of the company, asking him to come immediately to his office. Once in Mr. Jenkins' office, he was informed that he was being discharged effective as of the end of that day. Mr. Jenkins stated that he had been dissatisfied with Ralph V.'s performance for a long time and had been contemplating this move for many months. Ralph V. was stunned and visibly shaken. He protested that he did not believe that his work had been unsatisfactory and that he had worked many long hours over the past five years to meet the multitude of problems encountered in running the mill. Mr. Jenkins stated that his decision was final. In fact a new mill manager had recently been hired to take Ralph V.'s place. The new man was going to report on the following Monday. Acknowledging the abruptness of this termination, Mr. Jenkins offered the mill manager six weeks pay as a separation allowance.

Ralph had originally been hired five years previous as assistant mill manager. He was promoted to mill manager after one year when the old manager retired. The mill manager was in charge of all paper manufacturing operations in a mill employing 500 people. The functions of operations, maintenance, production control, and quality control were under his jurisdiction. Organizationally, the mill manager reported to the vice-president of the fine paper division, who in turn reported to the executive vice-president of the corporation. Ralph V. had originally been hired from the outside by Mr. Jenkins. He came well recommended.

A few days later in discussing Ralph V. and his termination the personnel manager said privately:

> He was a very affable guy. Very talkative and outgoing. He was popular with his foremen. Whenever I visited his office on business I found it difficult to get away because he had so many stories to tell that did not really relate to the job. Ralph also took pride in counseling and coaching foremen, group leaders, and hourly workers. There was many a man who probably should have been discharged for poor work or violation of plant rules whom Ralph reformed and saved for the company. Ralph "cooked his own goose" however when he got into a serious argument with his immediate boss, Jake Richards, the vice-president of the division, about a year ago. Ralph was hired originally by the executive vice-president and he reported to him before Richards was employed. The new vice-president of the fine paper division was hired a little over a year ago to give the division more managerial attention and improve its profit picture. He became Ralph's immediate boss.

The director of engineering in commenting upon the situation made the following remarks:

> Ralph was just not on top of things. He tended to have a continuous stream of people in his office to get decisions on production problems and also to talk about social matters and trivia. He was active in various

fraternal and civic organizations in town and spent a great deal of time on the telephone handling these matters. In fact he also lost some normal job time handling these outside affairs.

Yet he was lax about planning, anticipating problems, and knowing what was going on in his own mill. Often times the foremen would run the production lines at only half or three-quarter speed because of troubles with the equipment or the product. Yet this could go on for a whole day or two and he would be unable to diagnose the cause of the trouble. Again, quality of the paper coming off the machines might be low, and Ralph would not take prompt corrective action. Also there were recurring problems with maintenance and housekeeping.

However, I do say that many of the problems in the mill were not fully Ralph's fault. He was not given the essential services he required to run a tight ship. He should have had more support from higher management.

One of the long service superintendents in the mill made these remarks about two months later:

Things aren't noticeably different under the new mill manager than they were under Ralph. The new man has many good ideas, but we still have frequent breakdowns of equipment, bottlenecks, and quality problems. I think Ralph was the "fall guy" for all that's wrong around here. Many of us have been wondering who is going to be fired next. I understand Jake Richards was determined to get rid of Ralph and never made an effort to help him.

The discharged mill manager, Ralph, was interviewed privately at lunch about two weeks later. He made these remarks:

I'm somewhat bitter about this whole thing. I was never given any real signals that this was coming. I had been in Mr. Jenkins' office just a few days before that Friday morning talking about various production matters. He did not act unusual at that time. As a matter of fact I always got along fine with Jenkins. I will agree that on a couple of occasions in the past he told me that he was displeased with production levels in the mill. But I did not take that to mean any strong criticism because he knew (or I thought he knew) that I was trying to run the operation with some equipment that was old and subject to serious breakdowns. Besides he didn't always let me hire the people I needed. I had very few foremen who were fully qualified.

I understand they hired my replacement behind my back and had been negotiating for months to get him.

I think Jake Richards was working on Jenkins for a long time to have him fire me—that is ever since he and I had the squabble about my refusing to fire one of the group leaders about a year ago.

Questions

1. Evaluate the way in which Ralph, the mill manager, was discharged.
2. Would you anticipate that the new mill manager would have any special problems upon commencing his new job?
3. What do you think of the method top management adopted to assure continuity of operations, namely, timing the hiring of the new manager to coincide with the discharge of the old one.
4. If an executive is performing unsatisfactorily, what action should his immediate superior take?

Suggestions for Further Reading

Ferman, L. A. and M. Aiken, "Mobility and Situational Factors in the Adjustment of Older Workers to Job Displacement," *Human Organization,* Vol. 26, Winter 1967, pp. 235-241.

Jennings, E. E., "Charting the Difficulties to the Top," *Management of Personnel Quarterly,* Vol. 6, No. 2, Summer 1967, pp. 13-21.

Kern, R. C., "Selection for Promotion", *Personnel Journal,* Vol. 46, July-August 1967, pp. 434-437.

McConkey, Dale D., "Ability vs. Seniority in Promotion and Layoff," *Personnel,* Vol. 37, No. 3, May-June 1960, pp. 51-57.

Odiorne, George S., "The Unpromotable Manager," *Manage,* Vol. 20, October 1967, pp. 46-49.

"Promotion from Within," *Personnel,* Vol. 44, January-February 1967, pp. 4-5.

Slichter, Sumner H., James J. Healy, and E. Robert Livernash, *The Impact of Collective Bargaining on Management,* Washington, D.C.: The Brookings Institution, 1960, Chs. 5, 6 and 7.

Steinmetz, Lawrence L., "The Unsatisfactory Performer: Salvage or Discharge," *Personnel,* Vol. 45, No. 3, May-June 1968, pp. 46-54.

Zaleznik, Abraham, "Management of Disappointment," *Harvard Business Review,* Vol. 45, No. 6, November-December 1967, pp. 59-70.

Training

13

To operate organizations, large or small, requires staffing with competent personnel. Our public educational system is primarily oriented toward teaching broad knowledge and skills to enable people to cope successfully with their environment, to support themselves, and to help advance the society as a whole. Generally speaking, it is not designed to teach specific job skills for positions in particular companies or organizations.

About a million and a half young people enter the labor force each year. Because the vast majority of these are not prepared to perform jobs in work organizations, they must be trained by their employers. Even those who have learned a technical or professional field of work at college must receive some initial training in the form of orientation to the policies, practices, and ways of their specific employing organization. Because the technology of our productive processes is developing at such a rapid pace, there is a need for continual retraining of experienced workers to perform new and changed jobs. The automation of recent years is but an advanced stage of the technological developments that have been taking place at an increased pace in recent decades.

Fifty years ago new workers were expected to pick up necessary job skills and knowledge from experienced fellow employees. The newcomers were typically called learners or helpers. Although it cannot be denied that this method of learning worked, it certainly didn't work well. It was quite haphazard and caused the learning process to be very slow. Many incorrect procedures were often acquired. Frequently old-timers would deliberately seek to protect their positions and status by hazing the new men and by confining the learners' activities to the menial parts of the work.

Large-scale systematic training activities in industry got their start during the periods of war production during World Wars I and II. Especially noteworthy were the Training-Within-Industry (TWI) and the Engineering, Science, and Management War Training (ESMWT) programs of World War II. The TWI program trained people in industry in procedures for teaching job skills to others (Job Instruction Training), in developing better work methods (Job Methods Training), and in industrial relations (Job Relations Training). The ESMWT program consisted largely of specialized technical courses offered by colleges and technical schools to employees in defense industries.

This chapter will explore the nature of training, objectives to be accomplished, organizational considerations in training, the learning process and learning principles, training methods, and training programs. Means of evaluating the effectiveness of training will also be discussed. The training and development of managers, which is a special and very important application of training principles, will be covered in Chapter 14, "Management Development."

Training Defined

Training is the organized procedure by which people learn knowledge and/or skills for a definite purpose. The objective of training is to achieve a change in the behavior of those trained. In the industrial situation this means that the trainees shall acquire new manipulative skills, technical knowledge, problem-solving ability, or attitudes. It is expected that the employees apply their newly acquired knowledge and skills on the job in such a way as to aid in the achievement of organizational goals.

Training is often distinguished from education. Education is thought of as being broader in scope. Its purpose is to develop the individual. Commonly education is considered to be formal education in a school, college, or university, whereas training is vocationally oriented and occurs in a work organization. Training usually has a more immediate utilitarian purpose than education. In practice, training and education frequently occur at the same time. This is to say that the distinction is not always necessary or appropriate. Some formal vocational school programs are quite immediately practical and job-oriented, whereas some executive development programs in industry cover fundamental principles and philosophy, are broad in scope, and certainly should be designated as education.

TRAINING IN THE ORGANIZATION

Tangible Benefits of Training

Training is a vital and necessary activity in all organizations. It plays a large part in determining the effectiveness and efficiency of the establishment. Let us now examine some of the major contributions that training can make:

1. *Reduced learning time to reach acceptable performance.* By having qualified instructors and carefully controlled learning situations, management in countless cases has been able to obtain shortened learning periods and higher productivity from new employees. For example, one industrial company had traditionally expected its new male employees to learn a skilled craft simply by working alongside experienced craftsmen. Typically it required two to four years (depending upon the particular occupation) to reach acceptable proficiency. A rapid expansion of the business forced the company to establish formal classroom courses to speed up the learning process. It found that new men were able to reach the desired performance levels within one to two years after initial hiring and in some cases in even less time.

2. *Improved performance on present job.* Training applies not only to new employees but to experienced people as well. It can help employees increase their level of performance on their present job assignments.

3. *Attitude formation.* A common objective of company training programs is the molding of employee attitudes to achieve support for company activities and to obtain better cooperation and greater loyalty. Some training programs, such as those concerned with the "economics of the business enterprise system," have this as their primary goal. In other cases, attitude molding is simply a by-product of the instruction process.

4. *Aid in solving operational problems.* Training of both supervisory and hourly paid employees can help reduce turnover, absenteeism, accidents, and grievance rates. For example, inept supervision is often a cause of employee dissatisfaction and grievances. Supervisory training in such areas as labor relations, leadership, human relations, and administration may improve supervisor-subordinate relationships. Other operational problems that training can help solve are low morale, poor customer service, excessive waste and scrap loss, and poor work methods.

5. *Fill manpower needs.* One manufacturing company found it impossible to recruit sufficient skilled machinsts and toolmakers. Hence it concluded that the best way to solve this manpower problem, in

the long run, was to establish its own apprentice training program. A number of small manufacturers in the wearing apparel industry in an Eastern city continually find difficulty in hiring adequate numbers of skilled sewing-machine operators. None of these firms has any type of organized training program. Yet a large company in the same city seldom is short of labor, because it operates a complete training school for sewing-machine operators. Consequently, it is able to recruit green labor and train these women to become experienced stitchers. When totally new skills are required by a company, it often finds it most practical to select and train from within the organization rather than seek the skilled personnel in the outside labor market.

6. *Benefits to employees themselves.* As employees acquire new knowledge and job skills they increase their market value and earning power. The possession of useful skills enhances their value to their employer and thereby increases their job security. Training may also qualify them for promotion to more responsible jobs. This, of course, increases their pay and status.

Organization for Training

In small companies (in manufacturing, a small company is generally considered to be one having under 500 employees), training is, to a great extent, of the on-the-job variety, and it is done by line supervision. Where personnel departments exist in these companies, the planning and coordination of training activities is typically one of the many responsibilities of the personnel manager. It is rare to find specialization carried to the point of having a separate training section within the personnel department.

On the other hand, the vast majority of large companies have a separate training section within the personnel or industrial relations department. This is the most common organizational arrangement for managing the training function. In a questionnaire survey of members of the American Society of Training Directors, Belman and Bliek found that 85 per cent of the respondents indicated that the training function was located, organizationally, within the personnel, industrial relations, or employee relations department. The other organizational locations were scattered among production, sales, office of the chief executive, and a separate division.[1]

The training section is properly considered a staff function. It performs in the areas of program formulation, advice, service, and control in regard to organization-wide training activities. Quite commonly in industry, training of sales personnel is the responsibility of the sales division

[1] Harry S. Belman and John E. Bliek, "Organization and Structure of the Training Function," *Journal of the American Society of Training Directors,* Vol. 13, No. 8 (August 1959), p. 24.

and is divorced organizationally from the personnel department. In a survey of 255 organizations in business, industry, and government, Belman and Bliek found that 118 establishments conducted sales training separately from all other training activities.[2] This means that it is commonly placed under the authority of the sales department itself. This is done partly because of tradition and partly because the problems in sales are considered to be distinctly different from those in the rest of the organization. For one thing sales personnel are usually geographically separated from the main company locations.

The staff training section must commonly perform the following functions: (1) determination of training needs, (2) development of overall plans, objectives, and assignment of responsibilities, (3) development of training programs in consultation with line executives, (4) collection and preparation of training materials, outlines, curricula, booklets, and audiovisual aids, (5) administration and instruction for certain courses (often orientation and supervisory development courses), (6) administration and coordination of apprentice, on-the-job, vestibule, and other courses, (7) training of line personnel and designated instructors to develop teaching skills, and (8) evaluation of effectiveness of training effort.

Line Training Responsibilities

Top line executive management (this may be the president or executive vice-president or a top division manager in a decentralized company) has the responsibility for authorizing basic training policies. Likewise it must review and approve the broad outlines of training plans and programs without, of course, concerning itself with details. It must approve the training budget. If, for example, the training director thinks it would be desirable to inaugurate a comprehensive executive development program, he would have to obtain the wholehearted support of the chief executive officer of the organization before he could undertake such an activity. It would be the training director who would formulate complete plans for carrying out an executive development program. However, these plans would have to be approved by top line management. A training director might feel that certain managers should be sent to one of the extended on-campus executive development courses given by a number of major universities. The actual selection of a person and the decision to release him from his present job for the duration of the course is a line management responsibility.

What are the training duties and responsibilities of lower line management? Foremen, general foremen, and office supervisors must be alert

---

[2] Harry S. Belman and John E. Bliek, "The Nature of Current Training Function Activities," *Journal of the American Society of Training Directors,* Vol. 15, No. 2 (February 1961), p. 37. In this survey 63 respondents stated that training for sales was not organized separately from other training, and 74 stated the question did not apply to their situations.

to recognize training problems that exist in their departments. They may participate in the creation of special tailor-made training programs to help solve specific problems in their units. They must bear direct responsibility for the successful conduct of an on-the-job training activity in their departments. If certain employees are to perform in the role of on-the-job instructors, the supervisor must insure that these employees have themselves been adequately trained in the principles of teaching. The supervisor must coach and counsel his subordinates in order to obtain adequate performance. In effect a supervisor is himself a trainer. He often is personally responsible for the orientation of new employees. He may conduct safety training meetings with his personnel. The supervisor selects, from among his subordinates, those who should participate in formal training programs. He is responsible not only for meeting production goals but also for developing his people.

Discovering Training Needs

Sometimes a manager decides to set up a training program because it is the popular thing to do and because other companies are doing it. Many companies have set up business games or gone into the use of teaching machines on no other basis than this. However a company can literally pour thousands of dollars down the drain unless it attacks its training problems on a systematic basis.

Training programs should be established only when it is felt that they can aid in solving specific operational problems. Therefore, the rational way of deciding what kind of training activity to undertake is to make an analysis of the entire organization (people, jobs, technology, and so on) to identify trouble spots where training may help.

It should be pointed out at this point that training is not a cure-all. If employee output is low, this may be corrected by better skill training. On the other hand the problem may not be one of inadequate training at all. It might be due to faulty material, process equipment, or engineering design. If it appears that the general caliber of the work force is low, this condition might be corrected by training. On the other hand it could be that the general wage level is so low that the company cannot recruit good employees.

The identification of specific problem areas in the organization can suggest ways in which training may help toward a solution. The following are ways of discovering training needs:

1. Identify organizational and production problems
   Low productivity
   High costs
   Poor material control
   Poor quality, excessive scrap and waste

      Excessive labor-management strife

      Excessive grievances

      Excessive violation of rules of conduct, poor discipline

      High employee turnover

      Excessive absenteeism

      Delayed production; schedules not met

2. Analyze jobs and men

      Job analysis

      Employee appraisal

      Testing

3. Collect employee and managerial opinions

      Interviews and questionnaires to obtain views regarding necessary and desirable training programs

4. Anticipate impending and future problems

      Expansion of business

      New products, new services

      New designs

      New plants

      New technology

      Organizational changes

      Manpower inventory—compare present manpower resources with forecasted needs

THE LEARNING PROCESS

Learning is really the core of the training process. When management installs a new training activity, it reasonably expects that through participation in this training employees will exhibit new or changed behavior. Indeed, *learning can be defined as that human process by which skills, knowledge, habits, and attitudes are acquired and utilized in such a way that behavior is modified.*

We know that a person has learned when he demonstrates it by performance. If John is studying German, he shows that he has learned by translating a passage in a book. A mathematics student, by solving written homework problems, has demonstrated that he has learned his assigned lesson. Likewise a welding trainee reveals that he has learned to make a pipe weld by actually doing it.

Principles of Learning

Psychologists, primarily through experimentation, have developed a number of important principles of learning. These are equally pertinent for application by training directors who administer programs, for classroom instructors who teach employees, and for supervisors who train employees on the job.

Motivation.   If trainees are not receptive to instruction, if they can see no reason to learn, then a training effort can hardly get off the ground. Adequate motivation is essential to the success of any learning situation. People are goal-oriented in their behavior. They will exert themselves to fulfill a felt need. For example, a man will work at gainful employment to obtain money compensation in order to buy food to allay hunger. In our advanced society, of course, people are motivated to satisfy many other higher needs besides the basic survival needs. People are motivated to fulfill social needs (love, belongingness, friendship, esteem of others, gregariousness) and egoistic needs (self-significance, self-expression, self-accomplishment, and independence). Learning is effective when the trainees perceive that they can satisfy some goal through participation in a training program.

There are two kinds of motives: intrinsic and extrinsic. In intrinsic motivation the work itself is satisfying to the individual. He takes pleasure in his work or schooling and derives a feeling of accomplishment upon successful completion of the work. Extrinsic motivation refers to the holding out of incentives or external rewards for the successful completion of a task. Such incentives may be praise from the boss or the instructor, higher pay, a bonus, prestige, better working conditions, and the like. Both types of motivation are important to the learning process. However, learning is quite difficult if the external incentives are available but intrinsic motivation is lacking. This situation can be illustrated by a college student who has chosen to enroll in an engineering curriculum because he knows that the salaries paid to graduate engineers are very good. However, this long-range goal is unlikely to motivate him to learn mathematics, physics, electronics, solid mechanics, and fluid mechanics if he dislikes these subjects. He may grit his teeth and force himself to get through these courses, but the learning will be quite painful. Conversely learning engineering is easy for the student who has the aptitude plus the intrinsic interest in this subject matter.

Both rewards and punishment play a powerful role in motivation to learn. A reward for a desired response serves to stimulate a repetition of that behavior. Thus students may receive praise from their parents for doing well in school, and this will motivate them to continue to do well. Punishment tends to inhibit a certain response, but it does not necessarily eliminate it. Mild punishment is effective if it is immediate and if the learner understands the reason for it. Supervisors and trainers must be very judicious in the way in which they administer punishment. If a learner has been doing poorly, it may cause him to alter his behavior to threaten him with a discharge or to bawl him out, but most generally such action will affect many other aspects of his behavior besides the learning situation. It may cause him to fear or resent his instructor or boss so much that he cannot concentrate upon learning the work at hand. Employees may learn to follow company rules of conduct because those who don't are clearly punished. But often an emphasis upon punishment by management is only effective as long as there is repeated punishment or the threat of it. Employees will concentrate upon avoiding punishment rather than doing the right thing. In the long run, people will learn to behave in a desired way if they understand the reasons for such prescribed conduct and if they are rewarded for such behavior.

What is the motivation to learn of the newly hired employee? Generally those responsible for teaching new employees find a great deal of built-in willingness to learn. The new man knows that he is on trial during the probationary period. He knows he can be fired readily if he displeases his superiors. In fact, he is often rather anxious during the initial learning period. At any rate new workers are usually highly motivated to learn the requisite job skills and knowledge. The trainer should, of course, explain how various parts of the learning program and assigned tasks are necessary to success on the job.

Experienced employees sometimes find it hard to understand why they should participate in further training. This is especially true if they have been out of school for many years and if they feel that things are going quite smoothly on their jobs. John Smith, who has been a factory foreman for twenty years and has successfully met his production schedules and kept costs in line, may be quite reluctant to participate in a series of supervisory training classes run by the personnel department. How can he be motivated to take an active interest in such a program? Although individual differences mean that people will vary in the way they respond to stimuli, certain general ideas can be offered. Supervisory training may show John Smith the foreman how to delegate more effectively, how to save more of his own limited time, how to read reports more quickly, how to understand his subordinates better, how to eliminate potential labor troubles, and how to administer the new labor agreement. Training may even better qualify him for promotion.

Knowledge of Results.   Somewhat related to motivation is knowledge of the learner's progress. Research experiments have demonstrated that people learn faster when they are informed of their accomplishments. After analyzing numerous research experiments concerning such diverse activities as line drawing, use of gun sights, dot-dash code receiving, and typing, Wolfle has concluded that it is essential that trainees be given knowledge of their efforts. He states that such knowledge should be automatic, immediate, and meaningfully related to the task at hand.[3] Thus in a training classroom students' examinations should be graded and returned to them so that they can know where they have erred and what they have done correctly. In on-the-job training the supervisor should inform the employee of his successes and failures so that he can adjust his efforts if necessary. People like to experience a feeling of progress. They want to know where they stand. If an instructor returns examination papers

[3] Dael Wolfle, "Training" in S. S. Stevens (ed.), *Handbook of Experimental Psychology* (New York: John Wiley & Sons, Inc., 1951), pp. 1267-1286.

to a class of students with only the raw scores recorded, this knowledge will be meaningless until they are told how all of the grades were distributed and how they stand in relation to expected performance. Learning is facilitated when the trainee has some criterion by which he can judge his own progress.

Learn by Doing.   It is extremely difficult for a learner simply to listen to a teacher explain how to do something and then be able to do it solely from the explanation. It is by actually performing the task that a student really learns. The greater the number of human senses involved, the more complete is the learning. If one is teaching a physical task, such as operating a machine or sharpening a tool, it is easy to see how practice can be provided. But what if one is teaching theories and concepts? Actually a variety of techniques are possible. Laboratory experiments can be devised. Written problems can be assigned. Case studies and role playing can be utilized. Although not constituting full learning by doing, oral discussion and debate help to strengthen the learning of ideas.

When learning a task by practice, is it better to combine the total time devoted to practice into one concentrated session, or should the practice be subdivided into small time periods? The available research evidence seems to favor spaced practice sessions. Experiments with massed as opposed to spaced practice for simple motor skills and memorizing show that learning is superior for that type of practice which has a series of short rest periods.[4]

Whole or Part Learning?   In secondary school, when children learn to memorize a poem they do it one (or a few) stanzas at a time. Is this the way employees should learn to perform work sequences—one step at a time? Whether whole or part learning is preferable depends to a certain extent upon the nature of the learner and of the material to be mastered.

However, certain generalizations can be made. If the material to be learned is simple, if the task has few operations, then whole learning is superior. Where the different parts of the material are logically interrelated into a large unit, then the whole method should be employed. On the other hand, if the knowledge to be learned or the task to be mastered is very complex and long, then it should be broken down into parts so that the trainee can learn one section at a time.

Usually where part learning is primarily employed, the whole procedure can be presented in broad outline at the beginning and then periodically thereafter to orient the trainee to the whole subject. In fact, whole and part learning can be intermixed in the same training sequence to gain the benefits of both approaches.

Is Theory Desirable?   Does the chemistry laboratory technician need

[4] See E. R. Hilgard, *Theories of Learning* (2nd Ed., New York: Appleton-Century-Crofts, Inc., 1956), p. 487. Also William McGehee and Paul W. Thayer, *Training in Business and Industry* (New York: John Wiley & Sons, Inc., 1961), p. 151-153.

to understand why chemical reactions occur as they do? Does the process operator in an oil refinery need to know why he must turn valves and adjust temperatures and pressures? Do workers perform better if they understand the principles underlying the work they do?

The prevailing weight of evidence shows that learning is faster and can be applied better to new situations if the trainees understand the principles involved. This was found to be true for boys shooting at targets that were underwater: a knowledge of refraction increased the accuracy of shooting. It was also true for college students who had to solve simple reasoning problems. Those who were told the principles upon which the problems were based did better than those who were simply given sample solutions to a few problems. Those who were given a series of problems in such a manner that they could derive their own principles did still better in future problems.[5]

From the foregoing it is clear that a man who understands the theory behind his work is in a good position to readily adapt to new problem situations as they arise. The man, however, who has simply been trained to perform as an automaton will be hopelessly lost when confronted with situations out of the ordinary. This principle of teaching theory as well as practice does not mean that we need a graduate electrical engineer to repair a television set. But it does mean that the TV repairman, for example, should possess a practical, working knowledge of electronics as it applies to television receivers.

In summary, employees should be taught sufficient theory to understand the principles and reasons underlying their work and to cope successfully with the general run of problems they may encounter.

Learning Motor Skills. In motor-skill work muscular movement is prominent, but it is under sensory control. Examples of motor skills are skiing, skating, swimming, carpentry, setting up and operating machine tools, welding, glass blowing, using hand tools, and operating a sewing machine. The instructor must show and explain the materials, tools, and equipment that he will use. He should then demonstrate how to perform the activity. If the activity is complicated, the instructor should break the operation down into logical components, explain the steps involved and then demonstrate. Next the learner should start practicing the operation. He should understand what he is doing and be able to explain the activity. The instructor should provide guidance and feedback. The learner must know if his performance is progressing properly or improperly. Generally after practicing for a period of time, a rest pause should be provided. Distributed practice periods are generally more fruitful than prolonged and concentrated practice.

Learning Concepts and Attitudes. This process is much more complex than learning motor skills. At one extreme is rote learning where a

[5] Dael Wolfle in S. S. Stevens, *op. cit.,* pp. 1277-1278.

person may have to memorize a poem, learn the names of the parts of a machine, or learn a computer language. At the other extreme one may learn for depth of understanding. There may be all sorts of interconnections and associations among the ideas he learns. He may learn the reasons why as well as beliefs, attitudes and philosophies. He may search for general theorems, truths, and laws.

There are many ways to learn ideas and attitudes. We can learn by trial and error and personal experience. We can read and observe. We can learn by listening and talking with others.

The learning of ideas is enhanced when the students participate actively in the process. They may work on problems and exercises and ask and answer questions. This may be both written work and oral discussion in class. It is especially valuable to encourage students to explore problems and issues in some depth so that they discover relationships and principles for themselves. It may save time if the instructor organizes all of the subject matter and explains it logically and clearly to his trainees. But, at least part of the time, opportunity should be provided for them to work on exercises, problems, and concepts and discover truths for themselves.

Indeed, a fundamental question in designing a classroom learning experience is whether to depend heavily upon the lecture method of instruction or to foster a high degree of group discussion and interaction. The answer to this question depends somewhat upon the objectives of the program of training or education. If the purpose is solely to provide information of a factual nature to the group, the lecture method, which is highly leader centered, is quite satisfactory. However if the material to be learned is subject to varied interpretation and is not precise or explicit, then group discussion, with a group centered method of conducting the class, is clearly superior. There is also evidence that retention of factual knowledge is greater in classes having a high degree of group-member interaction. This result appears to be caused by the learning reinforcement which comes from the testing of one's ideas with others and from the intellectual stimulation which this generates.

Courses whose purpose is to modify attitudes, facilitate behavioral adjustments, aid interpersonal relations, and promote self-insight are clearly superior when the trainer adopts a democratic, participative leadership style. High-member interaction is most conducive to these goals. A very authoritarian trainer tends to be ineffective in changing group attitudes, but a leader who generates high member involvement can more effectively modify opinions, prejudices, and emotions.[6]

A large component of the requisite knowledge and skills of the manager are in the area of human relations; hence a great deal of manage-

[6] A clear discussion of when to use leader-centered and group-centered training styles, based upon an extensive review of available research, is contained in Alan C. Filley and Franklin C. Jesse, "Training Leadership Style: A Survey of Research," *Personnel Administration,* Vol. 28, No. 3 (May-June 1965), pp. 14-21.

ment training is conducted by methods featuring high group interaction such as discussions, conferences, case studies, management games, and sensitivity training.

TRAINING METHODS

Those who administer training programs have a great choice of methods for imparting learning in trainees. The particular method selected is determined by considerations of cost, time available, number of persons to be trained, depth of knowledge required, background of the trainees, and many other factors. The following is a listing of the major training methods:

1. On-the-Job
2. Vestibule
3. Classroom Methods
   a. Lecture
   b. Conference
   c. Case Study
   d. Role Playing
   e. Programmed Instruction
4. Other Methods
   a. Demonstration
   b. Simulation

On-the-Job Training

The vast majority of all training carried on is of the on-the-job variety. Much of what passes for on-the-job training is extremely haphazard. For example, a young engineer fresh out of college took a position in a large corporation. He was immediately assigned to an application engineering job. For training he was told to read a stack of books describing company standard procedures and specifications. His boss assumed that by studying these he would learn his job. As another example, Bill was hired as a machine operator in a government arsenal. He was expected to turn out precision parts on milling machines and boring mills for military weapons. He had had machine experience in another company but had never worked on this specific product under these conditions. He was given no instruction by the foremen. What he learned he had to gain informally by asking help from experienced work associates.

How should on-the-job training programs be conducted? Primary responsibility rests with each departmental supervisor. If he understands training principles and methods and if he takes an interest in proper train- of new employees, chances are that it will be done properly. The training may be done either by the supervisor himself or by a designated experienced nonsupervisory employee. The person doing the training must be given recognition for his work. He must not consider training to be an unpleasant chore that interferes with production. The instructor must himself first receive training in the principles and techniques of instruction. It is the responsibility of the training department to teach all on-the-job instructors how to instruct.

The instructor must assemble all necessary equipment, procedure sheets, working materials, and training aids. He must break down the material to be learned into meaningful packages and present it to the employee in a manner appropriate to the job to be learned. In many instances he will actually demonstrate how the work is to be performed. He will carefully guide and observe the trainee as he performs the work. Correction will be given as required.

A variety of training aids and techniques can be used in conjunction with on-the-job training. Among these are procedure charts, pictures, manuals, sample problems, demonstrations, oral and written explanations, and tape recordings.

Suppose, for example, that a young man is being trained to become an employment interviewer in the personnel department. He may first be required to read textbooks and a company manual on interviewing. Next, his instructor, who should be a skilled interviewer, can explain the theory and practice of interviewing. The trainee can then actually sit in on actual job interviews conducted by the instructor. He will learn how the interviewing technique can be varied to fit changing situations. The trainee can then conduct his own interviews, with the instructor present to furnish suggestions at the conclusion. The interviews could be recorded on a tape recorder and analyzed later by both the instructor and trainee. There are additional ways in which learning can be facilitated. Both the instructor and the learner can interview job seekers successively, in private. Then they can compare notes and impressions. On a long-range basis an interviewer can compare his predictions of success with the actual performance of hired persons on the job.

On-the-job training is most appropriate for teaching knowledge and skills that can be learned in a relatively short time (a few days to several weeks) and where only one or at most a very few employees must be trained at the same time for the same job. If a great depth of theory must be acquired, then this can be accomplished more efficiently in a classroom. On-the-job training is useful for learning unskilled and semiskilled manual type jobs, clerical jobs, and sales work. For skilled, technical, professional, and supervisory jobs, the underlying educational background must be obtained by other means; however, the applied aspects of these jobs are quite generally learned right on the job.

On-the-job training has the advantage of permitting the trainee to learn on the actual equipment and in the environment of his job. He can actually experience a feeling of accomplishment as he produces useful products. If only a few are to be trained at one time, it is cheaper for the employer to resort to on-the-job training rather than to invest in a vestibule school or classroom setup. Quite often expensive manufacturing equipment cannot be duplicated in the classroom.

On-the-job training suffers from the fact that the instruction is often disorganized and haphazard. Learners are subjected to the distractions of a noisy shop or office. There is a tendency to slight the principles and theory in favor of immediate production.

Vestibule Training

Vestibule training is the term used to designate training in a class-room for semiskilled production and clerical jobs. It is particularly appropriate where a large number of employees must be trained at the same time for the same kind of work. Where it is used, there is a greater likelihood that management will have well-qualified instructors in charge. The emphasis tends to be upon learning rather than production. It has been used to train clerks, bank tellers, inspectors, machine operators, testers, typists, and the like.

In vestibule training an attempt is made to duplicate, as nearly as possible, the actual material, equipment, and conditions found in a real work place. Typically the learning time ranges from a few days to a few months. Theory can more easily be presented in a vestibule school than on-the-job. The learning conditions are carefully controlled.

Classroom Methods

Classroom instruction is most useful where philosophy, concepts, attitudes, theories, and problem-solving abilities must be learned. This means that a considerable depth of knowledge must be acquired. There are certain aspects of nearly all jobs that can be learned better in the classroom than on the job. Certain portions of company orientation and safety training can be accomplished most effectively in the classroom. Most commonly, however, we think of the various classroom methods being used for technical, professional, and managerial personnel where a considerable grounding in theories, principles, and concepts is necessary. Let us now examine some of the principal classroom instruction techniques.

Lecture.   The standard instructional method in colleges and universities, the lecture is a formal, organized talk by the instructor to a group of students. The lecturer is presumed to possess a considerable depth of knowledge of the subject at hand. He seeks to communicate his thoughts in such a manner as to interest the class and cause them to retain what he has said. Quite often the students will take notes as aids to learning.

The principal virtue of the lecture method is that it can be used for very large groups, and thus the cost per trainee is low. It can be organized rigorously so that ideas and principles relate properly one to the other.

However, the limitations of this method may outweigh its advantages. The learners are passive. It violates the principle of learning by doing. It constitutes one-way communication. There is no feedback from the audience. The presentation must be geared to a particular level of knowledge and may bore the advanced student and be beyond the capabilities of the slow learner. It tends to emphasize the accumulation of facts and figures; however, this does not mean that the learners will be able to apply their knowledge. If students are permitted to ask questions only at the end of the lecture, their points may then seem inappropriate. Because it is difficult to hold the full attention of listeners for a sustained period, lecturers are tempted to resort to anecdotes, jokes, and other attention getters. This activity may eventually overshadow the real purpose of the instruction.

The most fruitful way to use the lecture is to combine it with other techniques. Thus a teacher may conduct a class by the combined lecture-discussion method. He may then lecture only to add new information that the group does not possess. He may give formal reading assignments, present demonstrations, and show films.

Conference.   A conference is a small group meeting, conducted according to an organized plan, in which the leader seeks to develop knowledge and understanding by obtaining a considerable amount of oral participation from the trainees or students. It overcomes certain of the disadvantages of the lecture, because, here, students play very active roles. They are not passive. In fact, the very success of any conference is dependent upon contributions from the students. Learning is facilitated through building upon the ideas contributed by the conferees. The people, to an extent, learn from each other.

There are three basic kinds of conferences: (1) the directed conference (also called the guided or instructional conference), (2) the consultative conference, and (3) the problem-solving conference. The directed conference is most commonly used for training purposes, because the instructor has certain concepts he wishes the class to absorb, and he guides the group carefully to insure that they cover these ideas. Conferences are not limited to training purposes, however. They are frequently used in all sorts of organizations to attack operating problems by bringing to bear the pooled thinking of a number of people. For solving business problems, either the consultative or the problem-solving method may be used.

Let us examine some of the features of a directed conference used for training purposes. Because it depends for its success upon the active participation of the conferees, the size of the group must be limited to fifteen to twenty persons. The people should sit facing one another around a conference table rather than theater-style, as in an ordinary classroom.

The students should have some knowledge of the subject to be discussed before coming to the conference. This can be obtained from assigned readings or previous experience or both. The instructor introduces the topic and invites viewpoints from the group on problem areas related to this topic. He must, by the skillful use of questions, make sure that the class analyzes the topic thoroughly. Often he will record student responses on the blackboard. He will summarize progress made at pertinent points throughout the session. Points of disagreement will also be highlighted. In the directed conference the instructor or leader may introduce new material by occasional brief periods of lecturing.

In contrast to the lecture, the students play a very active part in determining the progress of the conference. They are not forced to submit passively to the instructor's viewpoints. They are expected to make assertive statements and to ask questions. They learn not only from the instructor but also from each other. It is rare for a trainee to become bored or to fall asleep in a conference, whereas this condition is common in the lecture. Interest tends to be high. The conference is ideally suited to tearing apart problems and issues and examining them from different viewpoints. It is an excellent procedure for reducing dogmatism and modifying attitudes. Because they have had a part in developing solutions and reaching conclusions, the conferees are often willing to accept these conclusions. The skilled conference leader is acutely aware that he must avoid imposing his opinions upon the group.

The principal limitations of the conference method are as follows: (1) it is limited to a small group, and (2) progress is often slow because all those desiring to speak on a point are generally allowed to do so. Irrelevant issues creep in easily.

The conference method is useful in training primarily for the development of conceptual knowledge and for the creation and modification of attitudes. Case studies are ideally suited to the conference format. This method is extensively employed in supervisory- and executive-development programs.

Case Study.   In the teaching of mathematics, it is almost universal practice for the instructor to assign problems for the students to work out to illustrate the principles previously taught. This method gives the student an opportunity to apply his knowledge to the solution of realistic problems. Likewise, this principle can be applied to the teaching of those subjects concerned with human affairs. Case studies are extensively used in teaching law, personnel management, human relations, labor relations, marketing, production management, and business policy.[7]

Cases can be used in either of two ways. First, as stated above, they can be used subsequent to the exposition of formal theory. In this way students must apply their theory and knowledge to specific situations.

[7] For a discussion of the case method in teaching management and human relations, see Kenneth R. Andrews and others, *The Case Method of Teaching Human Relations and Administration* (Cambridge, Mass.: Harvard University Press, 1953).

Second, they may be assigned to students for written analysis and/or oral class discussion without any prior explanation of pertinent concepts and theory. The students are expected to derive useful generalizations and principles themselves. This second approach places heavy demands upon the student. It requires that the students have a good deal of maturity and some background in the subject area.

The case study method is very popular in graduate professional schools of law and business administration. It is also frequently used in supervisory and executive training in industry.

Case discussions in class are usually conducted in a conference atmosphere. Students soon learn that there is no single answer to a particular problem. Engineers who are used to a right and wrong dichotomy are often initially frustrated in case discussions because the instructor does not tell them what is the right solution.

The case study method of instruction provides for learning by doing. Good cases are usually based upon real experiences and problem situations; therefore, student interest tends to be high. They are excellent for developing analytical thinking and fostering problem-solving ability. Narrowmindedness is reduced because the trainees soon learn that others have studied the identical problem and come up with different patterns of analysis and solution. Students must often defend their proposals in the face of keen criticism from others. The case method is an excellent means for integrating the knowledge obtained from a number of foundation disciplines.

Role Playing. Role playing is actually a technique that should be used in conjunction with some other instructional method such as the lecture or the conference. Originally developed by J. L. Moreno for group therapy for mentally disturbed people, it has been widely used for human relations and leadership training. It is primarily used to give trainees an opportunity to learn human relations skills through practice and to develop insight into their own behavior and its effect upon others.[8]

In role playing two or more trainees are assigned parts to play before the rest of the class. There are no lines to memorize and no rehearsals. The role players are provided with either written or oral descriptions of a situation and the role they are to play. After being allowed sufficient time to plan their actions, they must then act out their parts spontaneously before the group. Typical role playing situations are a supervisor discussing a grievance with an employee, a supervisor conducting a post-appraisal interview with an employee, an employment interviewer conducting a hiring interview, and a salesman making a presentation to a purchasing agent.

Role playing for developing human relations understanding and skills

---

[8] Excellent accounts of role playing are contained in Alex Bavelas, "Role Playing and Management Training," *Sociatry* (now *Group Psychotherapy*), Vol. 1, No. 2 (June 1947), pp. 183-191; Norman R. F. Maier, A. R. Solem, and A. A. Maier, *Supervisory and Executive Development: A Manual for Role Playing* (New York: John Wiley & Sons, 1957).

has a number of advantages. It provides an opportunity for students to actually put into practice the knowledge they have absorbed from textbooks, lectures, and discussions. It is learning by doing. They become sensitive to the way their behavior affects others. It helps people to appreciate other points of view as when roles are switched (that is, the boss plays the part of the worker). Knowledge of results is immediate, because the role players themselves as well as the class analyze and criticize the behavior of the players. Interest and involvement tend to be high.

Programmed Instruction.   One of the exciting developments to occur in the 1950's in the field of training was the advent of programmed instruction. The term *teaching machine* has also been applied to this type of learning. However, programmed learning or instruction is the preferred designation, because a teaching machine is only one device for this type of training. It can be carried out as well with a book or manual as with a machine. If a machine is used, it is simply a vehicle for handling the program. The most vital ingredient is the information that must be broken down into meaningful units and presented in the proper way to form a program.

The key features of programmed learning are (1) students learn at their own pace, (2) instructors are not a key part of the learning, (3) the material to be learned is broken down into very small units or stages, (4) each step logically builds upon those which have preceeded it, (5) the student is given immediate knowledge of results for each answer he gives, and (6) there is active participation by the learner at each step in the program.

Some types of programs take into account individual differences in background. If a student is unable to give the right answer to a question or a series of questions, he will be directed along a different branch of the program to provide him with the fundamentals he has missed.

To date programmed instruction has been used primarily for teaching factual knowledge, such as mathematics, physics, a foreign language, and the like. It has not been used to develop philosophical concepts, attitudes, clinical problem-solving skills, or motor skills. The cost of creating a single program is very great.

Experience with teaching machines and programmed instruction shows that there is a high level of learner motivation. The training can be done at odd times and in odd places. It does not have to be done in a classroom. Research studies concerned with the worth of programmed instruction have been generally favorable in their assessments.

Other Methods

Demonstration and simulation are other important instructional methods. Demonstrations may be carried out either on the job or in a classroom. Simulation is sometimes done in the classroom and sometimes in a laboratory type of situation.

Demonstration.   Of all the senses sight is one of the best for learning. A demonstration in which the instructor actually shows the trainees how to do something has wide application. It is one of the key steps in much on-the-job training. The instructor may show an assembler how to put something together, a tester how to test an engine, a stitcher how to sew a seam, and a pilot trainee how to manipulate controls in an airplane. A sales manager may show sales trainees how to deal with a potential customer and how to explain the performance features of his merchandise. Soldiers in the army receive much of their training by means of demonstration.

Demonstrations are usually combined with some other technique, such as a lecture, pictures, text material, and discussion. A demonstration is particularly effective for skill training. It has only limited usefulness for training management personnel. Because a demonstration emphasizes primarily knowhow, principles and theory must be taught by some other method.

Simulation.   A simulator is any kind of equipment or technique that duplicates as nearly as possible the actual conditions encountered on the job. The Link trainers used to train military pilots in World War II were simulators. Commercial airline pilots are taught to use new types of airplanes in realistic working models of the actual ship. Business games, to be described in more detail in Chapter 14, "Management Development," are a form of simulation. Many business games are worked in conjunction with an electronic computer. A typical business game consists of several teams that represent competing companies. The teams make typical management decisions concerning prices, production volume, research expenditures, and advertising effort to try to maximize their profits. The results of their actions are fed into a computer that has been programmed according to a particular model of the market. Feedback is prompt, so that the teams can learn the effects of their actions to improve their competitive business situations.

Trainee interest and motivation is normally high in simulation exercises because the actions taken closely duplicate real job conditions. Simulation is very useful (and even necessary) where on-the-job practice could result in a serious injury, a costly error, or the destruction of valuable material.

TRAINING PROGRAMS

Principles of learning and training methods are useful only insofar as they contribute to effective training in a specific program. We shall now examine the more important kinds of training programs found in work organizations. Because of the recent heavy commitment of the Federal government in manpower development, we shall start by a brief discussion of the government's role as it affects vocational and job-skills training.

Federal Manpower Programs

Commencing in the early 1960's the Federal government has taken an increasingly active role in national manpower planning and human resources development. It has established and administered a variety of training and retraining programs. It has also allocated funds to the states and to private industry for training efforts. The heightened interest by the Federal government was caused by the unemployment and hardship caused by technological change and automation and by the plight of the culturally deprived (the Negro and white poor) in our cities.

Of primary concern to private industry is the Manpower Development and Training Act of 1962. The original purpose of this law was to retrain experienced adult family heads who had been displaced by technological and economic change. Later the emphasis shifted to the disadvantaged. The MDTA provides basic education and training in both vocational schools and on-the-job in factories and offices for those who are unemployed and underemployed. Of particular interest to employers is the fact that Federal money is available to provide a stipend to trainees enrolled in on-the-job programs. This stipend is roughly equivalent in amount to unemployment compensation.

With the Economic Opportunity Act of 1964, the Federal government launched a comprehensive plan of antipoverty manpower programs. Notable among these are the Job Corps, Neighborhood Youth Corps, Work Experience and Training, New Careers, and Community Action Programs. Private industry can look upon these programs as one source of manpower for semiskilled and skilled occupations.

Orientation

Although proper orientation is easily and often neglected, it is essential for insuring that new employees get off to the right start. Although other terms, such as *induction* and *indoctrination* are also used, *orientation* is most accurately reflective of the real meaning of the process. *Orientation is the guided adjustment of the employee to the organization and his work environment.*

The objectives of orientation are multifold. In carrying out such a program management seeks to create favorable attitudes toward the company, its policies, and its personnel. It can instill a feeling of belonging and acceptance. It can generate enthusiasm and high morale. Quite frankly many employers seek to mold employees' attitudes and behavior so that they fit in well with the organization and accept management policies and ethos. A well-run orientation program may minimize the likelihood of rules violations, discharges, quits, grievances, and misunderstandings.

In most instances an employee is partially oriented before he comes to work for a company. He has heard about its reputation as a place to work and about its deeds in the community. In the reception area of the employment office, he may see company exhibits, copies of the house organ and other literature. In the employment interview he will gain many impressions about the benefits and the responsibilities associated with working for the organization. He will be informed of the job demands, working conditions, and pay.

After an employee is hired, both the personnel department and his supervisor play key roles in the orientation process. The relative part played by each depends upon management intention and the resources of the personnel department. In small companies, either having no personnel department or else having only a skeleton one, the major responsibility for new employee orientation falls upon the operating supervisor. Even in large companies where there are extensive personnel departments, there are certain orientation tasks that essentially belong to the employee's own department.

What is the role of the supervisor in orientation? He is responsible for making the newcomer feel that he is wanted and needed. He should pave the way ahead of time by informing present employees that a new man is going to work in their midst. He should give reasons for adding a new man, so that any suspicion or resentment is allayed. The supervisor should review, with the new employee, the nature of his duties, introduce him to each person with whom he will come in contact, and show him the department or work area and its facilities. In introducing him to other employees with whom he will deal, the supervisor should make it a point to explain the function of these individuals, so that the new man can properly deal with them in the future. Thus a factory production worker should become acquainted with his group leader, inspector, maintenance man, setup man, union steward, timekeeper, and the like. The employee should be told what is expected of him in terms of performance and conduct. He must know what he can expect from the company regarding pay, pay increases, promotion opportunities, holidays, vacations, and benefit plans.

The personnel department is responsible for seeing that the orientation program is initiated in the first place, and that it is carried out according to plan. It should train line supervisors in the performance of their orientation responsibilities. In some companies it exerts staff control over these lines supervisors by requiring them to fill out a check list form that shows that they have done specified orientation tasks for each new man.

Table 13-1 is a listing of important content information and actions that may be included in an orientation program. It includes fundamental things that should be done with each new employee. However, the list is not conclusive, since every organization will make adaptations to fit its needs.

TABLE 13-1   EMPLOYEE ORIENTATION CONTENT

Company history, policies, practices
Company products and/or services
Company plants and facilities
Organization structure (in general)
Employee responsibilities to company
Company responsibilities to employee
Pay treatment
Rules of Conduct
Tour of department
Work schedules
Collective bargaining agreement
Benefit plans—life insurance, medical, hospitalization, pension, unem-
    ployment
Safety program
Training opportunities
Promotion policy
Introduction to fellow employees
Establishment of a feeling of belonging and acceptance; showing genu-
    ine interest in new employee
Employee appraisal system
Work assignment

Experimental evidence of the value of proper orientation of new workers is reported by M. Scott Myers and Earl R. Gomersall, who conducted the research at the Texas Instruments Company. Interviews with about
400 factory operators who had been on the job only about a month dis-
closed that (1) they felt very anxious the first few days on the job; (2) hazing by older workers intensified their anxiety; (3) turnover of new people
was caused primarily by anxiety; (4) they were reluctant to discuss problems with their supervisors. As a result of this background information,
Myers and Gomersall devised an experiment with a control group and
an experimental group. The control group was given the conventional
two-hour orientation consisting of a briefing on hours of work, insurance,
parking, work rules, and the need to conform to the company expectations. The experimental group of new workers was given a full day's
orientation. This included the same two-hour orientation provided the
control group. But in addition they spent the remainder of their first day
in a conference room with the trainers. There was no work the first day.
Emphasis was placed upon getting acquainted with each other and the
company. They were encouraged to relax. Four key points were emphasized: (1) their likelihood of success in the job was very good; (2) they
should disregard hazing by older employees; (3) they were encouraged to
take the initiative in asking questions of their supervisors; (4) they were
told about their new supervisor and how he would behave. Then they were
introduced to the supervisor and training operators. What were the results

of this experiment? For the experimental group job-learning time was reduced, output was higher, and attendance was better. Waste and rejects were also lower for the experimental group. The researchers attributed this gain to lowered anxiety through better orientation. Supervisors were also aided in improving their role in the orientation process.[9]

Adult Basic Education

Prior to the early 1960's employers always assumed that it was the responsibility of the public school system to provide basic education in reading, grammar, speech, spelling, writing, and arithmetic. Indeed the public school system does have this responsibility. Companies never dreamed that they would find it necessary one day to provide this type of basic education themselves.

When the great nationwide effort was launched in the mid-1960's to provide jobs for the culturally deprived—those hard-core unemployed who lack education, job skills, and hope—businessmen found that a substantial portion of these people were grossly unprepared to enter an industrial environment and undertake job-skills training. Many were functionally illiterate. For a variety of reasons, including a need for more workers, government encouragement, and top management's desire to help combat urban ills, many companies have hired fair numbers of the hard-core unemployed. To prepare them for industrial work they have introduced a short course in basic education.

Typically, trainees are hired but possess reading and arithmetic skills at only the fourth or fifth grade level. The goal commonly is to raise these two or three grade levels so that the trainees can take semiskilled jobs that require them to follow verbal and written instructions, communicate effectively, read simple measuring instruments, and fill out production tickets and other forms.

Inasmuch as most industrial firms have no experience or expertize in operating basic education programs, they have turned to educational consulting firms. One such firm, MIND, was first set up by the National Association of Manufacturers as a research and development department in manpower training. Now independent, it uses programmed instruction and audiovisual materials plus regular teachers. A few of our very large corporations have staffed their own basic education training groups.[10]

[9] Earl R. Gomersall and M. Scott Myers, "Breakthrough in On-the-Job Training," *Harvard Business Review,* Vol. 44, No. 4 (July-August 1966), pp. 62-72.

[10] For descriptions of some basic education programs in industry see William A. Burcin, "General Skills Training Program," *Training and Development Journal,* Vol. 21, No. 12 (December 1967), pp. 9-11; "A Quick Way to Upgrade Your Blue Collar Workers," *Business Management,* Vol. 32, No. 5 (August 1967), pp. 34-38; Lee S. Gassler, "How Companies Are Helping the Undereducated Worker," *Personnel,* Vol. 44, No. 4 (July-August 1967), pp. 47-55.

Job Skills and Knowledge

When we speak of training for job skills and knowledge, we are not talking about any specific program. Rather we are referring to the variety of training programs, methods, and aids that have been established to answer particular training needs. Either on-the-job or classroom techniques may be employed. The subject matter will vary according to the training problem encountered. Although many who are unsophisticated regarding training tend to look upon it primarily for new employees, in actuality a vast amount of training effort must be continuously expended on further education and retraining of old employees. The content and demands of jobs change with time, the expectations of management change, and above all the technological revolution that is going on in our civilization means that old ways become obsolete and new skills must continuously be introduced. Quite frequently the best answer to a shortage of labor for particular kinds of work is to grow skilled workers from within.

Perhaps a few illustrations of common job-skill programs may be appropriate. In the cutting and packing department of a paper mill the foreman was plagued by low output, poor quality, and failure to meet schedules. He wanted to get rid of several of his workers. The assistant personnel manager asked him one day if he had ever actually taken the time to really train his people. The foreman said that no, he hadn't. Because they had been on the job when he took charge, he assumed they knew how to do their work. Working together, the foreman and the personnel man, developed an on-the-job training plan which drew heavily upon Job Instruction Training procedures of the Training-Within-Industry program of the World War II era. This training effort, when combined with improved work methods, was largely instrumental in raising the productivity level of the department to an acceptable level.

When the research laboratories of the American Telephone and Telegraph Company developed the No. 5 Crossbar type of dial switching equipment for central offices, the operating Bell Telephone Companies anticipated the need for capable switchmen to maintain this equipment. Therefore, they established schools to which they sent these craftsmen to take extended courses in the theory and application of this new equipment.

Apprentice Training

The apprenticeship system, which is a way of developing skilled craftsmen, is a descendant of the craft guild system of the Middle Ages. Indeed one can go further back into history with some justification. The Code of Hammurabi of ancient Babylon in 2,100 B.C. made explicit provision that artisans must pass on their skills to youth. The apprentice in America before the Industrial Revolution generally lived in the home of the master craftsman to whom he was indentured and received no wages but simply was given his room, board, and clothing. Boys became apprentices at an early age—typically at the age of 14. Apprenticeships commonly lasted for seven years. The training was entirely of the on-the-job variety. Much of the work was very menial and routine.

In 1937 Congress passed a national apprenticeship law, popularly known as the Fitzgerald Act. Its purpose is to promote the furtherance of apprentice training and to extend apprenticeship standards on a voluntary basis throughout the United States. A Bureau of Apprenticeship was established within the United States Department of Labor. The Act also reorganized and enlarged the Federal Committee on Apprenticeship. This committee has recommended certain essentials of an effective apprenticeship program. There should be a minimum starting age of 16, an approved schedule of work experience supplemented by at least 144 hours per year of related classroom instruction in subjects related to the trade, a progressively increasing schedule of wages, proper supervision of on-the-job training, and periodic evaluation of the apprentice's work.[11]

Apprenticeable trades are those requiring at least 4,000 hours (two years) of training experience through employment. Recognized apprenticeable trades exist in approximately 300 skilled occupations grouped by the United States Department of Labor under 90 general trade classifications. Typical occupations and their term of apprenticeship in years are airplane mechanic—4 years, carpenter—4 years, photoengraver—5-6 years, and rigger—2 years.

Quite frequently an employer can arrange through the local board of education in the community to have the related classroom courses given in a high or vocational school. The related classroom instruction for a machinist, for example, would include the following subjects: safety, industrial and labor relations, blueprint reading and sketching, mathematics, trade theory, and trade science (cutting tools, heat treating, welding theory, and so on).

The apprenticeship system in this country is very loosely organized. Each employer is free to run his program as he sees fit (union participation especially in the building trades is often necessary). But there is no requirement to conform to state or Federal standards for the various trades. Thus an apprentice graduate from Company X may have received vastly inferior training to that of a graduate from Company Y. Yet both have their papers and are considered journeymen craftsmen. Some employers still look upon apprentices as a source of cheap labor, and their time is often occupied with menial tasks. Yet properly run according to state and Federal standards, countless apprentice programs are turning out well-qualified journeymen. For these companies skilled-labor needs are being adequately met. The advantages of apprentice training to the

[11] Department of Labor, Bureau of Apprenticeship, *Apprenticeship Training* (Washington, D.C.: Government Printing Office, 1956), p. 6.

trainees are that they receive decent wages while learning and that they acquire a valuable skill which commands a high wage in the labor market. Skilled craftsmen in many industries earn as much or more than technicians, subprofessionals, and beginning professional employees, such as engineers and scientists.

Special Purpose Programs

A wide variety of courses and programs can be and are provided by organizations for their employees. Many corporations reimburse their people for part or all of the tuition for courses taken in local colleges and universities as well as in proprietary technical schools.

Safety training courses and meetings for hourly paid employees are almost universal among those organizations operating sound accident prevention programs.

Courses in public speaking and effective presentation are quite popular. A few organizations provide general education courses for their people.

EVALUATION OF THE TRAINING EFFORT

If management invests in training programs for employees, it understandably expects to see some tangible benefits derived therefrom. When a staff training director approaches top management for approval to establish a new training activity, the question reasonably can be asked as to the good the course will do and why the company should invest such and such a sum of money in it. In short the question is "How can we determine the value of a training program?"

Training directors, who are often placed in the position by top management where they must justify their existence, use a number of techniques to evaluate the effectiveness of training programs. Generally speaking, the usefulness of these methods is inversely proportional to the ease with which the evaluation can be done. One approach is to pass out a questionnaire to the trainees at the completion of the program to obtain their opinions as to its worth. Their opinions could also be elicited by means of interviews. Another approach is to measure the knowledge and/or skill that employees possess at the beginning of training and again at the completion of training. This is accomplished by administering the same examination (or an alternate form of a single examination) before and after.

The real purpose of training is to cause a change in employee behavior on the job and ultimately to improve the effectiveness of the organization. The aforementioned evaluation techniques do not measure employee behavior on the job. Thus if employees say they liked a course of instruction, this is not the real payoff. A comparison of before-and-after test scores does not really get to the point either. People may show that they have learned a lot on classroom examinations, yet they may not transfer this learning to the job.

A better way of measuring the worth of training is to use various indices of work performance and compare them after the course with values before the course. In this manner the output and quality of work of production workers, salesmen, stenographers, and other workers can be used for evaluation purposes. Though at first glance this seems to be a fruitful approach to the problem of evaluation, there is a basic flaw in the method. We have no way of knowing whether the training activity caused an improvement in the performance index or whether it was achieved as a result of a combination of other factors. An improvement might have been caused by better production planning, better supervision, new work methods, and improved materials as well as training. If we give a comprehensive training course to outside salesmen and at the end of a year we note that company sales have risen 10 per cent, how do we know whether this is due to the training or to higher consumer demand? If sales had declined during the year, does this prove that the training was worthless?

The most refined method for evaluating training (and one that avoids the errors of other techniques) is to measure performance before and after training for both a control group and an experimental group. This procedure can be accomplished by selecting two groups of employees that are approximately equivalent in education, experience, skill, job conditions, and performance. Subject one group to the training program, and give no training to the other (control) group. Some time after training is completed choose relevant performance measures, and compare results for the two groups. This method is somewhat cumbersome from the administrative standpoint; however, it is one of the most fruitful methods available. Unfortunately such a rigorous experimental approach to training evaluation is seldom carried out in practice.

Questions for Review and Discussion

1. What contributions can an effective training program make to a business organization?
2. What are the duties and responsibilities of the following for training?
    a. The training department
    b. Line supervision
3. How can one determine what kind of training programs to offer?
4. Discuss the following concepts as they affect learning:
    a. Motivation
    b. Knowledge of results
    c. Learn by doing

    d. Whole or part learning

    e. Teaching the theory underlying the work

5. What considerations should be evaluated when deciding whether to train employees on the job or in a classroom?

6. A company has decided to set up formal courses for selected groups of its employees in the subjects listed below. Of the various instructional methods available, which would be most suitable for each course?

    a. Statistics and probability theory

    b. Maintenance of electronic equipment

    c. An attitude building course on the American free enterprise system

    d. Motion and time study

    e. Operation of a nuclear reactor

    f. Industrial safety

7. Prepare a proposed orientation program for the following at a university:

    a. College freshman

    b. A newly hired departmental secretary

    c. A newly hired professor

8. What constitutes a thorough apprenticeship-training program? What are the strengths and limitations of the apprentice-training system?

9. Explain how you, as a training director, would evaluate the contribution and worth of the following training programs:

    a. Orientation for new employees

    b. Technical classroom course for engineers

    c. On-the-job training for machine operators

CASE PROBLEM

The Ajax Manufacturing Company is in a very competitive metal products business. It employs 4,000 people. Because the designs and prices for its products are quite similar to those of its competitors, it maintains its sales by emphasizing quality and service. About a year ago it lost two of its major customers, who had been dissatisfied with excessive manufacturing defects. The Ajax Company, upon studying the problem, decided that its basic engineering was sound but that carelessness and lack of quality consciousness on the part of production workers, inspectors, and manufacturing supervision were a prime cause of the trouble. Accordingly it established a quality-control training course to solve the problem.

    The course was given after working hours, from 7:00 to 9:00 P.M. each Thursday for ten weeks. Employees were not paid to attend. Technically attendance was voluntary; however, management intimated that employees who attended faithfully would have the fact recorded in their personnel records. This fact would be considered in future pay raises and promotions. The course was taught by a staff engineer from the Quality Control Department. Consisting mainly of lectures, the course was varied at times to include movies on quality control and some discussions. The course covered such topics as the need for high quality, "quality can't be inspected into a product, it must be built in," conditions affecting quality, costs of poor quality, inspection standards, inspection procedures and methods, statistical quality control, sampling inspection, and control chart procedures. The course was open to all interested employees in the plant, including supervision. Attendance at the early sessions averaged around fifty. Toward the end of the course it had declined to about twenty-five.

The training director made the following comment at the conclusion of the course. "Frank Smith (the instructor) did a good job of lecturing. He was interesting, informative, and spiced his talks with humor at appropriate times. It was not his fault that attendance fell off."

Questions

1. Do you think this training program was organized and administered properly?
2. Are there other training methods that could properly have been used?
3. Evaluate this approach to improving product quality.

Suggestions for Further Reading

Bass, Bernard M. and James A. Vaughan, *Training in Industry: The Management of Learning,* Belmont, California: Wadsworth Publishing Company, 1966.

Blake, Robert R. and Jane S. Mouton, "Training Traps that Tempt Training Directors," *Training and Development Journal,* Vol. 21, No. 12, December 1967, pp. 2-8.

Bolino, August C., "Manpower Development: Charges and Challenges," *Michigan Business Review,* Vol. 17, No. 4 (July 1965), pp. 31-37.

Corsini, R., M. Shaw, and R. Blake, *Role Playing in Business and Industry,* New York: The Free Press, 1962.

DePhillips, Frank A., William M. Berliner, and James J. Cribbin, *Management of Training Programs,* Homewood, Ill.: Richard D. Irwin, Inc., 1960.

Glaser, Robert (ed.), *Training Research and Education,* Pittsburgh: University of Pittsburgh Press, 1962.

King, David, *Training Within the Organization,* Chicago: Educational Methods, 1964.

Lynton, Rolf P. and Udai Pareek, *Training for Development,* Homewood, Ill.: Irwin-Dorsey, 1967.

McGehee, William and Paul W. Thayer, *Training in Business and Industry,* New York: John Wiley & Sons, 1961.

Odiorne, George S., "A Systems Approach to Training," *Training Directors Journal,* Vol. 19, No. 10, October 1965, pp. 11-19.

Ofiesh, Gabriel D., *Programmed Instruction: A Guide to Management,* New York: American Management Association, 1965.

Schmidt, Charles T., Jr., "Education: Can Business Do a Better Job?" *Management of Personnel Quarterly,* Vol. 7, No. 1, Spring 1968, pp. 36-39.

Stokes, Paul M., *Total Job Training,* New York: American Management Association, 1966.

This, Leslie E. and Gordon L. Lippitt, "Learning Theories and Training," *Training and Development Journal,* Vol. 20, No. 5, May 1966, pp. 10-17.

Management Development

14

There are few activities that captured the interest of management during the 1950's as much as that of management development and training. Companies realized that they had to establish systematic programs for manager development. The business stagnation of the 1930's, the shortage of talent during World War II, and the very rapid expansion of business organizations in the postwar years revealed an urgent need for capable managers to pilot business and industrial organizations.

There has been a recognition that qualified executives of the caliber and quantity needed throughout our society do not just emerge from the labor force without consciously planned action on the part of work organizations, large and small. When undertaking to establish a management development program, top management must fully understand just what it is trying to accomplish. What is management? What do managers do? What knowledge and skills must they possess? How can these best be acquired? What part does the individual play in the program? What are the merits of on-the-job development as contrasted with classroom training? We shall examine these and related topics in this chapter.

NATURE OF MANAGEMENT DEVELOPMENT

What Is Management Development?

Management development is a systematic process of training and growth by which individuals gain and apply knowledge, skills, insights, and attitudes to manage work organizations effectively. As explained in the previous chapter on training, training and the learning process really involve the implication that there will be changed behavior on the part of the individual. Managers develop not only by participating in formal courses of instruction but also through actual job experiences in a work environment. The role of the company is to establish the program and the developmental opportunities for its managers and potential managers. But it must be recognized that simply exposing employees to lectures, case studies, readings, job rotation assignments, and the like, does not guarantee that they will learn. An equal, and perhaps more important, counterpart to the efforts of the organization are those of the individual. There has been increasing recognition that the company can set the proper climate, but that the major effort must be made by the individuals themselves. Thus self-development is an important concept in the whole program for management development. The participants must have the motivation and the capacity to learn and develop. They must make the requisite efforts to grow.

What Is a Manager?

Before one can obtain an adequate understanding of the principles and procedures of management training and development, he must know what a manager is and what he does.

Management is a process of utilizing material and human resources to accomplish designated objectives. It involves the organization, direction, coordination, and evaluation of people to achieve these goals.

The word *manager* has been used in a variety of ways by industrialists and theorists. To some the term *manager* means top executive. To others a manager is any person who supervises other employees. In fact, one large manufacturing company uses the term without any status connotations. In this firm a manager may supervise a number of managers, and he, in turn, may report to a manager. Thus the organization structure contains a number of echelons, each level possessing the designation of manager. Another large company in the communications business even considers that all its engineers are members of management even though they may supervise no one.

The most commonly accepted view is to consider as members of management all those who coordinate and direct the activities of others plus all those administrative and staff people who deal with others outside their own group and who have a decided impact upon the organization. Thus all supervisors from a foreman up through a corporation president are decidedly managers. Administrative personnel such as assistants-to, planners, coordinators, executive assistants, and the like are also members of management even though they do not supervise other employees. They are members of the management team because their work is related to or affects management policies, practices, and actions. Usually, engineers and scientists are considered to be professionals but not managers.

Another way of understanding what managing is and what managers do is to examine the functions of management. The process of management consists of planning, organizing, staffing, leading and controlling. Planning encompasses looking ahead to the future, setting goals, and figuring out policies, procedures, and methods for accomplishing these goals. The cognitive and decision-making processes are heavily involved in planning. Organizing involves the breaking down of the total work to be done into jobs, groups, and departments and the establishment of workable relationships between these units. It includes such elements as grouping activities both by level and by type, setting up jobs, determining authority and responsibility relationships, setting up patterns of communication, delegating, and use of staff. Staffing refers to the process of recruiting and selecting people to run the enterprise. Leading is the motivation and direction of people to achieve a desired goal. It integrates the personal goals of the employees with the objectives of the enterprise. Finally the control function of management includes measurement of work performed, comparison of actual performance with a predetermined standard, and then the taking of corrective action, when necessary, to insure that performance meets standard.

Knowledge and Skills of the Manager

Although a foreman is just as much a manager as a top executive officer, the nature of his work and the skills he must utilize to do this work are different from those of a major executive. A foreman must devote a majority of his time to leadership activities. He must be an expert at applied human relations. He must motivate, communicate, direct, correct, discipline, coordinate, teach, and reward his subordinates. He must also be able to teach his men the technical aspects of the products and processes with which they must work. He must effectively solve routine technical problems of the work processes. A foreman primarily carries out directions from above. The scope of his discretionary power is quite limited.

Top executives need very little technical skills pertaining to the products and processes of the business they manage. To be sure, they must have an appreciation or general knowledge of the capabilities and limitations of these technical processes, but these are the men who hire others to design, install, operate, and maintain the facilities. Major executives devote much of their time to forecasting, policy formulation, and planning. They deal, to a considerable extent, with forces and people outside their own organizations. They are concerned with the economic, social, and political environment. They must be adept at integrating the various functional branches of an organization, such as production, sales, finance, and industrial relations. Top managers spend a high percentage of their time interacting with other people in group conferences and two-man face-to-face dealings. Executives not only exert their authority and power to get things done through their subordinates, but also they frequently seek to persuade and influence others outside their own hierarchical sphere.

In analyzing the skills needed by an administrator (manager according to our terminology), Katz speaks of three types: technical, human, and conceptual skills. Technical skill refers to proficiency in handling methods, processes, and techniques of a particular kind of business or activity. Human skill refers to the ability to work effectively with others and build cooperative group relations to achieve goals. Conceptual skill, as Katz describes it, is the ability to see the organization as a whole, to recognize interrelationships among functions of a business and external forces, and to be able to guide effectively the organization in consideration of the multitudinous forces affecting it. Coordination depends upon conceptual skill. Conceptual skills are concerned with the realm of ideas and creativeness. Technical skill is an essential ingredient of lower-level management, human skill is important at all levels of management, and conceptual skill is especially critical in top executive positions.[1]

Evolution of Management Development

It was not so many years ago that a man was selected to be a supervisor on the basis of his performance as a worker. There was a basic assumption that a man who was a high producer and who was at the same time loyal and dependable would be a capable manager of people. There was a further assumption that a man could acquire leadership skills and management abilities by serving long years as a craftsman or office worker. Both of these assumptions are false. Years ago industrial leaders did not understand that it was necessary to consciously plan the training and development of managers and potential managers. This lack of understanding of the problem was due, in large part, to the fact that most corporation presidents and top executives of a generation or two ago possessed only modest formal education and had achieved their positions by being members of a small group who had founded their own enterprises. They were owner-managers. They had achieved their own positions through inventive genius, ability as a promoter, financial power, or a combination of all three.

Causes for Interest in Management Development. The present high interest and activity in systematic management development programs commenced in the 1945-1950 era. It reached full bloom in the 1950's. There are a number of factors which explain this interest.

[1] Robert L. Katz, "Skills of an Effective Administrator," *Harvard Business Review,* Vol. 33, No. 1 (January-February, 1955), pp. 33-41.

The rapid rate of technological and social change in our society has made it imperative to have managers who are trained to cope with these developments. Among the manifestations of this change are automation, the fruits of accelerated research, electronic computers, intense market competition from foreign nations, new markets in emerging underdeveloped nations, enlarged voice and elevated role of labor, permanent cold war and defense industry-government relations, greater interest by the public and government in actions of business, and increased interdependency among elements of our society.

There has been a pronounced shift from owner-managed to professionally managed enterprises. Management has been recognized as a distinct kind of occupation consisting of teachable skills and a unified body of knowledge. Management can be described as an emerging profession. Professions consist of two kinds: the learned (law, medicine, teaching, and so on) and the artistic (acting, music, and so on). We are here concerned with the learned professions. A profession has the following characteristics.

1. It requires advanced, specialized formal education and training.
2. It requires the consistent exercise of discretion and independent judgment.
3. It is based on a deep and organized body of knowledge. Efforts are continually made to expand the knowledge through research.
4. The members of the profession have a keenly developed sense of ethics and public responsibility.
5. The members of the profession have a sense of common identity and purpose. There is a professional organization which seeks to advance the field and uphold professional standards.
6. It demands certain recognized standards of competence in terms of education, training, experience, and human performance.

It must be recognized that management is still an emerging profession. It is not full-fledged, because of the lack of recognized standards of competence, and because the members have not created or adhered to any generally accepted code of ethics. There exists great variation in the routes people take to become managers and in performance after they acquire their positions. But the point being made is that management has been acquiring more and more of the characteristics of a profession even though it has still not arrived there.

Within the past few decades there has been an ever-increasing amount of research-generated knowledge of the principles and techniques of administration. This applies both to general management and to its various functional fields, such as personnel and industrial relations, production, finance, marketing, and accounting. The universities through their schools of business, public administration, industrial management, and social science have carried on much of this research effort under both government and industry sponsorship. This newly acquired information has been favorably received by the industrial community, which has often sought to apply certain portions soon after it has been made available.

Another cause for interest in management development programs has been an increased recognition by business and industrial leaders of the social and public responsibilities of management. This has been coupled with very close ties between business and government via government defense contracts. This has demanded new awareness, sensitivity, and skills on the part of managers.

The initial surge of management development programs in the late 1940's was occasioned by a serious shortage of qualified executives because of the stagnation in our economy during the 1930's (when none were trained) and the rapid post-World War II expansion of industry.

The problems of management have become intensified because of the increasing size and complexity of most organizations in our society—governmental, industrial, commercial, and nonprofit public service ones.

Recent Trends. As the management development movement has evolved over the past two decades, certain shifts in emphasis have become evident.

The initial efforts of the late 1940's and early 1950's were directed toward the training and development of a chosen few hand-picked to fill key posts. This created an elite corps of "crown princes" and "fair-haired" boys. In more recent years industry has concentrated upon the development of *all* who are in management positions to improve performance on their present jobs as well as to provide a solid foundation for promotion. There has been recognition that the success of a business depends upon a total team effort.

The emphasis in the early years was upon sending men (and women in some cases) to formal classroom training courses both on the premises and away at universities and management institutes. However, there developed a recognition of the fact that this procedure often caused no change or improvement in behavior back on the job. This has led to a current emphasis upon both formal classroom training and on-the-job development. Although knowledge is obtained in the classroom, it is right on the job in the work environment that real management skills are developed and sharpened.

Because the capacities, abilities, experiences, and temperament of no two people are alike, organizations are concentrating upon tailor-making development programs according to individual needs. This places a great responsibility upon each man's superior to take an enlightened interest in the individual and to do a competent job of appraisal and guidance.

And finally there has been recognition that management development is not a one-shot affair. Rather it must continue throughout an executive's entire career. Very little in our modern world is stagnant; therefore, managers must continually educate themselves to successfully meet new challenges as they occur.

Start at the Top

Management training and development can succeed only when it pervades the entire organization and when it begins with top management. This is a fundamental necessity for any program of this type to be successful. However, in actual practice this simple idea has not been grasped by top business and industrial leaders. Many thousands of dollars are spent annually on foremen's training conferences throughout this country, yet much of this effort is fruitless. A management development program can succeed only in a climate of sound management from the top to the bottom of the organization.

The author has been personally involved in teaching numerous supervisory courses where top management has said in effect, "We think that the company could be improved if we could make better leaders of our supervisors and improve their management knowledge and skills." However, the realities of the situation are such that supervisors may learn the latest and soundest principles and techniques of management in the classroom but not be allowed to apply the knowledge on the job because, so often, higher management is unaware of and does not practice this pattern of management itself. The realities of the authority structure in industry are such that a supervisor must always conform to the demands of his superiors. If this pattern of leadership is in conflict with the principles that the supervisor learned in his management course, he may experience serious frustration and impared performance.

In a significant and pioneering research project aimed at evaluating the effectiveness of foreman-leadership training at the International Harvester Company, Fleishman, Harris, and Burtt found that foremen performed back on the job in a manner that conformed to the attitudes and behavior of their bosses. It their superiors rated high on what the researchers labeled a "consideration score," then the foremen also rated high on a "consideration score," and vice versa. Their ratings were irrespective of knowledge and attitudes developed during participation in the leadership course. The researchers concluded that foremen are more responsive to their day-to-day climate on the job than to any special course of training they may have taken.[2]

From this study and the evidence of other researchers, consultants, and management training specialists, it is clear that management training and development, to be effective, must begin with top executive officers

---

[2] Edwin A. Fleishman, Edwin F. Harris, and Harold E. Burtt, *Leadership and Supervision in Industry: An Evaluation of a Supervisory Training Program* (Columbus, Ohio: Bureau of Educational Research, The Ohio State University, 1955).

of a firm. As they acquire new insights and skills and as they begin to practice these in their work, they are in a sound position to launch formal development activities for members of middle and lower management.[3]

PLANNING AND ADMINISTERING THE PROGRAM

The inauguration of a management development program must be done by the chief executive officer of an organization, because it involves fundamental policy decisions, important actions by executives all down the line, and the expenditure, in some cases, of considerable sums of money. Ordinarily the planning and guiding of an executive development program is carried out by a committee composed of major executives, whereas the day-to-day administration is performed by the personnel department.

Let us now examine the essential ingredients of a management development program. The key elements are:

1. Analysis of organization needs
2. Appraisal of present management talent
3. Management manpower inventory
4. Planning of individual development programs
5. Establishment of training and development programs
6. Program evaluation

Analysis of Organization Needs

After the key decision to launch a management development program has been made, the first thing to do is organization planning. The organization structure must be studied to ascertain whether activities and functions are grouped properly. Forecasts must be made of the growth of the business. Projected new products and services must be identified. What will the organization consist of five or ten years hence in terms of functions, departments, and executive positions? Will any portions of the organization have to be reduced in size?

The next step is to prepare descriptions and specifications for all management jobs. The purpose is to obtain a record of the kinds of management work performed and the kinds of executives and administrators needed in the organization. It is necessary at this stage to highlight the kind of education, experience, training, special knowledge, skills, and personal traits required for each job. If the company already has in operation a comprehensive job-analysis program (as it should have), then it will be necessary at this point only to collect the job descriptions and job

---

[3] For additional information on the need for beginning management training activities with top management see Warren C. McGovney, "Start at the Top," *Advanced Management-Office Executive,* Vol. 1, No. 2 (February 1962).

specifications for all management activities, review them, and make desired summarizations.

Top management must make a policy decision as to whether it wishes to fill contemplated vacancies in executive ranks from within the organization or whether it wants to hire from the outside. This decision will depend to some extent upon the caliber and number of present personnel in comparison with projected needs. Most commonly companies hire on the outside to fill their lowest-level positions and then promote from within. In effect they grow their own executives except where they have a critical shortage of specialized high-level talent.

Appraisal of Present Management Talent

The purpose of this part of the program is to determine qualitatively what the organization now has in terms of management personnel. Each executive must analyze and evaluate each of the people reporting to him. He will analyze the performance of each management employee and compare it with expected performance. He will also analyze personal traits and make a value judgement of a man's potential for moving ahead. The principles and techniques of manpower appraisal are explained in Chapter 11, "Performance Appraisal."

Management Manpower Inventory

At this stage it is necessary to prepare an inventory of present management personnel. For each member of the management team, a card is prepared, listing such data as name, age, length of service, education, work experience previous to company employment, company experience, training courses completed, health record, psychological test results, and performance appraisal data. This information is often summarized and tabulated on business machine punch cards. If this data has been judiciously classified into categories, it then becomes possible to select via the machine all those individuals possessing a desired kind of background. For example, the machine may be set up to pick out the cards of all those who are under 40 years of age, who are college graduates, who have had at least 5 years' experience in the supervision of research and development projects, and who are rated above average by their bosses.

Some organizations go one step further than the preparation of a management inventory. They set up *replacement tables or charts* that show each individual, his background and rating, and projected promotions and transfers. Quite often this is prepared in organization-chart form with certain coding used to portray a man's rating and planned movement. For example, Mr. A, the plant manager may be 63 years of age and two years from retirement. Mr. B, the manager of manufacturing, may be 47, a college graduate, have 18 years of diversified plant experience, be rated outstanding in ability and potential, and be picked to fill the plant manager's position when Mr. A. retires. The replacement chart may also show that there are several capable executives who will be given serious consideration for the plant manager's post at the time Mr. A. actually retires.

Although the replacement chart is certainly a systematic way of mapping out plans for the utilization of management manpower, it must be recognized that conditions may change rapidly, so that the earmarking of individuals for particular jobs several years hence is highly speculative.

Planning of Individual Development Programs

This activity must be performed by each executive working cooperatively with each of his subordinates. The executive should be guided heavily by the results of the performance appraisal, which will indicate strengths and weaknesses for each person. Much has been said in recent years about the allegation that American industry has been molding a group of conformists and "organization men." In reality it is unwise to try to force every management person into the same mold. Each of us has a unique set of physical, intellectual, and emotional characteristics. Therefore, a development plan should be tailor-made for each individual. In setting up this development plan, each executive should give consideration to the expressed interests and goals of his subordinates as well as the training and developmental opportunities that exist within the organization.

If an engineering supervisor shows considerable potential and yet has spent all of his company career within the engineering department, then it makes sense to rotate him into such other activities as production, sales and finance to broaden him. Although it makes sense, up to a point, to correct an individual's weak points by exposing him to training opportunities that will help overcome these deficiencies, it must be remembered that once a person has reached adulthood, it is extremely impractical to try to change his basic personality and temperament. This will frustrate both the trainee and the trainer. The soundest approach is to build upon a man's strengths. Of course, this does not mean that we should not introduce new knowledge and experiences that a man lacks, nor does it mean we should not expose a "bull of the woods" foreman to a human-relations training course. But it does mean that a boss should not, by his counseling and coaching, attempt to remake his subordinates into his own image or try to force upon them a certain temperament and personality.

Establishment of Training and Development Programs

This step of the broad management development effort involves the setting up of well-conceived training and development opportunities on a companywide basis. The personnel department or its training section will establish certain training programs—such as leadership courses, management games, sensitivity training, courses with local universities, and so on—as needs, time, and costs dictate. Top management may wish to send certain individuals to executive development courses at universities. It may establish a companywide system of job rotation or of multiple management.

The personnel department executives must take an active part in keeping abreast of new developments in the field of management education and development. They must carefully study training needs and recommend to top management that certain specific programs be set up as conditions dictate. These staff officers must continually work with line managers to insure that they are developing their subordinates and that they are not denying qualified candidates the opportunity to participate in formal courses. The staff training executives should keep adequate records to audit and control the management development activities throughout the entire organization.

Program Evaluation

Many organizations have undertaken vast programs of management development. Since these involve large expenditures of time and money, top management justifiably would like to know whether it is receiving its money's worth. Has the training and development improved individual and organizational performance?

It is exceedingly difficult to obtain definitive proof that such activities have accomplished their given objectives. A group of supervisors may take a course in human relations and leadership. After the program is completed, some of these may exhibit subtle changes in attitude and behavior; however, it is difficult to measure these. An executive may attend an in-residence advanced management course at some university; yet it may be difficult to observe a significant change in his work after he returns to the job.

Although it is difficult, if not impossible, to obtain clear-cut, objective proof that development activities have—or have not—been successful, there are a number of sound procedures that can be used to obtain substantial and convincing evidence.

The most rigorous scientific approach is to set up a field experiment in which a control group and an experimental group are used. Both of these groups of managers should be as identical in all factors pertinent to the experience as possible. This, of course, is a tall order. Then the experimental group is given the training program, and the control group is not. Some time after the completion of the program, ratings and measures are taken of both groups to detect differences between them. The measures may consist of attitude surveys and gauges of performance, such as production, quality, and cost control. Although this method of evaluating a training and development activity is sound, it is also very expensive and difficult to administer.

There are other methods of evaluating management development activities. If a training course, say in methods and work simplification, were designed specifically to correct one operating problem, then a before-and-after type of analysis is practical. If, after completing such a course, supervisors initiate many more methods improvements than before, we can reasonably conclude that the course has been effective.

However, those developmental methods that are carried out on a day-to-day basis, on the job, are exceedingly difficult to evaluate objectively. How can one measure the effectiveness of appraisals, coaching, and counseling? Quite often one has to settle for opinions and judgments in a case like this. The central personnel staff can survey both executives and their subordinates to obtain their impressions of the benefits gained from these activities. To be sure, changes in the performance of both individuals and groups may occur while coaching and counseling is taking place, but one cannot be sure whether these changes are caused by this development effort or to other factors.

DEVELOPMENT THROUGH WORK EXPERIENCE

There are two principal methods by which people can acquire the knowledge, skills, and attitudes to become competent managers. One is through formal training and education courses; the other is through on-the-job experiences. Fifty years ago in the United States, almost all management development occurred on the job. (Most of the learning was unorganized and haphazard.) Around 1950, when the management development movement in industry was working up a "full head of steam," the major emphasis was upon taking men away from their jobs for a period of time so they could attend executive development and supervisory training classes.

Now it is recognized that both classroom and on-the-job training are important. Formal course work is invaluable for learning new knowledge, new techniques, and broader concepts. Yet real learning can occur only when the learner has an opportunity to practice and apply his ideas. This must be done on the job. It must be further recognized that a manager, by the very nature of his position, serves as a teacher for his subordinates. The authority structure of the organization and the responsibilities of a manager cause him continually to guide and mold the behavior of his subordinates so that they conform to his expectations.

Of the two influences, formal training courses and on-the-job development by the boss, the latter is the most powerful. Yet it is totally unsound to place sole reliance upon on-the-job development because many executives and managers are themselves unqualified to carry out this important task. They may lack the skill, the interest, or the patience. They may possess wholly faulty notions of administration, and for them to impose such ideas upon all of their subordinates would be tantamount to deliberately weakening the organization. Yet when on-the-job development is properly balanced with classroom training, and when both are carried out in an atmosphere of sound management emanating from the very top of the company, then we have a workable formula for management development.

We shall now examine some of the important techniques of management development.

Understudies

An understudy is a person who is in training to assume, at a future time, the full duties and responsibilities of the position currently held by his superior. It is a means of insuring that a fully trained man is available to take over the job of a manager when he leaves his post because of promotion, retirement, or transfer.

There are several ways of arranging for understudies. A department manager may pick one individual within his unit to become his understudy. He will then teach him his own job and let him grapple with the problems that confront the manager daily. Or the department manager may choose several of his subordinates who will act as understudies. They may take turns at filling their boss's job when he is absent because of vacation, a business trip, or illness. Or the manager may designate one of his subordinates to be his administrative assistant. This assistant will handle a great variety of administrative matters that his superior may choose to delegate to him. Quite often the choice of an understudy is not made by a department head alone; he must consult with his superior.

An understudy can gain the requisite experience to take over his boss's job one day in a number of ways. When the manager is handling his daily operating problems, he may discuss these with his helper to get his ideas and give him experience at decision making. He may assign the understudy to investigate and make written recommendations upon long-term problems. In other words the man may be assigned a project that is closely related to the work of his unit. There may arise occasions where the understudy can be assigned direct supervision of a two- or three-man task force. This will give him an opportunity to try out his leadership skills. The understudy may also be sent to important executive meetings in place of or in attendance with his superior. He may be called upon to make presentations and proposals before higher executives.

The understudy method is a practical and fairly quick way of training designated persons for greater management responsibilities. It emphasizes learning by doing. Motivation of the learner tends to be high. Further, it relieves the boss of some of his work load. It guarantees, to the organization, that it will not be placed at a serious disadvantage if an executive or supervisor should suddenly terminate his employment.

On the other hand, this technique has serious disadvantages. It insures that things will be done pretty much as they always have been. It does not infuse any new ideas into the unit. The understudy will have been picked in the first place because his way of thinking and acting is similar to that of his boss. Therefore, when he takes command, the understudy will tend to perpetuate existing practices—the bad as well as the good. The other major disadvantage of the understudy approach is that it destroys the incentive to get ahead for all the other employees in the unit who have not been made the understudy. The designation of one man as an understudy often seems to the others in the group to be an act of favoritism. This can cause jealousy and friction within the department.

Job Rotation

The transferring of executives from job to job and from plant to plant on a coordinated, planned basis is a popular means of development among industrial concerns. Under the typical arrangement a top management committee oversees the operation of the program and makes the final decisions on the reassignment of executives. When a supervisor or other management man takes a new post on such a program, it is no mere orientation assignment. He is placed in an important line or staff position where he must assume full charge and make regular management decisions. Quite often this executive on the rotational program will be backstopped at each location by experienced, permanent personnel who will exercise a steadying influence and keep things running if the individual experiences difficulty. Job assignments under a rotational scheme typically last from six months to two years. Some times the new job assignment will represent a promotion for the individual. The executives to whom these rotating men report evaluate their performance and funnel appraisal reports back to the central coordinating committee.

In the modern corporation a high proportion of the entry jobs for junior executives and engineers demand a considerable degree of technical knowledge and specialization. As a man increases in stature with time, he can never acquire the broad perspective and diversified skills needed for promotion unless he is deliberately taken out of his specialty and placed in different types of situations. In order to obtain the generalists who are ultimately needed at upper management levels, the enterprise must take action to provide a variety of job experiences for those judged to have the potential for major executive ranks. Job rotation answers this need. It also serves to break down departmental provincialism—the feeling that only my department is important and others' problems are not worthy of my concern. When a number of managers have served in each other's units, they can all understand the reasons why a certain function must be done in a particular way. Interdepartmental cooperation is enhanced. A frequent complaint in production departments of manufacturing companies is that the engineering departments design products that cannot be built economically. The sales department is also perceived as one that makes impossible delivery promises to customers. Engineering personnel frequently seek to bypass the purchasing department buyers. Purchasing resents this. If the key personnel in these departments are given an opportunity to grapple with each other's problems when rotated into the various units, then their understanding of the other fellow's situation is increased.

Job rotation injects new ideas into the different departments and branches of an organization. New concepts become infused and diffused throughout the enterprise. Under this system of management development, a man is not destined to end up in just one spot. He is equipped to step into any one of several executive posts in any of various functional divisions. Thus the organization gains management strength in depth.

However, job rotation is hard on those executives who are in the program, because they must periodically pull up stakes and move to a new location. Many of our large multiplant industrial giants have acquired the reputation of requiring their rising young executives to be continually on the move. This is upsetting to home and family life. It periodically tears the children out of school and forces them to make new friends in a strange town. The net result is such that the executive must, in effect, "marry" the company. He must look to the company for nearly every form of social and ego satisfaction.

Job rotation may undermine the morale and efficiency of the departments managed by these executives, especially if a whole parade of them go through in a relatively brief time span. The subordinate personnel must continually readjust their behavior to conform to new leaders. Sometimes the rotating executives are viewed as an elite corps, somewhat apart from the other personnel. Their attitudes and expectations set them off from the other supervisors and administrators. If sharp cleavages arise between these groups, then cooperation is impeded and frictions occur.

Coaching

It is quite common for consultants and researchers to find, upon interviewing employees and managers alike, that they are rarely told by their superiors how they are doing. Their bosses have not taken the time to sit down with them to discuss their performance on specific assignments or on their last few months' work. Yet, if properly done, coaching is something every supervisor can do; it costs little money; and it contributes toward improved performance by the individual and ultimately by the whole work group.

Coaching should be distinguished from counseling. Coaching is a procedure by which a superior teaches job knowledge and skills to a subordinate. He indicates what he wants done, suggests how it may be done, gives suggestions, follows up, and corrects errors. The objective is not only to teach and guide the subordinate in the performance of immediate assignments but also to provide him with diversified work so that he can grow and advance. Counseling, on the other hand, involves a discussion between the boss and his subordinate of areas concerned with the man's hopes, fears, emotions, and aspirations. It reaches into very personal and delicate matters. To be done correctly, counseling demands considerable background and ability on the part of the counselor. If carried out poorly, it may do considerable damage. Supervisors and executives, at times, must play the role both of coach and counselor. However, the coaching role is by far the most frequent.

A manager should recognize an obligation to take a decided interest in the training and advancement of those who work for him. His coaching responsibility can be implemented by doing a number of things. He can delegate more. He can assign not only the routine chores, but he can invite his people to tackle some of the more complex problems, which he may have felt could be properly handled only by himself. An executive can give his subordinates an opportunity to participate in making important decisions affecting the department. This can be done either on an individual man-to-man basis or else by a group conference of all management members in the department.

In dealing with his men, the executive-coach lets them know what he expects. He insures that there is common understanding between himself and each individual as to what authority the man has and what constitutes completed and acceptable work. The coach tells his men where they have done well and where they can improve. In discussing past failures, the manager is careful to suggest ways of overcoming the difficulty. A good coach is continually alert to find new assignments for his men so that they can gain a breadth and depth of work experience.

The effective coach avoids criticizing his subordinate's personality. He concentrates upon the work and the job. What constitutes a good or bad personality is a matter of opinion. Besides, it is extremely difficult to change another's personality. To do so would appear high-handed to many persons.

As a management development technique, coaching requires the least centralized staff coordination. Every executive can coach his men regardless of whether top management has set up any formal management development program. It can yield immediate benefits to the organization, the coach, and the man. It constitutes learning by doing. The learner can experience a feeling of progress. He can see the fruits of his efforts.

Although a great deal of emphasis has been placed upon coaching in management circles in recent years, as a management development technique, it cannot stand alone. It is primarily a device for insuring that individuals grow within the boundaries set by their jobs and their organizational units. The man cannot develop much beyond the limits of his own boss's abilities. The coaching technique is authoritarian. The implication is ever present that the boss knows best. He tends to indoctrinate his subordinates with his own work habits, beliefs, and frame of reference even though some of these may be quite faulty. Coaching works best when used in conjunction with periodic formal classroom instruction and other types of training.

Multiple Management

Multiple management is the designation given to the system whereby permanent advisory committees of managers study problems of the company and make recommendations to higher management. The concept of multiple management, or the junior board of executives system, as it is sometimes called, was pioneered by Charles P. McCormick in 1932 when he established his Junior Board of Executives at McCormick & Company in Baltimore. McCormick went on to set up a Factory Board, a Sales Board, and the Junior Sales Associates. Although originally appointed by the president of the company, the Junior Board itself now rates its own members and sets up a membership committee to appoint new members. For each succeeding term of office, some of the old members must be dropped and new people added to the Board. At McCormick & Company the various boards are granted wide latitude to investigate problems in different facets of the business. When a board has arrived at a solution to a problem, the members must agree unanimously before the proposal can be submitted to the Senior Board of Directors (which is the regular stockholder-elected board). This insures that problems are thoroughly worked out. It prevents the lower boards from dumping their problems upon the Senior Board. The latter board is under no compulsion to adopt proposals of the subordinate boards. These junior boards serve in an advisory capacity only. However, in the twenty-five years after the inauguration of the junior board program at McCormick, the Junior and Factory Boards combined had submitted more than 5,000 unanimous recommendations to top management. Only fifty of these were rejected.[4]

The junior-board-of-executives system has been used successfully by a number of companies in addition to McCormick & Company. Craf made a study of twenty-one companies that used this system of manager training. They ranged in size from 85 to 25,000 employees and were distributed in a variety of industries, such as petroleum, dairy products, food products, men's jewelry and accessories, and paper manufacturing. Craf emphasized that a junior board is different from the ordinary committee found in all businesses. Junior boards are formally organized under a set of bylaws. The members rate each other to decide which ones deserve to retain membership after their term of office expires and which should be dropped.

[4] Frederick J. Bell, "Highlights of Multiple Management" in Harwood F. Merrill and Elizabeth Marting (eds.), *Developing Executive Skills* (New York: American Management Association, 1958), p. 143-144.

Often board members are paid extra compensation for their service. Most importantly the boards do far more than merely discuss topics. Committees within the board are assigned definite projects by the chairman. They must conduct thorough investigations and submit written reports to the entire board. The junior boards ordinarily have broad authority to study nearly any phase of a company's business.[5]

As a management development technique, multiple-management—or the junior-board-of-executives system—has several advantages: (1) it gives board members an opportunity to gain knowledge and experience in aspects of the business other than their own specialty; (2) it helps identify those who have good executive talent. Multiple judgments are obtained on each individual through the board rating system; (3) the members gain practical experience in group decision making and in teamwork. Through the group interaction process they gain respect for the rights and views of their associates; (4) it is a relatively inexpensive method of development, and it permits a considerable number of managers to participate within a reasonable period of time.

In addition to the foregoing benefits for management development, junior boards certainly can and do make significant contributions to efficiency, productivity, and the human relations climate. In effect, they are a way of achieving better administration and a better enterprise.

FORMAL TRAINING COURSES

Formal training courses for managers can be conducted in a number of ways and under a variety of conditions. Several of the training techniques discussed in Chapter 13, "Training," find important application in supervisory and executive training. The conference method is probably used more than any other single technique. Role playing and written case studies are ideally suited for use within the conference type of classes. Extensive reading assignments in company literature, college textbooks, and journal articles are frequently given to middle and top management trainees. At the foreman level reading assignments tend to be light. Professional training specialists tend to feel that foremen, because the majority lack a college education and because they are not required to read extensively on the job, would be frustrated by long required-reading assignments.

The lecture method is employed in courses for all levels of management. However, it is rare to find any training course that consists entirely of lectures. Lectures are usually interspersed with discussions, films, case studies, role playing, and demonstrations.

Who does the teaching in management training courses? The answer is that practice varies considerably. Subjects dealing with the company,

[5] John R. Craf, *Junior Boards of Executives: A Management Training Procedure* (New York: Harper & Row, 1958).

its policies, and organization are often taught by either a major line executive or a member of the training staff. Quite often a business organization will engage professors from schools of business administration and engineering to teach courses in statistics, operations research, production planning, and methods engineering. Or these management techniques may be taught by specialists within the company who are professionally qualified in these topics. Those courses concerned with the particular processes and technology of the industry, for example, metalworking in the metal fabrication industry and food processing in the canning industry, are most generally taught by qualified engineers and technicians within the organization. College professors are often hired by companies to teach courses in human relations, organization theory, industrial relations, report writing, public speaking and reading improvement.

Subject Matter and Course Content

The essential subject matter appropriate for management training is as follows:

1. THE COMPANY OR ORGANIZATION
   a. Objectives and philosophy
   b. Policies and procedures
   c. Products and services
   d. Organization structure and organization dynamics
   e. Plant facilities
   f. Financial picture
   g. The labor agreement and union-management relations

2. MANAGEMENT PRINCIPLES AND TECHNIQUES
   a. Organization principles
   b. Financial planning and management
   c. Management information systems
   d. Production planning and control
   e. Methods analysis and work measurement
   f. Personnel management
   g. Wage and salary administration
   h. Cost analysis and control
   i. Statistics and probability
   j. Operations research
   k. Data processing
   l. Marketing
   m. Risk management

3. HUMAN RELATIONS (ORGANIZATIONAL BEHAVIOR)
   a. Fundamentals of human behavior
   b. Motivation

    c. Group dynamics
    d. Attitudes
    e. Conflict resolution
    f. Managing change
    g. Patterns of management
    h. Concepts of leadership
    i. Power, authority, influence
    j. Communication
    k. Personnel management responsibilities of supervision in such areas as selection, training, pay administration, counseling, appraisal, discipline, and grievance handling

4. TECHNICAL KNOWLEDGE AND SKILLS

These are peculiar to every type of business and to every type of work. Managers, of course, must have an adequate understanding of the technology, products, processes, and methods of their line of business.

5. ECONOMIC, SOCIAL, AND POLITICAL ENVIRONMENT

    a. Business ethics
    b. Economic system
    c. Relations with local, state, and Federal governments
    d. Community relations
    e. Social responsibilities
    f. Legal framework for business
    g. Business operations in foreign countries

6. PERSONAL SKILLS

    a. Speaking
    b. Report writing
    c. Conducting meetings
    d. Reading improvement
    e. Interpersonal skills, listening, feedback, communication

Any of these individual topics—for example, organization principles, statistics and probability, or reading improvement—might constitute an entire twenty to thirty (or more) classroom hour course. Because resources in any company are limited, the training department staff must decide in what subject areas the greatest needs lie. It can then establish courses to tackle these problems first.

The training needs of a newly appointed manager are somewhat different from those of experienced ones. The experienced man will need only a very light coverage of subject area 1 above, "The Company or Organization," whereas this is a logical starting point, and one that demands great emphasis, for the newcomer.

Emphasis Varies with Management Level. Although foremen, department heads, plant managers, and vice-presidents are all members of management, the nature of their duties and responsibilities differs rather substantially. The six main subject areas listed above ("The Company," "Management Principles and Techniques," "Human Relations," "Technical Knowledge and Skills," "Economic, Social, and Political Environment," and "Personal Skills") are necessary for all levels of management. However, certain topics are more appropriate for one level than another. For example, foremen are not directly involved in the economic, social, and political environment of a corporation, whereas vice-presidents are. Not only the content but also the depth of knowledge and skill vary according to the level and nature of the personnel involved.

Courses for top management will emphasize such subjects as economics, finance, organization theory, human relations, policy formulation, administrative controls, business operations overseas, the business man in politics, labor relations, and public relations. Because top executives, to a large extent, control their organizations' relations with the outside world, there is usually considerable time devoted to topics concerned with the economic, social, and political environment. Courses for members of middle management tend to contain elements of both top and lower-level management programs. They, of course, devote considerable time to human relations and personnel management principles because these are essential at all levels of management. Middle-level executives must often possess a solid grounding in such management techniques as cost analysis and control, data processing, production planning and control, and wage and salary administration.

Courses for first-level supervisors concentrate upon technical processes of the business, human relations, and personal skills. They tend to be immediately practical. They are closely related to the supervisor's day-to-day job.

Some courses for managers are designed simply to acquaint them with a particular field or technique. They learn how it fits into their total area of work, what it can do, and what its limitations are. For example, a course in operations research for plant managers, sales managers, and personnel executives would be of this type. It would orient them to this new and expanding applied mathematics and statistics technique. These managers would not be expected to become proficient in the use of operations research techniques. On the other hand, a company might give a very intensive course in operations research to all its supervisors in the engineering department, and it would expect them to acquire real proficiency in its application. A certain subject area may constitute one manager's day-to-day work, whereas another manager may need only an orientation type of knowledge of that topic.

University Nondegree Programs

As of 1960 approximately forty colleges and universities offered residential programs in management for executives employed in industry. These programs are given on the college campus, and in most cases the participants are sent by their companies. The employer pays full tuition and living expenses plus the man's salary. In addition to these broad coverage management programs—they are often called advanced management or executive development programs—there are literally scores of special purpose programs given by universities. In the discussion that follows, we shall confine ourselves to the broad, residential executive development programs.[6]

The first university executive development program was started in 1931 at Massachusetts Institute of Technology. This was the Sloan Fellowship program, which provided financial support for a few young industrial executives each year to spend a year of study in industrial management. The next program—and the first really large-scale one was started in 1943 by the Harvard Business School at the request of the United States Office of Education to train executives in war industries. Terminated at the end of World War II, this program was soon reactivated and modified by Harvard because of strong requests from private industry. The Harvard Advanced Management Program is 13 weeks in length and is for top level executives. The program is designed to handle two groups of about 160 men each year, one group starting in September and the other in February. Largely using the case method of teaching, the faculty offers the following courses in the program: Business Policy, Administrative Practices, Business and the American Society, Cost and Financial Administration, Marketing Administration, and Problems in Labor Relations.[7]

In 1959 Andrews sent a questionnaire to each of the 10,000 executives who had attended 39 formal university programs over the years. A sample of nonrespondents were followed up with direct interviews. Andrews found that 82 per cent of the 10,000 participants gave favorable evaluations to these programs as a group. The range of favorable evaluations for individual university programs was from 58 per cent to 92 per cent. The respondents stated that the effects of the programs upon themselves were (in rank order) first, increased confidence in own ability and capacity to improve performance; second, knowledge of aspects of business other than own speciality; third, the making of valuable personal acquaintances; and fourth, improvement of their understanding of human relations and dealing with people.[8]

It is extremely difficult to evaluate university executive development programs by rigorously controlled experiments of the before-and-after

---

[6] Information on university executive development programs is contained in the following: George V. Moser, *Executive Development Courses in Universities,* Rev.; Studies in Personnel Policy, No. 160 (New York: National Industrial Conference Board, 1957); Kenneth R. Andrews, "University Programs for Practicing Executives," in Frank C. Pierson *et. al., The Education of American Businessmen* (New York: McGraw-Hill Book Company, Inc. 1959; and Robert A. Gordon and James E. Howell *Higher Education for Business* (New York: Columbia University Press, (1959).

[7] George V. Moser, *op. cit.,* p. 36.

[8] Kenneth R. Andrews, "Reaction to University Development Programs," *Harvard Business Review,* Vol. 39, No. 3 (May-June 1961), pp. 116-134.

variety or of the "control and experimental" group type. No experiments of this type have been conducted. But most of the research that has aimed to get opinions of former participants and of their sponsoring employers has been favorable.

In discussing the content of these university executive development programs as a group, Gordon and Howel point out that the subject areas can be classified into three areas: financial management and control, management of human resources, and the nonmarket environment of the business firm. The nonmarket environment includes such subjects as relations between government and business and community responsibilities of the company. In addition to these three basic or core areas, courses in marketing, production, statistics, managerial economics, reading and speaking skills, and business policy are common.[9]

Management Games

A management game—also called a business game—is a classroom simulation exercise in which teams of students compete against each other or against an environment to achieve given objectives. The game is designed to be a close representation of real-life conditions. Often the controlling features of the game are expressed in the form of a mathematical model.

Although new to the business world, games have been used for many years by the military forces in a number of nations. War games were pioneered by the Prussian Army in the early nineteenth century. The first business management game was created by the American Management Association in 1956. It was formally used in management training at this organization's Academy at Saranac Lake, New York, in 1957. Computations were made on an IBM 650 computer. A noncomputer or manual game was developed in 1956 and described by Andlinger in 1958.[10]

Management games can be classified as either manual or computer. Calculations for manual games are made by hand or with a desk calculator, whereas calculations for a computer game are made on a high-speed electronic computer. Although a computer can handle more complex mathematical data in a very brief time period, there are many good manual games in use, and there appears to be no difference in educational value between the two types.

Some games are designed to teach students how to make top management decisions in an integrated manner. These games are called top management or total enterprise games. Others are designed to teach a particular functional field of management, such as production control, sales, materials control, and financial management.

Perhaps a better understanding of a management game might be gained

[9] Robert A. Gordon and James E. Howell, *op. cit.,* p. 297-298.
[10] G. R. Andlinger, "Business Games—Play One," *Harvard Business Review,* Vol. 36, No. 2 (March-April, 1958), pp. 115-125.

by describing one. The game developed by the International Business Machines Corporation is called the Management Decision-Making Laboratory. This is a top management game, processed by a computer. The game consists of three teams—each representing a company—that compete in four distinct geographical areas. Each team or company has its office and manufacturing plant in a "home" geographical area. All three companies compete on an equal basis in a fourth area, which is contiguous to the other three. Each company produces the same product. Each company tries to achieve a good financial position, to increase its assets, to make a good return on investment, and to place itself in a sound position for the future. Quarterly decisions are made by each team in regard to price, marketing expenditure, production volume and cost, research and development expenditure, and investment in additional plant capacity. These decisions are recorded on specially prepared forms, and the data is fed into a computer. The computer has been programed with a mathematical model that simulates a typical economic situation in the market. Thus participants find that sales volume increases appreciably with increases in marketing dollars up to a point of diminishing returns.

Of what value are management games as a training device? A game is a type of simulation exercise in which many, but not all, of the elements of a real-life situation are present. Students learn by analyzing problems, by using some intuition, and by making trial-and error type of decisions. The error of an unsound decision could be disastrous in a real business situation. But in a game an executive learns from his mistakes and has a chance to recoup his losses without harmful consequences. In some games players can even get a second chance to do something all over again if their first decision backfires. A management game has objective feedback of the consequences of business decisions. Feedback is prompt and this facilitates learning. Games also permit a telescoping of the time dimension. Actions that would consume months and even years in real-life situations can be telescoped to a few hours. All who have used management games, whether as students or instructors, agree that there is a high degree of ego involvement among the players. Interest runs high. It is actually fun to play these games. The players learn to organize themselves into a smooth-functioning team. They learn how to interact effectively with one another. Games provide instructors and researchers a wonderful opportunity to study the group process—patterns of communication, emergence of leaders, resolution of disputes, and development of friendship ties. A top management game provides functional specialists with an excellent appreciation of the realities and problems of managing a business as an integrated whole.

There are some limitations to games. The model upon which a game is built may be typical of a general kind of situation, yet it may not be realistic. Therefore, a learner executive may be lulled into a false confidence that he can apply the same action on the job as he did in the game. But this is not true. He can apply the same principles and patterns of analysis, but he cannot apply identical solutions. Management games, being relatively new, have not been rigorously validated as a training device. We do not know whether those who have been exposed to them actually improve or alter their behavior back on the job.

Management games cannot stand alone as a training method. They must be used in connection with organized theory, which may be given by readings, lectures, or conference discussions.

Sensitivity Training

Sensitivity training (often called T-group or laboratory training) is a method of training for the purpose of increasing human relations understanding and skills primarily by means of interactions within the framework of small group meetings. Work in this field has been pioneered by the National Training Laboratories which held the first laboratory training program at Bethel, Maine, in 1947.[11] While Bethel has continued to be NTL's principal laboratory training center over the years, this organization has also set up various regional and special training centers in other parts of the United States. Regional training and research centers have been set up at such universities as the University of California at Los Angeles, the University of Utah, and the University of Texas. Business schools at many universities conduct sensitivity training programs for managers from industry as well as for their own students. Many of our large corporations conduct in-company programs for their own executives and other employees. For a number of years the American Management Association's Executive Action Course has emphasized T-Group methodology.

The objectives of sensitivity training are to help people understand themselves better, to create better understanding of others, to gain insight into the group process, and to develop specific behavioral skills. Many people go through life never really understanding why they feel and act as they do. They do not really know how others feel about them. They are insensitive to the effects of their behavior upon others.

Employees give great deference to their bosses. A supervisor may, year after year, issue orders to his subordinates and criticize them without ever fully realizing that many of them may fear or hate him. If such a boss has an opportunity to participate in a sensitivity training course, he can be expected to gain important insights into himself and his effect upon others. Quite often trainees are upset about what they learn.

T-group programs also seek to improve communication skills. They help the trainee become an active listener—to really learn through listening. When engaged in conversation, many of us concentrate upon what we are going to say rather than upon what the other fellow is saying.

---

[11] The National Training Laboratories is affiliated with the National Education Association. Originally called the National Training Laboratory in Group Development, it became the National Training Laboratories in the early 1950's. In 1967 its official designation became the NTL Institute for Applied Behavioral Science.

Additional goals are to aid participants to work more effectively as group or team members and to perform leadership roles at times. Also one can see how informal groups coalesce, how people come to play different roles, how informal leadership may emerge, and how an organization actually takes structure and form. They can observe and experience interpersonal influence.

How is sensitivity training carried on? Although methods vary somewhat depending upon the specific orientation of the program, the core of most programs is the face-to-face, largely unstructured group (T-group). This group typically consists of from 8 to about 16 persons. At times there may be no leader, no agenda, and no stated goal for this small group. The group is left to its own devices to develop interaction and on-going experiences that serve as the real substance of the learning process. At other times the designated "trainer" introduces certain planned activities involving interaction between paired individuals and subgroups. The participants are encouraged to give feedback to each other on their personal feelings and reactions to what is happening in the group and on their reactions to one another's behavior. The emphasis is on the "here and now," not on the participants' experiences before they come to the program.

One or two professional trainers sit in with each T-group. However, the trainer tends to remain in the background. He does not lecture to them, does not rule certain conduct right and other conduct wrong, and does not pass out rewards and penalties (grades) as in conventional training courses. The role of the trainer sometimes seems ambiguous to the T-group members. At times he plays the role of a detached observer, at other times he acts as a group member, and at others he clearly introduces planned exercises for the group to engage in. His true role is to help the individuals and the group to learn from their own experiences in the group.

The emphasis in T-group work is not upon learning specific objective facts but rather upon gaining understanding of feelings, gestures, attitudes, and emotions—in short, sensitivity to oneself and others. There is a high degree of participation, feeling, and involvement in the typical session.

The following excerpt gives some of the flavor of a group session:

> "Today," Bob confided in his diary, "I was on the 'hot seat.' I felt quite tense and uncomfortable when the group started to talk about me, and I was glad when we later shifted to someone else. . . . Still, I knew they were on the right track. They were getting at the truth. . . . I was told that I am 'judgmental,' that I don't accept people for what they are . . . that I try to have them jump according to my tune. . . . This 'nugget of wisdom' is deeply disturbing, and I have, as they say, learned it at the 'gut level.' . . . Accepting others as they are (including acceptance of myself as I am), without judgment, is fundamental I guess to effective interaction."[12]

---

[12] Robert Tannenbaum, Irving R. Weschler, and Fred Massarik, *Leadership and Organization: A Behavioral Science Approach* (New York: McGraw-Hill Book Company, Inc., 1961), p. 133. Reprinted by permission.

In addition to the relatively unstructured T-groups, laboratory training also may include role-playing, intergroup competitive exercises, self-insight questionnaires, theory sessions with lectures, background readings, panel discussions, and training films.

What are the results of sensitivity training? One executive, a friend of the author, said that he felt his participation in this training was the greatest thing that had ever happened to him. His company had paid $1,000 plus expenses for the two weeks' course. He considered the money well spent and felt the company would still be ahead even if it had cost $10,000 for the course. In another company a supervisor recounted to the training director that for the first time, as a result of this training, he had been able to "reach" his 11-year-old son. Years before the father had been told by school authorities that his son had only modest intellectual potential; yet the man had continually condemned the boy for his poor academic showing. It was only after this father had acquired better insight into himself and his motives that he was able to listen to his son's problems and reach a sound basis for understanding.

For some, participation in sensitivity training is a traumatic experience. A few reach the breaking point emotionally under the pressure and from criticism by fellow trainees. Such situations demand alert action by the trainer, who will usually take the person out of the group, at least temporarily, to help him readjust.

> In one course a trainee, who was a major executive in a large corporation, developed a fixation upon a piece of broken plaster in the wall. He accused the group of deliberately cracking it to upset him. He had to leave the group, because the total situation was too upsetting emotionally.

Sensitivity training is a powerful tool for developing human relations understanding and skill. It must be conducted by professional leaders who are aware of its dangers as well as its advantages.

A limited number of controlled research experiments have been conducted seeking to determine the outcomes and results of sensitivity training. Paul Buchanan has reported upon a study made by Boyd and Elliss on the effectiveness of laboratory training in a Canadian hydroelectric power commission. A two-week laboratory program was compared with a traditional two-week course in administration for managers built around lectures and case discussions. Assessments were made after completion of the programs by interviewing the supervisor, two peers, and two subordinates of each participant. Of those who had attended the laboratory training, 64 per cent were judged to have changed their behavior, whereas only 23 per cent of those in the traditional or control group were observed to have changed. Furthermore, a much greater percentage of observers reported positive changes for the laboratory trained group than for the traditionally trained group. The laboratory trained people, in reporting upon themselves, stated that they now paid more attention to what others said, they felt they learned to make better contributions in group situations, and they gained in tolerance and flexibility.[13] Douglas Bunker obtained data on 346 persons who participated in Bethel, Maine, programs in 1960 and 1961. He obtained reports from others such as supervisors, peers, and subordinates who knew participants well. The principal changes noted were increased openness, receptivity, and tolerance of differences; increased skill in interpersonal relations and greater capacity for collaboration; and finally, improved understanding and diagnostic awareness of self and others.[14]

Sensitivity training, however, is not without its critics and without weaknesses. The emotional pressure and shock for some can be devastating. The T-group members, at times, pick on certain individuals unmercifully. Their psychological defenses are stripped away. Proponents of T-group training reply that people are being hurt every day on the job and in their daily lives. T-groups provide a low-risk atmosphere where people do not have to worry about saving face or worry that their behavior will affect them back on the job.

Another major area of criticism is that the openness, trust, and equalitarianism emphasized in laboratory training clashes head-on with the aggressiveness, autocracy, guile, secrecy, and interpersonal competition which is so prevalent in modern bureaucratic organization. The real business world is not permissive or democratic. People are often forced to do things they disapprove of. Thus the critics say that laboratory training does not equip its trainees for the hard realities of business life. But the proponents of laboratory education argue that the values which underlie their approach enable people to be more, not less, effective in their interpersonal relations and in organization life. They argue for a new set of values and a new way of behaving. Openness, trust, improved communication skills, greater self-insight, cooperation, team management, and participatory leadership have been shown to be viable.

It has also been argued that a two-week exposure to sensitivity training is unlikely to achieve really lasting improvements or changes in a person's interpersonal behavior. Remember that at age 30 or 40 a man's life style, personality, and characteristic responses are pretty well ingrained.

The Managerial Grid

The managerial grid created by Robert R. Blake and Jane S. Mouton is grounded in some of the same behavioral science values and methods as T-group or laboratory training. It utilizes small face-to-face groups

[13] Paul C. Buchanan, "Evaluating the Effectiveness of Laboratory Training in Industry," *Explorations in Human Relations Training and Research,* No. 1 (Washington, D.C.: National Training Laboratories, 1965).

[14] Douglas R. Bunker, "The Effect of Laboratory Education upon Individual Behavior." This article appears as Chapter 13 in Edgar H. Schein and Warren G. Bennis, *Personal and Organizational Change Through Group Methods* (New York: John Wiley & Sons, Inc., 1965).

as the basic learning mechanism. A grid seminar typically is of one week's duration. Each seminar is composed of a number of study teams of from five to nine members each. The teams are composed of a diagonal slice of a company, that is, persons from various levels of the corporation and from various functional specialties. However, no one participates in a grid seminar at the same time with his own boss or his immediate work colleagues.

The theoretical formulation underlying a grid seminar is the "managerial grid." This is a graphic way of expressing underlying assumptions and theories about ways of managing people in work organizations. Blake and Mouton have synthesized and summarized the salient features of current theory in organizational behavior. They postulate that managers may evidence a concern for production or a concern for people (or a combination of these) in their styles of management. The graphic representation in grid form displays concern for production along the abscissa or X-axis on a scale from 1 through 9. The ordinate or Y-axis expresses concern for people and is also on a scale of 1through 9. A management theory that exhibits a maximum concern for production and a minimal interest in people (9,1) is characterized by a high pressure, authoritarian style. The converse of 9,1 management is 1,9, which shows a low concern for production and a high concern for people. This has been labeled "country-club" management. Leadership that evidences a high concern for both people and production is labeled 9,9. This is held to be a most desirable pattern of management from the standpoint of conflict resolution, creativity, commitment, morale, and productivity. In addition to these three positions on the grid, there is the 1,1 theory of management wherein management basically abdicates its responsibilities for both people and productivity and the 5,5 theory wherein management compromises and adopts an "organization-man" strategy. These five basic theories of management can be supplemented by eight other positions or combinations on the grid to make a total of thirteen formulations.

In a grid-seminar each study team carries out a series of exercises and experiments. The participants, via self-study, have become well grounded in managerial grid theory. After each exercise the participants evaluate and critique their behavior. A major aim is to develop greater understanding of issues such as team organization, communication and commitment, strategy, planning, decision-making processes, and control. Other grid-seminar goals are to increase personal objectivity, improve teamwork skills, learn ways of managing conflict, and aid in identifying and evaluating the values and work culture of one's organization.

In contrast to sensitivity training, grid seminars do not emphasize personal introspection or a rather deep exploration of personal feelings, emotions, and attitudes. Grid seminars are much more applied in nature.[15]

[15] For a comprehensive discussion of the managerial grid by its creators see Robert R. Blake and Jane S. Mouton, *The Managerial Grid* (Houston, Texas: Gulf Publishing Company, 1964).

Management Development in Perspective

Management training and development are intimately related to the entire system of management practice in an organization. If administration is disorganized, haphazard, and faulty, then sound management development will be extremely difficult to accomplish. Executives and supervisors will learn, to a great extent, by precept and example while on the job.

Management development activities must be undertaken on behalf of and by all members of management, not just a chosen few. An organization stands or falls on the basis of the total efforts of the entire team. An effective, going concern cannot afford to neglect a large segment of its leadership in favor of an elite corps.

Those in charge of guiding the whole program can appropriately adopt an eclectic view toward the process. They must not place all of their eggs in one basket of, say, job rotation or coaching and counseling; rather they must establish a multidimensional program that reaches to every manager and educates in a variety of ways for a variety of specific purposes.

Questions for Review and Discussion

1. What is a manager and what does a manager do?
2. What elements constitute the management process?
3. What knowledge, skills, and abilities should a manager possess?
4. How do you account for the surge of interest by industrialists and business leaders in management development programs in the 1950's?
5. Is management a profession? Discuss.
6. Why is it necessary that management training and development activities be started with top executives first?
7. What are the essential components of a comprehensive management development program?
8. What role should the following play in a management development program?
   a. The president of the organization
   b. The director of industrial relations
   c. The training director
   d. Individual supervisors and executives throughout the organization
9. How can one determine the value of specific management training and development programs?
10. What is coaching? How should it be done? What are its strengths and limitations?
11. Prepare, in outline form, a curriculum for a comprehensive series of training conferences for:
    a. Foremen
    b. Vice-presidents of an industrial company

12. What is a management game?

13. What is sensitivity (T-group) training? What are its goals? What are some of the criticisms of sensitivity training?

14. What is the managerial grid, and what constitutes a grid seminar?

15. Which training techniques, of those discussed in Chapters 13 and 14, are most effective for accomplishing the following objectives?

    a. Impart factual knowledge

    b. Induce attitude changes

    c. Develop awareness of oneself and one's effect upon others

CASE PROBLEM

A Supervisory Training Course

James Westmore was contacted on the telephone by the Extension Director of State University Labor-Management Center. Westmore was a professor at a private university in a nearby city. The Director invited Westmore to teach a ten-session supervisory training course to the shop foremen at the Peerless Machine and Foundry Works. He suggested that Professor Westmore visit the personnel manager at Peerless to become oriented to the company and its problems.

The Peerless company employed 300 people and produced heavy iron and steel products. The personnel manager told Professor Westmore that he liked to take advantage of State University's services by having it give one course for the foremen every year on some aspects of supervision and industrial relations. The full cost of these courses was paid by State University as part of its extension program for industrial, labor, and public organizations.

Inasmuch as the company could not spare the foremen during the working day, the course was given one afternoon each week for ten weeks from 4 to 6 P.M. The foremen came directly to the course from their jobs. They received time and one half overtime for these extra hours. Because the company lacked training class facilities, the personnel manager arranged that it be held in the quarters of a fraternal club a few blocks from the plant.

This fraternal club was situated in an old house in a declining section of the town. A makeshift classroom was set up in the former dining room of this house. Old card tables were placed back to back to make a conference type layout. The blackboard consisted of an old slate supported by a card table and leaned against the wall. Light was provided by an old-fashioned chandelier from which several bulbs were missing.

On the Monday afternoon of the first class Professor Westmore found that he had to introduce himself to the class of sixteen foremen. The personnel manager had left word with one of the men to say that he was busy and could not make it. Because there was no chalk for the slate board, one of the foremen volunteered to go to the store to buy some.

Professor Westmore had prepared a course outline that contained the following topics: (1) Nature of a foreman's job, (2) What foremen expect from management, (3) What workers expect from their foremen, (4) Elementary aspects of organization, (5) Motivation, (6) Making work assignments, (7) Coaching, (8) Complaints and grievances, (9) Leadership, and (10) Discipline. He made weekly assignments of about 25 to 30 pages in a textbook on supervision. The classes were conducted on a lecture-discussion basis with some case studies used.

Professor Westmore noticed that the men were always late for the class although they seemed to be in and about the building. Finally at 4:00 P.M. on the third week he decided to explore the building. To his surprise he found most of the men drinking beer at a bar located on the second floor. In class the foremen.were courteously attentive on the surface but basically seemed unenthusiastic. In many of the discussions they stated that they had learned about various aspects of human relations and supervision in courses given to them by other instructors in previous years. Professor Westmore began to wonder if he had been hired to repeat instruction that had been given previously. The men said on more than one occasion that the ideas about leadership and human relations contained in the book and in Professor Westmore's talks were O.K. in theory, but they wouldn't work at the Peerless plant because of MacGregor, the factory manager. They claimed that MacGregor knew nothing about human relations and was tough to deal with, that the union always went directly to the personnel manager with the grievances, and that they, as foremen, had no authority. All discipline was handled by the personnel manager.

Westmore observed to himself that these foremen felt more like workers than members of management. They even dressed in blue jeans and shop work clothes. The pattern-shop foreman made the following statement to him one day: "I have worked here for twenty-five years and have been a foreman for fifteen. But maybe I should have taken a job somewhere else. One day I was standing on the street corner when a truck from the Acme Steel Company went by. The truck driver must have just gotten his paycheck, because he threw his checkstub out the window and I picked it up. He gets one hundred forty dollars a week, and that is lots more than I get as a foreman."

Questions

1. Was this training course launched properly?
2. What could foremen training accomplish in this company?
3. What do you think of the course content and method of instruction?

4. How do you account for the behavior of the foremen in this training program?

5. If you had free rein to make needed changes, what actions and what kind of management development program would you establish for this company? How would you carry out your program?

Suggestions for Further Reading

Andrews, Kenneth, "There Are Some Tricks Only Old Dogs Can Learn," *Columbia Journal of World Business,* Vol. 1, No. 4, Fall 1966, pp. 101-108.

Blake, Robert R. and Jane S. Mouton, *The Managerial Grid,* Houston, Texas: Gulf Publishing Company, 1964.

————, *Corporate Excellence Through Grid Organization Development,* Houston, Texas: Gulf Publishing Company, 1968.

Bradford, Leland P., Jack R. Gibb, and Kenneth D. Benne (eds.), *T-Group Theory and Laboratory Method; Innovation in Re-Education,* New York, John Wiley & Sons, 1964.

Ferguson, Lawrence L., "Better Management of Managers' Careers," *Harvard Business Review,* Vol. 44, No. 2, March-April 1966, pp. 139-152.

House, Robert J., *Management Development: Design, Evaluation, and Implementation,* Bureau of Industrial Relations, University of Michigan, 1967.

Houston, George C., *Manager Development: Principles and Perspectives,* Homewood, Illinois: Richard D. Irwin, 1961.

Hunt, J. G., "Another Look at Human Relations Training," *Training and Development Journal,* Vol. 22, February 1968, pp. 2-10.

Jerkedal, Ake, *Top Management Education: An Evaluation Study,* Stockholm, Sweden: Swedish Council for Personnel Administration, 1967.

Kibbee, Joel M., Clifford J. Craft, and Burt Nanus, *Management Games: A New Technique for Executive Development,* New York: Reinhold Publishing Corporation, 1961.

Klaw, Spencer, "Two Weeks in a T-Group," *Fortune,* Vol. 64, No. 2, August 1961, pp. 114-117 *ff.*

Levinson, Harry, "A Psychologist Looks at Executive Development," *Harvard Business Review,* Vol. 40, No. 5, September-October 1962, pp. 69-75.

Merrill, Harwood F. and Elizabeth Marting (eds.), *Developing Executive*

Skills: New Patterns for Management Growth, New York: American Management Association, 1958.

Schein, Edgar H. and Warren G. Bennis, *Personal and Organizational Change Through Group Methods: The Laboratory Approach,* New York: John Wiley & Sons, 1965.

Tosi, Henry and Robert House, "Continuing Management Development Beyond the Classroom," *Business Horizons,* Vol. 9, No. 2, Summer 1966, pp. 91-101.

Wikstrom, Walter S., *Developing Managerial Competence: Changing Concepts and Emerging Practices,* New York: National Industrial Conference Board, 1964.

Wilson, J. E. and others, "Sensitivity Training for Individual Growth— Team Training for Organization Development," *Training and Development Journal,* Vol. 22, January 1968, pp. 47-55.

UNDERSTANDING
AND
MANAGING PEOPLE

Understanding People

15

Human beings, as individuals, are very complex in their psychological make-up. When they interact with one another in groups and in large organizations, the complexities are multiplied. Scientists still have much to learn about the nature of man. However, as a result of systematic experimentation, observation, and clinical studies, behavioral scientists have developed insight into the nature and conditions of human behavior.

This chapter is essentially concerned with an analysis of the reasons people behave as they do, and with an explanation of various means by which management can stimulate and guide the conduct and actions of members of its organization. We shall explore the subject of human motivation and shall look into some important theories of motivation. Why do people act as they do? What do they seek out of life? Why do some have high levels of aspiration and others not? Do most human drives and wants form a consistent pattern? We shall delve into the subject of human adjustment and the concepts of adaptive and maladaptive behavior. What are the characteristics of behavior induced by frustration? How can one's job induce frustrations?

Finally, and most importantly, we shall discuss ways in which motivational principles can be applied by management in the work situation. The concept of integration of goals—the joining together of the drives and wants of employees with those of the organization for which they work—will be examined.

HUMAN BEHAVIOR FUNDAMENTALS

In his efforts to guide and direct others, the manager must first of all acquire an understanding of the nature of human behavior and why people act as they do.

Self-Concept and Personality

To understand another person, we must be aware of how he thinks and feels about himself. This image of himself which the individual holds may not be a fully accurate representation. Nevertheless, he will tend to behave in accordance with his own self-image. His actions are a function of how he views himself. His behavior will be logical from his point of view although it may not appear logical from our own perspective. Even though a person's knowledge about himself may be a little vague, he will strive at all times to be true to his own views of himself. Our opinion of this person may be quite an inaccurate picture of how he considers himself. To learn to understand him truly we must be less judgmental of his actions and more perceptive.

How does a person acquire his self-concept? The strongest influence is that in the home during one's formative years as a child. If a child is raised in a family where people are demonstrative, he will learn that this is approved behavior. If high but attainable standards of achievement are expected by his parents, he will tend to hold to such standards throughout life. Children in the family are rewarded or punished for all sorts of behavior. They learn to avoid physical and emotional pain and to repeat that behavior which gains approval and reward. In addition to the influences of the parents and brothers and sisters, are those of friends, associates, school teachers, and other authority figures in one's youth. As a child matures he gains a view of his personal worth on the basis of the way others respond to him and on the basis of his achievements. Thus a person's sense of personal worth is conferred on him as well as derived in relation to his accomplishments. Gradually as maturation takes place, the individual acquires rather definite beliefs about what his behavior, values, and goals ought to be. These become internalized.

In addition to self-concept everyone also acquires a personal view of his world. He perceives and responds to other people, places, things, and events. His personal frame of reference is an amalgam of his self-image, his behavior, and his perception of the world about him. His perceptions and preconceived notions of his environment help determine whether he will be bold or meek, optimistic or pessimistic, trusting or suspicious.

Based upon his self-concept and his view of the world about him, each individual develops an accommodation and a characteristic way of acting. He will always behave in such a way as to protect and improve his adequacy in his world as he sees it. His behavior is internally logical and consistent as he sees it.

In talking about *self,* we have in a sense also been talking about personality. Personality is the sum total of the physical, mental, emotional, and social characteristics of a person. It is the integrating process by which all of the physiological and psychological components of man are combined into the whole. Psychologists, in their research investigations, have devised many ways of quantifying bodily sensations, perceptions, intelligence, attitudes, and motives. However, these do not act singly. They are all contained within the unified whole of the person. Frank Edwards is the personnel director. It is not simply his intelligence alone nor his emotional state alone that is Frank Edwards. All of his attributes operate together to reveal his characteristic responses. The *self* and *personality* are one and the same. Personality is more than the sum of all the various attributes of a person; it is the organization of these parts. If we ask a person to change one undesirable part of his personality, say his hot temper, he may find this very difficult if not impossible to do because we are really asking him to change the fundamental structure of his personality.

When a human being is internally consistent within himself, we speak of him as having a well-adjusted personality. When he is externally adapted to his environment, we say he is well-adapted. When one is both adjusted and adapted, we say that he has an integrated personality.

A person may be at ease with himself but maladapted for his environment. Conversely he may get along well with others socially and in business but suffer from all sorts of internal tensions and anxieties in the process.

An individual continually strives to maintain his personality consistent and in balance. The basic parts of the adult personality are stable. In actuality we deduce an individual's specific personality from the stability of his characteristic way of behaving.

As a person matures, he gains more needs and abilities, and he also deepens many of those he already possesses. As new ideas, traits, and outlooks are gained, these are incorporated into the person so as not to upset his equilibrium. With maturation his private world expands. His perception of the world about him is always colored by his frame of reference and his self-image. Actually everyone, in a sense, lives in his own private world. The personality becomes complete and integrated only when it interacts with other people, things, and groups. The insolated individual cannot fully develop. We can understand ourselves only as we can understand others; conversely we can understand others only if we also understand ourselves.

Individual Differences

Beyond the more noticeable and obvious differences among people in physical appearance, voice, intelligence, race, language and general habits, are the less readily apparent differences in emotional responses to various stimuli, and in motives, attitudes, and modes of thought.

There are vast differences among people of different cultures and subcultures even though biologically they are the same. For example, one can observe great differences in the competence, behavior, and attitudes between the subculture composed of corporate executives and that of the culturally deprived. If a manager tries to operate various personnel programs for a group of poorly educated, culturally deprived people in a factory setting, he soon learns that they do not respond to the same kind of communications and incentives that he is accustomed to. The culturally deprived are not verbally oriented. Some are illiterate, and others read with great difficulty. They will not react to the discipline of the factory in the same way as middle-class employees. When applying for jobs, they do not think in terms of the long-run future and prospects for advancement. One personnel manager stated that he has interviewed hundreds of culturally deprived persons applying for laboring jobs in factories and that they very rarely ask about opportunities for promotion.

Even within the same social melieu we find considerable variation in the abilities, attitudes, and temperaments of people. If a manager gives identical projects to two engineers, he will find that their modes of attack may be quite different. People react to praise, criticism, promises, frustration, and the like quite differently. A challenging assignment may frustrate one man but stimulate another.

The manager must be perceptive. He must be ever alert to the world and personality of his subordinates, peers, and superiors.

Human Behavior Is Caused

Initially it is important to know that all human behavior has a cause (or causes). There is a reason for a person's behaving as he does. A stimulus is present to initiate behavior on the part of the individual. For example, physiological changes in the body accompanying the passage of time since a person has had his last meal will give rise to a feeling of emptiness and discomfort in his stomach. There will be a feeling of hunger. We call this a need or a feeling of tension inside the person. The person will normally then seek food to alleviate his hunger so that he can again experience a feeling of well-being. To generalize, we can say that one or more stimuli may interact with an individual. The person will then experience a state of tension such that he seeks to fulfill his need and reduce the level of tension and discomfort. He adopts a type of behavior he feels will satisfy his need.

The cause for human behavior constitutes an interaction between a stimulus (noise, light, a threat) and the person's own internal interpretation of that stimulus. Thus to one person a sound may be annoying, whereas another may consider it like soothing music. If one employee smiles at another, the second may view the smile as a leering smirk. On the other hand, someone else may consider it a smile of approbation. One's perception is determined by his background, personality, and the circumstances surrounding the event.

The actions of rational human beings are goal directed. Our behavior is aimed toward the fulfillment of basic wants, drives, and needs. The politician who does favors for his constituents hopes thereby to gain their votes at election time so that he can retain his office. The piece-rate worker in the clothing factory may work very hard to increase her earnings because she desires to buy a new coat or a car. It is important to understand that behavior is purposeful and that it is caused. People are not uncooperative just for the sake of being perverse. There are causes for such behavior. The successful leader is the one who can uncover these causes and take steps to correct them. Bawling out an uncooperative worker does not get at the cause. This constitutes treating the symptom only. If a patient complains of a sore throat, his doctor may prescribe aspirin to relieve the pain; however, such action does not correct the reason for the sore throat. Many times doctors treat only symptoms because medical science has not as yet found the cause and cure for a particular ailment (for example, prescribing pain relievers for arthritis). But the medical profession is constantly probing deeper for causes. Likewise the practicing manager must constantly dig beneath surface behavior to inquire of its causes.

MOTIVATION

Motives are the mainsprings of action in people. The leader who wishes to incite his men to reach an objective must hold out the promise of reward once the objective is attained. What rewards do people seek in life? The answer is that they seek to fulfill their wants, drives, and needs.

The term *motive* implies action to satisfy a need. The terms *need, want, drive* and *motive* are often used interchangeably by psychologists. Motivation can be defined as a willingness to expend energy to achieve a goal or a reward. Let us look at the figure below in order better to understand motivation.

Need	Behavior	Reward
Respect from others	Outstanding work on the job	Praise, pay increase, status symbols

Assume that an engineer in industry seeks to win the admiration and esteem not only of his boss but also of his fellow engineers. This feeling on his part is called a need or a motive. Although there are perhaps a number of ways of achieving this, let us assume that our engineer chooses to work unusually diligently on a particular design project so that it becomes evident to his supervisor that he has made a major contribution. The supervisor may then choose to reward the engineer for his performance with oral praise, with a pay increase at salary review time, with certain formal recognition in the company newspaper, or by means of a letter of commendation to higher management. Depending upon how the individual perceives these forms of reward, his original need may be wholly or partially satisfied.

The psychology of learning tells us about the law of effect which states that behavior that is perceived to be rewarding will tend to be repeated, whereas behavior which goes unrewarded or is punished will tend to be extinguished. This has great import for trainers, personnel directors, and managers. Over the long run they can induce desired behavior such as high quality workmanship, good attendance, loyalty, or initiative by their choice of rewards and the way they are administered. Unrewarded behavior tends to disappear as evidenced by the example of the high level engineer in the department of public works of a state government who told the author that he once worked out a plan for saving $250,000 for the government. He installed the plan on his own authority and then proudly informed his boss about his cost-saving. His boss showed not the slightest interest in this accomplishment. What his boss was interested in was new and bigger projects to expand the prestige of his department, not ways to reduce expenses. The engineer got the message and did not repeat his cost-cutting venture.

Classification of Needs

To understand human needs adequately, it is useful to classify them as to type. Thus we have innate or primary needs, such as food, shelter, water, rest to overcome fatigue, and so on. These are inborn needs. Generally speaking, they are not conditioned by experience. The innate needs are primarily physiological in nature. Gratification of these needs is vital to the survival of a human being as an organism.

The other major type of need is called an acquired or secondary need. These needs are dependent upon our experience. They are learned. They vary greatly from person to person and from one group to another. The need for a lady to wear white gloves and a hat at certain social gatherings in warm weather is certainly not inborn. It is culturally determined. It is acquired from her parents and friends. It is largely a manifestation of the desire to belong and be accepted by others. In the home the child feels a need to be wanted and loved. We are all familiar with the serious emotional problems that occur in children who are rejected by their parents: The same needs to be necessary, to be wanted, and to belong are present in adults. An employee can readily sense when his boss disapproves of him. If a supervisor or manager, by his attitude and actions, makes it apparent that he dislikes one of his employees, this usually causes anxiety, tension, and frustration in the subordinate. If the supervisor's attitude is readily apparent to the other employees, his attitude often has

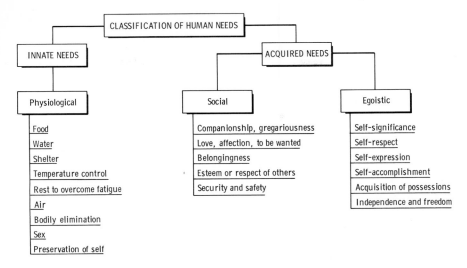

Figure 15-1.   A Classification of Basic Human Needs.

an effect upon their relations with the rejected employee. Refer to Figure 15-1 for a classification and listing of basic human needs.

The drive to obtain safety and security has several ramifications. Partly it is related to the innate physiological need for self-preservation. The aim is to avoid bodily harm, to avoid suffering, to continue to exist. The need for security is also social in context. The fact that one knows that others like him, respect him, and want him to continue to be a part of the group or organization, enhances his feeling of security. We can call it a feeling of emotional security. The struggle to achieve a measure of security is fundamental for most people. Some achieve financial security by means of hard work, superior ability, and fortuitous circumstances. Others turn to collective security from their group. Thus we have various health and welfare programs to provide a measure of security for eligible members. These may take the form of a pension plan operated by a private employer for his employees, a group insurance program paid for by union members' dues, or a comprehensive social security program provided by a national government for its citizens.

The egoistic needs are concerned primarily with a person's view or conception of himself. Satisfaction of these needs tends to enhance one's ego. Some writers refer to the egoistic needs as *personal* drives. They are often called the higher needs, because a person is seldom motivated to fulfill them until after he has first met his physiological and social wants. Business executives and political leaders tend to be strongly motivated to meet their egoistic needs. They have a drive for power, prestige, and status. They seek to make their mark in the world. They want to accomplish and achieve. They want others to hear their words. But persons of lesser fame also desire satisfaction of their personal needs. The bookkeeper with forty years' service who has labored long and hard in the back room of a merchandising establishment feels a warm glow when someone praises him, and he feels very important if his boss asks him for his advice on an involved accounting problem.

Hierarchy of Needs—Maslow

The psychologist A. H. Maslow has developed a widely acclaimed theory of human motivation in which he postulates that there is a definite rank order priority of human needs. Until the more basic wants are fulfilled, a person will not strive to meet his higher needs. Maslow classifies needs into five categories:

1. Physiological.
2. Safety, stability, and security.
3. Belongingness and love.
4. Self-esteem and the esteem of others.
5. Self-actualization, self realization, and self-accomplishment.[1]

The implications of the hierarchical nature of human motivation are important for an understanding of why people behave as they do. If a person has barely enough food, water, and shelter to survive, his entire energies are devoted to eking out an existence. He is not interested in status, prestige, or making his ideas known to others. He cannot afford the luxury of engaging in ego-enhancing activities. Once the basic physiological and safety wants are met, then people strive for companionship, belongingness, love, affection, and the esteem of others. When he has a superabundance of food, clothing, and shelter, the fulfillment of these needs no longer motivates our hypothetical man. He turns to his higher needs. The higher needs are social and psychological in nature. They are less concrete and more nebulous than the survival needs. Particularly when we concern ourselves with the egoistic drives, we find that full satisfaction seldom occurs. People can always take more recognition, more praise, more status, and more adulation.

Characteristics of Acquired Needs

The strength and pattern of the acquired needs vary considerably from one person to another. The boy who is raised on a farm in Iowa will tend to seek somewhat different satisfactions in life from the boy whose father is a corporation executive and who lives in the suburbs of New York City.

[1] A. H. Maslow, *Motivation and Personality* (New York: Harper & Row, 1954). See especially Ch. 5.

The former may cherish the values of family, neighbors, the soil, and the open air, whereas the latter may struggle hard to climb the corporate ladder and thereby achieve power and wealth. Management may concern itself with profits, costs, and efficiency, whereas the leaders of organized labor seek better wages, hours, and conditions for workers. Therefore, we can say that when people exist in different environments and when their experiences are different, the pattern and intensity of their motives will vary. Anthropologists have observed that among many peoples on earth the great urge to acquire more goods and possessions that is so characteristic of Americans is totally absent. Likewise competition serves successfully as a motivator for company salesmen and for college athletes, but it is far less successful as a stimulus to higher production for blue-collar workers in the factory.

Acquired needs vary over time for the same individual. A young breadwinner raising a family has an urgent need for a higher income, whereas the same person, after his children have reached adulthood, finds a lesser need for material rewards but may seek more leisure time or pursue cultural activities.

Learned needs do not operate upon a person singly. They occur in groups. The desire to achieve a higher income may be based upon one's desire for greater status and respect in the company and the community at large as well as the desire to obtain more of the material comforts of life. Very frequently a person is not fully aware of why he behaves as he does. He is not able to say "I do this because I seek security," His motives are often hidden from conscious recognition.

Level of Aspiration

The degree to which a person will strive to achieve and accomplish is determined by his level of aspiration. Failure tends to lower what one feels he can do, and success raises his sights. The person who repeatedly fails to reach his goal must lower his sights (or change his methods) or else experience deep frustration. On the other hand, one young industrial relations director who had risen very rapidly in the business world was a member of top management in his company, had a good salary, and enjoyed considerable prestige and acceptance both in his company and in the community. Upon being asked if he were now satisfied, he replied, "No." He aspired to continue to go up in the business world. He hoped to become president of his company and obtain higher and higher financial rewards. Repeated success in this case gave rise to continuously higher expectations.

There is another important determinant of one's level of aspiration. This is parental influence. Most of our values in life we gain from our parents. If a boy's father is a doctor, he would tend to experience considerable status anxiety if he were to hold only a minor clerical position as an adult. Conversely, if by example and preachment a father demonstrated that a foreman's job in a factory was the epitome of success, there would be a tendency for the son to let that be his standard of accomplishment.

One's associates also exert an influence upon the level of expectation. In seeking to win and maintain the approval of his friends, a person will try to behave as they do. In the factory individual workers tend to produce as much as the group to which they belong. If most of a college sophomore's friends own automobiles, he too will aspire to own one. If it is considered socially desirable for college freshmen to become pledged to a fraternity, then individual students will exert great efforts to achieve fraternity membership.

HUMAN ADJUSTMENT

Human adjustment is concerned with the way in which people react in the process of seeking to satisfy their needs. Some, whom we call well-adjusted individuals, are relatively successful in meeting and solving the myriad problems that the average person faces. We speak of them as possessing a mature personality. These persons are goal centered and adopt a flexible, resourceful, problem-solving form of behavior.

If an obtacle or barrier presents itself on the path to attainment of their goals, they are adaptive. They try other ways of relieving tension and satisfying their needs. They may intensify their efforts, they may reorganize their perception of the problem, and they may adopt substitute goals. Others, who are not so fortunate, may be poorly adjusted to meet the problems of life. They may exhibit what we call maladjusted or maladaptive behavior. They may be disorganized and unproductive in relieving tension and fulfilling their needs. Their actions take on the characteristics of frustrated behavior.

Now all persons cannot be conveniently classified into the two categories: (1) well-adjusted, or (2) maladjusted. People fall along a continuum. The terms are relative. Many persons whom we would ordinarily consider to be well adjusted may in a particular situation lose their tempers, swear, or develop a tension headache. When goal-directed behavior is successful it leads to a reduction of internal tension and a satisfaction of needs. However, all of us experience situations that irritate, annoy, and vex us. John may have missed his usual train on the way to work in the morning causing him to miss an important business contact. Or if the boss is in a grumpy mood, the entire office force may become apprehensive.

Defense Mechanisms

When motivated behavior encounters an apparently insurmountable barrier, and when a problem-solving approach fails to achieve the goal, then frustration occurs. All of us encounter situations where our self-integrity is threatened and we must find an outlet. We speak of the various forms of behavior that people may adopt in the face of frustration as *defense mechanisms*. Occasional resort to a defense mechanism as an outlet does not mean that a person is maladjusted. It is when frustration-directed behavior dominates one's whole life that we can say that a person is abnormal and needs expert help.

Now the barriers to the fulfillment of needs and wants can be both external and internal. If a boy who is sent to the store by his mother to buy a bottle of milk finds his way blocked by two neighborhood bullies, then the obstacle to the attainment of his goal is clearly external. If a salesperson continually repels potential customers because of his own antagonistic personality, then this barrier is internal to the salesperson. To a considerable extent the most difficult obstacles to surmount are those arising within the person himself. Likewise some barriers are "thing-type" obstacles, for example, it is too cold or the automobile has a flat tire. Others are "people-type" barriers. The most vexing type is that involving people. Executives whose jobs require that they try to persuade others to act know that this can be a very challenging assignment.

The defense mechanisms that people may adopt as an outlet from frustration can be classified into four broad categories:

1. Aggression
2. Withdrawal
3. Fixation
4. Compromise

Within each category are a number of subcategories. The particular form of reaction a person adopts depends upon his personality, the situation, and upon how he perceives the barrier. The frustration tolerance of people varies considerably. Some are much more susceptible to frustration than others. Different people will react differently under the same circumstances. Assume that four persons working in the same company for the same supervisor have each been expecting a salary increase on June 1. All are denied the increase on the same grounds, namely, that although their performance has been acceptable, it has not been good enough to justify a raise in pay. Besides, the company has been experiencing a poor year financially. One employee might become so incensed that he would immediately start looking for another job. Another might grumble, complain, and exhibit hostility toward his boss and the company. The third might decide that his best course of action is to apply himself even harder on the job so that his boss would surely reward his efforts the next year. And the fourth employee might see in this situation the need for the formation of a union in order to increase the bargaining power of himself and his fellow employees. He might then contact the nearest union office to see if it would undertake an organizing campaign.

Let us now examine the various forms of frustrated behavior. One of the most common forms is *aggression.* This is primarily an attack response designed to inflict injury or damage. We see aggression nearly every day in one form or another. It is readily apparent in children, where it usually takes the form of a physical attack (for example, hitting another child because he has taken a toy). With adults, physical violence as an outlet for frustration certainly occurs too (for example, violence on union picket lines to prevent strike-breakers from going to work). However, education and training have taught most adults in most situations to channel their aggressive impulses into nonviolent forms. Thus we find a person spreading rumors about another whom he dislikes or uttering vituperative remarks against the source of a frustration. In labor-management relations examples of aggression are the firing of a worker because he is active in organizing a union, or, on the employees' part, a deliberate slowdown in protest against the actions of the company.

Scapegoating is a form of aggression in which the aggressor attacks substitute people or objects. For various reasons he finds it inadvisable or perhaps impossible to attack the real source of his discontent, so he picks on some innocent person or object. The Nazi atrocities against the Jews in Europe in the 1930's and 1940's were a form of scapegoating.

There are a number of kinds of *withdrawal* reactions that occur. Basically when a person withdraws, he seeks either physically or mentally to avoid the obstacle or situation. Thus we find flights into *fantasy* and daydreaming. By so doing a person can obtain satisfaction through a temporary escape from reality. Physical *escape* or absence from the situation is another type of defense mechanism. The worker who continually changes jobs because of dissatisfaction with what he is doing at the time may simply be avoiding a sound appraisal of himself and a mature approach to his problems. *Regression* consists of adopting less mature, more childish behavior. Sometimes it signifies an attempt to return to the security and comfort of one's childhood. Symptoms of regressive behavior in adults are crying, pouting, horseplay, loss of emotional control, and homesickness. A continual longing for the good old days may be a reaction to frustration. Those who live in the past do so because the present is unhappy for them. Americans in recent years have tended to expel their elders from the family unit when they are less able to take care of themselves or when there is a lack of compatibility between adult sons and daughters and their elders. They are placed in old folks' homes. Yet we often note that these old folks really live in the past. Their conversations are filled with recollections of their youth when they were wanted, when they belonged, and when they were considered important by others.

Still another form of withdrawal is *resignation.* This involves giving up the struggle. After repeated failure the individual may cease trying. The downtrodden worker who has lost all hope of better things from his job may have simply resigned himself to his unsatisfactory existence.

Fixation, the third major type of frustrated behavior, consists of a compulsion to continue repeatedly a type of behavior that does not result in the attainment of a goal. It does not reduce tension. The person is figuratively hitting his head against a stone wall. Persisting in the old way of doing things, even when unsuccessful, may be the only recourse that some people know. They are afraid or do not know how to try something else.

Compromise reactions, the fourth major category, consist of *sublimation, rationalization,* and *projection.* Compromise involves altering one's objectives either actually or symbolically. Thus in sublimation an individual will adopt a substitute goal, or behavior, generally one that is on a higher ethical plane and socially more acceptable. *Rationalization* involves protecting one's ego by claiming that he really didn't want something anyway. It may take the form of giving false reasons for one's conduct. Alibiing is a form of rationalization. Sometimes a person finds his own thoughts or actions so intolerable that he ascribes them to another individual. Such an action constitutes *projection.* Examples of this can be found in the unfaithful husband who accuses his wife of infidelity or in the irritable person who accuses others of being irritable. The person who adopts this form of defense mechanism often believes his accusations to be true.

DISSATISFACTIONS ON THE JOB

In this chapter we have so far examined the needs and wants that human beings seek to satisfy in their quest for happiness and fulfillment in life. Then we have discussed ways in which people react when their motives and drives are blocked. We have discussed defense mechanisms and adaptive and maladaptive behavior. The employment situation provides abundant opportunities for need satisfactions for employees. Work can be meaningful; it can answer many (but not all) of workers' basic wants. Later in this chapter we shall examine ways in which management can create a working climate in which employees' needs are met.

Yet we find in every organization countless individuals and groups who are dissatisfied and frustrated. It is true that some may have been maladjusted when first hired. Others may have been emotionally mature, well-adjusted individuals at the time of hiring, but over the ensuing years they may have experienced so many insurmountable obstacles on the job (inadequate pay, difficult boss, lack of advancement, and so on) that they acquired serious tensions and anxieties. A third category consists of those who have encountered severe disruptions in their private lives off the job (for example, family or financial problems). In actual practice it may not be possible to ascribe a person's source of discontent and frustration solely to personal background, to the job situation, or to home pressures. It may be a composite of many influences.

There is little doubt that in our society a person's job exerts a powerful influence upon his well-being. A wage earner devotes about one quarter of his entire adult life to his job. His job establishes his economic and social station in life. Loss of a job can mean hardship and loss of status. The many anxieties and pressures encountered at work can have a profound effect upon one's personality and happiness.

Unfortunately much of the work in our society is performed under conditions where the employees experience boredom, monotony, anxiety, and frustration. The dissatisfactions with one's job situation may be classified into the following categories: (1) nature of the work, (2) job insecurity, (3) interpersonal relations, and (4) upward mobility and status.

Nature of the Work.   Much of the work performed in our industrialized society is perceived by the workers to be routine, repetitive, boring, and monotonous. Consider the very subdivided tasks carried out on the assembly line in an automobile factory. The process of tightening a few bolts upon cars that pass by in an endless parade is anything but stimulating. The same conditions exist in much white-collar office work—routine typing, filing, sorting, and recording of numbers. Boredom and monotony are not products just of twentieth century industrial life. Writers such as Adam Smith, Fourier, and Proudhon in the eighteenth and nineteenth centuries described and condemned excessive division of labor and its depressing effects upon man.[2]

Job Insecurity.   Although life is filled with insecurities (for example, injuries, sickness, insufficient income in old age), the principal one attributable directly to one's job is the threat of unemployment. In a free-enterprise business system there are periodic expansions and contractions in the economy. Over the long span there tend to be more years during which unemployment is high than years during which it is low. Even during periods of general business prosperity, there exist pockets of unemployment. Certain regions such as the coal areas of West Virginia and Pennsylvania have been chronically depressed. In the central urban sections of our large metropolitan areas, unemployment among Negroes has been persistently high. Unemployment hits the poorly educated and the unskilled most hard.

Another form of job insecurity is that caused by threats of discharge due to alleged ineffectiveness, personality clashes, rules infractions, and the like. Certainly some of these terminations are justified on their merits. Nevertheless, a great many employees are discharged every day throughout industry without benefit of due process procedures of administrative justice.

Interpersonal Relations.   A wide variety of dissatisfactions and tensions can be classified under this heading. There may be jealousies and rivalries between individuals in the same office. There may be conflicts between workers on "tight" piece rates and those on "loose" rates. But a primary one that is critical in all organizations is that between a man

---

[2] Georges Friedmann, *Industrial Society* (New York: The Free Press, 1955), pp. 129-132.

and his boss. An employee's immediate superior controls most of the rewards and penalties he receives from his job. He provides training and makes work assignments. He checks upon the quality of his output. He dispenses praise and criticism. The boss is largely instrumental in determining pay increases and promotions as well as transfers, demotions, and discharges. To a considerable extent the authority system makes the employee very dependent upon his supervisor. The employee, being aware of his position, tends to seek the approbation of his superior. Any feeling by the person that he is being mistreated, slighted, bypassed, or discriminated against can cause tension, anxiety, and frustration.

Upward Mobility and Status. A fourth major cause of dissatisfaction for employees is that associated with their inner aspirations—with their expectations from employment. Some people are satisfied with an average paying job that provides a reasonable measure of job security. They do not expect to gratify many of their wants and drives on the job. Instead they gain most of their satisfaction in life off the job, that is, through family, friends, social clubs, recreation, and leisure-time activities. On the other hand, there are others for whom their career is a way of life. They look to their work as a major source of fulfillment not only for their basic economic wants but also for some of their social, and most significantly, their egoistic drives. They have high aspirations. They seek continual raises in income, promotion up the organization ladder, and high status both within their organizations and in their communities at large. Those who fail to meet their self-established measures of success may experience real status anxiety. They may be frustrated because their upward mobility has been blocked.

ADDITIONAL MOTIVATION THEORIES

So far in this chapter, we have studied motivation by examining basic human needs and wants and by discussing Maslow's hierarchy of needs. Let us now turn to two other theories of motivation. The first has been formulated by psychologist Frederick Herzberg. It is a theory of motivation in the context of a work organization. That is, it is a theory of work motivation rather than a more general theory of human motivation. The other by Harvard psychologist David McClelland is concerned with achievement motivation, not only in the context of individuals but also in the context of achievement drives in entire societies.

Motivation—Hygiene Theory

In the late 1950's Professor Herzberg and his research associates conducted careful interviews with two hundred engineers and accountants who worked for eleven different companies in the Pittsburgh area. This research endeavor was designed to test the concept that man has two sets of needs: (1) his lower order needs to avoid loss of life, hunger, pain, and other deprivations and (2) his needs to grow psychologically. Included under his psychological growth needs are those of knowing more, seeing more relationships in what one knows, creativity, being effective in vague situations, maintaining individuality in the face of group pressures, and real growth through self-achievement.

The interviewers asked these men to tell about events in the course of their employment which caused them to feel a marked improvement in job satisfaction and also about those situations which caused a substantial reduction in job satisfaction. A great many probing questions were asked in each interview to pinpoint just how and why the people felt as they did and how their feelings affected their job performance and personal relationships.

When the results of the research were analyzed, the researchers found that one group of factors accounted for high levels of job satisfaction. These were labeled *motivators* because they seemed to be effective in motivating the individual to superior performance and effort. These factors were *achievement, recognition, work itself, responsibility,* and *advancement.* All of these satisfiers related to the job content.

Another group of factors, labeled *hygienic or maintenance* factors seemed to focus discontent with their work situation. However, these factors were seldom mentioned by the respondents as causing positive job satisfaction. These factors pertained primarily to the job context or environment. These factors were *company policy and administration, supervision, salary, interpersonal relations,* and *working conditions.*

M. Scott Myers has independently replicated the motivator-hygienic factor research at the Texas Instruments Company using as subjects scientists, engineers, manufacturing supervisors, technicians, and female hourly assemblers. His findings are very similar to—and essentially support—the original Herzberg conclusions.[3]

What are the practical implications of this research? The hygienic or maintenance factors provide an essential base upon which to build. If employees' wages, fringe benefits, working conditions, eating facilities, job rights, and status systems are inadequate, they will feel uneasy and discontent. They may complain openly about job conditions and company policies. They may even become very antagonistic toward the company. However, if all of these maintenance needs are taken care of adequately, the people will not necessarily work any harder. But these factors

---

[3] The original motivator-hygienic factor theory is presented in Frederick Herzberg, Bernard Mausner, and Barbara B. Snyderman, *The Motivation to Work* (2nd Ed., New York: John Wiley & Sons, Inc., 1959). For an account of Myers' independent replication see M. Scott Myers, "Who are Your Motivated Workers?," *Harvard Business Review,* Vol. 42, No. 1 (January-February 1964), pp. 73-88. For accounts of other replications see Frederick Herzberg, *Work and the Nature of Man* (Cleveland: The World Publishing Company, 1966), Chs. 7 and 8.

do serve as a base upon which to add the motivators to improve job performance.

It is true that certain people, in these studies, reported that they received job satisfaction solely from maintenance factors. Herzberg has asserted that such individuals show only a temporary satisfaction when hygiene factors are improved, they show little interest in the kind and quality of their work, they experience little satisfaction from accomplishments, and they tend to show a chronic dissatisfaction with various aspects of job context (such as pay, status, and job security).[4]

How can top management apply Herzberg's motivators—achievement, recognition, the work itself, responsibility, and advancement—in a practical way to create a high level of job performance? It must create a climate where employees and managers can reach satisfactions for their higher-order needs. Some of the specific leadership practices that it can institute are delegation of responsibility and authority, job enrichment, full utilization of employees' skills and training, establishment of an atmosphere of approval toward subordinates, granting of earned pay increases, and granting promotions when deserved.

Herzberg holds that motivation seekers are motivated by the nature of the work itself, have a higher tolerance for poor hygienic factors, and show capacity to enjoy their work.[5]

Although numerous researchers have independently replicated Herzberg's two-dimensional theory of work motivation, the theory does have its critics. Some scholars and researchers have commented that this two-factor explanation of job satisfaction is a great oversimplification of the whole motivational complex of the world of work. Also the Herzberg research technique does not include any statistical correlations between the *motivators* and actual job performance. Vroom has asserted that employees who are interviewed may attribute the causes of their satisfaction to their own achievements on the job while they ascribe their dissatisfactions, not to their own inadequacies, but to factors in the work environment (hygienic factors).[6] Some studies also show that hourly-paid blue-collar workers place more emphasis upon maintenance factors (such as pay and job security) than do higher-level employees. In effect maintenance or hygienic factors may be considered as motivators by blue-collar people.[7] Regardless of the criticisms, however, the motivator-hygienic

---

[4] Herzberg, *Work and the Nature of Man,* p. 90.

[5] *Ibid.*

[6] Victor H. Vroom, *Work and Motivation* (New York: John Wiley & Sons, Inc., 1964), p. 129.

[7] Critiques of the motivator-hygienic two factor theory are contained in Victor H. Vroom, *op. cit.,* pp. 127-129; Lyman W. Porter, "Personnel Management," *Annual Review of Psychology,* Vol. 17 (1966), p. 411; A. Kornhauser, *Mental Health of the Industrial Worker* (New York: John Wiley & Sons, Inc., 1965); and Orlando Behling, George Labovitz, and Richard Kosmo, "The Herzberg Controversy: A Critical Reappraisal," *Academy of Management Journal,* Vol. 11, No. 1 (March 1968), pp. 99-108.

factor theory of Herzberg has received considerable support from independent investigators. Although not all employees are motivated primarily by job content (we already know that humans are very complex and variable), the theory does provide a very useful way of analyzing work motivation and of predicting the probable employee responses to managerial leadership practices.

Intrinsic and Extrinsic Motivation

Intrinsic motivation is that which occurs while a person is performing an activity in which he gains satisfaction from engaging in that activity itself. This is internal reward. It is directly part of the job content. Extrinsic motivators are the incentives or rewards that a person can enjoy after he finishes his work. This is related to the job environment or an external reward.

Traditionally work has been viewed as necessary drudgery. Rewards came in the form of pay, which was enjoyed off the job; holidays and vacations, which were enjoyed off the job; cafeterias and lounges, which were enjoyed away from the job; and pensions, which were received after retirement from work.

Modern behavioral research has tended to emphasize that work itself can be satisfying. This has been postulated in the writings of Herzberg, just discussed, and of other behavioral scientists such as Rensis Likert, Chris Argyris, and Douglas McGregor.

Managers in some of our more enlightened corporations have been applying this concept by placing people on jobs for which they are trained and are interested, by new concepts of job design and work flow, and by gearing recognition directly to the job.

Although there are those enthusiasts for intrinsic motivation who would substantially downgrade all efforts toward extrinsic motivation, in reality both are necessary. If working conditions, wages, job security and fringe benefits are inadequate, a company will find it difficult to recruit and retain good people. Turnover, absenteeism, and grievances tend to be high where management ignores external forms of reward. Large bureaucracies, in both government and industry, tend to do quite well in meeting peoples' maintenance needs. What they so often lack is emphasis upon challenging assignments, an encouragement of innovation, and large rewards for achievement. By emphasizing job tenure, loyalty, and conformity, bureaucracies tend to repel those with an enterprising spirit and drive.

A sound motivational climate must provide both extrinsic and intrinsic motivators.

Achievement Motivation

Beginning in the 1940's, a group of researchers led by Harvard psychologist David C. McClelland began investigating the achievement motive in people. For a measuring instrument they used a projective test of personality, the Thematic Apperception Test. In this research, subjects were shown a series of pictures and then asked to tell a story about each picture. This technique reveals the inner dynamics of a person's personality. What does a man think about and what does he daydream about when he is not required to think about anything in particular? If a man spends his time thinking about doing things better—about building, creating, and doing—then psychologists say he has an achievement orientation. On the other hand if one spends his time thinking about his family and friends, he has an affiliation orientation. Of course the reader will recognize that most people are not entirely achievement-oriented or entirely affiliation-oriented. They posses some of each. But there are people who lean much more in one direction than the other.[8]

McClelland's research, which has now been carried on for many years, has uncovered some important things about achievement-oriented people. They actually tend to translate their thinking into action. They are not idle dreamers. They place great demands upon themselves. They are persistent and they are realists. They are not romantics.

For the achiever accomplishment is often an end in itself. This is comparable to the mountain climber who was asked why he continually tried to scale Mount Everest. His answer "Because it is there," has become classic.[9]

The achievement-oriented individual believes in moderate risk-taking. He is not a reckless-adventurer. Rather he takes calculated risks. He also tends to be very sanguine about his likelihood of success. He is persistent for the long-term pull. Such individuals also seek concrete feedback on how they are doing.

How do high achievement-oriented people get that way? Parental influence is paramount. The parents set high standards of accomplishment. They show warmth and encouragement. The father is not domineering nor authoritarian. Discipline is consistent and specific, but it is neither harsh nor all-pervasive. Overly disciplined children tend to be overregulated and docile. McClelland found that middle-class parents—managers, professionals, and entrepreneurs—tend to impart a decidedly stronger achievement drive than do lower-class parents.

People also acquire their achievement drive (or lack of it) from the culture and predominant values of the society in which they live. McClelland has charted the tendencies of many societies throughout the world and for different periods in history. He did this by coding the contents of the literature of a people. School books were especially useful. The values imparted to the youth are instrumental in shaping that nation's future.

---

[8] David C. McClelland, *The Achieving Society,* Princeton, N. J.: D. Van Nostrand Company, 1961.

[9] This statement was made by the British mountaineer George Leigh Mallory, who tried to scale Everest repeatedly in the early 1920's. Tragically he perished in 1924 when very near the top.

The United States scores high in achievement. Business careers offer abundant opportunities for realization of this motive. The Protestant ethic helped shape this orientation in the population. In recent years the Soviet Union has also scored high in the achievement motive. McClelland has found a positive coefficient of correlation of .53 between achievement scores derived from the literature of twenty-two nations and their subsequent economic growth rate.[10]

Unfortunately, the present stage of the development of psychological testing does not permit the accurate use of the Thematic Apperception Test or a similar test for picking high achievement-oriented employees. The TAT can be used for research purposes to distinguish among groups of people, but it cannot be used reliably and validly for individual prediction. However, personnel specialists can make general predictions by evaluating all the data available on job candidates. Past achievements are a reasonable guide to future performance if one really knows how to interpret this evidence.

After people are on the payroll, management bears the responsibility of establishing a leadership climate that encourages the achievement motive to thrive in the organization.

MORALE AND PRODUCTIVITY

For a great number of years, it has been assumed that a work force which possesses high morale is also likely to exhibit high productivity. It has seemed logical to managers that happy workers are also productive workers. Indeed this condition did hold for the Relay Assembly Test Room in the pioneering Hawthorne experiments conducted by Elton Mayo and his Harvard associates in 1927-1929. There was a definite correlation between their increasing productivity and the favorable attitudes that the girls had toward each other, their supervisor, and their environment.

However, recent research investigators have demonstrated that there is no simple relationship between morale and productivity. Enough instances of high productivity and low morale and of high morale and low productivity have been observed to cast doubt upon the once assumed direct relationship. The heart of the matter is that morale is a complex concept. It includes many facets.

Some writers have emphasized the satisfaction of needs as a dimension of morale. Others have stressed the social approach by concentrating upon group bonds and friendships. Still others have emphasized attitudes toward supervision, the work, and the organization. And finally other writers have concentrated upon the interaction of personality with the work situation. Recognizing that morale is multidimensional, let us define it as the *total satisfactions a person derives from his job, his work*

[10] David C. McClelland, "Business Drive and National Achievement," *Harvard Business Review,* Vol. 40 (July-August 1962).

*group, his boss, the organization, and his environment. It is also affect-
ed by his personality structure. Morale pertains to the general feeling
of well-being, satisfaction, and happiness of people.*

Productivity is output divided by input. Commonly the productivity
of an industry or of an establishment is measured by the total physical
or dollar volume of output divided by the man-hours of input for a given
time span. The productivity of a work group or of individuals is generally expressed in terms of the units produced during a given time period,
say a day, week, or month. Productivity of routine repetitive work is easy
to measure. But the output of creative and intellectual efforts is very difficult to measure. Thus professional and executive work accomplishments
may have a long time span before completion and considerable judgment
may be required to determine the real value of work done.

Vroom has tabulated the results of twenty investigations into the relationship between morale (job satisfaction in Vroom's terms) and job
performance. These studies were made by many researchers working
independently. They pertained to such diverse occupational groups as
insurance agents, bus drivers, female office employees, sales clerks, farmers, and supervisors in a package delivery company. Statistical correlations
between satisfaction and performance ranged from $+ .86$ to $- .31$ with
a median of $+ .14$ for all studies.[11] Thus there seems to be a low but
positive relationship between overall morale or job satisfaction and productivity of various work groups in general. Yet there are enough instances
of negative correlations to alert us to the fact that intervening factors may
be present.

For various reasons, productivity can be reasonably good while morale
is low. Many industrial plants are highly engineered. Output may be high
under machine-paced and assembly line conditions. Jobs may have been
carefully analyzed, improved, and subdivided by industrial engineers.
Materials and parts may flow smoothly from work station to work station.
In-process inventory may be kept at a minimum. Measured daywork standards may have been established for each worker's job. Under such conditions productivity of shop departments may be good even though employees dislike their jobs and their conditions of work.

Rensis Likert claims that the relationship between morale and productivity for complex and varied work such as research, engineering, and
life insurance selling tends to be moderately high.[12] It seems that where
the performance depends solely upon the man or the team and where
the job cannot be engineered, then those employees who feel favorably
disposed toward their job situation are also more likely to be motivated
to produce.

Situations where morale is high but performance is poor also occur
with some frequency. This discrepancy can occur where a pleasant, social,

---

[11] Victor H. Vroom, *op. cit.,* pp. 183-185.

[12] Rensis Likert, *New Patterns of Management* (New York: McGraw-Hill Book Company,
Inc., 1961), Ch. 6.

country-club atmosphere is encouraged or permitted by supervision. The people may gain considerable pleasure from coming to the office each day to meet their friends and socialize. But the motivation to produce may be minimal.

Actually job attitudes and morale can be quite positive for two reasons. The first has just been given above. Employees gain social satisfaction from interactions at the workplace. Working conditions and supervision may be good. Second, high morale may result from high motivation to produce. Much recent behavioral research has demonstrated that when a leadership and work-group climate is structured to generate high work motivation, then employee satisfactions and attitudes are often positive. In other words, management should put its eggs in the basket that creates a highly motivated work force. Good morale and job satisfaction are likely to follow. But if top management spends its efforts on morale building programs *only,* for instance, wages, working conditions, recreation programs, and financial benefits, it will become disillusioned when work performance remains low. It should not be assumed, however, that money spent on morale-building programs is necessarily wasted. Numerous investigations have demonstrated that there is a positive correlation between high morale and low turnover and low absenteeism. Worker loyalty and stability are important.

APPLYING MOTIVATIONAL CONCEPTS

We have, so far, discussed a number of basic concepts and theoretical foundations for understanding individual behavior, motivation, and reactions to blocking of motives. The executive must be able to apply his knowledge of human behavior dynamics to real work situations in order to elicit acceptable performance from his work force. There is no simple formula to tell the manager how to lead and motivate his people. The executive must be perceptive to the character of his people and the demands of the situation. He must be adaptable and flexible in applying motivational principles. Responses of employees are a function of the reward system and how they perceive the rewards as satisfying their needs.

The old fashioned simple logics of the "carrot and the stick" are inadequate. People will not necessarily produce better in response to the chance to make more money; nor will they perform better under threats to their job security.

Positive and Negative Incentives

The leader who wants his subordinates to adopt a particular form of behavior, for example, better attendance or higher output, can either offer rewards to them for successful fulfillment or threaten to apply penalties. The first utilizes positive incentives, whereas the second employs negative incentives. Both methods are widely used in practice. The auto-cratic approach is to rule through fear and force.

There are decided limitations to rule by threats, force, and fear. Such rule tends to generate only the minimum employee effort necessary to avoid punishment. People do not put enthusiasm into their work. Their efforts are directed toward "not getting caught" rather than doing what the leader desires. Second, the imposition of punishment frequently causes frustration to those punished. This manifests itself in maladaptive behav-ior that is not goal directed. The use of punishment does not teach people what *to do;* it highlights what not to do. Punishment also creates a hostile state of mind. Hostility may mean overt or passive resistance. Rapport between the leader and the led is then broken. The organization may suf-fer. In the world of work, in factory, office, and military, negative incen-tives are often used because this seems easy to the leader. It requires less effort to criticize and threaten than it does to teach and encourage desired behavior.

Positive motivation—both intrinsic and extrinsic—is generally the soundest choice in most situations. Rewarding good work develops a feel-ing of well-being in the employee. Reinforcement—the strengthening of the probability of a response—occurs and the individual will tend to contin-ue to exert energy to attain agreed-upon goals. There are of course some occasions when negative incentives are appropriate. Very young children often cannot understand the reasons why they must obey their parents. It is not always possible for the parent to create a positive incentive to induce his child to pick up his toys or to stop annoying the new baby. With adults there are certain emergency situations, for example, fire, panic, riot, where threat of punishment and force must be used to attain the de-sired behavior. Also in dealing with his group of employees the supervi-sor may find that positive rewards are effective for the majority, but that a few must be cajoled and threatened. In most instances the positive ap-proach would work even with the recalcitrant ones, however, the super-visor may not have time to develop it with certain individuals.

Integration of Goals

A desirable and somewhat idealized system of work motivation is to provide opportunities for need satisfaction through doing the job itself. The object of this pattern of motivation is to develop employee commit-ment to the objectives of the organization. Management sets up a system of rewards which causes high levels of job satisfaction at the same time that the employees are working productively to meet the objectives of their job, department, and plant.

Such a system of motivation is the essence of what Douglas McGregor called Theory Y management.[13] Rensis Likert has called it System 4 man-

[13] Douglas McGregor, *The Human Side of Enterprise* (New York: McGraw-Hill Book Com-pany), 1960.

agement.[14] It is at the heart of Herzberg's motivator-hygiene theory. This approach holds that people will exercise self-direction and self-control in working for objectives to which they are committed. They will become committed to working for organization goals to the extent that they gain real satisfaction from doing so. This style of leadership has sometimes been called "management by integration and self-control."

It emphasizes openness and trust, supportive supervision, and participation in decision making. It activates all motives—economic, social, and egoistic. To a considerable extent employees can gratify many of their drives for security, belongingness, status, self-expression, self-significance, and achievement right on the job.

This system of motivation works best in situations where the people have some freedom to exercise their own initiative, where they can see a direct connection between their efforts and the performance of their organizational unit, and where their work careers constitute a dominant focus in their lives. These conditions fit many executives. They are dedicated to their work and their organizations. They enjoy their jobs so much that the jobs do not seem like work to them. They adopt a proprietary interest in their companies. Not only is intrinsic motivation maximized but so is extrinsic motivation. These people exercise considerable influence and power. They can make things happen. They may command vast human and material resources. Their opinions mean much both in their organizations and in their communities. They enjoy prestige, high status, and high pay. They are operating at the high end of Maslow's hierarchy of needs.

Many other types of people in our society tend to enjoy this highly satisfactory motivational situation. This is true for many professionals such as college professors, attorneys, economists, engineers, and scientists. This integration of goals also tends to hold true for the self-employed and the small businessman.

However, it must be admitted that it is very difficult for workers on low level, repetitive jobs to experience this form of motivation. They may have been conditioned by past experience to expect no real satisfaction from their work. They may stay on their jobs and perform solely for their pay. Their jobs may have been so highly engineered or regimented that there is no opportunity for growth, recognition, and achievement. Presently we shall see how imaginative job design and work flow can often be used to really encourage a superior level of work motivation on routine jobs.

Job Design and Work Flow

As we have said many of the jobs in the world of work are perceived by job holders to be very uninteresting, boring, and monotonous. This

---

[14] Rensis Likert, *The Human Organization* (New York: McGraw-Hill Book Company, 1967).

dislike of the work itself may be quite apart from the fact that other aspects of the total working environment may be either pleasing or distasteful to the employees. What can be done with respect to the design of jobs and the flow of work to motivate employees and increase job satisfaction? There are a number of possibilities.

Job Enlargement. Job enlargement has been developed in recent years as a counteraction to the extreme specialization promoted by the scientific management movement. There are two kinds of job enlargement: horizontal and vertical. Horizontal job enlargement involves adding additional tasks to a short cycle repetitive job. Thus assemblers on a transformer assembly line may have initially been performing individual simple operations as the assembly moved along the line. The jobs can be enlarged by setting up work stations and having each worker build the entire unit. Thus each assembler will cable, wind, solder, laminate, and fasten the entire item.

Vertical job enlargement allows workers to do some planning and control functions in addition to the actual making or servicing routines. Formerly these functions would have been handled entirely by inspectors and supervisors. Of course it is possible to combine horizontal with vertical job loading. An additional variety of tasks may be put into a job at the same time that the employee is given certain planning and control duties. Frederick Herzberg asserts that vertical (or combined vertical and horizontal) job loading constitutes true *job enrichment.* By increasing the accountability of individuals for their own work, having them do a complete module of work, introducing more complex tasks, and granting authority to make job decisions, he maintains that many of the higher motives such as growth, learning, responsibility, and achievement are activated.

Herzberg has described an experiment in job enrichment using experimental and control groups. The subjects were stockholder correspondents of a very large corporation. Before job enrichment was introduced, indices of performance and satisfaction had been low. The jobs were enriched by having the correspondents sign their own letters, answer letters in a more personalized way, and by being personally accountable for the quality and accuracy of letters. Outgoing mail went directly to the mailroom without going over the supervisors' desks for checking. For this experimental group both the performance and job attitudes indices substantially increased over the course of the six-month study period. These measures were well ahead of those for the control group. The job enrichment group also evidenced a lower rate of absenteeism.[15]

One large-scale project in vertical job enlargement conducted at Texas Instruments involved 700 assemblers. It resulted in substantial cost re-

[15] For a fuller discussion of job enrichment concepts and experimental evidence, see Frederick Herzberg, "One More Time: How Do You Motivate Employees?," *Harvard Business Review,* Vol. 46, No. 1 (January-February 1968), pp. 53-62.

duction, less absenteeism and tardiness, and fewer complaints and personal problems.[16]

However, job enlargement is not a panacea. The response of employees to such restructuring depends considerably upon their attitudes toward work and the culture of the employee population one is concerned with. Some people like simple, straightforward jobs which carry no challenge. After an extensive analysis of the available research evidence, Hulin and Blood have postulated that worker response depends upon whether the workers are alienated or nonalienated from middle-class achievement values. They maintain that blue-collar workers in big cities are likely to be alienated and therefore will not respond to job enlargement. However blue-collar workers from rural areas and white-collar people from both urban and rural environments are likely to be motivated positively by job enlargement.[17]

Job Rotation.   Something akin to job enlargement can be obtained by periodically shifting employees from one job to another. This helps to overcome monotony on very routine, repetitive jobs. Maier has described an industrial application where job rotation helped relieve boredom. There were two jobs, solderers and dusters, in the central office of a telephone company. These were performed by women. The dusters had continuously to go over the equipment to keep it clean, and the solderers constantly looked for broken connections, which they then repaired. Morale was low, and turnover was serious. By permitting the women to exchange jobs every two hours, not only did morale improve, but also productivity increased.[18]

Rest Periods.   Rest periods, of course, are widely used in industry. For boring, monotonous work they not only relieve fatigue, but they also give the employees something to look forward to. They can talk with their associates, smoke, or have a soda.

Larger Units of Accomplishment.   To the inspector who visually examines objects as they come endlessly off the production line, his job can indeed be monotonous. However, by segregating the production units into batches or runs, he can achieve a greater sense of accomplishment when each batch is complete. Most of us have undertaken tasks that seemed endless. However, by establishing subgoals on the road to completion, we gain a sense of making real progress as we do our work. Examples occur in such activities as addressing Christmas cards, cutting the lawn, pulling weeds from the garden, or painting one's house.

[16] Earl R. Gomersall and M. Scott Myers, "Breakthrough in On-the-Job Training," *Harvard Business Review,* Vol. 44, No. 4 (July-August 1966), p. 63.

[17] Charles L. Hulin and Milton R. Blood, "Job Enlargement, Individual Differences, and Worker Responses," *Psychological Bulletin,* Vol. 69, No. 1 (1968), pp. 41-55.

[18] Norman R. F. Maier, *Psychology in Industry* (2nd Ed., Houghton Mifflin Company, 1955), p. 476.

Participation

Participation means the physical and mental involvement of people in an activity. Specifically, in the field of personnel management, the term has come to mean the involvement of employees in decision making. In this sense it means primarily mental involvement and ego involvement. Many managers speak loosely of developing participation in their employees. They exhort employees to "put their shoulders to the wheel," to help management cut costs, to attend company social functions, and to give generously to the Community Chest drive. These activities do not constitute true participation. Genuine participation includes those situations in which management actively encourages employees and lower-echelon managers to help make decisions regarding the business and the work. Although it is top management's job to set policy and establish overall goals, there is plenty of opportunity for subordinate members of the organization to participate in decision making in such areas as production methods, materials handling, cost reduction, safety, employee relations problems, and working conditions.

Participation in decision making can take many forms: consultative supervision, democratic supervision, multiple management, labor-management cooperation, suggestion programs, and others.

Chapter 19 will explore the subject of participation in depth.

Money as a Motivator

Money should be looked upon as one instrument among many for managing motivation. Managers in industry often tend to place major reliance upon pay, bonuses, and money incentives because it is easiest to manipulate. But the results do not always justify the efforts to use money as a motivator. There is abundant evidence that many blue-collar workers will deliberately restrict output even when working on a direct wage-incentive plan. The prospect of a steady income does not always induce the culturally deprived poor to work steadily.

Yes, pay is important for providing the material necessities of life. But it is most important for what it symbolizes to the recipient. To use pay effectively as a motivational tool the manager must study his people, the conditions under which they work, and the tasks they perform. Many jobs require close team cooperation. For such jobs an individual pay-incentive plan can be destructive of group cooperation. On the other hand, a wage incentive plan that rewards all members of the group for increased team output can be effective.

The value of money is determined by what people have learned to associate it with. For the young female secretary, a good salary symbolizes stylish clothes in abundance. For the young married father it represents a down payment on a home. For the executive who has just been promoted, a substantial pay boost tells him that his company superiors think highly of him. It is an index of progress.

McClelland points out that several research studies have revealed that persons who score high in achievement motivation on psychological tests do not work harder for the prospect of making more money alone. They are motivated by the love of accomplishment, interest in their work, and by success itself. The money comes afterward and of course is appreciated. On the other hand, people with a low achievement drive quite often will work for more money when it symbolizes something that they dearly want.[19] Such people tend to have no intrinsic interest in their work. But they will strive for the things money can buy such as a new automobile, a new television set, or a vacation cruise in the Caribbean.

There are of course some people who have almost an obsessive interest in money. From youth onward they have saved money and calculated how to make it multiply. Often times they go into business for themselves. Even after they have accumulated a large amount of money, larger in fact than needed to meet their desires for luxuries, they strive for more and more. For these people money fills some void in their lives. It may symbolize love and security or the affection that was missing in childhood. It stands in place of some deep-felt need of which the individual may not be fully conscious.

Competition

Competition as a form of motivation is widely used in our society. Examples that first come to mind for most of us are, perhaps, the competition that occurs in sporting events (both amateur and professional) and in games among friends, for example, a game of cards. In business, competition is most commonly used in sales departments. It is practically standard practice to have salesmen compete against one another for various awards and prizes. Another form of competition is that which takes place among members of the management hierarchy in most organizations for the prize of a promotion. Because there are fewer positions as one approaches the top of the organizational pyramid, the competition can get very intense and at times even vicious. If a number of people are striving for the same goal, and if that goal is attainable by only the one who wins, we know that such competition can motivate many people to give their maximum efforts.

However, competition has serious limitations when used within an organization. If, for example, all of the members of one department are competing for a single promotion, considerable jealousy and hostility are bound to develop among the employees. Mutual cooperation will

[19] David C. McClelland, "Money as a Motivator: Some Research Insights," *The McKinsey Quarterly* (Fall 1967), pp. 10-21.

be poor. So in this case individualistic competition will in most cases cause a destruction of teamwork. In this situation where people are competing for a promotion that can go to only one, the standards for selection of the winner can seldom be completely objective. Therefore, the losers may justifiably consider that bias and favoritism entered into the selection.

Another serious disadvantage of competition as a motivator is the frustration experienced by the losers. Any of the various forms of behavior induced by frustration may occur: aggression, regression, resignation, fixation, sublimation, and so on.

If the stakes are high, if the penalty for losing is great, then we find destruction of teamwork, lower morale, and frustration to be common consequences.

Cultural factors affect the attitude of different types of people toward competition. Blue-collar factory workers are less likely to respond to competition than executive and professional employees. Blue-collar employees often band together to protect themselves from the harmful effects of competition. Unions, for example, advocate seniority rules as a method of avoiding the loss of security that might occur as a result of competition.

Questions for Review and Discussion

1. Explain the meaning of the following concepts:
   a. Self-concept
   b. Personality
   c. Motive
   d. Defense mechanism
2. What are the basic needs of people? Distinguish between innate and acquired needs.
3. What are some of the characteristics of acquired needs?
4. Explain Maslow's hierarchy of needs.
5. Explain Herzberg's motivation-hygiene theory.
6. Distinguish between intrinsic and extrinsic motivation.
7. What are the characteristics of high-achievement-oriented persons?
8. Distinguish between morale and motivation. If workers have high morale, is their productivity also likely to be high?
9. How can individual motives and organizational goals be integrated?
10. Distinguish between horizontal and vertical job enlargement. How does job enlargement affect motivation?
11. Discuss the importance of money as a motivator.
12. Analyze the satisfactions you have obtained from the various jobs you have held. What differences do you note?

Simulation Exercise

Zif, Jay J., *Managing the Worker* (Creative Studies Simulation), New York: The Macmillan Company, 1970.

Suggestions for Further Reading

Behling, Orlando, George Labovitz, and Richard Kosmo, "The Herzberg Controversy: A Critical Reappraisal," *Academy of Management Journal,* Vol. 11, No. 1, March 1968, pp. 99-108.

Berelson, Bernard, and Gary A. Steiner, *Human Behavior: An Inventory of Scientific Findings,* New York: Harcourt, Brace & World, 1964, Ch. 6.

Friedlander, Frank and Eugene Walton, "Positive and Negative Motivations Toward Work," *Administrative Science Quarterly,* Vol. 9, No. 2, September 1964, pp. 194-207.

Gellerman, Saul, *Management by Motivation,* New York: American Management Association, 1968.

————, *Motivation and Productivity,* New York: American Management Association, 1963.

Herzberg, Frederick, "One More Time: How Do You Motivate Employees?," *Harvard Business Review,* Vol. 46, No. 1, January-February 1968, pp. 53-62.

————, *Work and the Nature of Man,* Cleveland: World Publishing Company, 1966.

————, B. Mausner, and B. Snyderman, *The Motivation to Work,* 2nd Ed., New York: John Wiley & Sons, 1959.

McClelland, David C., "Money as a Motivator: Some Research Insights," *The McKinsey Quarterly,* Fall 1967, pp. 10-21.

————, *The Achieving Society,* Princeton, N.J.: D. Van Nostrand Company, 1961.

Maier, Norman R. F., *Psychology in Industry,* 3rd Ed., Boston: Houghton Mifflin Company, 1965, Ch. 14.

Maslow, A. H., *Motivation and Personality,* New York: Harper & Row, 1954.

Myers, M. Scott, "Who Are Your Motivated Workers?," *Harvard Business Review,* Vol. 42, No. 1, January-February 1964, pp. 73-88.

Porter, Lyman W. and Edward E. Lawler, III, "What Job Attitudes Tell About Motivation," *Harvard Business Review,* Vol. 46, No. 1, January-February 1968, pp. 118-126.

Sorcher, Melvin and Herbert H. Meyer, "Motivating Factory Employees," *Personnel,* Vol. 45, No. 1, January-February 1968.

Vroom, Victor H., *Work and Motivation,* New York: John Wiley & Sons, 1964

Whyte, William F., *et. al., Money and Motivation,* New York: Harper & Row, 1955.

Group Relations
and
Informal Organization

16

Man is a social being; much of what he does is carried on through groups. People gather themselves into groups to satisfy their needs for companionship, friendship, recognition from others, a sense of belonging, and security. As a member of a group they can often achieve gains that would not be possible for individuals working alone. Membership in groups affects men's attitudes and behavior toward the employer, the supervisor, the union, the customer, and the work itself.

People do not behave as isolated, independent individuals. Rather their actions are strongly conditioned by the pressures, norms, and culture of the groups to which they belong. In the past, management has tended to direct employees without reference to group effects. Wage payment plans, methods changes, work-load assignments, discipline, and training activities largely ignored group influences. Supervisors were conditioned to deal with their subordinates essentially as individuals.

In this chapter we shall be primarily concerned with work groups, friendship groups, and informal social groups within the context of the larger work or business organization. These groupings of people can usually be identified in terms of their group consciousness; an interdependence in the satisfaction of their needs; interaction among the members; and, upon occasion, group action in a unified manner to achieve a goal. The network of informal personal and social relations which exist in any organization and which are quite distinct from those prescribed by the formal organization structure are known as the *informal organization*. The informal organization and the groupings of people into work and friendship groups are intimately related.

The perceptive manager can notice countless examples of actions that are primarily the products of the informal organization and informal work groups. A group of machine operators may walk off their jobs because of a commonly felt dissatisfaction with their pay classification. A foreman may issue an order and receive a negative response because the work group believes it to be impractical or even impossible to carry out. A rumor of a contemplated mass layoff may spread like wildfire throughout the plant. When employees sense an emergency, such as a fire or similar catastrophe, they may exhibit extraordinary team effort to overcome the crisis. Some people, managers and employees alike, bypass the formal channels of communication in order to get things done. Certain individuals are promoted rapidly because of their membership in certain cliques. These are but common examples of the impact that the informal organization and informal work groups can have upon the operation of an enterprise.

Informal work groups are an inevitable fact of life in any organization. Managers who do not understand group behavior and who are sometimes frustrated by apparent obstruction from these groups often try to break them up. However, new group alignments will most certainly form.

The successful manager is the one who understands the nature of group forces, who is perceptive to group action, and who can blend group goals with those of the formal organization.

THE STUDY OF GROUP BEHAVIOR

Although group action has always been a basic ingredient of mankind, it was not until the turn of the present century that writers and theorists began to devote their attention to this phenomenon in a systematic fashion. Among the early pioneers were Durkheim, Simmel, and Cooley. Most of the early writers analyzed group behavior in a philosophical and theoretical way. As a rule, they did not conduct systematic research studies and experiments.

The actual beginning of the study of group processes in an organized, scientific way occurred in the 1930's. Kurt Lewin, a social psychologist, has been credited with making some of the most significant contributions to research and theory in this area of inquiry. It was he who popularized the use of the term *group dynamics.*

Group dynamics, as a term, is generally used in more than one way. Basically it designates the forces and actions that occur within a group of people. Every group has its own special dynamics. Groups also interact with other groups. People act and talk with one another, they form friendships and antagonisms, they cooperate and oppose, they respond to leadership, they develop common sentiments and beliefs—these are the elements of group dynamics. The term *group dynamics* is also used to designate an area of scientific study. It is an interdisciplinary branch of the social sciences drawing upon the disciplines of psychology, sociology, cultural anthropology, and political science. Researchers in these disciplines have conducted a great deal of empirical research in recent years. They have studied such problems as change and resistance to change, social pressure, power, influence, leadership, conformity, cohesion, and group motivation.

Kurt Lewin came to America from Germany in 1932. Between 1937 and 1940, working with Lippitt and White, he conducted experiments at the University of Iowa with children under three different styles of leadership: democratic, authoritarian, and laissez-faire. Lewin is best known for his formulation of "field theory," in which the researcher concentrates upon an analysis of the totality of facts that determine the behavior of a person rather than initially studying isolated elements. Working from the whole, the researcher then progressively makes refinements and analyzes the component parts.

Sociometry.   Another who has pioneered in the study of group behavior is Jacob L. Moreno, who developed the sociometric method of analysis in the mid-1930's. Moreno's contributions apply to both research and therapy. He has developed such techniques as sociometric tests, psychosociodrama, and role playing. A *sociometric test* is a method of measuring the social structure of a group. The test is conducted by asking every member of a given group to choose one or more persons within that group on the basis of a stipulated type of choice. Most commonly the persons are asked to name those who are their best friends or those with whom they would rather work as a team. They may be asked to list their first, second, and third choices, or they may simply list all with whom they would like to be associated.

The data collected from a sociometric test can be plotted in the form of a *sociogram.* Those receiving the largest number of choices are designated as informal leaders or stars. Those receiving very few or no choices are called isolates or least accepted individuals. A subgroup or clique consists of three or more persons who mutually choose each other.

It should be pointed out that the sociometric test may ask any of a number of questions, such as: "Who is the most efficient employee?" "With whom do you deal most frequently?" "Who is least liked?" "With whom do you spend most of your time?"

Sociometric analysis helps one determine the size and number of cliques within a group, the level of cohesiveness, who the informal leaders are, patterns of communication, who may be in need of personal counseling, and the need for restructuring the group.

Interaction Analysis.   Men such as Conrad Arensberg, William F. Whyte, George Homans, Robert Bales, and Eliot D. Chapple have emphasized the importance of analyzing interaction among people within the group. They use such tools for analysis as activities, interactions, and sentiments. Whyte points out that it is necessary to determine who initiates activity for whom and the frequency and source of initiation of interaction. He classifies sentiments in terms of self-concept, evaluation of activities, personal identification, and ranking of people and things.[1]

Industrial Research: Hawthorne Studies

Our present-day knowledge of human relations in industry, and in particular of groups, had its foundation in the famous experiments conducted at the huge Hawthorne plant of the Western Electric Company in Chicago during the years 1927-1932. This research program was carried on jointly by researchers from that company and those from the Graduate School of Business Administration of Harvard University. The Harvard team was led by Elton Mayo.

The main portion of these experiments consisted of the following parts:

1. Relay Assembly Test Room.
2. Interviewing Program.
3. Bank Wiring Observation Room.[2]

In the Relay Assembly Test Room experiment, six girls experienced in assembling electrical relays were taken from a large shop department and placed, under observation, in a separate room. The investigators wanted to find out the effect of the introduction of rest pauses and changes in the length of the work day upon productivity. They also wanted to determine the attitudes of the girls toward their work and the company. An accurate count was made of each girl's production by the hour, day, and week by means of an electrical mechanism. The test room observer kept records of the weather, temperature, humidity, and large portions of the girls' conversations.

The entire experiment in this Relay Assembly Test Room lasted a little over two years. It was divided into 13 experimental periods. The first period consisted of the two weeks just before the girls were placed in the room, when a record was made of their output of relays to establish a norm for each girl. During succeeding experimental periods, which ranged in length from 4 to 31 weeks, rest pauses were introduced and a number of changes were made in the length of the working day and the work week. The trend of the hourly output for the girls rose throughout this whole experiment, ranging from 10 per cent for the girl with the smallest increase to about

[1] William Foote Whyte, *Men at Work* (Homewood, Ill.: the Dorsey Press and Richard D. Irwin, Inc., 1961), Ch. 2.
[2] The most complete and authoritative explanation and interpretation of these experiments is contained in F. J. Roethlisberger and W. J. Dickson, *Management and the Worker* (Cambridge, Mass.: Harvard University Press, 1939).

40 per cent for the highest. Because output had risen steadily from period 1 through period 11 (which consisted of a 5- instead of a 5½-day work week and 2 rest periods per day), the experimenters decided to return to the original conditions of work as a control. Accordingly period 12 contained no rest pauses, no special lunches, and a full-length work week. To the astonishment of the researchers, output did not drop to what it had been in the beginning. Both daily and weekly output rose to a higher level than ever before. In the last experimental period light lunches and rest periods in morning and afternoon were reintroduced as they had been in certain of the preceeding periods. Output remained at its established high level.

What accounted for this steady increase in production? The experimental control period (number 12) revealed that the rest pauses, lunches, and shortened work day and week were not causal factors.

The explanation lay in the changed psychological and sociological climate of the situation. The girls had far different attitudes toward their supervision at the end of the experiment than they had at the beginning. They stated that the work now was fun. They expressed resentment at the close supervision they had received in their former department; here they had very little control from formal line supervision. They looked with favor upon the test room observer and considered him as their supervisor though in fact he was not. Conversation was permitted freely, whereas it had been restricted in their regular department.

The girls knew that they were taking part in an important experiment. They had frequent discussions with members of management and the research team. They were consulted before each experimental change was introduced. A high level of group morale and teamwork developed through the course of the program. When one of them had a legitimate claim to feeling tired, the others would work harder to make up for her output on that day. The girls mingled together socially after hours. Absenteeism declined from an annual rate of 15.2 to 3.5 days per girl.

In summary, then, the mental attitude of the group was very favorable to high production and high group morale. They liked the new supervisory relationship, felt freer, were the center of attention from management and the researchers, and developed good group cohesiveness.

The next major phase of the Hawthorne experiments consisted of a mass interviewing program designed to find out employee attitudes toward their work, their treatment, company policies and practices, and supervision. Although a great deal of useful information was gained through this interviewing program (one thing found was that more complete information could be derived if the nondirective interviewing technique were used), the only part that concerns us here is that which led up to the establishment of the Bank Wiring Observation Room.

Many of the employee comments could best be interpreted in the light of an individual's social relationships within the plant and his immediate work group. The interviewers found that the social groups in shop departments frequently exercised very strong control over the behavior of their individual members. Restriction of output was a common phenomenon. Informal leaders emerged in these groups. Group members clung together to protect themselves from external influences that they perceived as unfavorable. There was punishment of workers who produced too much.

Bank Wiring Observation Room.   To obtain knowledge of informal social group relationships, the researchers established the Bank Wiring Room. The work group consisted of 14 men—9 wiremen, 3 soldermen, and 2 inspectors—who were engaged in the assembly of terminal banks for telephone exchanges. This observation room was kept in existence for about seven months. No attempt was made to change the conditions of work except that an observer was placed in the room. Wages were paid under a type of group incentive plan in which the output of these men was added to that of the entire department. The percentage by which the total output of the department exceeded the established standard was added to each man's base pay. In effect this was a group-standard-hour plan.

In this study it was found that the group as a whole had decided that two banks of equipment (6000 to 6600 terminals) was all that would be produced per day. This was considerably less than the men could have turned out if they had wanted to maximize their earnings as the designers of the plant-incentive system assumed everyone would do. The men had vague fears that unfortunate consequences would occur if they produced more than two banks per day. They created tight social control over those who produced either too much or too little. High producers were labeled rate busters, whereas low producers were labeled chiselers. These suffered social ostracism. They were "binged"—given a sharp rap on the shoulder or arm—for deviating from the group established level of output.

Although the workers had not been closely acquainted before they were assigned to this room, a strong informal organization soon developed among them. This operated as a mechanism to protect them against the demands of the formal company organization. The men did a number of things that were officially against company policy and rules. To relieve monotony, wiremen and soldermen traded jobs. Many of them put in claims for more daywork allowances than they were entitled to. Some deliberately overstated the amount of their daily production.

The fourteen employees divided themselves into two subgroups or cliques. Each clique had its own games and activities, which it carried on during lunch period, breaks, and lulls in the work. One clique considered itself to be of a superior status to the other. In general the members of this subgroup conformed most closely in output and behavior to the informally established standard for the whole group.

One wireman in the high-status clique emerged as the informal leader of the entire 14-man group. He was a skillful worker and one of the two men whose daily output conformed consistently to the group established norm. He was a key member of the superior clique. This person was the best liked by all in the room. There was a great deal of communication between him and the other workers. He had been successful at expediting a supply of wire, whereas others had tried and failed.

In summary, the bank wiremen formed a very effective social organization that served to provide security and protection for the members against outside management pressures and against internal deviation.

FORMATION OF GROUPS

All of us belong to groups of one sort or another. In some cases we may be rather passive group members, whereas in others we maintain strong bonds within the group.

We can classify groups into those that exist within the work organization and those that are outside or apart from it. Examples of groups that are essentially within the industrial or other formal organization are a local industrial union, a departmental group, and a job group. Other groupings may consist of those on the same shift, those of a common national origin, those of the same age, and those having the same length of service. Friendship groupings quite often cut across department and job boundaries.

People also belong to friendship groups outside the work organization. These may consist of a group of neighbors or a group united by some common recreational, social, or political interest. Quite often there is overlap between one's friendship group outside the company and one's work group within the work establishment. In fact, some employers encourage employees to develop social and recreational ties with the people they rub elbows with at the plant because they believe this practice helps build devotion and loyalty toward the company.

Of course, in addition to those informal social groupings of people outside the boundaries of the work establishment, we find that many people have membership in numerous outside formal organizations, such as a church, fraternal lodge, social club, women's club, and a political association.

Informal social groupings are not static. People come and go. Workers are transferred, promoted, and laid off. Technology and work flow are frequently altered by management. People's interests and attitudes toward one another change over time. As external changes take place in the environment, quite often the original driving force behind the group ties becomes weakened or destroyed. If the incentive system of payment for the Bank Wiring Room of the Hawthorne experiments had been abolished and replaced by daywork, it is quite likely that the tight group control over member's output would have been relaxed.

Formation of Work Groups—How and Why

A new employee in a department tends to feel lost and alone initially. The older employees, to him, may seem self-satisfied, competent, and clannish. But then as the newcomer's work puts him into contact with others, he finds that they start conversing with him. Perhaps they chat when relaxing over a soda or a smoke during a rest period. Or perhaps the new man tags along as the others go to the cafeteria for their coffee break. If some of the old-timers are outgoing and congenial, they may take the initiative to invite the new employee into their group activities. They may play cards during lunch hour, or they may take a stroll around the block. Gradually the newcomer feels accepted as a regular member of the unit. Some of the others may tell him shortcuts to do the job faster. They may inform him about the idiosyncrasies of their supervisor. And they may tell him about work routines, pay procedures, and special rules to be observed. Soon he begins to feel a full-fledged team member. He may sense that the others will help him when needed. He will now be in on the gossip and plant rumors. Our hypothetical employee may then form sound friendships with certain others in the unit who seem to have the same interests and outlook as he does.

Groups often form out of the reactions of people to their environment. Thus there is considerable need for close ties and teamwork when employees are paid under a group-incentive arrangement. On the other hand with individual piece work jobs, there will be greater competition and less cooperation. Those who work on similar machines, in the same location, at the same pay, and under the same supervision are bound to feel a oneness because they have common problems and interests. The people in the machine accounting section, for example, will tend to feel that they are something special and that their needs are distinct from those in other units. The very fact that people who do similar work tend to have similar backgrounds will promote a feeling of solidarity. Graduate engineers working in the engineering design department of a large aircraft manufacturer generally look upon themselves as professionals, and therefore they adopt a common view toward their conditions of employment.

Let us now look at the specific reasons why people band together into groups. Sometimes the participants themselves cannot always verbalize their own motives for doing so. They may often act spontaneously. But the causes are still present even if those most closely involved do not express their motives and expectations. We can consider the reasons people form groupings as *benefits or advantages* of group membership if we wish.

Companionship and Friendship.   By joining a group a person acquires companions with whom he can interact and share experiences. Group membership gives one a feeling of belonging—of having a place where he fits in. He has someone who will listen, often sympathetically, when he finds it necessary to "blow off steam" about some irritation. Very few people enjoy being alone for extended periods of time; instead most persons derive satisfaction from working or playing with others. How many of us would enjoy taking a vacation cruise to Europe alone? Dealing with others breaks the monotony of the work routine. For example, employees usually look forward to a coffee break when they can socialize with their friends.

Security and Protection.   Membership in a group provides a measure of security for the participants. Although they may have some disagreements among themselves, the group will close ranks to defend itself and its members from outside threats. If a member gets into trouble, he can usually count upon his associates in the group to speak up and defend him. Sometimes workers will cover up for one another's mistakes to prevent trouble from the supervisor. Sometimes we find that a particular work group has a favorable position in terms of working conditions, freedom from management pressure, and pay, and it will do everything in its collective power to prevent any decline in status.

Advance Group's Position.   Quite often a group of employees will take positive steps to gain benefits for themselves. Usually this will be accomplished through an informal group leader (or leaders) supplemented by a show of solidarity from the membership. A key production worker may ask the industrial engineer and the foreman for a more favorable piece rate. Meanwhile the other workers may demonstrate that it is "impossible" to meet standards by deliberately restricting their output. Or a group of engineers may feel acutely the need for positive status symbols. Therefore they may demand bigger desks, private offices, or the right to take longer lunch hours. They may press their immediate superiors for company sponsorship of their attendance at professional society meetings.

Help with the Work.   Innumerable situations crop up every day when an employee needs assistance or advice from a fellow worker to accomplish his job. The social isolate often sorely misses the little assists that could be given him by others. A maintenance mechanic forewarns a fellow craftsman about a ticklish repair operation that he has worked on previously. One salesman counsels another salesman on how to handle a difficult account.

> Fred had been out of work for three months. He felt very elated when he was hired as a machine-tool operator at a local factory. Having worked as a boring-mill operator about ten years ago in another company, he felt he would be able to pick up the necessary know-how to run other machines from his foreman or from an on-the-job instructor. But alas, when he reported for work he found that there was no instructor and his foreman adopted a sink-or-swim attitude. Fred was highly tense his first few weeks on the job because he felt inadequate to operate the variety of machines he was assigned to run. Fortunately, he made friends easily, and soon his fellow workers came to his rescue to show him how to index his machine, what speeds and feeds to use, how to select appropriate cutters, and the like.

Communication and Information.   A work group serves as a good means of disseminating information and keeping the members informed of what is going on. Facts and rumors transmitted by word of mouth generally travel fast. People find it advantageous to be in the know; it helps them adjust to new developments as they occur.

Types of Groups

Most of the groups with which we are concerned in this chapter are face-to-face ones. By *face-to-face* it is meant that every member can see and interact with all other members relatively freely. The members are located physically close to one another. In numbers the group may contain anywhere from three to twenty or thirty persons as a rough upper limit. However, as we shall see, there are several other kinds of closely related groups that also have a strong influence upon the operations and human relationships in a total work organization.

Various writers have sought to classify groups according to type or function. However, there is little agreement among them as to a universal classification scheme. In speaking of the informal organization of industry, J. A. C. Brown, a British psychiatrist and astute observer of the industrial scene, has divided groups into five distinct levels: (1) the total informal organization consisting of many interlocking groups, (2) large groups that have arisen over some issue of internal politics (for example, union and nonunion partisans), (3) primary group formed on the basis of similar jobs and the same work location, (4) small groups of two or three close friends, and (5) isolated employees who seldom participate in social activities.[3] Of course, the last category does not really constitute a group but is a level (albeit, the lowest) of social activity.

Informal groups can also be classified into the following categories:

1. Organizational unit group
2. Job or work team group
3. Friendship group
4. Pressure or interest group

An *organizational unit* group consists of all those employees under the authority of the same supervisor. It might officially be designated as a section, a unit, or a department. At the lowest level in an industrial establishment, a foreman typically supervises from ten to twenty-five workers. At higher levels in an organization, the span of control is smaller; it typically ranges from about four to twelve. All those working for one boss experience forces that tend to unite them. Having the same boss, they are all exposed to the same style of leadership. Being in the same department they all have the same mission (broadly speaking) in the formal organizational context. Thus all those in the purchasing department will tend to acquire the same outlook and will experience similar problems in dealing with outside vendors and internal company personnel.

Closely related to an organizational unit group is a *job or work team* group. In some cases these two types of groups coincide and are, there-

[3] James A. C. Brown, *The Social Psychology of Industry* (Middlesex, England and Baltimore, Md.: Penguin Books, 1954), pp. 129-130.

fore, synonymous. But often we find that three or four persons in the same department are assigned to work together as a team. Project teams are commonly set up to carry out engineering development and design assignments by carrying the work all the way from the research laboratory stage through to the time it is released for actual production. These teams are directed by a senior engineer or project leader. There may be several such teams within an engineering department. The team members often develop a high level of *esprit de corps*. Each member contributes a different skill to the total team effort. They tend to experience a strong sense of accomplishment; a sense of making significant contributions.

Friendship groups are not constrained by the boundaries of the formal organization structure. People may form attachments by reason of similar age, sex, marital status, education, ethnic factors, political beliefs, and the like. Friendship cliques are a universal phenomenon.

Pressure or interest groups seek to advance the position of their members. Sometimes they are embryo unions. They may seek higher wages, longer rest periods, better working conditions, better equipment, or looser piece rates. Often employees with no previous sense of unity will unite to protect what they have. Their efforts will be defensive. Thus a number of employees may learn that management plans to replace some of them with automatic equipment. Immediately they will develop a feeling of shared purpose—to resist the displacement.

Sayles devotes nearly a whole book to an analysis of pressure or interest groups. He states that unlike other social groups which tend to be small, interest groups may contain 100 or more workers. They are united by some shared feeling that their economic or social status can be protected or improved by joint action. Based upon his field research studies, Sayles has classified these interest groups into four types: (1) apathetic, (2) erratic, (3) strategic, and (4) conservative. The strategic groups had the highest level of grievance activity, highest degree of participation in union activities, and ranked second highest (conservative groups were the highest) in managements' eyes as satisfactory employees. The apathetic groups studied had the lowest number of grievances, least union activity, and ranked second lowest in managements' eyes as satisfactory employees. The erratic groups were judged to be lowest by management.[4]

STRUCTURE AND PROPERTIES OF GROUPS

Understanding of group behavior is facilitated when one has knowledge of the structure and characteristics of groups in general.

---

[4] Leonard R. Sayles, *Behavior of Industrial Work Groups: Prediction and Control* (New York: John Wiley & Sons, Inc., 1958).

Interaction

A characteristic common to all groups is that the members interact with one another. Broadly put, interaction is communication. But the communication does not always have to be oral. It can be in the form of a nod, a gesture, and a facial expression. Symbols can be a form of communication. It is by means of interaction that people are able to relate and adjust themselves one to another. Through interaction they are able to experience a feeling of group identification.

Activities

Nearly all groups do something. It is obvious that work groups carry on job-related activities. But friendship groups do something also. They may go to certain locations in the plant to converse, they may eat lunch together, they may ride together in the same car to and from their place of work. Within a group there is a differentiation of the type and amount of activity of the members. Some are constantly doing things, whereas others are more placid or even lethargic.

Norms

A norm is a group-established standard of expected behavior. Just as society in general has its common law, its taboos, and its beliefs as to what is right and wrong conduct, so too does the informal group. These standards of behavior are not written down, but they are often expressed orally. Sometimes a new employee learns by innocently violating the code, or perhaps he has been too independent to submit. The group enforces its standards by social pressure, ostracism, and occasionally physical violence.

Regulation of individual and group production is a very common practice in industry. The new man is told not to upset the balance of work flow, not to "kill" the job, not to try to make a name for himself, and not to work himself out of a job. If an employee tries to curry favor with his boss, most group members will censure him.

> I once gave a talk before the foremen's association of a certain company at one of its monthly dinner meetings. Seated at the head table were the president of the association (he was a foreman in the plant), the chairman of the board of directors of the company, and me. This association president obviously thought he could impress the chairman of the board, so he spent his whole dinner hour talking to him and reciting stories about the plant. He spoke not a word to me. The chairman of the board listened quietly for over an hour. During the intermission one of the front row foremen piped up so all could hear, "Joe, we all saw you apple-polishing Mr. Johnston, [the chairman of the board] ! Who do you think you are?" The man had thus been censured before everyone.

In a large manufacturing plant that employed a large number of machine-tool operators on three shifts per day, Sam worked for over a year on the second shift, where his work group had established a rigidly enforced norm or standard of eight completed units per eight-hour shift from each man. After Sam was transferred to the day shift he continued to turn out eight units. Three days later he was fired! He did not know that the day-shift group had established twelve units per day as the informal standard of output. Later Sam privately admitted that the evening shift had really put in only about five hours of work during the eight-hour shift.

College students have their own norms of classroom behavior. The eager beaver who sits in the front row and continually waves his hand to speak is frowned upon. In a recitation or discussion session, students never ask the professor a question just when the bell is about to ring. (The one who prolongs the class in this way is censured out in the hall afterward.) Except in those colleges having an honor system, it is generally considered a betrayal of the group to report a cheating student to the professor. However, if the professor himself catches a student who has clearly cheated, the professor's action is approved.

Informal Leadership

One (and often more than one) person may take on leadership roles in the group. The informal leader emerges from the group. He is not officially designated as the "boss" by management. He is not cloaked with the mantle of authority, as are supervisors and executives. He is not given a big desk nor a private secretary nor the power to hire and fire. Rather the informal leader guides and directs through persuasion and influence.

Sometimes leadership roles are diffused in the group. One man may be especially adept at being the spokesman for the group before management. Another may have a very wide range of outside contacts and may be looked up to as the one to arrange special outings and parties for the group.

Research into the nature of leadership has revealed that it does not consist of a set of special or outstanding traits. There is no such thing as the individual who will be the "natural" leader in all situations. The employee who is looked upon by his musical friends as a leader of their musical society, may not exercise any such position in the informal group at his place of employment. Leadership is dependent upon the relationship among a particular personality, a particular group of people, and a particular situation. The aggressive, militant agitator may be selected as a spokesman by a group of low-paid, discontented workers; yet a year later, if their lot has materially improved, they may reject him in favor of one with a stable, integrated personality who is good at getting along well with all.

After making an intensive analysis of leadership in small groups, particularly of William F. Whyte's street corner gang,[5] George Homans has made the following statement regarding the behavior of the leader:

> The leader is the man who comes closest to realizing the norms the group values highest. The norms may be queer ones, but so long as they are genuinely accepted by the group, the leader, in that group, must embody them. His embodiment of the norms gives him his high rank, and his rank attracts people: the leader is the man people come to; the scheme of interaction focuses on him. At the same time, his high rank carries with it the implied right to assume control of the group, and the exercise of control itself helps maintain the leader's prestige. This control he is peculiarly well equipped to wield by reason of his position at the top of the pyramid of interaction. He is better informed than other men, and he has more channels for the issuing of orders.[6]

It will be recalled from our explanation of the Bank Wiring Observation Room on pages 477-478 that the informal leader conformed very closely to the group established norm of output per day. This conformity with the norms has been found in a number of studies to be a mark of those with high status who at the same time enjoy a leadership position.

Cohesion

Most of us at one time or another have belonged to some groups that exhibited a high degree of "we" feeling, strong attraction of members for one another, and a willingness to help one another. On the other hand we also have been associated with groups where there existed internal apathy and even antagonisms among the members and where the members would not cooperate to achieve group goals. In fact, quite often, there was disagreement over the goals themselves. *Cohesion* is the term used to designate the attractiveness which the group holds for its members. It is another way of referring to group loyalty and solidarity.

It has been found that workers in highly cohesive groups exhibit less anxiety ("jumpiness," feeling of being under pressure for more production, and feeling lack of support from management) than do low cohesive groups.[7]

There are a number of factors that affect the degree of cohesion of a work group. The individual will exhibit a strong attachment to the group if it satisfies his needs. A man may feel that he obtains an economic advantage from group membership. He may gain prestige or security from it. If on the other hand his experiences with the group are neutral, negative, or frustrating, he will show little loyalty toward it or its members.

---

[5] William Foote Whyte, *Street Corner Society* (Chicago: University of Chicago Press, 1943).

[6] George Homans, *The Human Group* (New York: Harcourt, Brace & World, Inc., 1950), p. 188. Quotation by permission.

[7] S. E. Seashore, *Group Cohesiveness in the Industrial Group* (Ann Arbor, Mich.: Institute for Social Research, 1954).

If a person has high status and prestige in the group, he will be more devoted to it than will those with low status. This fact was determined in an experiment by Kelley, who deliberately created a prestige hierarchy by giving some members authority over others. He found that those who were low in status but had good expectations for rising were most attracted to the group. Those who were worried about a decline in their status or who were told they could not rise had low group loyalty.[8]

Cohesion is enhanced if management creates a climate where employees must cooperate with one another rather than compete against one another. For example, if management tells the employees that it is going to weed out all those having bad attitudes and poor production records, we can expect to see a dog-eat-dog situation develop among them. If employment opportunities are good elsewhere, many will quit.

A similarity in the personal and social characteristics of the group (sex, ethnic background, social class) enhances cohesion as does a similarity of pay, treatment by the boss, jobs, and nature of the work. On the other hand the group bonds can be destroyed by certain policies and actions of management. If certain workers are blessed with loose piece rates and others suffer from tight ones, this will divide the group. In the face of layoffs low and high seniority workers may become divided.

A threat from an outside force will generally unite a group. It has been continually observed that attendance at local labor union meetings is very poor. However, at the time of labor negotiations, if management seems to be making hard demands (for example, abolish union shop, abolish wage cost of living clause), then member participation suddenly soars, and the union commonly will present a solid front.

Social Pressure and Conformity

Group membership provides many benefits, but in return the group demands conformity to its way of thinking and acting. Highly cohesive groups are able to demand and enforce a greater degree of conformity from their members than are low cohesion ones. Other factors affecting the strength of the pressure to conform are the importance of group membership to the individual, the need for the group to achieve unanimous support in order to attain its goals, the certainty that sanctions will be invoked for deviation, and the degree of self-confidence of the individual. Self-doubters yield to group pressures easily.[9]

The principal reasons why groups demand conformity from their members are to maintain the security of the group and to help it achieve its goals. Rugged individualists, dissenters, and mavericks are viewed by

[8] Harold F. Kelley, "Communication in Experimentally Created Hierarchies," *Human Relations,* Vol. 4 (1951), pp. 39-56.

[9] Dorwin Cartwright and Alvin Zander (eds.), *Group Dynamics: Research and Theory* (2nd Ed.; Evanston, Ill.: Row, Peterson and Co., 1960), pp. 173-177.

the majority as destructive to the security of the whole. In actuality, the dissenters may have the best solutions to problems, but they are not usually perceived in this light.

Informal Hierarchy

Work groups, friendship groups, and interest groups often resemble a formal organization in their structure. That is, they have a hierarchy of status levels. Often the leader will have a few trusted "lieutenants" with whom he discusses his ideas before taking action. Communications to the rank and file are sometimes channeled through these subordinate leaders. Members acquire certain roles (for example, leader, straw boss, harmonizer, coordinator, and follower) on the basis of the group's response to their capacities.

Group Culture

Groups in industry develop their own cultures—their distinctive customs, beliefs, ceremonies, jargon, and ways of acting. These, at the same time, help cement the members to the group and sharpen the distinctions separating groups. To some extent the group culture is derived from the background (education, experience, national origin, social class) of the members. It is also derived from the particular nature of the group's environment at work.

It is common for some shop and craft groups to try out newcomers by hazing to see whether they can take it in their stride. Yet this practice is rare among white-collar groups. Certain occupational groups acquire a jargon that is incomprehensible to the outsider. Professional employees, such as scientists, physicians, and engineers, usually show consideration and loyalty to their profession. At times this conflicts with loyalty to their employers. Such things as publications, research contributions, recognition from their colleagues, and a general advancement of their group are vital to the professional. When management understands the culture of the groups it is dealing with, it is in a better position to predict behavior and facilitate changes that it deems necessary.

IMPACT OF INFORMAL GROUP RELATIONS UPON THE FORMAL ORGANIZATION

How does the fact that employees and managers maintain ties to various social groupings affect the operation of an industrial plant or a store or a bank? Do such group attributes as cohesiveness, norms, pressures toward conformity, and informal leadership help or hinder the achievement of the goals of the total organization? Let us now examine some of the more important influences of social and work groups upon a company or industrial plant.

Communications

People must have a frame of reference. They feel lost and insecure if they are kept in the dark. If management fails to keep employees informed regarding things that are important to *them,* the people will supply the missing data. This information is transmitted by word of mouth within a group and among groups via those persons having wide social contacts (that is, membership in numerous groups). What we are describing here is really the grapevine. It serves the useful purpose of helping to speed formal pronouncements from management to the far corners of the plant. It operates like a chain letter, which is to say, it has a multiplying effect. Informal communication modes and channels often serve to fill in meaningful gaps in orders from the big boss. If a trusted subordinate knows how his boss habitually thinks, he may give clarification and necessary amplification to orders when he discusses them with his work associates.

Of course, the great danger of informal communication is that it is often inaccurate. It can cause serious misunderstandings, errors, distortions, and clashes.

> Bill, a young engineer, had been expecting a promotion for some time. The company was expanding rapidly, and several of his associates with similar abilities, education, and years of service had been promoted in recent months. Promotions were always announced around the middle of the month, but because of the grapevine, everyone knew about them several days in advance. Several of Bill's friends told him that they heard authoritatively that his name was on the list to be announced on September 15. The rumors were so persistent that Bill took them to be true. He announced to his wife that he was going to be promoted. He even approached his boss to discuss his new job and status. Imagine his horrible shock when his supervisor told him that he had not been promoted and that no recommendation to that effect had been made.

Productivity

If employees display a strong level of attachment for their group—the group cohesiveness is great—they will tend to produce at the level established by the group. This level or norm may be either high or low from management's viewpoint. If there is a low level of cohesiveness, then there will be a great variation in production rates among the workers. But when the productivity of work groups having high and low cohesiveness are compared, a number of studies have revealed that those having high cohesiveness exhibit higher productivity on the average. By drawing upon the extensive researches of the Institute for Social Research of the University of Michigan. Likert explains the reasons why groups having high peer-group pride and loyalty (cohesive groups) are more productive. He notes that the workers in these groups are more cooperative in getting the work done, are more helpful toward one another, and help one another on their own initiative. He found that groups with high peer-group loyalty have lower rates of absenteeism than do low loyalty ones; they also have more favorable attitudes toward their jobs, and they have higher production goals.[10] It should be pointed out that these favorable results do not accidentally happen. They are strongly influenced by the way in which the supervisor leads the group. He must constantly strive to build up positive group sentiments and a spirit of cooperation. Most of all he must not perceive of the group strength as a threat to his position.

When England mechanized its coal mines after World War II, it adopted the longwall method of mining. In effect this broke up the two- to four-man work teams and substituted large teams of specialists. Whereas previously the small teams had performed all of the operations involved in extracting coal, the new method involved separate teams doing cutting, ripping, and filling operations. The complete cycle was completed in a twenty-four-hour period of three shifts. However, the teams were not integrated; they were not responsible for the complete process. If problems arose, one shift tended to blame the previous one for the trouble. The abandonment of the fully integrated small groups that were responsible for all phases of the work resulted in greater absenteeism, turnover, and sickness among the miners. Gradually through the years changes have been made to restore some small group work autonomy.[11] There is a great deal to be said in favor of organizing work so that it can be carried out from beginning to end by small face-to-face work groups. In this way the group can exercise internal controls over the members; the group feels responsible for satisfactory completion; and it senses a spirit of teamwork and a feeling of accomplishment.

Restriction of Output. There are many instances in which work groups do not have high output goals; instead they deliberately restrict output. The group exerts strong pressures upon its members to keep their output close to a group established standard. This phenomenon is common in factories operating with time standards and an incentive system of wage payment, but it occurs in daywork shops as well. Restriction of output occurred in the Bank Wiring Room in the Hawthorne experiments.

There are a number of reasons for group regulation of production. Primarily it is a protective mechanism. It prevents unusually skilled workers (these may even be newcomers to the group) from showing up to man-

---

[10] Rensis Likert, *New Patterns of Management* (New York: McGraw-Hill Book Company, Inc., 1961), pp. 34-36.

[11] E. L. Trist and K. W. Bamforth, "Some Social and Psychological Consequences of the Longwall Method of Coal-Getting," *Human Relations,* Vol. 4, No. 1 (1951), pp. 1-38.

agement those who are less skilled and slower. In other words it prevents management from weeding out slow workers. Under an incentive system it prevents rate cutting by management because of high earnings, and it serves to stabilize take-home pay from week to week. Restriction of output creates a feeling that all of the workers are equal, and it enhances group solidarity. Contrary to the expectations of managers, many employees under piecework do not seek to maximize their earnings. Instead they value the respect and friendship of their peers. They want to preserve their energies at the end of the day for outside recreational activities. In short they value the "social ethic" more than they do the "Protestant ethic." The accumulation of more and more money, for money's sake, is not a source of motivation to them.

Conduct and Discipline

Most work groups exercise a stabilizing effect upon the conduct of their members. If good relations have been established between the supervisor and the men and if the group respects the rules of conduct established by management, then this group discipline works in support of management's objectives.

> A number of foremen in a company which hires large numbers of young men (18 or 19 years of age) to do general construction work, including truck driving, have claimed that their work crews have always helped them to train and discipline these new men when they started to act like "cowboys" on the highway or to engage in horseplay when working at heights or with power equipment.

Of course, we find some work groups opposed to management policies. These groups engage in wildcat strikes (not sanctioned by the labor union), slowdowns, and other obstructionist tactics. These activities that obstruct sound conduct and discipline are primarily symptoms of frustration. The workers may feel seriously grieved over some element of pay, working conditions, work loads, the nature of their jobs, or treatment.

Conformity

There is little doubt but that group behavior engenders conformity. The person who criticizes accepted ways, the one who proposes quite different modes of action, is considered to be a potential threat to the security of the group. Friendship groups are initially formed by people who have much in common and who are therefore attracted to one another. Job and work related groups are formed according to the formal organization and technology of the enterprise. But even here we find that those who are drastically different in their beliefs, behavior, and dress often feel uncomfortable and gradually seek a location where they fit in better.

It is not only the small work and friendship groups that enforce conformity, but it is also the entire fabric of all organizations, large and small, that stifle individuality. In his book *The Organization Man* William H. Whyte, Jr., has eloquently exposed the harmful consequences of conformity in the modern business corporation.[12] He has written with particular reference to the ranks of management personnel. He complains not only that business organizations pressure their people to conform but that the individuals themselves readily accede. It is a fact that many large corporations pour a lot of money into orientation and communication programs designed to get their personnel to accept the company's "party line." Loyalty to one's boss and to the organization is often valued more than creativity and ability to get the work out. Rising young executives learn to ape the boss in order to get ahead. New attitudes and ideas are squelched. A premium is placed upon the type of fellow who gets along well with everyone and who doesn't rock the boat. Even wives of corporate executives are expected to fit the desired pattern.

INFORMAL VS. FORMAL ORGANIZATION

Most large organizations prepare and maintain charts that depict their formal structure. This work of structuring the organization is done by top management. The actual work of drawing the charts is carried out by personnel administrators, management engineers, or administrative specialists. Some of the very large corporations have separate organization planning departments. These organization charts show the names of the various functions grouped according to some practical arrangement. They often show the names of all management job holders in their proper position on the charts. They show lines of authority and accountability and formal channels of communication. Management personnel are neatly stacked into layers according to their level in the hierarchy.

Quite often, however, the abilities and personalities of individuals assigned to specific spots on the charts do not always match the written confines of their jobs. Some are power seekers and seek to build up their own empires. Some are very persuasive and influential, so that many come to them for advice and guidance. Still others are incapable of carrying out their assigned duties, so that the scope of their jobs shrinks. Others may be eager to step into the void. Quite often certain managers exercise influence far in excess of that defined by the formal organization chart and their own job descriptions.

Impartial observers are in a position to contrast the real organization (the way it actually operates) with the intended structural design.

[12] (New York: Simon and Schuster, Inc., 1956).

The technical problems involved in putting a defense plant into actual operation and production were very great. A number of totally untried major new techniques had to be devised. The technical director reported organizationally to the chief engineer, and he in turn was under the plant manager. Yet the technical director clearly "ran" the plant during its initial start-up period. Both the chief engineer and the plant manager freely came to the technical director's office to obtain counsel on major problems. Critical decisions regarding hiring, training, scheduling of overtime, manpower allocation, and quality standards were made by this man in addition to his regular engineering responsibilities.

Melville Dalton has described the striking contrast between the formal authority structure of the Milo Fractionating Center and the informal or unofficial structure.[13] Figure 16-1 is the official organization chart (simplified) while Figure 16-2 shows the chart as it actually operated in practice. As can be seen from our examination of these charts, the informal chart departs considerably from the planned or expected chart. Rees, who was superintendent of industrial relations, exercised a great deal of informal authority. He was young and had been sent to the plant from company headquarters to replace a weak predecessor, Lane, and

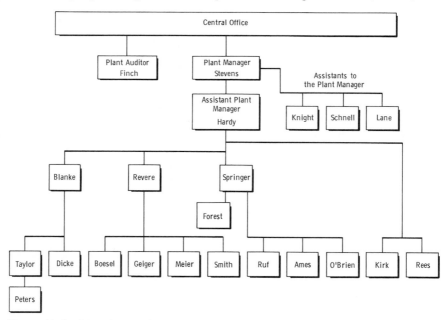

Figure 16-1. Milo Formal Organization Chart—Simplified. From Melville Dalton, *Men Who Manage* (New York: John Wiley & Sons, Inc., 1959). Reproduced by permission.

[13] Melville Dalton, *Men Who Manage* (New York: John Wiley & Sons, Inc., 1959), pp. 20-27. Milo is the disguised name of an actual company of 8,000 employees.

strengthen the industrial relations department. The assistant plant manager, Hardy, in actuality exercised power equivalent to that of the plant manager, Stevens. In executive meetings Stevens usually gave way to Hardy, who really dominated the discussions. Most questions from the group were directed to Hardy. Hardy's decision was most important on promotions. Stevens was a lone wolf and was disliked by many of the managers. Hardy had wide social contacts.

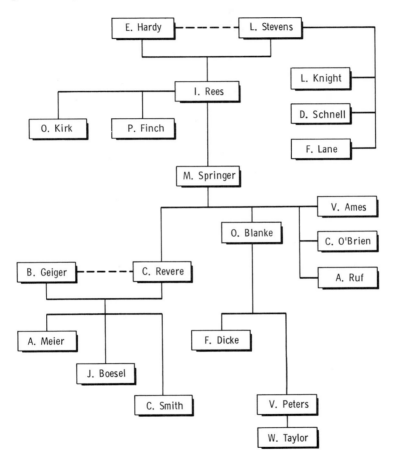

Figure 16-2. Milo Chart of Unofficial Influence. From Melville Dalton, *Men Who Manage* (New York: John Wiley & Sons, Inc., 1959). Reproduced by permission.

Blanke, Revere, and Springer were all superintendents and nominally equal in power and status. However, Springer was especially close to Hardy, and Blanke and Revere recognized this. Whenever they sought important favors from Hardy, they always first consulted with Springer.

Kirk, as head of production planning, and Finch, as chief auditor, were both very influential. They both had college degrees and varied job experience and sat with Rees at the table of Hardy and Stevens at the cafeteria by the latter's request. These three were the only staff managers invited to join Hardy and Stevens at lunch.

THE SUPERVISOR AND THE GROUP

An effective supervisor not only respects the individuality of his people (temperament, dignity, job assignment, and so on), but he also recognizes the group as a whole and the influences of the group on the individual. He must respect the values, norms, and loyalties of the group. He should dig beneath the surface to understand why the group has reacted in particular ways to his orders and activities in the past. In planning future actions he ought to consider the probable reaction of the group.

The successful supervisor is the one who is able to blend the forces within the group in such a manner as to channel them toward the goals of his department and of the total organization. He works with and through the group. He does not threaten it.

Relations with Informal Leader

The information-work-group leader may appear to the supervisor as a troublemaker, a ring leader, and a malcontent. Yet if he is removed from the group, usually someone else will come to the fore. This new leader may exhibit the same behavior as his predecessor. Why is this so? The answer lies in the fact that the leader is simply a reflection of the group he represents. The group chooses a leader who will represent its own interests.

The departmental supervisor can sometimes work with the group leader to obtain full cooperation from the group on certain difficult matters. This does not mean that a foreman or department head should channel his orders through the leader and make him a member of the management hierarchy. But it does mean that he can devote a little extra attention to winning his support when he senses that the employees may be reluctant to put their full energies into a project.

The department head can also use the informal leader as a supplemental channel of communication, both downward and upward. He can sound out this leader when he detects evidence of discontent.

The informal leader is an ideal person to bring new employees into the fold and help them feel accepted. This activity is most successful when done spontaneously without prompting from the supervisor.

In all of the foregoing actions, it is essential that the supervisor refrain from making the informal leader his favorite and that he does not compromise the latter's position by making him a "tool" of management. The best advice is to deal with the informal leader in a delicate and discreet manner.

Of course, there are some groups in which there is no informal leader. This is most likely where there is high turnover and no opportunity to form firm bonds. In other cases the leadership functions are dispersed among several persons.

Build a Team

To achieve high productivity and high morale, a supervisor seeks to build a smooth-functioning team. He wants the group goals and norms to coincide with management objectives. This is not an easy task. We shall have a great deal to say about leadership and supervision in succeeding chapters (Chapters 17 and 18). At this point our remarks will relate to the supervisor in his dealings with his work group. The following are some important actions that he can take to weld the group together into a team:

Go To Bat. If a departmental supervisor does not take the initiative to provide good equipment and working conditions, pay raises, promotions, training opportunities, and the like, for his men, then no one else will. Workers will respond to a boss who faithfully represents them within the context of the needs of the entire enterprise.

Foster Cooperation. Cooperation among men within the same department facilitates production and advances the entire group. Competition spurs individual effort, but it sparks jealousy, conflict, and a dog-eat-dog attitude. Playing favorites is one sure way to destroy cooperation among the employees. With this type of leadership, the workers conclude that it is more important to gain the boss's favor than it is to help one another get the work out.

Recognize Friendship Patterns. Some supervisors deliberately separate two employees because they do too much talking together. They feel it inhibits production. But the key issue is the level of production, not the talking. In the Relay Assembly Test Room of the Hawthorne experiments, the girls' productivity increased substantially in spite of the fact that they conversed much more than in their regular department. If teammates are selected on the basis of friendship patterns, there is every likelihood that cooperation and morale will be better. By making up teams of carpenters and bricklayers on a construction project according to their own sociometric choices, Van Zelst found that productivity increased and turnover decreased.[14]

Minimize Subgroup Antagonism. Antagonism between subgroups is admittedly a difficult thing to stop after it has developed to an advanced stage. But basically the supervisor must seek the cause of the conflict. He must be careful to avoid any type of treatment that would indicate

[14] Raymond H. Van Zelst, "Sociometrically Selected Work Teams Increase Production," *Personnel Psychology*, Vol. 5, No. 3 (Autumn 1952), pp. 175-185.

favored treatment of one subgroup over the other. At times it is necessary to shift people about within the department and even out of the department.

Consult and Encourage Participation. Within the last several years a great volume of research evidence has shown the value to be gained by supervising employees in such a way that they are given a voice in decisions about which they have knowledge and a definite interest. Various labels, such as consultative supervision, democratic supervision, and participative management, are used to designate this approach. This entire subject is taken up in Chapter 19, "Managing Through the Use of Participation."

STATUS

In some offices when employees are upgraded and given a higher pay classification and enlarged responsibilities, they are assigned to a bigger desk with a better chair at the head of the row of desks. In some work groups certain jobs have traditionally been considered more desirable and hence of higher prestige. Certain places in the company parking lot are reserved for major executives. In fact, their names are indicated on signs at their parking spots. Foremen in many industrial plants wear a white shirt and tie when they come to work. To be sure the tie may be loosened, the sleeves rolled up, and the shirt may become spotted with grease by the end of the day; but the foreman would not think of wearing a rough gray or khaki shirt to save his white dress shirts. What we are talking about here are status distinctions. What is status, and what is its significance?

Status is defined as the relative position in a group or organization; it is relative social rank. There are two types of status: formal and informal. Formal status is that which a person acquires or which is granted by the company he works for. It is related to his position in the formal hierarchy. It is sometimes called *derived* status. Going beyond the confines of the organization, we can say that a person born to wealth and power has a high level of derived status. Informal status is sometimes called *intrinsic* status. This is most closely associated with the informal organization and work groups. It is based upon a person's contributions to the purposes of the group. Thus one possessing high skill, or one who has extensive knowledge of the technology, or one who is especially helpful to his associates will be a high-status individual within that group. Going outside the employment situation, we find that people have informal or intrinsic status in social groups, recreational groups, and in the family. A man may perform a menial job in the mill and hence have low status there; but he may be a father and head of a family and have high status in his own home.

Quite often it is difficult to distinguish sharply between those status distinctions that have been deliberately established by management and those things that have simply taken on a status meaning because of the way people feel about a situation. For example, because of the nature of their work some employees may have to wear protective uniforms. Over a period of years the work group may ascribe a specific status meaning to the wearing of that uniform. Time clocks are used in factories to determine accurately the number of hours a worker has put in each week so that his pay can be computed. However, in most organizations the people have attached a meaning of low status to clock punching. They desire to get off the clock and be paid a weekly or monthly salary.

Criteria for Distinguishing Status

Status in the business organization is based upon a number of factors.

1. Kind of work and organizational position
2. Personal contributions
3. Conditions of work
4. Benefits and privileges
5. Status symbols
6. Sex and ethnic considerations

Kind of Work and Organizational Position. Occupations can be graded according to their social desirability and prestige. Generally speaking, those requiring little or no education and previous work experience are considered of low status, whereas those having high level prerequisites are high status occupations. Accordingly industrial organizations have a grading of occupations from unskilled at the bottom up through executive and professional work at the top. The level at which a person's job appears on the organization chart is an indication of his status. If he is not shown on the chart at all, this means that his job is either nonmanagement or that he is an hourly paid worker.

Personal Contributions. Some people perform their jobs in such an exceptional manner that their jobs take on increased significance. The job literally grows with the person. This person then occupies high status, and even after he leaves the job, it may still be considered highly by all of the other employees. In addition, by reason of a person's behavior and personality, he may achieve high status within the informal group.

Conditions of Work. This category covers a multitude of distinctions. Traditionally white-collar office work has been considered higher in status than shop work. Employees on the exempt payroll (not paid for overtime) are high status, whereas nonexempt jobs are of a lower status. By reason of their jobs, some employees may travel extensively and be granted liberal expense accounts. Staying at luxurious hotels and eating in expensive restaurants, they may consider themselves to have a high prestige thereby. The pay classification and working conditions (clean or dirty) are other status distinctions.

Benefits and Privileges.   Usually higher-level employees (managers, engineers, scientists) enjoy considerably more freedom to come and go than do production workers. The latter are pretty much tied to their machines. Managers can take long lunch hours and arrive late in the morning with apparent impunity. Of course, they may also have to work evenings and weekends, but this is seldom noticed by the envious blue-collar workers. A company car may be placed at the disposal of the president.

Status Symbols.   A great variety of things take on special symbolic meaning in terms of status.

> In the main office of an electronics manufacturing plant, a series of fine gradations of status had been purposefully established. Clerks and secretaries had single pedestal desks and sat on stenographers' chairs. Young engineers had slightly larger single pedestal desks and were assigned chairs similar in appearance to stenographers' chairs but slightly larger. Senior engineers, project leaders, and senior accountants had full-size double pedestal desks and swivel chairs. Desks were arranged in a series of long rows. As men moved up in pay and rank they gradually moved to the ends of the rows. Desk calendars of different sizes were assigned to people according to the rank of their jobs. Department heads occupied semiprivate offices located around the perimeter of this large office area. But they had partitions only about six feet high. Division heads had completely private offices but with transparent glass doors. The door to the office of the plant manager was completely solid so that no one could see through. All of the men in the huge office took their suit coats off and hung them in a special locker room every day. Yet the very top executives kept their suit coats on all day long. These served as a badge of their office.

Sex and Ethnic Considerations.   Despite the force of political pressure and laws which try to grant equality of pay treatment to men and women on the same jobs and equal opportunities to Negroes and whites, there are still status distinctions among these kinds of groups. It must be agreed, however, that these distinctions and barriers are gradually disappearing. Men do not like to be assigned to what they consider women's work. In many factories and in construction projects, Negroes are assigned to the most unpleasant jobs. Quite commonly an analysis of the organizational levels in a company will reveal that the upper levels are composed of one ethnic group (for example, Anglo-Saxon), whereas the lower levels are composed mostly of another.

Functions and Significance of Status

Status symbols and distinctions serve as a means of identifying and ranking people. They give us cues as to the appropriate way to act toward certain individuals. Thus enlisted men in the Army will salute an officer in uniform even though they have no direct dealings with him. His position entitles him to a salute. A man dressed in a business suit on the factory floor will be perceived by the workers in overalls to be a man of some authority in the company. They will tend to show him respect and deference.

People who have a certain status strive to maintain their position. They do not want to lose what they already have. It gives them a sense, too, of responsibility to live up to their level. Employees and managers alike will usually react openly to any actions that threaten to lower their status.

Status levels serve as incentives for employees to rise in the organization. Because the prestige and the privileges go with jobs higher up in the hierarchy, people will be motivated to achieve these rewards. A more impressive job title, a better office, better working conditions, one's name in the company telephone directory, these and many similar conditions are rewards bestowed upon those who have made important contributions and thereby earned a promotion.

Status helps promote group solidarity. This is particularly evident where all those doing similar work in the same location are treated the same. They wear the same clothes, work at the same kinds of machines, and have the same job titles. Status distinctions may arise or be made by management within the total department or organization. But where a small group feels that everyone is of equal status and that everyone has been making equal contributions, then the fact they are all awarded the same status symbol serves to promote group solidarity. Some local union leaders who have been elected from the ranks are careful to continue dressing as workers to preserve their working-class identity. This practice has been particularly evident in the C.I.O. type of industrial unions.

When making transfers, new work assignments, and other changes, managers should be careful not to violate the expectations and traditions of the employees regarding status. A promotion should actually carry with it higher pay and a better title if people have always expected it. To tell highly skilled craftsmen to devote a high percentage of their time to sweeping floors would be looked upon as an insult and perhaps even a demotion.

Do those who have a low status position in the structure resent the fact that others enjoy much higher rank? Is it wrong for a department head to eat lunch in the executive dining room while his direct subordinates must eat in the cafeteria? These status distinctions do not destroy morale if there are actual opportunities for those on the bottom to improve their position. If every man feels that upward mobility is possible and if he sees that others just like him are achieving higher status, then he will be satisfied. But if a man has fierce ambition to rise, and the situation prevents him from doing so, then he will experience frustration and anxiety.

Questions for Review and Discussion

1. What is meant by the term *group dynamics?*
2. What is a sociogram? How can it be constructed? Of what use is it?
3. What causes accounted for the gradual increase in productivity for over two years by the girls in the Relay Assembly Test Room of the Hawthorne Researches?
4. Why did not the men in the Bank Wiring Room increase their output as did the girls in the Relay Assembly Test Room?
5. Describe and account for the behavior of the men in the Bank Wiring Room. Why did they control their rate of production?
6. Why do employees join and form informal groups? What benefits do they derive from doing so?
7. Distinguish between a pressure (interest) group and a job (work) group?
8. Show how there may be considerable overlap and interlocking membership in groups in a company.
9. What is meant by the following terms?
   a. *Norm*
   b. *Interaction*
   c. *Cohesion*
10. Describe ways in which a work group may aid and hinder the accomplishment of management objectives.
11. What relationship has been found between strong peer-group loyalty and productivity? Explain.
12. Is conformity an inevitable consequence of participation and membership in a group?
13. Why do informal channels of authority and influence sometimes differ significantly from those intended by the designers of the formal structure?
14. Why is a thorough understanding of the dynamics of work group(s) vital to the supervisor?
15. What is status? How do status distinctions affect the behavior of managers and workers? What is the significance of status for those who manage an organization?

CASE PROBLEM[15]

The Industrial Finishes Company has been in business for fifteen years, and the majority of the personnel have been employed there since its inception. The company conducts research and develops industrial finishes to customer's specifications. This is highly technical work. However, the actual production of the finishes is quite straightforward and is handled by a group of eight operators. In addition to the production force, there

---

[15] The author expresses his appreciation to Richard W. Pollay, a former student, for providing the essential features of this case.

are six chemists, ten sales personnel, three general office workers, and four executives who are stockholders and officers of the corporation.

The officers of the company, the sales manager, and the chemists are assisted by three middle-aged women who handle all of the paperwork, secretarial duties, bookkeeping, and reception tasks. Two of these women have been with the company since its beginning, whereas the third has worked there for seven years. All three are considered very efficient and loyal by the management personnel. Although these women are well acquainted with all of the men in the office, they rarely have really associated with them on informal activities. They have chosen to take their coffee breaks and lunches with each other rather than accept the often proffered invitation from the men to join them.

A few months ago, the company hired a girl, age 22, to help with the ever increasing secretarial load. She also was expected to assist in general clerical tasks. This girl was very attractive, and she enjoyed the company of men more than that of women. Hence she associated with the men during coffee breaks and lunch hours and made little effort to become really accepted by the women. Office efficiency appeared to increase after she was hired, and the backlog of work was cleaned up. Her sociability enhanced the morale of the men.

However, there was growing unrest among the older women. They resented the new girl. Finally, after the traditionally jovial Christmas party, when the new girl was clearly the center of attention, the older women as a group went to see the company president. They stated that it was impossible to work with the new girl, she upset office morale, and they demanded that she be let go. If not, they would all resign.

The president tried to conciliate them but to no avail. He considered all three women to be especially competent and valuable employees. Inasmuch as the women had husbands who had good jobs he knew that they would suffer no real hardship if they quit. He also had received reports from the men that the new girl was doing excellent work.

Questions

1. What action would you take as president?
2. Evaluate the behavior of the new girl; the three middle-aged women.
3. Could this situation have been foreseen and avoided?

Suggestions for Further Reading

Bowers, D. G., and S. E. Seashore, "Peer Leadership Within Work Groups," *Personnel Administration,* Vol. 30, September-October, 1967, pp. 45-50.

Cartwright, Dorwin, and Alvin Zander (eds.), *Group Dynamics: Research and Theory,* 3rd Ed., New York: Harper & Row, 1968.

Collins, Barry E., and Harold Guetzkow, *A Social Psychology of Group Processes for Decision-Making,* New York: John Wiley & Sons, 1964.

Festinger, Leon, Stanley Schachter, and Kurt Back, *Social Pressures in Informal Groups,* Stanford, Calif.: Stanford University Press, 1963.

Fiedler, Fred E., "The Effect of Inter-group Competition on Group Member Adjustment," *Personnel Psychology,* Vol. 20, No. 1, 1967, pp. 33-44.

Golembiewski, Robert T., "Management Science and Group Behavior: Work Unit Cohesiveness," *Journal of the Academy of Management,* Vol. 4, No. 2, August 1961, pp. 87-99.

Hare, A. Paul, E. F. Borgatta, and R. F. Bales (eds.), *Small Groups: Studies in Social Interaction,* New York: Alfred A. Knopf, 1955.

Homans, George C., *Social Behavior: Its Elementary Forms,* New York: Harcourt, Brace, & World, 1961.

————, *The Human Group,* New York: Harcourt, Brace & World, 1950.

Litterer, Joseph A., *The Analysis of Organizations,* New York: John Wiley & Sons, 1965, Ch. 4-6.

March, James G. (ed.), *Handbook of Organizations,* Chicago: Rand McNally, 1965, Ch. 3.

Phelan, J. G., and R. Goldberg, "Personnel Implications of Recent Small Group Research," *Personnel Administration,* Vol. 30, July-August 1967, pp. 51-55.

Sayles, Leonard R., *Behavior of Industrial Work Groups: Prediction and Control,* New York: John Wiley & Sons, 1958.

Van Zelst, R. J., "Sociometrically Selected Work Teams Increase Productivity," *Personnel Psychology,* Vol. 5, No. 3, (Autumn 1952), pp. 175-185.

Leadership 17

A supervisor persuades his team of engineers that they must revise their procedures drastically in order to meet the scheduled delivery date in the space technology program. A young lady stenographer takes the initiative in making arrangements and getting the other girls to help in giving an office party for an associate who is moving to the West Coast with her husband. An engineer who senses strong discontent among his fellow engineers because they must constantly put in long hours of overtime discusses the matter with the others and agrees to act as their spokesman before the boss. A telephone lineman takes charge when his gang experiences difficulty running cable while the foreman is temporarily away from the job.

All of the foregoing acts are examples of leadership behavior. In the first situation the supervisor's leadership behavior was an integral part of his formal position of authority and command in the organization. In the other three instances the leadership acts were initiated by employees who volunteered their services. They exhibited actions of an informal leader. They were not endowed with formal authority by the organization.

Leading involves a close personal relationship. Face-to-face interaction is a major ingredient of leadership. It is the element of management that impels others to action. It is one of the essential functions that must be performed by all superiors and executives—that is, by all who direct the work of other people. Recalling the key functions involved in the process of management—planning, organizing, staffing, leading, and controlling—leading is one of the most difficult to evaluate, acquire, and measure. For centuries scholars have been speculating on the nature of leadership. Yet it has been only in recent years that researchers have conducted systematic investigations that have yielded fruitful results regarding the dimensions of leadership.

NATURE OF LEADERSHIP

Leading is the process of influencing others to act to accomplish specified objectives. A precise and comprehensive definition of leadership is that formulated by Tannenbaum, Weschler, and Massarik, who state that it consists of interpersonal influence, exercised in a situation and directed, by means of the communication process, toward the attainment of a specified goal or goals. They point out that leadership always involves attempts by a person (leader) to affect or influence the behavior of a follower (or followers) in a situation.[1]

The effective leader gets others (followers) to act. He may impel them to action by any of numerous devices: persuasion, influence, power, threat of force, and appeal to legitimate right.

The person who either is or presumes to be in a leadership position must transmit his feelings and exhortations to his followers by the process we call communication. Communication involves both the sending of messages and understanding by the receiver. The successful leader is the one who can appeal to his constituents in a meaningful way. He talks their language.

Among the objectives the leader seeks to have the group accomplish may be those of the larger organization, as when a foreman exhorts his workers to increase production to meet the schedule set by top management. The leader also is an agent of the led. He seeks to satisfy the needs of his followers. Thus a foreman may go to bat for his men to obtain higher pay classifications for them because both he and they honestly believe the higher pay rates are justified. It should be emphasized that the leader of a group in a formal organization has the dual objectives of representing the interests of his group to higher management and of getting his subordinates to work for the goals of the enterprise as a whole. The problem of leadership is further complicated by the fact that individuals within his group of followers may (and usually do) possess varied and conflicting goals. These may not always be compatible with the objectives of the total organization or of the immediate group.

Followership is intimately related to leadership. A man's attempted

[1] Robert Tannenbaum, Irving R. Weschler, and Fred Massarik, *Leadership and Organization: A Behavioral Science Approach* (New York: McGraw-Hill Book Company, Inc., 1961), p. 24.

leadership is only effective insofar as he is able to cause others to respond favorably to his initiation of action. In fact, the way in which a subordinate reacts to his boss' directives affects the latter's manner of leading. A supervisor may learn from experience that it is unwise to assign John and Henry to work as partners on a maintenance repair job because John has previously said that he will not work with Henry. Of course, the supervisor could threaten to discharge John unless he works with Henry. But he knows that forcing the two men to work together is folly because their incompatibility prevents effective work cooperation.

Quite often when workers are asked to make sociometric choices of their preferences of others in their work group as to who would make good leaders and who would be good followers, persons selected for positions of leadership are also chosen for followership positions. In practically every organizational hierarchy, a supervisor or an executive is at the same time a leader of his subordinates and a follower of his superior in the structure. In effect, in the modern business enterprise, leaders must also behave in the role of followers a significant portion of the time.

Special Case of Charismatic Leader

Although rarely encountered in an industrial or business organization where the process of leadership is bound by convention, custom, legitimate authority, and formal policies, it is perhaps instructive to take a side path for a moment to examine a type of leadership that derives primarily from great personal power and magnetism. This type of leadership is referred to as charismatic or the gift of grace. The charismatic leader is perceived by his followers to be endowed with infallibility and infinite wisdom. He is believed to be possessed with supernatural powers, to be endowed with a special divine or spiritual gift. He is above ordinary mortals. Mahatma Gandhi of India was such a leader, as were Adolph Hitler of Nazi Germany, and Nikolai Lenin of Russia.

The followers of such leaders seek physical and emotional security by placing utmost dependence upon these father figures. By emotionally identifying with the charismatic leader they gain the vicarious experience of power, status, and prestige.

These leaders exert a strong emotional hold over their followers. Frequently, but not always, they are gifted orators and rely upon the psychology of mass action to manipulate their followers. Usually such leaders are mystics to an extent. They are not capable of the logical, systematic, and orderly behavior required of the executive in administering a going organization. Charismatic leaders attract a personal staff of followers who are utterly devoted to them. Formal lines of authority and responsibility, delegation, and a logical grouping of functions are rarely to be found in the organization attached to charismatic leaders. When they pass from the scene, the system they created often dissolves into chaos.

FOUNDATIONS OF LEADERSHIP

For centuries writers, historians, and the public in general held to the notion that leadership was primarily exercised by great men, that they were "born" and not "made" (by education and training), and that real progress and change in civilization awaited the coming of such individuals.

Indeed even in the late nineteenth and early twentieth centuries in America, writers depicting the successes of our great industrial giants asserted that their position of authority and power derived mainly from their superior birth, superior ability, and superior personal magnetism. These powers were possessed by only a fortunate few.

> The power to generate great ideas, the power to command great armies, the power to make great discoveries in the fields of science, the power to move the world with tongue or pen, the power to originate and conduct great industrial enterprises and accumulate great fortunes—always has been and always will be the inheritance of the few.[2]

But such theories as the foregoing have been largely discredited as a result of the scientific investigation of leadership by modern researchers.

Traits, Situation, and Group

In selecting supervisors from within the ranks of a company, can management identify those employees who will be good leaders by the personality traits they exhibit? Is there a distinct leadership type? Do leaders as a whole possess traits that distinquish them from nonleaders?

Over the years innumerable investigators have sought to answer such questions as these. They have employed such methods as observation of behavior in group situations, analysis of biographical data, psychological testing of persons occupying leadership positions, and ratings by observers. It has been asserted that a commanding voice, vigorous health, tall stature, a striking appearance, and dominance are common characteristics of leaders. However, the fact of the matter is that to a considerable extent these studies have yielded a confusing and often contradictory array of characteristics allegedly possessed by leaders. It has been found that the traits claimed to be possessed by leaders are also widely exhibited by followers as well.

As a result of a comprehensive investigation of leadership, Stogdill concluded that the pattern of leadership traits differs with the situation. There is no single personality configuration that typifies a leader. He observed that the evidence strongly suggests that leadership is a relationship which

---

[2] F. O. Willey, *The Laborer and the Capitalist* (New York: National Economic League, 1896), p. 42. As contained in Reinhard Bendix, *Work and Authority in Industry* (New York: John Wiley & Sons, Inc., 1956), p. 259.

exists among people in a social situation and that a person who becomes a leader in one situation may not do so in a different situation.[3]

The fact that those who rise to positions of leadership are different persons from one situation to another can be reasonably understood if we note the demands made upon the leader and the group in varying circumstances. John may be an avid outdoorsman and a leader of his mountaineering club, where endurance, resourcefulness, knowledge of the wilds, and helpfulness toward one another are vital attributes. Yet in his employment situation as an engineer in a research and development group, where expert technical knowledge and creativity are prime skills, he may not stand out at all. Let us take another example. Bill may be especially adept at working with boys and organizing baseball teams and Boy Scout troops. This fact does not mean that he will be equally successful in the adult world of leadership.

There are three main variables to be weighed when one analyzes the leadership process: (1) a *leader* operating in a (2) *situation* in relation to the (3) *personalities, attitudes, and abilities* of the followers. The present state of knowledge is such that it is not now possible to define with precision the specific leader qualities required for effective performance in defined situations with particular types of followers. However, the general dimensions of the problem are known.

Different types of followers—the group that is led—respond to different kinds of leadership. Some have great initiative and self-confidence; they respond best when they can assert themselves and work on their own. Other subordinates by reason of their background and personality development must have everything structured for them. Otherwise they feel lost. They require close guidance. Some employees like to take on new and important responsibilities; others simply are willing to "put their time in" and are content to obtain all their satisfactions off the job. Some persons exhibit little identification with the goals of the organization. Again we find that some employee groups possess a high level of education. They accordingly will respond to a particular style of leadership that would be quite inappropriate for a group having little formal education.

There are innumerable situations in which leadership must operate. Variations exist in the nature of the tasks, organizational environment, time dimensions, and social and cultural environment. The relationship that a leader or supervisor has with his boss affects the way in which he deals with his subordinates. On the one hand, there may be mutual confidence and trust between them; on the other, the supervisor may him-

---

[3] Ralph M. Stogdill, "Personal Factors Associated with Leadership: A Survey of the Literature," *The Journal of Psychology,* Vol. 25 (January 1948), pp. 35-71. Added evidence of the view that leadership is specific to the situation can be found in an experimental investigation by Carter and Nixon. See Launor F. Carter and Mary Nixon, "An Investigation of the Relationship Between Four Criteria of Leadership Ability for Three Different Tasks," *The Journal of Psychology,* Vol. 27 (January 1949), pp. 245-261.

self feel insecure in respect to his boss. The insecure position of a supervisor is bound to transmit itself into his dealings with his subordinates.

Different jobs within the work organization require different abilities. The assertive, exuberant, outgoing, people-centered sales manager would find himself ill at ease and ill equipped to supervise a design engineering department. Likewise it should be apparent that the skills and behavior required by our industrial giants in the early twentieth century—the Rockefellers, Fords, and Carnegies—to found industrial empires were quite different from the coordinative and administrative skills needed by the present-day executive to guide a modern enterprise.

A business leader operating in a Latin-American cultural climate must behave differently from one operating the same kind of enterprise in New York State. Variations between these two environments exist in the customs and expectations of the people both within and outside the work organization.

Any Common Traits?

We have emphasized that there is no such thing as the "leader type." Different situations and different groups require different leadership abilities. Generally speaking there are considerable variations in the personality, ability, capabilities, and skills of successful leaders. Yet with all of the research that has been done into this problem, it can reasonably be asked whether there are not a few characteristics of successful leaders that the practical executive can give attention to when he is selecting subordinate leaders. The answer is that yes, there are some traits that appear in a majority of the investigations of leadership. But it should be remembered that although the statistical correlations between these traits and leadership ability are positive, the correlations are often low. The correlations also do not prove a cause-and-effect relationship. It may actually require one set of traits to achieve a position of leadership and another, but related, set of abilities to maintain that position.

Intelligence.   Studies of leadership tend to show that a leader has somewhat greater intelligence than his followers. However, he will not usually have a great excess of intelligence over the average of his followers.[4] A manager of scientists would have, on the average, somewhat higher intelligence than his followers. But a person possessing the level of intelligence of a typical Ph.D. in physics would have far too much to supervise successfully a gang of laborers. In a study of 468 managers in thirteen companies, Mahoney, Jerdee, and Nash found that effective managers were somewhat more intelligent (as measured by a standard mental abilities test) than less effective managers.[5]

[4] Stogdill, *op. cit.*, pp. 44-45.
[5] Thomas A. Mahoney, Thomas H. Jerdee, and Allan N. Nash, "Predicting Managerial Effectiveness," *Personnel Psychology* (Summer 1950), pp. 147-163.

Social Sensitivity. Because he deals constantly with others and achieves his own and group objectives through the efforts of other people, the successful leader must be accurately attuned to others. He must be aware of their feelings, goals, and problems. He must be able to sense and judge accurately human reactions in order to be able to influence others. The successful leader must also be able to sense the values of the whole group he directs. He must be socially perceptive.

Activity and Social Participation. A man is unlikely to rise to a position of leadership and is unlikely to maintain that position if he is passive, apathetic, and aloof. The successful leader tends to initiate action for others. He is awake, alert, and enthusiastic. He proposes, suggests, and coordinates. Leaders tend to participate actively in group functions. Because leadership actions involve influencing other people, a successful leader must be skilled in working with people. Stogdill has reported positive correlation in a large number of investigations between leadership and the traits of social activity, biosocial activity, and social skills.[6]

Communication Skills. Since a leader exercises his skills primarily by interacting with his subordinates and with others outside his group, he must be effective as a communicator. He need not be, in any sense, a silver-tongued orator; but he must have a sufficient range of communication abilities to transmit his messages accurately. Fluency of speech is especially important.

INFORMAL, ELECTED, AND APPOINTED LEADERS

In Chapter 16, "Group Relations and Informal Organization," it was pointed out that in the informal social groupings in a business enterprise certain members frequently rise to positions of prominence within the group. They are looked up to by the members, and they exert strong influence over group behavior.

It is because these individuals have achieved high status, are popular, and are respected that they are able to shape effectively the actions of the group. They lead through persuasion, influence, and prestige. But they possess no formal authority or power. They do not have an arsenal of rewards and penalties to dispense as do executives in a company. People follow them because they feel (at the time at least) that their own personal goals and those of the group can best be attained by cooperating with the demands made by the informal leader.

There are countless kinds of formal organizations in our society in which the leader or leaders are elected by the members of the organization. These are essentially voluntary associations. In a voluntary and democratic organization those who achieve positions of leadership are chosen because

[6] Stogdill, *op. cit.,* pp. 56-59.

they reflect the popular sentiment. Examples are labor unions, service clubs such as Rotary and Kiwanis, professional societies, social clubs, political groups, and veterans organizations. The members of these groups choose by the democratic process leaders whom they agree to follow for a specified term of office. In some of these groups, custom dictates that a different slate of officers (president, secretary, treasurer, and so on) shall be nominated and selected at each election.

Many of these voluntary organizations represent an activity which is only a fringe function to many of the members. They are ruled by an oligarchy. Only a small group take an active interest in the affairs of the association. The majority are only minimally involved. The members suffer little if they leave the organization. In these the leader cannot compel anybody to do anything. If the members are enthusiastic about the objectives and composition of the group, they may work hard and become quite dedicated. They are willing to follow a good leader. Others are apathetic. Even if some of the apathetic ones should be chosen or appointed to a minor office (they may seek it for the honor), the president of the group can get them to exert themselves only by moral persuasion. The possible rewards and penalties he has available are very restricted and mild.

Some voluntary organizations, such as labor unions and political associations, play a much more prominent part in the lives of their members. In these cases, elected leaders strive to build up a strong following of supporters so that they can continually be re-elected. In the case of unions, the leaders exert a powerful influence upon the jobs and economic well-being of their constituents. Some union leaders hold vast power because they control jobs via the union hiring hall. They likewise can appoint devoted followers to choice positions as business agents, organizers, and international representatives. Political leaders exert considerable influence especially when their party is in power. The granting of a host of government jobs to loyal supporters of the party (the spoils system) is a system of rewards the leader can use to maintain his position. Even the leaders of the party that is out of power usually have important "connections" so that they can do favors for their supporters and thereby maintain the active loyalty of the party membership.

In both informal work groups and friendship cliques in the factory and in voluntary associations, such as clubs, fraternal organizations and unions, leadership is essentially by consent of the membership. If the members feel that the leader is no longer effective in satisfying their goals, they can replace him.

Let us now contrast the foregoing with the case of the leader in a formal work organization. He may be a shop foreman, a manufacturing superintendent, or a plant manager. These persons are not selected by their followers. They do not govern with the consent of the governed.[7] They

---

[7] Except where there is tyranny, an executive cannot maintain his position, in the long run, of course, unless he satisfies both his superiors and his subordinates.

occupy a position of formal command, and their authority comes from the top down to a large extent. They are appointed by their superiors in the hierarchy. Their job tenure is at the pleasure of their superiors, not their followers. The appointed managers may demonstrate either good or very poor leadership ability. A manager may have obtained his position of command because his superiors observed that he exhibited the skills and behavior of a good executive. On the other hand, he could also have obtained his position simply through nepotism, "pull," or financial control of the organization.

In the formal work organization most employees just expect that they will have to follow orders from their bosses. In the ordinary, run-of-the-mill situation the manager really does not need to display much leadership ability. But it is for the more demanding problem, the delicate situation, that he must perform in the role of a real leader.

In contrast to informal group leaders and many elected leaders of voluntary organizations, the business manager possesses great power over his subordinates. He has at his disposal a whole host of rewards (promotions, pay increases, more attractive job assignments) and penalties (demotions, discharge, unpleasant job assignments, and the threat thereof). In addition to these, of course, he uses moral suasion, personal example, influence, and other tools of the informal leader.

AUTHORITY AND POWER

In the formal organization—whether it be industrial, commercial, government, military, or philanthropic—leadership takes place in conjunction with authority and power. In fact, these are to a degree necessary concomitants of leadership.

Authority

In Chapter 6, "Organization," authority was defined as the legitimate right to direct or influence the performance of others. During the first four decades of this century a number of writers on the subject of management and organization viewed authority as including both the *right* and the *power* to exact performance from other persons. Men such as Mooney and Reiley,[8] Fayol,[9] and Urwick[10] have expounded these views. These men and others who share similar conceptions have been designated by very recent writers as belonging to the "traditional" school regarding the subject of organization and management. This view of authority holds that the source of authority and of power is at the top of the hier-

[8] James D. Mooney and Alan C. Reiley, *The Principles of Organization* (New York: Harper & Row, 1939).

[9] Henri Fayol, *General and Industrial Management* (trans. Constance Storrs) (New York: Pitman Publishing Corp., 1949).

[10] Lyndall F. Urwick, *The Elements of Administration* (New York: Harper & Row, 1944).

archy and that it flows downward through the structure by edict. Subordinates comply because they are compelled to do so.

In recent years "behavioral scientists"—social psychologists, sociologists, social anthropologists, and political scientists—have taken a totally different view of authority. They hold that authority stems from a willingness of followers to accept orders from others. If they reject the attempt to exert authority from above, then the authority has not become effective. This conception of the nature of authority is well stated by Tannenbaum, Weschler, and Massarik.

> The real source of the authority possessed by an individual lies in the acceptance of its exercise by those who are subject to it. It is the subordinates of an individual who determine the authority which he may wield. Formal authority is, in effect, nominal authority. It becomes real only when it is accepted.[11]

This view of authority is shared by March and Simon and many other modern theorists.[12] There is a tendency for "behaviorists" to consider that employees are free either to accept or to reject the orders from their bosses. In actual fact in the typical work organization this freedom by the subordinate is so closely constricted that he has very little choice but to follow orders from above if he wants to remain in that company.

In medieval times in Europe authority was thought to stem from the divine right of kings, who parceled out some of this to feudal lords and the landed aristocracy. The peasants at the bottom of these socioeconomic systems had few rights and no authority. They occupied a decidedly subservient position, which was their expected lot in life. When they were impressed into military service, they found the discipline more rigorous, but the authority and power structure was similar to that experienced as civilians. Their military commanders were members of the aristocracy, and the chief military leader was usually the king who possessed absolute authority. Mostly the peasants were illiterate and of a decidedly inferior status. Thus the divine right of kings, custom, and tradition dictated obedience of subordinates to orders from above.

In modern-day United States—as in most constitutional democracies—authority in private business enterprises is often considered to stem from the sacred right of private property guaranteed by common law and the United States Constitution. Prior to the Emancipation Proclamation in 1862, slaves were considered to be private property. Managers and entrepreneurs have often felt that they possessed nearly absolute authority to do with their property as they saw fit. But the fact of the matter is that the public creates both the laws and the Constitution, and it can alter

---

[11] Robert Tannenbaum, Irving R. Weschler, and Fred Massarik, *Leadership and Organization: A Behavioral Science Approach* (New York: McGraw-Hill Book Company, Inc., 1961), p. 271. Quotation by permission.

[12] James D. March and Herbert A. Simon, *Organizations* (New York: John Wiley & Sons, 1958), pp. 90-91.

them to best serve the needs of the society as a whole. In reality, then, authority stems from the citizens and from society as a whole.

In communistic, totalitarian regimes private property rights are non-existent or else severely restricted. Here authority is considered to stem from the state and ultimately again from the people as a whole (or society).

Modified View of Authority

Both the "traditionalists" with their view that authority always comes from the top downward and the "behaviorists" with their belief that authority always depends upon acceptance of orders by the subordinates have tended to look at authority with too narrow and fixed a focus. The "traditionalists" have an authoritarian bias, whereas the "behaviorists" have a democratic bias. The fact of the matter is that most work organizations in our society are rather autocratically run. Yet they operate in a society where freedom, independence, the rights of the individual, and democratic government are cherished. These ideals plus the relatively high level of educational attainment in the United States—and in much of Western Europe as well—mean that the gulf between leaders and the led has progressively narrowed over the past century and a half. Educated subordinates have ideas of their own and often are able to shape and modify orders as they flow down the organizational hierarchy.

That authority rests, to an extent, upon its acceptance by followers can be observed in many situations. If workers in a factory disagree with an order to give up their coffee breaks, there are a multitude of ways in which they can nullify that order without actually resorting to open insubordination or a strike. A superintendent whom the employees hate may have little real authority and power over them because they follow only the letter and not spirit of his orders. Deliberate slowdowns, absenteeism, strikes, carelessness, and a loss of interest in the work can all be manifestations of employee refusal to accept absolute authority from above.

Yet everyone who has ever held a job knows that his boss holds tremendous power over his economic livelihood. The employer controls a large share of the rewards and penalties in the lives of working men. A pay increase or the threat of withholding one, a promotion or the threat of a demotion or discharge, a better work assignment or unpleasant chore, these and a score of other rewards and penalties are available to the employer to enforce compliance with his orders.

We can say then that authority partly stems from the top down and partly stems from the bottom up. There must be a consensus between leaders and followers. In any particular instant situation the authority and the power may be all on the side of the superior (or management). In this case the subordinate pretty much is compelled to do what he is told because the alternatives to compliance are too terrible to endure.

In other cases the subordinates may be in a position to exercise considerable influence over the way the orders from above are carried out and indeed over whether the orders are acted upon at all.

In addition to management and labor (superior and subordinate), we find that such outside agencies as the government can play a significant role in the exercise of authority within the business enterprise. Court action can stop labor strikes and can stop management efforts to circumvent competitive pricing. The authority of the employer to discharge workers is partly regulated by law. In addition, the community exerts forces and pressures upon both executives and employees altering their behavior in ways not accounted for by a simply unidimensional upward-downward continuum.

Power and Leadership

For leadership to be effective, it must be supported by some measure of power. This is true for both the formal work organization and the informal social group. A leader tries to influence the behavior of other people. He may give them instructions, he may coordinate activities of specialists, he may seek to reconcile conflicting views, and he may seek to impel them to greater efforts to achieve higher productivity.

What is power? Power is the ability to obtain dominance of one's objectives and methods. It often involves the capacity to employ force if necessary.

French and Raven have postulated that there are five bases or sources of power. Although an understanding of the nature of power is facilitated by this categorization, it should be pointed out that more than one power element is often at work in any given situation. [13] Their bases of power are (1) reward, (2) coercion, (3) legitimacy, (4) identification with the power figure, and (5) expertise.

The arsenal of rewards the executive in industry can dispense to get his men to work to achieve designated goals is well known. Positive leadership through rewards tends to develop a considerable amount of loyalty and devotion of subordinates toward their leaders.

Coercion is the application of actual force to secure one's way. In private industry, physical coercion is almost never used by management. But coercion is also punishment. And the business leader often obtains compliance simply by the threat (often implied) of demotion, transfer, layoff, or discharge. The supervisor who shuns and ignores a subordinate is also punishing him. So is the superior who berates his employees.

Legitimate power is analagous to authority in the organization wherein employees ordinarily accept orders from their supervisors because they accept the authority system when they decide to work for that company. Cultural values also provide a basis for legitimate power. Thus a father

[13] John R. P. French, Jr., and Bertram Raven, "The Bases of Social Power," in Dorwin Cartwright (ed.), *Studies in Social Power* (Ann Arbor, Mich.: Institute for Social Research, 1959).

in most societies throughout the world is looked upon as the head of the family. So that order and stability may be maintained, the members of an organization know that they must abide by the reasonable directives of their officially designated superiors in the hierarchy. Repeated failure to follow legitimate authority would invite chaos.

Sometimes a follower develops a strong emotional attachment to a leader. There is a feeling of oneness between the two. Thus the leader is able to influence and modify the behavior of the subordinate because the latter identifies strongly with the leader. This is called referent power or identification with a power figure. This type of power is less common in business and industry than any of the other four classifications.

Persons who possess a vast fund of knowledge and technical skill often have the power over others who are less well informed. Thus when the respected physician suggests that people should get vaccinations against flu, his advice is usually heeded by the majority. When the lawyer formulates a procedure for handling litigation, the layman company president tends to adopt his advice. Power based upon expertise is usually limited to a specialized area of activity—that of the expert's specialty, for example, law, engineering, physics, or medicine. The technical expert usually cannot extend his power to other spheres of activity.

SITUATIONAL FACTORS IN LEADERSHIP

Recognizing that there is no single most effective leadership style for generating good performance from the team or unit in all situations, one can reasonably ask what style works best in what situation. The human-relations-oriented leader may be most effective in one situation, whereas the hard-driving boss gets better results in another situation. The perceptive and successful leader may be able to diagnose accurately the demands of the situation and alter his behavior somewhat to meet varying situations. Alternately it might be possible to restructure the work environment so that a leader who feels comfortable practicing a particular leadership style can be most effective in a situation suited to him. Or perhaps the leader can be assigned to that job where his particular leadership style is most useful.

Some of the more prominent situational dimensions in determining leader effectiveness are as follows:

1. Leadership style
2. Followers' expectations
3. Organizational climate
4. Leader-group relations
5. Task structure
6. Power position of leader

Leadership Style

Some leaders are predominantly people centered, and others are mainly production centered. People centered managers have variously been characterized as employee centered, relations oriented, democratic, and permissive. The Ohio State University studies in leadership characterized such leaders as scoring high in "consideration."[14] Such individuals are interested in their people and are sensitive to what their followers think of them. They tend to be supportive and helpful. They "go to bat" for their people. They encourage suggestions from their subordinates.

The opposite style of leader is highly production or task oriented. He continually pushes for production. He is prominent in issuing orders, telling employees how to do something, checking performance, and announcing deadlines to be met. He tends to be autocratic. The Ohio State studies rated such a leader as scoring high in "initiating structure." This style of leadership is far more traditional than is the employee-centered style. It is exemplified by military leadership in its extreme form. This pattern is also widespread in private business and government bureaucracy.

Although much of the research in leadership has classified the leader's style as being either employee-centered or production-centered, it should be clear to the reader that leader styles in actuality vary along a continuum from an extremely autocratic form through to a very permissive, relationship-oriented form. But classifying leaders according to this dichotomy is convenient for discussion.

The really critical aspect of leader style is how he is perceived by his subordinates. A given supervisor may see himself as a kind, understanding, supportive leader when in fact his people view him as very hard driving and somewhat neglectful of their problems. Thus they will respond to him as a production-centered boss.

The question of leadership style in relation to its effects upon the followers and upon group performance has received considerable attention from social scientists.

An experiment that has been considered a classic in this field is that conducted by White and Lippitt under the direction of Kurt Lewin in 1938 at the State University of Iowa.[15] In the second of the two major Iowa experiments into leadership, four groups of ten-year-old boys were each exposed to three different styles of adult leadership—autocratic, democratic, and laissez faire. Four adult leaders were given advanced training so that they each were proficient in the different leadership styles. The groups of boys were organized into clubs to carry on various craft activities, such as carpentry, mural painting, wood carving, soap carving, and the making of plaster of Paris masks. In setting up these groups, the researchers tried to equate them in terms of scholarship and interpersonal

---

[14] Carroll L. Shartle, *Executive Performance and Leadership* (Englewood Cliffs, N.J.: Prentice-Hall, Inc., 1956), pp. 115-123.

[15] Ralph K. White and Ronald Lippitt, *Autocracy and Democracy: An Experimental Inquiry* (New York: Harper & Row, 1960).

relationships, such as sociometric attraction and rejection, leadership, quarrelsomeness, obedience, and social activity.

In describing the experiment, we shall concentrate upon the autocratic and democratic leadership patterns, because the laissez-faire style proved to be quite ineffective, as might be expected. In the autocratic situation all determination of policy was made by the leader; he dictated the activity steps one at a time; he dictated the particular work tasks and work companions of each member; he was personal in his praise or criticism; and he was aloof from active group participation. On the other hand, in the democratically led groups, policies were developed by group discussion. Activity perspective was gained during these discussions, and the leader gave alternatives when suggesting procedures. The boys were free to choose their own partners. The leader was fact-minded in his praise and criticism and tended to be a group member in spirit.

In the autocratic-leadership pattern the leaders spent a high portion of their time in giving orders, making disruptive commands, and in giving nonobjective praise and criticism. Conversely the democratic leaders spent much of their time making guiding suggestions, giving information, and encouraging the boys to make their own decisions democratically.

What were the results of this experiment? As far as achieving work goals, the democratic and autocratic groups were about equally efficient. The autocracy created much hostility, aggression, and scapegoating among the boys. Several boys dropped out during the periods of autocratic leadership. There was more dependence and less individuality in the autocracy. In contrast there was more group-mindedness and more friendliness in the democracy. There was more mutual praise, friendly playfulness, and readiness to share group property in the democracy.

Rensis Likert has summarized the findings of numerous investigations conducted by researchers at the Institute for Social Research of the University of Michigan. Studies were made in widely varied kinds of work such as clerical, sales, and manufacturing. Employee-centered supervisors were much more likely to be in charge of high producing sections, whereas production-centered supervisors predominated in low producing sections.[16] There were of course some situations (although in the minority) where production-oriented supervisory style correlated with high productivity. There are enough occurrences of this latter relationship appearing in various studies of leadership to alert one to the fact that many other factors besides leadership style determine the performance of work groups.

Followers' Expectations

The attitudes and responses of the members of a work team to their leaders have a decided bearing upon their performance. Vroom studied

---

[16] Rensis Likert, *New Patterns of Management* (New York: McGraw-Hill Book Company, 1961), pp. 9-11.

108 supervisors in a parcel delivery company. He found that those persons whose personality showed strong needs for independence and low needs for authoritarianism exhibited higher levels of productivity on the basis of a number of different measures when they were allowed to participate in decisions affecting their jobs. However, there was no clear-cut correlation between job performance and personality for those supervisors having high dependency needs, that is, low in need for independence and high for authoritarianism.[17] In Vroom's studies the supervisors were viewed as followers in their relations with their superiors in the context we are concerned with here.

Some followers, by reason of family background and the general subculture in which they have lived, may respond more favorably to democratic, employee-oriented leadership, whereas others will expect to be docile and to be told what to do and how to do it.

Organizational Climate

If a military officer were to be transferred to the position of academic dean in a university and if he were to try to impose a regimented existence upon the professors, he would meet with immediate resistance. They simply would not respond to this type of authoritarian leadership. He would end up being a dean without a school. Conversely it is difficult for a permissive, employee-centered, democratic leader to give full range to his characteristic style in a highly autocratic regimented organization. His contacts with his superiors, peers, and subordinates would operate to discourage this. He would not be encouraged to behave this way.

Leader-Group Relations

One of the most critical aspects of leadership effectiveness is the relationship between the group members and their leader. Is the leader accepted by his men? Do they like and trust him? Is he able to obtain their compliance without exerting a great deal of time and effort for each transaction? How readily do they respond to his attempts to initiate action?

The effectiveness of the leader and his group is poor if he and his men get along badly. Friction, hostility, and resentment can make results accomplishment difficult. Where the leader knows that his men resent him, he may still get compliance with his directives. However, he may have to resort to the use of power and other stratagems to induce performance. And group performance tends to be minimal in such circumstances.

Task Structure

Some jobs and departments are highly structured, and others are not. Much of the work performed by blue-collar workers in factories is quite

[17] Victor H. Vroom, "Some Personality Determinants of the Effects of Participation," *Journal of Abnormal and Social Psychology,* Vol. 59 (November 1959), pp. 322-327.

structured and engineered. The work routines are carefully planned and laid out by industrial engineers. Vast numbers of workers in industry perform machine-tending and parts-assembly operations where the routines have been carefully spelled out. The army of clerks in the nation's offices are also mainly engaged in specialized, structured tasks.

On the other hand, many jobs are and can be only loosely defined. The work is variable. Job procedures cannot be specified in advance. Decisions must be made as one goes along. Such is the work of managers, engineers, scientists, doctors, salesmen, professors, staff specialists, and many skilled craftsmen and technicians.

The leadership style that is most fruitful for unstructured work tends to be different from that for structured jobs. Actually the leaders' lot is easier when work procedures have been fully spelled out in standard operating procedures (S.O.P.'s) and the workers have been trained to do a repetitive type of job. The flow of work itself, for example, an assembly line, may serve as the initiator of action for each employee. When the subassembly reaches his work station, he has been taught to fasten part number 10936 with four screws. On the other hand, where the work is unstructured, the leader and his group together must develop ways of solving job problems. The application of power or dependency upon previous programming may be wholly inappropriate.

Power Position of Leader

The extent to which the leader can apply sanctions often affects his ability to obtain compliance from his followers. A manager in a company is endowed with many elements of power that help him get performance from his people. He can hire, fire, promote, and transfer (or effectively recommend these). He evaluates the performance of his people and grants or withholds pay raises. He is given legitimate authority and symbols of office by the organization. All of these elements of power can serve the leader.

At the other end of the scale, is the informal leader who must gain cooperation by persuasion. He holds his post because the members feel he is best able to represent their interests. However, he can be deposed easily.

Relationships Among Key Dimensions

It should be apparent by now that the question of which leadership style yields the best results is really determined by the conditions under which this leadership is operating. Task-oriented leadership may be more effective under some conditions and employee-oriented direction may work better under other conditions. Although all the answers have not been discovered as yet, major attacks upon this problem have been made. The most ambitious research in this field has been conducted by Fred

Fiedler and his associates at the University of Illinois. Fiedler's work has been going on since the 1950's.[18]

His investigations have sought to explain how certain situational factors in leadership are related. These factors are (1) leadership style, (2) leader-member relations, (3) task structure, and (4) leader power position. He and his associates have systematically investigated the performance of work groups under various combinations of these four dimensions. Among the groups studied have been athletic teams, church groups, consumer-sales cooperatives, factories, aviation cadets, open-hearth steel crews, supermarket grocery departments, and hospital nursing.

Fiedler has constructed a contingency model of leadership effectiveness based upon the degree of favorableness of the group-task situation. The favorableness of the situation is the degree to which the situation enables the leader to exert influence over his group. According to Fiedler, the most crucial element in leadership is the leader-member relationship, that is, the extent to which they trust him and will respond to him. Eight situational combinations have been studied and classified according to data from empirical investigations. These range from a situation most favorable to the leader (good leader-member relations, structured task, and strong power position) all the way to the most unfavorable situation (poor leader-member relations, unstructured task, and weak power position). For a summary of these eight combinations see Figure 17-1.

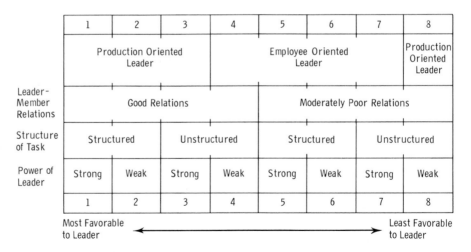

Figure 17-1. Chart Showing How Optimal Leadership Style Varies With Situational Elements. Group performance is good under all eight categories. Numbers 1 through 8 designate situational categories. Chart based upon data in Fred E. Fiedler, *A Theory of Leadership Effectiveness,* New York: McGraw-Hill Book Company, 1967, Chapter 9. Adapted with permission.

[18] Fred E. Fiedler, *A Theory of Leadership Effectiveness* (New York: McGraw-Hill Book Company, 1967).

Let us illustrate a few of the combinations depicted on the chart. In combination 1 the chart tells us that a task- or production-oriented leader achieves good results when he is fully accepted by his followers and has a strong power position and when the work is highly structured. This typology would fit an Army platoon in a basic-training camp wherein the officers held great power and the training exercises were fully detailed in advance. It would fit the case of a factory foreman supervising a group of female assemblers doing short-cycle tasks. In these cases we are assuming that leader-follower relations are satisfactory.

Employee-oriented leadership is most effective in environments where the work is unstructured and where the power position of the leader is less strong. Thus the chairman of a deliberative and planning committee may have to be quite supportive and permissive in order to obtain creative ideas from the members. Pressure tactics would be destructive here.

Category 8 depicts a situation where the power of the leader is weak, the task is unstructured, and the relations between leader and subordinate are not especially good. Such a case might occur when the group is placed in a very stressful situation that threatens their survival. A task-oriented leader is likely to get the best results even though he possesses little formal power. If the group accepts him as their leader, they will feel very dependent on him for their survival. There will be little time for him to develop a group consensus or to build warm relationships.

Implications of Situational Leadership

Personnel directors and others who must plan and build organizations should recognize the varied leadership requirements of different positions in their companies. Leadership skills can be learned. An important ingredient of management development programs is leadership training. Although many training programs have sought to increase the human relations consciousness of supervisors and this is all to the good, caution must be exercised such that all managers are not cast into the same mold. Self-insight is useful. Managers should be sensitive to and aware of their impact on others. They should be able to vary their responses to meet different situations and groups. However, training directors must remember that it is not only difficult but risky to try to change a person's personality structure. One can hardly expect to change a hard-driving production boss into a diplomatic, socially sensitive, participative group chairman.

Perhaps it is more fruitful to try to adjust the situation than to mold the leader. Thus task-oriented men can be assigned to highly structured departments. Free-rein leaders can be assigned to situations where the group members are self-actualized and the work is varied and challenging. In addition, it may be possible to adjust the power position of the supervisor. In some cases certain of the followers may advantageously be transferred to improve leader-follower relations. Those hostile to the department head may be shifted to units where they are more compatible with the leader.

LEADERSHIP—A CLOSING WORD

Behavioral scientists have discovered much over the past few decades regarding the leadership process. But a great deal is still either unknown or at best vaguely understood. The nature of the problem—to develop a unified, complete, and fully accepted theory of leadership—is extremely difficult. Yet considerable strides are being made.

Meanwhile, practicing leaders in the workaday world continue—as they have done since the beginning of time—to carry out leadership duties and responsibilities. The pragmatic executive may be highly successful as a leader without benefit of formal theory to guide him. Some managers achieve favorable results but cannot explain in a meaningful way how or why their leadership acts were effective. Others make serious errors that hinder their efficiency. Others are total failures as leaders but still may be quite capable in performing other functions of management.

As leadership theory becomes more sophisticated, educators and directors of management-development activities in industry can more fully integrate training in leadership into their programs.

Questions for Review and Discussion

1. Describe a situation you have observed (at work, college, fraternity, or social organization) where one (or more) persons in the group informally assumed leadership functions. Describe what functions the leader performed. How did he behave? Did the group accept his leadership acts?
2. What is leadership? Give a definition.
3. What is a charismatic leader? Why do people follow such an individual?
4. "A successful leader is an unusually talented individual who is endowed through birth and otherwise with those traits that induce others to follow him. He is born to command." Discuss and evaluate this statement.
5. Contrast the knowledge and skills required of a leader in the following paired situations:
   a. A leader of a pick-and-shovel labor gang and a leader of a group of research scientists
   b. A leader of a symphony orchestra and a leader of a mountain-climbing expedition
   c. A leader of a group of college professors (a dean) and a combat military commander in the army (a captain)

    d. A labor union leader and an industrial executive

    e. An elected president of a campus social organization and an appointed supervisor in industry

6. Are there any traits that seem to be common to successful leaders? Discuss.
7. What is the source of authority in the business corporation?
8. What is the relationship between leadership and power? What are the bases of power upon which leaders may depend?
9. What factors determine what particular style of leadership will be used or should be used? Explain the effect of each factor upon the leadership pattern.

CASE PROBLEM

Harold Evans has served as the president of the Central City chapter of a nationwide professional society for three months. His local chapter has a membership of 125, consisting largely of members of middle management from a score or more of industrial companies. Membership in this organization is entirely voluntary, although a number of the companies do sponsor (pay for) the memberships of some of their personnel.

The society has a program of activities that consists of the following: (1) a monthly evening dinner meeting at which there is a guest speaker, (2) major fall and spring all-day conferences on subjects of professional interest to the members, (3) occasional plant visitations, (4) other occasional functions of an educational and/or social nature.

This local chapter is governed by the elected officers, including Harold Evans and certain appointive committee chairmen. This group, known as the Executive Council, meets monthly to direct and decide the affairs of the chapter.

Harold has been perplexed by a number of serious problems during his short term of office. These are as follows:

1. The responsibility for obtaining a qualified speaker for each dinner meeting is assigned to a member of the local chapter. He in effect is in charge of all arrangements and the program for that meeting. Some of these meeting chairmen have failed to perform their assignments properly. One meeting had to be postponed two weeks because the meeting chairman failed to engage a speaker and failed to notify Harold of this predicament far enough in advance. Harold had to find a speaker himself and, in effect, run the meeting.
2. Attendance at dinner meetings has dropped off 25 per cent from the level of previous years.
3. The membership chairman has failed to follow up in contacting promising prospects who might be qualified and who might wish to join the organization.

4. One man who was assigned to set up an all-day conference involving several out-of-town speakers made serious errors of judgment and spent an excessive amount of money on brochures, speakers' fees, and luncheon costs. The man was very enthusiastic and worked hard. Harold does not want to criticize him severely because he may be crushed and then lose interest in the society.

Harold is a department head in his place of employment. When similar problems occur in his department he has the power, authority, and resources to demand good performance from his subordinates. But he recognizes that as president of an organization where people serve on a voluntary basis, he must employ a somewhat different approach to leadership.

Questions

1. What advice could you give Harold Evans?
2. How can he motivate the elected and appointed officers to give superior performance to the organization?
3. Analyze the authority and power position of the president.
4. Can Harold Evans employ autocratic methods to accomplish the objectives of the local chapter? Discuss.

Suggestions for Further Reading

Bass, Bernard M., *Leadership, Psychology, and Organizational Behavior,* New York: Harper & Row, 1960.

Bennis, Warren G., "Leadership Theory and Administrative Behavior: The Problem of Authority," *Administrative Science Quarterly,* Vol. 4, No. 3, December 1959, pp. 259-301.

Bowers, David G. and Stanley E. Seashore, "Predicting Organizational Effectiveness with a Four-Factor Theory of Leadership," *Administrative Science Quarterly,* Vol. II, No. 2, 1966, pp. 238-263.

Cartwright, Dorwin, *Studies in Social Power,* Ann Arbor, Michigan: University of Michigan Press, 1959.

Farbro, P. C., "Behavioral Science and Management Style," *Training and Development Journal,* Vol. 22, April 1968, pp. 61-66.

Fiedler, Fred E., *A Theory of Leadership Effectiveness,* New York: McGraw-Hill Book Company, 1967.

Hunt, J. G., "Breakthrough in Leadership Research," *Personnel Administration,* Vol. 30, No. 5, 1967, pp. 38-44.

Kuriloff, A. H., "Identifying Leadership Potential for Management" *Personnel Administration,* Vol. 30, November-December 1967, pp. 3-5, 27-29.

Sayles, Stephen M., "Supervisory Styles and Productivity: Review and Theory," *Personnel Psychology,* Vol. 19, No. 3, 1966, pp. 275-286.

Tannenbaum, Robert, Irving R. Weschler, and Fred Massarik, *Leadership and Organization: A Behavioral Science Approach,* New York: McGraw-Hill Book Company, 1961, Part I.

White, Ralph K. and Ronald Lippitt, *Autocracy and Democracy: An Experimental Inquiry,* New York: Harper & Row, 1960.

Supervision   18

Supervision is the function of leading, coordinating, and directing the work of others to accomplish designated objectives. A supervisor guides his subordinates so that they produce the desired quantity and quality of work within the desired time. He must also see that their needs are satisfied and that his group achieves its objectives with a minimum of friction and a maximum of harmony. In short, a supervisor seeks to have his group accomplish the required work and likewise seeks to promote need satisfactions and high morale among his men.

A supervisor is a leader. It is by his actions that his men are motivated to work toward agreed-upon goals. Without leadership, whether it be of the formal or the informal type, a mass of people are uncoordinated and can accomplish nothing. Supervision is crucial to all organized endeavor. The behavior of a supervisor is vital for determining the level of productivity and morale of his work group. In one research investigation of the attitudes and motivation of 200 accountants and engineers employed in nine companies, supervision was found to be one of the chief causes for dissatisfaction. The dissatisfaction related to such aspects of supervision as incompetency, poor scheduling of work, lack of teaching ability, unfriendly relations, lack of support, and unwillingness to listen to suggestions.[1]

This chapter will examine the nature of the supervisor's job, his respon-

[1] Frederick Herzberg, Bernard Mausner, and Barbara B. Snyderman, *The Motivation to Work* (2nd Ed., New York: John Wiley & Sons, Inc., 1959). Chs. 8 and 13.

sibilities, his organizational position, problems and pressures on the supervisor, patterns of effective supervision, and the supervisor in the role of an interviewer and counselor.

Twenty years ago the types of supervisory behavior that accounted for success or failure were pretty much a matter of conjecture. Industrialists, writers, and management "experts" tended rather to generalize from their own experiences in describing how to be a successful supervisor. Few had real knowledge based upon research, and platitudes abounded. Although all the answers to effective supervision certainly have not been discovered as yet, we are on much firmer ground now, because a great deal of really significant research has been conducted by a number of organizations since the late 1940's. The question of what type of behavior makes for effective supervision can be answered with a reasonable degree of assurance.

NATURE OF SUPERVISOR'S JOB

One of the most precise definitions of a supervisor is that contained in the Labor-Management Relations Act of 1947 (Taft-Hartley Act). Section 101, Subsection 2 (11) defines a supervisor as "any individual having authority, in the interest of the employer, to hire, transfer, suspend, layoff, recall, promote, discharge, assign, reward or discipline other employees, or responsibility to direct them, or to adjust their grievances, or effectively to recommend such action, if in connection with the foregoing the exercise of such authority is not of a merely routine or clerical nature, but requires the use of independent judgment." In formulating this labor relations law the United States Congress decided that foremen and supervisors should be considered, in effect, as members of management and that they should not be entitled to representation elections and bargaining unit certifications conducted by the National Labor Relations Board, as are nonsupervisory employees. Because foremen are direct representatives of the employer in dealings with the rank-and-file worker, Congress evidently felt that it would be inappropriate for foremen and office supervisors to be union members as well.

Common parlance has tended to restrict the use of the term *supervisor* to those individuals who direct the activities of others and who are also in the lower ranks of the management hierarchy. If we divide the organization structure of a typical company into three levels of management—top, middle, and lower—then the word *supervisor* would apply to those at the lower level. In a very large corporation this lowest level would typically consist of two or three organization levels. Common job titles are foremen, assistant foreman, general foreman, and superintendent. For office and white-collar work the title *supervisor* is used, never foreman. The generic term is *supervisor,* and this can be properly used to apply to persons in charge of production workers as well as those in charge of office workers.

Now in reality, whenever a man-boss relationship exists supervision is involved. The president of a corporation guides and directs the activities of his immediate subordinates— the vice-presidents— and they in turn supervise the division heads. So we can say that the supervisory function is carried out at all levels in the organizational hierarchy. It is usually true that a corporation president deals with his vice-presidents in a somewhat different way than a foreman deals with machine operators. Vice-presidents work more independently, and their actions are not checked so closely, for example. Personal leadership is not quite so large a part of a chief executive's job as it is a foreman's. But the differences in the supervisory responsibilities and skills of a top executive differ from those of a foreman more in *degree* than they do in *kind*. The principal emphasis in this chapter is upon the supervisory level; however, it must be noted that many of the insights relating to *patterns of effective supervision,* covered later in this chapter, apply equally well to higher level managerial leadership.

Duties and Responsibilities of a Supervisor

If we were to make an on-the-spot analysis of the activities of a supervisor during a typical work week, what would we find? Although we would find some variation from department to department and from company to company in the degree of emphasis devoted to the various supervisory tasks, we would find rather surprising agreement in the list of functions which a supervisor must perform and for which he is responsible. In a very hazardous industry, safety would require a great deal of attention from a foreman, whereas in a nonhazardous one this would be a minor part of his job. However, the maintenance of safe working conditions and adherence to rules of safety is definitely a requirement of the latter's job, just as it is with the foreman in the hazardous factory.

Let us now examine the particular duties and responsibilities of a supervisor. You will note that these items are classified as "duties and responsibilities." There would not be enough hours in the day for a supervisor to perform personally all of these items himself. Therefore, in many instances he is responsible for seeing that these tasks are carried out by one or more of his subordinates. Thus he may delegate to one of his men the task of requisitioning materials and supplies or of instructing a new employee in the details of his job. Certain essential leadership functions, such as appraising, counseling, and disciplining, should not be delegated.

The order of appearance of the following duties and responsibilities does not indicate relative importance. They are all essential. For purposes of classification, certain responsibilities are listed under the heading "Personnel Management and Human Relations." However, it must be emphasized that in carrying out practically all of the other responsibilities such as production, quality, and costs, the supervisor must deal with people and exercise human relations skills. It is really not possible, in the day-to-day activities of a supervisor, to make a strict line of demarcation between those duties involved in getting out the production and those involved in personnel management.

Production
    Requisition materials and supplies
    Expedite the flow of materials and supplies
    Plan utilization of machines and equipment
    Schedule flow of work through department
    Assign employees to operations and jobs
    Check progress of employees
    Help employees clear production problems
    Maintain records of production
    Meet production schedules

Maintenance
    Check equipment for correct operation
    Order repairs to equipment
    Maintain clean and orderly working environment

Methods Improvement
    Devise new and improved work methods
    Cooperate with staff groups such as industrial engineering in developing and installing better methods and procedures

Quality
    Insure that quality standards are met
    Analyze quality reports and take corrective action on defective work
    Inspect incoming materials
    Act on changes in quality standards
    Cooperate and coordinate with quality assurance, engineering, and inspection personnel

Costs
    Control and reduce costs
    Analyze budget
    Determine causes for variances from standard costs and budgeted costs and take corrective action

Personnel Management and Human Relations
    Request additional employees as needed
    Make final employee selection decision
    Orient new employees to their environment, the requirements of the organization, and their rights and privileges
    Train employees
    Provide face-to-face leadership

Appraise performance

Coach and correct

Counsel employees

Recommend pay increases, promotions, transfers, layoffs, and discharges

Enforce rules and maintain discipline

Settle complaints and grievances

Interpret and communicate management policies and directives to subordinates

Interpret and communicate employee suggestions and criticisms to higher management

Motivate subordinates; provide rewards for good performance and behavior

Eliminate hazards and insure safe working practices

Develop own skills and abilities through self-development activities and participation in company training programs

Cooperate and coordinate with personnel department in administering the company personnel program within own department

POSITION AND PROBLEMS OF THE FOREMAN

Evolutionary Changes Since 1900

The position and status of the foreman in American industry has undergone a number of evolutionary changes since the 1900 era. A foreman is the head of a department or section involved in production or maintenance operations (as distinct from white-collar office activities). He supervises, typically, anywhere from five to forty blue-collar, rank-and-file workers.

In the early twentieth-century the shop foreman possessed a great deal of power over the production processes and the lives of his men. He was a direct representative of top management and was charged with getting the production out on time with whatever methods he knew. His authority over the job, tenure, pay, work loads, and advancement of his men was supreme. In that era, foremen were picked from among the ranks of the workers because they were tough, aggressive, and technically competent. No importance was attached to administrative and human relations skills.

During succeeding decades a number of forces emerged to alter significantly the nature of the foreman's position in industry. The size of industrial establishments became greater. Productive technology became more complex. Greater task specialization was adopted. The scientific management movement of Frederick W. Taylor inaugurated the trend toward the splitting off of technical specialties from the line supervisor's job. Taylorism was particulary evident in regard to the establishment of production planning and control and industrial engineering departments. Commencing around 1920 personnel departments began to appear throughout industry. At first these took over the hiring and firing function from the foreman. Later they began to administer training, benefits and services, and safety functions. With the rise of unions in the mass-production industries during the late 1930's, these personnel departments were often given the authority to handle disciplinary problems and settle grievances. These functions had all previously been handled exclusively by foremen. Thus it can be said that the growing trend toward functionalization—the creation of ever more staff specialists—has resulted in a reduction in the authority and status of the foreman.

Starting in the late 1930's and early 1940's, top management tended to develop an interest in "good human relations." This was sparked by the results of the famous Hawthorne experiments at the Western Electric Company and many other factors. In selecting a worker for the position of foreman, management began to give consideration to leadership ability, human-relations skill, ability to get along with others, communications skill, and the like. The "bull of the woods" foreman was becoming a thing of the past. In recent years, in many of the more advanced companies there has been a trend toward making the foreman a true department manager. Although he must deal with a host of staff personnel (accountants, personnel specialists, industrial engineers, and so on), he is granted considerable authority for final decision making in matters affecting the performance of his department. Through participation in formal management training programs, the abilities and competence of foremen are being elevated.

Organizational Position

Within the management hierarchy the foreman occupies a unique position in that he supervises nonmanagement personnel, whereas all the other managers direct other managers. His job is unique because the attitudes and expectations of rank-and-file workers are quite different from those of managers. The workers have less upward mobility. They perform more narrow, restricted jobs. They possess less education. To a considerable extent they obtain fewer need satisfactions on the job. They tend to gain most of their ego satisfactions through off-the-job activities. The foreman is the connecting link between management and labor. It is through him that the policies and directives of upper management really become operational.

A true foreman, being a supervisor, does not perform direct productive work. He does not do the same kinds of tasks as his subordinates. If he did he would be called a working leader, a group leader, or a working foreman. Generally speaking, the only occasions when a foreman does direct production work are when he must help out in an emergency and when he is instructing an employee by demonstrating the proper way to perform a job.

Pressures on the Foreman

Being a front-line leader of men at the point where all prior management planning and decision making is translated into the actual fabricating of a product or the rendering of a service, the foreman is a key man in the organization. Yet he is subjected to unremitting pressures from a number of sources. See Figure 18-1 for a graphic representation of the demands and forces impinging upon the typical foreman.

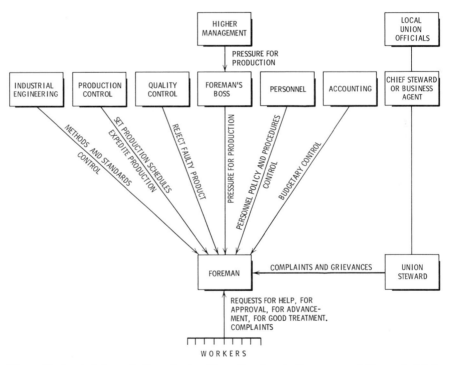

Figure 18-1. A Schematic Organization Chart Showing the Pressures and Demands Made upon a Manufacturing Foreman by His Boss, His Subordinates, Staff Departments, and the Union.

First and foremost the foreman must please his immediate line superior in the organization. There is a tendency in industry for line superintendents and production managers to be primarily interested in getting out the production. The foreman often interprets this pressure as a demand to meet the production goals even if it is necessary to sacrifice human values in dealing with his men. He knows he will be called upon the carpet if there are delays in meeting scheduled delivery dates or if his costs are excessive, but he also knows that there is less likelihood of criticism from above for overriding human relations values.

The various specialized staff departments, such as industrial engineering, production control, and personnel, exist to help line departments do a better job. They provide technical knowhow and specialized services and guide and regulate the activities of line departments. However, to the foreman the behavior of people from these departments often appears as intrusion, interference, and trouble. The industrial engineer tells him how his operations must be performed as well as how fast individual workers must work; the production control specialist tells him on what dates he must complete certain work and then rides herd on him to see that he meets these due dates. Quality control sets quality standards and rejects certain items as unsatisfactory. The personnel department sets hourly wage rates for his subordinates, hires workers for his department, and sometimes overrules his decisions on grievances filed by the union. Accounting establishes budgets and standard costs, and the foreman's line boss criticizes him if he exceeds these estimates.

A foreman is also subjected to pressures from his immediate subordinates. The employees expect supportive, favorable treatment from their foreman. They want him to help them with their work problems and to go to bat for them to obtain necessary tools and equipment, pay raises, promotions, better working conditions, and the like. Basically they want their supervisor to help them obtain satisfaction for many of their physical, social, and egoistic needs insofar as these can be provided in the work environment.[2]

If employees are represented by a labor union their problems, complaints, and grievances are brought to the foreman's attention with persistence backed by power. Most unions will not dally long if they do not receive satisfaction from the first-line supervisor. They will go over his head to higher line management or to the personnel department. Sometimes the foreman finds that his decisions on grievances are overruled by the personnel department, and sometimes he is criticized by line management for having too many labor problems.

Background, Outlook, and Status

Foremen quite generally acquire their positions as a result of promotion from the ranks of the workers. In other words, a foreman was pre-

[2] Documentation of this point, based upon a research investigation, can be found in Edwin A. Fleishman, Edwin F. Harris, and Harold E. Burtt, *Leadership and Supervision in Industry* (Columbus, Ohio: The Ohio State University, 1955), pp. 59-60. It was found that workers expected the ideal foreman to rate high on a "consideration" score. They preferred less "initiating structure" on the part of their foremen.

viously a blue-collar worker himself. Whereas in years gone by management tended to promote the skilled worker who was at the same time hard-driving, aggressive, and company-minded, nowadays managers are more sophisticated. They know that skill as a worker does not necessarily mean skill as a supervisor. In picking a man to be foreman, companies look for administrative ability, leadership, and human-relations skills, as well as technical ability.

In recent years many of the large companies engaged in manufacturing technical products have tended to hire college graduates for jobs as foremen. Usually this is looked upon as a beginning job for a young man who will rise in operating management. In many cases young engineers and business administration graduates are assigned jobs in production supervision as part of their company training programs. This practice of utilizing college graduates for careers in production management means that promotion opportunities for hourly production workers are materially reduced, and it also means that noncollege foremen find it exceedingly difficult to meet the competition for advancement to higher levels in the organization. In essence it means that the majority of these up-from-the-ranks foremen can go no higher in the organization.

Although from a formal standpoint foremen are considered as part of management, in actual practice they are often closely identified with the hourly employee level. In a study of the traits differentiating the various levels in an industrial organization. Ghiselli has found that foremen are much more like production workers than they are like middle and upper managers in regard to intelligence, supervisory ability, initiative, self-assurance, and occupational level. Ghiselli feels that these differences partially explain why some companies prefer to recruit college graduates for middle and top management positions rather than promote from lower levels of management.[3] This accentuates the problem of lack of status experienced by many foremen in industry. They themselves expect and are expected by their superiors to behave like managers, but indeed their capacities and attitudes tend to militate against it.

In many plants the foreman is not really treated as a manager. He is primarily a transmitter of orders. He is somewhat like a policeman in that he simply enforces schedules, work methods, rules, and directives established by others. His authority and discretion are severely limited.

Although, many organizations have done an excellent job in providing the foreman with the status symbols of management—exempt payroll, a desk, an office, clerical assistance, participation in management training programs—others treat him as a glorified worker or a "pusher." He may wear a blue collar, punch a time clock, and for his office have little more than a high stool and table in the corner with a bare light bulb sus-

---

[3] Edwin E. Ghiselli, "Traits Differentiating Management Personnel," *Personnel Psychology,* Vol. 12, No. 4 (Winter 1959), pp. 535-544.

pended overhead. Here he may have a clip board hanging from a nail in the wall where he keeps the day's work tickets.

If a reduction in force occurs due to production cutbacks, the foreman is vulnerable to being "bumped" back to a production job as an hourly paid worker. Foremanship is not a profession like engineering or law. A man may have worked his way up to this position with one employer, but if circumstances cause him to seek employment in a different industry, chances are he will have to start at the bottom as a worker. Then too a foreman lacks the protection against arbitrary treatment that a union affords the production worker in the factory. For the hourly worker layoffs are by seniority, and discharges are almost always appealed by the union. His pay raises are uniform and regulated by the union contract.

Implications of the Foreman's Position

The net result of all of the foregoing facts regarding the position and problems of the typical foreman in industry means that he is not secure in his status. He does not have a full measure of control over the departmental operations for which he is held accountable. He is subjected to a multitude of pressures from higher management, his workers, the union, and from staff departments. Being insecure he must be cautious. He has to play it safe. He is ever perceptive to the feelings and inclinations of his boss; yet he cannot succeed as a leader if he ignores the needs of his subordinates. As an individual he is readily replaceable. He cannot be fully self-confident. He does not always know where he stands.

PATTERN OF EFFECTIVE SUPERVISION

The behavior of a supervisor of a work group is vital for determining the accomplishments of that group. We shall now examine those kinds of supervisory behavior that tend to yield high productivity in his section or department. We shall also be interested in noting the kind of actions that cause high morale among his subordinates. It will be recalled from the discussion of leadership in Chapter 17 that research attempts to isolate a set of human traits that correlate with successful leadership have indicated that considerable variability exists among the traits of effective leaders. So it is also with supervision. A supervisor is essentially a leader of a primary work group. However, when researchers study the behavior (not personality traits) of successful and unsuccessful supervisors, they discover some very significant differences between the two groups.

Some of the most comprehensive and significant research into patterns of supervisory behavior has been conducted by the Institute for Social Research of the University of Michigan. These investigations commenced in 1947, have been carried on over a number of years, and have been conducted in a wide variety of organizations and industries. In evaluating supervisory effectiveness, the Institute has used criteria such as productivity (output per man hour), job satisfaction, turnover, absenteeism, costs, scrap loss, and employee and managerial motivation.[4] Other organizations and individuals have conducted noteworthy research in this field as well. A few of these will be mentioned in footnotes at appropriate points.

Almost never does a research investigator find that one mode of supervisory behavior causes high productivity 100 per cent of the time whereas another mode causes low productivity 100 per cent of the time. Rather the general pattern of research will show that one particular mode of action will cause a certain result, say, 70 or 80 per cent of the time. Individuals, groups, organizations, and situations are so very complex that it is not possible to get a "black and white" solution to a problem. Nevertheless, in all of the results that are presented, the researchers did obtain data that was statistically significant when subjected to standard statistical tests.

General Supervision

A supervisor is more likely to achieve high output from his section if he practices general rather than close supervision. The University of Michigan investigations bear this out.[5] Those practicing general supervision allow their employees to exercise their own discretion more frequently, to set their own pace, and to work out details of their jobs by themselves. Those practicing close, detailed supervision watch their subordinates more closely, give frequent work orders, and check upon them continually. In different words, we can say that effective supervisors are skilled in the art of delegation. There was evidence in the tractor-manufacturing company studied by the Michigan researchers that employees receiving general supervision not only produced more but also had a higher level of satisfaction with their jobs, supervisors, and the company. This in essence meant that their morale was higher.

Delegation. Effective delegation is part and parcel of successful management. However, many executives and supervisors do not know how

[4] Rensis Likert, *New Patterns of Management* (New York: McGraw-Hill Book Company, Inc., 1961), pp. 5-6. Likert points out that studies have been carried out in the following industries: automotive, chemical, delivery service, electronics and electrical instruments, electric appliances and equipment, food, heavy machinery, insurance, paper, petroleum, public utilities, railroads, textiles, hospitals, and government agencies.

[5] Robert L. Kahn and Daniel Katz, "Leadership Practices in Relation to Productivity and Morale," in Dorwin Cartwright and Alvin Zander, *Group Dynamics: Research and Theory* (2nd Ed., Evanston, Ill.; Row, Peterson & Co., 1960), Ch. 29, pp. 554-570.

An intensive observation of twelve high-rated foremen compared with twelve low-rated foremen conducted by the General Electric Company supports this conclusion regarding the efficiency of general supervision. See Public and Employee Relations Research Service, *The Effective Manufacturing Foreman,* General Electric Company, 1957.

to delegate. Ineffective supervisors feel that they must hover over their men to make things come out right. They do not trust their subordinates to do a good job. They are of the school of thought that believes that the only way to get a job done is to do it yourself. Some supervisors are psychologically insecure. Subconsciously they fear that if they assign more freedom and responsibility to one of their men, the latter will develop to the point where he will outshine his boss. In other words reluctance to delegate is sometimes an indirect way of keeping good men down.

When a man is promoted from the ranks of individual contributors to a supervisory position he must learn that his superiors will judge him, not on how much work he personally produces, but rather on how much his entire section, as a unified team, accomplishes. The supervisor can extend his knowhow and influence only by training his men adequately and then delegating tasks and responsibilities to them. The skilled delegator knows that individual employees will not perform an assignment in precisely the same way he would. But this does not bother him. He concentrates upon results. He carefully trains his men, teaches them the constraints within which they must operate (that is, company policies, procedures, and rules), sets job objectives, and then lets them perform on their own with reasonable latitude. He emphasizes objectives and results, not details.

The overworked manager who learns the art of delegation is at one and the same time able to relieve himself of some of his burden, increase the competence of his men, and raise the level of accomplishment of his unit. When should one delegate? A supervisor should delegate duties, authority, and responsibility to his people when he is overburdened (when there do not appear to be enough hours in the day to get his job done), when a subordinate has special skills and knowledge that means he can do something better, when it will aid in training subordinates, and when the activities can be done at less cost by subordinates.

Of course the supervisor who delegates work to one of his men does not give up his own obligation to see that the project is carried out properly. He is still accountable. Likewise, delegation is not a tool for dumping excessive work loads upon already overburdened employees. Furthermore, the supervisor cannot relinquish any of his essential leadership functions to one or more of his subordinates. For example, he must not grant the power to discipline his men to one of his subordinates.

Employee-Centered

Supervisors of high-productivity sections tend to be employee-centered in their manner of dealing with their subordinates, whereas supervisors of low-productivity sections tend to be primarily production-oriented in their attitudes and behavior. This fact has been determined over and over again in the various investigations conducted by the University of

Michigan group. It has also been verified by Walker, Guest, and Turner of Yale University, who made an intensive observational and interview study of foremen in an automobile assembly plant. Walker and his colleagues found that foremen who supplemented the compulsions of the assembly line with additional pressure through nagging, threatening, and demanding were least successful in getting results. On the other hand, those foremen who capitalized upon internal motivations and who built up a relationship of responsibility and respect were more successful in maintaining production, quality, and morale.[6] What is meant by the term *employee-centered*? This means that the supervisor takes a personal interest in his employees. He is supportive and helpful. He keeps them informed of matters important to them; he is available to talk over their problems, and he takes action as a result of these problem discussions.

The employee-centered supervisor respects the dignity of his men as important human beings. He is understanding of their problems. When they make mistakes he is primarily interested in showing them how to prevent a recurrence of the problem rather than in punishing them.

It may seem an anomaly that those supervisors who push the hardest for more production are least successful, whereas those who emphasize the building of good human relationships achieve higher output. How can this be explained? First of all it should be pointed out that the employee-centered leader is also interested in achieving high production. But he achieves this goal, not by driving his men, but by being supportive and helpful. Sensing that they have a "good" boss, the employees are motivated to respond favorably by producing more and by taking an interest in their work. On the other hand, employees working for a production-centered boss know that he takes no interest in them and that he looks upon them merely as tools to get the production out. They are most unlikely to respond favorably to his style of leadership.

Employees working under a climate of employee-centered leadership tend to have higher morale than those experiencing pressure-oriented leadership. They experience greater satisfaction of their wants and drives in their dealings with their supervisors and in their work environment.

Identification with Employees and Management

Sometimes when a man is made a supervisor, he feels that he must give up any loyalty he previously had for the workers and now becomes a 100 per cent company man. He feels that he must look at every issue through the eyes of higher management alone. In actuality this is an erroneous conception of the role of supervisor. A supervisor can only achieve real

---

[6] Kahn and Katz, *op. cit.,* pp. 562-565; also Rensis Likert, *Motivation: The Core of Management,* Personnel Series No. 155 (New York: American Management Association, (1953), pp. 3-21; Charles R. Walker, Robert H. Guest, and Arthur N. Turner, *The Foreman on the Assembly Line* (Cambridge, Mass.: Harvard University Press, 1956), p. 143.

results through the willing cooperation of his employees. Of all the management personnel in the organization, he is in a position to appreciate their problems best. If he will not effectively represent their interests in the councils of management, then no one else will (except, perhaps, for union representatives in a unionized organization). The really effective supervisor pulls for his men or both his men and the company, rather than for himself or the company only. Further, these supervisors were judged by higher levels of management to be more promotable than those who pulled only for the company or themselves.[7]

Concentrates upon Management Functions

Quite often a supervisor feels that he can increase the total volume of output of his section by pitching in and doing direct production work. In fact, such action is entirely consistent with prevailing notions among people in general, that a good leader must get his hands and clothes dirty and participate equally with his men to accomplish mutual goals. This is the vision of historical military combat commanders and of frontiersmen in the American West in the nineteenth century.

Contrary to common beliefs, those leaders who are in charge of the most productive sections do not themselves perform physical production type of work. Instead they concentrate their activities upon the management functions of planning, organizing, leading, and controlling. In short, they behave like supervisors, not hard-driving or superior workers.[8] Now group leaders and working foremen *do* perform direct production work, but they are not really true members of management. A working leader (or working foreman) is an hourly paid employee who receives extra compensation for performing certain, limited supervisory duties. These may occupy 20 or 30 per cent of his time, typically. Ordinarily these duties consist of such things as assigning workers to operations, clearing difficulties, checking on quality and quantity of output, answering technical questions, and instructing new workers.

The true manager sees that the physical work gets done, but he does not do it himself. Now this does not mean that a supervisor or manager is idle. Far from it. But he devotes his time to planning, anticipating and preventing crisis, coordinating the work of others, motivating, coaching, training, deciding, organizing, measuring performance, and taking corrective action where necessary.

Researchers at the University of Southern California found that the most effective supervisors in terms of productivity of their groups and other

[7] F. C. Mann and J. Dent, *Appraisals of Supervisors and Attitudes of their Employees in an Electric Power Company* (Ann Arbor, Mich.: Institute for Social Research, 1954).

[8] Kahn and Katz, *op. cit.,* pp. 555-558. They point out that supervisors having the best production records play a more differentiated role than those having a poor output record. This means that they do different work than that of the rank-and-file worker.

measures of performance did more planning and advance planning than less productive supervisors. Advance planning was distinguished from ordinary planning in that it dealt with factors not entirely within the foreseeable future. Ordinary planning was concerned with materials availability, scheduling, and the like. These effective supervisors looked more favorably upon the usefulness of paperwork also.[9] In reality unsuccessful supervisors tend to be heavily occupied with "putting out fires." Their work day consists of one crisis after another. Not only is this a terrific drain upon their energies, but it does not achieve good results. In the General Electric study of foremen, it was found that the least effective foremen spent their time primarily in finding solutions to immediate production problems, whereas the more effective foremen devoted more of their time to the planning-ahead type of activities.[10] The successful supervisor foresees possible difficulties. His plans call for actions by himself and his men in such a way that these obstacles are avoided or overcome. He is in reasonable control of people and situations because he plans ahead.

Rounding out the picture of the greater concentration of effective supervisors upon management functions is the finding in the General Electric study mentioned above that effective foremen devoted a higher portion of their working time to contacts with staff and service personnel. In this particular study they spent 32 per cent of their time with these functional specialists as against only 20 per cent for the ineffective foremen. In other words, successful supervisors find that they can gain real benefits by working closely with such individuals as the industrial engineer, quality assurance engineer, maintenance foreman, and the personnel manager. The ineffective supervisor often feels that staff personnel interfere with his work, whereas the highly productive one gains materially from his dealings with them.

The Organizational Hierarchy

The relationships between a supervisor and his men and between that supervisor and his boss have a profound effect upon productivity and morale. We shall now examine the relationship between effective supervision and power, influence, and authority.

Power, Influence, and Authority. Authority refers to the legitimate right to do something oneself and to expect performance from others. In the typical work organization we often think of authority as residing at the top of the structure and being parceled out in successive delegations and redelegations to managers and supervisors in the lower echelons. Authority is something that often is spelled out in black and white in an organization manual and in position descriptions. Power and influ-

---

[9] A. L. Comrey, J. F. Pfiffner, and W. S. High, *Factors Influencing Organizational Effectiveness: A Final Report* (Los Angeles, Calif.: University of Southern California, 1954).

[10] Public and Employee Relations Research Service, *op. cit.,* p. 5.

ence, on the other hand, are less precise than authority. They are more informal, less capable of direct measurement, and dependent more upon human relationships. A supervisor may be said to have influence with his boss if he has a rather clear voice in decisions made by the boss. If the boss consults his subordinate on important matters before taking action and if he gives his subordinate considerable latitude to run his own section as he sees fit, then we can say that the latter has influence with his superior.

The general pattern which has emerged from a number of research investigations is that the effective supervisor exercises considerable influence both upward in his dealings with his boss and downward in his dealings with his men.

In an investigation of employee attitudes and morale in a large Midwestern electric light and power company, Pelz found that the amount of influence that a supervisor was able to exert with his own superior in the organization was a key factor in determining the degree of employee acceptance and satisfaction with him. Ordinarily employees will respond favorably to a supervisor who sides with them and exhibits social closeness. However, Pelz found that supportive and helpful behavior on the part of the supervisor was effective in raising his men's morale only if the supervisor actually had considerable influence with his own superior. A supportive supervisor who has little influence upward tends to cause a lowering of satisfaction among his men.[11] It can be hypothesized that this supportive behavior raises their hopes only to have them later dashed to the ground when the men discover that their supervisor cannot deliver the goods because he lacks power and influence with the "big boss."

But supervisory influence affects much more than morale. It has a positive correlation with productivity in a department or work group. Likert, in reporting on a study in thirty-one geographically separated departments in a company operating nationally, states that there existed a positive relationship between departmental productivity and the amount of influence actually exercised by the department managers (as well as higher echelons of management) as perceived by the nonsupervisory employees. This investigation did not pertain to influence with one's superior only (as did Pelz's study) but to the total influence that the manager had in running the affairs of his department. It was dependent upon his ability to build a smooth-functioning team and develop mutual loyalty among his men, as well as his ability to get results in his dealings with his superior.[12]

In the investigations of the University of Southern California group, it was found that effective supervisors were on good terms with their own superiors and were confident of support from above. They tended to be successful in obtaining approval of requests for pay raises and other bene-

[11] Donald Pelz, "Influence: A Key to Effective Leadership in the First-Line Supervisor," *Personnel*, Vol. 29, 1952, pp. 209-217.
[12] Likert, *New Patterns of Management, op. cit.,* pp. 55-58.

fits for their men. They also felt that they had been granted authority sufficient to meet their responsibilities.[13]

We sometimes hear supervisors complain that they have not been given enough authority to really get things done right. They feel that they lack power. How does a supervisor obtain sufficient authority, influence, and power? To some extent the formal authority is doled out to a supervisor from above. In this sense he has little real control over the amount he possesses. However, in the overall, a man has a great deal to do with the total amount of authority, power, and influence he is able to exert. I have observed two managers working in the same organization. One was afraid to make decisions and was afraid of his boss. He tended to act like a messenger boy who devoted his time to transmitting messages from above. His men readily sensed his impotency. On the other hand, the other manager, who reported to the same executive as the first one, had an air of confidence in his manner. He concentrated upon building up relations with his superior in such a way as to be given wide discretionary latitude to get things done. He was an effective organizer and delegator. He clearly demonstrated to his superior that his department was achieving desired results. On day-to-day affairs he usually assumed that he had sufficient authority to make a definite decision, whereas the other manager tended to be unsure of himself and to run to his boss for permission to do something.

In general a supervisor can build up his influence with his superiors by trying to establish a basis of personal compatibility, by demonstrating that he has confidence in himself and his men, by careful fact finding and planning before presenting a program to his superior, and by building a record of successful accomplishment in his department. An executive will tend to grant greater authority and autonomy to a subordinate supervisor who has demonstrated his own competence than to one whom he continually must bail out of trouble. When it becomes evident to the nonsupervisory employees that their supervisor has considerable support and influence with higher management, then they will tend to respond positively to his leadership. In addition to this, the leader can concentrate upon building loyalty, channels of communication, and teamwork within his section. By effective delegation, by building up his men and their jobs, and by displaying confidence in their abilities, he adds to their influence as well as to his own.

Communications

Relations among people are almost impossible without communication. As one might expect from common-sense reasoning, successful supervisors are much better communicators than unsuccessful ones. In the typical business firm information, directives, and instructions from the top tend

[13] John M. Pfiffner, "The Effective Supervisor: An Organization Research Study," *Personnel,* Vol. 31, No. 6 (May 1955), pp. 530-540.

to flow much better downward through the organization than do ideas, suggestions, and complaints from the bottom up. The good supervisor strives not only to interpret management to his men but also to interpret the needs and interests of his people to higher management. In addition, the *way and manner* in which one communicates is just as important as *what* one communicates. Thus a supervisor may talk to his men in such a manner as to cause misunderstanding and to evoke antagonism and apprehension. On the other hand, he may convey essentially the same factual data but do it in such a way as to create a favorable impression in his people.

In the General Electric study of the differences in the behavior of successful and unsuccessful foremen, mentioned earlier, it was found that better foremen initiated fewer contacts but spent more total time with persons when they did initiate a contact. Likewise, when contacts were initiated by others, they spent more time in each contact. Better foremen engaged in more two-way conversations on job-related matters. Poor foremen spent more time seeking information, whereas higher-rated foremen spent more time answering requests for information.[14]

Strong Group Relationships

Some supervisors and managers tend to feel that they are primarily directing a collection of separate individuals. They deal with each of their subordinates as individuals and tend to downplay the relations of their men with each other. They seek to build strong lines of communication and loyalty between themselves and each individual worker, but discourage bonds among the men in the group. These supervisors foster competition among the men for those rewards that they can dispense. This competition, although it may increase individual performance temporarily, tends to create mistrust, conflict, and lack of cooperation among the employees in their dealings with one another.

In direct opposition to this foregoing pattern of supervision, the available evidence shows that the best supervisors are those who strive actively to build up strong group pride and cohesiveness. Although groups having strong bonds of attachment among the members are not always high producers, they tend to exhibit high production more frequently than do loose-knit, low cohesive groups. This fact was brought out in Chapter 16, "Group Relations and Informal Organization." The fostering of group pride and loyalty also contributes to higher employee satisfaction and greater morale.

In their analysis of workers and foremen in connection with automobile assembly-line production, Walker, Guest, and Turner found that the most successful foremen were those who were able to develop strong group relations. They generally had to overcome a number of difficul-

---

[14] Public and Employee Relations Research Service, *op. cit.,* p. 16.

ties standing in the way of good group relations. Principal among these problems were the physical layout of the moving conveyor line, the high noise level, and frequent shifting of the men from one work station to another. However, the successful foremen built up a pattern of group relations in such a way that the men displayed initiative in helping one another. Interactions between the foremen and the workers were more often reciprocal than unilateral. This meant that when a foreman talked with a worker, he often asked a question and listened to a response rather than just gave an order. In addition, key operators often served as channels of communication.[15]

From this and other studies it is apparent that there is a great deal to be gained from efforts by supervisors to create strong group motivation, loyalty, and solidarity. Of course, interests and drives of the group should be channeled toward department and organizational goals.

The supervisor can build group relations by first of all thinking of his employees as being group members rather than isolated individualists. He can hold periodic meetings with all of the members of his department. These meetings should not be used to lecture to the employees nor to give them a pep talk to increase output. Instead they should be used for a free interchange of views between the supervisor and his people and among the people themselves. Group *esprit de corps* can be fostered by the supervisor who goes to bat for his group for deserved pay raises, good working conditions, and needed tools, equipment, and supplies. He should encourage his employees to help one another. He should engender a feeling of group responsibility for the success of the whole section or department. He should be careful not to play favorites nor to discriminate against any individuals in his department.

TRANSMITTAL OF SUPERVISORY STYLE

In adopting a style of supervision, a foreman or manager tends to follow the lead of his boss. This is a tendency, but, of course, there are numerous exceptions in individual cases. Why is this general tendency true? The answer lies in the authoritarian nature of most commercial, industrial, and other kinds of work organizations. It is somewhat of a human tendency for a manager to think more highly of those of his subordinates who think and act as he does and to disapprove (not only privately but sometimes openly) of those who are different. So the manager often gives more support and rewards (praise, help, encouragement, promotion, pay raises, and more interesting assignments) to those who behave just like he does. In a very rigid, autocratic relationship the subordinate supervisors quickly sense this feeling on the part of the boss. Therefore, they

---

[15] Walker, Guest, and Turner, *op. cit.,* pp. 131-135.

tend to conform to the pattern of behavior that they know will please their superior.

In an investigation into the effects which participation in a supervisory training course (concerned mainly with human relations and leadership) had upon the later behavior of foremen, an Ohio State University research team found that the style of leadership practiced by the foremen's bosses was more influential in determining their behavior than were the material and attitudes they had learned in the course. If a foreman's superior scored high on a consideration score (that is, supportive and interested in his subordinates), then the foreman also tended to score high in consideration. If the foreman's superior scored high in "initiating-structure" behavior (that is, close controls and pressure upon the foreman), then the foreman himself tended to behave that way toward his subordinates.[16]

Findings by the University of Michigan researchers support the general conclusion that supervisors guide and lead their men in a manner similar to the way they are treated by their superiors in the organization. In studies in an insurance company, an agricultural equipment company, and a railroad, factors such as closeness of supervision, employee orientation, use of pressure, and relative amount of freedom were largely conditioned by the way the supervisors themselves were led by their immediate superiors.[17]

So we can see that attitudes and leadership practices tend to start at the top in an organization and are transmitted down through the chain of command. This means that a supervisor is not completely free to adopt the pattern of supervision that research data and his own personal experience may tell him he should follow. It also means that any attempts to introduce a different pattern of supervision must start with the chief executive officer and other top executives. They must practice effective supervision themselves before it will be truly possible for the subordinate echelons to do the same thing.

SUPERVISOR AS A COUNSELOR

Counseling consists of a private interview between the counselor and someone who has a problem. The aim is to increase understanding into the nature of the problem on the part of both the counselor and the counselee so that real progress can be made toward a solution. The principal emphasis in counseling is upon helping an employee solve human adjustment and emotional problems. Counseling has also been used in many companies to provide factual information to the employee on such matters as company personnel practices, promotion opportunities, financial aid,

---

[16] Fleishman, Harris, and Burtt, *op. cit.* Ch. 6.
[17] Kahn and Katz in Cartwright and Zander, *op. cit.,* pp. 560-564.

legal aid, training opportunities, and the like. However, the providing of factual knowledge and specialized technical advice is, strictly speaking, not really counseling. This giving of factual data to an employee can be more properly designated as an employee information service, orientation, or education. Rather straightforward principles of communication are involved here. On the other hand, counseling requires a different frame of reference, a different approach, and additional skills.

What are appropriate applications for employee counseling? First of all it is useful for individual employees. If there are groupwide or plantwide problems of high turnover, low morale, frequent work stoppages (strikes), and absenteeism, then individual employee counseling is not the answer. (However, depth interviews with a selected sample of employees may help uncover the causes for such widespread difficulties.) Bearing this in mind, then, counseling can help effect solutions involving individual problem employees. It may be that the person is maladjusted. He may exhibit a chronic chip on his shoulder. He may constantly challenge orders from his boss. He may engage in frequent clashes with his fellow employees. Or he may be excessively aloof. He may be the type who apparently seeks to stir up trouble by circulating false accusations and rumors.

The individual in need of counseling may have been, in the past, a very valued and efficient employee, but in recent months his performance may have declined seriously. The counseling technique is very useful in dealing with employees who have complaints and grievances, in handling discipline problems, in adjusting disputes between two employees, and in helping a person become aware of and correct his shortcomings. It should be remembered that while this discussion has been expressed in reference to *employee* counseling, *supervisors and managers* themselves are often in need of real counseling help too.

Background of Counseling in Industry

Historically counseling in industry was first performed, not by line supervisors, but rather by specially trained staff counselors who were usually attached to the personnel department. One of the components of the famous Hawthorne experiments conducted at the Hawthorne Works of the Western Electric Company was the mass employee interviewing program carried on from 1928 to 1931. The nondirective method of interviewing was developed during this program. In 1936 Western Electric launched a formal and permanent program of employee counseling using this nondirective technique. During World War II a host of manufacturing companies set up counseling services in their industrial relations departments, primarily because of the influx of large numbers of new workers, mostly women, into defense industries. These counselors dealt with a host of problems relating to housing, household finances, child care, vocational guidance, marital relations, and adjustment to the factory environment. Most of these programs were abandoned after the war, although many companies continued to give lip service to the idea.

At present only a small number of companies (mostly very large corporations) maintain full-time trained counselors on their staffs. A few employ psychiatrists and clinical psychologists, occasionally on a full-time basis.

There has been a decided trend toward having counseling performed by the supervisors and managers in the various operating departments rather than by specially trained staff specialists. There are a number of causes for this shift in emphasis: (1) It is costly to employ full-time, professionally trained counselors attached to the industrial relations department. (2) The emphasis in these programs was mainly upon getting employees to change their attitudes and learn to make adjustments in their outlook so that they could accommodate to an existing situation. This approach tended to overlook the fact that there may have been a real need to make changes in the situation itself (for example, rate of pay, work load, job assignment, treatment by the supervisor). (3) It ignored the vital role that the employee's own supervisor can and should play. If an employee is in trouble and if it has any connection (either directly or indirectly) with his behavior at work, then his supervisor has a key interest in that trouble. These problems which the employee encounters may have an effect upon his output, quality of work, attendance, and general well-being. These matters should be of concern to his immediate superior.

Role of the Supervisor. The current thinking, then, is that the supervisor should bear primary and initial responsibility for counseling his people. To do this he must be trained in the principles and practice of nondirective interviewing. In addition, he must also have received, through company-sponsored courses, education in elementary principles of the nature of human behavior (for example, goal-centered behavior, motivation, defense mechanisms, frustrated behavior, and the formation of attitudes). Because he is closer to and knows his men better than any other management representative, the supervisor is in a good position to counsel. However, it is essential for him to recognize his limitations, that he is not a professionally trained counselor, and that he cannot hope to solve deep-seated emotional disturbances. He must know when to refer the person to someone who is more professionally qualified and who has the time and resources to tackle serious cases. Thus the supervisor may refer a person to a company psychologist or to an outside physician, social worker, or religious specialist.

The Counseling Process

The principles and practice of nondirective interviewing for industrial counseling were developed in the Hawthorne researches and by Carl

R. Rogers and his followers.[18] The objective is to help the person being counseled to obtain a clear understanding of the nature of his problem and to help him develop a means for solving it. The counselor tries to get the employee to acquire greater insight into his problem. In a strict sense, in a nondirective interview the counselor gives no diagnosis and no direct advice. Rather he seeks to guide the interviewee by skillful questioning in such a fashion that he can figure out his own approach to a solution. The theory is that a directed solution—one that is forced upon a man—will not be accepted. The counselee has a different make-up—consisting of both inherited and acquired traits—than does the counselor. His frame of reference and personality may be quite different. Therefore, a course of action that a supervisor would adopt if he were in the employee's shoes may be quite incompatible with the latter's personality and abilities. Besides, a man who creates a course of action for himself is more likely to follow it than if he is told to do so.

In actual practice the strict dictum that the counselor should do no diagnosing and give no advice is often modified by the practical supervisor. The pure approach is most successful when used by a professional counselor who has almost unlimited time to work with his client for long hours and upon repeated occasions. The typical factory supervisor just does not have this much time available. In addition, every employee may not have the intelligence nor the educational background to work out his own problems even with gentle guidance. He may really need more directed help, properly given. But the general approach of the nondirective counseling interview can be successfully used by the line supervisor.

The supervisor adopts a friendly, patient, understanding attitude. He puts the person at ease and seeks to establish a feeling of rapport. The past relations between the supervisor and his men determine in large part whether they feel free to discuss their personal problems with him. If in the past the supervisor violated any confidence, if remarks made by the employee have been used against him at a later date, or if any information obtained during the interview was used to undercut the man, then an impenetrable barrier will have been created by the boss.

The proper counseling technique is essentially a listening one. Because most managers and supervisors are in the habit of telling others what to do on the job, this is a difficult role for some to play. The counselor seeks to draw the other person out. He asks neutral questions. He does not moralize, preach, or admonish. In fact, the quickest way to shut off the flow of words from the individual is to criticize or condemn. This immediately puts him on the defensive and he must defend his self-image. Rather the supervisor is the sympathetic listener and helper. He must not pass moral judgment upon the ideas expressed by the employee. He will show that he is interested in what the interviewee is saying by responding with

[18] F. J. Roethlisberger and W. J. Dickson, *Management and the Worker* (Cambridge, Mass.: Harvard University Press, 1939), and Carl R. Rogers, *Counseling and Psychotherapy* (Boston: Houghton Mifflin Company, 1942).

such comments as "Yes," "I see," "That is interesting," "Tell me more." Often the supervisor will simply repeat the last phrase or sentence made by the employee but express it in the form of a question. This is then an invitation to elaborate.

The initial phase of the typical interview is one of establishing rapport. Then comes the catharsis or release of pent-up tensions. The employee unburdens himself and often feels better because he has had a sympathetic listener. Then together the interviewer and the interviewee start to examine the facts of the problem. By the skillful use of questions the supervisor causes the employee to explain more facts and ramifications of the situation. With the nature of the problem fully explored the two can work together to evolve a solution.

Solutions to problems can take many forms. The individual may simply adopt a more positive attitude toward a new company rule that may have seemed quite objectionable. Or the man may have been led to acquire real understanding of the importance of coming to work on time. Or in the discussion the supervisor may himself have acquired new insights into the employee and may realize that he had not appraised him fairly when making the last performance appraisal. Or if the man had not been making the progress he had expected, he may learn during the counseling interview that he really must acquire more education or alter certain of his work habits.

EFFECTIVE SUPERVISION—CONCLUDING OBSERVATIONS

The general picture that has been painted of the successful supervisor, in this chapter, is that he practices general supervision (not detailed), is a good delegator, is employee-centered, is supportive and helpful toward his subordinates, is a good counselor, keeps his men well informed, does not bear down upon them, and concentrates his own attention upon planning, coordinating, and leading rather than doing direct production work himself. Further, he fosters good group relations. This pattern of supervision tends to achieve high productivity and high morale.

This pattern of supervision is most successful in the long run, among employees where the work offers intrinsic job satisfaction and where the work is varied in character. It appeals more to employees who have strong drives for self-accomplishment, self-expression, and independence. On the other hand, some people are content simply to put their time in on their jobs and to work in a situation where their work operations are highly regulated and engineered through industrial engineering techniques and close supervision.

As a broad generalization the principles and practices described in this chapter tend to be employed more often when supervising white collar, sales, engineering, scientific, and managerial employees and hourly employees in certain industries where the work is highly varied and does not permit close control than they are for supervising workers doing routine, repetitive production work in factory or office. The prevailing practice in mass-production industries over the years has tended to be in the direction of high-pressure supervision, close control of the worker (for example, he must ask his boss for permission to leave his immediate work station), and precise work standards. Now in this type of highly engineered situation, high productivity can be achieved by either the high-pressure, highly engineered approach *or* by the pattern of supervision described in this chapter. There is some evidence that the high-pressure, highly engineered approach will achieve good results in the short run, but at the sacrifice of human resources and human values.[19] The pattern of supervision depicted in this chapter will achieve high productivity and maintain or enhance human resources in the long run.

Questions for Review and Discussion

1. Describe the nature of a supervisor's job. What are his duties and responsibilities?
2. Describe the evolutionary changes that have occurred in regard to the position and status of the foreman in industry since 1900.
3. Why is a first-line supervisor unique in his position as a member of management? What are the pressures and forces impinging upon the first-line foreman in a typical factory?
4. What is meant by the term *employee-centered?*
5. Enumerate and describe those supervisory practices that tend to yield high productivity among the work group or section.
6. If a supervisor concentrates upon personally performing direct production work, how may this affect the performance of the whole section? Why?
7. How can a supervisor acquire or increase his influence with his superior?
8. Why is there a tendency for supervisory styles to be transmitted downward through the organizational hierarchy?
9. Why has there been a decline in industry in the use of staff personnel counselors attached to the industrial relations department?
10. Describe the supervisor's responsibility for employee counseling.
11. Explain the principles of the nondirective interviewing method of counseling.

CASE PROBLEM

Mr. Johnston, a new man from another department of the company, was appointed as supervisor of the instrumentation repair and calibration

[19] Likert, *New Patterns of Management, op. cit.,* Ch. 5.

section. This section was part of a large development-engineering and manufacturing laboratory.

The people in the section consisted of three engineers and nine highly skilled technicians. Their job was to repair and calibrate all electronic laboratory equipment and special manufacturing test equipment, most of which was originally designed by the development engineering group.

Mr. Johnston was introduced to the group by Mr. Wheeler, his predecessor, during the last two days of the latter's stay on the job. Mr. Wheeler emphasized the difficult nature of repairing the highly complex electronic equipment. He also noted that in his opinion the human relations aspects of the supervisory job were the most important ones. He felt that letting people work independently and at their own pace would result in their learning from their own mistakes.

During his first few weeks on the job Mr. Johnston made no changes in established procedures but concentrated on getting acquainted with the people, watching them work, and sometimes working with a technician or engineer to find the cause of a difficult instrument repair problem.

He soon realized that the total amount of work performed was rather low. There remained always a huge backlog of repair and calibration work to be done. Yet relations with other departments requesting the work were fairly good. In fact, people from these departments did not hesitate to bring in personal television or radio repair work.

Mr. Johnston found that by working together with someone in his group, the trouble in a piece of equipment was usually located more quickly. He concluded that the men were not working very efficiently nor exerting their highest efforts.

Rather than telling them his opinion, he decided to require individual rather than group reports on a weekly basis. These reports were to include the number of instruments repaired, causes of trouble, and the time spent on each piece of equipment, as well as a detailed explanation of the calibration activities of the individual.

Mr. Johnston was pleased to notice an immediate increase in the total number of instruments repaired with a resulting reduction in the backlog of work.

However, there seemed to develop a more strained and formal atmosphere between the supervisor and the group.

Two months later, two technicians who had been in the section five and eight years respectively, requested a transfer to another department in the company. They cited the pressure of work as a reason for the request.

Mr. Johnston realized that the request might be due to his increased demands on his people.[20]

---

[20] The author expresses his appreciation to Carl H. Rosner for the essential features of this case.

Question

What steps should he take to retain the new, higher level of performance and also restore the friendly atmosphere and high morale previously present in the section?

Suggestions for Further Reading

American Management Association, *Leadership on the Job: Guides to Good Supervision,* New York: American Management, Association, 1966.

Dickson, W. J. and F. J. Roethlisberger, *Counseling in an Organization: A Sequel to the Hawthorne Researches,* Boston: Harvard University, Graduate School of Business Administration, 1966.

Hopper, Kenneth, "The Growing Use of College Graduates as Foremen," *Management of Personnel Quarterly,* Vol. 6, No. 2, Summer 1967, pp. 2-12.

Indik, B. P., B. S. Georgopoulos, and S. E. Seashore, "Supervisor-Subordinate Relationships and Performance," *Personnel Psychology,* Vol. 14, No. 2, 1961, pp. 357-374.

Kell, B. L. and W. J. Mueller, *Impact and Change: A Study of Counseling Relationships,* New York: Appleton-Century-Crofts, 1966.

Likert, Rensis, *The Human Organization: Its Management and Value,* New York: McGraw-Hill Book Company, 1967.

———, *New Patterns of Management,* New York: McGraw-Hill Book Company, 1961.

Patten, Thomas H., Jr., *The Foreman, Forgotten Man of Management,* New York: American Management Association, 1968.

Pfiffner, John M. and Marshall Fels, *The Supervision of Personnel,* 3rd Ed., Englewood Cliffs, N.J.: Prentice-Hall, Inc., 1964.

Sartain, Aaron Q., and Alton W. Baker, *The Supervisor and His Job,* New York: McGraw-Hill Book Company, 1965.

Walker, Charles R., Robert H. Guest, and Arthur N. Turner, *The Foreman on the Assembly Line,* Cambridge, Mass.: Harvard University Press, 1956.

Wikstrom, Walter S. *Managing at the Foreman's Level,* Studies in Personnel Policy No. 205, New York: National Industrial Conference Board, 1967.

Managing Through the Use of Participation

19

The maintenance superintendent in a steel mill calls a foreman into his office to obtain his suggestions on the most efficient and safest way to dismantle an obsolete overhead crane. A service-engineering manager in the home office of an electronic data processing manufacturer calls a meeting of his engineering staff to discuss ways and means of improving service for installations of equipment on customers' premises. Ideas are freely submitted by the engineers. A standing committee composed of both union and management representatives in a machine tool manufacturing company reviews cost reduction and methods improvement suggestions submitted by rank-and-file employees. These three examples illustrate some of the kinds of participation activities that occur in industrial enterprises.

Participation is the term used to designate the process by which people contribute ideas toward the solution of problems affecting the organization and their jobs. The people exercise some degree of influence in the decision-making process. Participation is ego and task involvement of an individual or group. It includes not only the physical contribution of the person but also his intellectual and emotional involvement in the affairs of the organization.

When managers establish means, on either an informal or a formal basis, for obtaining help from subordinates in the making of plans and decisions, they are tapping the knowledge and creativity of others. Because managers can't possibly know all the answers to all the problems and issues

553

connected with the work of their departments, they can often obtain valuable advice and assistance from their subordinates. The process of participation brings into play the higher drives and motives of man: the drives for self-expression, accomplishment, autonomy, and self-assertion. It lets the employees know that their contributions are sought and appreciated. Great benefits to the company and its members can derive from such leadership; however, participation is not a cure-all nor necessarily the most appropriate style of management for all circumstances.

Some writers have proposed that participatory management has positive values over and above its effects upon productivity and morale. In a society such as that in the United States, where the concepts of political democracy and the rights and duties of the individual to take an active part in the affairs of his country are cherished, it is held that the environment at one's place of employment should be fully compatible with these democratic ideals. To put the matter more directly, democracy should be practiced in the factory and office as well as in the outside civic and social life of American citizens. In point of fact, most business and industrial organizations tend to be quite authoritarian in the internal relations between superiors and subordinates. The system is rather autocratic. Yet this is a basic contradiction, because the executive who practices autocratic leadership at the office preaches the need for maintaining individual freedom in the American society as a whole. To him it is self-evident that men should have to say-so in the shaping of laws and policies that affect them. But often this executive does not know how to apply this democratic value system to his own company. Therefore, many spokesmen maintain that participation programs in work organizations derive positive support from the cultural heritage prevailing in the United States of America.[1]

ROLE OF PARTICIPATION IN THE ORGANIZATION

Participation is appropriate for all levels in the organizational hierarchy. In practice in industry it takes place only rarely at the level of the blue-collar and white-collar nonsupervisory employee. Many executives have the notion that these people would have nothing worthwhile to contribute. Participation activities via committees and meetings occur more often at middle and upper levels of management and with professional and technical groups of employees.

A program of management in which employees are invited to contribute ideas and suggestions concerning the running of the business must be distinguished from a system of democratic government. In a democracy the citizens—the people—set up their own governing body and

[1] For another statement of this proposition see Walter Sikes, "The Paradox of Participation," *Personnel,* Vol. 39, No. 1 (January-February 1962), pp. 35-38.

make their own laws through elected representatives. The people have the power at stated times to elect, re-elect, or reject their representatives and executive leaders. However, in a work organization the employees do not select their leaders. Supervisors and managers are appointed from the top of the organization. Only in a very broad sense do these managers rule with the consent of the governed. If a manager is totally ineffective as a leader, he may be removed by his superior in the organization because he observes that this manager cannot win the support and co-operation of his subordinates. But the subordinates do not directly exert control over their supervisors and managers.

Now when a manager consults his subordinates and shares some of his decision-making authority with them, he does this voluntarily. He still retains the final authority and most of the power to make and implement these decisions. He can rescind his sharing of decision making at any time.

Most of the participation methods and programs that exist in business and industry are discretionary on management's part. Management almost never has established a formal organizational arrangement in which it shares the actual final authority and power for deciding and taking action with its employees.[2]

Pseudo Participation

For the past twenty years writers, researchers, and social scientists have been giving speeches and writing articles about the values that can be gained from participation programs. Some executives have picked up some of these concepts and sought to apply them in their own plants and offices. Quite often the net result of their efforts has been programs that contain a few surface elements of participation but no genuine, true sharing of decision making.

Some managers speak of developing a "sense" of participation in their employees. They exhort them to get their "shoulders to the wheel and all push together." They try to persuade their people to work more enthusiastically to perform jobs and activities designed and regulated exclusively by management. This type of participation is task involvement but not ego involvement. It is not true participation.

In conducting meetings with subordinates, ostensibly for the purpose of joint consultation and problem solving, some managers seek primarily to manipulate the group. The executive has a preconceived plan he wants his men to support wholeheartedly. He opens up the problem for

[2] There are some exceptions to this statement. In a few instances employees have achieved seats on the board of directors of corporations. In this sense they share in the exercise of authority to make top level policy decisions. Also collective bargaining between management and union is a form of participation in which authority to regulate wages, hours, and other conditions of employment is shared equally between management and the elected representatives of the employees.

discussion and invites suggestions from the group. But he is careful to lend his support only to those ideas that agree with his own views and to diplomatically veto those he dislikes. Sensing the power of his position, his subordinates gradually tend to voice approval for those ideas they know will please the boss.

Now there are occasions where a supervisor or an executive must sell his decisions to his subordinates. And there are occasions where he clearly is going to make the final decision, but he wishes to obtain ideas from his men before doing so. But in both instances he must be honest with himself and his subordinates. He must let it be known just what their roles are to be. He must not delude himself and his people into believing that there is going to be genuine participation if in fact he merely wants to play upon their emotions to gain support for a plan he is going to install anyway.

Barriers to Participation

There exist a number of barriers to effective participation in the typical business organization. Perhaps first and foremost is the power structure of the organizational hierarchy.

An employee knows that his boss judges him in regard to his performance and day-to-day behavior. He knows that his supervisor makes decisions regarding pay raises, promotions, and work assignments. Likewise, the boss can dispense a host of punishments (subtle and overt) to keep his men in line. Fully realizing their position, subordinates tend to speak less freely in the presence of the boss. Their ideas tend to be couched in terms that will support those views which they know the boss already possesses. It is perhaps human nature for a person to feel more at ease in the presence of those who agree with him than among those who challenge him. Managers are no exception to this generalization.

If a group of people are called together to participate in a problem-solving conference, their responses will vary appreciably, depending upon whether the meeting is led by the boss or whether it is led by a peer or colleague. Assuming that both individuals are skilled conference leaders, the leader who is an organizational equal to the rest of the participants will tend to obtain more spontaneous participation from the conferees. On the other hand, in the presence of their superior the men will tend to give deference to his views. The wise manager who is leading a problem-solving discussion will carefully refrain from announcing his own personal opinions if he wishes to obtain genuine, uncolored contributions from his subordinates.

A vivid illustration of the effect that the power position of an executive can have upon the outcome of a problem-solving conference is contained in the following description of a meeting of branch managers from the marketing department of a company:

Most of the participants were branch managers from the company's marketing department, gathered from distant field offices around the country. Some were headquarters and staff people from the home office: functionaries and experts in budgets, customer relations, advertising, and other specialized fields.

Presiding as conference leader was an administrative assistant to the head of the marketing department. The chief himself was seated in a chair removed from the conference table in a row reserved for guest speakers, observers, and others not directly involved in the proceedings. The chief had designated his assistant to act as conference leader because the agenda was devoted to the operating problems and needs of the branch managers. He said he thought the expression of ideas would be freer and group participation greater if he refrained from active direction of the discussions, so he withdrew himself from the chairmanship in the interests of improved upward communication.

Also seated at the side among the guests and observers were two representatives of an outside consulting organization which provided certain professional services for the marketing department and, in particular, for the group of field managers. These two outsiders were scheduled on the program to present some preliminary plans for the services they proposed to offer in the ensuing year.

The time came for reviewing these outside services and considering the group's recommendations concerning them. The conference leader called on the outsiders to make their presentations. Each one of them got up, and with blackboard and flip charts, explained their proposals in detail. Two basic alternatives were offered for adoption or appropriate modification, which for the sake of simplicity we shall call Plan A and Plan B. The outside spokesman concluded his presentation with a comment that either alternative was suitable from his point of view, and that determination of a final plan should be based on the conferees' actual needs and interests inasmuch as the service was being purchased by the company solely for their use in the branch offices.

The outsider then sat down, and the conference leader led the group into a discussion of the pros and cons of each alternative plan, continuing for several minutes until it became evident that consensus was shaping in favor of Plan A. Sensing closure, and wanting to get on with other items on the agenda, the conference leader asked for a show of hands to formalize acceptance of Plan A. Of the two dozen or more present, all but three or four raised their hands.

Up to this point, the chief had been sitting silently on the sidelines, observing. Now he cleared his throat and briefly cautioned the group that he "hoped to see complete agreement here, and not ride over minority points of view too hastily."

This change in the atmosphere gave everyone pause to reflect on their proceedings. The conference leader reacted first. Being close to the chief on a day-to-day basis, he may have been more finely tuned to the reality of the situation. In any event, he asked for restatements and clarification of the Plan B proposal and "less hasty reconsideration by the group of the merits of both plans." After a few minutes of such exploratory discussion, consensus seemed to be turning in the direction of Plan B. Again the conference leader asked for a show of hands. This time, the group decision was indeed reversed. Only three or four people raised their hands for Plan A; the rest voted for Plan B. Presumably encouraged by this popular endorsement of his own apparent position, the chief arose and in confident good humor proceeded to make his point of view abundantly clear. He delivered a 3-minute lecturette in support of Plan B, complimenting the group on their good judgment, and adding "but I don't want to impose my own views on you men. The decision is really yours, since it's your program out there in the field.[3]

Another barrier to participation is a manager who has an authoritarian personality. Some executives feel that they are destined to lead, whereas others are destined to follow. The very idea of consultation with subordinates is anathema to them. Such personalities will not take suggestions from others. They cannot tolerate any possibility of ideas that might challenge their doctrines.

Upon graduation from college I took a job with a large manufacturing corporation. My first several months were devoted to job rotational training assignments in a number of departments. The section supervisor in one of these departments appeared to be highly intelligent and creative. During an informal conversation with this supervisor at lunch one day, I remarked that he had a great number of original ideas regarding the work operations of the section. I asked him, "How did you acquire so many good ideas? Did you obtain some from your subordinates?

The supervisor replied in a shocked tone, "From my employees? Never! A good supervisor never consults his subordinates. I was hired to be boss of this section. This means that I must make all the decisions. Just remember that if a boss asks for advice from his men he loses respect."

The atmosphere and climate of the society in general may constitute a barrier to participation. Although democratic ideals pervade the social fabric of the United States, the British Commonwealth, and many countries of Western Europe, in many other nations the general populace just naturally expects to be passive. The social and economic gulf between the ruling class and the masses of people is often great, and mass public education is lacking. When peasants take jobs in factories, they may actually have little knowledge and no original ideas to contribute. Having been raised for generations to accept their lot in life and to simply follow traditional modes of behavior, these employees tend to accept a nonparticipative life in business organizations as the natural or ordinary mode of existence. Furthermore, in underdeveloped nations, physical survival occupies nearly 100 per cent of the average individual's time; therefore, he has no energy left over for ego-satisfying drives, such as participation in decision making.

[3] From Norman R. F. Maier and John J. Hayes, *Creative Management* (New York: John Wiley & Sons, Inc., 1962), pp. 45-47. Quotation by permission.

A final barrier to participation that manifests itself in many situations is the pressure to conform to the common beliefs of the group and the organization. This phenomenon occurs in both the informal friendship and work groups that exist in most work organizations and also in the larger framework of the work organization itself—the factory, the government agency, the bank, or the department store. To a considerable extent this pressure for conformity is imposed by the organization—both the formal and informal—in order to preserve its existence and to maintain stability and security. Too much autonomy, individualism, and creativeness is perceived by the group as a threat. The prevailing notion of "don't rock the boat" develops in the group and the organization.

RESEARCH INTO PARTICIPATION

Since the 1930's, and especially in more recent years, a considerable number of experiments have been conducted with industrial and other types of work groups to determine the effects of employee or follower participation upon such variables as productivity, morale, group attitudes, turnover, and grievance rates. As was discussed in Chapter 17, "Leadership," an early classic experiment was conducted by Lewin, White, and Lippitt at the State University of Iowa in 1938 to determine the effects of autocratic, democratic, and laissez-faire leadership upon groups of boys. Let us now review the highlights of some other investigations.

Piece-Rate Production Workers

In the Harwood Manufacturing Company, which produces wearing apparel, management decided to modernize its production methods. It sought to reduce in-process inventory, attain more flexible control of production, reduce costs, and improve quality. Rather significant changes were to be made in the methods of materials handling and in processing the goods at all three of the company's plants. The objectives were decided by management, as were the major aspects of the engineering changes. Participation took the form of a great number of meetings between management and small groups of workers who were involved in the various changes. Most of the employees involved in these changes were women who were paid under a piece-rate incentive system. Because the changes required skilled engineering knowhow that the workers did not possess, management decided that the participation would have to be limited to questions and answers and discussions related to the working out of details of the changes. In the ordinary situation management can expect rather strong and widespread opposition from piece-rate employees when their work methods, time standards, and working procedures are changed. However, in this company the participative meetings combined with a program of temporary pay subsidies (retraining allowances until the operators learned the new work methods) achieved highly satisfying results in terms of both productivity and morale. Two different products were involved in the change. For one of these products, average productivity one year later was about 10 per cent greater than before the change was made. For the other product the average productivity was unchanged. However, for both products direct-labor costs were 10 per cent lower because of the engineering improvements. Employee turnover rates, as measured by voluntary resignations divided by the average employment, declined in all three plants. One might have expected turnover to increase if there were considerable employee resentment over the methods changes and consequent piece-rate changes. There did occur a temporary increase in the number of piece-rate grievances, but management did not consider the fifty grievances during the year 1956 excessive in view of the fact that there had been 1,300 piece-rate changes during the course of the program.[4]

Office Employees

One of the experiments conducted by the Institute for Social Research of the University of Michigan involved the study of 500 clerical employees in four parallel divisions. Each division was organized the same way and did exactly the same kind of work. The supervisory and managerial personnel of each division were given a training program of about six months' duration before the actual experimental changes were introduced into each division. In two of the divisions a participative climate of leadership was established. This meant that the supervisors practiced more general (as contrasted with close) supervision and used group methods of leadership wherein subordinates could actively participate in making decisions related to their work. In the other two divisions a pattern of management called the hierarchically controlled program was installed. This pattern called for close supervision and the making of decisions at the higher levels of the organization. In these two divisions all jobs were time studied by the methods department and standard times were established. The program lasted for one year. What were the results of this experiment? At the end of the year, productivity had increased an average of 25 per cent for the two hierarchically controlled divisions and 20 per cent for the two participative divisions. But the increases in productivity in the hierarchically led divisions were accompanied by negative reactions in terms of loyalty, attitudes, interest, and involvement in the work. In the participative divisions the employees' feeling of responsibility to see that the work was accomplished increased after the introduction of partici-

---

[4] John R. P. French, Jr., I. C. Ross, S. Kirby, J. R. Nelson, and P. Smyth, "Employee Participation in a Program of Industrial Change," *Personnel,* Vol. 35, No. 3 (November-December 1958), pp. 16-29.

patory leadership. When the supervisor was away temporarily, the employees kept right on working. Just the opposite reactions occurred in the hierarchically controlled divisions. Employees in the participative divisions held more favorable attitudes toward high-producing workers, believed that their managers became "closer to them," and considered that their supervisors "pulled for them" to a greater extent than did those in the hierarchically controlled divisions. Turnover increased in the hierarchically led program throughout the experimental year.[5]

Telephone Employees

In the late 1940's Wickert conducted a study of operators and service representatives of the Michigan Bell Telephone Company. He specifically studied those hired during the period January 1945 to February 1948. A comparison was made between the attitudes and characteristics of that group of these employees who were still on the payroll at the time the study was conducted and those who had been separated from the company. A notable finding of this study was that those who had stayed with the company showed a more favorable attitude toward supervision, and this was particularly derived from the fact that they had an opportunity to make decisions on the job. They felt that they were making an important contribution to the success of the company. Most commonly those who had left the company stated (via questionnaires and interviews) that they had little chance to make decisions on their jobs.[6]

Sewing Machine Operators

Fleishman made a study of the way in which workers in a women's dress factory reacted to frequent changes in work details caused by the introduction of new dress styles. The subjects of his study were 60 sewing machine operators working in a unionized garment factory. They were paid on a piece-rate basis. Rates were bargained between union and management. A major problem in this operation was that output and piece-work earnings on new styles were always low. It generally took about seven weeks for output to reach a satisfactory level. When new styles were introduced, the girls typically complained vigorously about the fairness of the piece prices.

To determine the effects of participation upon rate of recovery of output when a new style was introduced, management set up matched experimental and control groups. The experimental group determined the sequence of operations, the bundling procedures, and pricing of individ-

[5] Rensis Likert, *New Patterns of Management* (McGraw-Hill Book Company, Inc., 1961), pp. 62-69.

[6] F. P. Wickert, "Turnover and Employees' Feelings of Ego-Involvement in the Day-to-Day Operation of a Company," *Personnel Psychology,* Vol. 4 (1951), pp. 185-197.

ual operations. The control group did not participate in planning their work. The results revealed that the participation group achieved a high rate of output almost immediately after introduction of the new style. They also retained this high level of output when shifted back to a style previously worked upon. Fleishman concluded from his investigation that attitudinal factors rather than skill factors were the major contributors to the customary drop in output and later recovery in output when a new style was introduced.[7]

Research in Perspective

A considerable number of scholars, researchers, and writers have described and reviewed research studies in the field of participation. Viteles has delved extensively into this subject in his book *Motivation and Morale in Industry.*[8] One of the principal themes throughout Marrow's book, *Making Management Human,* is the subject of participation. Marrow, the president of the Harwood Manufacturing Company, describes a number of group decision-making experiments conducted in his plants into such problem areas as resistance to change, turnover, and employee attitudes. His book constitutes a strong endorsement for participation as a method of management.[9] Another proponent of participatory management is N. R. F. Maier. After reviewing some of the significant research done in the area of democratic leadership and advantages thereof, Maier goes on to explain how to train supervisors to use methods of leadership requiring group decision making.[10]

Vroom, upon reviewing the available research, has stated that there is substantial evidence for the belief that participation in decision making does increase productivity. When workers have influence in making decisions that they are able to carry out, productivity tends to be higher than when the level of influence is low.[11]

Some Counter Views. Participation does not always increase productivity. In the Lewin, White, and Lippitt experiments with children, there was no demonstrated superiority of the democratically led group over the autocratically led group as far as productivity was concerned. The superiority for the democratic group was in terms of attitudes and interpersonal relations.

---

[7] Edwin A. Fleishman, "Attitude versus Skill Factors in Work Group Productivity," *Personnel Psychology,* Vol. 18 (1965), pp. 253-266.

[8] Morris S. Viteles, *Motivation and Morale in Industry* (New York: W. W. Norton & Co., Inc., 1953). See especially Chs. 9 and 23.

[9] Alfred J. Marrow, *Making Management Human* (New York: McGraw-Hill Book Company, 1957).

[10] Norman R. F. Maier, *Principles of Human Relations* (New York: John Wiley & Sons, Inc., 1952).

[11] Victor H. Vroom, *Work and Motivation* (New York: John Wiley & Sons, Inc., 1964), p. 226.

Harold Leavitt has argued that managerial styles ought to be differentiated. Where the nature of the tasks are such that they can be highly programmed, they should be. But where the work is complex, variable, and requires creativity, then a more democratic style with looser controls is most advantageous. Leavitt has noted that in laboratory experiments on the college campus, autocratic control yields better solutions on certain problems but that morale tends to be higher and there is greater flexibility in meeting novel problems under egalitarian and decentralized control. He has also asserted that the proponents of participation have been too eager and have claimed the general superiority of participation for all situations.[12]

PARTICIPATION EVALUATED

After all the available evidence has been gathered, weighed, and digested it appears that participation by subordinates in decisions that affect their work yields rather clear-cut benefits in terms of attitudes and morale. People become "ego involved" in decisions in which they have had a part. They acquire a greater sense of responsibility for making the agreed-upon course of action succeed. Participation is an effective countermeasure for apathy.

Participation also facilitates acceptance of change. People resent change that is imposed upon them unilaterally. How are they to know whether their interests have been properly considered? In a conference discussion when the people work out the nature and mechanics of a proposed new system, they can analyze all the possible objections and ramifications and decide for themselves whether it is feasible.

The evidence on participation is rather clear-cut also in terms of its effects upon morale. The very act of consulting a subordinate means that the boss values the man's knowledge and abilities. This is a form of recognition. Being more closely identified with their jobs and with the organization, employees are less likely to quit, to be absent, or to express serious discontent.

Employee development is substantially enhanced by participatory management. One of the principal reasons for having the junior boards of executives system in many companies—the McCormick & Company plan is perhaps best known—is that it serves as an excellent means of training and developing managers for more important job assignments. Participation programs give subordinates an opportunity to work on projects and problems that they would ordinarily never encounter under conventional authoritarian management until after they had actually been promoted to higher positions.

[12] Harold J. Leavitt, "Unhuman Organizations," *Harvard Business Review,* Vol. 40, No. 4 (July-August 1962), pp. 90-98.

On the key question of performance (productivity and quality of decisions), the weight of evidence tends to favor participation as a managerial style. More commonly than not group performance is superior when the group has had real influence in shaping the decisions affecting their sphere of activities. However, this result is not always true. Sometimes in group meetings the people are more concerned with maintaining good social relations with their peers and with their superior. They are reluctant to engage in the constructive conflict of ideas that is necessary to resolve critical problems. In some circumstances, also, the needs of the organization may clash with the needs of the people. The best quality decision might be to transfer or lay off employees. Yet these people themselves are hardly going to advocate a course of action that clearly threatens their security or survival.

CONDITIONS FOR EFFECTIVE PARTICIPATION

Participation is not a magic solution to all the problems encountered in managing a business. Nor can it be used willy-nilly. Procedures for utilizing participation have their time and their place. Let us now examine the factors that determine how, when, and where participation can be effectively and practically employed.

Characteristics of Subordinates

Independence Needs.   Research has demonstrated that subordinates who have strong needs for independence react more favorable toward the opportunity to participate in decision-making activities than do those who have low independence needs and who score high on an authoritarianism measuring scale. By "need for independence" it is meant that the employees have strong drives to express themselves in their work, to exercise their own judgment, to assert themselves, and to figure things out for themselves. Thus participation appeals to persons having this type of personality structure more than it does to those having little interest or desire to exercise their own initiative and assert their independence.[13]

Desire to Participate.   This characteristic is related to the preceding one. Some employees and supervisors are quite content to operate in a frame-work where practically all the decisions are made for them. They are content to work in a rigidly structured environment. But for participation to succeed, the people must become interested in the wider ramifications of their jobs, their departments, and their organization. They

[13] Victor H. Vroom, "Some Personality Determinants of the Effects of Participation," *Journal of Abnormal and Social Psychology,* Vol. 59 (November 1959), pp. 322-327. The subjects of this investigation were 108 first-, second-, and third-line supervisors in a large company whose basic activity was the delivery of packages from stores to private residences.

must want to contribute. They must be motivated in that direction. Of course, proper leadership can stimulate this desire. Employee attitudes toward participation are not immutable. A positive urge in this direction can be cultivated over a period of time by management.

Intelligence and Knowledge.   Subordinates must possess a certain minimum amount of intelligence and knowledge for any participation program to succeed. In other words they must first be capable of contributing, and then they must have something worthwhile to contribute. Because management sets the selection standards for employment, it can control the level of intelligence (generally) of those it puts on the payroll. In the short run, employees may lack the necessary information, background, and knowledge to make worthwhile contributions in any program of participation in decision making. However, information and training programs instituted by management can, in the long run, substantially raise the level of knowledge of the work force so that it can make useful contributions.

Organizational Climate

It would be pretty difficult for a foreman, on his own initiative, to launch a comprehensive program of consultation or democratic supervision with his men if he were the only foreman in the entire company who was so inclined. The employees would tend to misunderstand and misinterpret his efforts. If this foreman's boss were unsympathetic, he would tend to feel that the foreman was abdicating his leadership authority and responsibility, didn't know his own job, and was generally wasting time.

Basically, then, participation is most likely to succeed when top management (starting with the board of directors and the president) believes in it, encourages it, and practices it in its day-to-day relations with subordinate executives. The pattern of management established at the very top of an organization tends to be transmitted down through successive echelons to the lowest-level supervisors. Executives tend to reinforce and support those of their subordinates who think and act as they do and penalize those who do not conform to their modes of action.

Problem Must Be Appropriate

An indecisive supervisor who cannot make decisions on routine administrative matters should not waste the time of his subordinates by calling meetings to get opinions on these run-of-the-mill problems. A manager is paid to run his department, to apply his knowledge and judgment, and to make decisions affecting his unit and its employees. It would be ineffective for him to, in effect, look upon his subordinates as a senate continuously in session to help him resolve daily problems. Participation should be utilized for those situations and problems that are important and that have a material impact upon the people involved and the organization.

A manager should not waste the time of all of his subordinates if a particular problem clearly concerns only one or two of his men. He should bring into the picture only those who have an interest and a legitimate concern for the topic. Of course, there are some occasions where employees and managers may not themselves be directly involved in a problem area, but the executive in charge values their counsel or wants them to be informed of what is going on.

Training for Participation

Not only do managers need to learn how to delegate, consult, lead conferences, encourage suggestions, and so on, but also employees need to learn how to work cooperatively and effectively in such situations. If a shop supervisor calls a meeting of all his machine operators and service personnel to figure out better production methods and ways of cutting costs, the employees must be told just what their roles are to be. Is the supervisor simply calling them together to have them serve as a sounding board for a program he has already designed? Or does he want them to assume the major share of the responsibility for improving methods? Will the supervisor be bound by any consensus decision? How should the group view vigorous dissent by a minority? Does the boss expect the men to do advance preparation before coming to the meeting? How does he expect them to behave in the meeting? What is the role of the union steward?

The point being made here is that management cannot switch from an authoritarian to a participative pattern of leadership overnight and expect employees to respond instantly to the new program. They must be taught just what is expected of them and how they are expected to perform. If employees have been expected to be yes men for years, they cannot suddenly transform themselves into independent, thinking, creative people.

Scope of Authority and Responsibility

Managers should generally invite participation from their subordinates only on problems within their sphere of authority and responsibility. It would invite frustration for a low-ranking supervisor in a shop department to call his people together to arrive at decisions regarding company wage or vacation policy because this is clearly beyond his power to control. Policy questions are primarily the responsibility of top management. It would be very pertinent, however, for the supervisor to invite participation regarding such subjects as work flow, methods, quality, safety, cost control, employee discontents, and housekeeping.

There are some exceptions to the foregoing principle. Sometimes participation programs are set up to create ideas and proposals at lower levels in the organization. These must then be transmitted up through several levels in the structure before a final authoritative decision can be made. In this case the participation may serve as a method of upward communication, as a way of uncovering information and trouble spots that would be otherwise overlooked, and as a means of developing subordinates. In this case the supervisor of the employees who developed the proposal may have to recommend it to his superior before it can be adopted. However, if the participation program is to operate in this way, it is vital that the people involved understand fully just where the final decision-making authority resides. Quite commonly under the multiple management—junior board of executives—system the board has far-reaching authority to delve into any and all functions of the business (for example, marketing, production, industrial relations, engineering, research), but the decisions of the board are viewed only as recommendations to top management, which renders the final binding decisions.

Time Available

Emergency situations may preclude any consultation with others. A decision on a rush shipment of goods, a tactical action in a strike, a pressing action to meet a short deadline, and an act to avert serious damage to equipment or injury to personnel, may clearly require authoritarian behavior.

TYPES OF PARTICIPATION

As an aid to understanding the various kinds of participation programs and activities that can be carried on, it is useful to classify them into two broad categories: (1) informal and semiformal methods, and (2) formal programs.

Informal and Semiformal Methods
  A. Individual
  B. Group
    1. Consultative Management
    2. Democratic Management

Formal Programs
  A. Junior Boards of Executives
  B. Collective Bargaining
  C. Union-Management Cooperation
  D. Suggestion Plans

Informal and Semiformal Methods

The informal and semiformal methods essentially involve relations between a supervisor (or manager) and his subordinates. These participation activities tend to take place at rather unscheduled or irregular intervals (although sometimes they occur as frequently as daily). When a specific issue or problem arises, the boss may discuss the matter with one or more of his direct subordinates. In some departments in some organizations, the manager may schedule regular weekly or biweekly meetings with his staff. These meetings may be partially for the purpose of passing on information and directives to the people and partially to involve them in group discussion and decision making.

Individual Participation.   When a subordinate initiates actions and issues for his boss and when they jointly discuss operating problems almost as equals, then we can say that there exists a very high degree of individual participation between subordinate and superior. Consider the following illustration between a salary administrator and his boss, the industrial relations director:

SALARY ADMINISTRATOR
(ENTERING OFFICE OF
INDUSTRIAL RELATIONS
DIRECTOR):

Frank, I have been studying salaries paid to engineers and scientists by the majority of companies that hire our kind of personnel in the entire Eastern half of the United States. My analysts have just about completed a survey and tabulation of salaries and supplementary benefits paid to engineers and scientists on an occupation basis. Our initial figures show that we are lagging behind the market by about 10 percent. I strongly recommend an upward revision of salaries and salary structure.

INDUSTRIAL RELATIONS
DIRECTOR:

Yes, Bill, we have been sensing difficulty in attracting and retaining high caliber men. I believe you are right. Are you ready to make specific recommendations at this time?

SALARY ADMINISTRATOR:

By the end of the week I shall be able to submit to you a detailed proposal regarding a new pay schedule and a proposed upward adjustment in salaries. My purpose now is primarily to alert you to the situation.

INDUSTRIAL RELATIONS
DIRECTOR:

Thanks, Bill. As soon as you have your report complete we can go over it jointly

and then make a definite recommendation to the President.

Contrast the foregoing situation where there is a high degree of individual participation, with the following way of handling the same salary
problem.

INDUSTRIAL RELATIONS DIRECTOR (SPEAKING TO HIS SECRETARY):	Miss Hanson, please get Bill Worth on the phone and tell him to come to my office right away.

A few minutes later.

INDUSTRIAL RELATIONS DIRECTOR:	Hi, Bill, sit down. Have you finished the salary survey yet?
SALARY ADMINISTRATOR:	Yes, I have the data here.
INDUSTRIAL RELATIONS DIRECTOR:	I want you to compute our average salaries for each occupation and each salary grade and compare them with those paid by the other companies. We want our average to be about equal to the market. Prepare a report which shows just what changes we would have to make in each occupation and for each employee to bring ours in line. Then bring all the figures to me so that I can decide just what recommendation to make to the President. Try to have the figures by Friday.
SALARY ADMINISTRATOR:	Yes, Frank. I will have them for you by then. Do you want me to prepare a set of complete recommendations regarding pay and supplementary benefits?
INDUSTRIAL RELATIONS DIRECTOR:	No, I want your figures, and I will draw up the recommendations.

It is clearly evident that in the second situation the industrial relations
director was confining his salary administrator to a narrow sphere and
that he wanted very little participation from him. Individual participation can occur when a manager invites one of his men to come to his office to get the man's ideas regarding a new assignment; it can occur when
the manager walks through his department to discuss with one of his men
at his work station ways of performing the job; and it can occur when
a subordinate seeks out his boss to exchange views on a new project. The

manager who delegates a great deal of responsibility to his subordinates and who practices general and supportive supervision is, in effect, establishing a climate in which his employees feel free to make important decisions regarding their work. This is a form of individual participation.

Individual participation can be very effective, but it has its limitations when compared with group participation, such as consultative and democratic management. In group discussion the process of free association can take place. A thought contributed by one man sparks an idea in another, and so on in a chain-reaction fashion. Because there are more minds involved in a group discussion, the possibility of generating more and better ideas is considerably greater than in individual participation. Furthermore, there is less likelihood, in group participation, of overlooking the interests of particular branches of the business. Personnel specialists, production specialists, and financial specialists all have their own ways of viewing the same issue. Therefore, a problem-solving conference that includes representatives from all interest groups is more likely to develop a solution that is practical and with which all concerned can live. Two people with limited knowledge and perspective, such as boss and a single subordinate, might easily agree upon a solution to a problem, but they are more than likely to overlook significant aspects if they do not bring other informed people into the picture.

Consultative Management.   Consultative management (often referred to as consultative supervision) is a system of management whereby the executive or the supervisor calls a meeting of his subordinates, whenever the situation requires, to obtain group ideas toward the solution of operating problems.[14] The manager presents a problem to the group and invites their questions, suggestions, ideas, and criticisms. Consultative supervision can take either of two principal forms. In one case the manager may have already arrived at a tentative decision, and he presents it to his employees for review and discussion. He clearly indicates that his decision is subject to change. In the other form the manager may have no clear decision in mind beforehand. He presents a problem to the group, invites suggestions and analysis, and then makes a final decision, taking into account the opinions and contributions of the group.

It should be pointed out that in consultative management the manager does not transfer final decision-making authority and power to his subordinates. He definitely makes the final decision on any question presented to the group. The subordinates must be informed as to the role they are to play. They must not be deluded into thinking that they, as a group, are being given the authority to make the final decision to commit their entire organizational unit. Now as a matter of practical consequences, in the majority of cases, the manager will tend to adopt the decision

[14] Mr. H. H. Carey is generally credited with having developed the term *consultative management* (or *supervision*). See H. H. Carey, "Consultative Supervision and Management," *Personnel,* Vol. 18, No. 5 (March 1942), pp. 286-295. Also George V. Moser, "Consultative Management," *Management Record,* Vol. 17, No. 11 (October 1955), pp. 438-439.

that has evolved in group discussions and that represents a consensus. Because he is consulting his subordinates, he must value their collective judgment. Therefore, on only rare occasions will he find it necessary to render a final decision that is clearly in opposition to the tenor of the group's feeling. The practice of consultative management will fail if on repeated occasions the manager finds it necessary to announce to the group that he will have to overrule the consensus decision of the group. Both they and he will lose confidence in the process if this occurs often.

Democratic Management. Democratic management (or supervision) is similar to consultative supervision except that the primary decision making responsibility is shifted from the supervisor to the entire group. When the supervisor invites his subordinates as a group to participate in making decisions regarding operating problems, he serves primarily as a conference leader. He plays an important part in shaping the course of action, but his role is essentially that of chairman of the conference rather than that of boss and final authority.

Democratic management is actually somewhat of a radical departure from traditional leadership as practiced in the typical work organization. To institute a system of democratic supervision in a company requires a substantial departure from common modes of thinking. Managers must be willing to share decision making with subordinate levels in the hierarchy, and they must believe that subordinates have the capabilities to make worth-while contributions. Supervisors and foremen cannot effectively institute democratic supervision on their own initiative. The program must start at the top of the hierarchy. Top management must believe in it and practice it.

When a supervisor convenes a democratic problem-solving meeting of his employees he chooses problems that are appropriate for group analysis. Quite often he possesses knowledge not possessed by his subordinates. Therefore, if they are to share the authority for shaping courses of action, he must serve as a resource person and impart that information to them. The supervisor does not relinquish his authority and control; rather he shares it with his people. They are taught to adopt a fully responsible point of view. In serving as a conference leader and chairman, he seeks to develop, if possible, a consensus. He tries to reconcile opposing points of view. He does not seek votes and simply adopt the majority view as a routine procedure. Often a minority has a better solution to a problem, and if given a chance it may win over the majority. Of course, it is not always possible, or necessary, to obtain unanimous agreement on every issue.

In a democratic setup the members function as a close-knit team. Each employee is heavily involved in team thinking and activities. He is kept well informed of the activities of his associates. The supervisor is clearly the most influential person in the section, but he leads by persuasion, influence, and group consensus rather than coercion.

A supervisor who practices democratic leadership does not do so only at those times when he is conducting problem-solving conferences with his group. He does not revert back to autocratic behavior afterward in his day-to-day behavior with his men. Of course, there are occasions on which he must give orders. But he is permissive in his behavior. He seeks feedback and suggestions from his men. Whereas the autocratic boss seeks to build loyalty from each employee, as an individual, toward himself, the democratic supervisor seeks to build cooperative relations and loyalty among all the members of the group toward each other as well as toward himself.

Informal and Semiformal Participation in Perspective.   Individual participation and consultative management are widely practiced in industry at the top and middle levels of management. The actual extent of this in any particular company depends largely upon the inclinations of the executives themselves. Consultative management involving subordinates as a group is rather uncommon at the bottom level of the organization (that is, between office or factory supervisors and the workers). True democratic supervision is a relatively recent innovation, and it has not become widespread. To some extent it is practiced in upper levels of organization through committee structures and on boards of directors.

Practically any supervisor or executive can practice individual consultation on a face-to-face basis at his own discretion. But for complete and continuing consultative and democratic management practices to thrive, active approval by top management is essential. Indeed, it should not only give vocal approval, it must actually practice one or the other of these forms of management.

Actually the term *democratic supervision* is not precisely accurate because industrial enterprises, commercial concerns, and most other types of work organizations are not democracies. The employees do not choose their leaders. They do not set up the corporation in the first place. Whereas a political leader in a democracy is dependent upon the electorate for his continued job tenure, in a corporation a manager primarily is beholden to those above him in the hierarchy. He does not answer to his subordinates (at least directly he doesn't) but rather to his boss. Most of the rewards a business executive receives at his company are bestowed from the top down.

A problem that confronts the supervisor who wants to practice democratic supervision is that a great many direct orders come down from above, and he must insist that his men obey. These may be orders derived from top management, which has the broad view and which must institute companywide actions. The supervisor can effectively carry on democratic leadership on problems only within his area of control. Therefore, part of the time he must behave somewhat autocratically when transmitting orders from above and part of the time democratically. Thus the practice of genuine democratic management is extremely difficult.

Formal Participation Programs

Formal participation programs require that a formal organization structure be established to carry them out. There tends to be a degree of continuity and permanence to these programs. Certain of the participants acquire formal positions and titles over and above their regular jobs as employees and managers. Thus, as a member of a junior board of directors, an engineering department manager may serve as the chairman of the junior board for a year. When the board is in session, he behaves as the board chairman, not as the engineering manager.

Junior Boards of Executives. The junior board of executives system, by which standing committees of managers carry out studies and make recommendations to top management, is also known as multiple management.[15] The idea of junior boards of executives was first installed in American industry by Charles P. McCormick in 1932 at McCormick & Company in Baltimore, Maryland. This system of management has since spread to a number of other companies. Most commonly these boards are composed of members of middle management, with there being some system by which members are rotated into and out of the board. In most companies new board members are selected by present board incumbents through an election procedure. Also present board members merit-rate or appraise one another to decide who is to be retained for the next term of office and who will be dropped. In a few companies board members are appointed by the president of the company.

Generally these junior boards of executives have wide latitude to undertake the study of practically any type of problem area affecting the company's business. Within the board itself there will be committees that carry out investigations in project areas. Typical topics for investigation are company organization, executive compensation, automation, foreign markets, personnel policies, warehousing operations, and use of wage incentives. When the board has reached a decision, a recommendation is sent to top company management, which can accept or reject the proposal.

A junior board of executives can be looked upon as a standing advisory committee to top management. It is a type of "senate" representing middle (and in some companies lower) management in the conduct of the business. The selection of the board members and the choice of subjects for investigation is determined by the board itself. There is little or no dictation from the president of the company regarding the conduct of the board's business. A prime requisite for success of the junior board of executives system is top management support and encouragement for the whole concept.

Collective Bargaining. Collective bargaining, which occurs when a

---

[15] See Chapter 14, "Management Development," for an explanation of multiple management as a method of strengthening the organization and developing executives.

union represents the employees, is a type of participation program distinctly different from all the other participation methods. Collective bargaining is not instituted by management (except in special circumstances), whereas all of the other programs of participation are discretionary on management's part. Bargaining relationships usually commence as a result of a union organizing campaign and an election conducted by the National Labor Relations Board to determine whether the employees wish to have a union represent them in negotiations with the employer over such matters as wages, hours, and other conditions of employment. Although it must be admitted that in some instances a union and an employer may sign an initial labor agreement over the heads of the employees (that is, without a National Labor Relations Board election to determine employee sentiments regarding unionization), and it must be further agreed that a few unions are not democratically run, in the vast majority of cases unions do solicit member opinions at regular meetings regarding bargaining demands to be made upon the employer and regarding the handling of day-to-day problems in the shop. The Labor-Management Reporting and Disclosure Act of 1959 (Landrum-Griffin Act) contains strong provisions to ensure union democracy.

Thus it can be accurately said that employees through their elected leaders do participate on an equal basis with company representatives in negotiating labor agreements, in administering the agreement, and in processing grievances. The local union leaders, who are usually company employees as well, help make decisions regarding pay rates, seniority rules, pension plans, order of layoff, vacations, holidays, grievance procedures, benefit plans, and hours of work.

All sorts of bargaining relationships exist among companies and their unions in the United States. In some there is clear conflict. The union has forced itself upon an unreceptive employer, or the union has been very aggressive toward the company management. In others a clear balance of power exists and an atmosphere of mutual respect and accommodation prevails. In some cases relations between management and the union are harmonious, and there may even be cooperation on the mutual problems of production, costs, and market competition in addition to those directly relating to employment relationships.

Union-Management Cooperation. Over the years the term *union-management cooperation* has come to mean a formal program of cooperation and consultation between management and union to solve production problems jointly and to devise improvements in plant efficiency for the mutual benefit of both the company and the employees. It is usually carried on through the mechanism of joint union-management committees at the department, plant, and company-wide levels. Generally the ideas generated in these committees are looked upon as suggestions to management. This means that management can accept or reject the proposals, and therefore it still retains most of its traditional prerogatives.

However, a management that is unusually sensitive about placing a wall around its inherent rights is unlikely to enter into a union-management cooperation program. The spirit of cooperation, conciliation, and give and take must prevail in order that a program of union-management cooperation can succeed.

Cooperation programs can be classified into two categories: (1) nonincentive type, and (2) pay incentive type. Well-known and long-standing examples of the nonincentive type are the plans of the Baltimore and Ohio Railroad, the Canadian National Railways, and the Tennessee Valley Authority. The best-known example of the incentive type is the Scanlon Plan.

The TVA plan was started on the initiative of, local union leaders of the Tennessee Valley Trades and Labor Council in the early 1940's. The committee structure consists of 25 joint plant committees, plus a central joint committee to cover the entire TVA system. The union members of the plant committees are job stewards. Both workers and management personnel are invited to submit suggestions to these committees. The TVA plan has been unusually successful. The number of suggestions submitted per 100 employees has tended to increase over the years. It was 14 per 100 employees in 1948, and that figure had risen to 31 by 1958. The percentage of labor-saving suggestions has also risen with the passage of years.[16] A 1965 study by Patchen of the TVA experience in terms of its impact upon employees revealed that this program of labor-management consultation increases employee feelings of solidarity with the organization and with management and that it increases employee acceptance of work changes. The workers viewed work changes, not as something imposed upon them, but rather as products of joint consultation.[17]

The Scanlon Plan (named after the late Joseph Scanlon, who originated the plan in the late 1930's) contains an incentive feature whereby any reduction in plant payroll costs below an agreed-upon standard or norm is passed on to the employees (or shared with them) in the form of a bonus. The standard is expressed as total payroll cost divided by the sales value of the product. Each department has a two-man committee composed of one management and one union representative (usually the foreman and the shop steward). It reviews suggestions obtained from the employees of that department. A larger plantwide screening committee acts upon the suggestions from all the departmental committees. Where it has been installed, the Scanlon Plan has generally worked well. It depends for its success upon a genuine spirit of cooperation. Experience has shown that with such a program the workers are more willing to accept tech-

[16] Sumner H. Slichter, James J. Healy, and E. Robert Livernash, *The Impact of Collective Bargaining on Management* (Washington, D.C.: The Brookings Institution, 1960), pp. 862-863. For coverage of the whole subject of union-management cooperation see Ch. 28.

[17] Martin Patchen, "Labor-Management Consultation at TVA: Its Impact on Employees" *Administrative Science Quarterly,* Vol. 10, No. 2 (September 1965), pp. 149-174.

nological change than in the typical company. There is a greater interest by the workers in the problems of management, the employees tend to help one another to a considerable extent, and foremen actively seek (instead of resent) suggestions for improvement from the workers.[18]

Although the idea of union-management cooperation is very appealing, it has not actually achieved widespread acceptance in American industry. Workers sometimes fear that by initiating cost-cutting suggestions they may actually contribute to their own layoff as a result of these increases in efficiency. Union officials sometimes feel that cooperation programs may weaken their position for vigorously pressing for wage increases and other gains at contract negotiation time. Some company executives tend to fear that union-management cooperation will open the door to a union invasion of traditional management prerogatives and that the union may ultimately be able to exercise a veto power over certain management actions.

However, the actual experience of many programs demonstrates that union-management cooperation can be very successful. It depends fundamentally upon a mature and cooperative attitude on the part of both union and management and acceptance by management of the legitimate place of the union in the company-employee relationship. If one party is very insecure in its relations with the other party, then union-management cooperation is unlikely to succeed.

Suggestion Plans.   A suggestion plan is a formalized system established by an employer to encourage employees to submit ideas that will result in improvement for the business and the organization. The payment of monetary awards for accepted suggestions is a fundamental feature of these plans.

Suggestion plans are not a recent development. The first plan in the United States was that instituted by the Yale and Towne Manufacturing Company at Stamford, Connecticut, in 1880. In 1894 the National Cash Register Company began its plan. Other early plans were Eastman Kodak and Bausch and Lomb in 1898, General Electric (1905), and Westinghouse (1910). All of these plans are still operating successfully. In the year 1957 Westinghouse estimated that it saved $1,446,505 on suggestions, while paying out $295,905 in awards to employees.[19]

A well-run suggestion program can achieve a number of real benefits for the organization. It provides an additional avenue of upward communication. This is especially important, because higher management, in many organizations, is insulated from the problems and viewpoints of the employees. It provides a means by which employees can achieve some mea-

---

[18] For a fuller explanation of the Scanlon Plan see Ch. 25, "Incentives Based Upon Cooperation," where it is treated as a plantwide wage incentive plan based upon the idea of cooperation.

[19] "How to Keep a Suggestion Plan Successful," *Management Record,* Vol. XXI, No. 2 (February 1959), p. 42.

sure of participation in the affairs of the business. A suggestion system is looked upon by some people as a technique for improving employee relations and morale. A primary gain from a properly conducted program is the significant reduction in production and operating costs that can accrue. In addition, employees receive money awards and recognition from management.

Although there is considerable variation from organization to organization as far as the mechanics of their suggestion plans are concerned, the essential features of most plans have much in common. Typically companies will recognize those ideas that will achieve measurable dollar savings in labor and/or material costs through new methods, procedures, materials, and equipment. They also welcome ideas proposing improvements in safety, housekeeping, employee relations, public relations, and those that aid the organization in general. For these latter types it is usually not possible to calculate a definite dollar benefit that will accrue to the organization from adoption of the suggestion. In this case, token awards are granted.

Suggestions are put in writing on special blanks supplied at convenient locations throughout the working area. These are then dropped into suggestion boxes. They are processed by a suggestion secretary, who may be a member of the industrial relations or industrial engineering departments. Many companies utilize the services of suggestion investigators, who collect all of the facts needed to evaluate the ideas adequately. Final decisions on whether to accept, reject, or defer judgment until later are generally made by a suggestion committee, which is usually composed of middle management individuals. Cash awards are computed on the basis of net annual savings in material and labor costs. Commonly an employee will receive an award equal to a percentage (often 10 or 15 per cent) of the first year's net savings.

As a means of developing employee participation and involvement in the thinking required to run an organization, a suggestion plan is less comprehensive than consultative management, democratic supervision, and union-management cooperation. It relies almost entirely upon written communication. There is little or no opportunity for groups of people to put their heads together to jointly evolve an idea and a plan. If an employee's idea is rejected because the suggestion committee misunderstood his meaning, there is little chance for him to explain it in face-to-face discussion.

Some critics point out that it is organizationally unsound because the upward flow of suggestions bypasses the first-level supervisor. He is cut out of the picture. In many companies he resents the fact that his men are initiating methods and production ideas for top management review. By contrast, however, consultative and democratic management and union-management cooperation puts the foreman on the team by heavily involving him in the participation program.

The record does reveal, though, that many suggestion plans have operated successfully for years. They are a source of motivation. Employees with initiative and ideas can be identified. They can obtain significant monetary rewards. The strength of an organization is increased by developing meaningful contributions from workers as well as management. Definitely worthwhile cost savings have accrued to innumerable companies year after year.

Questions for Review and Discussion

1. What is mean by the term *participation?* Distinguish between genuine and pseudo participation.
2. Traditionally why is participation carried on more frequently at higher levels in a business organization than at the foreman-worker level?
3. What are the advantages of participation to the organization? To the individual employee?
4. Give some examples of situations where it would be inadvisable to invite participation from subordinates?
5. "The position of a leader is weakened if he consults his subordinates. They tend to acquire doubts as to his command of the situation, and this causes him to lose control." Discuss this viewpoint.
6. A department manager in a research laboratory asked each of his subordinates as individuals to submit to him in writing proposals for new projects that should be undertaken in the future. After reviewing each man's report, the manager selected two projects and announced at the next department meeting that he had decided that these were the ones that would be carried out during the forthcoming year. There had been no discussion with the researchers regarding their proposals. Evaluate this as a form of participation.
7. Compare individual boss-subordinate participation with group consultation between the supervisor and his entire group of subordinates. Give consideration to such factors as skills required of the supervisor and subordinates, capacity for generating ideas and reaching conclusions, nature of problems that can be discussed, time involved, and so on.
8. Distinguish between consultative and democratic management.
9. Do you think that the junior board of executives system can be successful at the level of foreman and office supervisors? Discuss.
10. In what ways does collective bargaining differ from the other kinds of participation activities and programs discussed in this chapter?
11. What is meant by the term *union-management cooperation?* What forces have impeded the adoption of these programs throughout industry?

12. Explain how the typical suggestion plan operates in an industrial establishment?

Suggestions for Further Reading

Coch, L., and J. R. P. French, "Overcoming Resistance to Change," *Human Relations,* Vol. 1, No. 4, 1948, pp. 512-532.

Lawrence, Lois C., and P. C. Smith, "Group Decision and Employee Participation," *Journal of Applied Psychology,* Vol. 39, October 1955, pp. 334-337.

Leavitt, Harold J., "Unhuman Organizations," *Harvard Business Review,* Vol. 40, No. 4, July-August 1962, pp. 90-98.

Maier, Norman R. F., "Assets and Liabilities in Group Problem Solving: The Need for an Integrative Function," *Psychological Review,* Vol. 74, No. 4, 1967, pp. 239-249.

Marrow, Alfred J., D. G. Bowers, and S. E. Seashore, *Management by Participation,* Harper & Row, 1967.

Marrow, Alfred J., *Making Management Human,* New York: McGraw-Hill Book Company, 1957.

McCormick, Charles P., *The Power of People,* New York: Harper & Row, 1949.

Newport, M. Gene, "Participative Management: Some Cautions," *Personnel Journal,* Vol. 45, No. 9, 1966, pp. 532-536.

Sikes, Walter, "The Paradox of Participation." *Personnel,* Vol. 39, No. 1, January-February 1962, pp. 35-38.

Strauss, George, "Some Notes on Power Equalization" in Harold J. Leavitt (ed.), *The Social Science of Organizations: Four Perspectives,* Englewood Cliffs, N.J.: Prentice-Hall, 1963, pp. 41-84.

Tannenbaum, Robert, Irving R. Weschler, and Fred Massarik, *Leadership and Organization: A Behavioral Science Approach,* New York: McGraw-Hill Book Company, 1961, Ch. 7.

Thompson, Arthur A., "Employee Participation in Decision Making: The TVA Experience," *Public Personnel Review,* Vol. 28, No. 2, April 1967, pp. 82-88.

Communication

20

An organization cannot function without communication. Communications tie together the component parts of an organization and impel people to action. In order for group and organizational activity to take place there must be communication among the participants.

Within a work organization communication serves several functions. (1) It transmits information and knowledge from person to person so that cooperative action can occur. (2) It serves to motivate and direct people to do something, as when a supervisor induces subordinates to undertake a project. (3) It helps to mold attitudes and impart beliefs in order to persuade, convince, and influence behavior. (4) It helps to orient people to their physical and social environment. Without such orientation, people (employees and managers) would be lost. They would be unable to gain perspective or to place themselves properly in their environment. In addition to these four functions, which are primarily related to communication in a work organization, communication also serves auxiliary functions, such as entertainment and the maintenance of social relations among human beings.

For the manager, skill in speaking, listening, reading, and writing is vital. His environment and his job are primarily involved in language and communication. He is continually interacting with other people via conferences, interviews, and telephone conversations. He is heavily occupied reading reports, letters, documents, and special studies. Top and middle level executives typically devote 60 to 80 per cent of their total working hours to communicating.

One observation study of foremen in a Midwestern corporation showed that they spent approximately 50 per cent of the work day in some form of oral communication either in speaking or listening. Of the total time devoted to communication, 60 per cent was with subordinates, 30 per cent was with their superiors, and 10 per cent was with others on their same level in the company.[1]

Communication is the transfer of information and understanding from person to person. It is essential in studying communication that we realize that it involves more than just the transmission of messages from one person to another. A man may receive a message but not comprehend its meaning. For communication to take place, the sender of the message must actually get through to the receiver. In other words, the receiver must *understand* (although, of course, he does not necessarily have to agree with the content or the point of view expressed).

Elements of Communication

The basic elements involved in the process of communication are an *information source, encoding, transmission, reception,* and *decoding.* The information source is a person who possesses knowledge or opinions that he desires to send to another person. So he expresses his ideas in some form (encoding). He may do this by speaking, writing, drawing a picture, or signaling with a physical motion. The message is then transmitted to someone else (or a group). The transmission may be by sound waves through the air, as in face-to-face voice communication, by handwritten or typewritten words on paper, or by physical movements that are seen by the receiving person. Reception takes place when the person for whom the message is intended hears the oral communication or sees the written or graphic communication. He then decodes the message by grasping meaning and understanding from it. In any communication situation something may occur to interfere with the full and accurate carrying out of the communication process. The encoding may be faulty, as for example when a person uses the wrong words or improper sentence structure to express his ideas. The transmission step may cause distortion in such a way that the message is not received in the same way it was sent. An example of this would be an altering of a policy directive from the president of a company as it filters down through the chain of command. The receiver of a message may misinterpret it because he has a totally different frame of reference from that of the sender.

The transfer of meaning from one person to another is accomplished by the use of *symbols.* A symbol is that which represents or stands for something else. Thus the symbols of communication are words both oral and written, a two-dimensional diagram or picture or a three-dimension-

---

[1] D. T. Piersol "Communication Practices of Supervisors in a Mid-Western Corporation," *Advanced Management,* Vol. 23, No. 2 (February 1958), pp. 20-21.

al model, and such human actions as gestures, facial expressions, and other physical movements.

Channels of communication are the pathways used to transmit information and understanding. A channel is a route. We can say that the chain of command is a channel, as is also the grapevine. The grapevine constitutes an informal channel of communication wherein messages are transmitted by word of mouth from friend to friend and from worker to worker. Communications between departments or between two companies constitute other channels. A channel should be distinguished from a technique or *vehicle* for communication. Vehicles are the specific means by which messages are transmitted, such as written reports, letters, books, meetings, interviews, lectures, conversations, manuals, and the like.

A *network* consists of the paths over which communication travels among people. It is the organization chart or road map showing the communication routes.

COMMUNICATION FUNDAMENTALS

So that the student of management can apply his talents effectively in communicating in work organizations, it is desirable that he become familiar with the more important basic principles and problems of human communication. We shall now examine some of the more important communication fundamentals.

Words Do Not Have Meaning in Themselves

A word is just a symbol—a sign to represent a thing, an action, or a feeling. Through the process of education and socialization we learn to assign meaning to words. Those raised in the same neighborhood and who attend the same schools and participate in the same institutions will tend to associate the same meaning to a particular word-symbol. Those raised in the same culture and in the same country will associate the same *approximate* meanings to words, but there will be varying interpretations, perhaps, among different regions.

Words Mean Different Things to Different People

In attempting to communicate with one another, we often find that the person to whom we are talking assigns a different meaning to our words than we intend. This can lead to all sorts of trouble. Let us look at a few examples.

Whereas the old-style factory foreman used to bark orders at his men in a bull-of-the-woods fashion, the modern shop supervisor tends to be more polite. He will say to a worker, "Joe, will you handle this repair job for me?" If Joe is new to the industrial scene, he may interpret this as a question that gives him an option to say no. But in reality the *will you* phrase usually means "you will," and it is simply a courteously expressed order.

If a person comes from the Midwest he uses the word *pop* to order a carbonated soft drink. But along the East coast of the United States, such a beverage is called soda. To the Midwesterner soda is made with carbonated water, flavoring, and ice cream. Likewise a milk shake to a Midwesterner contains a scoop of ice cream, milk, and flavoring, whereas along the Atlantic Seaboard to obtain such an item at a soda fountain one must order a frosted.

The magnitude of the problem can be appreciated by noting a simple statistic. For the 500 most commonly used words in the English language, there are a total of over 14,000 dictionary definitions. What causes this confusing situation? There are several reasons. The way in which the general public actually uses a word primarily determines its meaning. Over the years words take on new meanings. They tend to be applied to new situations. Sometimes old meanings become unused and hence obsolete. Also regional differences arise in the meanings given to words. In different sections of the country, different ethnic groups predominate. The religions, customs, industries, and mores of the people will vary from place to place. These factors give rise to varying interpretations of words. Still another reason for differences in the meaning of words is that scientists and professional people strive to develop precision of language within their fields of knowledge so that they can communicate with each other. Thus the technical meaning of a word may be quite different from the ordinary or popular meaning.

How can we overcome the difficulties imposed by variation in the meaning of words? One good way is for the listener to gain clues from the context of the communication. The context is the whole situation in which a word is used. If we are at a baseball game and a friend speaks of the score, we would know that he is referring to the number of runs made by each team and not to a musical score, which would show instrumental and vocal parts written on staffs.

The speaker or writer can reduce the possibility of misunderstanding by using synonyms for the word in question as he expresses himself. He can express the same thought in more than one way. He can paraphrase. An excellent way to determine whether a listener understands our words is simply to query him. Invite him to express himself. Get feedback.

Perception of Reality Differs

If two people experience the same phenomenon, there is a natural human tendency for them to think that each perceived it in the same way and came to the same conclusions. But such is frequently not the case.

What we perceive is governed by our needs, wants, and drives. To a considerable extent people perceive what they want to perceive. A person's behavior is not governed by the bare, objective facts of the physical and social world around him; rather it is determined by how he structures and interprets the perceived phenomenon. We interpret the world about us in accordance with our background, attitudes, prior knowledge, and experiences accumulated since birth.

One's frame of reference has a powerful effect upon how he perceives a problem situation. This has been illustrated by an experiment described by Dearborn and Simon. Twenty-three middle-management personnel from a variety of departments were enrolled in a company executive training course. A case study, 10,000 words in length, was given to them to analyze. When they appeared at the class session they were first asked to write down a brief statement of what they considered to be the most important problem facing the company described in the case. Five out of six of the sales executives saw the problem as one of sales, marketing, or distribution. Only five out of the remaining eighteen executives saw the problem in this way. The three executives from the public relations, industrial relations, and medical departments perceived the major problem to be one of human relations, employee relations, or teamwork.[2]

Consider some other examples that can often occur in industry. A company policy pronouncement that all employees will be reviewed annually for merit increases may be interpreted (wishfully) by most of the employees to mean that they can count on receiving a raise in pay every year.

A manufacturing manager makes the following statement: "Twenty-five per cent of our employees are terminated before the end of their six months' probationary period." The employment manager considers this to be a high figure and interprets it as a reflection on his ability to select new workers. The local union president sees in this statement the "fact" that the company deliberately discharges people before the end of six months to prevent them from joining the union and increasing the union's strength. The research investigator in industrial relations would tend to want to look behind this figure of a 25-per-cent termination rate before he made any conclusions. What portions of it are due to discharge, layoff, and quits? How do these figures compare with other departments, plants, and companies? Are the differences significant? In making the statement in the first place the manufacturing superintendent may have meant that he has high standards, demands good performance from his people, and therefore weeds out all poor and mediocre employees.

There are several approaches that can be adopted to reduce the difficulties imposed by selective perception. Steps can be taken to provide an adequate background of facts and events so that the various people involved will be brought to a more common level of understanding. Adequate opportunity must be allowed for two-way discussion to clarify points

[2] De Witt C. Dearborn and Herbert A. Simon, "Selective Perception: A Note on the Departmental Identifications of Executives," *Sociometry,* Vol. 21, No. 2 (June 1958).

of misunderstanding and disagreement. The communicator should be sensitive to the frame of reference and point of view of the receiver. He should get to know the receiver ahead of time. What are the recipient's problems and needs? How will these color his reception of information?

One reason many companies spend so much money on employee orientation programs, indoctrination, house organs, economic education, and the like, is that they want to develop company loyalty and a common frame of reference among all the employees. They attempt to develop an air of receptivity to company pronouncements. Although such company programs can be properly criticized because they tend to create unquestioned obedience and support for the "company line," it cannot be denied that well-run programs do improve internal communications and cooperation.

Emotions Affect Understanding

To a great extent people "think with their hearts, not with their minds." On the day that it was announced, several years ago, that fluorine would be added to the public water supply (to reduce tooth decay) in Newburgh, New York, numerous citizens telephoned the city officials to complain of dizziness, headaches, and other ailments from the fluorine in the drinking water. But in point of fact none had been added to the water on the first day, because of technical difficulties. The complainers had reacted emotionally to the very idea of fluorine in the water.

Some top executives react very negatively to the idea of a "general pay increase." For years now unions have been extracting across-the-board wage increases from corporations for the hourly employees. When someone suggests to a company president that he should grant a general increase to all salaried personnel to maintain equity, he often reacts very strongly with a statement that all increases to these white-collar groups will be based strictly on merit. Such persons are emotionally opposed to the idea of a general pay increase and believe that only people who deserve them should be granted a raise. They forget that often it is necessary to raise everybody's salary just to be able to attract and retain labor in a tight labor market or in a time of a rising price level.

In a 1960 study of worker reactions to words in company communications, the Opinion Research Corporation found that the workers reacted favorably to the term *union shop* but negatively to the phrase *compulsory union membership.* The word *strike* was approved as an acceptable means to an end, whereas the phrase *work stoppage* implied irresponsibility on the employees' part.[3]

It is rarely possible to eliminate emotions as a factor in communication. But it is possible for the sender of the message to learn ahead of time

[3] Verne Burnett, "Management's Tower of Babel," *Management Review,* Vol. 50, No. 6 (June 1961), pp. 4-11.

of the attitudes and biases of his audience so that he can express his ideas in such a way that the true meaning is comprehended by the receiver.

Facts Must Be Distinguished from Opinions

Opinions are easy to acquire, and most people are ever ready to proclaim their viewpoint. Facts are much harder to come by. We must analyze, study, investigate, and collect statistics to arrive at facts. Now many speakers attempt to achieve an air of authority by expressing their opinions as if they were facts. "The welfare situation is bankrupting the country." "High taxes cause inflation." The unsophisticated listener may endow such a speaker with greater expertise than he really possesses. Often this is just what such a speaker hopes for.

The careful speaker and writer will clearly distinguish his assertions of opinion from his statements of fact. If he is expressing merely an opinion or an inference, he will say, "I believe that such and such is the better way," or, "I perceive," or, "It seems to me." Quite often the context of a remark makes it clear to the listener that a speaker is merely giving his opinion.

The great difficulty with failing to separate opinions from facts is that many will consider an opinion to be a fact, act accordingly, and arrive at an erroneous conclusion.

Quite commonly a fact to one person is not a fact to another. One of the principal causes of the deep-seated struggle between the free world and the communist world is that what one side considers to be basic facts regarding freedom, human rights, human progress, and economics is rejected by the other.

Feedback

Much of the communication that takes place in this world is one way. It travels from the sender to the receiver only. The sender does not know the reactions of his listeners. Do they understand? Do they agree? disagree?

The primary teaching technique that has been used in colleges for centuries is the lecture. This comprises communication in one direction only. Company bulletins, newsletters, loudspeaker announcements, orders, and procedure manuals are forms of one-way communication. How effective is communication in one direction only? Does the listener really understand? Let us turn to a research experiment for an answer to the question.

Leavitt and Mueller have conducted experiments involving communication from person A to person or persons B, both with and without any flow of messages back from B to A. In effect they measured the value of feedback in a human communications system. In this experiment groups of students were expected to reproduce on paper certain geometric patterns upon receipt of oral instructions from the instructor. In one of the problems the students were asked to reproduce a pattern composed of six rectangles arranged in a particular way, one to the other. There were four levels of contact between instructor and students. (1) Zero feedback in which instructors and students could not see one another and communication was solely from instructor to students. (2) The instructor and audience could see one another, but no speaking by students was allowed. (3) A yes-no situation in which students could say only yes or no to questions from the instructor. (4) Free feedback, in which students were allowed to ask questions freely and interrupt the instructor as they wished. When graded on a scale of accuracy of reproduction from 0 to 6, it was found performance was poorest with zero feedback, better with a visible audience, still better with a yes-no condition, and best with free feedback. However, the total time to complete the instruction was greatest with free feedback and lowest with zero feedback.[4]

As a result of this and related experiments, several important conclusions emerge. Two-way communication is more accurate in terms of developing understanding than one-way communication. Two-way communication consumes more time than one-way communication. With two-way communication the receivers (for example, students, workers, subordinates) are more sure of the correctness of their judgments and actions. When the receiver has an opportunity to question and speak back to the sender, he sometimes will express his feelings openly and critically. He may be quite frank in his statements toward the sender.

Sometimes a person in a position of power, such as a supervisor, a teacher, a parent, or a military officer, will issue orders and instructions but allow no back talk. He does this ostensibly to save time, to maintain discipline, or to achieve efficiency. But more often he really denies his followers the opportunity to express themselves (feedback) because he fears he will lose control. He cannot tolerate any critical comments from his followers. He does not want to hear that perhaps his directions were not the wisest nor the clearest nor the most appropriate. Thus one who seeks to preserve the appearance of maintaining absolute authority will often seek to prevent feedback from his followers.

For the proper management of an organization feedback is essential. In face-to-face contacts with his men, a supervisor can encourage them to express their questions and suggestions. He can adopt a receptive frame of mind and learn to be a good listener. The president of a company is often isolated from the true problems occurring in the plant. He must take the initiative to establish a genuine and successful upward flow of information from the lowest levels in the organization. The methods of obtaining a flow of upward communication in the organization are discussed later in this chapter.

[4] Harold J. Leavitt and Ronald A. H. Mueller, "Some Effects of Feedback on Communication," *Human Relations,* Vol. 4 (1951), pp. 401-410.

Communication Networks

The paths or channels of communication among people as well as the direction of the communication have an effect upon group performance and morale. This has been demonstrated by the research of Alex Bavelas and others at the Massachusetts Institute of Technology. Consider the three networks shown in Figure 20-1. The dots represent people, and the lines represent paths of two-way communication. For an industrial analogy consider that Network I is a leaderless group of five in conference to solve a problem. Network II is a five-man organization with two levels of supervision. A is the manager, E and B are supervisors, and D and C are employees. Network III is an engineering group consisting of four engineers and one supervisor.

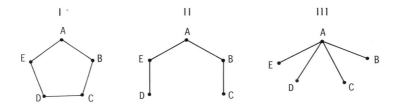

Figure 20-1.   Communication Networks.

When given exactly the same problem, Networks II and III are both fast and accurate at working out solutions, whereas Network I is slow and accuracy is poor. However, morale is very high in Network I, whereas it is poor in II and very poor in III.[5]

Heise and Miller, working in a laboratory situation with students at Harvard University, set up three experiments for communication among just three persons with five possible networks of communication for each three-man group. Each person was required to reach a solution to the problem. Communication was by talking, not writing. The networks varied in the sense that full two-way communication was permitted among all three persons in one net, whereas only certain individuals could initiate conversation in other nets. Experiment 1 called for the exchange of isolated words to reproduce a master list. Experiment 2 required the building of sentences, whereas experiment 3 required the forming of as many anagrams as possible from a list of six given words. The measure of efficiency in the first two experiments was the time to complete the tasks, whereas in the anagram experiment it was the number of words constructed within ten minutes.

[5] Alex Bavelas and Dermot Barrett, "An Experimental Approach to Organizational Communication," *Personnel,* Vol. 27 (March 1951), pp. 366-371; see also M. Glanzer and R. Glaser, *Techniques for Study of Team Structure and Behavior, Part II* (Pittsburgh: American Institute for Research, 1957).

In experiment 1 a closed chain in which only one-way communication was possible between any two persons was the least efficient, and the closed chain where all members talked and listened to each other was most efficient. In experiment 2, where close coordination of the group activity was required, it was found that the most efficient net was the one that required one man to serve as the focus of communication—that is, persons B and C had two-way communication with person A but no communication with each other. In the anagram problem communication was not really necessary to the solution; hence there turned out to be no real difference in efficiency among the networks studied.[6]

This series of experiments by Heise and Miller demonstrates that there is no one communication pattern that is most efficient for all types of situations. It depends upon the complexity of the problems, the range of alternatives available to the group, the attitudes of the members toward one another, the availability of information among the members, and a number of other factors.

Communication networks in an industrial concern are clearly much more complex than those employed in the foregoing experiments. Considerably more research remains to be done in this area. Yet these experiments have demonstrated that for a particular set of circumstances regarding a problem situation there are certain networks that are more productive than others. They also show that group morale is strongly determined by the pattern of communication.

Actions Speak Louder Than Words

This is an era in which the art and science of communications has reached an advanced stage. Motivational researchers are able to tell an advertiser what type of slogan is most likely to appeal to consumers. Public relations experts are employed by politicians to improve their image with the voters so that they can get elected. Big business spends millions on public relations programs to develop the desired "corporate image." With all this emphasis upon words, slogans, atmosphere, image, and public relations, there is a tendency for many executives to become enchanted with such illusion making to the point that they neglect the substance. Yet in the final analysis an employee will judge his boss on how well he is treated, not on the boss's promises. A person may buy a product the first time because of a slick slogan, but he will become a steady customer only if that product performs to his full satisfaction.

Basically, then, actions must conform to promises. A public relations consultant cannot generate a lasting positive image of a corporation if that firm's behavior in its relations with its customers, employees, stockholders, and the community is unsavory. Deeds must match words.

[6] George A. Heise and George A. Miller, "Problem Solving by Small Groups Using Various Communications Nets," *Journal of Abnormal and Social Psychology*, Vol. 46 (1951), pp. 327-336.

Status and Propensity to Communicate

If people in an organization have some degree of freedom to choose the persons with whom they will communicate, they will deal with people in their own immediate work group and with other people who occupy positions of higher status than they do. They will avoid dealing with persons possessing lesser power, lower level positions, and inferior status.

> Bill, a personnel specialist, had worked in a small field office for a federal government agency for two years. Group cohesiveness and morale were high. Then he was promoted to a job in Washington, D.C., at the headquarters of his agency. Here he found a rigid caste system stratified according to pay grade and rank in the agency. Although his job required frequent dealings with persons holding higher-level positions, he soon noticed that these same persons snubbed him on informal occasions, such as during lunch, coffee breaks, and at chance meetings in the hallways. These persons would associate only with others at their same level in the organization or with persons having higher status and influence.

> The *Management Society* in the city is composed of about 100 junior executives, nearly all of whom are college graduates. The organization holds monthly dinner meetings to which eminent persons are invited to speak on topics of professional interest to the membership. In addition the society organizes several all-day conferences throughout each year. Most of the members are under forty years of age and hold staff positions in the lower and middle ranks of management in their respective companies. It has been observed over the years that as members are promoted into upper-middle and top management positions, they drop out of active participation in the *Society*. Eventually they give up their membership entirely. It has also been noted by the active leaders that their efforts to recruit new members from the ranks of top management are generally unsuccessful.

The events in the two foregoing examples can be explained by the fact that people communicate to achieve their goals and to satisfy their needs. Both within and outside the business organization, they communicate with their peers because they share common problems, experiences, and outlook. The contacts are satisfying. In addition to this, many people have strong ambitions to get ahead, to be promoted, to achieve higher social status, and to raise their level of living. Therefore they seek to make the "right" contacts and to impress the "right" people. This means that they look upward. They consciously try to form social bonds with people of power and influence who might do them good in their careers. They are reluctant to mingle with people of lower position and status, because these could contribute nothing to their careers or standing in the community.[7] An exception to the foregoing analysis applies, of course, to communi-

---

[7] For further discussion of this point see Jay M. Jackson, "The Organization and Its Communications Problem," *Advanced Management,* Vol. 23, No. 2 (February 1959), pp. 17-20.

cation between a supervisor and his immediate subordinates. A super-visor communicates frequently and extensively with his men in order to accomplish results. Further, the effective supervisor knows that he is ap-praised by his own superior according to how well he is able to motivate his people to produce and how well his section, as a unit, meets established goals.

Abstruseness and Vagueness

One graduate student whom I advised during the course of the prep-aration and writing of his master's thesis had a propensity for writing in an abstruse and vague fashion. Throughout his thesis he made frequent mention of the theories and concepts of prominent researchers and writ-ers in the field of his thesis. Yet he expressed the ideas so vaguely and, at times, inaccurately that it was very difficult to comprehend his train of thought and the points he was trying to make. By conducting a thorough interview with him, I learned that the real reason for the vague mode of expression was a lack of basic preparation and understanding of the top-ics he was attempting to write about. In reviewing samples of other pa-pers that this student had written, I saw that he could be very clear and concrete when he was writing about topics with which he was thorough-ly familiar. The solution to this graduate student's problem was to have him do much more extensive study and reading in the fundamentals of his chosen thesis topic.

Thus it is that we find that a person expresses himself in a vague, ab-struse, and incomprehensible fashion when he himself does not really understand that which he seeks to explain. Clarity of thought and clar-ity of language go hand in hand. Generally if someone is unable to express his thoughts clearly in words (either oral or written), he really has formed only a fuzzy and hazy notion of the idea in his own mind.

Face-to-Face Communication Is Important

If you want to sell an idea, to persuade and influence someone else, the best way to do it is to visit the other fellow in person and engage in a face-to-face conversation. Have you ever witnessed a political speech in person and then read the verbatim text of that same speech in the news-paper the next day? It usually appears dry and dull by comparison.

What ingredients are present in face-to-face communication that are missing in the written form? In an interview, a meeting, or a conversa-tion, we can percieve the tone of voice, the facial expressions, the ges-tures, and the emotions of the other party. All of these things serve to transmit meaning.

Immediate feedback can take place with face-to-face communication. The speaker can determine what effect his words are having upon the receiver and make modifications as he sees fit. Feedback can occur with written communication also, but the response is delayed, often for several days or even weeks.

In the work organization what should be the respective roles of written and verbal communication? Contacts between superior and subordinate should be predominantly face-to-face. Contacts among members of a work team should be essentially of the oral face-to-face type. Persons in higher levels of the organization should be accessible to nonsupervisory employees and members of lower management. If we want significantly to influence the behavior of another person (for example, salesman-customer, supervisor-subordinate, company negotiator-union president), we should employ personal contact. But the human memory can be very misleading. Therefore, such face-to-face communication should often be followed up and supplemented with written agreements, procedural manuals, memoranda, engineering specifications, labor-management agreements, and the like. It is particularly necessary to use written communication where the content is lengthy or involved. Written communication serves as a permanent record. It can be referred to again and again as required.

If a company adopts a no-smoking rule for the shop, would it be sufficient to simply mimeograph a brief statement to that effect and post it on all factory bulletin boards? The answer is that such a procedure probably would not have the desired effect. If this rule represented a change from a long-standing policy that permitted smoking, the employees would want to know the reasons for the change. Does management really mean what it says? Does the rule apply to all employees? To foremen? Does it apply only at certain times and in certain places? These and similar questions can best be answered by direct oral communication between supervisors and their men. The written bulletin board notice is necessary because it insures consistency throughout the company, and it is a permanent record. But actual implementation depends upon oral communication.

COMMUNICATION IN ORGANIZATIONS

A central problem in many companies is communication failures. The symptoms may range from an inability to meet promised delivery dates for finished goods to poor labor-management relations. Quite often a management problem is due to a number of causes, but communications breakdowns compound the issue.

University of Michigan researchers have investigated superior-subordinate communication among high-level management personnel in five companies. They interviewed fifty-eight superior-subordinate pairs of managers in regard to their extent of mutual understanding and agreement on four factors: (1) job duties, (2) human requirements to fulfill the job demands, (3) possible future changes in the job, and (4) obstacles and problems encountered in doing the job. The investigators found a low level of agreement between the superiors and their subordinates regarding the four factors in general. It was only in the area of job duties that the superiors and subordinates agreed more often than they disagreed. On all the other three factors they disagreed more often than they agreed.[8] When it is considered that superiors and their subordinates should be in frequent face-to-face contact with one another and that understanding between the two should be good in order to accomplish the desired results, then such findings certainly demonstrate and typify the seriousness of the problem. If high-level managers are in such a state of disagreement it may be expected that the consequences of such a situation may be magnified as one goes down the chain of command.

A survey of 500 engineers in industry revealed that there was considerable dissatisfaction expressed with the effectiveness of upward communication. Twenty-nine per cent of the engineers said that their supervisors do not pass suggestions upward, 16 per cent said their ideas get filtered when they are passed on, and another 16 per cent felt that management was not interested in suggestions. There was a prevailing feeling that if their suggestions might somehow get through to higher management, there was a strong chance that the originator of the idea would lose credit anyway.[9]

The foregoing two research studies typify the kind of communications difficulties that are prevalent in industrial and other types of work organizations. Such failures can be significant causal factors in problems of low employee morale, poor interdepartmental cooperation, poor quality, duplication of effort, excessive grievances, and poor employee performance.

Communications in the Hierarchy

According to all accepted theories of management and organization, the flow of communication should be the strongest and fullest downward and upward through the chain of command. Although many other channels must be utilized to achieve the organizational goals, none can take the place of the vertical flow from president to vice-president to superintendent to supervisor to employee, and vice versa. In a sense many of the other channels, such as company newsletters, bulletin board notices, and suggestion plans, are only supplementary to the primary channels through the hierarchy. Yet, as we have already seen, serious difficulties occur in the day-to-day operation of communications between superiors and their subordinates.

[8] N. R. F. Maier, L. R. Hoffman, J. J. Hooven, W. H. Read, *Superior-Subordinate Communication in Management,* Research Study 52 (New York: American Management Association, 1961), pp. 1-38.
[9] "Communications and the Engineer—1: How Engineers Rate Company Communications," *Machine Design* (April 11, 1963), pp. 148-152.

Occupying positions of power and authority, managers are accustomed to originating orders that they expect their subordinates to carry out. Ordinarily the kind of response or upward communication they expect to receive consists of oral or written reports of progress toward the goals they have set. In the ordinary course of events, managers do not want nor expect subordinates to originate action for them. They may have read the literature of modern management, which says that communication should flow upward as well as downward in the organization. But the type of upward information they are looking for primarily is answers to their questions, reports of work successfully completed, or explanations for failures. Generally speaking, managers do not actively seek out information from lower level supervisors and workers pertaining to their complaints, problems, criticisms, or proposals for change.

Despite the foregoing, managers often pride themselves in the belief that they really do know what is going on out in the shop. They like to feel that they are "on top of things" and that they maintain accurate and quick sources of information throughout the plant.

Sometimes an executive insulates himself from problems in the plant because he will not listen to his subordinates.

> Howard S., the factory superintendent in a small manufacturing company, stated that he was able to get in to see the company president (his immediate boss) only about once every two weeks. "I spent a half hour with Mr. A. this morning. I told him about all the problems on which action must be taken in order to keep the plant running. I told him about the patched-up equipment we are trying to turn out products with. I told him about the leaky roof, the broken conveyor, the lack of adequate maintenance men, and the need for extra janitorial help. I could see that he didn't want to hear about these problems. He was fidgeting with letters on his desk, fussing with the desk pen and the calendar, and even looking out the window."

> In this same plant Edward J., the maintenance foreman, made the following comment. "Mr. A. [the president] doesn't pay any attention to Howard [the superintendent] or to any of us foremen. The place could be falling down around our ears, and he wouldn't listen to our problems. The only ones Mr. A. pays attention to are Frank B. [chief engineer] and Bill B. [the treasurer]. Those two eat lunch with the President every day, and they are always hanging around his office."

In the foregoing illustration we can see that a barrier existed between the company president and his superintendent. Upward communication was not effective. The president listened to his chief engineer and to the treasurer but not the superintendent. This actually is a problem of influence. Close relations had been established among the president, chief engineer, and the treasurer. He had confidence in their ideas and judgment but not in his superintendent.

Good News Only.   Because subordinates are ever acutely conscious of their dependence upon the boss for their job tenure, pay raises, promotions, and general well-being in the company, they do everything they can to protect and enhance their image in his eyes. This means that they try to tell him about the good things that they do or the good things that happen in their departments and cover up the bad things that happen. If a supervisor's men are discontented with his leadership, he will do everything in his power to prevent this fact from becoming known to his boss.

Insulating Layers.   Large companies have many levels of management. Between the president and the worker on the factory floor, there may be seven or eight levels of management. This makes communication through the chain of command necessarily slow and cumbersome. Inevitably many messages get lost along the way. Those that get through are often distorted so that the original meaning is lost. Policy directives are materially altered through successive interpretations as they travel down the chain of command. Employee suggestions and complaints often are stopped or distorted on the way up.

One solution to these problems is to reduce the number of levels in the organization. This can be accomplished by a wide span of supervision. This means that each supervisor and manager has many men reporting to him instead of a few. Hence fewer managers are needed, and fewer levels of management are necessary. Another (often closely related) way is to decentralize the authority and decision-making powers. Instead of the chief executive officer holding on tightly to the reins of office and getting involved in relatively small problems, he can delegate more authority to subordinate departments and groups so that they can solve their own problems. This means that greater autonomy is granted to the constituent parts of a business organization. Thus there are fewer levels of management between the rank-and-file employee and a key decision maker in his division.

SYSTEMS OF COMMUNICATION

Multiple methods of communication must be utilized in any organization. The choice of any one method depends upon the purpose to be accomplished and the likelihood of success for that mode. Quite often it is judicious to use more than one method to convey the same information so that one can reinforce the other.

Below are shown the principal methods of downward, upward, and horizontal communication within an organization.

DOWNWARD
1. Oral, face-to-face communication through the chain of command. Includes private contacts between superior and subordinate and group meetings conducted by the superior.
2. Written communication. This includes management bulletins, bul-

letin board notices, policy and procedure manuals, house organs, letters to employees, written performance appraisals, and employee handbooks.

3. Personal contacts between higher managers and lower-level employees. This may take the form of direct bypassing of intermediate levels or of informal chatting as the manager walks through the shop.

UPWARD

1. Reports of performance. This includes reports on production, costs, quality, morale, profits, special projects, and the like.
2. Meetings with superiors, consultative management.
3. Open-door policy
4. Suggestion plan
5. Attitude surveys
6. Grievance procedure
7. Periodic meetings between union and management officials.[10]

HORIZONTAL

1. Work flow contacts, both oral and written, between persons on the same level in the structure.

Downward Communication

In instituting formal mass communications to employees, top management should exercise care so as not to ignore or cut out the intermediate supervisors. It can be very frustrating to a supervisor to learn that his men have been told about an important company event before he has. If a great deal of communication is routed from a plant manager directly to the employees, then the men will assume that the plant manager is the key individual to whom they should go with their problems. The supervisor will become superflous.

To prevent such a state of affairs from developing, supervisors should receive all information before it is given out to the employees. If there is to be a change in the organization, a plant expansion, a general pay increase, or a layoff, the members of supervision should be told first. If a printed notice, rule, or handbook is to be distributed to all employees, an excellent approach is to have the foreman hand these out to the workers. This preserves his status and position. Of course, the supervisor should receive a briefing ahead of time on the content so that he can intelligently answer employee questions.

A great deal of information in any organization must be transmitted to employees. For example, the personnel department may publish information pertaining to new personnel programs, wage changes, organ-

---

[10] This might also be classified as a form of horizontal communication. But it seems more appropriate to list it under upward communication, because the problems initiated by the union are generally ones that manifest themselves at lower levels and are first brought to the attention of union officials by rank-and-file workers.

ization changes, promotions of individuals, rules and the like. The question arises as to just what method of communication is most effective from the standpoint of accuracy of understanding on the part of the receivers? Are bulletin board notices sufficient?

One study has shown that when management wishes to communicate purely factual information that is noncontroversial and where the purpose is informative rather than persuasive, then a combination of oral plus written communication is best. Dahle studied the transmission of factual information that was deemed important by both communicators and receivers. He conducted experiments in three different settings: a university (communication from faculty to students), an industrial plant, and a large mail order house. He investigated five methods: (1) oral plus written, (2) oral only, (3) written only, (4) bulletin board, and (5) grapevine only (as a control group). Understanding was measured by an objective test derived from the content of information transmitted. The oral-plus-written method ranked first in effectiveness, with the oral-only method a very close second. The bulletin board and grapevine methods were poorest, and the "written only" method was intermediate.[11] This research in effect, casts doubt upon the value of such prevalent media as bulletin board announcements, leaflets, and pay check envelope inserts when used alone. To get its messages across to employees, management should hold meetings, have question and answer sessions, *and* use carefully prepared written messages that go to every employee individually.

Upward Communication

The upward flow of information in most companies tends to be much less adequate than is the downward flow. Higher management frequently is not aware of the true state of affairs in the shop. It tends to have fairly adequate and prompt data on shipments made, production data, costs and quality, but it is commonly in the dark regarding employee dissatisfactions, criticisms, and ideas. It does not know whether a supervisor in the engineering department has played favorites in the allocating of pay raises. It may fail to provide the opportunity for that new production coordinator to initiate some of the good ideas he has brought with him from his last place of employment. It may not know that there is festering discontent in the machine shop over the issue of working conditions.

Certain methods can be used to provide an upward flow of information. If the employees are unionized, a formal grievance procedure will be established. This provides a means for workers and their union representatives to present complaints and grievances to the department foreman first, and then if satisfaction is not obtained, the issue can be taken

[11] Thomas L. Dahle, "An Objective and Comparative Study of Five Methods of Transmitting Information to Business and Industrial Employees," *Speech Monographs,* Vol. 21 (March 1954), pp. 21-28. Reprinted in Redding, W. Charles and George A. Sanborn, *Business and Industrial Communication* (New York: Harper & Row, 1964), pp. 311-322.

to successively higher levels of management. Since the union as an institution may possess considerable power, individual employees usually are not fearful of lodging a complaint against management, because they feel that the union can protect their jobs adequately.

Recognizing that nonunion employees also need an outlet for their frustrations, some companies have set up grievance procedures for these people. Because there is no union steward or chief steward to represent the employee, a grievance procedure in a nonunion company usually means that the individual simply has the right to go to his supervisor and then to higher levels of management if satisfaction is not obtained at the supervisory level. Some nonunion companies have adopted an open-door policy. This means that an employee with a serious complaint has a right to visit the chief executive officer to discuss his problem. Usually he is expected to have gone to his immediate supervisor initially, and then, if satisfaction has not been obtained, he is expected to have skipped the intermediate levels of management and submitted his problem directly to the top official. Because of the imbalance of power and status between the executive and the worker and because of the uneasy position this puts the immediate supervisor in, the open-door policy frequently does not function as its advocates expect.

In many collective bargaining relationships the top local union officials meet regularly (usually weekly or semimonthly) with the director of industrial relations and other management officials to review and discuss common problems. Quite often these meetings are set up for the ostensible purpose of settling grievances that could not be resolved at the lower levels. But generally these meetings evolve into a wide ranging discussion of issues and ideas. They can serve as an excellent means for foreseeing potential trouble spots and taking preventive action. Not only do such meetings serve as a medium of upward communication, but they also serve as a medium of horizontal communication between two equivalent organizations. Commonly the union leaders will transmit information down to the rank-and-file employees regarding agreements reached and items discussed. Management must be very careful that it keeps its supervision fully informed of action taken at such meetings. A foreman's position can be considerably weakened if his subordinates have been informed about important decisions by the union before he has heard it from his superior.

Horizontal Communication

If an engineer in the industrial engineering department has business to transact with a foreman in a production department, he clearly has a right to deal directly with him. The extent to which the two can make binding decisions to adopt a new course of action depends upon the scope of authority each possesses. Generally higher management expects such interdepartmental coordination and cooperation to go on extensively.

The degree to which coordinate individuals in separate divisions or departments of a company can make commitments depends upon the philosophy and policies of top management. If the policy of the organization is one of centralized control of decision making, then the subordinate managers and supervisors will have to consult their superiors regarding every little issue. On the other hand, if the policy is one of decentralization and a liberal delegation of authority and responsibility, then these subordinate personnel will have wide latitude in initiating important actions.

THE GRAPEVINE

The word *grapevine* is applied to the communication system of the informal organization. The informal organization—which can be charted just as a formal organization can—is composed of all the friendship, work, and special interest groups within the company. Information can travel like wildfire through the informal organization because of the multiplying effect which occurs when one person talks to several others and each of these then tells several more, and so on.

Managers often become annoyed because the grapevine spreads rumors and stories that are wholly false. They feel this disrupts morale and employee confidence in management. Management can take affirmative steps to minimize rumors, but it should not and cannot eliminate the grapevine.

The grapevine is a normal concomitant of the social interaction among people. People will talk, socialize, converse, gossip. Such activities are necessary to develop group cohesion and a feeling of belonging among the individual members. Further, such informal communication serves the valuable function of orienting newcomers to the work routine and of keeping each other informed of important matters within the work group. It supplements communication from the boss.

Rumors are often spread via the grapevine. A rumor is a story that is not authentic or accurate although it may have some elements of truth present. Rumors can be devastating, because they can excite people without justification. Rumors thrive when people are confused and unclear about their position, when they are anxious, when they feel they have no control over their destinies, and when they are insecure.

> Rumors were prevalent in the Army camps and battle areas of World War II because the soldiers were uncertain about their very day-to-day existence. They lived in a state of tenseness and anxiety. Secrecy needs often prevented telling them where they were going, when, and why.

The best way to minimize rumors is for management to do a good job of supplying immediate and accurate information to employees at all times on subjects that are important to them. They must know where they stand

and where they can expect to go. By establishing a stable organizational environment in which employees feel accepted and secure, management will go a long way toward preventing rumors. People cannot live in an environment that is unstructured. If management does not provide the structure, then the employees will, even if some of their structure, based on rumors, is inaccurate.

Questions for Review and Discussion

1. Define the term *communication*. What takes place when one individual communicates with another?
2. Explain why words mean different things to different people. How can the communications troubles caused by this fact be solved?
3. Why is it that two people who witness the same phenomenon often perceive it quite differently and arrive at varying interpretations?
4. What is meant by the statement *People think with their hearts, not their minds?* How does this make communication difficult?
5. Explain the value of feedback to successful communication.
6. What has been learned about communication networks as a result of laboratory studies?
7. If one must choose between written and face-to-face oral communication, why is it that face-to-face is often preferable? What are the values of written communication?
8. Why does not information flow upward through the hierarchy as well as it flows downward? Are there ways of overcoming this problem?
9. What is the "grapevine"? Does it serve any useful purposes?
10. What can be done by management to minimize the creation and spread of rumors?

CASE PROBLEM

You are the safety director of the Clair-Mor Manufacturing Company, a firm that produces metal stampings and small machine parts on a job-order basis. Total employment at the one plant location is 1,100. The production and maintenance employees are represented by a union.

For several years the company has experienced a high accident rate. To combat this problem the initial efforts have been directed toward a better program of machine guarding and plant maintenance. This had tended to reduce the severity of the accidents, but it has not materially reduced the frequency of occurrence of work injuries.

An analysis of the work injuries over the past year reveals a high percentage due to improper use of hand tools, improper operation of machines, poor housekeeping, and failure to follow established safety rules.

In addition to this, you have investigated the literature in the field of industrial safety and learned that research studies have shown that employee knowledge, attitudes, and emotions have a powerful influence on accident rates.

You have decided that the key to the reduction of accidents is the launching of a comprehensive employee education program. The difficulty of the problem is accentuated by the high rate of employee turnover due to periodic layoffs. Because the wage level is somewhat lower than rates paid by other companies in the community, many quit to take better jobs elsewhere.

Top management is serious about reducing the accident rate and has promised to give you ample support. You have decided that one good way to educate employees in safety is to have each foreman conduct a brief safety meeting with his men once a month. However, in proposing this idea to the foremen you find that they object to this added burden. They claim that they are too busy, and in addition, they do not know what to talk about to their men.

Questions

1. How would you accomplish your objective of educating the employees in safety? What channels and methods would you use?
2. How would you deal with the problem posed by the foremen who object to conducting safety meetings?
3. To which group (top, middle, or lower management personnel, staff personnel, or workers) would you direct your safety communications?
4. What would be the content of your communications?

Suggestions for Further Reading

Anderson, J., "What's Blocking Upward Communications?," *Personnel Administration,* Vol. 31, No. 1, 1968, pp. 5-7.

Berlo, David K., *The Process of Communication,* New York: Holt, Rinehart and Winston, 1960.

Haney, William V., *Communication and Organizational Behavior,* Rev. Ed., Homewood, Ill.: Richard D. Irwin, 1967.

Hayakawa, S. I., *Language in Thought and Action,* New York: Harcourt, Brace & World, 1949.

Lee, Irving J. and Laura L. Lee, *Handling Barriers in Communication,* New York: McGraw-Hill Book Company, 1960.

Melcher, A. J. and R. Beller, "Toward A Theory of Organization Communication," *Academy of Management Journal,* Vol. 10, March 1967, pp. 39-52.

Redding, W. Charles, and George A. Sanborn, *Business and Industrial Communication,* New York: Harper & Row, 1964.

Rogers, Carl R., and Fritz J. Roethlisberger, "Barriers and Gateways to Communication," *Harvard Business Review,* Vol. 30, July-August 1952, pp. 46-52.

Thayer, Lee, *Communication and Communication Systems,* Homewood, Ill.: Richard D. Irwin, Inc., 1968.

Vogel, A., "Why Don't Employees Speak Up?," *Personnel Administration,* Vol. 30, May-June 1967, pp. 18-24.

Discipline

21

Discipline is essential to all organized group action. The members must control their individual urges and cooperate for the common good. In other words they must reasonably conform to the code of behavior established by the leadership of the organization so that the agreed-upon goals can be accomplished.

If the membership of any organization, whether a club, company, union, or nation, will not abide by some code of rules or laws, then that organization faces imminent collapse. Anarchy and chaos ensue. The world was presented with the tragic spectacle of anarchy, mutiny, violence, and disintegration in the Congo after it was declared a free and independent nation by the Belgian government in 1960. At that time the people of that country were not prepared to govern themselves.

In the work organization, skill in achieving a healthy state of discipline is an important qualification for the supervisor. Some supervisors have the knack of developing a willing conformance with the rules of the plant among their men. The men cooperate, conform, and regulate themselves almost without their noticing any ostensible imposition of authority by the supervisor. On the other hand, other supervisors can rule only, it seems, by frequent resorts to threats and punishment. And with still other supervisors the men do as they please and violate plant rules apparently with impunity.

The vital importance of discipline in personnel management is attested to by the fact that disciplinary issues constitute the largest single category of grievance cases going to arbitration under the procedures of the American Arbitration Association. A study in 1956 of 1,000 cases showed that 25 per cent concerned discipline, 21 per cent seniority, 12 per cent job evaluation and work assignments, 6 per cent arbitrability, 5 per cent overtime, and 5 per cent vacations. All other categories were each under 2 per cent.[1]

The Meaning of Discipline

Webster's Dictionary gives three basic meanings to the word *discipline*. First it states that it is training that corrects, molds, strengthens, or perfects. The second meaning is that it is control gained by enforcing obedience. The third meaning is punishment or chastisement.[2] If we combine meanings one and two we can say that discipline involves the conditioning or molding of behavior by applying rewards or penalties. The third meaning is more narrow in that it pertains only to the act of punishing wrongdoers.

The first dictionary meaning will be treated in this chapter under the heading "Positive Discipline." This is the kind of discipline that all managements should seek to create. Positive discipline is actually broader and more fundamental than the dictionary phrase *training which molds, corrects, strengthens, or perfects* implies. Positive discipline involves the creation of an attitude and an organizational climate wherein the employees willingly conform to established rules and regulations. It is achieved when management applies the principles of positive motivation, when sound leadership is exercised by supervision, and when the entire organization is managed efficiently. It is unfortunate that actual practice over the years in industrial, military, and school organizations has not granted sufficient recognition to this positive or constructive aspect of discipline. If the leaders devote enough time and effort to developing a willing conformity to accepted modes of behavior, then there is only infrequent need for resorting to force or the threat of force to keep errant individuals in line.

The second meaning of discipline encompasses the use of penalties or the threat of penalties to cause people to obey orders and to live up to the rules of the game. Often force is employed. This is the kind of discipline exercised by sea captains over sailors since the earliest days of civilization and the kind used in military forces the world over. This form of discipline is explained in this chapter under the heading "Negative Discipline."

In all organizations, regardless of whether positive or negative discip-

---

[1] J. Noble Braden, "From Conflict to Cooperation," *Proceedings of the Sixth Annual Labor Relations Conference* (Morgantown, W.Va.: Institute of Industrial Relations, University of West Virginia, 1956), pp. 46-47.

[2] *Webster's New Collegiate Dictionary* (Springfield, Mass.: G. & C. Merriam Company, 1953), p. 236.

line is utilized, some individuals will, upon occasion, break the rules. They are then brought to see the error of their ways and the need for improving performance by applying some form of punishment. This is the third dictionary meaning described above. Under the concept of positive discipline the punishment is administered to correct and rehabilitate, not to injure. Under the concept of negative discipline the punishment is for retribution and to scare others so they will not commit the same crime. Administering the program, handling violators, and assigning penalties is covered in this chapter under the heading "Administering the Disciplinary Program."

APPROACHES TO DISCIPLINE

Because the objective in any organized group endeavor is to develop in the participants such an attitude and behavior that they conform to established norms of conduct, the question is how this can be achieved. On the one hand, those in charge can rule with an iron hand, punish rule violators severely, and, in general, force the members to obey and conform. This mode of leadership has variously been called negative discipline, punitive discipline, autocratic discipline, or rule through fear. The other approach is to develop in people a willingness to obey and abide by the rules and regulations. They do so because they want to, not because they are afraid of the consequences of disobedience. This form of discipline has been called positive or constructive discipline. Let us now examine the methods and implications of each type of discipline.

Negative Discipline

This is basically the "big stick" approach to leadership. In industry this brand of disciplinary control was prevalent in the handling of hourly workers prior to the widespread growth of unions in the late 1930's. The union movement has been very successful in providing a considerable measure of security for the workers by granting them protection against arbitrary treatment by management. Disciplinary penalties are often appealed through the grievance procedure. If necessary these may be taken to arbitration for impartial review.

Of course, unions represent only a minority, albeit a large minority, of the employed persons in this country. The threat of punishment is employed by many managements to keep people in line. Although it may be infrequent that a man is suspended or discharged, the power of the boss to impose such penalties is kept ever present in the employees' minds. Written warnings may be handed out extensively to those who fail to meet the established standards of production or to those who are absent from work. The foreman may threaten individuals who do not respond as he expects. And of course during periods of business recession, the likelihood of being weeded out is prominent in employees' minds (especially in those companies where management has considerable discretion in whom it terminates).

The basic fallacy in negative discipline is that it achieves only the minimum performance necessary to avoid punishment. The people are not given a say-so in formulating the rules, and they are not taught the reason why. They are taught only that they will be punished if they break a rule. The rule-through-fear approach puts the emphasis upon avoidance of punishment, not upon enthusiastic, wholehearted cooperation.

Those who base their leadership upon rule-through-fear count upon making an example of violators. Public knowledge of the punishment (usually severe) is expected to serve as a deterrent to others. Yet in the whole history of crime, punishment has never been demonstrated to be an effective deterrent. The man who breaks the rules does not plan that far ahead. He is not thinking of the possible consequences. He is thinking only of his immediate wants.

As a philosophy of management for the long run and for the vast majority of followers, the practice of rule-through-fear can have only limited success. But this does not deny that for certain subordinates at certain times power and force may be the only answer. Some employees, as a consequence of their background and personality development, may respond only to the supervisor who uses a policy of "be tough."

Positive Discipline

Positive discipline, often called constructive discipline, consists of that type of supervisory leadership that develops a willing adherence to the necessary rules and regulations of the organization. The employees, both as individuals and as a group, adhere to the desired standards of behavior because they understand, believe in, and support them.

Discipline must take the form of positive support and reinforcement for approved actions. This is fundamental to all learning. Punishment may be applied for improper behavior, but this is carried out in a supportive, corrective manner. There is no vindictiveness. The aim is to help, not harm, the individual. The supervisor lets it be known that he approves of the violator as a person but that he is training the man in regard to a specific action.

A necessary prerequisite for positive discipline is communicating the requirements of the job and the rules and regulations to the employees. Every man must know, when he is hired and henceforth, just what management and his immediate supervisor expect of him. The performance standards (that is, work loads) must be fair, attainable with reasonable effort, and consistent from job to job. The rules likewise must be reasonable and few in number. Supervision must communicate the kind of positive behavior expected of employees rather than dwell upon an exhaustive list of detailed prohibitions.

In creating a climate of positive discipline, the supervisor seeks to build in his men a sense of personal responsibility and self-discipline. He applies principles of positive motivation and enlightened leadership. He recognizes individual differences among his subordinates and varies his methods and appeals as necessary.

When people are well trained so that they know how far they can go and what the limits of tolerated conduct are, they acquire a sense of security. They know the rules of the game, and they know where they stand.

In orienting a new person to his job and the company, the supervisor should explain what work performance is expected and what help is available to achieve it. He should then discuss the principal standards of behavior expected. This will ordinarily include such items as good attendance, notification when justifiably absent, punctuality, cooperation with the supervisor and fellow employees, standards of morality and honesty, and wakefulness throughout the work shift (no sleeping on the job). Particular circumstances in certain shops may require special no-smoking and other safety regulations.

To achieve constructive discipline, the supervisors must set a good example.

> To minimize the possibility of catching fingers in moving machine parts, a long-standing company safety rule prohibited the wearing of finger rings in the production departments. Yet it proved impossible to achieve compliance with this order, because many of the foremen themselves persisted in wearing rings.

> The college has a rule prohibiting smoking in all classrooms. Not only does smoking create a fire hazard, but the butts and matches create a special housekeeping problem for the janitorial staff. Yet certain professors disobey the rule and smoke while conducting their classes. Following their lead the students do likewise.

Group Responsibility. If a foreman takes the proper steps to build a cohesive, loyal work group, he will find that the group members will generally act to support and augment his disciplinary efforts. To do this he must first recognize the existence of the informal group and consult with his subordinates as a group in departmental meetings. He can lead discussions covering the plant rules and regulations as well as the need for them. The people can discuss how these apply to them in their own work situation. If the group, as a group, understands and believes in the rules, it will often exert social pressure upon its members to insure that they live up to the rules. The group in an informal way may supplement the supervisor's efforts in such areas as prevention of horseplay, achieving good attendance, doing one's fair share of any team work, and controlling the length of coffee breaks.

Honor systems in colleges are forms of group (student) discipline carried out on a *formal organized* basis. The student body is indoctrinated with the values of integrity and honesty in taking examinations, preparing term papers, and even in other spheres of life. The students themselves are expected to report any violators of the honor pledge, and judicial proceedings are handled by a student court or honor board. The faculty does not judge alleged violators nor does it mete out punishment. The student honor board does this.

Private industry rarely, if ever, entrusts the maintenance of discipline to an *organized* employee group. Elected union leaders are generally reluctant to take disciplinary action against any members who have violated company rules.[3] Management almost universally considers the maintenance of discipline to be a management prerogative and responsibility. It is reluctant to share this responsibility with its union. If management in a nonunion company were to believe genuinely in the value of employee-enforced discipline and were therefore to establish an employee organization to handle it, it would run the risk of violating the Taft-Hartley Act's prohibition against an employer-dominated union.

ADMINISTERING THE DISCIPLINARY PROGRAM

Even under the best of conditions and with excellent supervisory leadership and employee training, somebody is bound to step over the traces now and then. When this happens what action should management take? Are there in existence any generally accepted principles to guide management? Will certain measures be more effective in correcting the errant employee? Will certain actions have harmful repercussions upon future discipline in the organization?

Administrative Justice

Well-established principles and procedures for the handling and adjudicating of civil and criminal offenses against society have evolved in our legal system over a great many years via both common and statute law. Although administrative justice within private organizations has not developed to as advanced a state as in the public law field, certain powerful forces have been operating to create a body of fairly well accepted principles and procedural requirements.

Probably foremost as a positive force in this direction has been the impact of unionization upon employers and the work force. The presence of a union in a company means, almost invariably, the installation of a formal grievance procedure and generally arbitration as the final step in settling unresolved grievances. It is now about 35 years since unions

---

[3] Of course, they will discipline the members who break union rules.

have become widespread in industry. We have accumulated 35 years of arbitration experience that has hammered out certain guidelines for the administration of employee justice within the organization. One might say that we have developed an industrial code of common-law principles and precedents. The essence of the matter is that establishments should follow "due process" procedures.[4]

It is important to note that disciplinary procedures and grievance procedures interact. Discipline administered by the first-line supervisor is one principal cause for later grievance appeal by the employee and the union. The disciplinary penalty may have been applied for a variety of alleged infractions such as tardiness, absenteeism, low output, excessive defective work, intoxication on the job, insubordination, horseplay, or violation of safety rules. If management takes proper care to administer its discipline fairly and with due concern for procedural safeguards which are designed to protect the rights of the parties, then there is less likelihood of subsequent charges by the employee or union of injustice or discrimination.

Another force that has stimulated the adoption of sound administrative justice and "due process" has been the growing bureaucratization of modern organizations. Systematic, formal procedures have been established to preserve the soundness of the organization and to protect the rights of the members. Employees often spend their entire work careers with one or two organizations. They must be assured that they will be treated fairly by management. They cannot continually quit to escape oppressive conditions.

Still another force leading to the practice of administrative justice has been the modern human relations movement that has emphasized concern for individual dignity and rights, sound leadership and managerial climate, positive motivation, and a concern for job satisfaction and the well being of employees.

It is paradoxical to note that although collective bargaining has had a powerful influence upon the handling of discipline in industry, labor-management agreements contain very little on the subject. It is very rare to find the company rules and regulations with their accompanying penalties shown in the labor agreement. Traditionally management initiates the disciplinary policy and administers the program. The employees and the union have the right to submit a grievance if they do not like the way a case has been handled.

As far as contract language is concerned, most contracts merely state that management has the right to discipline, suspend, or discharge for *just cause* and that employees have the right to submit grievances if they consider an action unfair. Just cause means for good and sufficient rea-

---

[4] This designation has been applied to industrial discipline by Orme W. Phelps in his *Discipline and Discharge in the Unionized Firm* (Berkeley and Los Angeles: University of California Press, 1959), pp. 2-4.

son.[5] Some contracts specify the powers of the arbitrator in ruling on discipline cases. Usually he can reverse a penalty if he does not believe there has been just cause for the punishment. He can also modify penalties that he considers too severe for the offense. Even where the contract language is silent on these matters most arbitrators assume that they have the right to do the foregoing things.

Principles for Administration of Disciplinary Action

In administering discipline and penalizing employees, management must constantly be aware of the dual objectives of preserving the interests of the organization as a whole and protecting the rights of the individual. Unless sound policies are adopted and orderly procedures followed, there is a danger that management will look at a case solely in terms of its own needs at the moment rather than in terms of the needs of the employee as well as the organization. Short-run expediency might prevail over long-run considerations. Let us now examine the principal ingredients of a sound disciplinary system.[6]

Definite Policy and Procedure

It is the responsibility of top management to give serious consideration to the need for achieving a healthy state of discipline throughout the organization. It must decide what kind of behavior it expects from its employees and how it hopes to achieve this. Presumably the objective is to create a positive, constructive form of discipline through sound leadership and adequate training of all employees.

Top management must carefully think out the issue of the role of the first-line supervisor in the disciplinary system. Because of the need for consistency of action throughout the company and because the union will generally appeal the penalty over the foreman's head if it is dissatisfied, most industrial concerns have tended to centralize a considerable amount of authority in the hands of the industrial relations (or personnel) director.

This can be carried too far however.

> The personnel manager of a small manufacturer proudly displayed his book of rules and penalties and announced (to the author in an interview), "I handle all disciplinary problems in my plant. The foremen bring the violators to my office, I listen to both their stories, collect further evi-

---

[5] In determining whether an employee has been disciplined for "just cause," arbitrators consider the following three factors: (1) Did the employee in fact commit the improper act? (2) If he did, should he be punished for his behavior? (3) Does the penalty assigned by management fit the nature of the offense?

[6] The reader may wish to gain further information and other views on this topic by examining the due process procedures explained by Phelps, *op. cit.,* pp. 2-4, 141-143.

dence where necessary, and then announce my decision. The foremen in this plant are not able to make proper judgments regarding these cases. Therefore, I handle the whole thing."

With such a policy as followed in the company above the foremen are bound to lose respect and control of their men.

The need to maintain consistency of action throughout the organization is not incompatible with the need to preserve the authority and position of the foreman. How can this be done? The foreman must be fully instructed regarding the rules and regulations, behavior expected from employees, progressive disciplinary penalties, and the rights of all parties—management, employees, and union. The foreman should be given the authority to issue oral and written warnings on his own. For cases that he thinks are serious enough to warrant suspension and discharge, he should consult his line superior or the industrial relations director before taking action. This not only insures consistency of action throughout the company but also prevents a worker from being fired because of capricious or ill-considered action by the supervisor. In these more serious cases, after all the pertinent facts have been brought out and a decision agreed upon, the first-line supervisor should announce the action to the affected employee.[7]

To insure that the discipline policies and procedure are carefully formulated, that no essential elements are overlooked, and that members of management will support the program, there is considerable merit to involving representatives of middle and lower management in the process of developing the system.

Communication of Rules

Employees must have knowledge of the rule before they can be held accountable. Arbitrators have rescinded penalties where such was not the case.

The most commonly used method of informing employees about company rules is to include a list of the rules, penalties, and explanations thereof in the employee handbook. This is usually handed to a person at the time he is hired. This can be followed up with oral explanations of the more important rules during the initial orientation program. Usually this explanation is given in the department by the man's supervisor. The reasons behind the rules should also be explained. This explanation of the company rules should not be a drab recitation of the "Articles of War" (as is given to soldiers in the Army); rather it should be an explanation of the more important companywide rules and those special ones (for

---

[7] For a discussion of the role of the industrial relations director in discipline (based upon a survey) see Charles A. Myers and John G. Turnbull, "Line and Staff in Industrial Relations," *Harvard Business Review,* Vol. 34, No. 4 (July-August 1956), pp. 113-124.

example, no-smoking rules) to fit the particular circumstances in that department.

In addition to the statement in the handbook and the explanation by the supervisor, the list of rules and penalties may be posted on the bulletin board.

Burden of Proof

The principle of law underlying the English and United States legal systems, that an individual is presumed innocent until proven guilty, applies to industrial discipline cases as well. The burden of proof is upon the employer to show that the worker is guilty of the alleged offense. The degree of proof tends to vary with the seriousness of the charge. If there is serious doubt, arbitrators tend to give the employee the benefit of the doubt.

Consistency of Treatment

This is one of the most important principles and one that is too easily ignored. Management must not punish one man for an offense and ignore the same offense committed by another (often, more favored) employee. This kind of inconsistency can happen because supervisors in different departments have different standards of what they expect and have different tolerance limits when employees deviate somewhat from the standard. Thus one supervisor may overlook the occasional taking of a few pencils by an office employee, whereas another considers such action to be stealing and grounds for discharge. In addition to this, a supervisor may have a grudge against one of his men and seize upon any plausible pretext to punish him, whereas a more favored employee may be granted wide latitude.

The best way to achieve consistency of treatment and application of the rules is through supervisory training courses and by consistent action by higher management on a day-to-day basis as cases are brought up.

Consider Circumstances of the Case

The need for consistency does not mean that two persons committing an identical offense must always receive identical penalties. The background and circumstances of each case may call for differential treatment. But consistency does require that both employees know that they have violated a rule. Management must not condone an infraction by one and not the other. Both must be handled with equal gravity. But it is in deciding the severity of the penalty, or indeed whether there should be any punishment at all, that management must grant due consideration to the full circumstances surrounding each case.

Company policy may specify that any employee who is absent for five consecutive days without notifying the company as to his reason is automatically terminated. Such discharge may actually be invoked in the case of a worker who has had a bad record of unjustified absences. However, a long-service employee with a good employment record may suffer no penalty at all when it is demonstrated that he was absent and did not call in only because he had gone to his hunting camp on an island in the north woods for the weekend and had become bound in by severe storms and a breakdown of his motor launch.

Therefore, extenuating circumstances can modify or dismiss a penalty in a particular case.

Progressive Penalties

Industrial disciplinary penalties have become fairly well standardized as a result of custom and practice. In ascending order of severity these are as follows:

1. Simple oral warning.
2. Oral warning that is noted in the person's employment record.
3. Written warning noted in employment record.
4. Suspension from the job, usually varying in length from one day to two weeks.
5. Discharge.

Sometimes demotion is used as a penalty as is, also, the withholding of a scheduled pay increase. In industrial employment a monetary fine is almost never employed, although this practice is very common in professional team sports, such as baseball, football, and hockey.

In accordance with the concept of positive, corrective discipline, only oral or written warnings are assigned for minor offenses. For the average person such knowledge is sufficient to prevent a repetition. If minor offenses occur again and again, the penalty becomes more severe. A very serious first offense (such as stealing a substantial amount from the employer) usually brings immediate discharge.

The slate is normally wiped clean at the end of one or two years. This makes sense. There is no justification for holding against a man, in perpetuity, his indiscretions of past years if he has reformed himself in the meantime.

Reasonable Rules and Standards

The rules and standards of conduct should be reasonable. The plant conditions and management climate must be such that they are capable of attainment. Thus if a supervisor plans to penalize an employee who does not produce up to standard, he must first of all determine wheth-

er the standard of output is attainable by the average employee and whether the individual is capable of producing to standard.

> One plant has rather poor working conditions. The employees consis-
> tently break a company rule against littering the stairways with trash and
> bottles; yet the rule is difficult to enforce, because there are no lunch
> room or locker room facilities. Hence the employees have no other place
> to eat lunch or to take their rest breaks.

Right of Appeal

Whether a person has actually committed an infraction of the rules
may be a matter of opinion in certain instances and depend upon the frame
of reference of the person making the accusation. For example, if a man
disagrees with his boss vigorously on how to carry out an assignment, does
this constitute insubordination? For this reason the accused employee
should always have the right to appeal to higher authority. Even if the
man is truly guilty as charged, it may be best to hold a full hearing before
higher authorities to satisfy all parties to the case that the employee has
been justly treated.

Now it is a well-established principle of law that a man must not be
judged by his accuser. The prosecution and judicial functions must be
separated. The judge should not be a party to the dispute or issue. But in
work organizations this principle is not fully adhered to. Line managers
usually determine whether a violation has occurred, decide its severity,
and invoke a penalty against the involved employee. If the employees
are represented by a union, a worker who feels that he has been disciplined unjustly can appeal the case through the successive steps of the
grievance procedure. He may, if the union officials think he has a strong
case, have the full power of the union behind him. Presumably as the
case is appealed to successively higher levels of managers, these will
take a more detached and broad view than would the man's immediate
supervisor. Yet higher executives know that they must first of all preserve the organization. When in doubt they often tend to back up their
subordinate supervisors in order to help them maintain their authority.
A supervisor whose decisions are frequently reversed by higher management soon loses the respect of his men. The first genuinely neutral review
of a discharge case comes if the union takes it all the way to arbitration.
The arbitrator serves as a judge or impartial umpire. Of course, the mere
fact that a case can be appealed to arbitration causes both the union and
company to sit back and examine a case from all sides to judge in advance how an arbitrator *would* decide such an issue if it were actually
brought to him.

Nonunion companies can also set up a formal appeals procedure. However, arbitration is practically never used as a final step. The chief exec-

utive officer serves as the final appeal step. His objectivity and impartiality will largely depend upon his philosophy of management, his personality, and the circumstances in the particular situation. A distinct separation of the judicial review from the executive function would require wholly different organizational arrangements than exist in most business firms.

RULES AND PENALTIES

Sound management requires that a reasonably comprehensive list of rules and regulations be adopted and reduced to writing. This should be done initially when management formulates its disciplinary policy. The very existence of a carefully developed schedule of rules signifies that management has given reasonable consideration to its disciplinary program. If a company has never thought out its disciplinary code, it can some day find itself in the very awkward spot of creating a rule after someone has done something that displeases management. In civil affairs a person cannot be prosecuted for a law that was legislated only after he committed an act.

Below is a listing of most of the common rules adopted in work organizations. They are grouped into two broad categories: (1) minor or moderate offenses, and (2) serious offenses. Of course, the specific situation in a particular establishment may cause an offense listed as "minor or moderate" to be so serious as to justify discharge. Thus this listing should be viewed as illustrative only. It should also be noted that circumstances in a department or plant may require the adoption of many special rules. Safety rules are a good example of items that must be tailor-made to the situation:

I *Minor or Moderate Offenses*

Oral or written warning may be assigned for first offense; penalties will become progressively stiffer with repeated violation. Eventual discharge can result.

    a. Habitual tardiness
    b. Unexcused absence on one or more scheduled work days
    c. Failure to report accidental injury
    d. Leaving job or work area without authorization
    e. Loafing
    f. Individual gambling on company property
    g. Fighting
    h. Horseplay
    i. Unauthorized selling or canvassing on company property
    j. Sleeping on the job

   k. Smoking in a prohibited area
   l. Failure to obey safety rules
  m. Reporting for work or being on duty while intoxicated
  n. Clock-punching of another's time card
  o. Concealing one's defective work
  p. Work output below standard
  q. Excessive defective work due to employee's own errors

II *Serious Offenses*
   First offense can bring suspension or discharge

   a. Malicious damage or destruction of company property
   b. Gross insubordination
   c. Gross immoral, indecent, or disgraceful conduct
   d. Stealing
   e. Carrying concealed weapons
   f. Promotion of gambling on company property
   g. Attacking another with intent to seriously injure or maim
   h. Deliberate falsification of company records

A Uniform, Published Scale of Penalties?

Opinion differs as to the desirability of fixing in advance a uniform scale of penalties for the various offenses. Those who oppose such a practice claim that the circumstances of each case are different, and it is impossible to decide ahead of time an appropriate penalty that would fit every instance of a particular offense. In some cases extenuating circumstances would justify a lighter penalty, whereas in others a harsher penalty might be called for. Is it as serious for a file clerk to sleep on the job as it is for a plant guard or watchman? If stealing is grounds for a discharge, would it be fair to fire an office worker who takes a few wooden lead pencils?

There are some powerful arguments in favor of adopting a schedule of penalties for each offense. It insures consistency of treatment throughout all divisions of a company. Consistency is also achieved over time. An offense today is treated the same as the same offense a year ago. Employees have memories and equitable treatment appeals to them. Employees know where they stand and what to expect if they kick over the traces. A published list of penalties adds an aura of legitimacy to management enforcement action. Excessive or unusual penalties cannot be put into effect by ill-tempered or vindictive supervisors.

A written scale of penalties can be wholly compatible with the logical need for giving full consideration to the severity and circumstances of each offense. Consider the following example:

PENALTIES AND OCCURRENCES

Offense	First		Second		Third	
	Min.	Max.	Min.	Max.	Min.	Max.
Loafing on job	oral warning	1-day suspension	1-day suspension	3-day suspension	3-day suspension	discharge

With each occurrence of the act of loafing, management has reasonable latitude in choosing a penalty. If a man were caught loafing when the work demands were very light, he might be given a simple oral warning by his supervisor. On the other hand, if products are coming off a production line and an operator is making no effort to handle his assigned items and this causes damage or serious delay, he might be suspended without pay for a full day for the first occurrence.

Demotion as a Penalty

Strictly speaking, demotion should rarely be used as a form of discipline. The question usually arises when an employee fails to perform his job adequately. Should he be demoted in rank and assigned to a job that he will do properly? The answer to this question depends upon whether the man does not perform his job up to standard because of a basic lack of ability or because of negligence and lack of motivation. If the cause of the trouble is lack of capacity or ability, he may very properly be assigned to a different job at the same or lower pay. But such action is not discipline. This is not a disciplinary problem and should never be treated as such.

On the other hand if a man can do the job but deliberately will not do a fair day's work, this is a proper subject for discipline. But demotion is not the answer. If there is a clash of personalities between the man and his supervisor, he may be transferred, but this is not ordinarily classed as discipline. If the man has a bad attitude, a demotion is unlikely to improve it. The answer is to apply progressive, corrective discipline in the man's present job.

Discharge as a Penalty

Discharge is the supreme punishment in industrial discipline. Some writers have called it industrial capital punishment. Where progressive penalties are assigned for repeated minor offenses, the threat of discharge often serves to "sober up" errant workers. Discharge may be the only feasible course of action in the case of employees whose behavior is so bad as to make their presence in the plant a threat to other employees or to the effective operation of the business.

The history of arbitration of discharge cases shows that management has been too prone to fire a man without sufficient justification. An analysis of 1,055 discharge grievances that were taken to arbitration, in the period 1942 - 1956, as reported in the Bureau of National Affairs' *Labor Arbitration Reports,* revealed that management's action was upheld in only 41 per cent of the cases and was reversed or modified in 59 per cent.[8]

Arbitrators are reluctant to order discharge unless the evidence is incontrovertible and unless efforts at correction have been tried and have proven unsuccessful. Discharge is particularly grave for a worker with considerable length of service, for he loses his accumulated pension and group insurance benefits plus extended vacation rights. With rigorous employee selection procedures and a careful weeding out of undesirable workers during the initial probationary period, management can almost eliminate the need for discharges of permanent employees.

An interesting ramification of the question of discharge is the issue of whether management can or should dismiss workers who are involved in off-the-job criminal behavior. If an employee is accused of some criminal act such as assault and battery, theft, armed robbery, embezzlement, or organized gambling can the employer justifiably fire the man. In the absence of a union, the employer pretty much has free rein in the matter. For organized plants arbitrators have been called upon to wrestle with such cases and have been gradually developing broad criteria to guide decisions. They have tended to uphold the right of the employer to dismiss employees for off-the-job criminal behavior when it can be shown that the continued presence of the individual on the job would adversely affect the employer's business or would disrupt relations with fellow employees. Thus if an employee had been accused and convicted of aggravated assault with intent to rob, this probably would be viewed as just cause for discharge because the fellow employees could be endangered by the man's presence in the plant. Of course arbitrators look at the totality of the circumstances such as the man's past record with the company, any history of previous convictions, and the nature of his job.[9]

Questions for Review and Discussion

1. Why is discipline necessary to any organized group activity?
2. Distinguish the various meanings of the term *discipline.*
3. Evaluate the implications and consequences of maintaining discipline by force or the threat of force.
4. What is positive or constructive discipline? What are the goals of the supervisor in instituting a pattern of positive discipline? How can positive discipline be achieved in a work force?

[8] J. Fred Holly, "Considerations in Discharge Cases, " *Monthly Labor Review,* Vol. 80, No. 6 (June 1957), pp. 684 - 688.
[9] For further discussion of this matter see John W. Leonard, "Dismissal for Off-the-Job Criminal Behavior," *Monthly Labor Review,* Vol. 90, No. 11 (November 1967), pp. 21 - 26.

5. Do you think the local union leadership can or should be brought to play an active part in the disciplinary process in a company?
6. Describe the impact of collective bargaining and arbitration upon the handling of disciplinary problems in industry.
7. What should be the role of the first-line supervisor in handling employees who break the rules?
8. Do you think the dual goals of maintaining consistent treatment of all employees and adjusting the penalty to fit the circumstances of the particular case are compatible? Discuss.
9. Why are penalties often of the progressive type?
10. What should be the rights of an employee who has been charged by his supervisor with a rules violation?
11. Do you think a company should adopt a uniform scale of penalties for all offenses? Should these be announced to the employees?
12. Discuss the use of demotion as a penalty.
13. Under what circumstances should discharge be used as a penalty?

CASE PROBLEMS

Problem 1

Frank is an operator in a textile mill. Recently his foreman told him that the company was starting a regular program of monitoring the static-eliminator bars mounted on all carding machines.[10] The operation was to be performed monthly and would require about eight hours time each month. The work involved an inspection and cleaning of the bars plus wiping of each bar with special paper that was then sent away to a laboratory for measurement of any radiation leaking from the unit.

Frank refused to do this new work. He stated that he had been hired as a machine operator, not as a maintenance mechanic or radiation technician. He said that the maintenance mechanic job paid twenty cents more per hour and that such work was outside his job classification. Further, he had heard via the grapevine that it was hazardous to touch the static-eliminator bars.

His foreman told him that he must either perform the duties assigned to him or face immediate discharge. The work was not of a higher skill than his regular job, and it occurred only once per month. The foreman further explained that handling these bars was not hazardous, because they had been used in the mill for two years and no one had been injured from the radiation yet.

Frank still refused to do the work and said he was going to see his union steward. With that the exchange between the foreman and the worker terminated.

[10] A static-eliminator bar is an aluminum bar containing a strip of foil that is composed of a radioactive substance. The emission of certain rays from the foil prevents the fibers in the product from clogging the machine.

That afternoon the foreman went to see his superior, the superintendent, about the matter. The superintendent viewed it as a clear case of insubordination, for which immediate discharge was provided in the rules. He advised the foreman to send Frank to his office, at which time he, the superintendent, would give the man one last chance to comply or be discharged.

Questions

1. Do you think this case involves a straightforward issue of insubordination? Are there any other important issues involved?
2. Can a man ever justifiably refuse to carry out a direct order from his supervisor? Discuss.
3. How would you handle this case if you were the superintendent?
4. What course is open to an employee who feels his boss has given him an order that he cannot or should not carry out?

Problem 2

The ZYZ Company employs a large force of draftsmen of various classifications. The draftsmen are represented by an independent draftsmen's union at this company. The job title of Detailer 3 is an entry classification ordinarily assigned to new, relatively inexperienced detail draftsmen. Normally at the end of one year a Detailer 3 is upgraded to Detailer 2 if his work is satisfactory and if he demonstrates that he can do the slightly higher-level work of a Detailer 2.

On March 12, 1963, Mrs. Mary M., a Detailer 3 hired on January 8, 1962, submitted the following grievance to her superior:

> I request that my rating be changed from Detailer 3 to Detailer 2. I have been doing Detailer 2 work for about six months. I have always turned in jobs on time and in cases of rush work I have always had them in before they were promised. The designer that I work for and my drafting representative (union representative) both agree I am doing Detailer 2 work.

In discussing this grievance her supervisor made several assertions. He stated that he hired Mrs. Mary M. with the understanding that her job would involve a lot of short-promise work. A person doing such work must have a good attendance record. He said that she told him that her home problems would not interfere with her job.

The supervisor went on to say that he had spoken to her three times for talking too much and about her habitual tardiness. On February 26 he gave her a written warning notice because of excessive lateness, excessive absenteeism, and too much social conversation on the job.

The supervisor further stated that she was capable of doing Detailer 2 work. In fact, she has been doing some of it for the past six months. When she is on the job, the quality of her work is entirely satisfactory. The problem is that she is late and absent entirely too much. When she is here she talks too much with the other employees.

The absence record for Mrs. Mary M. is shown below:

5/8/62	½ day	Son sick
5/23/62	1 day	Out of town
6/14-15/62	2 days	Personal business
7/16/62	1 day	Illness in family
8/20/62	½ day	Alleged personal illness
8/29/62	½ day	Alleged personal illness
9/20/62	1 day	Personal illness
10/29/62	½ day	Car trouble
11/19/62	1 day	Car trouble
12/10-11/62	2 days	Illness in family
1/2/63	1 day	Personal business
2/18/63	1 day	Illness in family
2/24/63	1 day	Personal business

The supervisor said he would not promote a person with such a record.

Questions

1. Since Mrs. Mary M. has already demonstrated that she has done Detailer 2 work, do you think she should be upgraded?
2. If you were her supervisor, how would you handle this employee?
3. If one's actual work performance is of a higher grade level, does this justify a promotion regardless of excessive tardiness, absences, and talking on the job?
4. How appropriate is a denial of a promotion as a means of discipline?
5. If you were the manager in charge of the drafting department, how would you resolve this problem?

Suggestions for Further Reading

Gragg, Charles J., "Whose Fault Was It?," *Harvard Business Review,* Vol. 42, No. 1, January-February 1964, pp. 107-110.

Handsaker, Morrison, "Arbitration of Discipline Cases," *Personnel Journal,* Vol. 46, No. 3, March 1967, pp. 153-156, 175.

Heisel, W. D. and R. M. Gladstone, "Off-the-Job Conduct as a Disciplinary Problem," *Public Personnel Review,* Vol. 29, No. 1, 1968, pp. 23-28.

Huberman, John, "Discipline Without Punishment," *Harvard Business Review,* Vol. 42, No. 4, July-August 1964, pp. 62-68.

Jones, Dallas L., *Arbitration and Industrial Discipline,* Ann Arbor, Michigan: University of Michigan, Bureau of Industrial Relations, 1961.

Leonard, J. W., "Dismissal for Off-the-Job Criminal Behavior," *Monthly Labor Review,* Vol. 90, No. 11, November 1967, pp. 21-26.

Maier, Norman R. F., "Discipline in the Industrial Setting," *Personnel Journal,* Vol. 44, No. 4, April 1965, pp. 189-192, 213.

Pfiffner, John M. and Marshall Fels, *The Supervision of Personnel,* 3rd Ed., Englewood Cliffs, N.J.: Prentice-Hall, 1967, Ch. 7.

Phelps, Orme W., *Discipline and Discharge in the Unionized Firm,* Berkeley and Los Angeles: University of California Press, 1959.

Shiffer, Richard L., "Some Guides for Administering Discipline," *Personnel,* Vol. 38, No. 1, January-February, 1961, pp. 32-38.

Slichter, Summer H., James J. Healy, and E. Robert Livernash, *The Impact of Collective Bargaining on Management,* Washington, D.C.: The Brookings Institution, 1960, Ch. 21.

Stessin, Lawrence, *Employee Discipline,* Washington, D.C.: The Bureau of National Affairs, 1960.

Grievance Handling 22

In the course of human events in even the best-managed company, employee discontents, gripes, and complaints will certainly arise. Thus an employee may feel that his foreman assigns him to do all the dirty and heavy jobs. A clerk-typist may discover that the new girl—also a clerk-typist—has just been hired at a salary five dollars a week greater than she is getting after a full year on the job. She goes to see her supervisor about her own salary. An hourly production worker may have been handed a written disciplinary warning by his foreman because he refused to work overtime last Saturday. The worker thinks it is unfair to be disciplined for this, and he goes to see his union steward.

The foregoing are but brief examples of the myriad situations that can give rise to employee anxiety and complaint. For the sake of justice to the individual and the smooth functioning of the whole organization, it behooves management to get at the root of employee dissatisfactions and to take corrective action wherever possible.

NATURE OF COMPLAINTS AND GRIEVANCES

If some problem or condition bothers or annoys an employee or if he thinks he has been unfairly treated by someone, he may express his discontent to someone else. When he vocalizes his dissatisfaction, we can then designate such action a complaint. Usually, but not always, when a person "sounds off" about something that bothers him, he hopes that the listener (a fellow employee or his supervisor) will do something to correct the difficulty.

But an unexpressed dissatisfaction can be just as worthy of consideration by the supervisor as the spoken complaint. Just as an untreated wound can cause dire consequences for a human being, so can a festering discontent in the shop lead to grave results.

There are many reasons why an employee may keep his problem "bottled up" inside himself. He may simply have a high tolerance limit for frustration. Or he may feel that the conditions may soon change in such a way that the problem will then be corrected. He may have found from past experience that it does no good to complain to his supervisor. Sometimes a person may even feel that others will criticize or condemn him if he complains. By establishing a sound and healthy relationship with his men—one of mutual trust and confidence—the supervisor can do much to dispel employee fears and encourage free expression of feelings.

What Is a Grievance?

Viewpoints as to just what consitutes a grievance vary among personnel management and industrial relations authorities. According to some a grievance is any discontent or sense of injustice, expressed or not, felt by an employee in connection with his employment in an organization. This is a very broad conception. Such a definition includes all states of dissatisfaction or unhappiness whether they have been vocalized or not and whether they can be substantiated by facts or not.

A very narrow definition of a grievance is that adopted in many unionized companies. Here the labor policy may hold that a grievance is genuine only if there has been some alleged violation of the labor agreement. According to this view the only rights possessed by employees are those specifically spelled out in the contract; hence they can legitimately grieve only issues involved in the application and interpretation of the union-management agreement. As we shall see later in this chapter, such a narrow view has serious weaknesses. It is akin to a housewife's sweeping the dirt under the rug and pretending it doesn't exist.

Still another way of viewing this issue is to consider the act of expressing one's dissatisfaction with his supervisor as a complaint. It only becomes a true grievance if the supervisor is unable to settle the problem satisfactorily and then the employee appeals the case to the next higher level of management according to the steps in a formal grievance procedure. Thus some labor-management agreements specify that a complaint that has not been settled on the basis of informal discussion between foreman and worker must be put into writing and then submitted to the second step of the grievance procedure, at which point it becomes a true grievance.

The concept that will be used throughout this chapter is that a *grievance is any dissatisfaction or feeling of injustice in connection with one's employment situation that is brought to the attention of management.* This is a reasonably broad definition, but it does exclude the unexpressed dissatisfaction. It is difficult for management to act on an employee's problem if he does not call the matter to their attention. The emphasis on management's part should be to create a proper leadership climate, so that employees who feel they have a justifiable complaint feel free to inform management of this fact.

WHY HAVE A GRIEVANCE PROCEDURE?

Some employers, especially in nonunion companies, take the view that there is really no need for establishing a formalized grievance-handling system. They hold that all their first-line supervisors are trained to hear employee complaints and to take prompt action to settle them. As a further argument they add that the company is well managed, it has an enlightened human relations program in operation, and employees are generally satisfied, because very little evidence of dissatisfaction or complaint ever reaches the ears of top management. Of course, to the informed student of personnel management such contentions do not really prove much.

Why is it desirable that work organizations adopt a formal means for handling employee grievances? There are a number of sound reasons.

All employee complaints and dissatisfactions are, in actual practice, not settled satisfactorily by the first-level supervisor. There are many possible reasons for this. The supervisor may lack the necessary human relations skill to deal effectively with his people. He may lack the authority to take the action that is really necessary to properly solve the problem. He may even agree with the substance of the employee's grievance but know, from past experience, that it is futile for him to try to get higher management to act. Some supervisors may suppress the expression of grievances by their men. In those cases where the employee feels that his immediate supervisor has discriminated against him, he may feel that the supervisor can never, during a grievance discussion, fairly and objectively judge him and the situation. In this situation the employee must be able to appeal his case to some higher official.

Another justification for having a formal grievance-handling system is that it brings employee problems to the attention of higher management. The procedure serves as a medium of upward communication. Higher management becomes more aware of employee frustrations, problems, and expectations. It becomes sensitive to employee needs and well-being. Therefore, when higher management is formulating plans that will affect employees (for example, a plant expansion or contraction, company reorganization, or installation of new labor-saving machinery), it will have become fully cognizant of employee needs and reactions; hence complaints and grievances will be less likely to arise.

A grievance-handling system serves as an outlet for employee frustrations, discontents, and gripes. It operates like a pressure release valve on a steam boiler. Employees do not have to keep their frustrations bottled up until eventually seething discontent causes an explosion. They have a legitimate, officially approved way of appealing their grievances to higher management. If dissatisfied with initial attempts to iron out the difficulty with the foreman, employees do not have to feel that they are going over their boss's head surreptitiously, as often happens in plants lacking a grievance procedure.

The existence of an effective grievance procedure reduces the likelihood of arbitrary action by supervision, because the supervisors know that the employees are able to protest such behavior and make their protests heard by higher management.

The very fact that employees have a right to be heard and are actually heard helps to improve morale. An employee's conception of his problem may be quite biased. He may even lose his case. But the very fact that one or more management representatives have listened attentively to his story serves to demonstrate that the individual worker is important to management and somebody cares about him. That the act of listening to employee complaints can in itself improve employee morale was demonstrated in the famous Hawthorne research experiments at the Western Electric Company in the early 1930's. In the comprehensive employee interviewing program that was launched as a part of this research, it was observed that the general level of morale improved as a result of the program of interviewing employees about their complaints, problems, hopes, and ambitions even though nothing was immediately done to corect the conditions brought up by the workers. A helpful listener or counselor can often aid the employee to view his problem in a new light and sometimes help him solve his own difficulty.

NEED FOR A JUDICIAL BODY IN WORK ORGANIZATIONS

The issue of the handling of employee grievances regarding management actions or oversights reaches to the heart of a basic deficiency in modern work organizations. It is a well-established principle of democratic government that there be a clear separation of legislative, executive, and judicial bodies within government. No one branch of the government should serve dual roles nor dominate another branch. In work organizations line executives decide when employees have violated the rules of the organization, decide whether a man is guilty or innocent, select the penalty, and administer the penalty. They even sit in judgment upon their own actions when employees protest that something has been done unfairly. Now in the lowest ranks of any organization supervisors must, in the interests of efficiency and the maintenance of order, administer discipline and handle employee complaints and grievances. But when employees appeal a decision of their immediate superior to some higher level in the structure, a clear need for an impartial and independent judiciary becomes necessary. Under most existing systems employees must take their appeals to higher line executives. Although these executives may be more detached and broader in their outlook, they certainly cannot be wholly impartial. Their position in the organization causes them to seek to preserve the authority of their subordinate line supervisors. In many companies the first-level supervisor will not answer an employee's grievance until he has first consulted his immediate superior. Thus both of the lower levels of supervision really think as one on the typical grievance.

It is only when a grievance is appealed to an impartial arbitrator (as provided for in most collective bargaining agreements) that we can say a truly impartial and independent judicial body is being brought into the picture. But as we shall see later in this chapter, arbitration is rarely used in nonunion establishments.

The problem of the establishment of a judicial review body or system in business has just not been met. Indeed, most managers are hardly aware of the problem, because they have accepted, without question, the traditional ways of settling disputes by informal discussion between man and boss as the principal and, often, only approach to the problem.

One approach to the establishment of a judicial review system was the establishment of a public review board by the United Automobile Workers Union in 1957.[1] This board is composed of independent and eminent citizens to which members of the union can appeal their grievances against decisions of union leaders. The decisions of the Board are final and binding.

Approaches such as this might be tried in a business corporation. Because there is practically no past experience in this realm, there needs to be some experimentation to find out what specific organizational arrangements will work best. The members of a judicial body or review board might be appointed by the board of directors of a corporation for a fixed term of office, say five years. Or they may be appointed by an employer or trade association to serve all member companies. If the members of the board served on a part-time basis, held other regular full-time jobs, such as that of college professor, attorney, or consultant, and were appointed in the manner just described, we could expect the board to function with a good deal of independence.

A great variety of methods might be used as far as manner of appoint-

[1] See the booklet published by the United Automobile Workers Union entitled *A More Perfect Union. The U.A.W. Public Review Board—Why, What, How.* Detroit, U.A.W. Publications Department, 1960.

ment of the members, term of office, means of hearing cases, method for removal, and means for implementing decisions is concerned. The simple point being made here is that there is a clear need for the establishment of a judicial system within work organizations. The specific means for achieving this objective will depend upon the circumstances and the philosophy of top management in the particular organization involved.

Some very fruitful insights into the issue of appeal systems established unilaterally by management (as opposed to those bilaterally bargained between union and management) have been provided by William G. Scott.[2] Scott studied appeal systems in nonbusiness organizations such as unions, the United States government, the Roman Catholic Church, and the United States Army, and business corporations in six major industrial categories. Scott concludes, on the basis of his research, that appeal systems tend to be established in large organizations which must of necessity formalize their personnel handling procedures. His data also support the proposition that organizations establish grievance procedures for their members where there exist, by rule or common practice, restrictions upon the freedom of the members to leave that organization if they find conditions unsatisfactory. Certainly in the Roman Catholic Church and in the military, members are not free to leave at will. And increasingly in both the government service and in the modern corporation, employees tend to make a career with the employer. Accrued fringe benefits operate in such a way as to reduce labor mobility. Although he grants that formal appeal systems may be established as a by-product of unionism and in recognition of the influence of industrial humanism (the modern human relations movement) upon managerial thought and practice, Scott has ascribed the most powerful influence to be that of the process of bureaucracy. Large complex organizations must adopt, for the sake of effectiveness and justice to the members, formal administrative justice systems.

GRIEVANCE SETTLEMENT FOR UNIONIZED EMPLOYEES

It is when a union organizes the employees that demands are made by the union to establish a formal grievance procedure. Practically all labor-management agreements contain procedures for the handling of grievances.[3] It is understood by union and management alike that the signing of a labor contract does not automatically take care of all labor-relations

[2] William G. Scott, *The Management of Conflict: Appeal Systems in Organizations* (Homewood, Ill.: Richard D. Irwin, Inc. and The Dorsey Press, 1965).

[3] A study made in 1951 of 2,850 labor-management contracts by the Bureau of Labor Statistics showed that 94 per cent outlined definite grievance-handling procedures. Most of the remaining ones referred to but did not specifically describe a procedure. James Nix, Rose Theodore, and Dena Wolk, "Grievance Procedures in Union Agreements, 1950-51," *Monthly Labor Review,* Vol. 73, No. 1 (July 1951), pp. 36-39.

problems that will arise during the life of the agreement. Therefore, a grievance procedure provides one means of settling such difficulties.

With the presence of a union, employees know that it is fully legitimate to submit complaints and grievances to management. Often the union officials will encourage the expression of grievances. This may be done to bring to the surface all underlying discontents, to demonstrate to management that all is not well in the plant, to identify issues that can strengthen the union's hand, or to show the employees that the union can successfully help them achieve their needs and wants on the job. The economic and social power of the union commonly serves to prevent lower-level supervisors from taking punitive action against those workers who have submitted grievances against management actions.

The Grievance Procedure

The general pattern for handling grievances in unionized establishments has become rather standardized, although specific details, of course, vary from company to company.

Because management is presumed to possess full authority to operate its business as it sees fit (subject of course to legal, moral, and labor agreement controls), the reasoning is that a grievance represents a request by an employee, group of employees, and/or the union for a change in some management action or lack of action. In effect management administers the business and applies the provisions of the union-management agreement. If the employees or the union do not like the way this is done, they must submit a grievance according to the procedure outlined in the labor agreement.

Figure 22-1 shows a typical multistep grievance procedure for a medium- or large-sized company.[4]

There is considerable variation from company to company and union to union in the titles of the officials who handle the grievances above the first step. On the employer side some companies prefer to keep their industrial relations personnel in the background, acting in a purely advisory role. If such is the case, then only line management positions (such as superintendent, plant manager, and president) would deal directly with the union officials. In actual practice the trend in most companies is to have the industrial relations office play a major role in the handling of grievances at the higher steps. The industrial relations office consults closely with line officials, but it tends to carry the major burden for dealing personally with the union officials. In effect line management delegates the grievance-handling portion of its responsibilities to the staff industrial relations department. A primary reason for this is the need for

---

[4] The procedure for a small company would be very similar except that one or more of the middle steps would be omitted.

STEP	REPRESENTING THE EMPLOYEE OR UNION	REPRESENTING THE EMPLOYER
FIRST	EMPLOYEE ALONE OR UNION STEWARD ALONE OR BOTH TOGETHER	EMPLOYEE'S FOREMAN OR SUPERVISOR

If foreman's action is not satisfactory, the grievance is expressed in writing and appealed to second step.

STEP	REPRESENTING THE EMPLOYEE OR UNION	REPRESENTING THE EMPLOYER
SECOND	CHIEF PLANT STEWARD OR BUSINESS AGENT	SUPERINTENDENT OR INDUSTRIAL RELATIONS OFFICE

If management's action is considered unsatisfactory, union may appeal to third step.

STEP	REPRESENTING THE EMPLOYEE OR UNION	REPRESENTING THE EMPLOYER
THIRD	PLANT GRIEVANCE COMMITTEE (International Representative may assist)	INDUSTRIAL RELATIONS DIRECTOR OR PLANT MANAGER

If management's action is considered unsatisfactory, union may appeal to fourth step.

STEP	REPRESENTING THE EMPLOYEE OR UNION	REPRESENTING THE EMPLOYER
FOURTH	REGIONAL OR DISTRICT REPRESENTATIVES OF INTERNATIONAL UNION	TOP CORPORATE MANAGEMENT

If management's action is considered unsatisfactory, union may appeal to fifth step.

STEP		
FIFTH	ARBITRATION BY IMPARTIAL THIRD PARTY	

Figure 22-1. A Typical Grievance Procedure for a Medium- or Large-sized Company.

achieving uniformity of action in implementing company labor policy and in administering the union-employer agreement. In a large company considerable trouble could result if each of the scores of superintendents, managers, and department heads freely exercised his own judgment in answering grievances. Unions press for uniformity of treatment of employees throughout the entire organization. The labor contract commits the employer to essentially the same objective. Theoretically a company's policy and the labor agreement can be administered soundly and equitably by line managers if they are properly trained and can freely call upon the industrial relations department for advice. But actually labor relations problems are quite often technical, especially when one considers the important legal aspects. This technical complexity of the problem coupled with the potential serious consequences (slowdown or strike) of an error in the handling of a case has led many companies to assign major authority to the industrial relations department.

Well over 90 per cent of all collective bargaining agreements provide for arbitration as the final step in the grievance procedure. This is the peaceful method of settling an unresolved grievance. The alternative, which still exists in some agreements, is a strike. The subject of arbitration will be covered later in this chapter.

Initial Grievance Presentation. Section 9(a) of the Taft-Hartley Act of 1947 provides that employees have the right to present grievances to their employer and to have them adjusted without the intervention of the bargaining representative (the union) as long as the settlement is not inconsistent with the terms of the labor agreement. It also states, however, that the bargaining representative has the right to be present at such adjustment. The net result of this legal stipulation is that most collective agreements state that the employee may present his grievance alone or jointly with the union steward, or he may have the steward present it for him.

The position of most unions on this matter is that they want to be actively involved in the initial discussion with the foreman to discourage individual bargaining or the making of special private deals. They also feel that trained and experienced stewards can achieve more favorable results than an employee can alone. The union may also choose to screen out complaints that the steward feels are unjustified.

Many managements prefer to build up a solid bond of trust between a foreman and his men in such a way that the men will always feel free to bring up problems privately with the foreman. Some managers feel that the shop steward should enter the picture only if this private discussion between foreman and worker does not achieve a satisfactory settlement. Some managers further feel that there are times when the steward will attempt to magnify or expand the grievance for union political reasons.

Time Limits. Time limits on the appeal by the union to the next higher step and on management for its answer at each step appear quite commonly in labor agreements, especially in large companies. For its part management has sought to avoid heavy costs for retroactive pay in discharge and layoff cases as well as prevent the union from bringing up old issues for political purposes. Of course, unions want a limitation on the length of time management can take in deciding a case at each step to prevent deliberate stalling and possible serious hardship to an aggrieved worker. Typically the time allowed for a foreman to answer a grievance is one or two days. At the higher steps in the procedure, the time for management to prepare an answer is generally one to two weeks.

Union and management representatives are generally in agreement on the value of time limits for the efficient handling of grievances.[5] However, it is sound practice to extend the limits by mutual consent when

---

[5] See *The Grievance Process,* Proceedings of a Conference, March 23-24, 1956 (East Lansing: Labor and Industrial Relations Center, Michigan State University), p. 60.

requested by either party for a specific case. It is perhaps self-evident that from time to time cases arise where extensive investigation, fact finding, and consultation make a short time limit impossible to meet.

Special Grievance Procedures

It has become rather common practice to set up a special grievance procedure to handle those problems for which the foreman is not well equipped. These are generally grievances concerning industrial engineering techniques or those having a broad companywide impact or serious policy implications.

If a worker has a grievance concerning the fairness of the time standard on his operation or concerning his job-evaluated wage rate, this may be taken directly to a joint union-management committee that deals solely with such problems. Joint union-management job evaluation committees are very common in the steel industry. Nowadays many unions have specially trained personnel qualified to handle time-study, wage-incentive, and job-evaluation problems. Although the factory foreman is not an industrial engineer and may not be qualified to handle this type of grievance, he certainly should be fully informed that such grievance action over a job in his department is being processed. In fact, it is probably a good idea to route *all* grievances initially to the foreman so that he can always know what is going on in his department. Then grievances for which a special procedure has been established can be automatically routed by the foreman to the appropriate step or joint committee.

The Clinical Approach to Grievance Handling

A fairly common view, especially among business executives, is that the labor agreement is a legal document that spells out the rights and obligations of the company, the union, and the employees. In complaining about conditions in the plant, the employee really has a right to submit a grievance concerning only those matters that have been specifically covered in the contract. In short, the contract specifies the rights of the union and the employees; hence an employee can grieve only about some alleged violation of these rights. According to this conception of the grievance process, an employee who claims that he should be classified into pay grade 7 instead of his present grade of 6, on the basis of enlarged job responsibilities, would have a legitimate grievance, because the labor agreement specifically covers the matter of job classification. On the other hand an employee who complains that his foreman has picked on him and called him nasty names would have no right to submit a grievance, because there is no provision in the contract covering such an issue.

The procedure just described has been called a legalistic approach to grievance handling. Many union-management agreements conform to

this narrow concept of what is a proper grievance by stating that a grievance must be an issue that *relates to the interpretation and application
of the agreement.* Other kinds of complaints are ruled out as being ille-
gitimate or unjustified.

Benjamin Selekman has stated eloquently the argument for adopting
a clinical rather than legalistic approach to the handling of grievances.
The emphasis in the clinical approach is upon getting to the root of the
employee's dissatisfaction regardless of whether his grievance, as expressed, fits some narrow mold as defined by the labor agreement. Selekman points out that emphasis should be placed upon the problems of
treating grievances rather than upon the mechanics of accepting or dis-
missing them. In answer to the question "When is a grievance not a
grievance?" Selekman says, "Never."[6] Although the grievance on its surface may not fit a strictly defined mold of what constitutes a legitimate
grievance according to a contract definition, it behooves management to
make every reasonable effort to find out what is bothering the employee
in order to take steps to rectify the trouble. Discontent, unhappiness, and
unrest do not disappear just because a supervisor pronounces them
irrelevant and outside the scope of the contract.

A further argument for following a clinical approach is that numerous
problem situations are bound to arise that were not foreseen at the time
the company and union negotiated the contract. These trouble spots cannot be swept under the carpet until it is time to bargain the next agreement one or more years later. The labor law of the United States (for example, Taft-Hartley Act) requires bargaining between management and
union at all times to settle joint problems. This supports what common
sense tells us anyway, namely that there must be a good faith attempt to
solve difficulties and disputes as they arise. The grievance procedure provides an effective instrument for accomplishing this objective.

In conformity with this liberal view of grievance handling, foreman
and higher management personnel should wholeheartedly undertake to
investigate and act upon *all* grievances. If a grievance cannot be tied to
some provision of the labor agreement, it can certainly be judged according to psychological or sociological principles, principles of equity and
justice, or according to established personnel policies of the company.
This all inclusive approach to grievancies can be applied at all steps of
the procedure save the last one—arbitration. Because arbitrators' decisions are generally final and binding and because management and the
union, as a rule, do not choose to have arbitrators legislate for them by
creating new policies and contract provisions, it seems reasonable that
at this last step the arbitrator be empowered to settle only questions of
contract interpretation or application. Hence use the clinical approach

---

[6] Benjamin M. Selekman, *Labor Relations and Human Relations* (New York: McGraw-
Hill Book Company, Inc., 1947), Ch. 5.

through all the lower stages of the grievance procedure, but be legalistic at the final arbitration step.[7]

Must Grievance Be in Writing?

In order to process grievances through the higher steps of a grievance procedure, it is probably wise to require that they be reduced to writing. Since the number of individuals who must discuss and decide multiplies as a grievance is appealed to the higher stages, it makes sense to reduce the likelihood of varying interpretations by expressing it in writing. If this is done, there is little chance that the president of a company will render a decision on a grievance that no longer bears any resemblance to what the worker complained about in the first place.

Yet at the foreman-worker-steward level actual labor relations experience demonstrates that grievances are handled most satisfactorily if they are not first put in writing. This is a long-established truth, but sometimes it has to be rediscovered periodically. A few years ago the International Harvester Company and the United Automobile Workers Union were besieged with a tremendous backlog of formal written grievances. To solve this serious problem, management and union officials decided to change the procedure. Henceforth, as many grievances as possible were settled on the foreman-worker-steward level before they were put in writing. Only if settlement at this level failed, would the grievance be written down. The main feature of the International Harvester plan was to settle grievances on the spot, promptly and informally. If help from higher management or union officials was necessary, they were brought into the discussion promptly. Union stewards were given full opportunity to participate in the discussions to preserve and maintain their positions in the eyes of the worker. This revised procedure has been outstandingly successful in settling grievances quickly and in reducing the huge backlog of written grievances.[8]

Why is it preferable to settle grievances at the first level, informally, without requiring that they be expressed in writing? Many employees cannot express their problems accurately and completely in writing. A briefly stated grievance on a written form is devoid of the human feeling and attitudes that often lie behind the issue. Some people are afraid to commit their complaints to writing. They are afraid they will be labeled as malcontents. But they are perfectly satisfied to talk over the matter informally with their foreman and/or their steward. The process of expressing every grievance in writing is unduly cumbersome. It often serves to magnify a simple problem.

[7] This is essentially the approach recommended by Harold W. Davey in his *Contemporary Collective Bargaining* (2nd Ed.; Englewood Cliffs, N.J., Prentice-Hall, Inc., 1959), pp. 119-121.

[8] *Grievance Handling—A Case Study of a New Approach* (New York: Industrial Relations Counselors, Inc., 1961).

A reasonable procedure is to require that only those grievances that cannot be settled at the first, or sometimes even the second, step be then stated in writing.

Role of the Supervisor

The first-line supervisor in whose department a grievance originates should take the major responsibility for trying to reach a settlement that is acceptable to all parties concerned. However, all too often in actual practice his role becomes a minor one. When unionization became widespread in the mass production industries in the 1930's and 1940's top management in many companies feared the consequences of faulty action by foremen in handling grievances, so it centralized all grievance-handling authority in the industrial relations department. On paper the foreman was the first step in the grievance procedure. In practice the industrial relations department answered all grievances. This could be done in a number of ways. In one way the foreman might actually give an answer to the worker and/or steward, but it would be an answer he obtained as a result of consultation with the industrial relations department. Sometimes foremen would get in the habit of rejecting any and all grievances, and these would then be appealed to the industrial relations office, which appeared in the second or third step of the procedure. Often the local union would sense that the foremen were powerless and would skip the first step and immediately take its cases to the office that had the authority. In this same vein the plant industrial relations director of a large corporation once said to the author somewhat proudly, "For each and every grievance, I write out the answers that my foremen give to the union. I would no more trust them with such an important responsibility than I would a child."

It is fully sound to have a special grievance procedure for such technical matters as industrial engineering disputes and to enter a grievance at a higher step in the regular grievance procedure if it has broad policy implications for which no precedents have been established. But for practically all other types the foreman must be granted the necessary authority to make at least an initial settlement on his own. He must be fully trained in labor policy, contract interpretation, and human relations so that he can properly carry out this responsibility. In recent years many companies have swung around to this way of thinking.

In the face-to-face dealings between the aggrieved employee and the foreman, the foreman must listen attentively in order to obtain the man's full story as he sees it. Depending upon the nature of the grievance and the circumstances, this may be an ideal occasion for the supervisor to employ the nondirective technique of interviewing. This technique is most appropriate if the supervisor perceives that there may be underlying causes related to the psychological or social adjustment of the individual to his work environment.

Because worker grievances are often intimately related to the activities and pressures involved in getting out production (for example, work assignments, transfers, work loads, job classifications, overtime distribution) the foreman is in the best position to make a full investigation of the facts of the problem. He can collect written data and examine records as well as interview union representatives, employees, and management staff personnel to compile a full account of the facts and history surrounding a case. When a supervisor does not feel sure of himself, he should certainly consult his immediate superior or the industrial relations department. But he should never become merely a messenger boy, a front, or a figurehead. Grievances tend to be settled most expeditiously and to the satisfaction of all parties concerned in those companies where the front-line supervisor plays an important role.

Role of Shop Steward and the Union

The position of a union steward is a difficult one. One of his prime duties is to represent workers and the union in the processing of grievances. Shall he look upon himself as a shop lawyer who goes to bat for every worker on each and every complaint? Shall he make no attempt to reject those he honestly believes have no merit? In most industrial unions the steward is elected by his fellow employees in the department where he works. They are his friends. If he wants to keep his steward's position and get re-elected, he has a powerful urge to simply go to bat for his colleagues on all complaints.

Yet there are serious disadvantages to this approach. A steward is a union leader, and he has to stand up and be counted on important issues. He must be strong enough to say no when the facts demand such a position. Most union leadership manuals for stewards tell them to perform, at least partially, a judicial role in handling employee grievances. A union's position vis-à-vis the company can be seriously weakened if it loads up the grievance machinery with a lot of cases which are so weak that the union loses them at the higher stages.

Sometimes the union steward concludes that he has a thankless job. He may overextend himself to push faithfully a large number of worker grievances to a successful conclusion. Yet once he tells the men that they are wrong on an issue and he cannot in all fairness push their complaint, he often finds that they are vitriolic in their abuse of him.

Actually much of the legalism that has crept into collective agreements and union grievance-handling procedures has been created by union leaders to insulate themselves from rank-and-file pressures.

Political struggles within a union often have a profound effect upon the number of grievances submitted and upon the vigor with which union officials push them. If there is a sharp contest for some important union office, the competing candidates will often try to demonstrate how much they can do for the rank and file by vigorously digging up issues and pursuing them to a successful conclusion. Pressure tactics such as slowdowns and brief walkouts may even be employed to force management to back down. The same kind of grievance activity may take place if the union which is "in" the company is being threatened by an outside union that seeks to win bargaining rights and unseat the incumbent union.

GRIEVANCE ARBITRATION

If a dispute cannot be settled by discussion, negotiation, and compromise between the union and management, it is now almost standard practice for it to be taken to arbitration. The widespread practice of using arbitration as a means of settling unresolved grievances is a relatively recent phenomenon. Prior to 1940 only a small percentage of labor agreements provided for the use of arbitration. A principal force contributing to greater acceptance of arbitration was the National War Labor Board during the years of its existence from 1942 to 1945. It adopted a firm policy of recommending and in many cases ordering the inclusion of arbitration provisions in labor agreements. Added to this pressure has been the recognition by both labor and management that arbitration is the preferable way of handling unresolved disputes. If arbitration is not employed as the terminal point in a grievance procedure, the alternative for the union is either to call a strike or to accept managements' decision. Arbitration, in effect, promotes labor peace.

There are two basic ways of employing an arbitrator. One is the permanent arbitrator or umpire system, and the other is the *ad hoc* (from the Latin, meaning "for this case alone, or special") system. Some large corporations, such as General Motors and United States Steel, and certain trade associations, such as the needle trades in New York City, employ full-time arbitrators on a salaried basis. When the case load is heavy there is some justification for having a permanent arbitrator. Further he can become expert in the particular problems of the industry, and there is no delay in engaging his services. Notwithstanding these considerations, however, the most common method is to engage arbitrators on an *ad hoc* basis. An *ad hoc* arbitrator will hear either one case alone, or he may hear several cases during the course of one or two days. An advantage of the *ad hoc* system is that the individual can be selected on the basis of his expertise for the type of case to be heard.

The procedure for selecting an arbitrator is commonly spelled out in the labor agreement. Often the arbitrator is selected from a panel of qualified arbitrators listed by either the Federal Mediation and Conciliation Service or by the American Arbitration Association. If the two parties are unable to agree upon an individual, the contract will often state that an arbitrator shall be appointed by one or the other of these agencies.

It is almost universal practice for the union and the company to share equally the arbitrator's fee for his services.

Labor agreements generally specify that the decision of the arbitrator shall be final and binding upon all parties concerned—the company, the union, and the employees. Further they state, usually, that the arbitrator shall have only the authority to interpret, apply, or determine compliance with the provisions of the union-management agreement. He shall not add to, subtract, or alter the provisions of the agreement. This simply means that the parties expect the arbitrator to act in the role of judge and not a legislator.

An arbitration hearing is a quasijudicial process. It may be conducted quite formally, or the entire process may be rather informal. The desires of the arbitrator himself and the custom of the parties determine whether the hearing will be run formally or informally. But even a formal hearing ordinarily is much less strict and structured than is a hearing in a court of law.

Quite often after the hearing has concluded both the union and the company will file a post-hearing brief with the arbitrator to summarize facts and arguments of each side. Typically then the arbitrator has thirty days to make his decision and prepare his award and supporting opinion. The award is the decision of the arbitrator upon the issue submitted to him. The opinion summarizes the positions of the two parties and explains the reasoning of the arbitrator in arriving at his decision.

GRIEVANCE SETTLEMENT FOR NONUNION EMPLOYEES

Only a small minority of companies have squarely faced the problem of providing a mechanism for handling grievances for their nonunion employees. A 1954 survey by the National Industrial Conference Board of 495 companies employing a total of 923,435 hourly workers revealed that 284 of these companies employed hourly workers who were not represented by a union. Only 21.5 per cent of these companies had a formal grievance procedure for such people. In a survey conducted at the same time and pertaining to nonexempt salaried personnel, the Board found that only 39 (or 8.6 per cent) out of 454 companies had a grievance procedure for these employees.[9]

Further and more recent survey evidence on the prevalence of grievance procedures for nonunion employees in private business is provided by William G. Scott who sent questionnaires to 1800 companies in six different industries in the early 1960's. Of 793 replies received, only 275 companies (35 per cent) had some kind of a program for handling employee complaints. However, only 91 of these 275 companies had a formal

[9] *Peronnel Practices* in Factory and Office, Studies in Personnel Policy, No. 145 (New York: National Industrial Conference Board, 1954), pp. 56 and 109.

grievance system. The remainder had informal arrangements that were mostly rather loosely applied "open door" policies.[10]

By and large American managements have chosen either to ignore the problem of providing a means for solving a nonunion employee grievances, or they have relied upon quite informal measures. But the need for programs in the nonunion sector of the working force of business firms is nevertheless pressing.

Approaches to the Problem

In comparison to the well-defined procedures and the extensive experience of American industry in grievance handling for unionized employees, the procedures for nonunion personnel are either nonexistent, or else they are ill-defined, vague, and seldom employed. We shall explore the various approaches that have been or can be instituted for nonunion people.

Personnel Counseling. Some companies have employed specially trained personnel counselors who are attached to the personnel department. Their mission is to talk to employees who are troubled or have a problem and help them find a way to resolve it. Although not primarily designed to handle complaints and grievances, personnel counseling certainly has applications in this area. For reasons discussed in Chapter 18, "Supervision," personnel counseling by staff counselors has never been popular in American industry except during the World War II period.

Instead of the staff approach to counseling, the line supervisors can be trained in the theory and techniques of nondirective interviewing and counseling. Such a program has much to commend it. This can be an effective approach for the supervisor to uncover and help solve employee dissatisfactions and complaints. Yet counseling alone cannot be considered to be a complete grievance-handling mechanism. If the supervisor and the man cannot achieve a satisfactory resolution to the problem, what happens then? There must be a system for involving other and higher levels of management personnel in the program. There must be a way of appealing a supervisor's final decision.

Open-Door Policy. Many top executives who have a genuine concern for the well-being of their employees have set up an open-door policy to solve employee grievances. The open-door policy means that any rank-and-file worker has a full right to go to the office of the chief executive officer of that company or plant to discuss his complaint. Under such a program, the executive promises to make himself available for such contacts with the men. He further implies that he will investigate every

---

[10] William G. Scott, *op. cit.,* pp. 56-89. Scott surveyed companies in these six categories: manufacturing, finance, retail, transportation, extractive, and public utilities. The 91 companies with formal programs represented only 11 per cent of the total of 793 that responded to the survey.

grievance and take appropriate action. Although some open-door programs permit the employee to go immediately to the chief executive with his problem, it is much better to require that he discuss the issue with his immediate superior first. This procedure will solve the majority of grievances at the bottom level and will keep the supervisor fully informed of what is going on in his own department.

Although on the face of it the open door policy may seem like a good system to some, it seldom works out successfully in practice. There are a number of reasons for this. The social and organizational distance between the worker in overalls and the company president in the thick-carpeted office is so great that the worker is generally fearful of going to see the "big boss." He feels that he may not express himself well or that the "big boss" may not understand his point of view.

If the president should overrule the first-level supervisor, the latter will tend to lose face in front of his men. If the president does not act judiciously, he can seriously weaken the position of the supervisors.

If an employee feels that he has been mistreated by his foreman, he may get the action reversed by appealing to the chief executive. But the worker may find that although he has won that particular case, in the long run his supervisor may bear resentment against him and put him in an even worse position than he was originally.

From a practical standpoint the top officer of a company does not have sufficient time to 'hear frequent worker complaints and then conduct a full investigation. This is something that can be more effectively done by subordinate managers and supervisors.

The Inspector General Method. The military system of providing a means of correcting injustices by having a representative from the Inspector General's office visit each unit once per year to hear and investigate soldiers' grievances is an approach that is rarely employed in private industry. One large company that for many years had an open-door policy decided to establish a special vice-presidential position to relieve the president of the load of hearing and investigating worker grievances. This vice-president visits every plant at least once per year and more often if necessary. He in effect performs the functions of an inspector general in the military establishment.

Ombudsman. The concept of an ombudsman to process complaints of citizens against the government was first devised in Sweden in 1809. Finland also established this office in 1809 as a protector of the people. But it has not been until the 1950's and 1960's that the concept has really spread throughout the world. In its most precise meaning an *ombudsman* is an independent and politically neutral officer of a governmental legislature. His function is to handle appeals by ordinary citizens against the executive bureaucracy. He has the power to investigate, has access to government documents, has the right to prosecute officials for illegal acts, and can publicize his findings.

In its more general and looser meaning, the term ombudsman has recently been applied to any official of an organization charged with the responsibility of investigating and settling member complaints. The inspector-general system of the military is a form of the ombudsman. The State University of New York at Stony Brook in 1967 appointed three faculty members as ombudsmen to handle both faculty and student grievances.

Although this concept is just now beginning to be applied to nongovernmental organizations, its success in government-citizen relations in the Scandinavian countries reveals that it is certainly worthy of trial in private establishments.[11]

Multistep Grievance Procedure. Some companies have established official multistep grievances procedures patterned somewhat after those for union personnel. The last avenue of appeal is generally the chief executive officer of the company, or of the division, if the company is composed of semiautonomous divisions. Arbitration is seldom provided for. There are a number of reasons for this. Management is unwilling to dilute any of its powers by having an outside party review (and perhaps reverse) its decisions. The individual employee is often ill-equipped to prepare adequately and to present his case before the arbitrator. He generally cannot afford to pay one half the arbitrator's fee, as is customary in unionized establishments. If management assumes the burden of assigning a man to represent the employee and if it pays the full cost of arbitration, then the claim that both the company and the individual are on an equal footing before the arbitrator can no longer be made.

Although there are plausible reasons why arbitration is not more widely used, there is still considerable justification for having some impartial and independent agency serve as a final judicial body to review the decisions of top management. Some writers have proposed a board of review or a board of neutrals. Such a board might be established by the board of directors of a corporation, or it might be established by an employer or trade association to serve all the member companies.[12]

The personnel management literature contains a number of references to multistep procedures for nonunion people. In most of these procedures the employee can appeal his case to successively higher levels of managers in his direct chain of command. The industrial relations department usually plays a key part in the proceedings. Sometimes this office is the

[11] For an explanation of the ombudsman concept in government see Stanley V. Anderson (ed.), *Ombudsmen For American Government?,* prepared by the American Assembly, Columbia University (Englewood Cliffs, N.J.: Prentice-Hall, 1968).

[12] See, for example, Walter V. Ronner, "Handling Grievances in a Non-Union Plant," *Proceedings of the Fourteenth Annual Meeting of the Industrial Relations Research Association* (Madison, Wisc.: IRRA, 1961), pp. 306-314; Dale S. Beach, "An Organizational Problem: Subordinate-Superior Relations," *Advanced Management,* Vol. 25, No. 12 (December 1960), pp. 12-16.

next step of appeal after the supervisor. In others, a representative from industrial relations acts in an advisory capacity to the employee and may even serve as the latter's advocate if he thinks the employee has a justifiable complaint.

In order for a grievance system to work successfully in a nonunion organization, the employees must be assured, by both pronouncement and actual experience, that there will be no retaliation against them for submitting and pushing a case up through the successive steps in the system. Because of the great imbalance of power between management and the worker, employees tend naturally to have a deep-seated fear of retaliation by the boss or the other members of management. In fact, this is one of the principal reasons grievance procedures for nonunion people are seldom used. The danger is that top management will thus delude itself into thinking that everyone is content, because few if any grievances are submitted.

Questions for Review and Discussion

1. What is a grievance?
2. Why is it desirable that all work organizations have an established system for hearing and adjusting employee grievances?
3. What are the arguments in favor of establishing a judicial body within corporations and other work organizations with a clear separation of powers between the executive and judicial branches of the organization?
4. Explain how an employee's grievance would be processed through the grievance procedure in a typical large unionized company.
5. According to modern organization theory the industrial relations department should act primarily in a staff capacity. Is this principle violated if this department appears at the second or third step of the formal grievance procedure and takes on major responsibility for answering grievances? Discuss.
6. What is meant by the "clinical approach" to grievance handling? Contrast it with the legalistic approach. What are the arguments in favor of using a clinical approach?
7. Should all grievances be put in writing before management acts upon them? Discuss.
8. Discuss the proper role of the foreman in grievance settlement. Why has the foreman become powerless and a mere figurehead in grievance handling in some companies?
9. Describe the role of the union steward in grievance handling. What pressures play upon the steward?
10. Briefly describe the process of grievance arbitration. Include in your discussion the method of selecting an arbitrator, his authority, method of compensation, and hearing procedure.

11. Why do you think most companies have done little or nothing to establish a grievance-handling system for their nonunion employees?
12. What is the open-door policy? What are its merits and shortcomings?
13. Why is arbitration rarely employed as the final step for grievance handling for nonunion employees?

CASE PROBLEMS

Problem 1

The ABC Textile Company employs 550 production and maintenance workers who are represented by a union.

The grievance procedure in the union-employer agreement provides that the aggrieved employee and/or his union steward shall first submit the matter to the department foreman. If it is not settled at this step, it must be put in writing on a standard grievance form and submitted to the plant superintendent. Representing the union at this second step is the local union grievance committee and/or the business agent. The third step is the company president and a representative of the international union. The fourth and final step consists of binding arbitration. The company personnel director acts in an advisory capacity to plant management at all stages. In actual practice he is particularly instrumental in shaping the decision on a grievance at the second, or superintendent, step of the procedure.

During the past three months the following cases arose:

1. The company had been plagued with chronic worker absenteeism. The procedure for keeping track of absences was to have each foreman record the names of all those who were absent each day in a notebook. In an attempt to correct the problem, the superintendent and the personnel manager made a quick check of the various foremen's notebooks and then discharged six of the most serious offenders. The union immediately filed a grievance charging discrimination because some of the six men who had been fired had better attendance records than some other workers who remained on the payroll. At the second step of the grievance procedure, management decided to reduce the penalty to a one-week suspension without pay. In commenting upon the case later, the personnel manager said he expected that worker attendance would improve since the employees had learned that management was serious about improving attendance and that serious offenders might be discharged. However, several of the foremen grumbled that the incident had undermined their authority with their men because management had backed down. They said that the six men involved were poor performers and should have been fired.

2. A foreman in one of the production departments asked a machine operator to operate a different machine to fill in for a worker who was
absent that day. When he refused, his foreman told him to punch out
his time card and go home. He would not be paid for the rest of that
day. The union filed a grievance in the man's behalf charging a violation of the labor agreement. According to the contract the machines
and processes are grouped into categories. An employee cannot be
assigned to a machine outside his category without his consent. In this
particular case the machine involved was outside the employee's regular category. However the skill and knowledge requirements for the
two different machines were essentially the same. Also the rate of pay
for both operations was the same. At the second step of the grievance
procedure, management decided that the foreman had erred and the
man was paid for the time lost.

3. A man wearing canvas sneakers was told by his foreman not to come
to work again dressed in sneakers. Rather he must wear leather shoes
as a safety measure to protect his feet against cuts and wounds from
wire, nails, sharp projections on machines, and floor splinters. Before giving this oral warning, the foreman had consulted the superintendent and received full approval for his action. Despite the
warning the man appeared for work the next day again wearing
sneakers. He was sent home immediately, without pay, for the rest
of the day. When he appeared for work the following day he was
wearing leather shoes. However, the union filed a grievance charging discrimination because some workers in other departments had
worn sneakers and had not been disciplined. The grievance was
rejected at the first two steps of the grievance procedure and is
now pending at the third step.

Many of the foremen complain that they repeatedly lose face in front
of their men because higher management gives in too frequently in the
face of union pressure in grievance cases. The union business agent has
claimed that management provokes most of the grievances by its own
actions.

Questions

1. What seems to be wrong here? What measures should be taken to improve employee-management-union relations?
2. What do you think of the foremen's complaints about "undermining
their authority" and "losing face in front of the men"?

Problem 2

Henry M., a machine-tool operator, recently received a suggestion award
of $200 for a cost-cutting idea he had submitted three months previous-

ly under the regular suggestion plan. In writing his suggestion and explaining it to the engineering department, he had received some assistance from his foreman. According to the rules of the suggestion system, foremen are not eligible to receive cash awards for any suggestions they personally make in connection with their departments. The making of methods improvements and cost reductions is considered part of a foreman's normal job responsibility.

Shortly after Henry M. submitted his suggestion, his foreman hinted that the other men usually gave him a bottle of whiskey when he did little favors for them. Henry M. made no reply but privately resented the behavior of his foreman.

In recent weeks nearly all of the other men in the department have been called in to work Saturdays at overtime rates. Henry finds that his name is always omitted from the list. Last week on Wednesday afternoon the names of all twenty men appeared on the Saturday work list, including Henry's. But on Friday afternoon his foreman told him that he would not be needing him on Saturday, because his job activity was well covered by the other machine-tool operators. This foreman hinted quite strongly that for a bottle of scotch Henry's chances of working Saturdays regularly would certainly improve.

Because Saturday work means nearly thirty dollars, Henry is tempted to submit to this request for a payoff, but his wife is indignant and refuses to permit it.

The company is not unionized, and to Henry's knowledge there is no formal grievance procedure. Henry is thinking of going to the general foreman to expose the foreman's demand for a payoff.

Question

1. What would you do if you were in Henry's place?

Suggestions for Further Reading

Chamberlain, Neil W. and James W. Kuhn, *Collective Bargaining,* 2nd Ed., New York: McGraw-Hill Book Company, 1965, Ch. 6.

Corzine, James E., "Structure and Utilization of a Grievance Procedure," *Personnel Journal,* Vol. 46, No. 8, September 1967, pp. 484-489.

Drought, Neal E., "Grievances in the Non-Union Situation", *Personnel Journal,* Vol. 46, No. 6, June 1967, pp. 331-336.

Fleishman, Edwin A. and Edwin F. Harris, "Patterns of Leadership Behavior Related to Employee Grievances and Turnover," *Personnel Psychology,* Vol. 15, Spring 1962, pp. 43-56.

Harrison, S. C., "Preventive Medicine for Labor Disputes," *Personnel,* Vol. 44, May-June 1967, pp. 59-64.

Kuhn, James W., *Bargaining in Grievance Settlement,* New York: Columbia University Press, 1961.

McKersie, Robert B., "Avoiding Written Grievances by Problem-Solving: An Outside View," *Personnel Psychology,* Vol. 17, No. 4, Winter 1964, pp. 367-379.

Repas, Bob, "Grievance Procedures Without Arbitration," *Industrial and Labor Relations Review,* Vol. 20, No. 3, April 1967, pp. 381-390.

Scott, William G., *The Management of Conflict: Appeal Systems in Organizations,* Homewood, Ill.: Richard D. Irwin and the Dorsey Press, 1965.

Selekman, Benjamin W., *Labor Relations and Human Relations,* New York: McGraw-Hill Book Company, 1947, Ch. 5.

Slichter, Sumner H., James J. Healy, and E. Robert Livernash, *The Impact of Collective Bargaining on Management,* Washington, D.C.: The Brookings Institution, 1960, Chs. 23-26.

Stone, Morris, *Labor Grievances and Decisions,* New York: Harper & Row, 1965.

IV

FINANCIAL COMPENSATION

Wage and Salary Administration

23

Wages, as a means of providing income for employees and as a cost of doing business to the employer, constitute one of the most important subjects in the field of personnel management. Wages provide a source of motivation for employees to perform effectively. The wage rate offered is one of the most important considerations to a person who is contemplating taking a new job.

Formerly wage rates in organizations, whether in industry or in government and nonprofit institutions, tended to be established in a haphazard fashion, with little consideration given to consistency within the organization according to differentials in job requirements or to consistency with prevailing wages paid in other establishments. The movement in industry for the development and adoption of sound principles and practices of wage and salary administration had its infancy in the 1920's and 1930's, expanded greatly during and immediately after World War II, and in the 1950's became more mature with the general acceptance of the ideas and methods initiated earlier.

This chapter explores the subject of wage and salary administration in the individual organization, giving consideration to principles and practices.

Viewpoints of Wages

Employers consider wages as a cost of doing business. They are interested in labor cost per unit of output (whether the work is a unit of product or a unit of service). Wages, viewed broadly, constitute the largest single cost item for most firms. Even for the firm in which raw materials purchased from suppliers may amount to over half of the total unit costs, it may be seen that to the supplier himself much of his costs were labor, and so on back to the original source of the raw material. When an employer contemplates an adjustment of his wage level, he considers the effect upon his total costs in relation to income. Through experience, employers have learned also that to attract and hold competent employees in a free labor market they must pay adequate wages and pay one worker properly in relation to other workers within their establishments.

On the other hand, employees view wages as a means of providing for their wants and needs according to certain general standards that they may consider. They may believe that they should get paid as much as others receive for doing the same kind of work in the same organization or in other companies in that locality of which they may have knowledge. They may believe that they should get paid according to the union scale or enough to maintain a differential over those doing work requiring less skill, experience, and education. Other informal criteria that employees adopt to judge the adequacy of their pay are whether it is enough to support themselves and their families at a level comparable with their friends; enough to save a certain portion in the bank; and enough to keep up with increases in the cost of living.

Labor Costs and Wages

It was stated previously that the employer primarily looks upon wages as a labor cost to himself (and not—it may be added—as income to the employee). If, due to union pressures or a shortage of labor, the employer raises his wage level across the board, his labor costs per unit of output will also rise in the same proportion. But if he can increase productivity—that is, output per unit of labor—then he can reduce the impact of the increase in labor costs and may even cancel it out. Likewise, consider two firms manufacturing identical products in the same locality with firm A paying wages 10 per cent higher than firm B for the occupations involved. Does this mean that firm A's labor costs per unit of product are 10 per cent higher than B's? No, it does not necessarily mean that. A's productivity may be greater than B's, so that it costs him no more to produce a unit than it does B. This greater productivity may be due to more advanced technology, better management, more competent employees, and so on. Conversely it may be stated that an organization paying low hourly or weekly wages to its employees does not necessarily enjoy low labor costs.

Wage and Salary Administration

The term *wage and salary administration* has come to be accepted as the designation for that field of endeavor concerned with the establishment and implementation of sound policies and methods of employee compensation. It includes such areas as job evaluation, development and maintenance of wage structures, wage surveys, wage incentives, wage changes and adjustments, supplementary payments, profit sharing, control of compensation costs, and other related pay items.

The term *wage* is commonly used for those employees whose pay is calculated according to the number of hours worked. Thus the weekly paycheck will fluctuate as the number of hours actually worked varies. The word *salary* applies to compensation that is uniform from one pay period to the next and does not depend upon the number of hours worked. *Salaried* often implies a status distinction, because those on salary generally are white-collar, administrative, professional, and executive employees, whereas wage earners are designated as hourly or nonsupervisory, or blue-collar. Some of the distinctions between wage earners and salary earners have tended to disappear in recent years because wage earners in some organizations do receive full pay if they are absent for such reasons as sickness, whereas salaried employees, especially at the lower levels, often receive overtime pay when they work over the standard work week. In this book the word *wage* will be used as the general term and will include salary except where it is desired to highlight salary in its more specific context.

Haphazard Wage Administration

Although it is my intention in this book to emphasize the positive, something can be learned by examining incorrect practices of wage administration. Although all of the glaring errors referred to here may not occur in one organization, many of them do. The reason for these errors is that management often has been so engrossed in matters of production, sales, and finance that it has given scant attention to proper wage and salary management. In some organizations jobs of a low level of difficulty and responsibility are paid more than those having high job requirements. Personal wage rates are quite common, especially in smaller firms. In this case, wages are assigned to the personality without regard to the type of work he is performing. Nonsupervisory employees may be receiving higher pay than their own immediate supervisors. Allied with this wrong is the prevalent failure to maintain an adequate differential between first-level supervision and hourly paid wage earners. This problem is complicated by incentives and overtime pay for the hourly paid employees. In some marginal business firms and in many nonprofit organizations, employees are paid at or close to a minimum subsistence level. This means, in effect, that the employees are subsidizing their employer and permitting him to keep operating. Another weak practice followed in some organizations is that of promoting an employee to a position clearly having higher job requirements and then failing to grant a wage increase. The practice of paying women lower wages than men for performing work that is identical in all respects is defended by a few but condemned by most.

RATIONALE OF FINANCIAL COMPENSATION

To design, from scratch, a comprehensive program of financial compensation for an organization requires that the designer have a rationale—a set of goals and underlying principles about compensation and how it should work. In actual practice compensation programs in the majority of establishments have grown up over the years by additions, patches, and trial and error—but without any overall grand design. Nevertheless, whether programs have been consciously planned or whether they have grown by trial and error, we can take a detached view and analyze what on-going programs seem to be designed to accomplish.

There are four principal goals which compensation programs may seek to accomplish.

First they seek to serve a labor market function of allocating people among firms according to the perceived attractiveness of jobs as expressed by the rate of pay and associated pay supplements. Thus wage and salary levels are an adjunct to employee recruitment. Firms must be reasonably competitive in their rates to entice job applicants to the employment office door.

Second, carefully designed compensation programs—with job evaluation, pay scales, and employee classification procedures—enable management to control wages and salaries and control labor costs. Supervisors are not allowed to pay their people above the job rate. Many firms carefully control the distribution of rates within a given rate range. Tight controls may be placed upon the frequency and size of pay increases. A tight table of organization may be constructed for each department. Thus a particular department manager may be permitted to have only so many machinists first class, technicians second class, and so forth. He cannot pad his payroll or build an empire.

A third major objective of wage and salary programs is to keep employees content, to minimize quitting, and to reduce employee complaints and grievances due to inadequate or inequitable wage rates. It is hoped that a rational program of pay administration can satisfy employees that their pay is fair and that favoritism and discrimination have played no part in the allocation of money. If there is no union in the company, management may hope that when the employees are reasonably satisfied with their pay they will have little desire to invite a union in. Basically we are saying that management is using pay as a satisfier or as a hygienic factor. A satisfier (hygienic factor) must be distinguished from a motivator. A satisfier affects the feeling of well-being and contentment. If a satisfier such as pay is inadequate, employees may grouse, complain, quit, or agitate for a union. On the other hand, if the pay is perfectly proper and adequate, they may not be motivated to work any harder. A motivator, on the other hand, is something that induces one to consciously change his behavior.

A fourth and final goal of compensation is to induce and reward better performance. In other words, pay is looked upon as a motivator. It is a deeply cherished belief among American managers, generally, that increases in pay should be granted primarily on the basis of merit. Those who produce more should be paid more. Superior output and superior creativity must be rewarded. American business executives have asserted this loudly and often from Chamber of Commerce and National Association of Manufacturers platforms, via internal house organs for their employees, and to assembled union leaders. Executives have often railed against the leveling effect of union-imposed, seniority-dominated job and pay structures.

In brief then wage and salary programs can have four major purposes (1) to recruit people to the firm; (2) to control payroll costs; (3) to satisfy people, to reduce quitting, grievances, and frictions over pay; and (4) to motivate people to superior performance. The weight of evidence shows that goals 1, 2, and 3 are accomplished reasonably well in the better managed organizations but that goal 4—motivation—is very poorly accomplished.

Patton studied the actual distribution of pay rates of thousands of nonunion salaried employees in a conglomerate type corporation. He compared performance ratings with the positions of the people within their pay-grade ranges. He found that length of service and age were much stronger correlates of a man's pay than his proficiency rating. He found that people with extensive years of service almost invariably drifted into the top quarter of their rate ranges regardless of their efficiency rating.[1] Lawler found a similar result in his study of the compensation of managers in a variety of organizations. There was very little relationship between their pay and their rated job performance. Yet the top executives of these firms claimed that pay was administered as an incentive.[2] In one large national company Mason Haire found very little correlation between past performance (as measured by salary) and recent raises in pay for middle and top managers. He concluded that raises were almost randomly distributed.[3]

Piece-rate and other incentive schemes for factory workers are widely used and are supposed to induce superior output. Yet widespread restriction of output exists in American industry. This phenomenon will be dealt with more fully in Chapter 24, "Wage Incentives."

Can pay be used as a motivator? Yes it can. Frederick Taylor and his

[1] Thomas H. Patton, Jr., "Merit Increases and the Facts of Organizational Life," *Management of Personnel Quarterly,* Vol. 7, No. 2 (Summer 1968), pp. 30-38.

[2] Edward E. Lawler III, "The Mythology of Management Compensation," *California Management Review,* Vol. IX, No. 1 (Fall 1966), pp. 11-22.

[3] Mason Haire, "The Incentive Character of Pay," in Robert Andrews (ed.), *Managerial Compensation* (Ann Arbor, Mich.: Foundation for Research on Human Behavior, 1965), pp. 13-17.

followers who constructed the scientific management movement looked upon the worker pretty much as an "economic man." They viewed money motivation as paramount. Elton Mayo discovered the social and belongingness motives of man in the world of work. Recent behavioral scientists have emphasized the needs for power, achievement, and self-actualization. Some management practitioners and some of the interpreters of the behavioral writers have erroneously understood these human scientists to say that money is not and cannot be a motivator. This is not what they actually said.

They actually said that there are many bases for motivation: money, job security, emotional security, respect, social acceptance, power, achievement, and so on. They said that money was erroneously viewed as *the* prime mover in the past. They downgraded money as a motivator but did not eliminate it. At times nonfinancial incentives are most important to the individual. At other times economic incentives occupy the spotlight. For the young professional who is raising a family and who has just entered industry, the need for more money to pay off a home mortgage, for the material wants of his family, and later to educate his children, may be very pressing. Yet at other times in his life cycle the goals of recognition, status, and achievement may be most important to him.

Pay is important for providing the material necessities of life, yes. But it is also important for what it symbolizes. For some people money symbolizes security. For others it represents success. High pay may permit one to join the country club and the yacht club. If the boss grants one a sizeable pay increase, this may show the subordinate that the boss likes him and approves of his behavior.

Pay, especially earned and deserved pay increases, can satisfy higher order needs. Pay can be a motivator if geared to achievement.

In actual fact though, in industry, pay administrators and top management policy setters have given only lip service to the concept of pay as an incentive. The overwhelming emphasis, in practice, has been upon designing and operating wage and salary systems that would keep people satisfied and insure continued membership in the organization. And both workers and managers alike have observed this to be true, too often. The clerical employee who works her heart out soon finds that she gets an increase of 5 dollars per week, whereas her co-worker who slacks off much of the time gets a 4-dollar increase. The extra dollar wasn't worth the effort. The same is true for exempt personnel. The engineer who created three patentable designs over the past year is rewarded with a 700-dollar increase, whereas the plodders and the followers receive 500 dollars. The union wins a 6 per cent across-the-board increase for the production workers. To insure equity for the nonunion salaried personnel, management budgets 6 per cent that is to be distributed selectively on the basis of merit. But when all the raises have been granted, employees get to comparing paychecks. They soon conclude that, although individual differences exist, the major thrust has been an across-the-board increase. Rigidly drawn salary structures, narrow pay ranges and close limits on the frequency and amount of pay increases all serve to reinforce the control and the equitability functions of a pay system. This also dampens any motivational impact of pay. The goal of equity to keep people satisfied is overriding and perhaps with considerable justification. Many times the contribution of individuals cannot readily be identified as in team activities or in process-paced work. The appraisal of human performance is highly subjective. Management may not always be able to justify significantly different pay to employees assigned to similar duties. General economic conditions, supply and demand for labor, changes in competitive rates and in the cost of living—these all may necessitate a general across-the-board pay increase. There may then be very little left over in the budget for selective motivational increases in pay for deserving individuals.

Although specific research evidence is lacking on just how pay can be allocated so that it has the greatest motivational impact, it is probable that the size of a man's increase must be large in proportion to his base pay; that the increase must be determined by an appraisal plan perceived to be fair by all concerned; that the increase be in some reasonable relationship to the value of the man's contribution, both in size and timing; and finally that the entire pay-for-performance plan have the full approval of management and the groups of employees involved.

PRINCIPAL COMPENSATION ISSUES

Discussion of the multitude of topics and problems of wage and salary administration can be most conveniently organized around seven distinct but related issues. These are as follows:

1. Pay levels. This refers to whether the entire structure is high, average, or low. It is determined by competitive rates in the labor market and industry, financial strength of the company, management policies and other factors.
2. Internal pay structure. This concerns the hierarchy of pay rates, pay grades, and job classifications. Normally job evaluation constitutes the heart of this process.
3. Individual pay assignment. This involves classifying people into job titles and pay grades. It also means determining how much money each person is entitled to if the pay grades comprise a range of pay for each grade. Performance appraisal, a topic covered in Chapter 11, is intimately tied to the process of individual pay assignment in those organizations that relate pay to performance.
4. Pay by time or by output. Most people are paid by the hour, week, or

month according to elapsed time on the job. However some people are on piecework and are paid according to units of output. This topic is covered in Chapter 24, "Wage Incentives."

5. Special problems of Salesmen, Managers, and Professionals. This topic is covered in Chapter 26, "Compensation for Salesmen, Managers and Professionals."

6. Fringe Benefits and Pay Supplements. Such items as insurance, pensions, paid vacations, bonuses, profit sharing and the like are properly considered part of total employee compensation. They are a part of the company's labor costs, and they constitute part of the attractiveness of a job. These topics are covered in Chapter 25, "Incentives Based Upon Cooperation," and Chapter 28, "Benefits and Services."

7. Control of Wages and Salaries. Wage and salary administrators have devised a variety of techniques for regulating payroll costs. A table of organization may dictate just which job classifications are permitted in each operating department of the business. Job classifications may be audited annually to insure that the job descriptions and pay grades accurately reflect the current level of work performed. Incentive earnings may be reviewed to detect loose incentive rates. Pay increases may be carefully budgeted or limited.[4]

WAGE CRITERIA

The determination of the wages for jobs and people has reached the stage where it can be very logical, consistent, systematic, and explainable, but it is not an exact science and never will be. For one reason the give and take in the labor market and the forces of supply and demand prevent this.

Let us now examine those factors that help establish wages in individual organizations. These factors do not operate alone but usually work together in determining wage rates, levels, and wage increments.

Prevailing Wages

Most firms decide whether their wages are right or not by ascertaining what other firms are paying for the same class of work in the same labor market or sometimes in the same industry regardless of where located. Although the firm can attract labor by paying somewhat less, in the long run it has to come reasonably close to its competition in order to obtain labor in sufficient quantity and of proper quality. The familiar economic price determinant of *supply and demand* is really intimate-

---

[4] A complete explanation of control of wages and salaries is outside the scope of this book. The interested reader can consult David W. Belcher, *Wage and Salary Administration* (Englewood Cliffs, N.J.: Prentice-Hall, Inc., 1962), Ch. 20.

ly related to the prevailing wage concept. If the supply of a particular labor skill, say that of a machinist, becomes scarce, the buyers bid up the price in the labor market, and the prevailing wage rises. Likewise the reverse can happen. If an organization finds that it is unable to attract and retain the labor it desires, it may be that its wage level is too low.

Ability to Pay

The ability of the employer to pay affects the general level of wages in an organization relative to the prevailing level in the labor market or industry. It does not establish rates for individual jobs or people, as such. Within the same industry, firms that are enjoying good sales and profit pictures over the long run tend to pay higher wages than do those which are having difficulty making ends meet. Marginal type firms usually pay wages lower than the average for their labor market or industry. This factor is one of the major reasons why nonprofit hospitals and educational institutions pay relatively low wages.

Cost of Living

By the mid-1960's an estimated two million employees were working under union-employer agreements in which wages were adjusted automatically up or down in conformance with changes in the Consumer Price Index prepared by the Bureau of Labor Statistics of the United States Department of Labor. Such union contract provisions are commonly called escalator clauses. Used in this way, the purchasing power of employees' wages is maintained approximately constant, regardless of changes in the general cost of living for the country as a whole. Where there is no automatic formula for adjusting wages according to the cost of living, individual employees, unions, and employers nevertheless do give consideration to these changes and use the fact that prices are rising or falling to bolster their positions in wage discussions and bargaining.

Related to the cost of living is the concept of a "living wage." How much money does it cost a wage earner and his family to live per year at an adequate level of living? In an extensive research program, the United States Department of Labor studied what it would cost a city worker, his wife, and two children to live per year at a moderate living standard in the Autumn of 1966. This moderate standard of living was designed to satisfy prevailing standards of what is necessary for health, efficiency, the nurture of children, and for participation in community activities. It is neither a minimum subsistence budget nor a luxury budget. This average cost for this hypothetical family of four living in urban areas in the United States in 1966 was $9,191 per year. This figure includes costs for food, housing, clothing, transportation, personal care, medical care, recreation, insurance, and taxes. It varies somewhat from city to city. For example the cost was $10,141 in Boston, $10,195 in New York and North-eastern New Jersey, and only $8,028 in Austin, Texas.[5]

Generally employers do not favor using the concept of a living wage as a guide to wage determination, because they prefer to base wages upon employee contribution rather than need. Also they feel that the level of living prescribed in worker-budget studies is open to argument and is somewhat a matter of opinion.

Productivity

The key to the high standard of living that we in the United States enjoy in comparison with many other peoples of the world is our high level of productivity measured in terms of goods and services per man-hour of labor. Estimates for the economy as a whole and for particular industries are made by the United States Departments of Labor and Commerce. Quite accurate calculations can be made for individual companies. Economists have ascertained that productivity in the United States over the past several decades has increased on the average of 2.3 to 2.4 per cent per year.[6] This is an average, for in some individual years it may not increase at all, whereas in others it may leap ahead at a rate of 3 per cent or 4 per cent or more. For convenience productivity is measured in terms of output per man-hour. This does not mean that labor is the primary cause for the gain. Technological improvements, better organization and management, the development of better methods of production by labor and management, greater ingenuity and skill by labor, and other factors are responsible for this gain. The gain from this increased productivity can be passed on to labor in the form of higher wages, to the stockholders in the form of higher dividends, to the organization itself in the form of retained earnings, or to the customer in the form of higher quality and lower prices. Insofar as wage determination is concerned, higher productivity makes it possible for higher wage levels to prevail. A manufacturing concern run entirely by human labor with no mechanization whatsoever would not be able to pay as good wages as one that was highly mechanized with all the latest refinements. This assumes, of course, that the productivity of the machinery is greater than that of the human labor alone.

Productivity can be looked at in another way also. When operating under a wage-incentive system in a plant, greater productivity by individual employees is recognized in the form of higher wages. Increased skill and effort causes higher productivity, which results in higher earnings.

[5] Bureau of Labor Statistics, *City Worker's Family Budget for a Moderate Living Standard,* Bulletin No. 1570-1 (Washington, D.C.: United States Department of Labor, Autumn 1966).

[6] Bureau of Labor Statistics, *Trends in Output per Man-hour in the Private Economy,* 1909-1958, Bulletin No. 1249 (Washington, D.C.: United States Department of Labor, December 1959).

Bargaining Power

When employees organize a union for purposes of collective bargaining with their employer, they often are able to obtain larger wage concessions than they would as unorganized individuals. The economic benefits to be gained by a strong organization are certainly attested to by the results achieved by many of the large and powerful labor unions in this country. Although a good argument can be made that forcing wages up faster than increases in productivity causes unemployment (as many believe has occurred in the coal industry) or higher prices and inflation, nevertheless, for those remaining on the payrolls a real gain is often achieved as a consequence of stronger bargaining power. Although the problem of comparing union and nonunion wage levels is a complicated one, occupational wage data compiled by the Bureau of Labor Statistics in 1946 and 1947 for 902 occupations in union and nonunion establishments revealed that in about 87 per cent of these occupations average rates in union establishments exceeded those in nonunion organizations.[7]

Job Requirements

For ascertaining the relative value of one job to another within an organization, measures of job difficulty are frequently used. This is the basis for the many job-evaluation plans in use in industry. Jobs are graded according to the relative amounts of skill, effort, responsibility, and job conditions required. The subject of job evaluation will be examined in detail later in this chapter.

Observations Concerning These Criteria

These factors which determine wages do not operate in an isolated, distinct manner. Rather several criteria usually interact at the same time to influence wage determination. For example, ability to pay and productivity are very closely related. In manufacturing, one company may have greater profits and lower costs because it has developed and invested in labor-saving machinery that has increased its productivity. Job requirements are listed as a wage criterion. One element of this is skill. High-skilled jobs pay more than low-skilled ones within the same company. But probably the reason more money is assigned to a high-skilled job is that there are fewer people available to fill such jobs (supply and demand).

[7] Bureau of Labor Statistics, Wage Structure, Series 2, Bulletin Nos. 27, 31, 32, 35-38, 40-44, 46-52, 55, 57, 59-64, (Washington, D.C.: United States Department of Labor, 1947-1950), and W.S. Woytinsky, *Employment and Wages in the United States* (New York: Twentieth Century Fund, 1953).

WAGE POLICY AND PRINCIPLES

The wage policies of different firms vary somewhat. Marginal companies pay the minimum necessary to attract the required amount and type of labor. Often these companies pay only the minimum wage rates required by Federal or state law. With these rates they tend to be able to recruit only marginal labor.

At the other extreme some organizations pay well above the going rates in the labor market. They adopt such a policy because they seek to attract and retain the highest caliber labor force obtainable. By paying high rates, management is able to demand superior performance from its employees. Some managers believe in the economy of high wages. They feel that by paying good wages they can attract superior workers who will produce more than the average worker in industry. This greater production per employee, in effect, means greater output per man-hour. Hence labor costs may turn out to be lower than those existing in firms hiring only marginal quality labor.

Some companies also pay high wage rates because of a combination of favorable product market demand, superior ability to pay, and bargaining power from a strong union. This situation characterized the basic steel industry during the 1940's and 1950's.

We have been talking about the extremes to this point. It is fair to say that the vast majority of companies seek to be competitive in their wage program. That is to say, they aim to pay somewhere near the going rate in the labor market for the various classes of labor they employ. Realistically they expect to employ a reasonably good quality of labor and to pay people fairly, with respect to one another, so that the employees feel they are paid properly. They do not want wage inequities to be a source of employee discontent. Thus most firms give major weight to two wage criteria: job requirements and prevailing rates of pay in the labor market. Other factors, such as changes in the cost of living, supply and demand, ability to pay, and productivity are accorded subsidiary status, although special circumstances (for example, the firm has been losing money for several years) may force one of these factors to the fore in the short run.

A generally sound policy is to adopt a job evaluation program in order to establish fair differentials in pay based upon differences in job content. Employees are in a reasonably good position to judge whether their jobs are paid correctly in relation to other jobs in the plant. Job evaluation insures internal consistency of wage rates within the plant. External consistency—that is, reasonable equality with going rates paid by other companies in the community—can be achieved when a firm periodically surveys community rates and adjusts its general level of wages as required.

Principles of Wage and Salary Administration

The field of wage administration has been sufficiently well developed so that certain generally accepted guidelines and principles can be formulated.

1. There should be a definite plan in which differences in pay for jobs are based upon variation in job requirements, such as skill, effort, responsibility, and job conditions.
2. The general level of wages and salaries should be reasonably in line with that prevailing in the labor market. In some instances equality with pay levels in the industry is used instead of the labor market. The labor market criterion is most commonly used.
3. The plan should carefully distinguish between jobs and employees. A job carries a certain wage rate, and a person is assigned to fill it at that rate. Exceptions sometimes occur in very high-level jobs in which the job holder may make the job large or small, depending upon his abilities and contributions.
4. Equal pay for equal work. If two jobs have equal job difficulty requirements, the pay should be the same regardless of who fills them. This principle does not prevent having a rate range with individuals receiving different compensation within the range.
5. An equitable means should be adopted for recognizing individual differences in ability and contribution. For some concerns this may take the form of rate ranges with in-grade increases; in others it may be a wage incentive plan; and in still others it may take the form of closely integrated sequences of job promotion.
6. There should be a clearly established procedure for hearing and adjusting wage complaints. This may be integrated with the regular grievance procedure, if one exists.
7. The employees, and the union if there is one, should be adequately informed about the procedures used to establish wage rates. Every employee should be informed of his own position in the wage or salary structure. Secrecy in wage matters should not be used as a cover-up for a haphazard and unreasonable wage program.

ORGANIZATION FOR WAGE AND SALARY ADMINISTRATION

Although in very small organizations the owner or manager will handle all the problems in this area, larger concerns need the specialized knowledge of staff personnel. In an organization of, say, 200 to 300 employees, the personnel manager might very well handle all of the wage administration duties himself. Large concerns require the full-time services of one or more staff persons for this work. Usually the manager of wage and salary administration (the titles of director and supervisor are also in common usage) reports to the director of industrial relations. This manager may have one or more job analysts reporting to him, depending, of course, upon the work load.

Some firms look upon this field of endeavor more as engineering than personnel work; consequently they locate the function somewhere in the engineering department. They believe that greater accuracy and objectivity can be obtained by utilizing an engineering approach to the problem.

In terms of functions, the wage and salary administrator formulates and recommends compensation policies and procedures, develops and operates the job evaluation program, establishes and maintains wage and salary structures, conducts wage and salary surveys, insures compliance of wage policies and practices with federal and state laws, and may participate in the administration of a wage incentive program and the employee appraisal program.

Role of Operating Management

Operating supervisors and executives play a key part in wage administration. This is as true for a manager of engineering or a director of research as it is for a production supervisor. Let us use a production supervisor as an example. He is closely involved in providing information for job analysis. Job descriptions and specifications should be submitted to him for approval as to accuracy and completeness. His decisions are instrumental in classifying employees under his supervision into the various job titles that have been assigned to his department. He must explain the wage administration system to his subordinates and inform them of their job titles, classifications, and rate range. He appraises his subordinates and makes recommendations for wage increases within the framework of policies and procedures prevailing in his organization. In many companies it is the responsibility of the supervisor to notify the wage and salary unit of changes in job content as they occur. Complaints and grievances regarding possible wage inequities must be initially handled by him.

JOB EVALUATION

Job evaluation is a formalized system for determining the relative money value of jobs within an organization. It involves the analysis of jobs for the purpose of writing job descriptions and specifications, rating of these jobs through use of a job evaluation plan, and conversion of relative job values to definite wage rates.

Historically early attempts at job analysis and job evaluation were begun for the Civil Service Commission of Chicago in 1909 and shortly thereafter at the Commonwealth Edison Company in Chicago. A prototype of the modern systems of job evaluation was developed in 1924 by Merrill R. Lott, who created the first real point system for use by the Sperry Gyroscope Company. In 1926 Eugene Benge and Associates developed the factor-comparison method for the Philadelphia Rapid Transit Company.[8]

The adoption of job evaluation programs by industrial concerns spread in the late 1930's and became very widespread by the late 1940's. Factors inducing companies to adopt wage rationalization programs were the rise of industrial unions in the 1930's, decisions of the National War Labor Board during World War II, and internal recognition by management of the need for orderly, logical means for establishing wage rates. Management has learned that it must have some means for explaining how it has arrived at wage-rate decisions when it is negotiating with unions.

Figure 23-1 explains in chart form the various elements of job evaluation and their interrelationship.

Certain basic principles must be followed when evaluating jobs. First it must be noted that those who are doing the evaluation must rate the

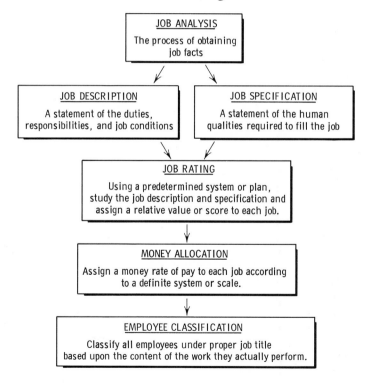

Figure 23-1.   The Elements of Job Evaluation.

[8] E. Lanham, *Job Evaluation* (McGraw-Hill Book Company, Inc., 1955), pp. 6-8.

job, not the employee. In deciding how much money a particular job is worth, there is always a temptation to be influenced in one's judgment by the qualifications and caliber of the individual who is presently performing the work. But he may be either over- or underqualified. It is the assignment of those doing the rating to be guided by the requirements of the job. It may be that an error has been made in placing individuals on particular jobs, but this is a responsibility of supervision and the personnel department.

A second guide to keep in mind is that wherever possible, the pooled or combined judgments of several persons should be employed in evaluating jobs. Job evaluation is a systematic, orderly, logical way of setting rates of pay within an organization or company; however, it is not exact measurement, it is grading or rating. The decisions of a number of qualified persons will reduce the likelihood of serious errors.

A third factor to bear in mind is that the accuracy of job rating is determined primarily by the accuracy of the basic job facts available. A comprehensive program of job analysis must serve as a basis for any job evaluation program.

JOB EVALUATION SYSTEMS

There exist in current usage four main types of job evaluation methods or systems. These are as follows:

Nonquantitative systems
  1. Ranking or job comparison
  2. Grade description
Quantitative systems
  1. Point
  2. Factor comparison

Although it is true that various practitioners and management consultants have from time to time developed modifications of one or a combination of two or more systems, the basic ways of evaluating jobs can be fully analyzed and understood by concentrating our attention on these fundamental types.

Ranking System

The ranking or rank-order system is suitable for small companies having a limited number of jobs. Although theoretically the method could be used for large organizations as well, it then becomes much too cumbersome for attaining a reasonable degree of accuracy. As for all four systems, accurate and complete job-analysis data is fundamental to the success of the ranking method. The procedure involves obtaining descriptions for all of the jobs under consideration and ranking these from low to high job requirements. If the organization is small, with only two or three departments involved, management can satisfactorily dovetail the jobs from the departments to come up with a master list, as illustrated below:

High Job	12. Electrician		6. Drill-Press Operator
Require-	11. Toolmaker		5. Punch-Press Operator
ments	10. Machinist		4. Spray Painter
	9. Millwright	*Low Job*	3. Materials Handling Man
	8. Fitter	*Require-*	2. Laborer
	7. Assembler	*ments*	1. Floor Sweeper

Presumably the jobs will already have wage rates attached to them; the ranking system is being used to judge whether these are equitable. By arranging the jobs in an array such as this and with a committee of competent management personnel, necessary adjustments can be made in wage rates to correct any apparent discrepancies.

However, the ranking method has serious disadvantages that limit its usefulness. Judgments are frequently strongly influenced by present wage rates. The ranking process does not tell one how far apart the jobs are in job difficulty and content. The procedure is very cumbersome when jobs from a larger number of departments must be dovetailed together. The procedure likewise does not provide any means for recording on paper the substantiations for the ratings. Its principal virtue is that it is easy to apply to organizations having no more than, say, fifteen to twenty jobs.

Grade Description System

The grade description system, also called the classification system, is the one used for classifying jobs in the United States Civil Service. Essentially it involves dividing up the job hierarchy into a number of pay groups or grades, developing written definitions for each grade, and then assigning every job to a particular grade.

In order to construct a grade description scale, the basic information must come from descriptions of all the jobs involved. As in much job evaluation work it is best to use a committee to take advantage of pooled judgment in arriving at decisions. The committee must actually set up a rank-order list of a large representative sample of all the jobs in the organization, giving consideration to duties, skills, abilities, responsibilities, and other differentiating qualities. These jobs are then grouped into classes or grades that represent different pay levels ranging from low to high. By analyzing the job descriptions for those jobs slotted into each grade, common types of tasks, skills, knowledge, responsibilities, and job conditions can be identified and written in somewhat general language, so that these statements then become grade descriptions. When these have been developed for all grades they can then be used as a standard for assigning all other jobs to a particular pay grade.

Below are printed the first three grade descriptions for what is called the General Schedule (GS) covering professional, scientific, clerical, and administrative positions of the United States Government as defined in the Classification Act of 1949.

General Schedule

> Grade GS-1 includes all classes of positions the duties of which are to perform, under immediate supervision, with little or no latitude for the exercise of independent judgment, (1) the simplest routine work in office, business, or fiscal operations, or (2) elementary work of a subordinate technical character in a professional, scientific, or technical field.

> Grade GS-2 includes all classes of positions the duties of which are (1) to perform, under immediate supervision, with limited latitude for the exercise of independent judgment, routine work in office, business, or fiscal operations, or comparable subordinate technical work of limited scope in a professional, scientific, or technical field, requiring some training or experience, or (2) to perform other work of equal importance, difficulty, and responsibility, and requiring comparable qualifications.

> Grade GS-3 includes all classes of positions the duties of which are (1) to perform, under immediate or general supervision, somewhat difficult and responsible work in office, business or fiscal operations, or comparable subordinate technical work of limited scope in a professional, scientific, or technical field, requiring in either case (a) some training or experience, (b) working knowledge of a special subject matter, or (c) to some extent the exercise of independent judgment in accordance with well-established policies, procedures, and techniques; or (2) to perform other work of equal importance, difficulty, and responsibility, and requiring comparable qualifications.

The assignment of a wage rate for each grade can be accomplished by taking an average of the existing rates for all the jobs in each grade or by following a procedure similar to that of the point system, which will be described later in this chapter.

In assessing the merits of the grade description system, we can see that it is a definite improvement over the ranking method, because here we have a fixed written scale against which to compare all jobs. The process of rating jobs in the grade description system involves a job-to-scale comparison. Because jobs often change in content over a period of time, one can readily see that the use of a scale is more durable and standardized. Also jobs are grouped into pay grades for administrative simplicity. A serious fault of the classification plan is that the grade description must of necessity be rather general and abstract in order to be applicable to a great variety of jobs. Also, like the ranking method it provides no way of weighting the compensable factors that make up jobs. How does one determine the worth of one job having high-skill requirements and low-job hazards in comparison with one having high hazards and low skill?

Point System

The point system is, by a wide margin, the most commonly used method of job evaluation in the United States. It is more complicated than either of the preceding two that have been described. If a company chooses to adopt the point system, it can either select a universal type of plan, such as that developed by A. L. Kress for the National Electrical Manufacturers Association, or it can tailor-make a plan to suit its own particular needs. If the decision favors a custom-designed plan, the company can either have personnel from within its own organization do the work (commonly this would be either the personnel department or the industrial engineering department), or it can engage an outside management consultant to plan and direct the installation. Initial discussion here will explain how to rate jobs by using a point plan which has already been established in an organization. After this some important considerations involved in constructing a point plan will be given.

Every point plan consists of a number of compensable job factors or characteristics. These can be classified under the four headings of skill, effort, responsibility, and job conditions. Examples of factors or job attributes that are frequently used are listed below.

FACTOR CATEGORIES

	Skill	Effort	Responsibility	Job Conditions
Factors	Education	Physical	For preventing	Working
	Experience	demand	monetary loss	conditions
	Training	Visual effort	For direction	Hazards
	Judgment	Concentration	of others	
	Analysis	Mental effort	For machines	
	Mental	Muscular	For materials	
	complexity	coordination	For safety	
	Manual	Alertness	of others	
	dexterity		For policy	
	Adaptability			

Of course, no single plan utilizes all these factors. Eight to twelve factors are common. Each factor is subdivided into degrees that define the relative amount of that factor that may be required for each of a series of jobs. Thus experience, which is almost universally employed as a fac-

FACTORS			DEGREES			
	1	2	3	4	5	6
Skill						
1. Knowledge	7	17	30	47	70	100
2. Training and Experience			(See Chart Below)			
3. Complexity of Duties	9	20	36	56	84	120
4. Contacts with Others	7	17	30	47	70	100
Responsibility						
5. Responsibility for Trust Imposed	6	14	26	40	60	---
6. Monetary Responsibility	9	20	36	56	84	120
7. Performance	4	10	18	28	42	60
Effort						
8. Mental or Visual	4	8	15	24	35	---
9. Physical	0	4	9	16	25	---
Job Conditions						
10. Working Conditions	0	6	14	25	40	---
GROUP LEADERSHIP						
11. Responsibility for the Work of Others 14						

****

CHART FOR TRAINING AND EXPERIENCE

1.	Up to and including 3 months	9
2.	Over 3 months, up to and including 6 months	19
3.	Over 6 months, up to and including 9 months	28
4.	Over 9 months, up to and including 12 months	35
5.	Over 1 year, up to and including 2 years	62
6.	Over 2 years, up to and including 3 years	82
7.	Over 3 years, up to and including 4 years	97
8.	Over 4 years, up to and including 5 years	108
9.	Over 5 years, up to and including 7 years	123
10.	Over 7 years, up to and including 10 years	134
11.	Over 10 years	140

1. KNOWLEDGE

Education is the basic prerequisite knowledge that is essential to satisfactorily perform the job. This knowledge may have been acquired through formal schooling such as grammar school, high school, college, university, night school, correspondence courses, company education program, or through equivalent experience in allied fields. Analyze the requirements of the job and not the formal education of individuals performing it.

Figure 23-2. The Point Plan of Job Evaluation for Nonexempt Salaried Positions of the Allis-Chalmers Manufacturing Company. The names of all rating factors and points assigned to every degree are shown above. This and the following pages show the definitions of the factors and degrees for the first four factors only. Reprinted by permission.

POINTS

1st Degree

    Requires ability to read, write, and follow simple written or oral in-
structions, use simple arithmetic involving counting, adding, subtracting,   7
multiplying and dividing whole numbers, etc.

2nd Degree

    Requires ability to perform work requiring advanced arithmetic involving
adding, subtracting, dividing, and multiplying of decimals and fractions;
maintain or prepare routine correspondence, records, and reports. May   17
require knowledge of typing or elementary knowledge of shorthand, bookkeeping, etc.

3rd Degree

    Requires specialized knowledge in a particular field such as advanced
stenographic, secretarial or business training, elementary accounting
or general knowledge of shop practice and manufacturing methods,   30
blueprint reading, shop specifications, basic principles of production
control, welding, chemistry, electricity, etc.

4th Degree

    Requires ability to understand and perform work requiring general
engineering principles, commercial theory, principles of advanced
drafting; knowledge and application of general accounting fundamentals.
Originate and compile statistics and interpretive reports; prepare   47
correspondence of a difficult or technical nature. Requires a broad
knowledge of complicated shop procedures and processes, purchasing,
accounting, general sales work, foreign trade, labor laws, time study,
etc.

5th Degree

    Requires ability to understand and perform work of a specialized or
technical nature. Examples are work involving use of all type of
drawings or specifications in which application requires theory or
analysis of design or principles involved; use advanced formulas for
determining relationships; apply highly specialized technical theory   70
in determining causes of and correcting design or operating
difficulties; knowledge of theory and practices in accounting and
finance, business administration, chemistry, physics, journalism, and
related technical or specialized fields.

6th Degree

    Requires knowledge in a highly advanced and specialized field in order   100
to understand and perform work requiring creative endeavor.

2. TRAINING AND EXPERIENCE

Experience is the length of time usually required by an individual with the specified
knowledge to acquire the skill necessary to satisfactorily perform the duties of the job.
Where previous experience is necessary, time spent in related work or in lesser
positions, either within the company or with other organizations, shall be considered
as contributing to the total experience required to effectively perform the job. This
consideration will be based on continuous progress by an individual and will not include time spent on jobs due to lack of promotional opportunities.

Figure 23-2. (Cont'd)

		POINTS
1.	Up to and including 3 months	9
2.	Over 3 months, up to and including 6 months	19
3.	Over 6 months, up to and including 9 months	28
4.	Over 9 months, up to and including 12 months	35
5.	Over 1 year, up to and including 2 years	62
6.	Over 2 years, up to and including 3 years	82
7.	Over 3 years, up to and including 4 years	97
8.	Over 4 years, up to and including 5 years	108
9.	Over 5 years, up to and including 7 years	123
10.	Over 7 years, up to and including 10 years	134
11.	Over 10 years	140

3. COMPLEXITY OF DUTIES

This factor appraises the complexity of job duties, such as the amount of judgment required in the making of decisions; analyzing problems and situations; planning of procedures and determining methods of action; and the extent to which initiative and ingenuity is required to successfully complete the job.

POINTS

1st Degree

   Work is routine consisting of simple repetitive operations, such as filing, sorting, duplicating, copy typing, etc., performed under immediate supervision or where little choice exists as to method of performance.   9

2nd Degree

   Perform work from detailed instructions or where variation in procedures are limited. Work is semirepetitive requiring minor decisions and some judgment in analysis of data or situations from which an answer can readily be obtained.   20

3rd Degree

   Perform work where procedures are of a varied or diversified nature within a well-defined field under direct supervision. Requires initiative and independent judgment to analyze data or situations and determine solutions to problems within the limits of standard practice.   36

4th Degree

   Plan and perform complex work where only general policies or procedures are available in an established field requiring their application to cases not previously covered. Job duties involve working independently toward general results, devising new methods, and modifying or adapting standard procedures to meet new conditions. Requires analytical ability, initiative, and exercise of judgment to obtain solutions to problems and make decisions based on precedent and company policy.   56

Figure 23-2.   (Cont'd)

POINTS

5th Degree

   Plan and perform highly complex or technical work where no procedures
or standard methods are available. Duties require a high degree of
originality, initiative, and independent action to deal with complex factors   84
difficult to evaluate or the making of decisions based on conclusions for
which there is little precedent.

6th Degree

   Final analysis and judgment in planning and co-ordinating the work of a
large group or department. Requires initiative and aggressiveness;   120
original and creative planning and formulation of policy.

4. CONTACTS WITH OTHERS

Contacts with others is the extent to which the job requires co-operation and tact in
meeting, dealing with, or influencing people, whether by telephone, correspondence, or
personal contact. Consider the frequency and importance of contacts, the tact required
to maintain harmony and efficiency within the company and good will of the general
public.

POINTS

1st Degree

   Contacts usually limited to persons in the same section or department.   7

2nd Degree

   Contacts with persons outside the department or occasionally outside the
company, furnishing or obtaining routine information only.   17

3rd Degree

   Regular contacts with other departments or other companies, furnishing
or obtaining information or reports, under conditions requiring the use   30
of tact to obtain co-operation and maintain good will.

4th Degree

   Contacts with other departments or other companies, involving carrying
out company policy and programs and the influencing of others, where
improper handling will affect operating results; or involving dealing with   47
persons of substantially higher rank on matters requiring explanation,
discussion, and obtaining approvals.

5th Degree

   Contacts inside or outside the company requiring a high degree of
tact, judgment, and the ability to deal with and influence persons   70
in all types of positions.

6th Degree

   Contacts with persons inside or outside the company on matters of
company policy, difficult adjustments, or the settling of controversial
matters, where adverse conditions make it essential that the highest   100
caliber of diplomacy and tact be used to obtain favorable decisions
or maintain good will.

Figure 23-2. (Cont'd)

tor, might be subdivided into five degrees: first degree, zero up to three months; second degree, three up to six months; third degree, six up to twelve months; fourth degree, one year up to three years; and fifth degree, three years and over. A scale of points is assigned to the degrees of each factor. Every point rating plan consists of factors with definitions for these factors, and each factor is broken down into degrees with written definitions for every degree. Figure 23-2 shows part of the point plan of the Allis-Chalmers Manufacturing Company. In rating a job, the proper degree for every factor is selected, and the corresponding points are tabulated to obtain a total score.

This point sum corresponds to a particular wage or salary grade level, which in turn signifies a particular wage.

The process of developing a new point plan is rather involved. Initially a significant sample of the jobs for which the plan is to be used must be analyzed and job descriptions and specifications prepared. Usually one plan is designed for hourly paid production or shop type jobs, another for clerical jobs, and a third for professional, technical, and managerial jobs. Those developing the plan must decide what job attributes or factors the employer wants to pay for (that is, what factors are significant for the type of jobs under consideration). Then these factors must be rather precisely defined. Each factor is then divided into a number of degrees, degree definitions are developed, and then the factors must be given a weighting. For example, experience is generally weighted much heavier than physical effort. After the weightings have been arrived at, point progressions must be given to the degrees for each factor. Although judgment plays a part in setting up the point scales, certain statistical techniques (notably linear correlation and multiple correlation methods) are often employed in addition. The method used to convert points to money will be discussed later in this chapter under the heading "Establishing the Pay Structure."

The strengths of the point system are numerous. First of all, it breaks jobs down into factors or attributes, and this is certainly an aid to evaluation. The factors are fixed and preweighted in such a way that all those doing the rating are forced to consider each job on the same factors and in the same way. The margin for differences of opinion, which is quite great in both the ranking and grade description methods, is considerably narrowed. The likelihood of continuing or pyramiding errors over a period of time is minimized, because new jobs are rated against a fixed scale rather than against other jobs. The job-rating substantiation sheets, which are customarily used, provide a means for permanently recording the reasons for each rating. (Figure 7-5, on page 201, shows a job rating and substantiation sheet for the job of a secretary.) Also points permit a ready and logical conversion to money. The principal disadvantage of the system is its greater cost of development and installation as compared with ranking and grade description. However, the greater accuracy possible with its use usually justifies the larger expenditure of time and effort.

Factor Comparison System

Being the second most popular system after the point method, the factor comparison method is often used for evaluating white-collar, professional, and managerial positions, although it is equally suitable for grading others as well. It is essentially a combination of the ranking and point systems. Like the rank-order method it rates jobs by comparing one with another; like the point system it is more analytical in the sense of subdividing jobs into compensable factors, and final ratings are expressed in terms of numbers. Actually ratings give us money directly.

In examining this method, we will first see how to rate jobs in an existing installation—that is, after the plan has been established. Figure 23-3 shows a job comparison scale or ladder diagram containing key jobs. This together with the job descriptions and specifications for these jobs constitutes the tools necessary for rating. Key jobs serve as standards against which all other jobs are compared. A key job is defined as one whose content has become stabilized over time; whose wage rate management officials agree is presently correct (if a union is involved, it too must agree as to the correctness of the rate); and which is important to the organ-

CENTS PER HOUR PER FACTOR	MENTAL REQUIREMENTS	SKILL REQUIREMENTS	PHYSICAL REQUIREMENTS	RESPONSIBILITY	WORKING CONDITIONS
90	Electronic Tech. Tool Maker	Tool Maker Machinist			
85	Electrician			Inspector Electronic Tech.	
80	Machinist	Electronic Tech.		Tool Maker	
75	Inspector	Electrician		Electrician	
70					
65		Engine Lathe Oper.	Laborer	Machinist	
60		Turret Lathe Oper.	Assembler Fork Lift Oper.	Engine Lathe Oper.	Laborer Fork Lift Oper. Floor Sweeper
55	Engine Lathe Oper.		Turret Lathe Oper. Electrician		Assembler
50		Inspector	Machinist Floor Sweeper	Fork Lift Oper.	Machinist
45	Turret Lathe Oper.			Turret Lathe Oper.	Turret Lathe Oper. Tool Maker
40	Assembler Fork Lift Oper.		Tool Maker Engine Lathe Oper.	Assembler	Engine Lathe Oper. Electrician Inspector
35		Assembler Fork Lift Oper.			
30			Inspector		Electronic Tech.
25			Electronic Tech.		
20	Laborer Floor Sweeper	Laborer Floor Sweeper		Laborer Floor Sweeper	
15					

Figure 23-3.   An Illustration of a Job Comparison Scale for Shop Type Jobs—Factor Comparison Methods.

ization. A job is important if a large number of persons are performing it or if it represents a significant skill in the company. Many may wonder how we can know whether the present wage rates for key jobs are correct. Information to help guide these decisions can be obtained by making job-to-job comparisons and by conducting an area wage survey.

The factor comparison method customarily has about five compensable factors on which all jobs are rated. This is considerably fewer than the point system, but is nevertheless sufficient, because they are each defined more broadly. It is not absolutely necessary that the particular ones given in Figure 23-3 be the only ones that are used, nor need they be confined to five in number. The ones listed in this example are generally employed in this method, however.

In rating a new job, it is necessary that it be compared with all the other key jobs, one factor at a time. It is then assigned a money value in cents per hour for each factor according to the point on the scale at which this job best fits. This process is repeated for all of the other factors. The total money value obtained by adding the selected amount for each one individually is the wage rate for the job being evaluated. Essentially, then, the process of rating involves comparing the job description and specification for each job to be rated with all of the descriptions for the key jobs, working one factor at a time.

One may properly ask where this job comparison scale comes from, so we shall now turn our attention to the problem of constructing a particular factor comparison plan. Because it requires the use of key jobs from within the company for which the plan is being established, it must always be tailor-made. It is not possible to use a universal type of plan, as may be done with the point system. Let us examine Figure 23-4 to learn how to build a factor comparison scale. This is a very simplified exam-

	Mental Requirements		Skill Requirements		Physical Requirements		Responsibility		Working Conditions	
	R	M	R	M	R	M	R	M	R	M
$3.25/hr. Electrician	1	85	1	73	3	53	1	75	3	39
$2.60/hr. Engine Lathe Operator	2	55	2	66	4	38	2	60	4	41
$2.30/hr. Assembler	3	40	3	36	2	63	3	36	2	55
$1.94/hr. Laborer	4	23	4	20	1	67	4	21	1	63

Figure 23-4. A Factor Comparison Work Sheet Used in Setting Up the Key Job Rating Scale. *R* stands for rank; *M* stands for money. Rank number 1 is for the job having the highest amount of the factor, and 4 is the lowest.

ple, for in actual practice twenty or more key jobs are used, the number depending upon the total number of jobs involved.

The work should be done by a committee of executives and administrators to take advantage of pooled judgment. The first step requires a ranking of the jobs, one factor at a time, until all of the rankings have been agreed upon for all five factors. Then working horizontally, the present wage rate is allocated among all the factors. It will be remembered from what has been stated earlier that a characteristic of key jobs is that, by means of some other criteria, management is satisfied that the wages are correct. After all of the horizontal distributions among the factors have been completed, the money assignments must be reconciled with the vertical rankings. Thus if a particular job, such as the electrician, is ranked number one on mental demand, it should receive more money than the engine lathe operator, which is ranked number two. When all discrepancies have been ironed out and the rating committee is in agreement, these key jobs can then be placed in the comparison chart as depicted in Figure 23-3. This key job comparison chart is analogous to the factors and degrees with corresponding points in the point system.

Advocates of the factor comparison system point out that it is flexible and has no upper limit on the rating that a job may receive on a factor (the point system does have ceilings on the factors). Another advantage of this method is that it utilizes few factors and thereby reduces the likelihood of overlap—that is, two factors measuring the same quality. The procedure of rating new jobs by comparing with other standard or key jobs is logical and not too difficult to accomplish. Set against these, however, are certain disadvantages. The use of present wages for the key jobs may initially build errors into the plan. Likewise, the content and, therefore, the value of these jobs may change over a period of time, and this will lead to future errors. In other words, the standard is not fixed.

Time-Span of Discretion

Based upon work which he did at the Glacier Metal Company in England over a span of fourteen years as a researcher-consultant, Elliott Jaques has constructed a strikingly different system for determining rates of pay in an organization. Although his system has been rarely adopted and is quite controversial, it is rather ingenious and does provide considerable food for thought.

Jaques uses three instruments in his system: (1) time-span of discretion, (2) equitable work-payment scale, and (3) standard-earning progression curves.

The time-span of discretion of each job is measured by the maximum period of time during which the use of discretion is authorized and expected, without review of that discretion by a superior. Really this constitutes a one-factor job evaluation scale. Time-span of discretion is analogous to "responsibility for decision-making." Jaques claims that his system involves work measurement not job rating or evaluation (by judgment). Measuring the time-span for a job can be illustrated by the case of machine-shop work such as turning, milling, grinding, drilling, and boring. The time-span is the time in hours (or days) from which an error, for example, wrong dimension or too much material left on the part or too rough a finish, by one operator goes until it is detected by the next operator in the sequence of work or by the inspector or supervisor. The same principle applies to professional and managerial work. Instead of a few hours or days, the time-span for this level of work often is months or even years. Analysis here is more complex because of multiple-task roles. In analyzing work, the job analyst does not concentrate upon the level of skills and experience required as in job evaluation, rather he centers his attention on the kinds of activities and points of managerial review.

The equitable work-payment scale was constructed from interviews with people in over 1000 jobs in many companies. Jaques asked people what they considered to be fair payment for their work irrespective of their present rates of pay. From this information he plotted a curve of level of responsibility (time-span) on the abscissa and weekly pay on the ordinate. Jaques has claimed the existence of an unrecognized system of norms of fair payment among the working population. Even though engaged in different work, people having jobs with similar time-spans responded similarly in regard to pay. Changes in the general level of wages in the country require an adjustment to the equitable work-payment scale.

Standard earning progression scales were derived by studying the achieved earnings of some 250 persons over their work career histories. He then plotted a series of smoothed curves from ages 20 to 65, these curves representing different earnings trends for people of differing capacities. To determine a proper pay progression for an individual over his career, it is necessary to go through the steps in the "standard payment and progression method." This involves determining the time-span bracket for each job holder and assigning the equitable wage or salary bracket. Then a graphical plot is made of each person's actual earnings progression over the past years to date. Next the manager, once removed, makes a potential progress assessment for the man based upon his work performance and history. Pay adjustments are made in accordance with movements in the countrywide wage index. The immediate manager assesses the man's performance for the immediate period and then maintains or adjusts the man's pay from the level set by the particular potential progress scale. If ever the level of work in the job undergoes a permanent authorized change, it will be necessary to alter the pay bracket accordingly. Also if it is determined by the manager, once removed, that the man was assigned to either too high or too low a wage progression scale, he can be assigned to another scale. These decisions are periodically reviewed in the light of the individual's work performance over time.[9]

[9] For a fuller discussion of this theory of wage payment see Elliott Jaques, *Equitable Payment* (New York: John Wiley & Sons, Inc., 1961.)

ESTABLISHING THE PAY STRUCTURE

Regardless of which method of job evaluation is used, the ultimate objective is to ascertain the proper rates of pay for all the jobs. In other words the job structure must be priced. Because both the ranking and grade description systems are qualitative and do not arrive at number designations for the job ratings, the procedure for conversion to money is somewhat more inexact and may be handled in a variety of ways. For ranking, the existing rate may be compared with the new rankings and discrepancies corrected. It might be well to decide upon certain key job rates that are fair and correct, and then the other rates can be adjusted and slotted into the hierarchy. Under the grade description system the jobs can be tabulated together with their present rates. Then judgments can be made as to proper rates for the grades. It will be recalled that the jobs are already grouped into grades; therefore, it may be considered sound to compute the arithmetic means of the present rates and let that serve as the new grade rate. These means could be adjusted by judgment to make a smooth or straight line progression from grade one to the highest grade.

The factor comparison system of conversion to money is quite simple because the method itself establishes pay directly in the rating process. Because it is desirable for administrative convenience to group jobs together into pay grades, averages of the newly determined rates can be found to give a figure for each grade.

With the point system a graph is plotted of all the points on the abscissa and the existing or old rates of pay on the ordinate. If the existing rates are reasonably correct and if the rating of the jobs under the point plan has been done carefully, we can expect these points to fall along a trend line with very little dispersion. On the other hand, if the existing structure is loaded with inequities and errors, we will find considerable dispersion or scatter from the trend line. There are a number of procedures available to ascertain the best-fitting trend line. The two most common are to draw it by eye, carefully trying to insure that about the same number of points fall below as above the line. The other principle method is to use the statistical technique of "least squares." This is the most accurate way of finding the best fitting straight line. For a straight line, $Y = a + bX$, where a is the Y intercept and b is the slope of the line, it is necessary to solve these two normal equations to determine the value of these constants.

$$\Sigma Y = Na + b\Sigma X$$
$$\Sigma XY = a\Sigma X + b\Sigma X^2$$

In these equations N is the number of jobs, Y is the wage for each job, and X is the point value. It must be noted that even if the points actually fall along a curve, these equations will give us the very best-fitting straight line. A similar statistical procedure can be used to find the best-fitting parabola, for example, if visual inspection leads one to suspect that the points would more faithfully be represented by such a curve. It would be best to consult a statistical textbook for the details of the exact procedure involved.

Figure 23-5 shows a trend line that has been drawn for a plotting of present wage rates against job evaluation points for 17 hourly paid jobs. Our objective is to use this graph as a work sheet for constructing a wage structure with jobs grouped into labor grades. In this illustration vertical dashed guidelines have been drawn in order to divide the points into five groups or grades. Horizontal lines have been drawn through the midpoints of the trend line in each grade in order to arrive at a single rate of pay for each grade. This would be the simplest kind of structure, as shown in Table 23-1.

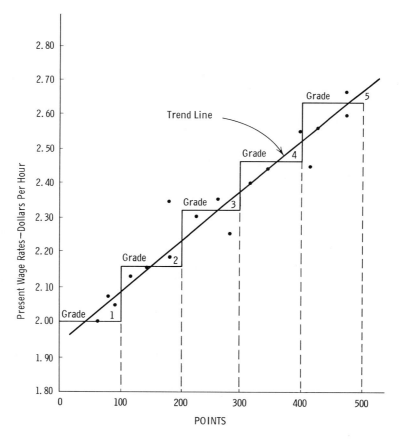

Figure 23-5. A Graph Showing a Trend Line Drawn Through a Plot of Points vs. Wage Rates for 17 Jobs with Single Rate Grades Constructed Thereon.

TABLE 23-1

Grade	Point Range	Hourly Wage Rate
1	0 - 100	$2.00
2	101 - 200	2.16
3	201 - 300	2.32
4	301 - 400	2.47
5	401 - 500	2.63

Commonly a range of money is established for each wage grade. The content and difficulty of the job is used to decide into which grade the job falls. The skills, abilities, and length of service of the different employees on each job determine how much money within the grade limits a particular employee receives.

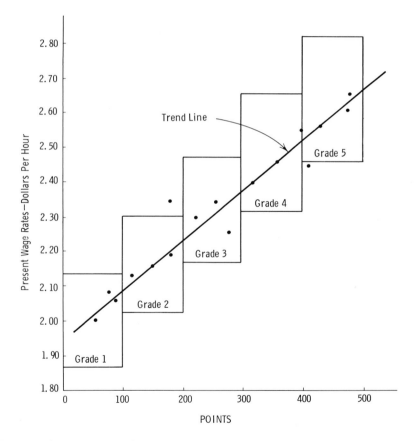

Figure 23-6. A Graph Showing a Trend Line Drawn Through a Plot of Points vs. Wage Rates for 17 Jobs with a Rate Range Established for Each Grade.

TABLE 23-2

Grade	Point Range	Hourly Wage Range
1	0-100	$1.87-2.13
2	101-200	2.02-2.30
3	201-300	2.17-2.47
4	301-400	2.31-2.65
5	401-500	2.46-2.82

Figure 23-6 is an example of how a rate range can be set up using the same data as in Figure 23-5. In this case we have five wage grades and a vertical spread of approximately 14 per cent from the minimum of each grade to the maximum as shown in Table 23-2. It will be noted that the structure provides for overlap between adjacent grades. This means that the maximum rate for one grade level is higher than the minimum rate of the next higher grade. This type of arrangement is almost always used for white-collar, professional, and administrative types of jobs. It is also sometimes used for hourly paid jobs, although in this latter case single or flat rates for each grade level are often employed. The reason for having overlapping rate ranges is that they provide greater flexibility for management in transferring an employee from a job in one grade to a job in an adjacent grade without changing his pay. This is especially true for temporary transfers. In addition, overlapping ranges are practically necessary if one wishes to have a reasonable vertical spread from minimum to maximum within each grade to properly compensate employees as they increase in skill and contribution during the years they may be assigned to a particular job.

Flat or single rates for each grade are useful for administrative simplicity and in situations where the differences in merit and contribution of all employees assigned to particular jobs are slight. Unions usually demand wage uniformity within each grade in order to eliminate favoritism and discrimination in pay treatment of employees. It must be admitted that the rating of the worth of employees by their supervisors is a rather subjective process in many instances.

Over- and Underpaid Employees

Whenever a new pay structure is adopted, management is inevitably faced with the problem of how to deal with those employees whose present rates are outside the limits just established. If single rates for the grades are used, then the vast majority of employees will be off the line. A rate range system, especially with wide limits, will reduce the number of adjustments that must be made. One approach to the problem is immediately, upon installation of the new structure, to raise all employees whose present rates of pay are below the new minimum for their particular grade up to that minimum. Because a primary purpose for the adoption of a job evaluation program is to eliminate inequities, this solution seems sound. Should a great number of jobs require increases thereby making the cost to the employer quite expensive, it might be practical to raise them in steps over a period of a few months. "Red circle" is a designation usually applied to those employees who are receiving more than the maximum for their grade. Mechanistically one might argue that these rates should be immediately lowered to their proper level. However, this would tend to cause a hardship for the employees affected. It certainly is no fault of theirs that management has decided to adopt a job-evaluation program. They did not set the job rates in the first place. A reasonable solution would involve informing the "red circle" employees that they are being paid more than the proper rate, that they personally will continue to receive the same pay as they are now getting, but that all new persons assigned to their jobs will be paid within the grade limits. Thus as employees are promoted to higher level jobs, and as some may eventually leave the company for reasons of retirement, resignation, and layoff, these wage rates will in the course of a few years fall into their proper slots. In addition to this solution to the problem, some organizations, when raising the entire wage structure across the board due to union bargaining or other reasons, will not grant any increases to "red circle" employees. Thus the structure will catch up to these, and eventually they will fall within their proper limits.

Employee Classification

Regardless of which system of job evaluation is used, a decision has to be made regarding the job title to assign to every employee in the organization. For clear-cut, easily definable jobs the problem of employee classification is easy. If an employee operates a single-spindle, sensitive drill press and does nothing else, his title is self-evident, and his pay is tied to his job title.

However, many concerns have job families, such as the typist, clerk-typist, stenographer, secretarial group. A girl employed in an office may do typing, take dictation by shorthand and transcribe it, answer the telephone, sort and distribute the mail, compose routine letters for her boss, and so on. Shall she be classifed as a stenographer or as a secretary? The pay differential may be $10 to $15 per week. The decision is of vital concern both to the employee and the employer. An additional example from the skilled trades should serve to emphasize the point fully. It is common in many factories to have such occupational sequences as millwright A and millwright B or machinist A and B, with the A designation receiving the higher pay and requiring somewhat greater skill and responsibility than the B.

The decision on classifying employees is ordinarily performed by the departmental supervisor with aid and counsel from the wage and salary administrator. The problems of wage control and justice for the employees are involved here. The decisions are not always black and white. An employee will often believe that he should receive the higher title, whereas his boss may think otherwise. It is at this point that the accuracy and thoroughness with which the job analysis program has been conducted comes under scrutiny. I believe that if those in charge of the job analysis program are not able clearly and precisely to describe differences between two jobs (such as machinist A and machinist B), then in fact they should be treated as one and the same. If a company wishes to pay employees different rates to reward those having superior merit, then it should do this through a performance appraisal program geared to rate ranges in its structure. But artificial job distinctions can cause only dissension.

Present Rates or Prevailing Market Rates

It should be emphasized that the entire preceding explanation concerned with establishing the pay structure has involved using existing wage rates as the basis for the new wage plan. Essentially the objective (in theory) is to iron out existing inequities and have all the rates fall upon a line when money is plotted against job difficulty points as in Figures 23-5 and 23-6. Because jobs are grouped into grades and special action is required for "red circle" rates, this theoretical goal is not achieved. However, the thoughtful reader may well question the wisdom of using present wages as a basis for building a better wage structure. If the level of the present wages is approximately correct and all that is required are some moderate adjustments of individual rates, then this procedure is sound. But if all the existing rates are out of line with the average rates prevailing in the labor market for the same class of work, then clearly it is folly to spend a large sum of money to install a job evaluation plan when the critical step of conversion to money results in the wrong answer.

A choice of one of two approaches can be used when existing rates are far apart from market averages. The first involves setting up a new structure based upon present wages, as has been already described. Then if the resultant wage rates are clearly below the average paid in the community, a policy decision must be made by top management. If it wishes to be fully competitive in the labor market, then the structure must be raised so as to achieve this goal. But the important point being emphasized here is that with such a solution the question of internal wage equity and the establishment of the structure is being treated separately from the question of the proper level and slope to the wage-trend line. The second alternative requires that wage rates for key jobs be surveyed in the labor market and that these rates be plotted against job evaluation points on the same graph as the one showing existing company rates against points for all jobs. With this approach management is called upon to make a decision as to which trend line it wishes to use as a basis for constructing its grade levels. It may indeed choose to compromise between the present company line and the trend line for the area average key job rates. If this second alternative method is utilized, the structure is established directly upon the particular trend line selected.

ADMINISTRATION OF PAY WITHIN RANGES

It is almost universal practice to provide for a range of pay rates for each pay grade for clerical, administrative, professional, and managerial employees. Sometimes rate ranges are used for hourly workers as well, but often single rates are adopted in response to union pressure for uniformity of treatment of all employees. The rationale for paying people classified into the same grade different rates (within the limits of the grade) is that pay should closely reflect the value of a man's contribution. It must be admitted that among a group of people all of whom are classified into pay grade 12, for example, there is likely to be a considerable variation in the quantity and quality of work produced.

The size of pay increases to advance an employee through his range may be based upon either predetermined fixed-step rates or upon individual decisions related to the individual employee's merit. Steps are commonly employed for hourly and clerical employees in industry. The pay schedules for government employees at the federal and state level are usually set up with predetermined steps. Public school teachers also have definite steps in their pay schedules. Where no definite steps are used, as is usually the case with administrative, professional, and managerial personnel, the industrial relations office and top management often will assign percentage limits to the pay increase. Thus the smallest increase might be 2 per cent, and the largest might be 10 per cent.

There are basically three methods of determining pay progression through a rate range: (1) length of service, (2) merit, or (3) a combination of merit and length of service.

Progression by length of service is also called automatic progression. For example, the progression for clerical employees in pay grade one might be as follows. Hiring rate— $80.00 per week. At the end of six months all persons would automatically be raised to $85.00 per week. At the end of the first year the rate would be $90.00. From then on all girls in this grade could expect an increase of $5.00 per week each year until they have reached the maximum of $105.00 for that grade. In this example the length-of-service progression has used predetermined step rates. This combination is very common in industry.

In actual practice many length-of-service increases are only semiautomatic. The individual employee must exhibit at least average work performance to receive his increase on schedule. If his performance is unsatisfactory, he may be denied an increase. The compensation policy of most organizations having length-of-service increases specifies that a man cannot be repeatedly denied his increase. If his supervisor can definitely establish that a man's performance is decidedly unsatisfactory on a continuing basis, he must be discharged or else reassigned.

Where the salary policy states that progression within a range is based solely upon merit, the company must have some formal program for periodically appraising the performance of all employees on a regular basis. Some firms have clear-cut formulas for translating an individual's performance rating score to a definite pay increase. Other companies are quite informal about the whole process. They leave both the frequency and the size of the pay increase pretty much up to the individual manager.

Especially in large organizations the problem of administering pay increases for thousands of people on a fair and honest basis has caused many managements to give some recognition to length of service. Philosophically most executives are opposed to the seniority principle, but when dealing with a very large work force, they are often forced to grant some recognition to this factor. One way of handling this problem is to count years of service as one factor in the rating plan used to set salary increases. Another method is to provide for automatic progression (length of service) to the midpoint of each range and merit progression above that point. Only those whose performance is decidedly above average can receive pay increases above the midpoint.

Those managements that are firmly committed to the merit principle are often plagued by the problem of general versus merit increases. If the union has succeeded in bargaining an across-the-board increase for the hourly workers, how should the white-collar and professional people be treated? The only proper way to handle this problem is to make a clear distinction between an adjustment to the entire pay structure and individual pay increases within the structure. The entire structure may be raised every two or three years because of economic factors, competitive rates in the labor market, the need to maintain equity between hourly and white-collar rates, and so on. If the structure is raised, all employees will receive pay increases. Some may be granted additional increases because of superior merit. If the structure is unchanged, then all raises will be on merit alone.

UNION CONSIDERATIONS

Some international unions as a matter of policy oppose job evaluation, whereas others accept it fully. Examples of two unions that typify the opposing viewpoints are the International Association of Machinists, which is against it, and the United Steel Workers of America, which has worked cooperatively with the basic steel industry in developing and administering a point-rating plan.[10]

To a certain extent union viewpoints and policies are shaped by the experience they have had with job evaluation in their industries. If it has seemed to help the unions achieve their goals, they tend to favor it; if, on the other hand, there has been considerable conflict between management and the union over wage-rate criteria and procedures, the unions often oppose it.

The most basic union criticism is that job evaluation is or may be utilized by management as a substitute for collective bargaining over individual wage rates. It means the adoption of a formula in place of bargaining power and judgment at the bargaining table. The unions often claim that job evaluation is not scientific and that personal opinion plays a large part in arriving at the various rating decisions. In addition to the broad objections unions also sometimes claim that it ignores problems created by labor-market supply and demand, dead-end jobs having no promotion sequence, traditional craft distinctions, and wage problems created by irregularity of employment in a company. Despite the criticisms, many unions do see in job evaluation the opportunity for making systematic, consistent, explainable decisions on wages for jobs. And if these favorably disposed unions are granted a reasonable degree of participation in decision making,they will tend to support it.

According to the National Labor Relations Act of 1935, an employer is required to bargain rates of pay with the union that has been certified as the sole and exclusive bargaining agent for its employees in a particular bargaining unit. Because a company cannot avoid negotiations over wage rates for individual jobs with its union, the question resolves itself into whether the job evaluation procedure that management uses shall be open to joint participation. It would be futile for an employer to spend a great sum of money installing a plan only to have the union refuse to accept the resultant job rates so determined. Before the program is initially established, union and management must agree upon the desirability of job evaluation and the general procedures to be followed. Various degrees of union participation may exist. It may range from simply a periodic review by the union of the work that management is doing in developing a program to full partnership participation all the way from the analysis of jobs through to pricing the job structure. Likewise in operating a going program, participation can range from a union review of the rates established by management (if the union is dissatisfied it will turn in a grievance) to equal partnership through a joint union-employer evaluation committee that rates all jobs. There is no single answer to the ques-

[10] International Association of Machinists, *What's Wrong with Job Evaluation* (Washington, D.C., The Association, 1954); Robert Tilove, "The Wage Rationalization Program in United States Steel," *Monthly Labor Review,* Vol. 64, No. 6 (June 1947), pp. 967 - 982.

tion of union participation. It depends primarily upon the attitudes and relationships between the two parties.

WAGE SURVEYS

If the wage policy of a firm is to keep competitive in the labor market, that is, to pay rates which are at least approximately equal to those prevailing in the community, then it must collect accurate wage and salary data and make changes in its pay structure as may become necessary. Whereas job evaluation establishes pay differentials based upon differences in job content, wage-survey information provides a means by which management can determine whether its entire wage level is proper.

There are actually several purposes for gathering data, periodically, regarding area-wage rates. This information is necessary when installing a new wage structure based upon job evaluation. After the pay structure has been initially installed, it must be examined periodically (usually annually) in the light of current area-wage data to determine whether an adjustment in the general wage level is necessary. In preparing for contract negotiations with a labor union, management is well advised to gather wage data in the area, the industry, and from other firms organized by the same union. Wage-survey information is also useful for determining the going rates for particular jobs about which a problem has arisen. Management may suspect it is overpaying certain jobs, or it may experience difficulty in staffing others because of inadequate pay.

In collecting wage data, management wants to find out the going rates for its various jobs in the area from which it recruits labor. This area is its labor market. A labor market is defined as a geographical area within which employers recruit workers and workers seek employment. It is usually thought to consist of a central city or cities and the surrounding territory in which persons can change their jobs without changing their place of residence. This definition is particularly appropriate for hourly and clerical workers. On the other hand, the labor market for engineers, scientists, and executives tends to be much greater in scope. These kinds of personnel are more mobile than lower-level employees. They are much more likely to relocate if they can find a good job in another city even though it may be far removed from their home town. Thus salary statistics for these higher-level personnel tend to apply to large geographical regions and sometimes even to the country as a whole.

Sources of Wage Data

Although conducting one's own survey will probably yield the most satisfactory and accurate results, this rather costly procedure is not always necessary. There are other sources of reliable information. If a company participates in a survey conducted by another organization to the extent of providing actual pay information for its own jobs, it is usually provided with a summary of the results of the survey. In many cities employers pool their efforts and conduct one annual survey to meet the needs of the group. This is most often accomplished through a personnel managers' professional association or through the local Chamber of Commerce. Employer trade associations are also important sources of wage and salary information.[11] Likewise the Bureau of Labor Statistics of the United States Department of Labor conducts surveys at regular intervals in the larger labor markets in the United States. The major disadvantage of relying upon published and association data rather than upon one's own survey is that the jobs one is particularly interested in may not be reported. Therefore, a saving in cost can be gained at a sacrifice of comprehensive coverage of the information a company desires.

Planning and Conducting the Survey

Because it is generally impossible for a company to find other jobs in the area that are exactly comparable to all of its own jobs, the problem resolves itself into one of selecting representative jobs from within one's own organization. Thus for an organization having 300 jobs, 40 or 50 jobs might be chosen for survey purposes. The jobs chosen must be distributed across the board from low to high job content. A reasonably large number of employees must be assigned to each of these survey jobs.[12] The jobs selected must be important to the company, and their content must be reasonably stable over time. They must appear quite commonly among other companies within the survey area.

It is most important when surveying area-wage rates to recognize that job titles alone are insufficient for making comparisons. Each job title must be backed up by a brief job description, so that it is possible to compare accurately the job of, say a junior accountant in company A with the same job in company B, even though company B may use a different job title.

Because managers recognize quite well that the basic wage rate is not the only factor that determines its attractiveness to job seekers, they also generally collect information regarding prevailing fringe benefits and personnel practices. This kind of information is very necessary if the company finds itself negotiating with a union regarding such items as pensions, health insurance, and vacations.

A survey of fringe benefits and personnel practices will typically include such items as overtime and premium pay policy; paid holidays; vacation

---

[11] See, for example, N. Arnold Tolles and Robert L. Raimon, *Sources of Wage Information: Employer Associations* (Ithaca, N.Y.: The New York State School of Industrial and Labor Relations, Cornell University, 1952).

[12] These surveyed jobs are sometimes called key jobs.

practices; shift differentials; level of benefits and employer's share of costs for pensions, group life insurance, health insurance, and sick-leave pay; and employer-financed services, such as recreational and social programs.

Questions for Review and Discussion

1. Explain why prevailing wage rates within a labor market are such an important factor influencing wages in individual companies.
2. What are reasonable goals for a comprehensive program of employee compensation? Why does compensation seldom really motivate improved performance?
3. In the United States private industry generally bases its wage-rate decisions upon the nature and level of the work the employees do. Can you think of other ways of deciding how much to pay individual employees? Evaluate these.
4. If you had the task of persuading union officials in your organization to agree to the adoption of a job-evaluation program, what arguments would you give?
5. A company president makes the statement that he sees no need for introducing a job evaluation plan into his company. He feels that if he conducts an annual wage survey and adjusts his own rates accordingly, there will be no need for a costly job rating program. Do you agree or disagree? Why?
6. What criteria could you develop that would serve as a guide to decide the amount of vertical spread to be used for a pay structure having pay ranges for each grade?
7. What guides can you develop to aid in deciding how many grades should be employed for a given pay structure? What are the relative merits of many versus few grades?
8. Many companies have a practice of keeping wage and salary policies, rates, structures, classification, and so on, secret. How much information would you provide the employees? Explain.
9. Explain the process involved in evaluating a given job using a point plan. Using a factor comparison plan.
10. Compare the point system with the factor comparison system on the following factors:
    a. Factors used
    b. Degrees used
    c. Method of expressing final rating
    d. Usage of key jobs
    e. How ratings are recorded and explained
    f. Flexibility for meeting changing conditions and significantly different types of jobs

11. An industrial engineer makes the statement that his company is the only one in the area that has placed employees in certain occupational categories on wage incentives. He further states that their average earnings working under the motivation of such an incentive are equal to the daywork average of other companies in the area for the same jobs. Do you agree that his rates are fair and equitable with such a criterion?

PROBLEM

Wage Lines and Wage Structure

The data in Figure 23-7 shows the job titles and points assigned to these jobs under a newly installed point plan of job evaluation. The jobs are of the nonsupervisory office and technical type. The wages shown are the present average weekly wages in this company and the average wages paid in the same labor market for these jobs as found from a carefully conducted area survey.

JOB TITLE	NUMBER OF EMPLOYEES	POINTS	PRESENT AVERAGE WEEKLY WAGE	AVERAGE WAGE IN AREA
Clerk, Mail	2	93	$ 70.00	$ 73.00
Typist	3	98	71.00	76.00
Clerk, Typist	3	118	71.00	79.00
Bookkeeping Machine Operator "B"	2	123	81.00	78.00
Switchboard Operator	2	128	89.00	77.00
Stenographer	5	145	85.00	86.00
Clerk, Billing	2	148	78.00	75.00
Clerk, Payroll	3	153	90.00	91.00
Bookkeeping Machine Operator "A"	2	163	91.00	94.00
Secretarial-Stenographer	7	168	92.00	98.00
Bookkeeper	2	178	94.00	96.00
Secretary	8	196	103.00	108.00
Buyer, Assistant	1	208	112.00	117.00
Nurse	2	216	95.00	112.00
Cashier	1	223	110.00	121.00
Draftsmen, Layout	12	256	120.00	135.00
Accountant, Assistant	3	266	135.00	144.00
Draftsman, Design	4	321	152.00	163.00

Figure 23-7.   Chart of Job Titles, Points, and Wages.

You are to plot a graph of points versus present company wages. You can show the average area rates on the same graph or on a separate one. By the method of "least squares" or some other appropriate procedure, obtain trend lines for both the company rates and the area rates. Then construct a wage structure having a rate range for each grade. This problem requires decisions to be made on which line to use, how many grades, the vertical spread in money within the grades, action to be taken on jobs now payed above and below the newly established limits, and method of in-grade progression.

Suggestions for Further Reading

Adams, J. Stacy, "Wage Inequities, Productivity, and Work Quality," *Industrial Relations,* Vol. 3, No. 1, October 1963, pp. 9-16.

Bassett, Glenn A. and Harlow A. Nelson, "Keys to Better Salary Administration," *Personnel,* Vol. 44, No. 2, March-April 1967, pp. 23-30.

Belcher, David W., *Wage and Salary Administration,* 2nd Ed., Englewood Cliffs, N. J.: Prentice-Hall, 1962.

————, "Ominous Trends in Wage and Salary Administration," *Personnel,* Vol. 41, No. 5, September-October 1964, pp. 42-50.

Brennan, Charles W., *Wage Administration,* Rev. Ed., Homewood, Ill.: Richard D. Irwin, 1963.

Fleuter, Douglas L., "A Program for Controlling Wage and Salary Costs," *Personnel,* Vol. 42, No. 1, January-February 1965, pp. 60-65.

Groenekamp, W. A., "How Reliable are Wage Surveys?," *Personnel,* Vol. 44, No. 1, January-February 1967, pp. 32-37.

Jaques, Elliott, *Equitable Payment,* New York: John Wiley & Sons, 1961.

Kindig, Fred E., "Wage and Salary Administration—A Philosophy of Management," *Personnel Administrator,* Vol. 12, No. 4, July-August 1967, pp. 10-14.

Langsner, Adolph and Herbert G. Zollitsch, *Wage and Salary Administration,* Cincinnati, Ohio: Southwestern Publishing Company, 1961.

Lanham, Elizabeth, *Administration of Wages and Salaries,* New York: Harper & Row, 1963.

Patton, John A., C. L. Littlefield, and Stanley A. Self, *Job Evaluation,* 3rd Ed., Homewood, Ill.: Richard D. Irwin, 1964.

Sibson, Robert E., *Wages and Salaries: A Handbook for Line Managers,* Rev. E., New York: American Management Association, 1967.

Taylor, George W. and Frank C. Pierson, *New Concepts in Wage Determination,* New York, McGraw-Hill Book Company, 1957.

Tolles, N. Arnold, *Origins of Modern Wage Theories,* Englewood Cliffs, N.J.: Prentice-Hall, 1964.

Wage Incentives

24

As we have seen, the previous chapter has examined and explained the factors that determine wage levels in an organization—factors such as supply and demand for labor, comparable wage rates in the community, ability to pay on the part of the employer, productivity, and union bargaining power. Individual job rates within the organization can then be established through a method called job evaluation, wherein a determination is made of the relative amounts of skill, effort, responsibility, and job conditions for all jobs. Then a rational formalized pay structure can be established.

Wages to employees for services rendered can be paid according either to the time worked or to the amount of work produced. Those whose pay is based upon time are paid a certain sum of money per hour regardless of how productive they may be—this is commonly called daywork or time work. Usually employees receive their paychecks once each week, and pay is calculated according to the number of hours the particular employee worked during that week. If, on the other hand, pay is computed according to how much work is produced (units, pounds, dozens, assemblies, tons, and so on) and if employees can earn extra money for producing more than a certain quota or norm, we say that this is a wage-incentive-payment method. If top management decides to adopt a wage-incentive program, its objectives are generally to reduce unit labor costs by increasing manhour output, to raise worker income without increasing labor costs, and to acquire a means of effectively controlling the production process.

Features that most incentive plans have in common are measurement by management of the amount of work done, establishment of a quota or standard output, and the utilization of a formula for relating pay to production or performance.

This chapter is devoted to an analysis and explanation of direct wage incentive programs for hourly paid workers. In Chapter 25, "Incentives Based Upon Cooperation," we shall examine plant or companywide incentive programs based upon the concept of teamwork and joint cooperation among employees, management, and the union. In Chapter 26 we shall discuss compensation and incentive programs for salesmen, professionals, and managerial personnel.

Wage Incentive or Daywork?

Of the 11.25 million production and related workers employed in manufacturing in 1958 in the United States, 27 per cent were paid on an incentive basis. There is considerable variation from industry to industry. In men's and boy's wearing apparel, the portion was 71 per cent on incentive pay; for cigars it was 66 per cent; for women's outerwear it was 63 per cent; and for blast furnaces, steel works, and rolling mills it was 60 per cent. At the other end of the scale we find that fewer than 10 per cent of the production and related workers were on incentive pay in such industries as aircraft and aircraft parts, bakery products, beverages, commercial and newspaper printing, industrial chemicals, sawmills, and millwork. The proportion on incentive during the years 1945 and 1946 was approximately the same as in 1958.[1] Since 1959 there has been some indication of a decline in the number of manufacturing plants using direct wage incentives. Schultz has reported that 41 per cent of 751 plants surveyed in 1965 were using incentives compared to 51 per cent of 785 plants queried in a similar survey in 1959.[2]

The decision to place work on an incentive basis of payment depends upon a number of factors. In order to utilize this form of wage payment:

---

[1] L. Earl Lewis, "Extent of Incentive Pay in Manufacturing," *Monthly Labor Review,* Vol. 83, No. 5 (May 1960), pp. 460-463.

[2] Among the reasons for a decline in utilization of incentives are (1) automation and machine-paced processes reduce need for incentives; (2) labor costs have increased over the years in some plants due to loosening of rates and inattention to auditing of standards; (3) union pressures and grievances over rates and earnings have caused problems; (4) supervisors complain about added administrative burden caused by incentive installations; (5) some managers feel it is harder to maintain product quality standards under incentives; (6) it is very costly to set standards on short production runs and one-of-a-kind products. Such situations are multiplying; (7) the number of indirect employees is increasing while direct labor workers are decreasing. It is difficult to set standards on indirect labor jobs. See Gregory Schultz, "Plants' Incentives Slump Badly Over Last 6 Years," *Factory,* Vol. 123, No. 6 (June 1965), pp. 68-79; "Mitchell Fein vs. Gregory Schultz," *Factory,* Vol. 125 (July 1967), pp. 83-85.

1. The output of employees either individually or in groups must be measurable and suitable for standardization. By standardized we mean that the work methods, materials, tooling, and the operations are uniform from one unit or cycle to the next. If there is great variation in the work requirements themselves or in the conditions under which the work must be done from unit to unit, it may still be possible to measure the work in terms of time or some other criteria of performance, but any averages or norms so determined would be inherently of little value as far as standards go.
2. There must be a consistent relationship between the amount of skill and effort exerted by the employee and the output. Some processes are machine controlled entirely; thus greater employee application can have little or no effect upon production. It is true that even in situations like this, however, some companies set up an incentive or bonus plan so that the employees will be diligent in supplying and servicing the machine to avoid shutdowns.
3. The work can be readily counted and credited to the proper individuals. If the cost of determining how much each individual employee has produced at each step in a production process is excessive, the alternative is generally either to utilize a group or plantwide incentive plan or to use daywork.
4. There must be an opportunity for reducing the unit cost of the product or service. Or expressed in another way, an increase in productivity should be attainable. Indeed a primary reason for an employer even to contemplate the installation of a pay incentive is his expectation that it will result in increased productivity, improved performance and efficiency, and lower unit costs.
5. The employees (and the union if the employees are organized) must accept, support, and cooperate in this method of wage payment. The reward that employees can expect to receive from participation is higher earnings that they would receive under the daywork or timework method of payment. But if such support is lacking, the incentive program will rest on a shaky foundation. The opposition of the United Automobile Workers Union to incentives is well known, and this attitude led to the general decline in their utilization when the Union organized the workers in the automobile industry in the late 1930's. On the other hand, the prevalence of the piecework system in the men's and women's wearing apparel industries relates directly to the positive attitudes of the International Ladies' Garment Workers Union and the Amalgamated Clothing Workers Union toward incentives. Of course, in these latter cases long-standing tradition has played a large part also.

The five foregoing conditions indicate when the adoption of the incentive method of wage payment is practical and desirable. On the other hand, payment according to time worked is clearly preferable where these requirements cannot be met. Process-controlled operations, such as are found in most of the pulp and paper and chemical industries, are more properly paid by daywork. Most clerical, technical, engineering, and scientific occupations are not under incentives. However, salesmen are typically paid by commissions or at least by a guaranteed base salary plus a commission. Many organizations pay their top executives according to a salary-plus-incentive-bonus arrangement, because there is a rather close relationship between the performance of a company president, for example, and the profits of his company.

Thus where the work is inherently variable, where it cannot be accurately measured, standardized, and counted, where productivity is not closely related to employee skill and effort, where employees and unions strongly oppose incentive payment, and where the employer can realize no potential gain from wage incentives, it is preferable to employ time wages. Time wages have the added advantage of simplified payroll computation. Likewise employees can readily ascertain their earnings for a given pay period (the same statement cannot be made for many incentive installations). A primary disadvantage of time payment is that the labor cost per unit is variable. The employer cannot as readily control or fix his direct labor costs, since different workers on the same job receive the same pay regardless of how much they turn out.

Historical Development

Although payment by the piece or unit has been used for centuries—for example, craftsmen during the colonial era in America were typically compensated in this manner—wage incentives as we know them today, that is, those based upon careful and systematic work measurement—were originally developed by Frederick W. Taylor while employed at the Midvale Steel Company in the 1880's. Taylor is rightly called the father of the scientific management movement. He was hired as a consultant to the Bethlehem Steel Company during the years 1898 through 1901, where he had an opportunity to apply many of his ideas regarding time study and wage incentives. It was here that he conducted his well-known experiments in work methods and time study in connection with pig iron handling and the shoveling of iron ore.[3] Taylor emphasized the importance of the scientific study of work methods, careful measurement of productive effort by stop watch time study, selection and placement on incentive work of highly competent employees, and the payment of wages in direct proportion to output.

In the early years wage incentives tended to be applied to direct labor, production type of operations in factories. This type of activity is generally rather repetitive and standardized and thus susceptible to the setting of

---

[3] Those interested in the life and work of Taylor can read, F. B. Copley, *Life of Frederick W. Taylor* (New York: Harper & Row, 1923).

standard times and incentive rates. During more recent years industrial engineers have been extending incentives to maintenance, inspection, and service operations, such as tool room, machine repair, messenger service, janitorial work, product testing and inspecting, and the like. Because of difficulty of measurement, inherent variability, noncyclic nature of the work, and problems of controlling quality when under incentive motivation, operations of this nature have presented great challenges to the industrial engineer in his attempts to put them on incentive.[4]

WORK MEASUREMENT

Most commonly "time" is used as the standard for measuring performance of work that is on an incentive (time per piece, time per pound, time per assembly, time expressed as a percentage of maximum possible operating time for running mechanical equipment, and so on). Other bases or standards against which performance can be compared may also be used. The amount of finished or good product from a given quantity of material can give a standard expressed in terms of a percentage of maximum possible yield. Also, employees can be rewarded for a reduction in the usage of costly supply materials; in this case the standard is expressed as a budgeted money figure determined by accounting procedures. Or rewards can be tied to an improvement in quality, in which case the standard would be a permissible percentage of imperfections or rejects.

The time required to perform a given amount of work is, as was stated above, the most generally used measure upon which to base an incentive system. There are a number of methods available for establishing standards. These are (1) past performance, (2) bargaining between employer and union, (3) time study, (4) standard data, (5) predetermined elemental times, and (6) work sampling. Each of these methods will be discussed briefly.[5]

Past Performance

Industrial engineers almost universally agree that past performance is a poor way of deciding what future performance should be. The Halsey (50-50) gains-sharing incentive plan, which originated in the 1890's, used

---

[4] Examples of incentive installations for maintenance and service work can be found in the following articles: H. J. Moore, "Application of Direct Incentive to Maintenance Work," *Proceedings,* Fifth Annual Time Study and Methods Conference, sponsored by the Society for Advancement of Management and the American Society of Mechanical Engineers, 1950, pp. 94-101; Keith Boaz, "Incentives in the Warehouse," *Factory Management and Maintenance* (September 1953).

[5] Complete explanations of systematic work measurement methods can be found in such books as the following: Ralph M. Barnes, *Motion and Time Study* (4th Ed., New York: John Wiley & Sons, 1958); Delmar W. Karger and F. M. Bayha, *Engineered Work Measurement* (2nd Ed., New York: The Industrial Press, 1965); Benjamin W. Niebel, *Motion and Time Study* (Homewood, Ill.: Richard D. Irwin, Inc., 1955).

a standard based upon past performance. Standards derived from past performance when employees were on day work usually are much lower and easier to attain than those developed through time study and other engineered work-measurement techniques. Because no complete analysis has been made of work methods, delays, allowances, and of the skill and effort of those employees upon whom the past performance records are based, management cannot justifiably say what standard or normal performance should be.

Bargaining Between Employer and Union

Bargaining is the method followed in the men's and women's wearing apparel industries to a considerable extent. The facts upon which the negotiators base their judgments may be either past production records, their own experience, or actual time study. In the New York dress industry, as an illustration, samples of new dresses are submitted by employers to the price settlement department of the International Ladies' Garment Workers Union. The experts in this department analyze each garment in detail. Industrial engineers in the Union conduct time and motion studies to provide standard time information, which is then used as a guide by the rate experts in the determination of an actual money piece rate for each garment. Then these persons meet with representatives of the manufacturers. If agreement is reached, the matter is settled. However, if there is a dispute, the office of the permanent impartial chairman (arbitrator) is requested to assign an impartial adjuster to study the garment and decide upon a piece price. Although his word is usually taken as final, appeal may be made to the impartial chairman himself.[6] William Gomberg, formerly of the International Ladies' Garment Workers Union, has repeatedly stated his views that time study should be used only as a basis for negotiations.[7]

Time Study

The principal method used in industry to set work standards is stop watch time study. This was the method used by Frederick W. Taylor, and the stop watch still occupies a prominent part in the time study engineer's kit of tools. Indeed, the more modern and refined techniques of standard data and predetermined elemental times depend upon and are adaptations of basic time-study principles.

The basic task that is measured and standardized is the operation. An operation may consist of drilling four $\frac{1}{2}''$ diameter holes through a piece of $\frac{3}{8}''$-thick steel on a sensitive drill press; or in a garment factory it might

[6] Sumner H. Slichter, *Union Policies and Industrial Management* (Washington D.C.: The Brookings Institution, 1941).

[7] See, for example, William Gomberg, "Union Interest in Engineering Techniques," *Harvard Business Review,* Volume 24 (Spring 1946), pp. 356–365.

consist of sewing a pocket on a man's white dress shirt; or in the electrical industry it might consist of spray painting the case for a circuit breaker as it hangs suspended from an overhead conveyor. In analyzing an operation, the time-study engineer will subdivide it into work elements. He will seek to find the most efficient way to perform the work. In some cases extensive redesign of the work place layout and revamping of the hand motions may be in order. The training of the time-study engineer causes him continually to seek a better way to perform an operation or sequence of operations. Work simplification principles and techniques are a necessary and important part of the time-study engineer's approach to his work.

After the most efficient method has been developed (of course, in the future a still better way may be found), one or more qualified workers is timed with a stop watch while he is following the prescribed work procedure. A separate time reading is taken and recorded for each work element. Since different employees exhibit considerable variation in the pace at which they work, it is necessary for the time-study engineer to adjust the actual observed time by a percentage factor to arrive at the time it should take a normal worker exhibiting normal skill and effort to perform the given operation. This process of adjusting the observed time by a percentage factor to yield a normal or base time is called leveling or performance rating. There are a number of means by which time-study engineers are trained to develop a concept of what normal performance should be.[8] Thus if an operator spent 0.20 minutes to perform one element of his total operation and if the time-study engineer rated his performance (that is, skill and effort) at 20 per cent above normal, the normal time for that element would be 0.24 minutes (0.20 $\times$ 120 per cent). To the sum of the times obtained for the individual elements are added allowances to compensate the employee for necessary personal time, unavoidable delays, and for rest to overcome fatigue. The resulting figure is the standard time for the operation. Time-study authorities and practitioners claim that they can achieve an accuracy of plus or minus 5 per cent of the true standard time. The true standard, of course, is never really known. Several time studies of the same operation performed by different workers would represent samples taken from a population or universe (to use statistical terminology) whose mean or average is unknown. The sample averages would represent estimates of the true average for the universe. A well-known trade union spokesman has challenged the accuracy of management's time-study procedures.[9]

---

[8] Motion picture sequences of work operations that have been rated or judged by time-study practitioners are often used. The average ratings of many experienced time-study men are used as standards for guiding the judgments of time-study trainees. An example of this approach consists of the rating films of 24 typical manufacturing and clerical operations prepared and distributed by the Society for the Advancement of Management.

[9] William Gomberg, *A Trade Union Analysis of Time Study* (2nd Ed., Englewood Cliffs, N.J.: Prentice-Hall, Inc., 1955).

Standard Data

When similar operations have been studied repeatedly by means of stop watch time study, it soon becomes apparent that certain patterns and uniformity of times develop for individual work elements. By tabulating and classifying times taken from a large number of studies of similar work, the initial steps toward the development of standard data are made. By use of this data it is not necessary to make a stop watch time study in order to arrive at the proper standard time. What is required is that the engineer observe the job in question to fully comprehend what is involved (noting machine, workplace layout, parts, fixtures, and so on). By knowing what elements are required to perform the work, the engineer can select the standard times corresponding to these elements from tables of previously prepared standard data.

Predetermined Elemental Times

Predetermined elemental times are basically a form of standard data; however, the elements of work are of the general type or order called therbligs. Therbligs are elements of work that were first identified and analyzed by Lillian and Frank Gilbreth in their pioneering work in motion study. Therbligs are basic finger, arm, hand, and body motions, often called basic divisions of accomplishment. Reach, move, hold, grasp, position, preposition, inspect, assemble, and select are some illustrations of these elements. Use of ordinary stop watch time-study procedures does not permit the measurement of work elements as short as therbligs. Standard time values for these are obtained by studying a large sample of diversified operations with a timing device, such as the motion-picture camera, that is capable of measuring very short elements.

There are a great many different predetermined elemental time systems from which to choose. A considerable number have been developed as proprietary systems by industrial engineering consulting firms; others have been created by industrial companies for their own usage. Examples of such systems are Methods-Time Measurement (often called MTM), Work-Factor and Basic Motion Time Study. With the Methods-Time Measurement system, as an illustration, a reach of 10″ to an object in a fixed location or to an object in the other hand would take .000087 hours, which is equivalent to .0052 minutes.[10] In order to set a standard for an operation by using such systems, it is necessary for the engineer to make an extremely detailed analysis of the motions involved and to record these on paper. He must properly classify each motion and then take the time from a table of standard times. An ordinary operation having a work cycle of one minute could very well contain over a hundred basic elements of

[10] H. B. Maynard, G. L. Stegemerten, J. L. Schwab, *Methods-Time Measurement* (New York: McGraw-Hill Book Company, 1948).

work. The great advantage of using predetermined elemental times is that the process of establishing a standard requires that the engineer make a very detailed analysis of the motions involved. This procedure often uncovers inefficiencies and leads to significant improvements.

Work Sampling

One of the newest techniques of work measurement, work sampling requires that the engineer take a great number of observations of a worker at random times throughout the working day. He records precisely what the employee is doing at the time he is being observed. No stop watch is used. The objective is to find the frequency of occurrence of every work element. Even though the worker is not under observation constantly, by adequate random sampling of his activities, the engineer can ascertain within limits of accuracy that can be calculated statistically the percentage of time that he spends on each portion of the operation. Delays, allowances, and infrequently occurring noncyclic elements can also readily be measured this way. In order to set a standard by the work sampling procedure, it is necessary to level or rate the performance of the worker being studied (as is true with stop watch time study) and to count the actual number of units produced during the period under study. Advantages of work sampling are that it is possible to study a considerable number of different operations at the same time, the psychological problems presented by standing over a worker for a considerable period of time as in stop watch time study are avoided, and considerable statistical reliability can be achieved through the process of taking many observations over a period of several days.

ESSENTIAL REQUIREMENTS OF A SOUND WAGE INCENTIVE PROGRAM

Based upon the experiences derived from study of successful and unsuccessful programs in various industries through the years, writers, researchers, and others have concluded that if certain general principles or guides are followed by management in installing and administering a wage incentive plan, the chances for success are good. A successful plan is one that achieves its purpose. This is usually to increase productivity, reduce costs, improve efficiency, and increase employee earnings while at the same time maintaining or enhancing employee morale and employee relations.

1. Management, employees, and the union (if the employees are organized) should understand and support the incentive program. Since the procedures involved in methods analysis, time study, base rate setting, and bonus calculation when taken collectively are rather com-

plicated, explanations and training by management for employees and union leaders are essential. Discussion and participation with lower-level supervisors and union officials in the initiation and the development of the program is advantageous in creating the kind of support that is necessary for success.

2. Methods analysis of each operation should be undertaken before a work standard is established. The optimum methods and procedures for doing the work should be devised first. A standarized method should be followed. Employees must be taught how to perform the work according to this standard procedure.

3. The standard upon which the wage incentive is based should be arrived at by carefully applied work measurement techniques, such as time study, standard data, work sampling, or predetermined elemental times. If piece rates are bargained collectively between management and union, the decisions should be guided by engineered work measurement techniques. Standards should not be based upon past performance. If this were done, those employees who had loafed in the past would be rewarded with easy-to-achieve standards, whereas those who had previously given an honest day's work would be penalized with a difficult-to-meet quota.

4. Each job on incentive should have a guaranteed minimum or base rate. Even if output drops to a low level, the employee can depend upon earning at least a certain minimum amount of money. Normally this base rate will be determined by job evaluation. Differences in base rates among jobs will reflect differences in skill, effort, responsibility, and job conditions. Maintenance of proper differentials between these base rates will insure that employees on jobs having low requirements will not earn more than employees on highly skilled jobs when both are on incentive.

5. The work standard (whether it be expressed in time or money per unit) should be guaranteed by management against change unless there is a change in the method, tooling, equipment, materials, or design of the product. The employee must know that his work standard or quota will not be increased just because he starts to make large bonus earnings. The practice of rate cutting became acute during the early days of the scientific management movement because some employers felt that workers were making too much money and that somehow the rates had become "loose" or were incorrectly established in the first place. Rate cutting still occurs to some extent, but it is frowned upon. A change in the work standard is legitimate if the method of doing the job is altered. If management simplifies the operation in such a way that the time per unit is less than the previous standard, the worker should be able to earn as much money as before, provided he exerts equivalent skill and effort. If the employee, through his own initiative and ingenuity, figures out a better way, he should be rewarded.

6. It should be easy for employees to calculate earnings. Even with a complicated incentive formula, management with its specialized knowledge and calculating machines can generally compute employee earnings readily. However, employees need to be able to verify the payroll department's calculations. This builds confidence and trust in the program.

7. An effective grievance procedure must be available to handle dissatisfaction and complaints on the part of employees. Grievances over incentives usually are concerned with charges by the employees that the rate or standard is too "tight" (that is, too difficult to meet) or that there are too many holdups and delays due to machine breakdowns and interruptions in the supply of material.

TYPES OF INCENTIVE PAY PLANS

Although literally scores of incentive plans have been used over the past seventy years, only a few primary types are in common usage at present. Those that will be explained here are measured-daywork, piecework, standard-hour, and gains-sharing plans.[11]

Measured Daywork

The measured daywork plan is in the twilight zone between a true direct incentive plan and regular time payment or daywork. A work standard is set through time study or some other work measurement technique. The worker is expected to meet this quota. If he exceeds the standard or falls below, he still receives his regular hourly rate of pay. From management's standpoint, the plan has the advantage that unit labor costs are much more predictable than with ordinary daywork, because there is considerable emphasis placed upon meeting the standard. In some installations merit rating is employed. This is the classical and historical type of measured daywork. Every three months each person is rated on four factors: quantity of work, quality of work, dependability, and versatility. A high score yields an increase in hourly pay for the ensuing three months, whereas a low score results in a decrease in pay. The employee's rate of pay actually consists of two parts: a basic or guaranteed portion, which normally approximates 75 per cent of the total rate and the personal portion, which is subject to fluctuation every three months. As an incentive plan this particular type of measured daywork has the disadvantage that the reward for improved performance is not directly and proportionately related to that behavior. The pay adjustment is too re-

[11] Many of the numerous other plans were created by industrial engineering consultants. Some like the Taylor Differential Piece Rate plan are of historical interest but no longer in use. Other plans are the Gantt Task and Bonus, Rowan, Barth, Emerson Efficiency, Merrick, Hayes-Manit, and Dyer.

mote in point of time. Also the instrument for relating pay to perform-ance—that is, the foreman's judgment in merit rating the employee—is subjective. On the positive side the system does encourage (in fact, it requires) the foreman to become well acquainted with every employee in order to rate him. Also management has greater control over labor costs than is true under ordinary daywork.

There is another kind of measured daywork program that is becom-ing increasingly popular in industry. Indeed, it has tended to supplant the type just described. According to Slichter, Healy, and Livernash, the kind employing merit rating that adjusts the employees' hourly rate in accordance with his performance over a period of time has become quite rare.[12] More commonly at present measured daywork involves simply pay by the hour accompanied by control of worker efficiency by means of production standards. The hourly rate is not adjustable. Emphasis is placed upon the establishment of accurate standards of output through time-study, standard-data, or other procedures. Then pressure is placed upon the worker to meet the standard consistently. If his performance falls below standard, the industrial engineer and the supervisor investi-gate to determine the cause. If the materials, equipment, or process are faulty, corrective measures are taken. But if the worker is at fault, he is subject to disciplinary action (assuming the standard is fair and he has the basic capacity to do the work).

There is some evidence to indicate that measured daywork in contrast to piecework and other incentive plans results in less worker resistance to the introduction of changed methods. Also management encounters fewer union and worker grievances over the fairness of production stan-dards.[13] There is less likelihood of measured daywork causing sharp contro-versy between labor and management than with ordinary incentive ar-rangements, because there are fewer sensitive issues over which to clash.

Piecework

One of the simplest and most commonly used of all incentive plans is piecework. The standard is expressed in terms of a certain sum of money for every unit produced, such as $0.10 per piece or $0.77 per pound or $1.31 per dozen. The earnings of the employee are directly proportion-al to his output. This is what industrial engineers call a 1-for-1 plan—for each 1-per-cent increase in production the worker is paid a 1-per-cent increase in wages. If the basic hourly rate of pay of a given job is $2.40 (as established by job evaluation) and if the industrial engineer has set a stan-dard time of 1 minute per unit (therefore 60 units per hour), we find that the piece rate then becomes $2.40 per hour divided by 60 units per hour, which is equal to $.04 per unit. Although in the early days workers were paid

[12] Sumner H. Slichter, James J. Healy, and E. Robert Livernash, *The Impact of Collective Bargaining on Management* (Washington, D.C.: The Brookings Institution, 1960), p. 490.
[13] *Ibid.,* pp. 544 and 545.

only for the actual work they turned out, with no guaranteed minimum, modern practice requires the payment of a certain minimum wage if the employee has not produced enough units to meet that base. Thus, as in the example just cited, if the guaranteed minimum were $2.40 per hour and if the worker's output was less than the 60 units necessary to earn the minimum, he would still be paid $2.40 per hour. With straight piecework (without a guaranteed minimum) many of the risks of factory management are transferred to the shoulders of the employee, because even if there are production delays, faulty materials, and machine breakdowns, the direct labor cost per unit to the employer is fixed. Since the passage of the Fair Labor Standards Act by the Federal Government in 1938, all employers whose employees are engaged in interstate commerce or the production of goods for interstate commerce must pay a minimum hourly wage.

For a piecework plan that has a guaranteed minimum, Figure 24-1 shows graphically the relationship between output of an individual employee

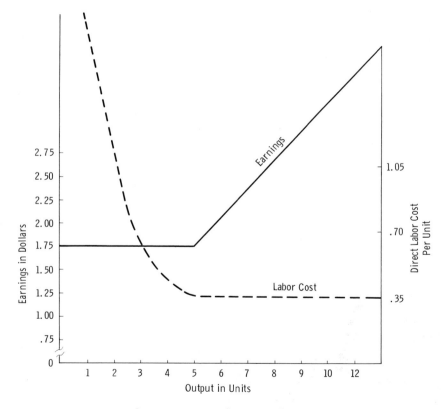

Figure 24-1. Piecework with a Guaranteed Minimum. The standard is $.35 per unit. For output of 5 units or less per hour the employee is paid $1.75 each hour. For 6 units the pay is $2.10, and so on.

and his total earnings. The direct labor cost to the employer per unit of output is shown on the ordinate at the right side of the graph and is portrayed by the dashed line.

The advantages of piecework are its simplicity and ease of understanding by the employees. It is eminently fair in its rewards, since earnings are directly proportional to output for all output levels in excess of standard. The guaranteed minimum protects the employee's basic income should output fall below standard due to production delays or inexperience on the employee's part. Cost accounting and control by management is facilitated by the fact that labor cost is constant for output above standard.

However, the piecework system does have serious disadvantages. If a general wage increase is put into effect for all employees, this necessitates changing all the piece rates on the books. This is a very cumbersome clerical task. Usage of piece rates for a group incentive where different employees have different hourly base rates is very cumbersome. Piece rates often lead to confusion in the minds of both management and labor in that time study is here linked rather directly with money rates. To insure objectivity, the money rate should be arrived at for every job by an evaluation of its relative amount of skill, effort, responsibility, and job conditions, whereas the standard time should be determined by an objective study of the quantity of work that can be reasonably expected from a normal worker working under standardized conditions. The money level and the work standard should be considered separately.

Standard-Hour Plan

Sometimes called the 100-per-cent bonus or standard time plan, the standard-hour plan expresses the work standard in terms of time. It features a guaranteed base rate that the worker receives if he fails to meet standard performance. This plan is very widely used, and it overcomes all of the disadvantages of the piecework plan while retaining its advantages. It is essentially the same as piecework with a guaranteed minimum, with the exception of the fact that the standard is expressed in time instead of money. As defined by the Society for the Advancement of Management, it is a pay plan in which the per cent performance over standard is rewarded by an equal per cent premium over base pay.[14] An example will reveal more correctly how the system works. Assume that the base rate for a job is $2.00 per hour and that the time standard for the operation upon which the employee is currently working is $\frac{1}{4}$ hour per unit. Pay would normally be calculated separately for each day. If 40 units are produced in one day, the employee would have earned 10 standard hours of pay, or $20.00. If the work day were 8 hours long, he would then

[14] Society for Advancement of Management, *Glossary of Terms Used in Methods, Time Study, and Wage Incentives* (New York: The Society, 1953).

have earned 10 standard hours of pay, although his clock hours were 8. His efficiency is thus 125 per cent. If, for some reason, the employees' output for the day were only 24 units (6 standard hours), he would be paid his base rate for the full 8 clock hours worked.

Advantages of this plan are that it is easy for employees to understand, and earnings are directly proportional to production above standard. A change in hourly wage rates for all employees has no effect upon the standards, because they are expressed in time units (rather than money units as in the piecework plan). It is readily suitable to group incentive applications where the group may include employees on various base rates. Further it facilitates the utilization of accounting controls and departmental measures of efficiency. There appear to be no disadvantages to this system; in fact, many companies, having tried other more cumbersome plans, have dropped them in favor of the standard-hour plan.

Gains-Sharing Plans

A gains-sharing plan is one in which the money rewarded for increasing output above standard is not in a direct proportion to the increment in production. The worker receives less than 1-per-cent increase in pay for each 1-per-cent increase in production. The "gains" are shared with the employer. All of the gains-sharing plans are based upon the premise of rewarding the employee for saving time in the performance of his job. Standards are expressed in terms of time. In one well-known plan, the Bedeaux plan, named after its creator Charles Bedeaux, 75 per cent of the gain went to the worker, whereas 25 per cent went to indirect labor and supervision. In 1940 this plan was revised so that 100 per cent of the gain went to the worker. In the Rowan plan, devised by James Rowan in 1898, the incentive was determined by the ratio of time saved to the standard time. Essentially this involved a variable sharing arrangement that changed continuously as output levels increased. The plan was difficult for the employees to understand and did not generate their enthusiastic support.

The Halsey 50-50 bonus plan was devised about 1890 before the advent of time-and-motion study. The standard, expressed in time per unit, was based upon past performance when the employee was working for daywork wages. Daywork output typically averages about 60 to 85 per cent of the "intermediate task," which is usually used as the standard for the piecework and standard hour plans. According to Lytle[15] 100 per cent performance under the Halsey plan is equivalent to 78 per cent under the standard hour of intermediate task scale; Mee[16] says it is equal to 62½

[15] Charles W. Lytle, *Job Evaluation Methods* (2nd Ed., New York: The Ronald Press Comany, 1954), p. 476.

[16] John Mee (ed.), *Personnel Handbook* (New York: The Ronald Press Company, 1950), p. 228.

per cent; and Loudon and Deegan[17] state it is 83 per cent. If the worker should complete the operation in a time equal to or greater than standard, he is paid his guaranteed base rate for the elapsed time. If he does it in less than the standard time, he is paid a bonus of 50 per cent times his hourly wage rate multiplied by the time saved. Note that in the standard hour plan he would be paid for 100 per cent of the time saved. A fundamental purpose of the sharing feature in the Halsey plan is to prevent the worker from "running away with the rate." Because no methods analysis or time study is done first, there is great incentive for the employee to figure out a better way of doing his job. This would cause the standard to appear "loose" as time goes by. But because he has to give one half of the reward for increased productivity to management, the employee soon feels that the increase in money income from a really great increase in output is not really worth the effort. So he tends to produce at a respectable but moderate level above standard. The Halsey plan is only infrequently used in industry at the present time. Industrial engineers strongly disapprove of basing standards upon past performance, and employees are not enthusiastic about sharing the fruits of their efforts with the employer.

Group Incentives

Group incentives for work that is measured and standardized can be paid under any one of the foregoing types of incentive plans. Earnings are determined from the total number of units produced by the group. However, the group approach does not obviate the necessity of analysis and standardization of each job within the group. Where the workers are quite interdependent and where clear cooperation and coordination is vital to success, a group incentive plan makes a great deal of sense. On a production line, where one employee cannot get ahead of the person who precedes him, a group plan may work well. If there are a number of different jobs within the group, each having a different basic hourly rate of pay, the standard-hour plan works quite well. Here the percentage increase in output above standard for the entire group can be added to the base rate for each employee to determine the amount of his bonus for that pay period.

HUMAN RELATIONS AND INCENTIVES

The usage of wage incentives in an industrial organization often achieves management's goal of higher productivity and lower direct labor costs. Further, the total cost per unit may very well decrease too. If a particular machine or work center has an overhead (or burden) costing rate of $5.00 per direct labor hour and if output is increased, then the overhead

[17] J. Keith Loudon and J. Wayne Deegan, *Wage Incentives* (2nd Ed., New York: John Wiley & Sons, Inc. 1959) p. 30.

cost per unit is decreased, because the overhead rate, within limits, does not go up if production rises. Employees too stand to gain from the installation of a wage-incentive system. Commonly their pay will average 20 to 30 per cent higher. So far, so good.

However, the introduction of incentives brings about many administrative and human relations problems that either are not present at all under daywork or are present to only a minor extent. A larger industrial engineering staff is needed to devise the incentive plan, set work standards, and develop controls. Greater attention must be devoted to obtaining accurate piece counts of each worker and to maintaining quality and safety standards. And above all serious human-relations problems are created. Of the 3,399 grievances cases handled by the American Arbitration Association in 1955, 23 per cent were caused by disputes over job standards, wage incentives, and time studies. In the period 1951 to 1956 more than 25 per cent of all man-hours lost from work stoppages were caused by disputes over measuring workers' performance.[18]

Role of the Industrial Engineer

The process of work measurement used to set standards generally requires that the engineer closely observe the detailed motions of the employee for a considerable length of time (anywhere from one half to a whole eight-hour day). The engineer often tells the employee to change his method of doing the work. To an experienced worker who feels he already knows his job well, this detailed observation and correction often causes tension and antagonism toward the engineer. But in reality this is only the start of a human relations conflict. The worker knows that the engineer is going to set a time standard on his job. This standard will determine his wages. If the rate turns out to be "tight," he will be unable to exceed standard performance, and he will only be paid his hourly base rate for the time he has actually worked. Workers tend to feel that if they can make the work look more difficult and take longer than really necessary, they can fool the engineer and thus get a "good" or a "loose" rate. However, the engineer is often aware of the worker's objectives, so he adjusts the actual observed time by a percentage factor to rate or level his performance. So if the employee stalls in doing his job and takes 5 minutes to perform a unit of work and if the engineer judges his skill and effort to be 75 per cent of normal, he will allow only 3.75 minutes for the operation. Sometimes in spite of his awareness, the engineer is "fooled," and he does establish a loose rate. On the other hand, if the resultant rate should turn out to be "tight," not only will the worker who has been studied be dissatisfied, but also his fellow workers who perform the same operation will blame him for the bad rate.

The industrial engineer, trying to do a professional job, is many times

[18] *Time,* (March 26, 1956), p. 94.

caught between two fires. There is pressure from higher management for greater efficiency, higher production, lower labor costs, and the placing of as many jobs as possible on incentive in a limited amount of time. If the engineer establishes "loose" standards, he is criticized by management. Because he is dependent upon management for his job tenure, salary increases, and progress in the organization, he must conform to management's expectations. However, there are pressures on the other side of the fence too. The workers will turn in rate grievances and express resentment against him if they are not satisfied with the standards. Since the engineer must frequently mingle with the employees, he seeks at least their passive goodwill and cooperation. If the employees should file a great number of grievances over the rates set, management may express dissatisfaction with the caliber of his efforts.

Restriction of Output

Restriction of output is a phenomenon that occurs with both union and nonunion employees and under both daywork and incentive situations. The problem is accentuated under an incentive system. Restriction of output means that informal group pressures and sanctions are imposed to prevent employees from producing as much as they are capable of. From the early days of the scientific management movement through to the present day, industrial engineers and management-engineering consultants have tended to believe that the installation of a wage-incentive program would cause employees to try to maximize their earnings by maximizing their production. Certain individual employees indeed do just this. They work to the limit of their endurance to earn as much money as possible. But the majority control their output; they do not produce as much as they could if they worked to the limits imposed by bodily fatigue. Usually they work well below this point. In one factory the employees in the punch press department systematically produced at 27 per cent above standard, never more. This restriction was achieved through group controls. When he was confronted with the evidence of restriction, the informal leader, who in this case was the shop steward, vehemently denied any planned effort on the employees' part to restrict work.

Why does this phenomenon occur? There are many reasons to explain it. First, employees tend to believe that if they earn more money than management thinks they should, the piece rate will be cut. Rate cutting is a practice that arose in industry many years ago. Ill-trained "efficiency experts" who served as consultants to employers often adopted this practice. At the present time all reputable industrial engineers and employers frown upon the practice. However, it still occurs often enough to arouse the employees' fears.

Even if the employer does not intentionally cut rates when earnings reach too high a level, sometimes a worker thinks he does. This comes about through the continued auditing and re-examination of operations that some companies undertake. In the effort to reduce costs still further, operations with established rates are many times restudied for further methods improvement, and then a new and lower rate is set. Strictly speaking the employee should have as good an earnings potential as before, but frequently management's motives are mistrusted. The employees may interpret this as a form of disguised rate cutting.

There are social reasons for restriction of output also. According to the logics of management and its engineers, employees should engage in individualistic competition, should work hard and take pride in doing a good day's work for their employer. Primary emphasis should be upon the acquisition of more money as the fruits of hard labor. This is considered a major virtue. Concern with the reactions of one's associates to this competitive drive for more and more should not bother the individual.[19] Yet many workers are not so strongly motivated in this direction. They are sensitive to what others in their work group think. They want to acquire and maintain the respect and friendship of their fellows. They feel that group acceptance, social participation, and group solidarity are important values. Those who seek to maximize their earnings by exceeding the group-imposed quota are labeled rate-busters. They generally are set apart from the group and its social activities. I was once employed in a shop where one employee beat up another worker because the latter was working too fast.[20] Rate restrictors sometimes feel that they are "shown up" in the eyes of management by the high output of the "rate-busters," and they resent the latter. Workers often believe that slow workers will be discharged. Thus in many factories there are conflicts between the restrictors and the rate-busters.

Wage Inequities

Work measurement techniques such as time study have a margin of error. Authorities claim that a well-qualified engineer can set standards that are within ± 5 per cent of the true or correct values. Many critics challenge this assertion. But regardless of this controversy, it is a fact that nearly every industrial establishment has a fair number of loose and tight rates. These may be caused by inexperienced engineers; by workers figuring out short cuts so that the rates become loose over a period of many months; or because the job conditions (adjustment of machine, quality of the materials, and so on) have changed with the passage of time. The fact that the earnings potential will vary significantly from one job to an-

---

[19] This philosophy is described by Max Weber in his book *The Protestant Ethic and the Spirit of Capitalism* (New York: Charles Scribner's Sons, 1930).

[20] The victim, only slightly bruised, was transferred to another plant. The aggressor was a local union committeeman. Management, not wanting to upset good union relations, took no disciplinary action against him.

other causes anxiety and jealousy among the employees. They naturally compete to get the jobs with "loose" standards.

Then there is the perennial problem of equity between the semiskilled
worker, who is on incentive, and the highly skilled employee, such as the
tool and die maker, who is paid by the hour. Industrial engineers find it
very difficult to put nonrepetitive, highly variable, and complex jobs on
incentive. In one electronics factory, male machine-shop craftsmen
went on a one-day strike because semiskilled women on incentive in the
same plant had higher take-home pay.

Fluctuations in Earnings

A common source of frustration to workers is the variation in earnings
from one week to another. This is prevalent in shops where there are short
runs, and new operations must be continually mastered; where workers
are transferred from one operation to another frequently; and where the
process equipment breaks down often (down-time). In job-order shops
where new and different products are continually being introduced, there
naturally is a lag from the introduction of new operations until they have
been placed on incentive. If workers are paid daywork rates for this in-
terim period, they will experience a temporary lowering of their pay.

Rewards for Methods Improvements

The typical incentive plan rewards employees for physically working
harder but gives them nothing for greater ingenuity and new ideas on how
to improve their jobs. If employees develop methods improvements that
make the work easier and reduce the time per unit, they are faced with
a dilemma. If they notify their supervisor or the industrial engineer of
the improvement, there is every likelihood that the operation will be
changed to conform to the better method. Then a new and lower time
standard will be established. Employees often feel that their "reward" for
passing on their ideas to management is a lower piece rate that will require
harder work to earn as much money as they obtained previously. Even if
the new rate should provide them with as much money as before the
change (equivalent earnings for equivalent skill and effort), they tend to
feel that they are exposing themselves to the risk of a tight rate. So we find
that in many shops workers devise jigs, fixtures, and other simple methods
improvements and keep them secret from management. By so doing they
can increase their incentive earnings substantially without increased
physical exertion. Or if they suspect that earnings of, say, 50 and 60 per
cent above base rate will arouse the industrial engineer's suspicions, they
use their labor-saving devices to give themselves more free time during the
working day.

Many companies attempt to solve this problem by encouraging employees to submit their proposals for methods improvements and cost reduc-

tions through a formal suggestion system in order to receive monetary awards. In theory this is fine. However, the typical suggestion plan pays the employee who submitted an idea 10 to 15 per cent of the first year's net dollar savings. Many employees conclude that they will make more money by concealing their ideas from management and thereby obtain higher incentive earnings through utilization of jigs and fixtures of their own making. The central problem, in summary, is this: Should an incentive plan reward employees only for the exertion of greater physical skill and effort, or should it reward them for their own ideas and initiative as well? Would it be better to incorporate rewards for ideas into the basic incentive plan itself, or should this objective be met by means of a separate program? Possible solutions are the payment of much more liberal awards under a suggestion system or the adoption of a plantwide incentive system, such as a Scanlon Plan. More will be said about the Scanlon Plan in Chapter 25.

Meeting the Human Problems Imposed by Incentives

Although no magic formulas exist that can solve the human problems imposed by incentives, there are certain sound approaches that, if followed, can ameliorate them. There is need for more research and experimentation to find full answers.

By assiduously applying the principles enunciated earlier in this chapter for the successful operation of an incentive program, some of these difficulties can be overcome or greatly modified. For example, employees' fears of rate cutting can be prevented by guaranteeing standards. Tight rates can be adjusted if an effective grievance procedure exists. Careful administration of the program can reduce fluctuations in earnings (for example, some firms pay the average incentive earnings that an employee has built up during the preceding three months when he is transferred to an unfamiliar operation or for machine down-time). If the employer adopts an easy-to-understand incentive system and if a training program is instituted to teach the employees how the plan operates, confidence will be built up and distrust and suspicion allayed.

Antagonisms between the industrial engineer and employees can be considerably reduced by a full recognition of the staff nature of the engineer's position in the organization. The employee is accustomed to having interaction originated for him by his foreman. In his approach to the employee for making a time study, the engineer should first obtain the authorization of the foreman. If the employees are represented by a union, the shop steward should be notified also. The foreman, steward, and engineer as a group would then approach the employee to explain the work measurement assignment in relation to his job. After the work standard has been determined, the engineer should present it to the foreman for his reactions and approval. It should be the foreman who announces the standard to the employee. The shop steward should also be informed of developments to obtain his reaction.[21]

There are still other possibilities for overcoming many of these human relations problems. Where employees are represented by a union, there is considerable merit to the idea of having a degree of union participation in the time study and rate-setting process. Union participation through union-employed time-study men and bargaining of piece rates accounts, in no small measure, for the full acceptance by the workers of the piecework method of payment in the garment industry. It is not here proposed that work standards and piece rates should be bargained throughout industry. Employers typically hold that setting of work loads is a management prerogative. The money paid for each job is, of course, a bargainable issue. However, there is considerable merit to the proposal that local union officials and stewards receive training in the fundamentals of time study and incentives—even to the point where the union would have one or more fully qualified time-study experts in its membership. Various procedures could be followed for implementing this. Standards set by management would be put into effect except for those that workers have found by trial to be incorrect or unjust. They would then file a grievance. If a restudy of the operation were deemed by both parties to be advisable, it would be carried out by both the industrial engineer employed by the company and the time study specialist working for the union. The dispute would then be resolved by a meeting of the minds of all parties involved: management as represented by the foreman and the industrial engineer and the employees as represented by the steward and the time-study specialist. Disputes unresolved at this level could be processed through the regular grievance procedure and eventually taken to arbitration if necessary.

The adoption of a plantwide incentive plan based upon the essential concept of cooperation between labor and management is another method of attempting to overcome the multitude of human problems created by wage incentives. The Scanlon Plan described in Chapter 25 is one well-known method. It does not involve individual job rates but rather a standard expressed in terms of labor costs as a percentage of the sales value of the product for the plant as a whole. Employee participation in reducing costs is actively encouraged. Teamwork and cooperation instead of individualistic competition is emphasized.

UNION ATTITUDES

Union viewpoints toward wage incentives vary considerably. Broadly speaking, unions tend to oppose incentive pay programs, although there

---

[21] A procedure very similar to this is proposed by William Foote Whyte in his book *Money and Motivation* (New York: Harper & Row, 1955), pp. 229-234.

are some notable exceptions. The high percentage of the workers in the men's and women's wearing apparel industries working under the piece-rate method of payment correlates highly with a positive acceptance of incentives by the unions involved. Piecework has been traditional in the needle trades for several generations. This fact coupled with the fact that in many cases piece rates are established through bargaining between union and employer accounts for the rather general acceptance in these industries. The Amalgamated Clothing Workers Union (men's wearing apparel) has, through the years, favored incentives, because only in this way could workers' earnings increase without increasing labor costs. If labor costs were increased, it would be difficult for unionized firms to compete in the product market with nonunion employers. The problem of competition from nonunion mines has also historically been a factor in the acceptance of the piecework system by the United Mine Workers Union.[22] The United Automobile Workers Union is officially opposed to wage incentives. So also is the International Association of Machinists.

There are numerous reasons for union antagonism toward incentives. Union spokesmen argue that individual incentives foster competition among workers. They pit one man against another. Those who are high, low, and average producers are readily identified. Management judges one employee by the achievements of another. If the employer offers the employees an opportunity to make a basic living wage only by exerting above average skill and effort under an incentive system (instead of an adequate daywork wage), the unions oppose such an arrangement. Unions also charge that piecework plans tend to transfer part of the risks of business ownership to the worker. With fixed-unit direct-labor costs the worker bears the brunt of production delays, inefficient scheduling, machine breakdowns, and so on.[23]

Unions also criticize the inequities caused by "loose" and "tight" piece rates. Foremen may reward friendly workers with jobs having "loose" rates (gravy jobs) while penalizing others through assignment to jobs having "tight" ones. Likewise inequality of earnings opportunity can divide union membership into opposing camps. Some departments in a plant may enjoy high earnings, whereas others may have low earnings even though base rates may be the same. Another major problem from the union viewpoint is the inordinate amount of time required by business agents and international representatives to handle disputes and grievances arising from the operation of incentive programs. They claim incentive plants require much more attention than do daywork shops.[24]

[22] G. F. Bloom and H. R. Northrup, *Economics of Labor Relations* (6th Ed., Homewood, Ill.: Richard D. Irwin, Inc., 1969), p. 149.

[23] Solomon Barkin, "Labor's Attitudes Toward Wage Incentive Plans," *Industrial and Labor Relations Review,* Vol. 1, No. 4 (July 1948).

[24] *Collective Bargaining Report,* AFL-CIO, Vol. 2, No. 12 (December 1957), pp. 75-76.

Questions for Review and Discussion

1. What considerations would guide your decision to pay employees according to an incentive pay plan or a daywork plan?
2. Give a list of occupations for which you feel it would be very difficult to develop a fully fair and equitable incentive plan.
3. From the standpoint of employees, what are the possible advantages of working under an incentive payment plan? Disadvantages?
4. After carefully weighing all the problems involved and the potential benefits and limitations, the management of a company has decided to adopt the incentive method of wage payment for as large a portion of its employees as possible. Explain how you would go about initiating and installing such a program. (In answering give consideration to administrative problems involved, employee reactions, union reactions, views of supervision, and so on).
5. Explain the meaning of the following:
   a. Time study
   b. Predetermined elemental time systems
   c. Standard hour plan
   d. Performance rating (or leveling)
6. What are the causes of organized restriction of output that often develops among work groups in industry? How can the problem be alleviated?
7. What problems are likely to arise under a system where piece rates are established through joint bargaining between management and the union?
8. In addition to training in the purely technical aspects of methods and time study, what other types of skills, knowledge, and abilities should methods-time study engineers possess?

CASE PROBLEM

The Automotive Supply Parts Company is a well-established, profitable manufacturing concern located in a large Eastern city. It makes a variety of products for the automotive industry. These are sold to the automobile manufacturers as original equipment and also sold through distributors throughout the country as replacement parts.

For several years the company has had a major portion of its production operations on individual incentives. A large, well-trained staff of industrial engineers is employed to analyze and improve production methods, standardize operations, and set time standards for individual operations by means of time study procedures. Base rates of pay for every job are bargained with a local independent union. A standard-hour-incentive plan is used throughout the plant. For output in excess of standard, the plan pays employees in direct proportion to the increase in productivity. Thus an employee whose average production for a day is 25 per cent above standard receives a 25-per-cent bonus above his base pay. If an operation is shut down due to a machine breakdown or lack of materials, the operator is paid his guaranteed basic hourly rate for the actual hours involved.

The incentive program works fairly well in most production departments of the plant. If an employee feels that a particular standard is unjust, he can file a grievance with the union time study stewards, who will investigate and retime the job if necessary. The union time study stewards (three in number) are members of the union who have been trained by management in the intricacies of the time-study system used. They are paid by the company but do in fact effectively try to look out for the workers' interests when a time standard is in dispute.

In one large department, the punch press department, which contains eighty employees, there is continual conflict over the operation of the incentive program. In fact, the average number of grievances over time standards emanating from this department each year is more than are filed in all of the other departments combined. The union steward in this department is very aggressive in presenting grievances to management. Those in the industrial engineering department feel that a large part of the continuing controversy over time standards is due to the rabid antagonism of this one union steward. They feel that he keeps the workers continually stirred up and suspicious of the integrity of the industrial engineering department. However, the employees feel that he effectively represents their interests, so they have repeatedly re-elected him to office throughout the years.

The employees complain that there is too much down-time, for which they receive only their base pay. They also do not like the fact that new operations or new parts are being continually introduced. Sometimes they must work several weeks on daywork wages on these new operations before the industrial engineer who is assigned to that department gets around to timing the work and placing it on incentive. They complain, through this steward, that the standards are too "tight." They can't make a suitable bonus. There is considerable animosity toward the industrial engineering staff members. One employee has stated, "Every time I see you time study guys, I get so mad I see red."

The departmental foreman, who firmly allies himself with the industrial engineer assigned to his department, makes a practice of demonstrating to workers who complain about rates that the rates are in fact fair and just. He does this by sitting down at a punch press, producing at a furious pace for perhaps five minutes, and then announcing that he has no trouble meeting the standard. They complain that he could not keep up such a fast pace all day long, as they must do.

For its part the industrial engineering department feels that the work standards in the punch press department are fair. The head of the industrial engineering department becomes very annoyed with workers who deliberately hold back production on an operation for which the rate is in dispute. He has noticed that on more than one occasion when the standard (expressed in units per hour) has been lowered as a result of a grievance and consequent retiming of the operation, then the employees have "gone to town" on the operation and produced far more than the original (disputed) standard. When workers restrict output on operations having rates they think are unfair, this also makes it very difficult, if not impossible, for the company to meet its production schedules.

On more than one occasion certain high producers (the rest of the workers call them rate-busters) have been physically shoved around and punched by other employees because the latter consider such activities detrimental to the security of group.

With the exception of the punch press department, relations between the top leadership of the union and management are reasonably amicable. The president of the union is an electrician who remains rather aloof from the constant strife in the punch press department.

In summary, then, the employees, led by an aggressive shop steward, feel that the work standards are too tight to make a decent incentive bonus. (They have averaged 23 per cent bonus over the previous six months' period on those operations having a time standard.) Further they claim that they receive only their base rate of pay for too large a portion of the time because of down-time and delay in establishing standards on new operations, and in general they resent the close controls that the incentive system imposes on their jobs. The industrial engineering department seeks to establish accurate standards, to prevent loose rates from being created, and to have the incentive system serve as an instrument of management control. It is willing to restudy operations over which grievances have been filed and make adjustments if they are fully justified. It never loosens a rate just because of worker and union pressure—only when the objective facts justify it.

Questions

1. Diagnose the situation presented in this case.
2. What can the industrial engineering group do to improve relations?
3. What can management do to alleviate the problem? What can the union leadership do?
4. Are problems such as these inherent in the operation of an incentive system?

Suggestions for Further Reading

Beach, Dale S., "Wage Incentives on the Wane?" *Personnel,* Vol. 39, No. 6, November-December 1962, pp. 47-54.

————, "Wage Incentives and Human Relations," *The Journal of Industrial Engineering,* Vol. XII, No. 5, September-October 1961, pp. 349-353.

Belcher, David W., *Wage and Salary Administration,* 2nd Ed., Englewood Cliffs, N.J.: Prentice-Hall, 1962, Ch. 14.

Brennan, Charles W., *Wage Administration,* Rev. Ed., Homewood, Ill.: Richard D. Irwin, 1963, Chs. 15-22.

Gelberg, Alfred, "How to Save a Failing Incentive System," *Management Services,* Vol. 3, No. 5, September-October 1966, pp. 31-34.

Karger, Delmar W. and F. M. Bayha, *Engineered Work Measurement,* 2nd Ed., New York: The Industrial Press, 1965.

Lanham, Elizabeth, *Administration of Wages and Salaries,* New York: Harper & Row, 1963, Chs. 13 and 14.

Lincoln, James F., *Incentive Management,* Cleveland: Lincoln Electric Company, 1956.

Loudon, J. K. and J. W. Deegan, *Wage Incentives,* 2nd Ed., New York: John Wiley & Sons, 1959.

Magnum, Garth, "Are Wage Incentives Becoming Obsolete?," *Industrial Relations,* Vol. 2, No. 1, October 1962, pp. 73-96.

Maynard, Harold B. (ed.), *Industrial Engineering Handbook,* 2nd Ed., New York: McGraw-Hill Book Company, 1963.

Niebel, Benjamin W., *Motion and Time Study,* 4th Ed., Homewood, Ill.: Richard D. Irwin, 1967.

Payne, Bruce, "Controlling White Collar Labor Costs," *Michigan Business Review,* Vol. 19, January 1967, pp. 10-19.

Schultz, Gregory V., "Plants' Incentives Slump Badly Over Last Six Years," *Factory,* Vol. 123, No. 1, June 1965, pp. 68-79.

Smalley, H. E., "Another Look at Work Measurement," *Journal of Industrial Engineering,* Vol. 18, March 1967, pp. 202-218.

Whyte, William Foote, *Money and Motivation,* New York: Harper & Row, 1955.

Incentives Based Upon Cooperation

25

The preceding chapter was concerned primarily with individual wage incentives where there is a direct relationship between the amount produced by the individual worker and his pay. For the most part, engineering work measurement techniques are used to establish the production standard upon which pay and output calculations are based. In this chapter we shall examine plant-and companywide incentive programs that have objectives somewhat broader in scope than the higher-output-per-unit-time objective of the traditional direct-wage-incentive installation. These plantwide and companywide incentives are based upon the concept of cooperation among employees, management, and the union (if the workers are represented by one).[1] The objectives may be manifold. Included among typical objectives are a plantwide reduction in labor costs or total payroll costs, reduction in material and supply costs, fostering of greater company loyalty, improved cooperation between labor and management, and lower turnover and absenteeism.

In this chapter we shall discuss three kinds of plant or companywide incentive programs. These are the Scanlon Plan, the Kaiser-United Steel Workers plan, and profit sharing.

[1] Group incentives are based upon the concept of cooperation among a group of employees. It seemed more appropriate to include these in the preceding chapter on direct wage incentives because they are based upon engineering work measurement techniques.

INCENTIVES AND LABOR-MANAGEMENT COOPERATION

An incentive system that departs considerably from commonly accepted notions of what an incentive plan should be is the one developed by Joseph N. Scanlon. The plan is generally known as the Scanlon Plan.[2] The late Mr. Scanlon was an official of the United Steelworkers of America in the late 1930's and early 1940's; later he joined the faculty of the Massachusetts Institute of Technology.

The plan consists basically of two parts: (1) a plantwide wage-incentive arrangement for which the standard is set by accounting methods and not by time study; (2) a program for implementing cooperation among the employees, the union, and the management to solve production and efficiency problems. This is accomplished through a unique suggestion plan. Although the details of the Scanlon Plan vary from one installation to another the essential features are the same. Even though the plan can work successfully in a nonunion company, Scanlon felt that if employees were represented by a union, the greatest advantages of employee participation could be obtained.

Labor Cost Norm and Incentive Bonus

Cost accounting records are examined to arrive at a labor cost norm. This norm is expressed as a percentage of the total sales value of the product shipped by the company. Usually direct and indirect labor as well as supervisory payroll are included in the figure for labor cost. Sometimes even executives are included in the incentive plan. Scanlon generally recommended that all employees from worker to major executive should participate. An example will show how the plan works. Assume that labor and management after a careful examination of accounting records arrive at a labor-cost norm of 40 per cent of the sales value of the product. This figure then becomes the standard for the ensuing year. Calculations are then made on a monthly basis. If cooperative efforts reduce the actual payroll costs below that 40-per-cent figure for any one month, the employees will then receive a bonus.

It has been found practical to reserve a portion of the monthly savings (25 per cent in Table 25-1) to balance against those months when the actual is in excess of the norm or standard. Likewise it should be pointed out that in some companies which use the Scanlon Plan, a certain percentage of the savings are retained by the company. If major changes

---

[2] Descriptions and analyses of the Scanlon Plan can be found in a number of articles and books. Among them are: William Foote Whyte, *Money and Motivation* (New York: Harper & Row, 1955); "Productivity and Incentive Pay," *Management Record,* Vol. 19, No. 10 (October 1957); Russell W. Davenport, "Enterprise for Everyman," *Fortune,* Vol. 41, No. 1 (January, 1950), pp. 55-59; F. G. Lesieur and E. S. Puckett, "The Scanlon Plan Has Proved Itself," *Harvard Business Review,* Vol. 47, No. 5 (September-October 1969), pp. 109-118.

TABLE 25–1

Sales shipped for month	$125,000
Less decrease in value of finished goods in inventory and in process	25,000
Total production value	100.000
Labor cost allowable (40%)	40,000
Actual payroll for month	36,000
Savings from improvement in production efficiency	4,000
Less 25% for contingency reserve	1,000
Net available for distribution to employees	$3,000

Each employee receives a bonus of 8.33 per cent for the month ($3,000 divided by actual payroll of $36,000).

occur in basic wage rates, in the selling price, or in the cost of raw materials or if the company invests in substantial technological improvements, a re-examination of the labor-cost norm may be made. A change in the percentage would be by mutual agreement between management and labor.

Suggestion Plan and Production Committees

It is through the suggestion plan that ideas are handled that make it possible to improve work methods, redesign products, reduce or simplify paperwork, and improve machine utilization. Every department has a production committee composed of a management representative (commonly the foreman) and an employee or union representative. The function of these committees is to process and evaluate employee suggestions. Some are accepted and put into effect at the department level. Those considered worthwhile for the entire plant or those involving major expenditures and changes are passed on to an administration or screening committee composed of an equal number of management and employee (or union) representatives. Suggestions approved by the screening committee are passed on to top management for a final decision. Because management is represented on the screening committee, it generally approves at this point. There are no individual awards under the Scanlon Plan. The payoff comes from cost-cutting ideas that benefit the organization as a whole and thus contribute to the plantwide bonus. Benefits of this participative form of suggestion plan are threefold. (1) It emphasizes cooperation between management and labor. They work together in production and screening committees to solve problems. (2) Teamwork means that often a problem that could not be solved by one person alone is successfully handled by the combined brains of a group. (3) Genuine participation by employees in the affairs of the business reduces the likelihood of restriction of output and resistance to change on their part. They tend to support that which they have initiated and designed.

It is interesting to point out the contrasts between the traditional type of suggestion plan used in industry and the type that is part and parcel of the Scanlon Plan. In the standard suggestion plan individual employees write their ideas on suggestion blanks and drop these in suggestion boxes scattered throughout the plant. The suggestion plan coordinator generally either assigns the suggestions to a specialist (such as an engineer) who then studies their feasibility, or he turns them over to a suggestion committee that evaluates them. If, after thorough investigation, management considers a suggestion useful, it will calculate the annual dollar saving that could be realized through adoption of the idea. Then a percentage of this amount will be awarded to the employee (usually in the form of cash but sometimes in merchandise). If an employee's idea is rejected, he generally is notified by means of a form letter.

So we see that in the traditional suggestion system the emphasis is upon the individual, whereas in the Scanlon Plan it is upon group cooperation and group sharing in the benefits. Formal written communication is utilized in the traditional plan, whereas social interaction and discussion is a key feature of the Scanlon method. In the traditional setup, first-level supervisors sometimes are jealous of workers who submit cost-cutting ideas, because they fear that higher management will criticize them for not thinking of the idea themselves first. This problem is not present under the Scanlon arrangement, because both supervisor and employee work together in the production committee to initiate ideas jointly.

Evaluation of the Scanlon Plan

The Scanlon Plan is not a panacea. Just as the success of other incentive plans depends to a large extent upon the way in which they are administered and upon the attitudes of the parties involved, so it is with the Scanlon Plan. This plan requires a high degree of mutual confidence and cooperation between labor and management. It places a premium upon group cooperation and the initiation of ideas among the employees. If individual workers are unproductive, they will still share in the bonus earned by the entire plant. If no bonus is earned for several months running (as happens in some companies), employee dissatisfaction can mount. The underlying philosophy of the Scanlon Plan is different from that of the traditional type of incentive program. It overcomes many of the inherent difficulties of the traditional approach, but it raises new problems.

KAISER-UNITED STEELWORKERS PLAN

On March 1, 1963, the Long-Range-Sharing Plan negotiated between the Kaiser Steel Corporation of Fontana, California, and the United Steelworkers of America was launched. During the 116-day steel-industry strike in the fall and early winter of 1959, Edgar Kaiser, Chairman of the Board of Kaiser Steel, negotiated a separate settlement with the union before the rest of the industry made its agreement. He proposed to David J. McDonald, then President of the Steelworkers Union, that a way be found to prevent the periodic crises and fixed bargaining positions at contract-negotiating time. A tripartite committee (containing company, union, and public members) was established to develop a long-range plan for the equitable sharing of the Company's progress among the stockholders, the employees, and the public. In creating such a plan this Long-Range Committee, as it was officially called, was expected to give consideration to safeguarding the employees from increases in the cost of living, promoting stability of employment, sharing the fruits from increased productivity, providing for necessary expansion, and assuring the Company's and the employees' progress.[3]

The Long-Range Sharing Plan was evolved over a three-year period by the committee. It was submitted to the workers in January, 1963, voted upon, and accepted by a 3-to-1 margin. The key features of the plan have been as follows:

1. An employment guarantee that protects workers from unemployment as a result of technological improvements. It does not, however, protect them against layoff due to a decline in the company's business.
2. A "sharing of the gains" plan in which employees receive 32.5 per cent and the Company receives 67.5 per cent of any cost reductions realized because of increased efficiency.
3. Increases in wage rates and fringe benefits that are equal to or greater than those bargained throughout the rest of the industry. The cost for such increases is taken from the employees' share of savings from improvements in productive efficiency, as described in 2 above.
4. A program for gradually eliminating direct-wage incentives.

Psychological theory of motivation, specifically Maslow's hierarchy of needs, tells us that people must satisfy their basic needs for survival, safety, and security before they can exert efforts directed toward satisfying higher-ranking needs such as accomplishment, self-expression, and self-actualization. In other words fear of insecurity must be removed before men can make really significant contributions in the areas of improvements, innovations, and changes. The designers of the Kaiser plan

[3] Additional information on the Kaiser Long-Range-Sharing Plan can be found in Harold Stieglitz, *The Kaiser-Steel Union Sharing Plan,* Studies in Personnel Policy, No. 187 (New York: National Industrial Conference Board, 1963); "Three-Year Review of Kaiser Steel Corporation—Steelworkers Long Range Sharing Plan," *Collective Bargaining Negotiations and Contracts* (Washington, D.C.: The Bureau of National Affairs, Inc., 1966), pp. 16:611-614; *Business Week* (March 4, 1967), pp. 149-150 and (January 27, 1968), p. 68.

recognized this psychological fact when they incorporated the employment security provisions into the plan. Workers whose jobs are eliminated due to methods improvements and automation are transferred to other jobs. If the rate of pay on the new job is lower than his old rate, he receives his old rate for at least one year. Then he is paid the rate for the new job.

Recognizing that they could not possibly foresee all the problems that would arise in the operation of the Plan, the Tripartite Committee has looked upon the Plan as a living document. Changes and improvements have been made as required.

Sharing the Gains and Cooperation

The sharing-of-the-gains portion of the plan provides that 32.5 per cent of any savings in production costs below those prevailing in 1961 shall be distributed to the employees. Part of the savings have been distributed monthly as a cash bonus. For example in August 1963 the average hourly worker received a cash bonus of $39, in September $73, in October $70 and in November $64. During the three-year period from March 1963 through February 1966, the average worker was paid a total of $1560 in bonus. This gains distribution has averaged $.31 for each hour worked during this same period. This bonus money has been an addition to wage rates that are generally equivalent to those paid in the rest of the basic steel industry.

The monthly bonuses have fluctuated according to the actual cost savings that have been generated. In 1967 these bonuses had declined to the point where there was persistent grumbling by union members. Accordingly in early 1968 a major revision in the plan was negotiated. The revision provided that all of the employees' share of cost savings would go directly into the monthly payouts. The "wage and benefit reserve" that had claimed a portion of employees' share was eliminated. This reserve had been originally created to provide a fund to match increases in basic wage rates and fringe benefits bargained in the rest of the steel industry. Since the 1959 negotiations Kaiser had not been a party to the industry-wide steel bargaining. Even with the elimination of this reserve fund in 1968, Kaiser agreed to match union gains won from the other steel companies. Kaiser now counts the added expense of this matching as a labor cost in computing the employees' share.

The 1961 standard against which future costs have been compared is the production cost of the finished product. It includes all variable labor and material costs and certain nonvariable labor, material, and supply costs related to the maintenance of the plant and equipment. It excludes selling, administrative and general expenses, depreciation charges, profit or loss from the sale of property or equipment, interest, taxes, and profits. The 32.5 to 67.5 per cent split was derived from the fact that historically, over a ten-year period, labor costs had averaged 32.5 per cent of production costs. Separate calculations are made each month for savings in material and supply costs and for savings in labor cost. Deductions from the total savings are made for any company expenditure for improvements in methods and technology and for maintenance and repair of existing facilities. This deduction, according to the agreement between the parties, must be the lesser figure of either one third of the actual reduction in cost resulting from the change in machinery or one sixtieth of the capital expenditure. No deduction is made for sums spent for expansion of plant capacity.

A few months after the long-range-sharing plan was inaugurated, a participation program to generate and process employee production ideas was set up. The Idea Proposal Program grants the people a mechanism to submit their suggestions for reducing costs, improving quality, and cutting accidents. In addition 31 joint management-union committees were established. Their mission is to reduce production costs. The acceptance rate on employee suggestions has averaged about 70 per cent, which is well above the rate for a traditional suggestion plan.

Direct Wage Incentives

The Kaiser Plan has provided a mechanism for the gradual elimination of direct-wage incentives. At the time the plan was launched in 1963, about 40 per cent of the workers were covered by incentives. In common with many other companies, Kaiser had experienced numerous difficulties with its wage-incentive program. One fourth of all employee grievances related to the operation of the incentive system. Some rates were very loose, and the company felt it was not obtaining the high production that it was paying for. Employee resistance to changes in methods and standards was very great. Added to all these factors was the fact that many employees on low-skilled jobs earned more than those on high-skilled jobs.

The program for the gradual elimination of incentives provided for an employee vote in each incentive unit. If they voted incentives out, they received a sizable lump sum payment to compensate them for loss of their customary incentive bonus. Upon voting for the elimination of incentives in their unit, the employees immediately began to participate in the sharing-of-the-gains plan. Those who voted to retain their incentive payments did not participate in the gains-sharing plan. By early 1966, 75 per cent of the work force was covered by the sharing plan.

PROFIT SHARING

The concept of a company sharing some of the profits of its business with its employees is not new. The practice had its beginning in America in the late eighteenth century and in England and France in the middle nineteenth century. Albert Gallatin, Secretary of the Treasury under Presidents Jefferson and Madison, initiated a profit-sharing plan in 1794 at his glass works in New Geneva, Pennsylvania. Horace Greeley had a plan for certain employees of the *New York Tribune*. Pillsbury Flour Mills in Minneapolis set up a plan in 1882. In 1887 the Procter and Gamble Company adopted a plan that is still in operation although in a revised form.[4]

Profit Sharing Defined

The first formalized definition of profit sharing was that adopted by the International Cooperative Congress, Paris, France, in 1889. It reads as follows: "Profit-Sharing is an agreement freely entered into, by which the employees receive a share, fixed in advance, of the profits."

The Council of Profit Sharing Industries, which promotes the profit-sharing movement gives the following definition: "Any procedure under which an employer makes available to all regular employees subject to reasonable eligibility rules in addition to prevailing rates of pay, special current or deferred sums based on the profits of the business."[5]

For those plans that defer the distribution of benefits to employees until some future date, the regulations of the United States Internal Revenue Service must be adhered to if the employer wishes to avoid paying a tax on the profit-share sums. Among these requirements are the following. (1) There must be a predetermined formula for allocating the funds to the participants. (2) There must be a trust fund established, and this must be used for the exclusive benefit of the employees or their beneficiaries. (3) The plan must be in writing and communicated to employees.[6]

A profit-sharing plan, then, distributes part of the profits of the business to the employees. The earlier definition of the International Cooperative Congress specifies that the plan must have a definite formula or method for determining the amount that goes to the employees. The definition of the Council of Profit Sharing Industries omits any mention of an agreement by which shares are computed. Thus under the latter's definition the percentage share going to the employees might vary from year to year. Presumably the exact amount would be determined by the board of directors. The great majority of plans actually do have a systematic formula for computing the employee's share. It is logical that greater faith and confidence will tend to be created where the employees know exactly how their shares are figured.

According to Lovejoy there were about 11,000 profit-sharing plans in

[4] Some of the many companies that now have profit-sharing plans are Bell and Howell Company; Dow Chemical Company; Eastman Kodak Company; Kellogg Company; The Kroger Company; The Lincoln Electric Company; S. C. Johnson and Son, Inc.; Sears, Roebuck and Company; and Tappan Stove Company.

[5] Council of Profit Sharing Industries, *Profit Sharing Manual* (Rev. Ed., Chicago: The Council, 1957).

[6] F. B. Brower, *Sharing Profits With Employees,* Studies in Personnel Policy, No. 162 (New York: National Industrial Conference Board, 1957).

operation in the United States in 1958.[7] The National Industrial Conference Board placed the figure at 10,000 for 1957.[8] The number of profit-sharing plans in existence was at a very low ebb during the depression of the 1930's. When there were no profits to share and indeed many firms were operating in the red, numerous plans were abandoned. But there was a strong resurgence during World War II, especially because of the excess profits tax on employers. Also these were looked upon as additional fringe benefits to help recruit and retain qualified employees. Since the end of the War, profit sharing has continued to be quite popular.

Objectives of Profit Sharing

Why would an entrepreneur or the board of directors choose to share some of the fruits of a business enterprise with the employees? Although in practice the motives are many and varied, a fundamental purpose is to create a sort of proprietary interest on the part of the employees in the business organization. The belief is that they will be more loyal and devoted. Presumably the prospect of a profit bonus at the end of the year will motivate the employees to work harder in the hopes of increasing the profits of the company. They will become more cost conscious, try to reduce waste and scrap.

Other objectives are to improve employee morale, enhance employer-employee relations, and aid the public relations image of the corporation. A few companies, particularly in the past, looked upon profit sharing as a means of paying low wages and yet providing for adequate total employee income when profits were good. This in effect introduced a flexible wage structure to correlate with the profitability of the company. The rigidities of adequate wages through good times and bad could be avoided. Experience has shown that such plans based upon low wages (below prevailing rates for the given class of work) are generally unsuccessful.

For those plans that defer the payment of benefits until some future date, the objectives are modified somewhat from the foregoing. These plans typically provide benefits upon termination of employment, retirement, death, or disability. The goals here are to provide some financial security to meet certain risks of employment and life. Also management frequently feels that putting off the payment of the profit shares until many years in the future reduces the likelihood of employees' leaving the company.

Types of Plans

Profit-sharing plans can be conveniently classified according to when the benefits are paid out to the employees. There are three categories:

[7] L. C. Lovejoy, *Wage and Salary Administration* (New York: The Ronald Press Company, 1959), p. 421.

[8] Brower, *op. cit.* p. 9.

1. Current Distribution—This is the oldest method historically and still quite popular. Under it benefits are paid monthly, quarterly, semiannually, and annually.
2. Deferred Distribution—Growing rapidly in popularity in recent years this arrangement sets up a trust fund with benefits to be paid out for such contingencies as retirement, permanent disability, death, and termination of employment. In some instances the money is set up as a savings fund with employees having the right to withdraw certain portions after having been on the payroll for a specified number of years.
3. A Combination Plan—Some organizations have attempted to gain the advantages of both the current and the deferred distribution plans by paying out part of the profit share in the year earned in cash to the employees. This is a tangible reward in the present that people can fully realize and appreciate. The rest of the money is placed in a trust fund to be paid out at some future date according to the provision of the plan.

A 1965-66 study by the Bureau of Labor Statistics of 12,771 establishments employing 8.9 million workers showed that 12 percent of plant workers and 22 percent of office workers were under some form of profit-sharing plan. Of these workers, 81 percent were under a deferred distribution type plan, only 8.7 percent were under current distribution, 7 percent were under combined plans, and 3.7 percent were under elective plans.[9]

Figuring the Share

Most often the share of the total profits to be distributed to employees as a whole represents a fixed percentage of corporate net profits. In some cases it is a percentage of profits before deduction for dividends and taxes, and in others it is a percentage after deduction for dividends and/or taxes. In some cases the sum paid to participants is expressed as a percentage of the dividends to stockholders.

After the size of the total fund for any one year is computed, the allocation to individuals must be made. Usually each person's share is based upon the amount of his annual earnings in relation to the total payroll of those participating in the plan. Very commonly, also, the size of the share is related to one's length of service as well as his wage level. Occasionally each person's portion is based upon a performance rating (merit rating) score assigned by supervision.

Requirements for a Sound Plan

Due to a relatively long history accompanied by many successes and failures of various plans, certain helpful guides can be offered to insure

[9] Engen Gunnar, "A New Direction and Growth in Profit Sharing," *Monthly Labor Review,* Vol. 90, No. 7 (July 1967), pp. 1-8.

a successful program. Profit sharing cannot be installed as a substitute for adequate wage rates. The wages paid must be comparable to the prevailing rates for the same class of work in the labor market. The profit share which is distributed to each employee must be something extra. Only then will it be an incentive; only then will it develop loyalty and a proprietary interest in the success of the business.

Before the plan is instituted the state of employer-employee relations must be satisfactory. Profit sharing cannot be expected to restore an unhappy situation. The entire personnel-management program should be up to date and sound. The company must already be doing the right things as far as wages, hours, working conditions, fringe benefits, supervisory climate, and employee communications are concerned.

There must be some profits available to distribute to the employees. If a company is unfortunate enough to have a number of years of financial losses or of very small profits, there will be discontent with the program. An occasional loss will not ruin a firmly rooted plan, but continued losses have been a major factor causing the abandonment of many plans.

If the employees are represented by a union, the full support and cooperation of this organization is essential for success. According to decisions of the National Labor Relations Board, profit sharing is a bargainable issue. An employer cannot install and operate a plan unilaterally if the employees' representatives choose to bargain the point.

American Motors—UAW Progress-Sharing Plan

In 1961 the American Motors Corporation and the United Automobile Workers Union bargained a profit-sharing plan that has been officially called a progress-sharing plan. At that time this action attracted considerable nationwide attention because people felt this might herald the beginning of a movement toward profit sharing in the automobile industry generally. Such did not prove to be the case. Also it had been uncommon in the past for profit-sharing plans to be negotiated with unions.

The plan had been initially proposed to the union by American Motors to reward employees if sales and profits should be good but to also prevent the company from being saddled with a heavy fixed wage burden equivalent to the pattern negotiated in the rest of the industry. The plan has been administerd by a joint committee composed of equal numbers of union and management representatives.

As originally designed, the plan was the deferred distribution type. The employees did not receive any year-end cash bonuses. The share going to the employees was used to pay for increased pension, life insurance, health insurance, and supplemental unemployment benefits above those existing in 1961. In addition, a portion of the individuals' profit share was used to buy common stock in American Motors. The stock was held for him in a trust account. In certain emergency situations, such as illness or prolonged layoff, the person could withdraw all or part of the stock in his account.

The share of the total profits that was allocated to the workforce was equal to 15 per cent of the profit before taxes but after 10 per cent of net worth had been deducted. Two-thirds of the 15 per cent share was used to pay for the pension and insurance benefits and one-third was for the purchase of company stock.

During the first two years of the plan, company profits were good, and there was reasonable satisfaction on both sides. But since those early days American Motors has experienced a poor profit picture with some years showing actual losses. This caused dissatisfaction among the workers.

In 1964 the plan was revised to provide for direct cash payments yearly in the form of added vacation allowances. No longer was the money used to pay for pension and insurance benefits.

The American Motors plan never lived up to its original promise. The company-union conferences provided for in the initial 1961 contract were not productive. No genuine spirit of labor-management cooperation every really evolved. Improvements in work output and worker motivation were not forthcoming.

Healy, Henderson, and others, in analysing the American Motors experience, have stated that a profit-sharing formula of and by itself is unlikely to produce a new labor-management relationship. The plan, standing alone, becomes merely a gimmick.[10]

Union Attitudes

There has been no official attitude of the trade union movement in the United States toward profit sharing. The viewpoints vary from one union to another. Generally speaking, however, union spokesmen are skeptical of profit sharing. They frequently distrust the motives of management in this respect. They feel that management may wish to wean the employees' loyalty away from the union toward the employer. They sometimes see profit sharing as the symbol of a paternalistic nonunion employer. Frequently unions have preferred a definite wage increase over the vagaries of profit-sharing benefits. In many instances union pressure has caused the abandonment of these plans. On the other hand, one survey has revealed that both unionized rank-and-file employees and local union officials who have had experience with actual operating plans have a high degree of preference for profit sharing.[11]

Some Conclusions on Profit Sharing

A fundamental weakness of profit sharing is that employees' earnings are tied to profits—something over which they have only modest control.

[10] James J. Healy (ed.), James A. Henderson and others, *Creative Collective Bargaining* (Englewood Cliffs, N.J.: Prentice-Hall, Inc., 1965), p. 49.

[11] Brower, *op. cit.,* pp. 64-65.

Profits are affected by general business conditions and the state of the business cycle, extent of competition, luck, caliber of top management, and other factors beyond the control of the employees. Of course, employees as a group do have some effect upon profits to be sure. But if top management wishes to adopt such a program primarily for its incentive aspect, then this objective can be only partially realized. Nevertheless the record through the years, while fraught with ups and downs, reveals that great numbers of programs have been successful. They satisfy management. They satisfy the workers.

SOME COMPARISONS AND CONCLUSIONS

In this chapter we have analyzed the Scanlon Plan, which is at the same time a plantwide incentive plan and a program of union-management cooperation. Other incentive and labor-management cooperation plans are in existence in the United States, but this is by far the most popular and well known. There are certain similarities between the Scanlon Plan and the Kaiser Steel Company plan. Both are designed to foster cooperation among employees, union, and management to improve plant efficiency and reduce production costs. In both plans employees receive part of the savings derived from a reduction in production costs. In both plans the standard against which future costs or savings are compared is an historical one based upon an accounting type analysis of the relationship between labor costs and other manufacturing costs. Both the Scanlon type plans and the Kaiser plan contain organized mechanisms for encouraging and evaluating employee cost-cutting ideas. It appears to be very difficult to achieve real cooperation between management and labor to improve productivity without such committees.

However, there are some important differences also. The Scanlon Plan uses total sales value of the product as the basis for establishing the labor-cost norm. This includes selling, administrative, and general expenses and salaries, depreciation charges, and material costs. The Kaiser plan excludes selling, administrative, and general expenses and salaries and depreciation charges but includes material costs. There is a direct incentive in the Kaiser plan for employees to reduce material as well as labor costs. The Kaiser plan guarantees employees against unemployment due to technological improvements. There is no such guarantee under the Scanlon Plan.

Profit-sharing plans are designed to foster increased employee concern for the welfare of their company, greater cooperation, greater cost-consciousness, and higher morale. No performance standard is adopted in profit-sharing plans as it is in Scanlon and the Kaiser plans. Theoretically it would be possible for employees to receive a bonus with both the Scanlon and Kaiser plans even if there were no company profits for that year. Employees, as a group, have more control over their bonus under both Scanlon and Kaiser plans than do workers in profit-sharing firms. The profit of a company may be more related to general market conditions than to internal labor productivity. The payoff with the Scanlon and Kaiser plans is monthly in the form of a cash bonus (if it has been earned), whereas the payoff under profit sharing is at the end of the year. The trend in recent years throughout the country has been toward deferred profit sharing, which means the money is used to finance pension and insurance benefits, hence the worker does not receive his money until several years in the future.

Questions for Review and Discussion

1. What are the relative merits of individual incentives based upon engineered time standards as compared with a plantwide incentive, such as the Scanlon Plan.
2. Explain the principal features of the Scanlon Plan. Do you feel it can be operated successfully in a large multiplant company?
3. Why do workers so generally resist methods and machine improvements installed by management? Do you feel that the employment security provision of the Kaiser plan is a necessary prerequisite to employee acceptance of technological change?
4. What might motivate an employer to install a profit-sharing plan?
5. Do you feel that a deferred profit-sharing plan will appreciably alter employee productivity or attitudes?

Suggestions for Further Reading

Engen, Gunnar, "A New Direction and Growth in Profit Sharing," *Monthly Labor Review,* Vol. 90, July 1967, pp. 1-8.

Healy, James J. (ed.), James A. Henderson and others, *Creative Collective Bargaining,* Englewood Cliffs, N.J.: Prentice-Hall, 1965, Chs. 3 and 8.

Industrial Relations Counselors, *Group Work Incentives: Experience With the Scanlon Plan,* New York, 1962.

Jehring, James J., "A Contrast Between Two Approaches to Total Systems Incentives," *California Management Review,* Vol. 10, Winter 1967, pp. 7-14.

Lesieur, Frederick G. (ed.), *The Scanlon Plan: A Frontier in Labor Management Cooperation,* New York and Cambridge: John Wiley & Sons, and the Technology Press, 1958.

Metzger, Bert L., *Profit Sharing in Perspective,* 2nd Ed., Evanston, Ill.: Profit Sharing Research Foundation, 1966.

Stieglitz, Harold, *The Kaiser-Steel Union Sharing Plan,* Studies in Personnel Policy, No. 187, New York: National Industrial Conference Board, 1963.

Torbert, Frances, "Making Incentives Work," *Harvard Business Review,* Vol. 37, No. 5, September-October 1959, pp. 81-92.

Walton, Richard E., "Contrasting Designs for Participative Systems," *Personnel Administration,* Vol. 30, No. 6, November-December 1967, pp. 35-41.

Whyte, William Foote, *Money and Motivation,* New York: Harper & Row, 1955.

Compensation for Salesmen, Managers, and Professionals

26

In this chapter we shall explore pay practices for salesmen, supervisors, executives, and professionals. These comprise the exempt group. The term *exempt* means that they are exempt from the overtime pay requirements of the Fair Labor Standards Act. Such persons may be classified as exempt if the nature of their job responsibilities meets certain tests and if their pay equals or exceeds certain minima established by administrative order of the United States Department of Labor.

The compensation issues and problems for each of these groups are unique, and they are distinctly different from those for hourly and office workers. Salesmen are on the road much of the time, they receive little supervision, and they have wide latitude in the way they operate. First-line supervisors bear important leadership responsibilities. They must possess good technical knowledge of the products and processes in their departments. They are largely judged on the results achieved by their departments, not on how much activity they personally demonstrate.

Top executives are involved in risk taking, allocating and budgeting resources, leadership, high-level decision making, reconciling conflicting interests, and relating to the world outside the corporation. The time span over which their decisions may bear fruit is generally quite long, often from one to ten years. In the professional group are included such jobs as engineer, physicist, chemist, mathematician, attorney, economist, psychologist, and biologist. The work of professionals is highly technical. It demands a high level of intellectual effort. Commonly they must possess advanced graduate-level college degrees. Their work tends to be quite variable in nature and difficult to measure. The work of a theoretical physicist, for example, generally defies measurement. On the other hand, the job of a test engineer might be quite accurately described and evaluated.

Salary administration for the exempt groups requires considerably more adjustment and accommodation for individual abilities and personalities than does wage determination for lower-level groups. For these higher-level groups, to a considerable degree, the "man makes the job."

COMPENSATION FOR SALESMEN[1]

Sales constitutes a major function in most businesses. Many organizations consider it to be a line activity along with manufacturing. The cost of marketing many products (for example, cigarettes, soaps, cosmetics, consumer appliances) is high. Salesmen, being out in the field, receive a minimum of supervision and work semi-independently. Financial motivation looms large in the typical salesman's mind. To achieve high sales volume, to control sales costs, and to reward superior performers, commissions and incentives have been a traditional form of payment for outside sales personnel.

The duties that the typical outside salesman performs may be classified in three categories: direct selling, indirect selling, and nonselling work. Direct selling includes visiting a prospective buyer, generally at the latter's premises, and endeavoring to influence him to purchase the products or services the salesman has to offer. He must have adequate knowledge of the potential customer's business and special needs in order to do an effective job. An interchange of information pertaining to quality, specifications, prices, terms of sale, and delivery dates takes place during the interview. Comprising indirect selling activities are providing technical advice to prospective or present customers, distributing and arranging displays and posters, caring for customer's stock, and handling complaints. Nonselling tasks are concerned with record keeping, making out reports to the home office, preparing expense accounts, and attending meetings and training sessions for all sales personnel. Nonselling activities relate primarily to communications, administrative matters, and controls between sales management and salesmen.

A variety of means are available by which management can measure the performance of salesmen. These are the volume of sales, expressed in terms of dollars or units or both; the gross profit or margin (difference between selling price and manufacturing cost) on items sold, especially where the salesman has discretion on prices quoted or items pushed;

---

[1] Some of the facts and ideas for this section on pay plans for salesmen have been drawn from Harry Tosdal and Walter Carson, Jr., *Salesmen's Compensation,* Vol. 1 (Boston: Harvard University Graduate School of Business Administration, 1953).

number of sales compared with number of calls; salary and expenses related to volume of sales; number of calls made per week; orders secured; general appearance, personality, and judgment. The weight given to the foregoing factors depends upon the nature of the business, types of customers, extent of competition, and other considerations.

A pay plan for salesmen must provide adequate income to attract and retain competent people. The level of earnings of the sales force of a particular company should equal, on the average, that which prevails for similar work in the same industry in the same geographical region. Most companies feel that of paramount importance is the need for the plan to motivate the individual to high levels of performance. It is only through sales that a business enterprise can exist. Therefore, most pay plans have a strong incentive feature. As in incentive plans for hourly paid workers, the best plans are easy to understand, and earnings are directly proportional to employee contribution. The plan must be fair to the salesmen and should not penalize them extensively for matters beyond their control. It should provide, as nearly as possible, for equal earnings potential among the various salesmen whose level of job requirements are approximately equal. Last, the sales pay plan should be economical to operate. It should be efficient. The input in terms of salaries, commissions, bonuses, and traveling expenses should not be excessive in comparison with the output (sales volume or profits).

When choosing a pay plan, top management basically has to choose among three types: salary, straight commission, and salary plus commission or incentive bonus.

Compared with the commission or the salary-plus-commision methods, salary plans provide the least incentive for high performance. It has been estimated that 20 to 25 per cent of all selling organizations compensate their personnel in this way.[2] The salary method has definite advantages. If the salesmen are expected to provide considerable technical advice and service (as is common in the industrial and technical equipment fields), they are more willing to devote the necessary time to this activity when they know their income is stable and secure. Generally speaking, where management expects its sales personnel to engage in considerable non-selling work, such as market analysis, service calls, visits to build goodwill, setting up displays and other sales promotion devices, and handling complaints, the salary pay plan works out satisfactorily. Indeed, these duties tend to be slighted under straight commission plans.

[2] *Ibid.*, p. 103. But in recent years there has been a noticeable shift away from both straight-commission and salary-only plans in favor of salary plus incentives. A 1966 survey of 191 manufacturing firms that set up new salesmen's pay plans after 1955 shows that 47 per cent had salary only plans before 1955 but only 14 per cent of the firms had such plans after revision. Fifteen per cent had straight commission plans before 1955, but only 3 per cent had such plans after revision. Salary-plus-incentive plans increased in popularity from 38 per cent of the firms to 83 per cent. See "Changing Patterns in Salesmen's Compensation," *Conference Board Record,* Vol. 3, No. 2 (February 1966), p. 37.

Further advantages are that salesmen are more willing to accept changes in territory; security and regularity of income is present; and the program is simple to administer. The major disadvantage of the salary method of payment is its lack of an incentive feature. Because salesmen work rather independently and are often far removed from their home office, it is difficult to overcome this problem by a good supervisory climate.

Straight commission plans are essentially the same as piecework plans for hourly paid workers. Under this arrangement the employer may pay all traveling expenses. In some plans there is no reimbursement for expenses, but commission rates are somewhat more generous. Commission plans are common in insurance, furniture, drugs, textiles, shoes, and wearing apparel industries. Such plans are a definite aid to new companies that may be inadequately financed because little selling expense is incurred until a sale is actually consummated. Commission plans provide maximum monetary incentive; poor performers tend to eliminate themselves. The premium is placed upon those possessing drive, initiative, and a strong liking for selling. The level of earnings of salesmen under commission plans tend, in general, to exceed that of persons on salary or salary-plus-incentive-bonus plans.[3] With commission plans selling costs are rather directly related to sales volume. On the other side of the coin, we find that there are serious disadvantages to commission plans. Fluctuations in earnings of the individual salesmen from pay period to pay period are often great. A man may suffer low pay due to factors beyond his control. Management finds that it has difficulty in getting nonselling and indirect selling functions performed. Customer service and missionary work of a long-term nature tends to be neglected. Less attention is given to records and report writing. The salesmen feel very independent, and the problem of control is greater than under the salary plan.

The majority of present-day plans combine a basic salary with a direct monetary incentive. This incentive may be in the form of a commission or a bonus. A bonus is distinguished from a commission in that it does not bear a direct mathematical relationship to sales volume. A bonus is a lump-sum payment for better than standard sales performance. The bonus amounts may be determined by judgment, but they are usually based upon a formula that takes into account several factors in the selling job. These combination salary-plus-incentive-payment plans combine the best features of salary and commission plans and eliminate most of their disadvantages. The principal limitation of these plans is their greater administrative complexity. But offsetting this is the greater security of income that the salesmen enjoy. Management can insist upon adequate efforts for the indirect and nonselling portions of the job. And still, a properly designed incentive plan can induce very high levels of output and reward salesmen accordingly.

[3] *Ibid.,* p. 133.

SUPERVISORY COMPENSATION

Job evaluation plans are widely utilized to determine the pay for assitant foremen, foremen, general foremen, and office supervisors. They are usually included in an evaluation plan for both lower and middle management. Sometimes technicians and professionals are rated with the same plan also. But it is unwise simply to extend the plan used to evaluate hourly jobs to encompass first-level supervision. The compensable factors should be different for the two groups. Typical job evaluation factors for supervisory positions include responsibility for supervision of others, number of employees supervised, relations with others, accountability, nature of decisions, technical knowledge, education, and planning.

Two important criteria are involved in setting the salary level for supervisors: (1) the prevailing rates in the area or in the industry, and (2) a proper differential above the highest-paid workers in the unit supervised. Because a foreman generally reaches his position by promotion from the ranks and because he is held accountable for the performance and results in his section, he should be paid a reasonable differential over his men. Since a supervisor is exempt from the overtime requirements of the Fair Labor Standards Act, he might earn less than his subordinates, should his unit work several hours overtime, unless he is paid a substantial differential.[4] Most authorities feel that first-level supervisors should be paid from 20 to 40 per cent more than the highest-paid jobs in their units.

Supervisory Incentives

A survey of 363 companies employing a total of 4.8 million persons in a wide variety of manufacturing and nonmanufacturing industries revealed that over half of these firms rewarded their first-line supervisors with a bonus or other extra compensation in addition to their basic salaries. Most of these were Christmas bonus programs and profit-sharing plans that were for rank-and-file and executive employees as well. Only thirty of the companies surveyed had developed incentive plans for the supervisors alone.[5] Nevertheless, real benefits can accrue to a company in the form of increased quality, lower costs, and greater interdepartmental and intradepartmental cooperation from the adoption of such an incentive plan. Supervisors themselves can gain higher earnings.

Essential Requirements for a Sound Plan. A supervisor, who is essentially a manager at the lower levels in the organizational hierarchy, has many and varied facets to his job. He is a leader of men. He must motivate

[4] Some firms pay rate and one half or rate and one quarter or some other ratio for supervisors who work scheduled overtime.

[5] N. L. A. Martucci, *Compensating First-Line Supervisors in Factory and Office,* Studies in Personnel Policy, No. 177 (New York: National Industrial Conference Board, 1960).

them and coordinate their efforts. He has responsibilities for employee training and development, maintenance of discipline, handling of complaints, communication, and numerous other personnel types of activities. He must see that his department meets production schedules, quality standards, and budgetary limitations. Equipment must be maintained and materials supplied in proper amounts. It is vital that the incentive plan not cause supervisors to neglect certain essential aspects of their responsibilities. A charge that could be fairly leveled at many existing plans is that they provide rewards for good performance in the cost and production portions of the job but totally neglect such important human dimensions as employee satisfaction, morale, loyalty, and relations between the supervisor and his subordinates.

Factors used to measure performance should be either wholly or to a large extent within the control of the supervisor. Assuming that the standards of performance are accurately set by higher management, a factor such as efficiency of direct labor (total output of all direct production employees in the department divided by standard or normal output) is to a significant degree controllable by the supervisor. On the other hand, supervision has only a very small influence upon the amount of absenteeism. If this factor is used, it should be weighted only very lightly.

In discussing supervisory incentive plans, Smyth gives additional guides for their administration: (1) the plan should apply to staff as well as line departments; (2) the great majority of the factors used must be subject to objective measurement; (3) the payments to the supervisors should be accompanied by a statement that explains how the incentive bonus was calculated.[6]

Typically the performance of supervisors who work on an incentive bonus arrangement is measured on a number of factors, generally from four to seven in number. Commonly used factors are (1) departmental budget efficiency, (2) production volume compared to scheduled volume, (3) quality of product or service, (4) accident frequency, (5) grievance rate, (6) maintenance of equipment, and (7) housekeeping.

EXECUTIVE COMPENSATION

Included in the category of executives are members of middle and top management. In the large multiplant company middle management would consist of department and division heads and plant managers, whereas top management would include the chairman of the board, president, all those reporting to the president, and perhaps the next level down as well.

Since 1950 the American Management Association has been conduct-

[6] Richard C. Smyth, *Financial Incentives for Management* (New York: McGraw-Hill Book Company, 1960).

ing surveys of executive compensation. Prior to this, executive pay in industry had been guarded by a wall of secrecy. These surveys have revealed a number of interesting relationships. First, large companies tend to pay their executives more than smaller ones. Second, the salary of the chief executive is instrumental in regulating the pay of subordinate executives. Third, the level of compensation for comparable positions among industries varies widely. Fourth, the pay level relationship among various management functions is reasonably constant from industry to industry.[7]

Arch Patton, who has written extensively on the subject of executive pay, claims that the great differences in salary levels among industries are directly related to the extent of competition in the product market and the nature of the decisions that influence profits (such as innovation and creativity). Surveys have indicated that executive pay in banking, life insurance, railroads, and public utilities is low compared to such ones as automobile, chemical, petroleum, and electrical. Patton relates the lower pay in the former group to a more sheltered competitive life, government regulation, centralized decision making, and a lesser need for innovation.[8]

There is disagreement in management circles and among writers on executive compensation as to the advisability of using job evaluation to establish an executive salary structure. It is certainly true at executive levels that the man makes the job. He lends his own distinctive pattern of interests, skills, and personality to his position. He shapes it in the way he feels most comfortable to operate. Thus the familiar job evaluation axiom "Rate the job not the man" does not fully apply to executive positions. When a company goes into the outside labor market to fill an executive position, a great deal of salary negotiation takes place. The resultant salary is determined largely by the need the company has for the executive, and his ability, previous earnings, and bargaining skill. The company would also try not seriously to upset existing salary relationships for present executives. But it might have to exceed some predetermined salary-grade ceiling.

Job descriptions for middle and top management are frequently called position guides or responsibility guides. They do not contain detailed

---

[7] Arch Patton, *Men, Money and Motivation* (New York: McGraw-Hill Book Company, 1961), p. vii. A *Fortune* magazine computer correlation analysis of the total compensation of the highest paid corporate officers of one hundred very large companies further substantiates Arch Patton's finding that the size of a company is a major determinant of top executive pay. *Fortune* correlated total compensation with five variables: sales, assets, net income, number of employees, and earnings-per-share growth rate (in 1957-1967). There turned out to be no meaningful correlation between growth rate (earnings-per-share) and pay. But the correlations of executive pay with measures of corporate size (assets, sales, net income, and employees) were very high. See "Performance Doesn't Pay," *Fortune* (June 15, 1968), p. 362.

[8] Patton, *op. cit.*, Ch. 3.

statements of duties and operating procedures. Rather they cover areas of responsibility, scope of authority, and relationships with other positions and organizational functions.

Although it is probably true that executive jobs cannot be analyzed, described, and evaluated with the same degree of exactitude and precision as hourly jobs, many organizations have successfully applied job evaluation techniques and created formal pay structures for executives. The techniques are different from those for hourly and office jobs, it is true. It is one thing to argue that executive salary determination is a complex problem and requires special methods. Most would agree with this. It is quite something else to argue that there is no need for a system or a procedure. Few would agree with this.

Where job evaluation plans are used, they are almost always tailor-made to the special requirements of the organization. Sometimes point plans are used, but most commonly combination point-and-factor-comparison plans are employed. One well-known plan is the guide chart-profile method developed by Edward N. Hay and Associates, a management consulting organization.[9]

Salary ranges typically provide a spread from minimum to maximum of from 30 to 70 percent. There is usually considerable overlap of one grade with the next higher one.

Executive Incentives

Incentive programs for executives in business firms can take the form of incentive bonuses that are directly tied to the profit record of the organization, bonuses for improved individual performance above standard, stock options, deferred compensation contracts, or executive fringe benefits. The latter three methods serve not only to attract and retain capable executives and to motivate them but also seek to save on the amount of income tax individual executives must pay. Because executives who receive high direct monetary compensation must pay a large percentage of it to the government under our progressive income tax structure, companies have tended to devote considerable (and perhaps too much) attention to tax-saving features of stock options, deferred compensation arrangements, and fringe benefits.

Incentive-Bonus Plans. In a survey of top-executive compensation, the National Industrial Conference Board found that 327 out of a total of 634 manufacturers had some kind of executive-incentive-bonus plan in operation. For the three highest-paid executives in each company reporting compensation amounts, the bonus payments averaged 35 to 40

---

[9] Edward N. Hay and D. Purves, "The Profile Method of High Level Job Evaluation," *Personnel* (September 1951), pp. 162-170; also by the same authors, "A New Method of Job Evaluation: The Guide Chart-Profile Method," *Personnel* (July 1954), pp. 72-80.

per cent of basic salary. For lower-level executive positions the percentage tended to be smaller.[10]

The primary objective of most bonus plans is to provide an incentive for major executives to enhance the profits of the company. Other goals that are sometimes stated are to encourage loyal and industrious service, reward initiative and resourcefulness, and attract and retain good managers. Inasmuch as the size of the incentive bonus fund is related directly to the amount of the company's profits, it is logical that those executives who are eligible to receive a share of this fund must occupy responsible positions that can effect the profit picture. Primarily, then, incentive bonus plans are for top management personnel and to some extent middle management people. In actual practice there is considerable variation among firms as to which executives are included. Some specify that all those receiving over a certain amount of annual salary are included, others set the lower limit in terms of salary-classification grade, and still others state that officers and division heads, or president, vice-presidents, and department heads are eligible.

The fund of money from which the bonuses are paid is usually a predetermined portion of the company's profits. For the Ford Motor Company the formula is 6 per cent of the company's profit before taxes reduced by 10 per cent of total capital investment.[11] Although in the majority of plans, a definite formula is used to figure the size of the fund, in some organizations the amount is discretionary with the board of directors. The advantage of the predetermined formula approach is that the executives know in advance what they are working for; therefore, this is likely to have a greater motivational effect. They can develop greater confidence in the plan, because they know the formula in advance. In the majority of the executive-incentive-bonus plans in operation, the funds range from 7 to 12 per cent of profits before taxes after deductions of from 5 to 10 per cent of invested capital have been made.[12]

The share of the fund distributed to each participant can be based upon the individual's performance, upon his salary level, or a combination of these. Where the amount is determined by performance, a systematic performance appraisal program must be utilized to judge fairly each executive. The judging is customarily done by a committee superior (in the hierarchy) to those being evaluated. Bonuses for the company president and vice-presidents are usually handled by a committee of members of the board of directors. If the administration of the executive appraisal program is carried out in a fully equitable manner, then basing the individual's share upon his performance can be expected to have the strongest incentive effect. In favor of relating the size of the bonus to each person's

[10] Harland Fox, *Top Executive Compensation,* Studies in Personnel Policy, No. 179 (New York: National Industrial Conference Board, 1960), p. 15.

[11] *Business Week* (December 31, 1955), p. 41.

[12] Smyth, *op. cit.,* p. 97.

annual salary, it can be said, however, that very close coordination and teamwork are essential to the success of a business enterprise, and it is often difficult to say that certain ones contributed differentially to the result. If accurate standards of performance cannot be established, it is probably sound to determine the size of the shares according to some objective system, such as level of salary.

The actual payment of the bonus can be either in cash or company stock. Because the value of the stock is considered income for federal income tax purposes, executives who are in the higher income brackets anyway find it dificult to pay this tax if the amount of stock bonus is large. This constitutes a serious disadvantage. The majority of companies pay the bonus entirely in cash, although some pay part cash and part stock.

Tax Saving Plans

Because executives' salaries place them in high income tax brackets, they are able to keep only a modest portion of an incentive cash bonus that they may have earned. Therefore, a number of plans have been devised to induce superior performance and at the same time permit the executives to retain a large portion of the payment.

Stock Options.   One device for meeting this problem is the stock option, which has become widely used since enactment in 1950 of Section 130A of the 1939 Internal Revenue Code. A stock option is a right to buy a specified number of shares of stock from one's corporation at a stipulated price within a definite period of time. The individual, however, is under no obligation to purchase the stock. Although stock options existed before the 1950 tax law change, this statute introduced certain liberalizing features which provide that the employee to whom the option is granted pays no tax on any profit realized until he sells his stock. The tax is paid on the basis of the capital gains rate instead of the individual income tax rate, if the option is issued and exercised in accordance with certain regulations of the law. The capital gains tax rate is one half the ordinary income tax rate up to a maximum of 25 per cent. For example, if an executive's income places him in a tax bracket of 40 per cent, his capital gains tax rate for that year is 20 per cent.

As a result of the tax law change in 1950, the stock option became a very popular compensation device for top executives in American corporations. There were certain limitations in the law that had to be met. A company could offer to any of its employees an option to buy stock at not less than 85 per cent of the current market value. If the market price subsequently dropped below the 85 per cent figure, then the option holder naturally would not have exercised his option. But if the market price should have increased he might decide to exercise his option. Thus if the market price were $100 per share at the time the option was offered and if two years later the price had advanced to $128, then he might have purchased the stock at the option price (which might have been anywhere between $85 and $100 per share). In order to obtain the tax advantages of the law, he had to keep the stock for at least six months. It can be seen that the executive holding the option right was in a favorable position to make a tidy profit because he could buy at a guaranteed price.

By the early 1960's articulate observers of the business scene and many members of the United States Congress began to criticize stock options because they gave very favored tax advantages to certain select individuals in our society. Some said that these executives thus evaded their fair share of tax responsibilities for the operation of our government.

To meet the objections, Congress, in the Revenue Act of 1964, established more stringent conditions for the use of stock options. These new rules do not affect options issued prior to January 1, 1964. Options issued after January 1, 1964, are called qualified stock options. The executive must hold his stock for at least three years after time of actual purchase before he can sell it if he wants to take advantage of the capital gains tax treatment. If he sells it before the three-year period has elapsed, then the difference between the option price and the market price at the time the option was exercised is treated as ordinary income. However, the excess between the market price when purchased and the market price when sold is still treated as capital gains. Another condition imposed by the new law is that options must be granted at 100 per cent of the market value. Previously they could be as low as 85 per cent. Also option prices may not be reset if the stock price drops in the open market.

The theory of a board of directors in granting stock options to top executives is that these provide a strong incentive to strive for long-term corporate growth. They will try to increase the profits of the company and will take a proprietary interest in the business.

A criticism of the practice of granting stock options to a few top executives is that it harms the interests of ordinary stockholders. The latters' relative equity is diluted when large amounts of stock are issued to option holders—this reduces the earnings per share paid to ordinary shareholders. Regular stockholders cannot buy shares in their own company at such favorable rates.

Since the mid-1960's there has been a noticeable decline in popularity of stock options as a significant part of the compensation of top corporate executives. Nowadays when companies set up new plans they grant smaller amounts to fewer people. The number of shares authorized for stock-option plans (according to one survey) expressed as a percentage of total stock outstanding in the companies studied, declined from 4.9 per cent in 1959 to 2.9 per cent in 1966.[13] There are several reasons for the decline of stock options. A major one is the stringency of the rules contained in the Revenue Act of 1964. Another is the fact that most executives must

[13] Jeremy Main, "An Expanding Executive Pay Package," *Fortune* (June 15, 1968), pp. 168-169, 356, 362, 365.

borrow funds to exercise their options. Rising interest rates have aggravated the problem. Personnel executives have concluded that many plans were too lavish and granted special favored treatment to a few. In addition the market price of some "blue-chip" stocks has declined such that no options have been exercised for several years.

Restricted Stock Plans.   Very recently, restricted stock-purchase and restricted stock-bonus plans have become very popular. Restricted stock plans are based upon a feature of the federal income tax law which holds that, when an employee receives property that cannot be valued, that property will not be taxed until it can be valued.

A restricted stock plan, whether of the purchase or the bonus type, works this way. The executive receives ownership of the stock immediately. However, he is not allowed to sell it for a designated period, say five years or possibly until his retirement. Another restriction might be that he would forfeit the stock if he should resign his job. The person need not pay any tax upon his shares until he is free to sell them. At the time the restriction expires, the executive pays ordinary income tax on the value of the stock at the time he first acquired ownership or at its current market value, whichever is less. Should he subsequently sell his stock, he pays capital-gains tax on the appreciation (if any) in the market value since the time he acquired the stock. An example will make this clearer. Under a restricted stock-purchase plan a manager may be given the right to buy X shares of his company's stock worth $75 each in 1970 for a special price of $40. If the restriction on sale of his stock expires in 1975, he pays ordinary income tax for that year on the difference of $35 per share. If he holds the stock for another year and sells at $125 per share, then he pays a capital gains tax on the $50 per share appreciation. If this had been a restricted stock-bonus plan he would have been awarded the stock by the company at no cost to himself. When the restriction was lifted in 1975 he would pay ordinary income tax on the full $75 a share.

Advantages to the individual of the restricted stock plan over stock options are that the executive actually owns the stock and can collect dividends while he waits for the price to rise. Also the executive generally does not have to borrow heavily to obtain the stock. An advantage to the company is that the plan may be so designed as to hold the executive to employment with the firm for an extended number of years. A restricted stock *bonus* is more costly to the corporation, however, than is a straight cash bonus because the firm cannot deduct the restricted bonus from its taxes as a business expense at the time it grants the bonus. It must wait until the restrictions lapse.

Deferred Compensation.   Certain advantages may accrue to the executive and to his employer from a deferred-compensation arrangement. By receiving a sum of money a number of years in the future, as for example after retirement, appreciable tax savings may be realized. Two primary means of accomplishing this may be available. Certain income may be taxed only at the capital gains rate, whereas other income received after retirement when one's level of income is normally lower would be taxed at a lower rate. The primary advantage to the company of deferred compensation is that it tends to assure that certain valuable executives will not leave the business.

There are three types of plans for which the United States Treasury Department regulations allow that taxes be paid by the employee only when he actually receives the compensation. These are pension, profit-sharing, and stock-bonus plans. If the benefit is received in one single sum, the recipient need pay only the capital gains tax rate up to a maximum of 25 per cent. The regulations specify that the plan cannot be for only a very limited group of top executives—a broader coverage of employees is necessary. It would be acceptable to include all of the salaried employees.

Another type of deferred compensation plan is one in which individual contracts are made to defer certain cash payments to some future time. Generally the amount is spread out over a number of years to keep the tax rate in a lower bracket. So that the executive does not have to pay an income tax on the benefit the year it is awarded, certain conditions of uncertainty about its receipt by the person must be provided for. Typical conditions are that he agrees (1) to relinquish his right to the money if he terminates his employment before a certain date, (2) not to work for a competitor while receiving the deferred pay, and (3) to be available for consultation and advice for the company.

Executive Fringe Benefits. A way of rewarding executives with compensation on which they do not have to pay income taxes is the provision of benefits and services that are paid for entirely by the company. Examples are group life, medical, and disability insurance, free medical service by the company doctor, payment of club membership dues, more liberal vacations, company automobiles, payment of education costs at universities and colleges, and the like. There is some question whether the discriminatory granting of these benefits to a chosen elite of top executives may not be destructive of internal morale in the organization. This may occur if the disparity between benefits for top executives and the rest of the employees is great.

COMPENSATION FOR PROFESSIONALS

In both absolute numbers and relatively, professional people in the labor force have increased greatly since 1900. Between 1950 and 1960 professional and technical employment expanded three times faster than did total nonagricultural employment.[14] This increase has been especially

---

[14] *Monthly Labor Review,* Vol. 84, No. 1 (January 1961), p. 13.

pronounced for engineers, scientists, and accountants. The work of a professional requires knowledge of an advanced type in a field of science or learning acquired by a prolonged course of specialized instruction and study. The work requires consistent exercise of discretion and judgment and is predominantly intellectual and varied in character.

When we speak of a professional employee, we generally mean one who is in a nonsupervisory position. He is an individual contributor. If a man is a supervisor in an engineering department or a research laboratory he may personally retain a professional identification, but strictly speaking he is a member of management. Where his company has separate compensation structures for managers and professionals, he would usually be included with the management group. However, group leaders and project leaders in an engineering department would ordinarily be classified with the professional group because their work is predominantly technical and not administrative in nature. They perform certain supervisory functions, but generally the major share of their time would be devoted to work as individual contributors.

Policy Considerations

The pay policies that an organization adopts for its professional employees are especially important in determining whether it can recruit and retain a competent staff. The pay policies also exert a strong influence upon the morale of the professional group. Engineers frequently strive to get promoted to managerial positions because they see this as the road to success in industry. The young engineer typically receives generous pay increases during his first few years after graduation from college. But then his increments become smaller and smaller. A leveling-off process has occurred. If the man has strong drives for achievement and upward mobility, he may actively seek a supervisory post. Now, this is a perfectly healthy action. Industry has large and expanding needs for supervisors and executives possessing a technical background. But too frequently we find that many men who possess great aptitudes for technical work and little or none for managerial activities seek a management position because it seems to be the road to success.

Many firms have sought to solve this problem by offering "parallel paths to success." They deliberately create high-level and high-paying positions to properly compensate superior engineers and scientists who can make their greatest contribution as individual contributors. In other words the salary structure for professionals goes as high as the middle or upper reaches of that for middle management. It must be recognized also that pay alone does not determine a man's satisfaction with his job. Engineers and scientists tend to want autonomy, an opportunity to determine the nature of their work and to make original contributions, and professional recognition.

Because the market demand for engineers and scientists is very high, because it exceeds the supply in certain occupations, and because professionals as a group are among the most mobile of all groups in the labor force, companies must give especial attention to questions of fair and adequate compensation.

The issue of salary compensation for professionals resolves itself into three separate problems. One is the question of salary structure, the second is the issue of individual pay determination within the structure, and the third is the maintenance of a proper salary level in comparison with that prevailing in the labor market.

Salary Structure

Some companies set up a salary structure for the professional employees in essentially the same way as for hourly and nonsupervisory office jobs. This means that they prepare detailed job descriptions, rate the jobs according to a point or factor-comparison method of job evaluation, classify the professional personnel into their appropriate job titles, and set up a salary structure with pay grades and rate ranges. The specific content of an individual's job determines his job classification and pay. If the content of his job is changed, strictly speaking, it should be re-evaluated to determine whether it should be placed in a higher or lower salary grade.

Implicit in this approach is the notion that the skills and abilities of the man occupying a professional job have no effect upon the nature and content of that job. Although this assumption holds true generally for hourly and clerical jobs, it frequently is not true for engineering and scientific positions. For the latter, not only does the individual tend to shape the job content according to his particular aptitudes and abilities, but also management gives consideration to the man in the job when handing out assignments and projects. The man to a great extent makes the job. Another problem with this traditional functional approach to salary determination is that the work of a professional employee tends to be highly variable as to its nature and complexity over a relatively short period of time. It cannot be standardized.

General Grade Descriptions. Realization of these difficulties has led some companies to abandon detailed functional job classifications and use very broad, general job classifications. Thus all engineers in a large engineering department might be classified into four categories, such as assistant engineer, engineer, senior engineer, and project specialist, regardless of the functional nature of their work. These classifications would be described in very general terms much as the General Schedule classifications of the Federal government. The use of such very general classifications, at one and the same time, grants considerable discretion to supervision and imposes a burden upon it to be fair in assigning individuals to pay classifications. When it adopts this approach to salary administration, management in reality is combining into one operation the question of salary structure and the question of an individual's pay. The reclassification of a man from, say, an assistant engineer to an engineer involves performance appraisal. The man classified as an engineer does essentially the same duties as an assistant engineer, only he does them better.

The disadvantage of this approach to the problem of salary determination is that the grade level descriptions are so vague and general that it often becomes simply a matter of opinion as to whether a man is called an assistant engineer or an engineer. Management cannot justify its assignment of a man to a particular grade with any degree of confidence. Discontent and complaints may easily arise.

Salary Maturity Curves.   There has been a trend in recent years for companies employing large complements of engineers and scientists, such as those firms in the aerospace industry, to use neither functional job descriptions or general grade level classifications but rather salary maturity curves.[15] Based upon salary survey data and internal company salary data and policy decisions, management sets up curves that relate salary to years since receipt of college degree or to age. An average curve is drawn for those who are judged to possess average proficiency, whereas other curves are drawn for those of above and below average performance. Job titles are then used only for identification and status distinctions. Figure 26-1 is an example of a salary maturity curve structure.

The use of salary maturity curves combines the issues of salary structure and individual pay allocation into one step. Those who employ them admit frankly that they cannot measure work content and create explainable job distinctions based upon differences in job duties. Differences in employee performance are accorded full recognition in the individual's resultant salary. The growing trend toward the use of maturity curves has been fostered partly because the data from many market salary surveys, such as those conducted by the Engineers' Joint Council, are expressed this way. The salary maturity curve approach dispenses with the artificial pay ceilings attached to pay grades in the traditional salary structure.

Individual Pay Determination

It is almost a universal practice for companies to pay professional employees according to their performance and potential within established limits. The principal exception to this rule is the practice of granting semiautomatic pay raises to young engineers, scientists, and other professionals, during their first year or two on the payroll. These raises are semiauto-

---

[15] Salary maturity curves are sometimes called career curves, professional maturity curves, or progression curves.

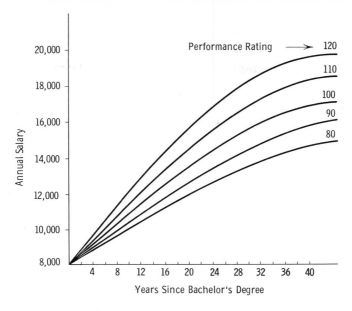

Figure 26-1. Salary Maturity Curves Which Relate Annual Salary to Years Since Graduation from College and to Performance Rating.

matic, because it is difficult for supervision to appraise their worth with confidence, especially if they move from training assignment to assignment within only a short time span. The raises for a few doubtful individuals may be held up for a while until management is sure of its judgments.

The conventional and still most common approach is to have several pay grades that overlap in salary. The maximum within each grade will typically be from 30 to 50 per cent above the minimum. In addition to individual performance, other criteria often considered in arriving at salary adjustments are length of service and amount of money that has been budgeted for salary increases for each department. These budgeted figures are related to top management attitude, company profitability, and prospects for the future of the business.

Where salary maturity curves are used instead of conventional pay grades, a man's salary adjustment in any one year is related to his years since graduation from college (or his age) and his performance rating score as arrived at by his supervisor. This has been described previously.

Equity with Labor Market

Because of the intense demand for professionally qualified personnel and because these people are quite mobile, management pays especial attention to keeping salaries competitive. This necessitates salary surveys, usually annually. The starting salaries for recent college graduates have been rising steadily year after year. There has been a continual upward pressure upon salaries for experienced personnel as well.

The standard approach has been to prepare a salary survey schedule that contains condensed job descriptions of key jobs within one's own organization and then to visit or mail questionnaires to other companies spread over a wide geographical area. These cooperating organizations then supply data on comparable jobs that they have. It is much more difficult to ascertain job comparability for these positions than it is for hourly and clerical jobs.

In recent years the Bureau of Labor Statistics of the United States Department of Labor has been conducting nationwide salary surveys for such occupations as engineer, mathemetician, chemist, and attorney. It expresses the survey results in the form of median salaries for various grade levels within each occupation.

The Engineers' Joint Council and several other professional organizations conduct surveys and express their data in the form of salary maturity curves classified according to years since receipt of the bachelor's, master's, and doctor's degree.

Questions for Review and Discussion

1. In what ways is the problem of determining proper compensation for the "exempt" group different from that for hourly and clerical employees?
2. What are the three basic methods of compensating outside salesmen? What factors must be considered when designing a compensation plan for salesmen?
3. Why do you suppose incentive plans for supervisors are not more widespread throughout industry?
4. Why are special incentive and bonus plans used much more often for top executives than for office workers, supervisors, and professionals?
5. What is a stock option? Why is it used? What are its advantages and disadvantages?
6. What is deferred executive compensation? Why is it used?
7. What are the relative merits of using functional job classifications, general grade classifications, or salary maturity curves to determine pay for professionals?

Suggestions for Further Reading

Andrews, Robert (ed.), *Managerial Compensation,* Ann Arbor, Mich.: Foundation for Research on Human Behavior, 1965.

Atchison, T. and W. French, "Pay Systems for Scientists and Engineers," *Industrial Relations,* Vol 7, No. 1, 1967, pp. 44 - 56.

Belcher, David W., *Wage and Salary Administration,* 2nd ed., Englewood Cliffs, .J.: Prentice-Hall, 1962, Ch. 19.

Carpenter, Russell B., "High Cost of Restricted Stock Incentives," *Harvard Business Review,* Vol. 46, No. 6 (November-December 1968), pp. 139 - 148.

Ewing, D. W. and D. H. Fenn, *Incentives for Executives,* New York: McGraw-Hill Book Company, 1962.

Foote, George H., "The Executive's Compensation and His Career Cycle," *Business Horizons,* Vol. 8, No. 1, Spring 1965, pp. 35 - 42.

Gellerman, Saul, "Motivating Men with Money," *Fortune,* March 1968.

Langsner, Adolph and Herbert G. Zollitsch, *Wage and Salary Administration,* Cincinnati, Ohio: Southwestern Publishing Co., 1961, Chs. 26 and 27.

Lawler, Edward, "The Mythology of Management Compensation," *California Management Review,* Vol. 9, No. 1, Fall 1966, pp. 11 - 22.

National Industrial Conference Board, *Top Executive Compensation,* Studies in Personnel Policy, No. 204, New York: National Industrial Conference Board, 1966.

Patton, Arch, *Men, Money, and Motivation,* New York: McGraw-Hill Book Company, Inc., 1961.

Patton, Thomas H., Jr., "Maturity Pay Curves in a Floating Labor Market," *The Quarterly Review of Economics and Business,* Vol. 7, No. 3, Autumn 1967, pp. 57 - 72.

Smyth, R. C., "Financial Incentives for Salesmen," *Harvard Business Review,* Vol. 46, No. 1, January-February 1968, pp. 109 - 117.

Weeks, David A., "A Fluctuating Paycheck for Managers," *The Conference Board Record,* Vol. 5, No. 4, April 1968, pp. 32 - 36.

V

SECURITY

Health and Safety

27

Over 2,200,000 disabling injuries and 14,200 accidental deaths occurred in 1967 in the course of employment in the United States. These occurred in the context of a total work force of about 75,000,000 persons. The National Safety Council has estimated that the total cost of these work accidents was 7.3 billion dollars for the year. This includes the value of lost wages, workmen's compensation insurance, medical-hospital insurance, fire losses, and administrative costs associated with work injuries.[1] Nearly 2 per cent of the work force is absent from the job due to illness (nonoccupational) on any one work day.[2] That these figures represent a serious problem in terms of human anguish, loss of income to affected workers, and cost to the employer must be evident from a moment's reflection. A half-century ago American industry did very little to protect the health of its employees on the job. Today a large portion of the companies (especially medium and large-sized ones) conduct extensive health and safety programs. Still there is much to be done among the majority of firms, both large and small, to improve the health of their employees.

The incentive for an employer to reduce work injuries and advance

---

[1] Source: *Accident Facts—1968 Edition* (Chicago: National Safety Council, 1968), p. 23-24. A disabling injury is one arising in the course of employment that results in death or makes the injured worker unable to perform his job on any one or more days following date of injury.

[2] Philip E. Enterline, "Work Loss Due to Illness in Selected Occupations and Industries," *Journal of Occupational Medicine,* Vol. 3, No. 9 (September 1961), pp. 405-411.

the health of his people is twofold. One is the humanitarian concern for the well-being of his employees. This means that he genuinely seeks to prevent human suffering and to maintain a safe, healthy environment. The other incentive is cost. It is more economical to maintain an accident-free plant and to have full attendance on the job than it is to have extensive lost time due to job-connected injuries and sickness. In point of fact, the real impetus for the introduction of health and safety programs throughout industry occurred because of the passage of Workmen's Compensation laws in the various states, principally between the years 1910 and 1925. These laws hold employers financially responsible for injuries incurred by their workers on the job regardless of the specific cause of the accident. The experience-rating provisions of these laws cause companies having high accident rates to pay higher insurance premiums than those having low accident rates. Industrialists and business executives may have deplored the human damage suffered in unsafe plants prior to the passage of these compensation laws, but they were actually prodded into action to a great extent only because of them.

Besides the efforts of individual companies, the work of such organizations as the National Safety Council and casualty insurance companies has done much to promote safety in employment. The Council's activities are primarily in the field of research, education, and the compilation and publication of information. Most states maintain safety inspection services within their departments of labor. In occupational health the Industrial Medical Association and the American Academy of Occupational Medicine (both composed of physicians employed in the occupational medicine field) are active in establishing, improving, and maintaining standards of medical care in industry. The Industrial Hygiene Foundation is active in carrying out research, rendering professional consulting service, and in disseminating information in the fields of industrial hygiene, toxicology, engineering, and environment control.

OCCUPATIONAL SAFETY

Accidents

What is an accident? Most of us tend to think of an accident as some event that causes a personal injury. But in point of fact an *accident is really an unexpected occurrence that interrupts the regular progress of an activity.* In effect it is any unplanned or uncalled for break or deviation from the expected. It is a negative or unfortunate event. Many accidents take place without an injury resulting. A man may stumble while walking along an aisle yet suffer no injury. A rigger may drop a tool and narrowly miss a worker below. Both of the foregoing are accidents without injuries. In common parlance most people consider the terms *accident* and *accident injury* to be synonymous. Actually there is no harm in this, and in the records of most companies only accidents resulting in injuries are shown. But pure chance plays a large part in determining whether a particular accident results in an injury or not. Employees, managers, and safety specialists alike must seek to minimize the possibility of any accidents taking place.

Computing Injury Rates

If both Company A and Company B each had 50 lost-time accidents in the same year, and if each employed an average of 1,000 people, one might conclude that their accident records were identical. However, this could be a totally erroneous conclusion if one plant worked a considerable amount of overtime during the year, whereas the other worked only a 35-hour week. It is the number of disabling injuries in relation to the total man-hours of exposure to possible injuries that provides the most meaningful measure of injury experience. The American Standards Association has developed standard formulas for measuring and recording injury rates.[3] Its system for handling accident data is used by the National Safety Council, government agencies, and practically all professional safety men in industry.

The ASA formulas give a measure of both the frequency and the seriousness of injuries. The standard injury frequency rate is the number of disabling injuries per 1,000,000 employee-hours worked. The formula is as follows.

$$\text{Frequency Rate} = \frac{\text{Number of disabling injuries} \times 1,000,000}{\text{Employee-hours of exposure}}$$

In Company A mentioned above (assuming an average work week of 44 hours and 50 work weeks per year) the frequency rate is 22.7. In Company B (on a 35-hour week) the rate is 28.6 disabling injuries (or lost-time accidents) per million man-hours worked. Both of these figures represent high injury rates.

The severity rate is measured as follows:

$$\text{Severity Rate} = \frac{\text{Total days charged} \times 1,000,000}{\text{Employee-hours of exposure}}$$

The total days charged is computed by totaling all the days lost due to work injuries and adding in the standard time charges that have been

[3] American Standards Association, Standard Z16.1—1954, *American Standard Method of Recording and Measuring Work and Injury Experience.* In 1966 the American Standards Association changed its name to United States of America Standards Institute. In 1969 the name was changed to American National Standards Institute.

agreed upon for deaths, permanent total disabilities, and permanent partial disabilities. For death and permanent total disability a scheduled charge of 6,000 days is used in each case. The loss of the end of an index finger (distal phalange), for example, would be counted as 100 days.

The principal reason every business establishment should compute its injury rates faithfully is that this practice provides a means of comparing accident performance within the establishment from year to year. A company can also judge whether its performance is good or bad in comparison with nationwide averages for its particular industry. Of the two measures, frequency and severity, the frequency rate is the more significant. It is the more sensitive indicator of performance. This is because the severity of a particular injury is largely a matter of chance. If a worker walks along a dimly lit aisle and stumbles and falls, the severity may vary from zero (no injury or only first aid) all the way to a fractured hip and weeks in the hospital. Efforts, of course, should be made to eliminate accident hazards that could cause very serious injuries. But the principle emphasis should be placed upon preventing all accidents. If there are few (or no) accidents, there will be fewer opportunities for serious injuries to happen.

Industry Injury Rates

For the year 1967 the National Safety Council reported that the average injury frequency rate for all industries was 7.22. The safest industries were communications 1.40, automobile manufacturing 1.64, aerospace 2.17, electric equipment 2.52, steel 3.10, chemical 3.55, textile 4.41, and cement 4.75. The most hazardous were underground coal mining 35.77, meat packing 19.63, marine transportation 18.51, lumbering 17.56, and transit 17.35.[4]

The injury rate of a particular company or industry strongly reflects the amount of money, time, and effort that management devotes to accident prevention. These factors override the hazards inherent in the industry. The basic steel industry is by its nature quite hazardous; so is the atomic energy industry. But in both industries top management has long since decided to carry on comprehensive safety programs that have resulted in very safe plants. Most work establishments that have bad accident records are in that unhappy situation because management has not been sufficiently motivated to take strong action to correct the problem.

---

[4] *Accident Facts, 1968 Edition* (Chicago: National Safety Council, 1968). It is of interest to note that the injury rates compiled by the National Safety Council are considerably lower than those compiled by the United States Department of Labor for the same industry categories. This is because the Council surveys companies which are more safety-minded, bases its data on a smaller sample, and includes fewer small companies (which have higher accident rates on the average). The Department of Labor surveys a larger and more representative sample of all companies throughout the country. Nevertheless, the rank order of the various industries is about the same in both surveys even if the absolute values differ.

Small Companies

Accident statistics reveal that small companies (generally those having fewer than 500 employees) have higher injury rates than large firms. Figure 27-1 shows the frequency rates for manufacturing in New York State classfied according to size of establishment. From examination it is apparent that small companies as a whole have poorer records than large ones. The reason for the somewhat better experience of companies having less than 50 employees is not known. However, it may be hypothesized that the owner or president can be in immediate face-to-face contact with practically all the employees every day. If an injury occurs he is immediately aware of the fact. In these small organizations all the employees are aware of the fact that the success or failure of the production, the quality, and the safety programs depend immediately upon their own efforts. In other words, the small size and the close relationship between owner and workers makes everyone feel responsible.

The unfavorable accident records for small businesses as a group is true for the country as a whole, not just for New York State. What are the reasons for this situation? The fundamental reason is that owners and top executives in small businesses are not as safety conscious and do not give as much effort to accident prevention as does management of large

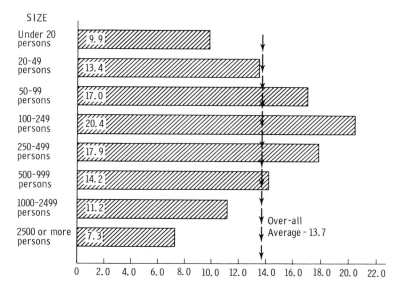

Figure 27-1. Injury Frequency Rates in Manufacturing by Size of Reporting Unit for New York State, 1966. Plotted from data in *Injury Rates in Factories, New York State,* 1966, New York State Department of Labor, Division of Research and Statistics.

firms. The typical small businessman does not even know what his accident frequency rate is. The only guide to the accident rate that he uses is the size of his workmen's compensation insurance premium. If his accident record becomes worse, his insurance carrier will raise the annual premium; if his record improves, the premium will be lowered. The typical small employer cannot afford to hire a full-time safety director and often he may not even have a full-time personnel manager. The pressing problems of production, sales, and finance overshadow, in his mind, the importance of accident prevention. Typically his accounting system does not isolate all those costs, into a separate category, that directly and indirectly are caused by accidents.

Cost of Accidents

In addition to the anguish and suffering experienced by injured employees, accidents are very expensive to the employer. Many executives simply look at their charges for workmen's compensation insurance and lose sight of the fact that the indirect costs of an accidental injury are considerably greater than the direct costs.

Accident costs are classified into two categories. First are the insured costs. The insured cost is the money paid for doctor and hospital bills, for weekly benefits while the injured employees are absent from work, and for any scheduled payments due to death or accidental dismemberment (for example, loss of a finger). This cost is readily apparent and is met by the insurance premium.

The second category of costs due to accidents is called the uninsured costs. Some authorities call these the indirect costs of accidents. These costs are not apparent to top management unless it assigns somebody to conduct a specific research project to isolate them. What are these uninsured costs? They include lost time of injured worker, lost time of fellow employees who render aid to the injured person, time spent by supervisory personnel to assist the injured man and to investigate the cause of the accident, lost production, possible damaged material or equipment, and administrative expenses to process paper work connected with the accident.

The ratio of the uninsured to the insured costs varies widely from factory to factory according to the particular situation. However, investigators have found that these uninsured costs tend to average about four times those of the insured costs. In other words the insured or direct costs represent only about 20 per cent of the total costs on the average.[5]

For some companies in high-risk industries the premium for workmen's compensation insurance may run as high as 15 to 20 per cent of payroll. If one estimates that the total cost for accidents in any one year is five

---

[5] See, for example, H. W. Heinrich, *Industrial Accident Prevention: A Scientific Approach* (4th Ed., New York: McGraw-Hill Book Company, Inc., 1959), pp. 50-51.

times this figure, it can be readily appreciated that the accident rate can spell the difference between profit and loss for a company.

In addition to the financial burden imposed by accidents upon a company, those workmen who are injured bear a substantial cost also. Most workmen's compensation laws specify a waiting period of one week before an injured worker can collect weekly benefits to make up for his loss of wages. Therefore, those who lose only one to seven days from work, receive no wage compensation whatever. The typical compensation law specifies that weekly benefits shall be only two thirds of the injured's wage up to a certain maximum. For permanent partial dismemberments the scheduled benefits are rarely adequate to compensate a worker for his future loss of earning power.

CAUSES OF ACCIDENTS

In order to prevent accidents from taking place it is necessary, first of all, to gain an appreciation of the causes of accidents. Accidents may at times seem to occur because of chance factors that are unavoidable. But digging beneath the surface one will find that in nearly every instance measures could have been taken to prevent the accident.

Accident causes can be classified conveniently into two major categories:

1. Unsafe chemical, physical, or mechanical conditions, and
2. Unsafe personal acts.

Examples of unsafe chemical, physical, or mechanical conditions are the following:

1. Inadequate mechanical guarding.
2. Defective condition of equipment or tools (for example, worn electrical insulation; cracked ladder, split drive belt).
3. Unsafe design or construction (for example, a pressure vessel that is too weak).
4. Hazardous atmosphere (for example, toxic substances in air, poor ventilation).
5. Inadequate or improper personal protective equipment.

Examples of unsafe personal acts are as follows:

1. Failure to follow established safe working procedures.
2. Horseplay, fighting.
3. Taking an unsafe position, such as under a suspended load.
4. Failure to use designated protective clothing.
5. Removing safety devices or making them inoperative.

Sometimes a physical or mental condition of the person involved may contribute to the accident. Thus a worker may be emotionally upset, inattentive, or fearful. Or he may be extremely fatigued or suffer some physical defect that makes an accident more likely.

Over the years attempts have been made by various groups to classify industrial injuries according to whether they were caused by an unsafe physical condition or by an unsafe personal act. Some of the earlier studies purportedly showed that 85 to 90 per cent of all injuries were caused by human error and only 10 to 15 per cent by hazardous conditions. If one did not study the matter further, one might jump to the erroneous conclusion that management could obtain the greatest gain from the dollars it spends on accident prevention by devoting its efforts to employee education and ignoring the engineering aspect of safety. But such is not the case. More recent analyses of accident statistics reveal that the vast majority are due to a combination of unsafe physical conditions and unsafe personal acts. Basically if the hazard were not present in the first place, an injury could not occur. The traffic safety records of the modern divided, limited-access superhighways furnish ample evidence that good engineering design can reduce accident rates significantly. The people who drive on these highways are no different from those who drive on ordinary roads, so the personal behavior factor is essentially constant for both superhighway driving and ordinary driving.

A sound industrial-safety program must emphasize both the engineering aspects of safety (hazard elimination) as well as employee education and training (showing people how to work safely in the presence of certain hazards).

Accident Proneness

For years industrial psychologists have been intrigued with the empirically observed fact that certain individuals have more accidents than could be expected on the basis of chance and that accident rates in factories could be reduced if accident-prone workers were identified and rejected during the employment selection process. Some of the earliest research to establish the fact of accident proneness was done by Greenwood and Woods in a British shell factory. Newbold also carried out one of the early investigations.[6]

Psychologists have given intelligence, aptitude, and personality tests to large numbers of people in a variety of occupations and industries. They have then correlated test scores with accident rates. The object has been to identify the specific traits that might be useful in predicting

---

[6] M. Greenwood and H. M. Woods, "The Incidence of Industrial Accidents upon Individuals with Specific Reference to Multiple Accidents," London, Industrial Fatigue Research Board, Report 4, 1919; E. M. Newbold, "A Contribution to the Study of the Human Factor in the Causation of Accidents," London, Industrial Fatigue Research Board, Report 34, 1926.

accident proneness. It has been shown that there is a definite relationship between accident rates and scores on motor sensory tests, emotional stability tests, muscular and perceptual speed tests, and visual tests in certain occupations. Above a certain minimum level there has been found to be no relationship between intelligence-test scores and accident rates.

A Balanced View of Accident Proneness. Despite the fact that the phenomenon of accident proneness does exist, many investigators and writers have been much too loose in their claims regarding the matter. It has been observed in many establishments that a small percentage of the workers have a high percentage of accidents; but this fact alone does not prove accident proneness. According to the laws of probability we would *not* expect all workers to have the same number of accidents. In any given year or other time period, some persons can be expected, by chance, to have several accidents, whereas others will have none. Mintz and Blum have done a scholarly job of setting the record straight regarding accident proneness. They conclude that this has been a much overemphasized factor and that it really accounts for only about 20 to 40 per cent of the total variance of accident records.[7] Willard Kerr claims that the factor of accident proneness really accounts for only 1 to 15 per cent of the total variance in individual accidents.[8] In actuality true accident-prone people are rather rare. To be accident prone, one must have a constitutional tendency to engage in unsafe behavior. What actually happens is that people who are apparently accident prone have only a temporary tendency toward frequent accidents, but if their performance were to be viewed over a long time span, it would be found that they settle down to an accident rate no different than that of the general population. Basically these people are in a transient stage. The group of accident-liable members is constantly gaining new members and losing old ones.

Thus although the theory of accident proneness seemed for many years to be a promising solution to the problem of work injuries, in actuality, when put in proper perspective, it contributed but little to the overall problem.

Arbous and Kerrich have added their voices to those who have rigorously reduced the significance of accident proneness as a causal explanation of accidents. They assert that both laymen and accident prevention specialists have continued to try to account for work injuries on this basis even though researchers have long since revealed the weaknesses in the argument. In contradiction to the concept of accident proneness that deals with the statistical experience of groups, they do say however that the individual clinical approach to accident proneness may have some merit. The clinical approach requires than an examination be made of

[7] Alexander Mintz and Milton L. Blum, "A Re-examination of the Accident Proneness Concept," *Journal of Applied Psychology,* Vol. 33, No. 3 (1949), pp. 195-211.

[8] Willard Kerr, "Complementary Theories of Safety Psychology," *Journal of Social Psychology,* Vol. 45 (1957), pp. 3-9.

individual accident repeaters from the standpoint of the whole man. This requires an investigation of each person's personality, emotional make-up, family background, physical condition, and so forth, in the context of the job demands and environment in which he works. Training, medical treatment, better supervision, and re-assignment all may be required to generate a change in the person's behavior. Such an attempt at individual diagnosis could be very expensive and has seldom been applied in practice, although the concept appears to have merit.[9]

Accidents and Environment

The physical, psychological, and organizational environment in a plant has a powerful effect upon injury rates. Keenan, Kerr, and Sherman correlated accident rates of 7,100 personnel in a large tractor factory over a five-year period. They found that a comfortable shop environment (good working conditions) was the single most significant factor relating to a low accident rate. These researchers believe that bad working conditions (noise, dirt, heat, and so on), although not directly causing accidents, cause worker tension and frustration. This physical frustration distracts the workers, causing them to have more accidents.[10] Many practicing safety engineers have for years felt, on the basis of experience, that plant housekeeping and decent working conditions are a positive encouragement to safety. Thus the research evidence supports this belief.

Substantial evidence exists to demonstrate that the total stress (internal and external) that impinges upon a worker has a strong influence upon his likelihood to have accidents. Internal stress consists of such conditions as disease, alcohol, anxiety, or worry, whereas external stress is built up from noise, heat, dirt, fumes, and excessive physical strain.[11] Positive action by management to maintain not only good working conditions but also good employee health (physical and mental) is bound to pay dividends in terms of fewer accidents and lower charges for workmen's compensation. The initial cost of establishing a good work environment and an occupational health program often discourages management from making the investment. Although one may fail to persuade top management to invest in such programs on the basis of their contribution to employee morale and the humanitarian objective, quite often the prospect of a long-term reduction in the cost of accidents may provide the impetus to adopt such a comprehensive program.

Management action in another broad area can have a very beneficial

[9] A. G. Arbous and J. E. Kerrich, "The Phenomenon of Accident Proneness" contained in Edwin A. Fleishman, *Studies in Personnel and Industrial Psychology* (Rev. Ed., Homewood, Ill.: The Dorsey Press, 1967), pp. 615-626.

[10] Vernon Keenan, Willard Kerr, and William Sherman, "Psychological Climate and Accidents in an Automotive Plant," *Journal of Applied Psychology,* Vol. 35, No. 2 (1951), pp. 108-111.

[11] Kerr, *op. cit.*

effect upon safety. When management directs the organization in such a way that employees have real opportunities to get ahead, to be promoted, to exercise some initiative and responsibility, to participate in controlling their own jobs, and to gain job prestige and other rewards, then accidents tend to be lower.[12] Thus it can be concluded that the positive, supportive, need-satisfying, autonomy-enhancing leadership that is quite generally advocated by modern researchers and writers in the field of human relations in industry is just as successful in promoting occupational safety as it is in promoting productivity, loyalty, and high morale. In other words the elements that constitute good management in other spheres of a business enterprise also constitute sound safety management.

Age, Training, and Work Experience

Available research evidence shows quite conclusively that young workers, untrained workers, and workers who are new on the job have substantially higher frequencies of work injuries than older workers, trained workers, and more experienced workers. Van Zelst investigated the effect of each of these factors separately in a large copper plant in Indiana. He found, for example, that the average monthly accident rate of about 1,200 workers declined steadily for the first five months on the job, after which the rate remained nearly constant for approximately a five-year period. When newly hired workers were given formal job training, Van Zelst found that the initial accident frequency was lower for this trained group and that the group declined to a normal expected level of accident frequency in three months instead of the five months for untrained employees. In the third and final part of his investigation, he found that a group of 614 persons of average age 29 years and 3 years job experience in the plant had a significantly greater accident rate than a roughly comparable sized group age 41 years, also with three years of job experience. Van Zelst observed that age actually had a stronger effect upon accident rate than did time on the job. He tentatively concluded that immaturity of the employees was a large factor in explaining the accident experience of young workers.[13]

Management can profit from findings such as these by instituting proper job-training programs, exercising special safety monitoring of new employees, and by giving attention to the possible immaturity of workers in making hazardous job assignments. A company with higher labor turnover is especially vulnerable to accidents. Management is well advised to take steps to reduce such turnover. A continuous parade of new workers is a sure invitation to a high injury rate.

[12] *Ibid.*

[13] R. H. Van Zelst, "The Effect of Age and Experience Upon Accident Rate," *Journal of Applied Psychology,* Vol. 38 (1954), pp. 313-317.

ESTABLISHING A SAFETY PROGRAM

Assume that a company has a high accident rate, high workmen's compensation costs, and no present safety program. What actions should be taken to establish and organize a workable safety program? Of course, the detailed procedure that would be followed would depend upon the circumstances of company size, number of plants, nature of the industry, production technology, and the attitudes of top management. But certain major actions that would have to be taken by nearly all organizations can be specified.

ESTABLISHING A SAFETY PROGRAM—KEY ELEMENTS

1. Objectives and policies.
2. Top management support.
3. Organization.
4. Establishing responsibility for safety.
5. Engineering.
6. Job safety analysis.
7. Analysis of accidents.
8. Education and training.
9. Enforcement.
10. Healthy work environment.
11. Adequate treatment of injuries.
12. Rehabilitation.

Objectives and Policies

When top management decides that it wants to take steps to obtain a safe organization, it must determine just how far it wants to go and what it wants to accomplish. Does it want to have a company that ranks with the best in its industry in terms of low injury frequency and severity? Or does it simply want a safety effort that will reduce workmen's compensation costs to a tolerable level. Is it willing to invest money sufficient to achieve a really nonhazardous plant? Or does it want to concentrate upon training the workers to cope moderately well in a basically dangerous environment? What policy will be adopted when a situation develops in the future in such a way that a production-oriented decision clashes with a safety-oriented decision?

Top Management Support

Top management sets the safety objectives and policies in the first place; and how top management chooses to support and implement its own policies is crucial to the effectiveness of these policies. It is top management that decides, ultimately, how extensive a safety organization to set up, the caliber of safety personnel that will be employed, and how much money, in total, it will invest in safety. The single most important element in the success or failure of any companywide program, whether it be safety, training, research, or maintenance, is the emphasis that is given to that program by top management.

Organization

The particular organizational arrangement that is adopted to carry out a safety program depends to a large extent upon the size of the enterprise. A company of 100 employees could not afford a full-time safety director. But it nevertheless must organize for safety. In such a small company the authority and responsibility for initiating a safety program must be assigned to some member of management. He must be granted enough time and resources to do an effective job. The production manager or a staff engineer may take on the responsibility of coordinating the safety program. This individual will need the full cooperation of all line personnel from the president down to the hourly workers. A small firm such as we are describing might advantageously engage the services of an outside consultant to provide the specialized knowledge and experience an endeavor of that kind requires.

Medium- and large-sized companies require the talents of a full-time safety director. In fact, a big corporation typically will employ a number of analysts, engineers, industrial hygienists, and safety inspectors in addition to the safety director. Simonds and Grimaldi suggest that as a rule of thumb one full-time safety specialist should be employed for each 2,000 employees.[14] Of course, if the work operations are especially hazardous, it might be necessary to have a full-time specialist for only 800 employees. Most commonly the safety director in a medium- or large-sized company reports to the director of industrial relations. Although a high portion of his time is devoted to administration, coordination, and training, a safety man should also have a sound technical background, since he must apply engineering principles and a knowledge of chemistry and human biology in eliminating physical and environmental hazards.

Inasmuch as it is clearly impossible for a staff safety man to implement a comprehensive safety program on his own, many companies obtain the participation of the other managers, supervisors, and workers by appointing them to safety committees. A policy and steering committee might be composed of top management personnel. Its function could be set to policies and general procedures, review safety performance, and apply the necessary support and "push" to those aspects of the overall program that are falling behind.

Many companies set up a committee headed by the safety director and composed of some or all of the factory line supervisors. One of the pri-

---

[14] Rollin H. Simmonds and John V. Grimaldi, *Safety Management: Accident Cost and Control* (Homewood, Ill.: Richard D. Irwin, Inc., 1956), p. 58.

mary responsibilities of such a committee is to analyze and evaluate potential accident-producing conditions and decide upon ways of correcting them. Commonly the supervisor's safety committee may review reports of periodic plant inspections often conducted by a safety inspector or a team of foremen) and decide whatever action appears necessary. The safety director can also use some of the sessions to educate the supervisors in safety via lectures, readings, case studies, movies, and the like.

Because the ultimate test of any safety program is the actual accident experience of the workers, their active participation must be secured. There are several approaches to this problem, and the committee method is but one. A committee of hourly employees may be set up in each production department to meet periodically with the departmental foreman. The men can help the foreman develop safe working procedures and uncover hazardous conditions. A principal purpose of the workers' safety committee is to develop favorable attitudes toward safety and educate them to work safely.

Another approach to the development of worker participation in accident prevention is the appointment of a worker as a safety observer in each department. Usually this position is rotated from man to man every few months. This is an excellent means of creating personal responsibility and identification with the safety effort. Although the safety observer carries out his regular job duties during his term of office, he is granted sufficient time away from his regular job to be of real assistance to his foreman in the area of safety.

Union-management cooperation in safety has much to commend it. Although the primary responsibility for maintaining a safe plant rests with management, additional help in carrying out this obligation can profitably be obtained from the local union leadership. A stable, mature collective bargaining relationship must exist between the two parties before such a cooperative venture can be reasonably inaugurated. Although union and management may clash over economic matters, their objectives should be identical in the sphere of injury prevention.

Establishing Responsibility for Safety

Some industrialists think that with the appointment of a safety director, they can "wash their hands" of all responsibility for safety and get on with their main business of obtaining high production, low costs, and adequate quality. Nothing could be further from the truth. The only way to achieve and maintain a safe plant is to place responsibility for safety on an equal status with responsibility for production, cost control, quality, and profit making. Whenever the responsibility for maintaining a safe plant is relegated to the position of a frill that can be attended to only after the more important objectives of production, costs, and efficiency are achieved, then injury rates will be excessive and will remain so until line management at all levels devotes adequate attention to accident prevention. If certain foremen or workers are not released to attend a safety meeting because they cannot be spared from the production floor, then the safety effort will suffer. If requisitions to design and install machine guards are put aside indefinitely because plant engineering has more "important" work to do, then again the safety program will deteriorate. In short, the basic responsibility for injury prevention rests with line management. It starts with the company president and goes vertically downward through the entire hierarchy (executive vice-president, plant manager, production superintendent, and foreman) to the actual worker.

What then does the safety director (and his subordinates) do? Is he not responsible for safety? Yes, the safety director bears very important responsibilities for injury prevention. But he serves in a staff, not a line, capacity. He basically serves as an innovator, organizer, creator, advisor, teacher, analyzer, investigator, stimulator, and (at times) a prodder. He must organize the safety program throughout the plant, collect accident data, investigate accidents, help develop engineering applications (guards, and so on), conduct safety training and information meetings for management personnel, analyze jobs to develop safe working procedures, and prepare instructional material for use by foremen in conducting meetings with their men.

The staff safety director rarely has line authority to order supervisors and workers to take a particular action in regard to safety. But he often acquires considerable influence in the establishment of plant safety policies, procedures, and the development of engineering standards for safety. He works closely in these areas with other line and staff officers. But because they recognize his proficiency and specialized competence in the field of safety, the views of the safety director are given considerable weight.

Engineering for Safety

Proper engineering to remove work hazards is fundamental to any organized safety effort. If one were to look at the typical mill of 1910 and compare it with the typical mill of the 1970's in the same industry, he would immediately perceive the vast advances that have been made in elimination and guarding of dangerous mechanical, electrical and chemical conditions. The typical mill of 1910 was a maze of exposed pulleys, belts, chains, gears, cutters, punches, and levers. Today technology has advanced to the point where many hazardous conditions have simply been designed "out" of the equipment and processes, and most of the remaining ones have been adequately guarded. But this statement should not be interpreted to mean that further engineering for safety cannot be done. Many factories are still behind the times as far as hazard elimination is concerned. New products, processes, and machines are constantly being designed, and full attention must be given to safety engineering in both design, layout, and installation.

The most foolproof way of engineering for safety is simply to eliminate the hazard from the machine, process, or structure. If, for example, a particular substance or material has been put into large heavy containers for movement from one operation to another throughout the plant (batch production) and if materials handlers have suffered many hernias and back injuries from lifting these containers, a basic engineering redesign of the production processes might eliminate the batch approach and substitute continuous process production. In this case the physical handling of the containers by human labor will have been eliminated because the material will flow from one piece of equipment to another by mechanical conveyor or by blowing the substance through large pipes.

If it is not feasible to carry out a basic redesign of the production process to eliminate the hazard, then the next stage is to design and install a guard to prevent workers from coming in contact with moving parts or point of operation elements. Thus gears on a machine are usually guarded to prevent human contact while the machine is in operation.

If it is not possible to eliminate the hazard or to guard the equipment itself, it may be possible to have the worker wear and use protective clothing and equipment. Thus construction workers and those working around overhead cranes generally wear hard hats, machinists wear goggles, and welders wear face shields and gloves.

Job Safety Analysis

Although job analysis for purposes of improving work methods, setting production standards, and determining rates of pay is carried on in many organizations, these investigations are rarely done for the purpose of isolating all the hazards and figuring out ways of overcoming them. But job analysis is useful both for hazard elimination and for developing safe work methods. Workers can thereby be trained to adopt these methods. Therefore, the safety director must set up a definite program whereby all the jobs will eventually be studied in great detail from the standpoint of accident prevention. This is a very time-consuming assignment. It makes sense to tackle the most hazardous jobs first to get under control those operations having the greatest likelihood of accidents. In certain situations it is practicable to teach foremen how to analyze the jobs in their departments from the standpoint of safety. This type of job study requires that the key work elements of each job be recorded on a sheet of paper, the potential health and injury hazards be identified, and the means for overcoming or avoiding them described. This approach to accident prevention when coupled with specific remedies and worker training can pay rich dividends in terms of lower accident frequency and severity. Instead of putting one's total effort into preventing a recurrence of an accident, this approach seeks to prevent it from happening in the first place by eliminating all possible causes.

Accident Analysis and Tabulation

Every accident that results in a personal injury, whether it be simply a first-aid case or a more serious disabling one, must be investigated by the injured employee's supervisor to ascertain the cause(s) and to determine what specific remedies are required to avoid a recurrence. He does this, of course, after the injured employee has been adequately treated and cared for. Although the primary reason for accident investigation is to find out what action must be taken to prevent a recurrence, accident information provides excellent case study material for use in training meetings. Figure 27-2 shows an accident report form made out by a foreman. This form records on one page all the essential information needed for identifying the injured employee, indicating the causes, applying preventive measures, and compiling injury statistics.

Although every accident must be investigated and reported by the foreman, a more intensive investigation should be conducted by the staff safety specialist for all but the very simple and elementary accidents. This is necessary so that he can be fully cognizant of the accidents occuring in his plant and so that he can apply his technical skill to uncover elements of the case possibly overlooked by the foreman.

The safety department should periodically summarize all injuries that have occurred and classify them by plant, department, shift, cause, type of injury, and whether disabling or not. Injury statistics are valuable for revealing where further effort must be exerted to achieve improvement in the safety performance, for comparing the record from one year to another, and for apprising management of needs for further action.

Education and Training

Safety education for all levels of management and for employees in a vital ingredient for any successful safety program. Education in this context concerns the development of proper perspective and attitudes toward safety. It deals with basic fundamentals and the reasons why. Training is more concerned with immediate job knowledge, skills, and work methods.

Top and middle management require education in the fundamentals of safety and the need for an effective accident prevention program. The costs of accidents, both human and dollar costs, must be brought to the attention of line management. Top management in large- and medium-sized companies does not need to concern itself with the detailed mechanics of accident prevention, but it must acquire a sufficient awareness of safety fundamentals so that it will actively support the work of the safety department and of middle and lower management in carrying out the program.

The safety director and his staff must undertake to provide extensive education and training for first-line supervisors. The supervisors must un-

```
┌─────────────────────────────────────────────────────────────────────────┐
```

FOREMAN'S ACCIDENT REPORT

Office Use

Non Disabling _____

Disabling (Lost time) _____X_____

Name of Injured ___John Jones___   Date of Accident ___January 15, 1962___

Job Title ___Machine Operator___   Time of Accident ___10:05 A.M.___

Department ___Carding___   Plant Number ___1___

Nature of Injury and Part of Body Affected   Cut off tip of middle finger, right hand

Describe the Accident (state what the injured employee was doing and the circumstances leading to accident. Mention tools, machines, and materials involved)
The stock became clogged in his machine as he was feeding it through. He shut off the
power and attempted to advance rolls by turning the pulley by hand. In doing so he
caught middle finger of right hand between belt and pulley. Momentum carried hand
around. He jerked hand away and cut finger tip off.

Unsafe condition involved (such as lack of guard, broken part, slippery floor, inadequate tool)   There should be a guard covering both pulleys and drive belt.

Unsafe employee act (such as not following instructions and safety rules) He should
not have attempted to advance rolls by turning pulley by hand. Should have pressed jog
button.

What steps are you taking to prevent similar injuries? 1. Have instructed all employees involved never to put hands on belt or pulley to advance rolls.
2. Initiated maintenance order to construct and install proper guard.

Did Employee go to Doctor? _Yes_   Doctor's Name _H. J. Hanks_   Date _1/15/62_

Hospital _____

Reviewed ___*T. R. Roth*___   Signature of Foreman ___*J.J. Fredericks*___
              Superintendent

Office Use Only

Temp. Total ___x___   Permanent Partial _____ Permanent Total _____

Started losing time _1/16/62_   Part of body _____Time Charge _____

Returned to work _1/19/62_   % Loss _____

Time Charged _3 days_   Time Charge _____

```
└─────────────────────────────────────────────────────────────────────────┘
```

Figure 27-2. A Report of an Employee Injury as Prepared by the Foreman.

derstand their key role in the safety effort, namely, that they are primarily responsible for preventing accidents (assuming they have adequate support from above). Each supervisor must conduct his own safety training for his employees. This takes the form of both individual on-the-job training and periodic safety meetings held right in the department. Sometimes supervisors feel that the safety director should be the one to conduct employee safety-training sessions. However, experience has shown that the supervisors should first of all be taught how to give safety instruction, and then they should do their own teaching. This practice strengthens the bond between supervisor and employee and makes it impossible for there to be any conflict between what a staff safety director might teach the men and what a line supervisor teaches by his day-to-day actions in dealing with the men.

At the employee level there are two principal objectives: (1) to develop safety consciousness and favorable attitudes toward safety, and (2) to achieve safe work performance from each employee on his job. To achieve these goals, a number of things must be done. At the time a man is hired, orientation by both the personnel manager and the man's supervisor should cover such areas as the need for safe work performance, the hazards in his own department and job, the necessity for prompt reporting of any personal injuries, desirability of reporting unsafe conditions to the supervisor, and the general causes of accidents. Each new worker must be taught how to perform his job safely. This frequently takes the form of on-the-job training. Instruction in safe working procedures must be integrated with instruction designed to achieve acceptable output and quality performance.

In addition to individual on-the-job training, successful safety practice in countless organizations has demonstrated the value of periodic safety meetings conducted by the supervisor. Among the topics that may be covered are the following: how to prevent accidents, accident causes, importance of good housekeeping, handling materials safely, first aid, machine hazards, fire prevention, use of hand tools, protecting the eyes.

Enforcement

The safety director helps to secure adherence to established safety policies, procedures, and regulations by periodically touring the plant to observe conditions and activities of the men. If he notices employees performing their jobs without wearing required protective equipment or if he observes faulty maintenance practices that could cause accidents, he will call these items to the attention of the departmental supervisor.

Immediate enforcement of standard operating procedures with respect to safety, of course, must be done by the line supervisor. When he observes employees who are not performing their jobs in the agreed-upon manner, he calls this to their attention and corrects them.

The enforcement aspect of safety must be done in a positive, supportive way. High pressure and a continual hounding of men leads to fear and resentment. With proper indoctrination and training there should seldom be need for punitive action for violation of company safety regulations. However, where individual employees deliberately refuse to cooperate, the regular disciplinary measures applied to other discipline offenses must be brought into play. The author has heard foremen say, "I am afraid to issue a written warning to any of my men because he will then go to the union and then I will have a formal grievance on my hands." In point of fact, if the foreman is sure of his facts in a particular case and is fair to the man, it is the rare union indeed that will try to obstruct a safety program. The goals of both union and management are fully compatible in the field of safety. A foreman must not evade his responsibility for safety by claiming he cannot obtain the cooperation of his men or cannot enforce discipline.

Healthful Work Environment

Not only does management have an obligation to create a safe plant to prevent injuries that occur at a specific point in time and place—that is, accidents—but it also must create a healthy plant environment to prevent occupational diseases. This means, for example, that the air must be free of contaminants, the temperature must be fully compatible to human existence, and toxic substances must be kept away from the body. Stated succinctly, the plant environment must be regulated in such a way as to be conducive to employee health, well-being, and morale. The subject of control of the work environment is covered in a later section of this chapter.

Treatment of Injuries

Every establishment, whether large or small, should have adequate facilities and trained personnel for rendering first aid to injured employees. The small company should have a clean, adequately equipped first-aid room. Its supervisory personnel and key hourly employees should receive first-aid training so that they are skilled in rendering help to the injured. Larger establishments have need for the full-time services of an industrial nurse and a physician. The providing of first-aid treatment is but a part of a comprehensive industrial health program as described in a later section of this chapter.

Rehabilitation

If an employee has suffered a serious temporary disabling injury or a permanent disability, it behooves the employer and the workmen's compensation insurance company to exercise every effort to rehabilitate that unfortunate individual. This includes helping him to learn how to care for his daily needs of living, learning how to acquire and reacquire useful job skills, helping him make a positive mental adjustment to his new situation, and then finding a new position for him in the company (if he cannot return to his old job).

Contests and Awards

Contests among the various departments of a company to achieve the best record in terms of freedom from lost-time accidents (or some other measure of safety performance) are quite popular with many safety men. Awards can take many forms: a dinner for all members of the winning department, a plaque to be displayed on the wall, or prizes such as a cigarette lighter, tie clasp, or cash to each employee. Many companies in the transportation industry make significant awards to those drivers who meet specified goals without an accident. Contests have their place as a means of arousing interest in safety. However, some safety directors lose sight of the fundamentals of safety and place practically all of the emphasis upon contests and gimmicks.

To encourage workers to wear hard-toe safety shoes, the safety engineer in one plant picks three names at random from the list of employees every month. He then personally visits each of these on the job to note whether he is wearing safety shoes. If so, he receives two dollars in cash on the spot. Now the chances of an individual being chosen are very slim, so as a motivator such a gimmick is rather questionable. If management has determined that safety shoes are a necessary form of protection for certain jobs, then it clearly must provide them and require that the employees wear them.

If a safety director places most of his faith in contests and attention-getting gimmicks, he will tend to neglect the fundamentals of hazard elimination, training, job analysis, and enforcement. The trouble with these contests and award programs is that they operate at the fringes. Safety must be an integral part of every worker's and supervisor's job. The prospect of having a chance to win a carton of cigarettes at the end of three months is unlikely to cause workers to think and act safely constantly.

ENVIRONMENT CONTROL—INDUSTRIAL HYGIENE

Simply stated the objective of an industrial hygiene program is the prevention of occupational disease. Stated affirmatively the goal is to create and maintain a work environment that is conducive to good health, good morale, and high production. An occupational disease is generally distinguished from an injury caused by an accident. Although the affected worker suffers in either case and the difference is immaterial to him, the distinction is often important under state workmen's compensation laws, because many states grant only limited coverage and benefits for occupational diseases.

Whereas an injury caused by an accident ordinarily occurs at a specific point in time and place and is unexpected or unforeseen, an occupational disease usually develops gradually over an extended period of time (weeks, months, or years) as a result of repeated or continuous exposure to toxic substances, microorganisms, air-borne contaminants, or stress-producing elements.

Only large companies (or smaller ones with obvious environmental hazards, such as the presence of radioactive elements) tend to have industrial hygiene departments. An adequate appreciation on the part of top management of the need for environmental control is a relatively recent development. Where this need is recognized and an industrial hygiene program has been established, it is most commonly located organizationally within the medical department. One survey of 175 companies that had such programs showed that the industrial hygiene function was placed under the medical department in 131 companies and under the safety department in 22 companies, with the remainder being scattered among personnel (direct reporting), medical and safety jointly, maintenance, and miscellaneous.[15]

The industrial hygienist must have training in such areas as physiology, biochemistry, environmental engineering, toxicology, biophysics, and psychology. In some cases the knowledge and skills required to solve particular environmental health problems are so complex that he must call upon the assitance of consultants. Industrial hygienists, by their education, are taught to recognize conditions that can cause deterioration of worker health and apply corrective measures before the fact.

Although it is unlikely that a particular plant would contain the whole spectrum of hazards that can cause occupational diseases, the following is a listing of the principal conditions that exist in industry in general:

1. Thermal environment that may cause heat exhaustion, heat stroke, heat cramps, or frostbite
2. High or low atmospheric pressure, such as encountered by divers, tunnel workers, fliers, and astronauts
3. Mechanical vibration, such as that caused by air hammers
4. Radiation consisting of both electromagnetic and ionizing radiation
5. Noise that can cause auditory damage and nervous tension
6. Air contamination. Inhalation is the most prevalent danger, but skin contact and ingestion also cause considerable illness. This includes such elements as gases, fumes, vapors, and air-borne poisons.
7. Skin diseases. According to the National Safety Council skin diseases

[15] Doris M. Thompson, *Company Medical and Health Programs,* Studies in Personnel Policy, No. 171 (New York: National Industrial Conference Board, 1959), p. 49.

account for the payment of more compensation dollars and hence cause more suffering than any other form of occupational disease.[16] Contrary to general belief these are not due to allergy so much as to primary skin irritants, such as solvents, acids, bases, and the like.

WORKMEN'S COMPENSATION

Contrary to most social insurance programs in the United States, workmen's compensation has been almost the exclusive province of the states rather than the Federal government. The first compensation law was passed by New York State in 1910.[17] By 1920 all but six states had passed such laws. Mississippi, the last state to do so, passed a compensation law that became effective in 1949.

Workmen's compensation laws place the financial responsibility for work injuries upon the employer without regard to who was at fault or who caused the accident. The costs associated with industrial accidents are considered simply as a cost of doing business that the employer must bear. Prior to the enactment of these laws, injured workers generally had little effective recourse. They had the right to sue their employer in a court of law to try to obtain compensation for wage loss, medical costs, and compensation for the damage suffered. However, workers fared very poorly in such court actions, because they possessed insufficient funds to pursue the cases and because the common law of the period favored the employer in such cases. This sad situation has largely been changed as a result of workmen's compensation legislation.

Benefits

All the compensation laws require that medical service be provided to injured employees. Although full medical treatment without any dollar limit is provided for in the majority of states, fourteen states specify a limit either in terms of time or money or both. This is unfortunate, because the dollar limits are quite low in many of these states. A disabled worker is generally in no position to assume the burden of his own medical bills for amounts in excess of, say, $1,000. All except two states grant coverage for occupational disease, although a considerable number limit the amount of medical payments to the affected employee.

In addition to medical benefits the laws provide partial recompense for

---

[16] National Safety Council, *Accident Prevention Manual for Industrial Operations* (4th Ed.; Chicago: The Council, 1959), Ch. 40, p. 29.

[17] This initial law was declared unconstitutional by the New York Court of Appeals. The tragic fire at the Triangle Waist Company in New York City in 1911 caused the State to amend its constitution and thereby acquire a firm law by 1913. The first law to take effect was Wisconsin's in 1911.

loss of wages during the period the worker misses from the job. In most jurisdictions the individual is paid 66⅔ per cent of his average weekly wage up to a designated maximum, which is typically between $50 and $60 per week. The imposed ceiling means that many injured workers will receive much less than two thirds of their average wage. To escape the administrative costs for handling short disablements and to discourage employees from feigning injury just to obtain a holiday, the majority of the states pay nothing to compensate for wage loss for periods of seven days or less. In other words there is a seven-day waiting period.

Permanent partial disabilities, such as the loss of use of an arm or the loss of the actual arm, are paid according to a specific schedule. For example, for the loss of a hand, in Wisconsin, benefits are paid for 400 weeks, whereas in Louisiana the person would receive 150 weeks of benefits for the same injury.

Administration and Financing

To make certain that funds are available to meet a company's obligations, the state laws require either that it carry compensation insurance or that it put up a bond to demonstrate financial responsibility if it wishes to be self-insuring. A company that is self-insuring pays all benefits required by the law directly out of its own pocket. Because only large companies can assume the risk involved in self-insurance, the majority of employers insure with either a state insurance fund or with a private insurance company.

The basic premium charged an employer is called the manual rate. This rate is based upon the various industrial classifications and occupations that exist in the establishment. This manual rate is uniform throughout the state and is set by the insurance-rating board. It is based principally upon the accident record of the particular industry group involved. This basic manual rate is adjusted upward or downward annually under a system called merit rating, to make the cost to the employer closely representative of his true charges for payments to his injured employees. Merit rating rewards the safe employer by lowering the insurance premium and penalizes the unsafe one by raising the premium. The merit-rating feature of the state laws is undoubtedly the most powerful stimulus to an employer to take positive, continuing steps to reduce accidents. When the pocketbook pinches, management acts. Two forms of merit rating are in current use. One is experience rating, which involves a raising or lowering of the premium in accordance with the risk's loss record for the thirty-six months immediately preceding the policy year. The other method is retrospective rating, which involves a review of the latest year's experience upon expiration of the policy. The premium is then adjusted up or down to correspond with the current loss experience. Under retrospective rating a company is more promptly rewarded for adopting a comprehensive accident prevention program. Under experience rating several years would have to elapse before the company could realize any real gain.

OCCUPATIONAL HEALTH

Historically, company health programs were inaugurated as a result of the passage of workmen's compensation laws with the attendant obligation to provide first-aid treatment for work injuries. Sometime later companies began to give preemployment physical examinations both to insure that those hired could meet the physical demands of their jobs and to prevent being charged with a compensation claim for a preexisting ailment. Company medical services then evolved to the point that if a physician was on the premises, it was only natural that he would be called upon to treat minor ailments not caused at work, such as colds, sore throats, skin disorders, headaches, and gastrointestinal upsets. Industrial medicine has grown to the point where the large corporation having a progressive personnel philosophy now takes positive steps to maintain good employee health off-the-job as well as on the job. Some companies have also established programs in the field of mental health. There has been a recognition by some corporate managements that it has a stake in the "whole man," not only his physical health but his mental health as well both on and off the job. This concern for the health of employees has not led to the establishment of company clinics to provide broad treatment of nonoccupational illness. Most generally it has taken the form of health information and education services, individual counseling by physicians, referrals to private specialists, and action by management to improve hospital and doctor services in the community. Not only do comprehensive industrial-health programs help the employees, but they also often result in reduced absenteeism, lower sickness insurance costs, higher productivity, and improved morale.

A comprehensive company health program will include the following features:

1. A professional staff of physicians and nurses.
2. Adequate facilities for emergency care of work injuries and for conducting preemployment and periodic medical examinations.
3. Proper first-aid treatment for occupational injuries and diseases. Serious cases are referred to private practice physicians and hospitals.
4. Preemployment medical examinations and periodic examinations for those exposed to special occupational hazards.
5. Reasonable first aid to employee for nonoccupational illness while on the job.
6. Information and education services for the personal health of employees.
7. Consultation with those suffering physical or emotional maladjust-

ment to the work situation. The company medical personnel may offer advice, refer the individual to a private specialist, work with the person's supervisor, or refer the man to an appropriate community agency.

8. Adequate and confidential medical records.
9. Cooperation by the company physician or medical director with those responsible for accident prevention and control of the work environment (industrial hygiene) to achieve an integrated employee health program.
10. Cooperation with public health authorities in regard to mass inoculations and other measures for the prevention of communicable diseases.
11. Advice and supervision, where necessary, to maintain proper company sanitation.

Although the foregoing health program is most feasible for the medium- and large-sized company, the small firm can carry out many of these elements by engaging the services of a qualified physician on a retainer or consulting basis.

MENTAL HEALTH IN INDUSTRY

Mental health can be defined as the state wherein a person is well adapted, has an accurate perception of reality, and can reasonably successfully adjust to the stresses and frustrations of life. At present very few companies are staffed with professionally trained personnel to conduct a mental health program. In a survey of 278 Canadian and United States companies, the National Industrial Conference Board found only 10 employing one or more part-time psychiatrists.[18] Spriegel and Mumma surveyed 567 companies and found that only 37 had a formal mental health program. They found that 15 companies employed one or more full-time counselors, 10 had full-time psychologists, and 7 had part-time psychiatrists.[19]

Emotional disturbances can be caused by the employee's interaction with his work situation or by his relationship to his personal environment off the job. Or they can be caused by a combination of both. Now whether a company employs psychologists and psychiatrists or not, it still can (and must) establish a healthy human relations climate through sound management, good supervisory leadership, and attention to the needs of its employees.

Sometimes line executives feel that the state of human relations and

[18] Thompson, *op. cit.,* pp. 42-43.
[19] W. R. Spriegel and Edwin W. Mumma, *Mental Health in Industry* (Austin: The University of Texas, 1962), pp. 6 and 31.

mental health in their organizations could be enhanced if only the problem employees—the malcontents, the frustrated, and the troublemakers—could be cured by referral to counselors, psychologists, or psychiatrists. But as an eminent psychiatrist, Temple Burling, has pointed out, the problems are in the relationships among people and not simply *within* the people themselves. In asking the specialist to cure his problem employees the industrialist is sometimes expecting him to cure them of their human nature.[20] Therefore, the major emphasis in any mental health program in industry should be upon the creation of sound supervisor-subordinate relationships, elimination of festering conditions that cause discontent, and the development of a favorable human relations climate. But even in the best-run plant some individuals will suffer from emotional disturbances. Supervisors should receive sufficient training in the psychological make-up of man to recognize when to refer one of their employees to the company physician or other qualified specialist for help. Inasmuch as the vast majority of companies do not employ professional talent qualified in the field of mental health, the company physician is often in a position where he must provide counsel and aid to emotionally disturbed employees.

It is not uncommon for a physical ailment to be aggravated and enlarged because of anxiety, worry, or abnormal pressures gnawing at an employee. The plant physician, though he is accustomed to treating essentially physical ailments, must learn to make a holistic evaluation of his patients. This is especially important where the patient appears to have repeated illnesses or injuries or a prolonged ailment that cannot logically be explained on the basis of physical medicine alone. Felton gives the example of a 35-year-old carpenter who developed pain in the lumbar area, with increasing stiffness of the back and lower extremities. Although examination by two neurosurgeons and an orthopedist failed to indicate a clear need for surgery, a psychological analysis revealed that the patient felt a clear "need" for surgical examination. Because he was going downgrade and walking was almost impossible, an exploratory operation was performed. The disks and back were completely normal and the patient recovered very quickly, with full use of his body and legs. The consulting psychologist learned that the patient's mother, when the same age as he, had had back trouble, had no surgery, and was an invalid in bed the rest of her life.[21] The carpenter had clearly felt that without surgery he would become a permanent invalid himself. Of course, an operation should not be used to cure every psychosomatic ailment, but the point being made is that all persons closely involved with a problem employee must search deeply to analyze the whole man to effect a solution. So-

[20] Temple Burling, "Psychiatry in Industry," *Industrial and Labor Relations Review,* Vol. 8, No. 1 (October 1954), pp. 30-37.

[21] Jean S. Felton, "Evaluation of the Whole Man," *Journal of Occupational Medicine,* Vol. 3, No. 12 (December 1961), pp. 579-585.

cial, psychological, family, cultural, ethnic, educational, financial, and physical factors may have to be taken into account to achieve a satisfactory solution.

Questions for Review and Discussion

1. What is an accident? Do all accidents result in injuries? Why must all be analyzed for an effective safety effort?
2. What is injury frequency? Injury severity?
3. For appraising the safety performance of a plant, which is more important, injury frequency or severity? Explain.
4. Why is the injury experience of small companies typically worse than that of large ones in the same industry?
5. Distinguish between the insured and the uninsured costs of accidents.
6. Are most industrial accidents caused by unsafe physical or mechanical conditions or by unsafe human acts? Discuss.
7. In the overall, what part do accident-prone people contribute to the total problem of industrial work injuries? Discuss.
8. How do the work environment and opportunities for recognition, advancement, and autonomy relate to accident rates in industry? Explain.
9. Enumerate the key elements of a complete safety program.
10. What part does line supervision play in achieving good safety performance in a plant? What are the responsibilities of the Safety Department?
11. What means can be used to develop safety consciousness among hourly employees?
12. What are the objectives of an industrial hygiene program? What kinds of skills and knowledge must an industrial hygienist possess?
13. Do you feel that an employer should be held financially responsible for any and all work injuries suffered by his employees? Discuss.
14. What is merit rating in workmen's compensation?
15. Outline the content of a comprehensive occupational health program.
16. What responsibility, if any, do you feel a company has in regard to one of its employees who becomes seriously emotionally disturbed at some time after initial employment?

CASE PROBLEM

The Textile Company, a family-owned business, is located in an old New England mill town. Although its early business was principally in woolen goods, in recent years it has shifted largely to synthetic fabrics. Profit margins have been modest, although the company has actually lost money only once in the past ten years.

The company employs 700 people of which 610 are hourly production and maintenance workers. The factory employees have been organized for many years by a union. The production facilities are situated in two old, multistory brick buildings having wooden floors. A few years ago a sprinkler system was installed throughout the factory and offices for fire protection.

The accident rate has increased significantly in recent years. You have just been hired as the company safety director. Until this point accident prevention had been the responsibility of the personnel manager. However, when the accident rate jumped and workmen's compensation costs soared, the company president decided that safety had to become the full-time responsibility of one man, at least until the situation could be brought under control. Your immediate superior is the personnel manager, who fully approved of the decision to hire a safety director, because he realized he did not have the time or background to do an effective job of accident prevention. The personnel department consists of the personnel director, yourself, and a secretary.

After you have been on the job for a week you discover the following facts and form impressions as follows:

1. Because production and employment have expanded about 25 per cent over the past two years, there are a large number of new workers on the payroll. Heavy layoffs occur every winter, during the slack season. Many of those laid off do not return when business picks up. This problem is accentuated by the relatively low wages paid to hourly workers.

2. Although the vast majority of all work injuries have been faithfully reported by the foremen, little post accident investigation has been done, and no attempt has been made to compute frequency or severity rates. The president became alarmed over the mounting accident rate only when the workmen's compensation insurance premiums mounted drastically. At present the company is paying a charge of 30 per cent over the manual rate for its industrial classification. Retrospective rating is used by the insurance carrier.

3. The safety program up to this time has been quite limited. A number of years ago the workmen's compensation insurance carrier provided good engineering and educational service, but the company president switched companies to obtain lower premium rates. The present program consists of a monthly safety meeting attended by all the foreman during lunch hour. The personnel manager, who has been conducting these meetings, has tended to criticize the foremen openly, as a group, for the poor accident record. Considerable resentment has developed over this issue. Each month a committee of three foremen (the membership rotates month to month) has had the responsibility for conducting a plant safety inspection. The findings of this committee were reported at the monthly foremen's meeting, at which

time the issues raised were discussed. In recent months this committee has ceased to function.

4. You have made a careful inspection of the plant. You have observed that in one of the departments the machinery is quite antiquated. It is driven principally by leather belting from overhead line shafting. Throughout the plant, layout of the machines and storage areas is poor from the standpoint of efficiency and smooth flow of materials. Although warehouse operations have been partially mechanized, within the manufacturing areas most of the handling of bales, cartons, and boxes is manual, with the aid of hand trucks and carts. Plant housekeeping is poor. Compressed air and water hoses tend to lie uncoiled on the floor. Spare machine parts are scattered on the floor in many areas of the plant. Machine guarding is minimal.

5. You have analyzed and classified all the work injuries for the previous year from the accident records. There were a total of 250 injuries including first-aid as well as lost-time cases. From the state of the records, it has not been possible to distinguish accurately between minor cases and lost-time injuries. The largest single category of injuries occured to hands and fingers which were caught between rotating machine parts. The second largest category of injuries was back ailments and hernias from lifting. The third most frequent was eye injuries from foreign particles becoming lodged in the eyes, and the fourth category could be directly attributed to faulty housekeeping.

The president and the personnel manager have promised full support for a reinvigorated safety effort. However, they look to you as a safety specialist and will leave most of the responsibility to you. Top management wants results.

Question

How will you go about establishing and organizing an effective safety program? What will be your first steps?

Suggestions for Further Reading

Cheit, Earl F., *Injury and Recovery in the Course of Employment,* New York: John Wiley & Sons, 1961.

DeReamer, Russell, *Modern Safety Practices,* New York: John Wiley & Sons, 1958.

Haddon, William J., E. A. Suchman, and D. Klein, *Accident Research: Approaches and Methods,* New York: Harper & Row, 1964.

Heinrich, H. W., and E. R. Grannis, *Industrial Accident Prevention,* 4th Ed., New York: McGraw-Hill Book Company, 1959.

Levinson, Harry and others, *Men, Management, and Mental Health,* Cambridge, Mass.: Harvard University Press, 1962.

McLean, Alan A., "Who Pays the Bill? A Clinical Perspective," *Journal of Occupational Medicine,* Vol. 9, No. 5, May 1967, pp. 244-250.

McMurry, Robert N., "Evaluating and Improving Mental Health: Who is Qualified?," *Journal of Occupational Medicine,* Vol. 9, No. 5, May 1967, pp. 215-219.

National Safety Council. *Accident Prevention Manual,* 5th Ed., Chicago: National Safety Council, 1964.

————, *Fundamentals of Industrial Hygiene,* Chicago: National Safety Council 1968. Contents of this booklet appeared as a series of articles in *National Safety News,* February through December 1967.

Parmenter, E. L., *Target: Zero Accidents,* Atlanta, Georgia: Textile Industries, Inc., A reprint of five articles from *The Textile Management and Engineering Journal,* 1967.

Shepard, W. P., *The Physician in Industry,* New York: McGraw-Hill Book Company, 1961.

Simonds, Rollin H., and John V. Grimaldi, *Safety Management,* Rev. Ed., Homewood, Ill.: Richard D. Irwin, 1963.

Trice, Harrison M., and James A. Belasco, *Emotional Health and Employer Responsibility,* Ithaca, N.Y.: New York State School of Industrial and Labor Relations, Cornell University, Bulletin No. 57, May 1966.

Vilardo, Frank, "Human Factors Engineering: What Research Found for Safetymen in Pandora's Box," *National Safety News,* Vol. 98, No. 2, August 1968, pp. 35-41.

Benefits and Services 28

Nearly every organization in this country provides its employees certain tangible benefits over and above the basic pay check. These benefits may supply financial protection against such risks as illness, accident, unemployment, and loss of income due to retirement. They may provide extra leisure, extra income, and a better work environment. Some benefits help fulfill the social and recreational needs of employees. Although benefits and services are not directly related to the productive effort of the workers, management often expects to aid its recruitment effort, raise morale, create greater company loyalty, reduce turnover and absenteeism, and, in general, improve the strength of the organization by instituting a well-conceived program in this area.

Although the term *benefits and services* is very widely used to designate this area of personnel management practice, other terms, such as *fringe benefits, employee services, supplementary compensation, indirect compensation,* and *supplementary pay* are also used. The frequently used term *fringe benefits* originated during World War II. Many management practitioners now object to this expression on the grounds that these benefits nowadays represent a very substantial portion of the total labor cost for a firm. They are no longer merely fringe costs or fringe items. They are important to management, employees, and unions alike.

The terms *benefits* and *services* are often used interchangeably and hence are considered synonymous by some writers. To others the word *benefit* applies to those items for which a direct monetary value to the individual employee can be rather easily ascertained, as in the case of a pension, separation pay, major medical insurance, or holiday pay. The word *service* applies to such items as a company newspaper, athletic field, Christmas party, or company purchasing service, for which a direct money value for the individual employee cannot be readily established.

Growth of Benefits and Services

With the exception of a very small minority of companies that had adopted progressive personnel programs in the 1920's, American industry, by and large, did not provide benefits and services for hourly paid workers prior to the World War II period.[1] Pension plans were rare before 1940. By 1960 about 20 million people were covered by funded private pension plans. Paid holidays and vacations were almost nonexistent before World War II; nowadays employees typically receive six to eight holidays per year and from one to four weeks of vacation annually, depending upon their length of service with a particular employer. Prior to 1940 very few employees were covered by hospitalization and medical insurance; now such protection is widespread throughout industry.

Benefits and services represent a tangible gain to employees that is either monetary or nonfinancial, depending upon the particular item involved. They also represent a labor cost for the employer. When viewed as a cost, the dramatic increase in benefits and services over the years can be appreciated by noting fringe-benefit cost data compiled by the Chamber of Commerce of the United States. Eighty-four identical companies have submitted cost figures every two years, starting in 1947 (The Chamber surveys over 1,100 firms biennially, but only 84 have responded to every survey). In 1947 total fringe payments averaged 22.1 cents per hour, whereas in 1965 they averaged 88.8 cents per hour. Expressed as a percentage of payroll, the figure was 16.1 per cent in 1947 and 28.1 in 1965. Because the sample of companies that have responded to the Chamber survey throughout the entire period is small, these absolute values are not accurate for industry as a whole. However, the upward rising trend is rather typical for industry in general.

The 1967 Chamber survey included a total of 1,150 manufacturing and nonmanufacturing companies. For this sample fringe benefits constituted 26.6 per cent of payroll. It has been estimated that in 1929 fringe benefit payments averaged only about 3 per cent of payroll for the nation as a whole.[2]

[1] Salaried white-collar and managerial employees fared slightly better, because they often received paid vacations.and were paid when they were absent because of illness. With these exceptions these employees generally received no more benefits and services than hourly workers during this period.

[2] The Chamber of Commerce figures include five categories of fringe benefits: (1) Legally required payments, such as Old Age, Survivors, Disability and Health Insurance, Unemployment Insurance, and Workmen's Compensation; (2) Pension and welfare payments; (3) Paid

Causes for Growth.   Several factors account for the significant increase in fringe benefits over the past thirty years. Public policy is perhaps one of the most fundamental reasons. The Social Security Act of 1935 requires employers to share equally with employees the cost of Old Age, Survivors, and Disability Insurance. Employers pay the full cost of unemployment insurance.

The great increase in fringe benefits in the United States has coincided with the growth of unionism. Union demands at the bargaining table have often forced management to grant additional benefits. Unionization combined with National Labor Relations Board and court interpretations of the Wagner and Taft-Hartley Acts, have broadened the scope of mandatory bargaining, so that management must bargain such issues as pensions, Christmas bonuses, vacations, profit sharing, stock-purchase plans, and group-insurance plans.

During World War II the wage-stabilization objectives of the federal government prevented direct hourly wage increases in many instances but permitted the creation of benefit programs. Wage increases tended to exert immediate inflationary pressures, whereas benefits did not, because the actual receipt of these was generally deferred to the future. During the World War II period the high corporation tax rates encouraged management to expand benefit programs, because monies so contributed were legitimate business expenses and hence not taxable. All of these activities during the war period occurred in a context of labor scarcity and keen employer competition to attract qualified people.

The advanced stage of industrialization in the United States, the increasing interdependence of the people, the vital need for getting and keeping one's job, and the general affluence and prosperity in the economy, all have served to make it both necessary and possible for employers to provide a measure of financial protection for workers against the risks of unemployment, sickness, injury, and old age.

TYPES OF BENEFITS AND SERVICES

There exists considerable disagreement among writers and among management and union spokesmen as to just what things to include within the meaning of benefits and services. The Chamber of Commerce surveys, mentioned earlier, are fairly inclusive in defining fringe benefits. This organization includes legally required payments; pensions, group insurance, separation pay, and so on; paid rest periods, lunch periods, wash-up time, and so on; payments for time not worked; and such other items as profit-sharing payments, Christmas bonuses, suggestion awards,

---

rest periods, wash-up time, and so on; (4) Payments for time not worked, such as vacations and holidays; and (5) Other items, such as profit-sharing payments and Christmas bonuses. See *Employee Benefits (Fringe Benefits) 1967,* Washington, D.C.: Chamber of Commerce of the United States, 1968.

and tuition refunds to employees. However, the Chamber of Commerce survey excludes "premium pay for time worked," a category included in many definitions of fringe benefits.[3] The National Industrial Conference Board includes four major classes of items in its definition of fringe benefits: (1) extra payments for time worked, (2) payments for time not worked, (3) payments for employee security, and (4) payments for employee services.[4]

Another analysis of the issue defines a fringe benefit as any kind of benefit that costs somebody something and is over and above the base rate of pay. At first glance this appears to be a very broad, all-inclusive definition, but the article then goes on to say that legally required overtime, unemployment insurance, and Federal Social Security payments are excluded.[5]

What to include under the meaning of the term *benefits and services* depends primarily upon one's purpose. If one wants to determine the full cost to a company, over and above the average straight-time hourly wage, of employing labor to operate the business, then he will adopt an all-inclusive definition. If one includes only those things that employees consider as benefits or those things that a company offers to recruit and retain qualified personnel, then a more restricted definition is used. Likewise, if one includes only those items subject to union-management negotiation, a rather narrow definition is adopted.

Some businessmen consider the following items to be employee benefits: rest periods, clean-up time, pay for time spent processing employee grievances, rest rooms, parking lots, accident prevention programs, salt tablets, drinking fountains, lunch facilities, locker rooms, first aid and health services, and special protective clothing. However, these things are directly associated with work and with the people who are necessary to operate any business. They are not frills in any sense. In a civilized society these things are an essential concomitant of any work organization. Hence they ought not to be classified as fringe benefits.

In most factories that operate a suggestion plan, awards are made to employees who submit acceptable cost-reduction ideas or other proposals that benefit the company. They should be treated as compensation for work produced in the same sense that incentive income under a piecework or wage incentive plan or a salesmen's commission plan is paid for extra production. These wage incentive arrangements are not considered fringe benefits. Likewise, a suggestion award should not be so considered either.

Extra pay for time worked (overtime, shift differential, holiday premium,

---

[3] The category "premium pay for time worked" includes overtime premium, holiday premium, shift differential or premium, and premium pay for working during a weekend.

[4] *Computing the Cost of Fringe Benefits,* Studies in Personnel Policy, No. 128 (New York: National Industrial Conference Board, 1952).

[5] "Fringe Benefits: Some Neglected Considerations," *Personnel* Vol. 33, No. 4 (January 1957), pp. 337 - 346.

and weekend premium) could be considered as a special benefit. On the other hand, it can be argued that these premiums are paid only to induce people to work at undesirable times and that they should be treated as pay for time worked. They may be considered a form of direct compensation. They are treated as a form of wages and not as a fringe benefit by Sargent.[6]

In accordance with the foregoing discussion, employee benefits and services may be classified as shown below. Under each of the four categories shown are the principal kinds of benefits and services commonly found in work organizations. However, this list is intended to be representative rather than exhaustive.

EMPLOYEE BENEFITS AND SERVICES

A. Employee Security (financial protection against certain risks)
  1. Legally required employer contributions
     Old age, Survivors, Disability, and Health Insurance
     Unemployment Insurance
     Workmen's Compensation
     State disability insurance
     Railroad Retirement Tax, Railroad Unemployment Insurance
  2. Pensions
  3. Life insurance
  4. Hospitalization
  5. Medical and surgical payments
  6. Paid sick leave
  7. Supplemental unemployment benefits, separation pay, and guaranteed wages.
  8. Accident insurance
  9. Contributions to savings plans
B. Pay For Time Not Worked
  1. Holiday pay
  2. Vacation pay
  3. Paid leave for personal business
  4. Military service allowance
  5. Jury duty pay
  6. Voting time pay
C. Bonuses and Awards (Not related directly to employee output)
  1. Profit-sharing bonus
  2. Christmas bonus
  3. Anniversary awards
D. Service Programs
  1. Social and recreational programs, such as parties, picnics, athletic facilities, clubs, and dances where financed wholly or partially by the employer.
  2. Special aids and services such as savings plans, credit unions, loan funds, scholarships for employees and their families, company purchasing service, medical treatment for minor sickness, subsidy for food service, discount on purchase of company products, employee newspaper.

[6] Charles W. Sargent, "Fringe Benefits: Do We Know Enough About Them?" *Personnel*, Vol. 30, No. 6 (May 1954), pp. 462-472.

WHY ADOPT BENEFIT AND SERVICE PROGRAMS?

What motivates individual companies to adopt benefits and services? Because there is practically no limit to how extensive an array of fringe benefits may be instituted, what determines a company's policy in this matter?

Most companies find that it is most beneficial to keep reasonably consistent with prevailing practice among all the companies in the labor market area. The more progressive companies generally conduct annual or biennial surveys of personnel practices and fringe benefits. This helps them to compete successfully for new employees and to retain those already on the payroll.

The need to have certain benefits in order to recruit employees is especially evident regarding the employment of technical and professional personnel. The opportunity to pursue advanced education programs at the master's and doctoral level is especially important to engineers and scientists. Hence companies frequently establish tuition refund programs and will even try to arrange special courses and programs with nearby universities. Again, to recruit and retain professional employees, many firms will pay the membership dues to the professional society of an individual's choice and will pay his expenses to attend out-of-town society conferences.

Many managements are sensitive to the needs and problems of their employees. They recognize that at times employees, as individuals, face crises that are beyond their resources to handle. Left to their own devices many workers would be unable to provide for themselves in their old age, to pay their hospital and doctor bills fully, or to tide themselves over extended periods of unemployment. They need help from other sources. To provide protection against the various risks of living, in our society, the employer pays part of the cost, the government pays a share, the individual worker pays part, and in certain instances private charitable groups also help out. There are two basic arguments for having the employer contribute toward employee-security programs. One is humanitarian. This means that the employer is genuinely concerned about the welfare of the people in his organization because they are human beings. This point of view can be bolstered by ethical and religious doctrines. The other argument is enlightened self-interest. The employer knows that anxieties, worries, and family crises that happen to a man outside his working hours tend to affect his job performance in the plant. Therefore, it is to the company's own advantage to help its people out, financially and with personal assistance, when adversity strikes.

Quite frequently management will establish certain benefits and services because it believes that these will enhance employee morale and create more positive attitudes toward the company. Morale refers to the total satisfactions, of all types, that people derive from the work situation. It relates to the personality structure of the individual, the social relations in the organization, the kind of supervision, the nature of the work, company policies and programs, and the incentives provided. Benefits and services make up part of this picture. If the morale is low because of harsh supervision or low wages, then the creation of a new pension plan or of a separation pay plan is not going to appreciably raise morale. But in the whole context of the system under which people work, the benefit and service program does have an effect upon morale. It is certain that if a company lags far behind the prevailing area practices on such important benefits as holidays, vacations, and economic security items, such as pensions and hospitalization, then the employees will be discontented.

Sometimes employers set up quite elaborate benefit and service programs that are designed to make the company the dominant institution in the lives of all its employees. The company seeks to provide for their economic, social, and psychological needs on a comprehensive basis. It may have social, recreational, and athletic programs and facilities for use by employees and their families. These may include such things as a country club, swimming pool, tennis courts, hobby clubs, dances, parties, bowling leagues, and the like. The benefits may include such things as a savings plan, stock-purchase plan, profit sharing, educational programs, the usual economic-security items, and a company small-loan fund. In addition, the company may provide medical counsel, legal aid, and personnel counseling. Subsidized company housing may be added for good measure. Such an elaborate program of benefits and services possesses the earmarks of a paternalistic employer. Some well-known American companies have been outstandingly successful with their paternalism. The intention of such a personnel program is to make the company the center of all the employee's lives (including the lives of their families as well). Top management believes that this will generate greater loyalty, greater cooperation, higher morale, and perhaps higher productivity. Top management also feels the people will have little inclination to unionize under such a paternalistic program. But, more and more, paternalism is becoming a thing of the past. People do not look upon their company as the one, mighty, all-encompassing institution in their lives. They want the opportunity to participate freely in the economic, social, recreational, educational, and political affairs of their community. In short they want to be free men and women.

Sometimes companies establish attractive fringe benefit programs in order to enhance their public relations image. The company may expect thereby to improve its market position and enhance product acceptance in the minds of the buying public. Presumably if the company is known as a good place to work, it must also make high quality products. (At least this is the theory.) The company may also expect to gain greater respect from the community because it has demonstrated a considerable measure of social responsibility by establishing a sound benefit program.

Union bargaining power is often the main reason a company adopts a particular benefit program. The automobile manufacturers granted a supplementary unemployment benefits program in 1955 in response to terrific union pressures for the guaranteed annual wage. The alternative was an extended strike. The liberalization of many existing programs is commonly due primarily to union economic power. A notable example is the considerable improvement in vacation benefits in recent years. In 1963, the United Steel Workers Union succeeded in obtaining from the basic steel industry a thirteen-week sabbatical leave every fifth year.

Criteria for Specific Benefits and Services

We have been considerating the major forces causing companies to establish and expand benefits and services in general. In the context of this general background, it is useful to enumerate the factors that top management must weigh when deciding to establish a *particular* kind of benefit or service.

Union Power.   If the employees are represented by a union, management cannot establish a benefit unilaterally. The issue must be bargained. Of course, a powerful union can sometimes force new and improved benefits upon a reluctant employer. In this situation management must weigh the increase in labor costs of the added benefit in comparison to the cost of a strike.

Cost and Ability to Pay.   This is generally one of the most paramount factors. For example, a pension plan can impose a substantial financial burden upon the company. In addition, this becomes a permanent commitment. The profitability of the firm and its prospects for the future are prime determinants of whether it can undertake the cost of a new program.

Tax Consideration.   Closely related to costs are taxes. Most benefits and services are legitimate company expenses. If the employees spend part of their pay to buy life insurance, annuities, and hospitalization and medical insurance, they must still pay federal income tax on this portion of their income. These costs are not deductible.

Need.   Does the contemplated program answer a real need? Is it necessary in order to recruit employees? Can the benefit or service be better obtained by the employees through the community as is sometimes true of social and recreational programs? Will the employees actually participate in the program?

Long-run Consequences.   Is the proposal program just a temporary fad? Will it operate in such a way as to support or hinder the entire personnel program? One employer instituted a company small-loan program, without interest charges, out of genuine concern for the welfare of its employees. If wanted to protect its employees from the loan companies, which often charge interest rates as high as 30 per cent per year. But the company was forced to abandon its loan program because of the ill will created when it made administrative decisions as to whether an employee's request for a loan was legitimate or not.

Sometimes during very profitable years or in order to meet a temporary employee-recruitment need, a company may offer a special benefit or service without looking very far to the future. If the profit picture or demand for labor changes, it may wish to abandon the program. However, by that time it may have become so much a part of the normal expectations of the employees that its abandonment would create severe ill will. Companies are ill-advised to adopt the gimmick approach to fringe benefits. They cannot be turned on and off like a water faucet.

SOME SIGNIFICANT BENEFIT AND SERVICE PROGRAMS

Space does not permit an explanation of all of the multitude of benefits and services that exist in industry. The ingenuity of managers and of union spokesmen combined with the variety of special circumstances that apply to particular companies means that there is an almost endless list of benefits and services that have been created. We shall concentrate upon only certain of the more important ones.

Life Insurance

Group life insurance is one of the oldest and most widespread types of employee benefit. The first group life insurance policy written by an insurance company was for the Pantasote Leather Company of Passaic, New Jersey, in 1911.[7] As of 1961, 43.5 million employees were covered by group life insurance. This represented 61 per cent of the civilian labor force in that year. And 81 per cent of the nonagricultural labor force was covered.[8]

Group insurance, which includes life, health, and pensions, operates according to principles different from individual insurance. With group insurance the insurance company makes no selection of individuals whom it will insure. The insurance carrier sets its premium according to the characteristics of the group as a whole. Most insurance companies require a certain minimum number of persons in the group, typically twenty-five people, to guard against adverse selection of risks and to achieve lower administrative costs. The group to be insured must have been formed for some purpose other than to seek group insurance protection. This is to avoid a group made up solely of those in poor health or who might, for some other reason, represent expensive risks.

---

[7] Robert I. Mehr and Emerson Cammack, *Principles of Insurance* (Homewood, Ill.: Richard D. Irwin, Inc., 1961), p. 553.

[8] "Group Life Insurance, 1961" *Management Record,* Vol. 24, No. 11 (November 1962), p. 5.

Group insurance is lower in cost than individual insurance for several reasons. The sales agent receives a lower commission percentage, because selling effort and service is lower. The employer handles certain of the administrative work of processing claims. The cost of collecting premiums is lower than for individual policies, because the employer pays a single sum for his entire group.

In writing group policies the insurance company generally requires 100 per cent coverage of the group if the employer pays the full cost and 75 per cent participation if the employees pay part of the cost. This rule is followed to prevent *only* unhealthy or high risk employees choosing to be covered.

Group life insurance is written without a physical examination and usually ceases when a person terminates his employment with the company. Usually it is term insurance. This means that it has no cash surrender or paid-up value and no loan provisions. If the employee leaves the group, he is given the opportunity to convert his coverage to an individual policy without furnishing evidence of insurability. He must pay a premium based on his then attained age.

Benefits are generally either the flat amount type or the graduated type. Where the life insurance plan has been negotiated with a union, it generally provides for a fixed amount of insurance, say $5,000, for all employees regardless of their pay bracket. Plans established by management, where there is no union, generally relate the amount of insurance to the individual's annual pay. Pay brackets are set up, and typically the insurance will range in amount from 100 to 200 per cent of annual income.

Health Insurance

There are a number of forms of health insurance. Disability income insurance provides a weekly payment to the employee to make up partially for the wages he loses when he is ill and unable to work.[9] Hospital expense insurance pays all or part of a person's hospital bills. Surgical insurance pays for surgical service performed by doctors. Medical insurance pays for physicians' bills other than for surgery. Comprehensive health insurance, sometimes called major medical insurance, provides coverage for hospital and physicians' service up to $10,000, $15,000 and even greater amounts for any single illness.

Both insurance companies and Blue Cross and Blue Shield groups are active in the health insurance field. Blue Cross is the name applied to hospital-bill insurance plans organized by the American Hospital Association. These plans are organized on a regional or statewide basis. They are coordinated on a nationwide basis by the Blue Cross Commission.

---

[9] Such plans are more prevalent for hourly paid workers than for salaried personnel. For the latter the employer generally pays the individual his regular salary when he is absent due to illness, at least for a moderate period of time.

Blue Shield plans are organized by physicians for the payment of doctor bills. The Blue Cross and Blue Shield organizations deal with their clients on a coordinated basis generally. Most states consider these organizations to be nonprofit in nature; hence they are entitled to certain tax exemptions.

Blue Cross plans provide a specified type of service regardless of variations in rate schedules from one hospital to another. Most commonly they will pay the full cost of semiprivate accommodations. Insurance companies, on the other hand, pay benefits up to a certain maximum for each day in the hospital and up to a certain maximum for supplementary services and for outpatient care.

Approximately 55 million persons are covered by Blue Cross plans in the United States, whereas 50 million are covered for hospital expenses under plans underwritten by insurance companies.[10]

Pensions

The Social Security Act, passed in 1935, provides basic retirement income benefits to those who have worked in covered employment for a specified number of years. Over 90 per cent of the labor force are covered by old-age insurance under the law. But the benefit levels provided are insufficient to support retired workers adequately; hence they must augment the payments received from the government with money drawn from individual savings or from a pension plan administered by the employer or both.

Slightly over one third of the labor force are covered by group pension plans operated through employers.

How much does it cost a retired couple to live? The United States Department of Labor surveyed the annual costs in both large metropolitan areas and nonmetropolitan areas in the autumn of 1966. The labor department constructed a retired couple's budget for a husband and his wife, age 65 or over, who are self-supporting and living alone. This budget represents a moderate standard of living that provides for the maintenance of health and social well-being and participation in community activities. Inasmuch as two thirds of retired couples in the United States are home owners and living in homes that are mortgage free, the budget calculates the cost of housing for 65 per cent of the couples as home owners and 35 per cent as renters. The average annual cost for this moderate budget is $3,869 for the United States as a whole. For metropolitan areas the cost was $4,006 per year, whereas for nonmetropolitan areas (those having a population of 2,500 to 50,000) the cost was $3,460. The budget includes food, housing, transportation, clothing, recreation, personal care, medical care, and charitable contributions. Income taxes are excluded

[10] Mehr and Cammack, *op. cit.,* p. 563.

because retired persons at this income level generally do not pay income taxes. [11]

In evaluating average budgets, one must be aware of the fact that the circumstances of a particular retired couple may vary significantly from that specified in the Department of Labor budget. Thus it should be viewed only as a rough guide.

Eligibility and Retirement Requirement. Quite generally employees must have worked for their company for a certain period of time before they can participate in the program—that is, before they are officially members of the plans—and money-credit is assigned to their accounts. Such a rule is adopted to avoid administrative and, in insured plans, cancellation charges for short-service employees who are not likely to stay on the payroll permanently. Often a person must have accumulated a minimum number of years of service before he is eligible to retire on pension. Some plans deny an individual a pension if he has first been hired after a certain age, such as 55 or 60.

Employees are usually expected to retire at age 65. Benefits are usually calculated on the basis of retirement at this age. Most plans allow an employee to retire voluntarily at an earlier age but at a reduced pension. The personnel policies of a large share of the work organizations of this country make retirement mandatory at age 65. However, there has been a growing recognition among managers, personnel specialists, industrial physicians, and behavioral scientists in recent years that many people are not ready or willing to retire at 65. People differ greatly in their rates of aging. Many argue that if a man, age 65 years, is still vigorous and has much still to contribute to his work, it is advantageous for the individual and the company to let him continue.

Benefit Formulas. There are a wide variety of methods in use for determining the amount of monthly (or yearly) pension a person receives. Generally the principle is followed that the larger one's wage and the greater the number of years of service, the larger will be the pension benefit.

A very popular formula specifies that the individual shall receive 1½ per cent (the usual range is from 1 to 2 per cent) times his years of service with the company times his average pay for all those years. Thus an employee who received an average wage of $500 per month for 30 years would receive a monthly benefit of $225 using the 1½-per-cent rate. Because a man's wage level tends to be low during his early years of employment and because he grows accustomed to a higher standard of living in the years immediately preceding retirement, many plans base the calculation upon the average income during his last five years of employment. This will yield a larger pension that would result from averaging the wages over all years of employment.

---

[11] Jean C. Brackett, "A New Budget for a Retired Couple," *Monthly Labor Review,* Vol. 91, No. 6 (June 1968), pp. 33-39.

The money-purchase plan is another way of establishing the benefit for an employee. This type of plan has been used widely under group annuity plans underwritten by insurance companies. The employer contributes a definite percentage of the employee's pay into a retirement fund. Usually with this type of plan the employee contributes a percentage of his pay also. When he retires the principle and interest accumulated in his account are used to provide a monthly retirement benefit. This money may be used to purchase an annuity from an insurance company. Money-purchase-plan trust funds can also be worked out with mutual fund investment companies, banks, and trust companies. The actual amount of pension that an employee receives is determined by his total income, the percentage contributed by the employer and/or the employee, his sex, and the number of years' participation in the plan.

A considerable array of other formulas are used in addition to those just described. Some provide for a flat benefit regardless of earnings prior to retirement and regardless of length of service. Some pay a fixed percentage of previous average wage. Some make adjustments for the amount of Social Security benefits received. Many have a minimum pension even if an individual's benefit figured according to the formula would place him below that figure. Some firms have a basic plan figured according to one formula and a supplementary plan (usually a person may participate in this one at his discretion) figured with another formula.

Methods of Financing.   A pension plan may be either unfunded or funded. The term *funded* means that money is set aside into a special fund to pay future obligations. An unfunded plan is also referred to as a pay-as-you-go program. Pension benefits are paid out of current income from the company.

The pay-as-you-go plan is extremely risky, and the results can be disastrous if the ability of the company to continue paying into the fund should become impaired. The pension programs negotiated between the United Mine Workers union and the companies in the bituminous and anthracite coal industries are of this type. The pension program in the anthracite industry has been in particularly bad straits. Pension payments come from the Anthracite Health and Welfare Fund, which was first established in 1946. This fund is financed by employer payments of 70 cents per ton of coal mined. Over the intervening years there has been a drastic decline in hard coal production; hence payments into the fund have also declined. In 1946 hard coal production stood at 61,978,710 net tons, whereas in 1960 it was only 17,721,113 tons. In addition many coal mine companies have defaulted on their payments to the fund. Although the pension was originally established at $100 per month, in 1954 the figure was cut to $50. In 1961 a temporary reduction to $30 per month was made. This has meant privation and hardship to retired mine workers.[12]

[12] Data regarding the United Mine Workers fund taken from *The Scranton Tribune,* August 16 and 17, 1961.

Funded plans are much safer from the standpoint of financial solvency than unfunded ones. There are two types of funded plans: trusteed and insured. A trusteed plan is administered by trustees who may be appointed by the company or jointly by the company and the union. Sometimes a bank or trust company will administer the fund. In any case an actuary must be engaged to determine the amount of money that must be set aside each year to meet current and future pension obligations. He will base his calculations upon such factors as the average age of the work force, rate of turnover, and expected interest earned by the fund. The fund should be irrevocable so that no portion thereof can be siphoned off by the employer or union for other purposes.

Insured plans are underwritten and administered by an insurance company. The premiums paid to the insurance company are used to buy annuities for each employee when he retires.

Vesting Rights. The term *vesting* refers to the right of an employee to receive the money contributed by the employer for his pension should the individual terminate his employment before retirement. Years ago the majority of pension plans granted no vesting rights to workers who were permanently laid off or who quit. In the last few years there has been a pronounced trend toward granting vesting rights after a specified number of years on the payroll. Typically anywhere from three to twenty years may be required.

The reasons for not granting vesting rights are twofold. In the first place, a larger pension can be granted for a given cost if it is known that a significant portion of the employees will not be on the payroll when they reach retirement age. Second, employees are less likely to quit after they have acquired a considerable number of years of service if they know they will lose their pension rights. This factor saves the company the cost of hiring and training replacements.

But the arguments in favor of vesting are somewhat more convincing than those against it. The primary purpose should be to provide a reasonable measure of economic security during retirement. Many employees are laid off permanently through no fault of their own. They should not lose the money credited to their account each year during their employment with a company. If a man is unfortunate enough to lose his job at an advanced age, he may find himself without any pension (other than Old Age Insurance under the Social Security Program) if he has acquired no vesting rights. As far as voluntary quitting is concerned, this is a fundamental right of people in a free country. Our business system is based upon the idea of a free labor market. Workers must be free to change jobs to better their situation. Employers must be able to offer inducements in the labor market to entice workers away from other firms if the ranks of the unemployed are insufficient to meet their needs. A pension plan is a poor instrument for reducing voluntary quitting in a company. Much better alternatives are available.

Employment Security and Unemployment Pay

During the years 1931 through 1940, the percentage of the civilian labor force that was unemployed never dipped below 14 per cent. In 1933, 24.9 per cent of the labor force was unemployed. Prior to 1935 there was no Federal or state unemployment insurance program in the United States.[13] The Social Security Act of 1935 provided for joint Federal-state cooperative programs in the unemployment insurance field. Basically this law provided an incentive for all the states to pass laws which met the Federal standards. All the states passed unemployment insurance laws by 1937. The cost of the program is born by a payroll tax of 3.1 per cent, which must be paid by employers. Four tenths of 1 per cent is paid to the Federal government, which in turn remits most of this money to the states to pay the cost of operating their programs. The remaining 2.7 per cent goes to the states to pay weekly benefits to unemployed workers. If companies have stable employment records, their premium rates may be reduced below the 2.7 per cent figure, and if they have heavy layoffs, their premium may go above that amount.

In 1967 the maximum weekly benefit paid to the unemployed worker ranged from a low of $30 per week in Mississippi to a high of $68 per week in Hawaii. Most states pay benefits up to a maximum of 26 weeks, although a few states go as high as 30 to 39 weeks.

The Federal-state system of unemployment insurance provides the basic level of protection in this country. However, the benefit levels are low (they vary considerably from state to state), and benefits are paid for only a limited period of time. To supplement this government system, many companies have established programs that help ease the financial burden borne by the unemployed worker. The vast majority of these programs have been instituted as a result of union-bargaining demands. Hence they are negotiated plans.

During the late 1950's and the early 1960's, unemployment developed into a chronic national problem. During the years 1958 through 1964, unemployment averaged about 6 per cent of the civilian labor force. Although there is far from universal agreement as to what constitutes a normal or average level of unemployment, government economists have tended to view 4 per cent as the figure above which national concern must be shown and government action is necessary.

We shall examine three kinds of programs that have been developed in industry to solve partially the problem of unemployment. These are supplemental unemployment benefit plans such as were first started in the automobile industry in 1955, separation or severance pay plans, and guaranteed employment or guaranteed wage plans.

Supplemental Unemployment Benefits. About 2 million employees

---

[13] Wisconsin passed an unemployment insurance law in 1932, but it did not come into full operation until after 1935.

in the automobile, steel, farm equipment, can manufacturing, rubber, and glass industries are covered by supplemental unemployment benefit plans. These plans are given this label because they add to the amount of money an unemployed worker receives from the regular state unemployment compensation program to bring his total benefit up to a specified percentage of his regular wage.

There are two types of SUB plans, the insurance fund and the individual account or income-security plans. The latter is found principally in the glass industry; most of the other are insurance fund plans.

In the insurance fund type of plans, the company contributes a certain number of cents per hour (typically 5 or 6 cents) to a trust fund. Company contributions continue until the trust fund reaches a designated maximum level.[14] If withdrawals to pay benefits reduce the amount in the fund below this level, then company contributions are resumed. The liability of the employer does not extend beyond the assets in the fund and the cents per hour contribution. Benefits vary somewhat from industry to industry. The Ford Motor Company plan, bargained with the United Automobile Workers Union in 1967, is typical of the automobile industry generally. It stipulates that after December 1, 1968, a laid-off worker shall receive 95 per cent of his weekly after-tax pay less $7.50. The $7.50 reduction takes into account work-related expenses such as transportation, lunches, and work clothing that are not incurred during a layoff. In the rubber industry benefits are set at 80 per cent of straight-time weekly earnings. The duration of benefits received depends upon the individual's length of service and the trust fund position (the amount in the fund compared to its maximum). In the automobile industry the maximum duration is 52 weeks. In the rubber industry those with less than 5 years of service are entitled to 52 weeks of benefit. This scales up to 4 years of benefit for those with 25 years or more of service. To be eligible to collect benefits, a man must meet the state requirements for receiving state unemployment compensation. SUB is paid for a genuine layoff or reduction in force. Employees are not paid if suspended or discharged for cause or if out on strike.

The individual account plans, also called income security or savings plans, provide for an individual account being established for each employee. A definite number of cents per hour (usually 10 cents) is contributed to the account for each hour worked. Each worker has a vested right to the money in his account, and he may withdraw it when he is laid off, is sick, retires, or leaves the company. These plans are in no way related to the benefits received under state unemployment compensation.

Despite early predictions that SUB plans would add a heavy administrative burden to the shoulders of management, actual experience since 1955, when they were started, has shown that the administrative prob-

[14] In some plans once the maximum fund position is reached, company contributions are used to provide a bonus for employees.

lems have been relatively minor. The administrative costs to the companies have been reasonable and moderate.[15]

SUB plans are of greatest value to employees possessing a moderate amount of seniority. Very low-seniority workers obtain either no benefits or else benefits of very limited duration. Long-service workers are rarely laid off anyway, so they have little need for a SUB program.

Separation Pay.   The National Industrial Conference Board has estimated that between 40 and 60 per cent of manufacturing firms employing 1,000 or more persons have some kind of separation pay arrangement.[16] To receive separation pay, the termination of employment must usually be permanent, it must be initiated by the company, and it will not be paid if the individual was discharged for just cause. At the time of layoff, it may not be known whether it will be permanent or not. Hence many plans specify that after a certain number of weeks, if a man is still on layoff, he may draw his separation pay. Many plans will grant separation pay if a person is discharged because he lacks the physical or mental qualifications to do the job. Most plans require at least one year of service before a person is eligible to receive the benefit. The amount of pay is related quite directly to a man's length of service. Upon termination a person would typically receive one week's pay for each year of service. Individual plans may, of course, vary considerably from this pattern.

Guaranteed Employment and Wage Plans.   So far we have been talking about private company and union plans to provide payments to unemployed workers. Now we shall talk about plans designed to keep people on the job or to provide them with a guaranteed annual wage.

These plans are few in number. The best-known plans are those of George A. Hormel & Company, the Nunn-Bush Shoe Company, and the Procter & Gamble Company. These have been in existence for over thirty years. In 1963 the Kaiser Steel Corporation and the United Steel Workers adopted their Long-Range Sharing Plan, one part of which provides protection against technological unemployment.

The Hormel Company is a meat-packing concern in Minnesota. About 80 per cent of the employees are covered. These employees are assured 52 regular, almost equal, weekly pay checks each year regardless of the fact that their hours of work may fluctuate somewhat from week to week. Overtime over 40 hours in one week is paid at straight time under the guaranteed annual wage provisions of the Fair Labor Standards Act. The wage guarantee plan is combined with a standard hour incentive payment plan.

The Nunn-Bush Shoe Company has a flexible wage plan combined with guaranteed employment. Those having five or more years of service are

[15] For an explanation of the Ford Motor Company's program for administering its SUB plan see W. C. Hampton, "Administering an SUB Plan: The Ford Experience," *Personnel,* Vol. 34 No. 1 (July-August 1957), pp. 76-83.

[16] Harland Fox and N. Beatrice Worthy, *Severance Pay Plans in Manufacturing,* Studies in Personnel Policy, No. 174 (New York: National Industrial Conference Board, 1959).

guaranteed 52 weeks employment a year. Those having less service receive a lesser guarantee. Each worker is assigned a yearly wage. He receives $\frac{1}{52}$ of this each week. The total labor cost of the company is standardized, on the basis of past experience, as a certain per cent of the value of production for the year.

The Procter & Gamble plan guarantees 48 weeks of employment each year to all hourly workers having at least two years of service. Subtracted from this 48 weeks is time lost due to holidays, vacations, disability, voluntary absence, and emergencies. The company also has the option to reduce hours of work to 75 per cent of normal. This plan makes no guarantee of a definite annual wage.

The Kaiser Steel Company employment-guarantee plan is but a part of a much broader program that is also designed to share the savings derived from cost reductions and to replace the individual wage incentives with the companywide gains-sharing, cost-saving plan. The employment-guarantee plan (our only concern in this chapter) is designed to provide protection against technological unemployment. This plan grants a flat guarantee that any employee having 26 weeks of service or more, whose lack of work can be attributed to changes in work practices, methods, or technology, shall be entitled to continued employment. The job may be eliminated, but the man stays on the payroll. If another job is available, he is assigned to it. If not, he is placed in the labor reserve pool, where he may do all sorts of work. The man is guaranteed against any loss of income for a full year even if he must take a lower-rated job.

How can Kaiser offer such a guarantee when the very purpose of improving technology is to reduce costs. The answer is that the company lets normal attrition—quits, retirements, deaths, and discharges—take care of its need for fewer workers. Annual turnover has averaged from 5 to 15 per cent of the work force at Kaiser.

The employment security plan does not guarantee a man employment if there is a general decline in company production and sales. Kaiser has a supplemental unemployment benefits plan and severance pay to help such workers. Therefore, management must make a determination of the number of people displaced by technological advances and the number displaced by a general business decline. This is done by making a physical count of persons displaced by a specific change in methods and equipment plus a comparison between the number actually employed at any time and a standard number that would have been employed had there been no technological change. The standard used is the number of employees required to produce a ton of steel during 1961.

Credit Unions

A credit union is a cooperative association designed to promote thrift among its members and to make loans to the members. Over three quarters of the 21,000 credit unions in the United States are employee credit unions. This means that the employees are all members of the same company. Credit unions hold about 10 per cent of all outstanding installment credit in this country.

The first credit unions were started in Germany over 100 years ago. Edward A. Filene, the Boston merchant, was primarily responsible for introducing credit unions to the United States about sixty years ago. He and his associates were instrumental in persuading many of the states to pass legislation so that credit unions could obtain state charters. In 1934 Congress enacted the Federal Credit Union Law. Credit unions are classified as nonprofit cooperatives and are tax exempt. Credit unions may be chartered by either a state or the Federal government. In recent years the credit-union movement has been expanding rapidly.

The organization and operation of a credit union is fairly simple. A group of people having a common bond obtain a charter to operate as an independent corporation. Officers are elected each year by the members. All, except the treasurer, must serve without pay. An employee can become a member by paying a nominal fee and buying one or more shares, which are usually priced at five dollars. The money paid for shares constitutes savings for the members. Members may take out loans at interest rates that are about in line with those charged by commercial banks but are decidedly lower than those charged by consumer and sales finance organizations. Typically members receive about 4 per cent interest on their shares.

Credit union officers look upon their organizations as service agencies. Their objective is to help their members; it is not to make a profit. The percentage of loan applications they approve tends to be higher than for other financial institutions, yet their loss ratios are extremely small. Despite their liberal attitude toward granting loans, very few credit unions fail because of capital deficiencies. The survival record of credit unions was better than other savings institutions during the Great Depression of the 1930's.

Although credit unions are organized and operated primarily by a group of employees, they can be classified as a company "benefit and service" because management often supplies free office space, because gentle encouragement for their formation is often given by management, and because credit unions are most often identified with and formed by the employees of a single company.

Social and Recreational Programs

The extent of social and recreational programs can range from companies that have a simple Christmas party each year to those that provide a vast array of athletic facilities, hobby clubs, socials, and family get-togethers. Such activities can be expensive. The question can be asked as to the good they do. Do the employees really want them? Do they participate just to please the boss or not at all? Do they actually build good will for the company?

Most often when top management decides to organize and support such activities, it hopes to generate a greater feeling of belonging, to improve morale, and to develop greater company loyalty. It recognizes also that people form close friendships among their work associates and that they often desire to engage in social and recreational activities as a group, a department, or a company-identified club.

If the whole thing is not overdone, social and recreational programs can benefit both the company and the employees. But such activities must not be forced upon the people. Experience reveals that they are most successful when the interested employees play an active part in organizing and running the activities. The summer picnic must be organized by the people who want to have one. The company softball or bowling leagues must have genuine employee participation in their organization and operation.

The question of whether the company should foot the entire bill for company-sponsored activities can be argued. Some companies use revenue from food and cigarette vending machines to finance such programs. In a sense this can be considered employee money too. As a general principle the most successful programs are those in which the people contribute time and effort as well as a share (even if modest) of the monetary cost.

Holidays and Vacations

The historical trend in the American economy has been one of decreasing hours of work and greater leisure for the working man. In 1850 the work week averaged 70 hours in nonagriculture establishments; by 1956 it had declined to about 41 hours.[17] By 1967 the workweek hovered around 40 hours per week.

Prior to 1940 paid vacations for hourly workers in private industry were uncommon. If they received a vacation it was usually for one week without pay. Office and managerial personnel generally did receive a one- or two-week paid vacation in that era. Nowadays the practice of granting paid vacations in commerce and industry (as well as in government service) is nearly universal throughout the country. Hourly workers typically receive a one-week paid vacation after one year of service and two weeks after two or three years of company service. Both hourly paid and office workers tend to receive three weeks paid vacation after ten or fifteen years of company service and four weeks after twenty or twenty-five years.

[17] "The Workweek in American Industry, 1850-1956," *Monthly Labor Review* (January 1956), pp. 23-29.

...eople spend
...raises important philosophical and sociological issues about the role of work and leisure in the life of man.

Historically, in ancient, medieval, and preindustrial times, work was the lot of the slave, serf, peasant, and artisan. Economically productive work lacked prestige. Work was decidedly frowned upon and avoided by the aristocracy and upper classes. Leisure was the "steady state" for the privileged classes. The Protestant Reformation changed all this. Productive work acquired a positive moral value. Work became a virtue, idleness a sin. Indolence was decadence. This glorification of hard work was a necessary concomitant of the industrialization process which began in Western Europe and the United States in the late eighteenth century. In the present-day world the attitude that the masses of the people in a nation hold toward gainful employment, work, and achievement is crucial in determining whether that nation advances along the avenue of industrialization or whether it remains in the throes of primitive poverty.

For the United States in the latter third of the twentieth century, modern technology has bestowed its fruits abundantly in the form of a higher and higher standard of living and in increased leisure time. This leisure time is not always completely free time. It may be partly consumed in commuting to and from work from far-away suburbs. But to a greater extent than ever before, people have options in what they do with their time.

The great unanswered question is how people will use their greater leisure. Will it be used in such a way as to advance the cultural level of mankind? Or will the free time be debilitating? Will it promote uplift or decay? With shorter hours and longer vacations, people can acquire more education. They can cultivate their mental and physical talents via col-

[18] James N. Houff, "Supplementary Wage Benefits in Metropolitan Areas," *Monthly Labor Review*, Vol. 91, No. 6 (June 1968), pp. 40-47. This Bureau of Labor Statistics study covered 12.9 million nonsupervisory plant workers and 3.6 million nonsupervisory office workers.

lege courses, adult education courses, painting, sculpture, music, and reading. Or they may simply pursue more recreations: television, golf, boating, camping, and travel. They may turn to more social and organizational functions or to hobbies and crafts. Or they may wile away their hours by engaging in drinking, gambling, and narcotics.

The pace of modern industry is very fast. The discipline of the industrial system is tough. This life induces more tensions and pressures than the rural and small town pattern of a century or two ago. Rest and recuperation are a necessary element of one's time off the job.

We do not as yet have the perspective of history to tell us whether people in an advanced industrialized society will use their new found leisure constructively so as to build their civilization or destructively so as to weaken it. The masses now can enjoy the leisure that once was the province of only the rich. Indeed there is some evidence that roles are becoming reversed. The upper classes in society now are expected to make a positive contribution to their world by work achievements. Work accomplishments are central to the life of entrepreneurs, executives, professionals, and public officials. They are the leadership elite in our society. High social status and abundant leisure no longer go hand in hand.

At the plant-worker level there is some evidence that leisure is viewed very positively by the people themselves. Klausner studied the reactions of Kaiser Steel Corporation hourly employees to their 13-week sabbaticals. The men themselves stated that they were happier on vacation than at work, they felt closer to their families, and they felt no need to take other jobs while on their extended vacations. The vast majority spent at least part of their vacations traveling. The workers reported that the vacations helped them as individuals and improved their outlook on life. Despite the strength of the Protestant ethic, there is some evidence in this study of steelworkers that they view work as only a means to living and not a goal in itself.[19]

Questions for Review and Discussion

1. What factors have caused benefit and service programs to grow substantially since the period around 1940?

2. Do you believe that benefits and services should be considered a part of compensation that employees have earned by working at their jobs, or do you feel that they represent something extra that the employer is giving his employees?. Justify your position.

3. Classify and give examples of the principal kinds of employee benefits and services.

4. What factors motivate the top management of a company to adopt

[19] Dr. William J. Klausner's study was reported in *Business Week* (November 26, 1966), pp. 166 - 168.

benefit and service programs? What factors must be weighed when deciding whether a particular program should be established? What long-range considerations should be evaluated when contemplating the creation of a new benefit program?

5. For a given cost for a particular group insurance program, why might it be cheaper for the company to pay the cost than for the employees to do so?

6. In what ways does group insurance differ from individual insurance?

7. Distinguish between health protection provided by the Blue Cross and Blue Shield organizations and that provided by private insurance companies.

8. Do you feel that the average wage earner could save sufficient funds to support himself and his wife during retirement so that a company pension program would be unnecessary? How much would it cost two persons to live, on the average, during retirement?

9. What are the relative merits of a pay-as-you-go versus a funded pension plan?

10. What does the term *vesting rights* mean in reference to pensions? What are the arguments for and against granting vesting rights?

11. Why has there been growing interest in the creation and expansion of employment-security and unemployment-benefit programs in recent years?

12. Explain the principal features of supplemental unemployment benefit plans.

13. What is a credit union? What is its purpose?

14. Describe the Kaiser Steel-United Steelworkers program for employment security.

15. What issues does increasing leisure raise for modern life? Do you think work is central to the life and satisfaction of the average worker?

Suggestions for Further Reading

Allen, Donna, *Fringe Benefits: Wages or Social Obligation,* Ithaca, New York: New York State School of Industrial and Labor Relations, 1964.

Dankert, Clyde E., Floyd C. Mann, and Herbert R. Northrup (eds.), *Hours of Work,* New York: Harper & Row, 1965.

Deric, Arthur J. (ed.), *The Total Approach to Employee Benefits,* New York: American Management Association, 1967.

Dickerson, O. D., *Health Insurance,* Rev. Ed., Homewood, Ill.: Richard D. Irwin, 1963.

Eilers, R. D. and R. M. Crowe, *Group Insurance Handbook,* Homewood, Ill.: Richard D. Irwin, 1965.

Employee Benefits (Fringe Benefits) 1967, Washington, D.C.: Chamber of Commerce of the United States, 1968.

Greene, Mark R., *The Role of Employee Benefit Structures in Manu-facturing Industry,* Eugene, Ore.: School of Business Administration, University of Oregon, 1964.

Houff, James N., "Supplementary Wage Benefits in Metropolitan Areas," *Monthly Labor Review,* Vol. 91, No. 6, June 1968, pp. 40-47.

McGill, Dan M., *Fundamentals of Private Pensions,* 2nd Ed., Homewood, Ill.: Richard D. Irwin, 1964.

Pickrell, Jesse F., *Group Health Insurance,* Rev. Ed., Published for S. S. Huebner Foundation for Insurance Education, University of Pennsylvania by Richard D. Irwin, Homewood, Ill., 1961.

Sheifer, Victor J., "White Collar Pay Supplements," *Monthly Labor Review,* Vol. 89, No. 5, May 1966, pp. 496-502.

Tumbull, J. G., C. A. Williams, Jr., and Earl F. Cheit, *Economic and Social Security,* 3rd Ed., New York: Ronald Press Co., 1967.

Zollitsch, Herbert G., "Fringes—Benefits or Burdens?," *Personnel,* Vol. 41, No. 4, July-August, 1964, pp. 54-59.

VI

PERSPECTIVES

Personnel Management in Perspective

29

The process of managing any organization requires knowledge and skills in the economic, technical, and human relations spheres. The effective manager must possess real understanding of the nature of man, the determinants of interpersonal effectiveness, and the ramifications of intergroup relations.

The key to organization building is to invest in human resources. This is true whether we are talking about a university, an industrial corporation, a city government, or a military force. Many top executives are ignorant of this vital concept. They concentrate their attention so heavily upon the technical phases of the business (such as the details of new product development, financial controls, or marketing) that they neglect investment in their people.

How does an organization invest in human resources? There are many ways. At an elementary level it consists of investment in a decent, healthful, and safe working environment. Beyond this it means offering attractive wages and job opportunities so that the establishment can attract competent employees. If management pays wages well below competitive rates, it cannot hope to build a really vigorous organization. The viable company devotes continuous attention to the education and training of its employees. I have observed time and again that differences in this one dimension—education and training—correlate significantly with the degree of effectiveness and success of organizations. Emphasis upon the development of people means such things as comprehensive in-house training, reimbursement of employees' tuition costs at neighboring colleges and universities, sending managers and engineers to professional seminars, circulating professional and technical journals within the company, and sending executives to advanced-management university programs. Investment in human resources also means providing a day-to-day climate where people are encouraged to make decisions and accept responsibility. It means supportive supervision and effective appraisal and coaching. Fundamentally, effective management depends upon the existence of an underlying philosophy that people-centered and achievement-oriented management is what really counts.

We have shown in this book that the practice of personnel management comprises two stems. The first is that component—the management of people at work—which pervades the entire organization. The president cannot hire a personnel director to handle all the human problems of management so that he can concentrate upon financial and technical activities. Personnel management and general management are intimately related. Operating executives cannot abdicate their very considerable responsibilities for selecting, developing, motivating, and leading people as they carry on their daily activities.

The second main stem of personnel management is that carried on and guided by the staff personnel department. This work entails the development and dissemination of personnel policies, provision of specialized services and counsel to the whole corporation, and the application of control measures to regulate the human resources climate. The work content of the personnel office is centered in such prime functions as organization and manpower planning, employment, labor relations, health and safety, education, benefits and services, and pay administration. Many who study the field of personnel, organizational behavior, and industrial relations intend to make it their vocation. It holds promising career opportunities. Let us now look into personnel work as a career.

PERSONNEL—INDUSTRIAL RELATIONS AS A CAREER

Those desiring to pursue careers in personnel and industrial relations should obtain a college education. This field has not achieved the degree of specialized professionalism that medicine and law have. Thus there is no single pattern of education that is specified for entry into this career. Nearly all of the universities and many of the colleges in the United States offer courses and integrated programs of study in personnel management, industrial relations, and organizational behavior. Administratively these programs are given in schools of business administration, industrial management (or administration), and industrial relations. In addition to majors in personnel, industrial relations, and organizational behavior, students ought to obtain a thorough grounding in general studies with special emphasis upon the social sciences (sociology, psychology, and economics). In the applied business administration field they ought also to take courses in statistics, data processing, finance, production, business policy, and the social and legal environment of business. For those who wish to pursue careers in technical industries, a baccalaureate degree in engineering followed by a master's degree in business administration is a very sound educational plan. Some who wish to specialize in labor relations and collective bargaining may study liberal arts or business administration at the undergraduate level and then go to law school for their graduate work.

Beginning or entry level positions in this field are such jobs as job analyst, employment interviewer, personnel trainee, training specialist, and labor-relations specialist. Actually, for the recent college graduate there are several routes for entry into personnel work. He may be hired by a company directly into one of the entry-level positions. Some of our larger corporations such as the General Electric Company and others have formal training programs in employee relations. Another very common route is for the young college graduate to be hired initially into some other activity such as manufacturing or operations and then transfer to the personnel-industrial relations department within a few years. This latter approach has the advantage of orienting the individual to the technology of the company, to its policies and to its people.

Position Levels

In the large corporation there are three principal levels of positions in personnel-industrial relations. First there is the specialist level. The specialist level includes the entry-level jobs previously mentioned plus the professional specialists such as physician, nurse, psychologist, safety engineer, labor lawyer, and personnel researcher. Many of the professional specialist positions require advanced education and training. In prestige, rank, and salary certain of these such as the physician, psychologist, and labor lawyer are equivalent to middle management in the large company. The second or next level of positions consists of the managers in charge of the various functional branches of personnel. Thus we find the manager or supervisor of labor relations, the manager of employment, and the manager of wage and salary administration. In the organization hierarchy these people are part of middle management. In addition to their managerial abilities, they must possess considerable knowledge and skill in the functional personnel specialty they are supervising. A manager of employment must know a great deal about sources of supply, selection testing, interviewing, job specifications, manpower planning, and selective placement.

The third level of position in personnel in the big company is the top management or major executive level. The executive in charge of personnel-industrial relations is designated most commonly as the vice-president of personnel, vice-president of industrial relations, or director of industrial relations. He typically reports to the president of the organization or to an executive vice-president. He is involved in policy formulation and administration and coordination with all major units in the corporation. He guides the development and installation of major personnel programs.

In the smaller company there would be fewer jobs and fewer levels in the personnel department. Generally one would find the director or top executive position plus certain of the functional positions. There would be less division of labor. One individual might handle all employment and training tasks. Another might be responsible for pay administration and labor relations. In the really small organization the personnel department might consist of only the manager of personnel plus his secretary.

Job Opportunities and Salaries

For those who have a reasonable amount of experience in personnel work, say three to five years or more, job opportunities are quite good. One need only read the advertisements in the *Wall Street Journal* or the *New York Times* to learn about job openings for labor relations manager, recruitment specialist, compensation manager, vice-president of employee relations, and a variety of other personnel occupations. Personnel opportunities with state and Federal governments are also rather abundant. Those lacking either special experience in the field or specialized education find it somewhat difficult to enter this career.

Salaries for entry-level positions are essentially the same as those offered business administration graduates generally. This is a little lower than beginning pay for engineers and scientists. Supervisory and executive posts in employee relations command pay that is essentially equivalent to that paid other managerial positions of similar rank within the organization. Salaries for these managerial jobs correlate highly with the size of the company. The top personnel executive in a small company (under 1,000 employees) will typically be paid from $14,000 to $20,000 per year. But in the large corporation their salaries will lie in the $20,000 to $40,000 range with a few going even higher.

Status and Professionalism

In many companies the personnel-industrial relations director serves as a key member of the top management group. Often he enjoys vice-presidential status. In many companies the personnel director serves as a key advisor to the president and to the whole top management team. He carries great weight in shaping personnel policy, labor policy, formulating executive development programs, and in designing employee and executive compensation plans.

In the area of professionalism, personnel practitioners have made considerable progress. Educational programs at the university level have been mentioned previously. There are a number of professional associations that are national in scope. Among these are the Industrial Relations Research Association, the Society for Personnel Administration, American Society of Personnel Administrators, the American Society for Training and Development, and the Personnel Division of the American Management Association. Active in most of the major metropolitan areas are local personnel managers associations.

Yet there is another side to this whole picture. In far too many situations, and especially in medium- and small-sized organizations, top management staffs the personnel department with individuals of only modest capabilities and skills. Too often a man gets the position of personnel manager because he is loyal, has worked for the company a long time, is familiar with company traditions, and gets along well with others. Such an individual generally looks upon his job as one of hiring and firing workers, keeping records, and administering the cafeteria, charity drives, and company parties and picnics. One can usually recognize whether the personnel manager and his staff are assigned a low status when the personnel functions for the executive, professional, and sales groups are handled by someone else attached to the chief executive's office and if collective bargaining is handled by the company's legal counsel.

When placed in proper perspective, the executive in charge of the personnel-industrial relations function should be of major executive caliber and should serve as a member of the top management team. His counsel should play a significant part (along with that of those in other functional parts of the business) in shaping decisions pertaining to company expansion or contraction, new facilities, plant relocation, organization planning, personnel policy, labor policy, executive development, and community relations policy.

The responsibility for insuring that the chief personnel executive sits in the halls of top management rests both with the personnel profession and with chief executive officers throughout industry. The personnel profession must continuously strive to educate and train its members for higher standards of competence, and it must educate top management upon the values and contributions of personnel management. In staffing the personnel-industrial relations department, the chief executive officer must select men with demonstrated professional competence and then give them the necessary support to be really effective.

Is personnel-industrial relations a distinct profession in the same sense as engineering and law? Or is it but a part of the broader, emerging profession of management. Does a manager who has been successful in marketing, production, or general management necessarily possess the qualifications to be a successful personnel director? Have the technical and knowledge requirements for personnel management grown to the point where only those who have had college preparation plus specific work experience in the field are qualified to assume the responsibilities of personnel director? In selecting individuals to manage engineering, accounting, and research functions, top management invariably chooses those who have professional education and work experience in these respective fields.

The author finds that the specialist and first-level supervisory positions in personnel-industrial relations are coming to demand specialized professional training. Thus, in this sense, personnel-industrial relations work is becoming a distinct profession in itself. On the other hand, the position of director of personnel-industrial relations demands skills, abilities, and aptitudes that are common to nearly all top-management work. Thus, at this level in the organization, the position requires general management talent. A top-level manager should consider that his profession is management. He may be equally effective in various managerial posts at this level. However, the executive in charge of the personnel-industrial relations function should have had considerable professional education and experience in personnel work before being placed in his position.

WHERE DO WE STAND?

As we come toward the end of this book, it is pertinent to review briefly the accomplishments of the personnel field to date and to highlight some of the principal unsolved or persistent problems that must command the attention of researchers, theorists, and practitioners in the future.

In discussing the current state of progress, it should be borne in mind that we are making broad generalizations. The actual stage of advancement in particular institutions deviates rather widely from the levels to be depicted. Specifically many companies do fall rather far short of the levels described.

Personnel Practices

The practice of personnel management in business and public institutions has grown from infancy to young adulthood in the past sixty years. For the most part organized hiring, training, and wage administration programs were nonexistent sixty years ago. Most of these functions were done very haphazardly by line supervision. The organized safety movement was just getting started in 1913. Pensions and health insurance were provided by only a handful of companies throughout the nation. Paid vacations for hourly workers generally did not exist.

Today employee selection is handled by means of planned interviews, validated selection tests, medical examinations, and background investigations. Management recognizes that new employees do not learn well by looking over the shoulder of older workers, but rather they must go through a planned training effort. Management also recognizes that long years of experience as an individual contributor do not automatically qualify one for promotion to supervision. Nowadays both potential and practicing supervisors are given classroom and on-the-job training in management fundamentals. Rational wage determination via job evaluation, formal pay structures, and wage surveys has become well accepted throughout industry. The field of industrial safety has now reached the point where the work place, especially in large companies, is safer than the home. Seven to nine paid holidays and two to three weeks paid vacation per year are now commonplace. Four weeks vacation after fifteen years of service is becoming increasingly popular. Comprehensive medical and hospitalization insurance, paid partially or entirely by the employer, is now widespread. Group life insurance, weekly disability benefits, pensions, and separation pay have all become well established by the 1970's.

Personnel Research

A great deal of research—both university and company based—has been conducted over the past thirty to forty years. Research findings are available in many areas of concern to the people-oriented manager. To identify just a few, significant research-based knowledge has been developed in the areas of absenteeism, motivation, morale, performance appraisal, the problems of the professional employee in industry, organization design, communication, accident causes, industrial toxicology and medicine, and pay incentives.

Some of the larger corporations have established their own research units to conduct investigations into human resource areas. Prominent among these is the Behavioral Research Service of the General Electric Company. Texas Instruments, Procter and Gamble, and General Motors also have units devoted to behavioral and personnel research.

The problems encountered in such research are complex and the results obtained are occasionally contradictory; nevertheless, substantial progress is being made. Managers nowadays need rely less and less upon trial and error and rule of thumb.

Education in Personnel, Industrial Relations, and Human Relations

Professional education has been mentioned previously when we discussed personnel-industrial relations as a career. Required courses in organizational behavior and administration are now an established feature of most graduate programs in business administration. Emphasis is also placed upon human resources through courses in labor economics, labor relations, and personnel management.

Nondegree advanced-management programs given at leading American universities for practicing executives from industry and government devote considerable emphasis to the human aspects of administration.

Union-Management Relations

Up until the late 1930's union-management relations, for the most part, featured labor spies, strikebreakers, discharge of union sympathizers, picket line violence, uncompromising employers, and militant union leaders.

Today, thanks to a generous assist from Federal labor legislation, organized labor has won its battles for recognition and acceptance as equals in dealings with management spokesmen. The old-time deep-seated hostility on the part of management and militancy on the part of union officials has largely disappeared. To the casual observer the modern sophisticated union official is indistinguishable from his management counterpart when seated around the conference table.

The union movement has largely won most of its long-time struggles for decent wages, shorter hours, safe and healthful working conditions, seniority and job rights, a voice in work load determination, and employee security benefits. Disagreements arising over the administration and interpretation of the labor agreement are settled peacefully by use of voluntary labor arbitration.

Human Relations

For many years now executives have taken an interest in applied human relations because they know it contains the key to a successful, smooth-functioning organization. Whereas formerly human relations practice in industry consisted principally of applied common sense (and everyone's common sense told him something different) and whereas the verbalization of a business leader's human relations philosophy often consisted of platitudes, nowadays there is greater understanding of employee motivation, informal group relations, morale, employee attitudes, cultural variables, leadership, and communication fundamentals. Management education programs and the dissemination of practical knowledge from the behavioral sciences have contributed to improved human-relations practice in industry and government. But a great deal more needs to be accomplished in this area.

Employee and Job Rights

Historically in the United States the individualistic ethic caused society in general and employers in particular to worship property rights and not employee rights or job rights. The individualistic ethic has been a system of values derived from the Protestant ethic, the American frontier, and concepts of personal liberty, private property rights, and freedom of contract.

The unilateral right of an employer to hire and fire at will and to operate his business as he saw fit was largely assumed and unchallenged.

But in recent years private business and industry has begun to accord greater protection, security, and rights to employees. This change has developed as a consequence of protective labor legislation, unionism, and a changed social attitude on the part of management. As a consequence of the Civil Rights Act of 1964 (Title VII Equal Employment Opportunity) and of the Age Discrimination in Employment Act of 1967, it is illegal for employers to discriminate against individuals in regard to hiring, compensation, or terms of employment because of race, color, religion, sex, national origin, or age.

The presence of unions has resulted in greater job rights for workers. Layoffs and sometimes promotions are determined by seniority. An employee can appeal his grievances through a formal grievance procedure and even get a hearing before an impartial arbitrator. Discipline and discharge must be handled by due process procedures.

The labor-relations law of the land prevents discrimination or discharge solely because of a man's union activities. In recent years court decisions have tended to grant greater recognition to job rights in cases of plant shutdowns and relocations.

The foregoing comments do not mean that employers cannot discharge a man for just cause. No one is guaranteed absolute job security regardless of his transgressions. Likewise, job security for those in policy-making positions and for all ranks of management and for many nonunion personnel is sometimes no greater than that required by law. Discharge due to clashes in personality, caprice, and whim still occurs with some frequency among these groups.

CONTINUING PROBLEMS AND NEEDS

Let us now review some of the major problems and needs concerning the management of people at work that demand serious attention.

Human Relations

Starting with the famous Hawthorne research studies in the late 1920's and early 1930's, a great deal of empirical research has been conducted in industrial human relations. Much of this research has generated significant and useful knowledge. Though it has been disseminated fairly widely, there remains a considerable gap between this knowledge and actual practice in business and industry. The state of the art of supervision, leadership, discipline, communication, counseling, and the related functions involved in managing people in a work organization is still surprisingly crude in many enterprises. Brusqueness, crudeness, arbitrary discharges, disregard of employee needs, poor leadership, continual strife and related difficulties are endemic to many, many establishments.

But although knowledge of human relations and organizational behavior has advanced considerably during the past thirty years, this scientific discipline is really only in its infancy. No well-accepted general theories have been developed. Much of the research tends to be highly descriptive and of the case study variety. Many of the conclusions reached in these studies are applicable only under the very specific circumstances of the organization studied. These statements do not deny that much useful work has been done or that a scientific research method is not followed by many. But there is a danger of repetition and coming back to the starting point all over again. There is a clear-cut need for comprehensive theories of organizational behavior and for substantial empirical evidence to support these theories.

Tannenbaum, Weschler, and Massarik have listed six major human relations areas requiring additional research emphasis. These are (1) an understanding of the factors underlying interpersonal effectiveness, (2) the dynamics of change of attitude and behavior, (3) criteria for evaluation of performance, (4) intergroup relations involving conflict and cooperation, (5) the effect of cultural variables, and (6) the individual in the organization.[1] To these can be added needs for much more basic and applied research in work motivation, job design, organization design, the role of money as a motivator, alienation of certain segments of the population from the world of work, and the problems of the increase in leisure time.

Ethics and Values

The whole field of ethics and values in management and in human relations practices in work organizations has received insufficient attention. Sporadically, as a result of such scandals as the price-fixing conspiracy in the electrical manufacturing industry in the early 1960's, there has been isolated public interest in ethics, social responsibility and standards of conduct. Hardly a day goes by but we read in the business journals about stock manipulations, conflict of interest transactions, and fraud perpetrated by buccaneer businessmen. But these affairs concern mostly stockholders, government suppliers, and customers in relation to top executives.

There needs to be much more searching examination of values within the organization, that is, of values and standards of conduct among

---

[1] Robert Tannenbaum, I. R. Weschler, and Fred Massarik, *Leadership and Organization: A Behavioral Science Approach* (New York: McGraw-Hill Book Company, Inc., 1961), pp. 12-15.

managers, employees, and union. What are the value implications of the internal struggles for power within the organization? Can executives justify the sabotaging of another person's career in order to advance their own? Is it right for top management to seek to destroy the very union that the employees have chosen, in a democratic election, to represent them in dealings with management? Have the psychological testers invaded the individual's privacy too deeply?

What should management do with the faithful, long-service employee who can no longer cope with an enlarged and complex job? Changes in technology and advances in the state of an art often proceed faster than some engineers and supervisors can accommodate. Should management discard these people? Or should it give them a sinecure and design the organization so that the work flows away from them?

Should private business bear social responsibilites for helping the culturally deprived and the hard-core unemployed to obtain meaningful jobs?

How can ethical standards be adopted, accepted, and enforced? How can they be upgraded? Do managers as a leadership elite have a mission to develop higher standards of conduct? Or is their day-to-day behavior merely a reflection of the prevailing standards of society?

The Individual and the Organization

Peter Drucker has stated that a business corporation is only one institution in the lives of employees. He says it is a partial institution existing for very limited purposes. Other institutions in the lives of people exist for much higher purposes. But top management tends to demand total loyalty and involvement on the part of the employees. Drucker claims that this is not compatible with the dignity of man.[2]

Chris Argyris has stated that there is a basic lack of congruence between the needs of healthy individuals and the demands of the formal organization. This tends to cause frustration and human conflict.[3]

The demands of the formal organization are for stability, order, obedience, conformity, and cooperation. The members of any organization must, to a point, submerge or at best blend their goals to the goals and needs of their organization. The organization cannot tolerate too much personal freedom, creativity, and independence. The strict discipline of the big organization tends to be very stifling. The needs of the individual for knowledge, self-accomplishment, self-expression, recognition, and autonomy are frequently denied.

Related to the foregoing is the excessive dependency of the subordinate upon his "boss". The boss controls his subordinate's livelihood. He controls his jobs security, advancement, pay, and state of well-being on

---

[2] Peter F. Drucker, "Human Relations: How Far Do We Have to Go?," *Management Record*, Vol. 21, No. 3 (March 1959), pp. 78-84.

[3] Chris Argyris, *Personality and Organization* (New York: Harper & Row, 1957), Ch. 9.

the job. The authority structure tends to be very autocratic. This can lead to excessive fawning of subordinates toward their bosses. Many court favor and flatter. Many become yes men. And such behavior occurs all up and down the channel of command from worker to vice-president.

These pressures are fundamentally a manifestation of the increasing trend toward bureaucratization of modern mass society.

Union-Management Relations

Although the days of open warfare between organized labor and management have happily passed into history and although countless relationships have matured into a cooperative atmosphere, to a considerable extent, the picture bears many of the characteristics of an uneasy truce. Much of American management has never really accepted unionism as a necessary and permanent institution. They yearn for the day when management can rid itself of the interferences and challenges caused by unionism. Many managements feel that they know what is best for their employees and that union leaders do not truly represent the interests of their constituents.

For their part many union leaders have not altered their philosophy, derived from the days of violence and conflict, to conform to the realities of the 1970's. They have not been sufficiently adaptable to meet the problems of a newer age. At times they have ignored the long-range consequences of their actions upon the prosperity of business, wage-price levels, and employment. Organized labor has been slow to advance educated young men with new ideas to positions of leadership.

The question of the role of unionism as an American institution and of the relationship between management and organized labor is still in a state of flux. This situation is likely to continue for some time.

Public Employee Bargaining. By the mid-1960's those working in government became restive and began to organize into unions at a fairly rapid rate. Contracts were quietly bargained with various agencies of the Federal government. But at the local level in schools and municipalities, the public has witnessed spreading crises and work stoppages. Public officials and union leaders have not had much experience of working with one another. The issues are complex. Frequently the agency that bargains the contract—the executive branch—does not have the authority to appropriate the funds to pay for the settlement. This is a legislative function. Although strikes are almost universally banned by law in public employment, these employees, having felt a sense of injustice, have struck on numerous occasions anyway. The problem has been particularly acute in the schools.

That public employees have a right to engage in collective bargaining few now deny. However, creative solutions are needed to develop a viable structure of bargaining relationships.

The Professional Employee

For decades the literature of personnel management has concentrated upon the hourly worker. The personnel programs of industry have been slanted in this direction. Most empirical research has been devoted to the factory worker.

But the ranks of the engineer, the mathematician, the chemist, the physicist, and the accountant have been swelling in industry. The needs, goals, problems, and orientation of the professional are somewhat different from those of the blue-collar worker. They are also different from those of managers. The professional in industry remains a fertile ground for research and discovery.

Equal Employment Opportunity

The problems of the chronically underemployed and unemployed Americans came dramatically to the attention of the public in the 1960's. Rioting in the cities shocked and frightened many citizens. The problems of the disadvantaged—especially the Negro—are many and complex. The long-term solutions must be worked out cooperatively by all institutions and all races in our society. Private business has a stake in this process.

The Federal government and many state governments have been encouraging private employers to go beyond merely nondiscriminatory employment policies. They have pressed to get employers to affirmatively bring into their workforces substantial numbers of Negroes and other disadvantaged peoples.

A number of issues have been created by the thrust for equal employment opportunity. Some managements have responded with mere tokenism. Some have hired a very few Negroes and widely publicized this hiring. Such a practice might be called window-dressing. Other companies have entered into the process wholeheartedly. At what point do affirmative efforts to hire Negroes become discriminatory against white job seekers? What about white citizens who are disadvantaged? Should hiring standards be deliberately lowered? How far can private businesses safely dilute their workforces in terms of lower employee qualifications and still remain viable and competitive?

Work and Leisure

Up until very recently the United States has been a work-oriented society. An analgam of factors caused this spirit. Among these have been: (1) prevalence of the Protestant ethic; (2) historic liberalism with its emphasis upon personal liberty, private property, and freedom of contract; (3) the character of the European immigrants who settled this nation; (4) the emphasis upon self-reliance and the entrepreneurial spirit; (5) the discipline of the industrialization process; and (6) the imperatives imposed by the Western frontier in nineteenth century America.

There have been increasing signs in recent years of a shift in attitudes and values away from work as a central orientation toward leisure and toward the pursuit of pleasure. Mechanization and the unparalleled productivity of our industrial system have made affluence and leisure available to more and more people. The trend toward pleasure-seeking is evidenced in the phenomenal growth of our leisure-based industries. The widespread use of narcotics and of alcohol is another manifestation of pleasure-orientation. The social ethic is supplanting the individual ethic.

How do these trends affect the work organization? Will they affect achievement motivation at the work place? Will our jobs become less central to our lives in the future? Will other institutions occupy a greater focus for the masses of people?

Questions for Review and Discussion

1. Discuss careers in personnel-industrial relations. Include fields of specialization, qualifications for employment, and status of personnel-industrial relations within the organization.
2. Is personnel-industrial relations a profession in itself or is it but a part of the larger (emerging) profession of management?
3. Explain how the prevailing practices in "the management of people at work" have matured over the past half-century.
4. Give and discuss current and emerging problems in the management of people at work.
5. Do you feel that the mass of Americans are becoming less work-oriented and more leisure-time and pleasure-oriented? Discuss.

Suggestions for Further Reading

Argyris, Chris, *Personality and Organization,* New York: Harper & Row, 1957.

_____, *Integrating the Individual and the Organization,* New York: John Wiley & Sons, 1964.

de Grazia, Sebastian, *Of Time, Work and Leisure,* New York: The Twentieth Century Fund, 1962.

Finley, Robert E., *The Personnel Man and His Job,* New York: American Management Association, 1962.

Golembiewski, Robert T., *Men, Management, and Morality,* New York: McGraw-Hill Book Company, 1965.

Kornhauser, William, *Scientists in Industry: Conflict and Accommodation,* Berkeley and Los Angeles: The University of California Press, 1962.

McFarland, Dalton E., *Cooperation and Conflict in Personnel Administration,* New York: American Foundation for Management Research, 1962.

Selekman, Benjamin, *A Moral Philosophy for Management,* New York: McGraw-Hill Book Company, 1959.

Spates, Thomas G., *Human Values Where People Work,* New York: Harper & Row, 1960.

Warner, Kenneth O. and Hennessy, Mary L. (eds.), *Public Management at the Bargaining Table,* Chicago: Public Personnel Association, 1967.

INDEXES

Name Index

Anderson, Stanley V., 641
Andlinger, G. R., 427
Andrews, Kenneth R., 390, 426
Appley, Lawrence A., 6
Arbous, A. G., 764
Arensberg, Conrad, 474
Argyris, Chris, 35, 52, 458, 823

Babbage, Charles, 23
Baitsell, John M., 108
Bakke, E. Wight, 35
Bales, Robert F., 35, 474
Balzac, Honoré de, 179
Bamforth, K. W., 489
Bancroft, Gertrude, 18, 20
Barber, E. S., 349
Barkin, Solomon, 713
Barnard, Chester I., 160
Barnes, Ralph M., 695
Barrett, Dermot, 588
Barrett, Richard S., 269
Barry, Carol A., 18
Bavelas, Alex, 588
Bayha, F. M., 695
Bayroff, A. G., 323
Beach, Dale S., 641
Beal, Edwin F., 102

Beebe, Leo, 302
Behling, Orlando, 231, 457
Belcher, David W., 656
Bell Frederick J., 421
Belman, Harry S., 377, 378
Bendix, Reinhard, 506
Benge, Eugene, 663
Bennett, George K., 264
Bennis, Warren G., 432
Berniger, Joseph, 238
Bills, Marion A., 238
Binet, Alfred, 262
Bingham, W. V., 274
Blake, Robert R., 52, 433
Bliek, John E., 377, 378
Bloch, Joseph W., 363
Blood, Milton R., 466
Bloom, Gordon E., 137, 713
Blum, Milton L., 249, 763
Boaz, Keith, 695
Brackett, Jean C., 797
Braden, J. Noble, 604
Bray, Douglas W., 352
Brenner, Marshall H., 306
Brinker, Paul A., 121
Brower, F. Beatrice, 725
Brown, Douglas V., 108

Brown, J. A. C., 481
Brown, Paula, 325
Buchanan, Paul C., 432
Bunker, Douglas R., 432
Burcin, William A., 397
Burkey, Lee M., 225
Burling, Temple, 781
Burnett, Verne, 585
Burtt, Harold E., 411, 533, 545

Caldwell, Nat, 109
Cammack, Emerson, 794, 796
Cannell, Charles F., 274
Carey, H. H., 570
Carson, Walter Jr., 734
Carter, Launor F., 507
Cartwright, Dorwin, 35, 486, 536, 545
Carzo, Rocco Jr., 35, 36
Chapple, Eliot D., 474
Ching, Cyrus S., 109
Clark, Gerald E., Jr., 293, 294
Comrey, A. L., 540
Cook, Morris L., 24
Copley, F. B., 694
Cowden, D. J., 256
Cozan, Lee W., 321
Craf, John R., 422
Cronbach, Lee J., 249, 268
Croxton, F. E., 256
Cullison, W. E., 121
Cummings, Laurie D., 290

Dahle, Thomas L., 597
Dale, Ernest, 166
Dalton, Melville, 349, 492, 493
Darwin, Charles, 49
Davenport, Russell W., 719
Davey, Harold W., 634
Dearborn, DeWitt C., 584
Deegan, J. Wayne, 706
Dent, J., 539
Deutsch, A. R., 230
Dickson, W. J., 34, 475, 548
Doehring, C. F. W., 28
Dooher, M. J., 233
Drucker, Peter, 54, 166, 823
Dunlop, John T., 14

Eastman, George, 39
Eells, Richard, 44
Eilbirt, Henry, 27
Emerson, Harrington, 24

England, G. W., 76
Enterline, Philip E., 755

Fayol, Henri, 35, 511
Felton, Jean S., 781
Ferber, Robert, 275
Fiedler, Fred E., 520
Filene, Edward A., 804
Filipetti, George, 24
Filley, Alan C., 385
Fleishman, Edwin A., 238, 411, 533, 545, 562, 764
Fogel, Walter, 291
Ford, Henry, 12, 165
Ford, Henry II, 217, 287, 299
Form, William H., 233
Fox, Harland, 741, 802
Frederikson, Norman, 267
French, John R. P., 329, 331, 332, 333, 514, 560
Friedmann, Georges, 15, 454
Fry, D. E., 264
Fuller, S. H., 108

Gainer, Marion, 231
Galbraith, John K., 44, 45
Gallatin, Albert, 725
Gandhi, Mahatma, 505
Gantt, Henry L., 24
Gardner, Burleigh B., 173
Gassler, Lee S., 304, 397
Gellerman, Saul W., 35, 270, 352
Georgopoulos, B. S., 317
Ghiselli, Edwin E., 53, 274, 534
Gilbreth, Frank, 24, 188
Gilbreth, Lillian, 24, 188
Gitlow, Abraham L., 16
Glanzer, M., 588
Glanzer, R., 588
Golden, Clinton S., 110
Gomberg, William, 696, 697
Gomersall, E. R., 396, 397, 466
Gompers, Samuel, 22, 115
Gordon, Robert A., 426, 427
Gottier, Richard F., 269
Graham, Gene S., 109
Graicunas, V. A., 172
Grant, Donald L., 352
Greeley, Horace, 725
Greenwood, M., 762
Gregory, Charles O., 117
Grimaldi, John V., 767
Guest, Robert H., 35, 538, 544

Guion, Robert M., 269, 271, 302
Gunnar, Engen, 727
Gustad, J. W., 274

Habbe, Stephen, 249, 305, 322
Haberstat, R. W., 238
Haggerty, H. R., 323
Haire, Mason, 53, 653
Hamel, Harvey R., 18
Hammurabi, 398
Hampton, W. C., 802
Hanson, Philip C., 333
Harbison, Frederick H., 6, 14
Hardesty, D. L., 352
Harris, Edwin F., 411, 533, 545
Hay, Edward N., 740
Hayes, John J., 558
Healy, James J., 353, 355, 575, 702, 729
Heinrich, H. W., 760
Heise, George A., 589
Henderson, James A., 729
Herzberg, Frederick, 35, 52, 455, 456, 457, 458, 464, 465, 526
High, W. S., 540
Hilgard, E. R., 383
Hitler, Adolf, 505
Hobbes, Thomas, 48
Hodgson, James D., 306
Hoffman, L. R., 593
Hollander, E. P., 314
Holly, J. Fred, 618
Homans, George, 35, 474, 485
Hooven, J. J., 593
Houff, James N., 17, 806
Howell, James E., 426, 427
Hoxie, Robert F., 24
Hulin, Charles L., 466

Indik, B. P., 317

Jackson, Jay, 590
Janger, Allen R., 74, 77
Jaques, Elliott, 675, 676
Jefferson, Thomas, 725
Jensen, Vernon H., 115
Jerdee, Thomas H., 508
Jesse, Franklin C., 385
Johnson, Lyndon B., 217, 287, 295, 299
Johnston, Denis F., 17
Jones, W. S., 352

Kahn, Robert L., 274, 536, 538, 539, 545
Kaiser, Edgar, 722
Kallejian, Verne, 325
Karger, Delmar W., 695
Kassalow, Everett M., 91
Katz, Daniel, 536, 538, 539, 545
Katz, Robert L., 408
Kay, Emanuel, 329, 331, 332, 333
Keenan, Vernon, 764
Keller, Suzanne, 292, 293
Kelley, Harold F., 486
Kendall, W. E., 240
Kennedy, John F., 30, 91, 219, 295
Kephart, Newell C., 274
Kerr, Clark, 14
Kerr, Willard A., 250, 763, 764
Kerrich, J. E., 764
King, Martin Luther, Jr., 286, 287
Kirby, S., 560
Kirchner, Wayne K., 315
Kirkwood, John H., 271
Klausner, William J., 807
Koontz, Harold, 5, 6
Kornhauser, Arthur, 457
Kosmo, Richard, 457
Kress, A. L., 667
Krick, Edward V., 186
Krislov, Joseph, 90

Labovitz, George, 231, 457
Lanham, Elizabeth, 663
Lawler, Edward E., III, 653
Leavitt, Harold J., 586, 587
Lenin, Nikolai, 505
Leonard, John W., 618
Lesieur, F. G., 719
Levitan, Sar, 299
Lewin, Kurt, 474, 516, 559
Lewis, John L., 22, 87, 89, 98
Lewis, L., Earl, 692
Likert, Rensis, 35, 44, 52, 458, 461, 463, 464, 489, 517, 536, 538, 541, 550, 561
Ling, Cyril C., 26
Lippitt, Ronald, 474, 516, 559
Livernash, E., Robert, 353, 355, 575, 702
Lopez, Felix M., Jr., 267
Lott, Merrill R., 663
Loudon, J. Keith, 706
Lovejoy, L. C., 726
Lytle, Charles W., 705

McClellan, John, 90, 124
McClelland, David, 294, 455, 458, 459, 460, 468
McCormick, Charles P., 421, 573
McCormick, Ernest J., 189, 263
McDonald, David J., 722
McGehee, William, 383
McGovney, Warren C., 412
McGregor, Douglas, 35, 50, 52, 328, 331, 458, 463
Machiavelli, Niccolò, 48
McKamy, Kent, 302
McLain, Gerald A., 271, 302
McMurry, Robert N., 274, 278
Madison, James, 725
Magnum, Garth L., 296
Mahoney, Thomas A., 508
Maier, A. A., 391
Maier, Norman R. F., 391, 466, 558, 562, 593
Main, Jeremy, 743
Mallory, George L., 459
Malm, F. T., 228
Mandell, Milton M., 233, 278
Mann, F. C., 539
March, James G., 35, 512
Marrow, Alfred, 562
Marting, Elizabeth, 233, 421
Martucci, N. L. A., 737
Maslow, A. H., 448
Massarik, Fred, 430, 504, 512, 822
Mausner, Bernard, 456, 526
Mayfield, Eugene C., 273, 274
Mayfield, Harold, 302
Maynard, H. B., 186, 698
Mayo, Elton, 34, 35, 460, 475
Meany, George, 22, 98
Mee, John, 705
Mehr, Robert I., 794, 796
Merrill, Harwood F., 421
Meyer, H. H., 329, 331, 332, 333
Mill, John Stuart, 23
Miller, Delbert C., 233
Miller, George A., 589
Mintz, Alexander, 763
Mitchell, William, 179
Mooney, James D., 35, 511
Moore, B. V., 274
Moore, David G., 173
Moore, H. J., 695
Moreno, Jacob L., 391, 474
Morsh, Joseph E., 196
Morton, Robert B., 333

Moser, George V., 426, 570
Mouton, Jane, 52, 433
Mueller, Ronald A. H., 586, 587
Mumma, Edwin W., 309, 780
Munsterberg, Hugo, 27
Murray, Philip, 22
Myers, Charles A., 6, 14, 71, 108, 611
Myers, M. Scott, 456, 466

Nash, Allan N., 508
Nelson, J. R., 560
Nelson, Roberta J., 76
Newbold, E. M., 762
Newman, William H., 5
Niebel, Benjamin W., 186, 695
Nix, James, 628
Nixon, Mary, 507
Nixon, Richard M., 298
Northrup, Herbert R., 111, 137, 713

O'Donnell, Cyril, 5, 6
Owen, Robert, 23

Parker, B. T., 238
Parker, V. D., 110
Patchen, Martin, 575
Patten, Thomas H., Jr., 293, 294, 653
Patton, Arch, 332, 739
Pelz, Donald, 541
Pfiffner, J. F., 540, 542
Phelps, Orme W., 609
Piersol, D. T., 581
Pierson, Frank C., 426
Platt, Robert, 363
Pollay, Richard W., 500
Porter, Lyman W., 457
Puckett, E. S., 719
Purves, Dale, 740

Raimon, Robert L., 687
Randle, C., Wilson, 137
Raven, Bertram, 514
Read, W. H., 593
Redding, W. Charles, 597
Reiley, Alan C., 35, 511
Reisberg, Donald J., 315
Reuther, Walter, 22, 98
Rickover, Hyman, 180
Rockefeller, John D., 438
Rockefeller, Nelson, 91
Roethlisberger, F. J., 34, 475, 548
Rogers, Carl R., 548
Ronner, Walter V., 641

Roosevelt, Franklin D., 89, 219, 295
Roosevelt, Theodore, 169
Root, Elihu, 169
Rorschach, Hermann, 268
Rosner, Carl H., 551
Ross, I. C., 560
Rothaus, Paul, 333
Rundquist, E. A., 323
Russell, J. T., 252
Ryscavage, Paul M., 19

Sanborn, George A., 597
Sargent, Charles W., 790
Sayles, Leonard R., 482
Scanlon, Joseph, 575, 719
Schein, Edgar H., 432
Schultz, Gregory, 692
Schwab, J. L., 698
Scott, Walter Dill, 273, 309
Scott, William G., 628, 638, 639
Seashore, Stanley E., 317, 485
Selekman, Benjamin M., 40, 55, 108, 633
Shartle, Carroll L., 516
Sherman, William, 764
Sikes, Walter, 554
Simmonds, Rollin H., 767
Simon, Herbert A., 35, 512, 584
Slichter, Sumner H., 353, 355, 575, 696, 702
Sloan, Alfred P., 166
Smith, Adam, 23, 49
Smith, Burk M., 225
Smyth, P., 560
Smyth, Richard C., 738
Snyderman, Barbara B., 456, 526
Solem, A. R., 391
Spates, Thomas G., 41, 42
Spencer, Gilmore J., 237
Spencer, Herbert, 49
Spriegel, W. R., 309, 780
Stagner, Ross, 271
Stegemerten, G. L., 698
Stevens, S. S., 382, 384
Steiglitz, Harold, 77, 722
Stogdill, Ralph M., 507, 508, 509
Stone, Harold C., 240
Summer, Charles E., Jr., 5

Taft, Philip, 127
Taft, Ronald, 315
Tannenbaum, Robert, 430, 504, 512, 822

Taylor, Erwin K., 321
Taylor, Frederick W., 3, 24, 25, 26, 35, 188, 530
Taylor, George, 91
Taylor, H. C., 252
Thayer, Paul W., 383
Theodore, Rose, 362, 365, 628
Thompson, Doris M., 776, 780
Thompson, Stewart, 46
Thorndike, Robert L., 256
Thurstone, L. L., 263
Tiffin, Joseph, 238, 263
Tilove, Robert, 685
Tolles, N. Arnold, 687
Tolman, William H., 26
Tosdal, Harry, 734
Trist, E. L., 489
Truman, Harry S, 89
Turnbull, John G., 71, 611
Turner, Arthur N., 538, 544

Ure, Andrew, 23
Urwick, Lyndall F., 172, 511

VanZelst, Raymond H., 495, 765
Viteles, Morris S., 238, 562
Vroom, Victor H., 457, 461, 518, 562, 564

Wadsworth, Guy W., 322
Wagner, Robert, 118
Wales, Hugh, 275
Walker, Charles R., 35, 154, 538, 544
Walton, Clarence, 44
Ward, Lewis B., 250
Ware, F. L., 250
Watson, Thomas, 39
Webb, Beatrice, 115
Webb, Sidney, 115
Weber, Max, 13, 49, 174, 709
Weisbrod, Burton A., 289
Weschler, Irving R., 325, 427, 504, 512, 822
Wherry, Robert J., 321
White, Ralph K., 474, 516, 559
Whyte, William Foote, 35, 474, 475, 485, 712, 719
Whyte, William H., Jr., 238, 269, 491
Wickersham, Edward D., 102
Wickert, F. P., 561
Wikstrom, Walter S., 352
Willey, F. O., 506

Wolfbein, Seymour L., 296
Wolfle, Dael, 382, 384
Wolk, Dena, 628
Wonderlic, E. F., 263, 278
Woods, H. M., 762
Worthy, James C., 154
Worthy, N. Beatrice, 802
Wortman, Max S., 137

Woytinsky, W. S., 659

Yanouzas, John N., 35, 36
Yoder, Dale, 76
Young, Harvey A., 111

Zander, Alvin, 35, 486, 536, 545
Zif, Jay J., 79, 146, 182, 470

Subject Index

Accident(s)
  and age, training, and experience,
    765
  causes of, 761-762
  costs, 760-761
  and environment, 764-765
  proneness, 762-764
Accident prevention. *See* Safety,
  program
Achievement motivation (McClelland),
  458-460
Administrative justice, 608-610
Adult basic education, 397
AFL-CIO, 97-101
American Arbitration Association,
  637, 707
American Management Association,
  32, 429, 738
American Motors-United Automobile
  Workers profit-sharing plan,
  728-729
American Telephone and Telegraph
  Company and assessment
  center, 351-352
Application blank, 236-238
Appraisal, performance
  applications of, 311

defined, 310
interviews, 326-331
methods, 315-323, 331-333
problems in rating, 324-326
by results, 331-333
trends and perspectives, 333-337
Arbitration, dispute settlement
  method, 139-140
  grievance, 637-638
Assessment centers
  for selection and promotion, 350-
    352
Authority
  defined, 159
  dual, 170
  and influence, 159-161
  and leadership, 511-515
  modified view of, 513-514
  and power and influence, 540-542
  relative to responsibility, 162
  source of, 159-160

Barriers to hiring
  credentials, 222-224
Benefits and services
  defined, 786-787
  growth of, 787-788

Benefits and services *(Cont.)*
  reasons for, 791-794
  types of, 788-790
Blue Cross, 795-796
Blue Shield, 795-796
Bumping on layoffs, 364-365
Bureau of Labor Statistics
  and cost of living data, 657-658
  and wage data, 659, 687, 750
Bureaucracy, 173-180
  advantages of, 177-178
  disadvantages of, 178-180

Career curves, salary. *See* Salary
    maturity curves
Case study, as training method, 390-
    391
Clinical approach to grievances,
    632-634
Collective bargaining,
  characteristics of, 115-116
  defined, 115
  joint committees, 131-132
  labor and courts, 117-118
  legal framework of, 116-127
  multi-employer, 128-130
  negotiating the agreement, 130-132
  and participation, 573-574
  strikes and settlement, 139-141
    arbitration, 139-140
    conciliation, 140
    fact-finding, 140-141
  structure for, 127-130
  subject matter of, 132-133
  substantive issues, 133-139
    grievance handling, 138-139
    job rights, 137-138
    management rights, 135-136
    union security, 134-135
    wages, 136-137
Communication
  defined, 581
  feedback, 586-587
  fundamentals, 582-592
  grapevine, 599-600
  networks, 582, 588-589
  in organizations, 592-595
  systems, 595-599
Compensation
  executives, 738-745
  professionals, 745-750
  salesmen, 734-736
  supervisors, 737-738

Competition, as motivation, 468-469
Complaints and grievances, 623-625
Conference, as training method,
    389-390
Conformity, 490-491
  and social pressure, 486-487
Consideration score, of supervisors,
    545
Consultative management, 567, 570-
    571
Cost of living and wages, 657-658
Counseling, personnel, 545-549
Credit unions, 803-804
Critical incidents appraisal, 321
Culturally deprived, employment of
  action by private business, 299-306
  culture of poor, 292-294
  government action for, 294-299
    Civil Rights Act, 295
    Economic Opportunity Act,
      297-299
    Manpower Development and
      Training Act, 295-296
  who are the deprived?, 289-294

Daywork, 692-694
  measured, 701-702
Defense mechanisms, 450-453
Delegation
  defined, 161-162
  dynamics of, 162-163
  and effective supervision, 536-537
Democratic management, 567, 571-
    572
Demotion, 365-366
  as discipline, 617
Discharge, 366-367
  as disciplinary penalty, 617-618
Discipline
  administration of, 608-615
  defined, 604-605
  and discharge, 71
  negative, 605-606
  positive, 604, 606-607
  rules and penalties, 615-618
Dissatisfactions on the job, 453-455
Due process in discipline, 609

Eastman Kodak Company, 576
  and employment of disadvantaged
    persons, 303-304
Employment management, 26-27
Engineer's Joint Council, 748-750

Environment control, industrial hygiene, 775-777
Ethics and managerial philosophy, 40-42
Ethics and values, 822-823
Executives, compensation for, 738-745
Exempt from overtime requirements of Fair Labor Standards Act, 733, 737

Fair employment practices, 218-222
legislation and executive orders, 219-222
and selection testing, 270-271
Fair Labor Standards Act and minimum wage, 703
Forced-choice appraisal, 320-321
Foreman, position and problems, 530-535
Frequency, injury, 757-758
Fringe benefits. *See* Benefits and services; *see also* specific type of benefit or service

General Electric Company, 73, 177, 331, 332, 333, 543, 576, 815, 819
General Motors Corporation, 177, 637
and employment of the disadvantaged, 304-305
Grapevine and communication, 599-600
Grievance(s)
arbitration, 637-638
clinical approach to, 632-634
defined, 624-625
handling, 138-139, 623-646
nature of, 623-625
settlement for nonunion employees, 638-642
settlement for unionized employees, 628-637
Group
appraisal method, 323
relationships and supervisor, 543-544
Group dynamics, 473-474
Groups
formation of, 478-480
impact upon organization, 487-491
structure and properties, 482-487
and the supervisor, 494-496
types of, 481-482

Guaranteed employment and wage plans, 802-803

Halo effect, in performance appraisal, 324
Hard-core unemployed. *See* Culturally deprived, employment of
Harwood Manufacturing Company, 559-560
Hawthorne studies (experiments)
and complaints, 626
and counseling, 546-549
described, 475-478
and development of human relations, 34
early human relations interest, 531
and human relations research, 821
Health and safety, as personnel function, 70-71
Health insurance, group, 795-796
Health program, company, 779-780
Holiday practices in United States, 805-806
Hormel, George A. and Company, guaranteed annual wage, 802
Human relations
accomplishments over years, 820
and Hawthorne experiments, 34
meanings of, 33
needs, 821-822
and organizational behavior, 33-36

Incentives
based upon cooperation, 718-732
executive, 740-745
supervisory, 737-738
wage, 691-717
Incentives, positive and negative, 462-463
Incentive wages. *See* Wage incentives
Individual differences, 443-444
Individual and the organization, 823-824
Industrial hygiene, 775-777
Industrialization, 7-15
benefits and costs, 13-15
modern system, 10-13
Influence
and authority, 159-161
supervisory, 540-542
Informal leadership, 484-485, 509-511

Informal organization, 472-473
vs. formal organization, 491-494
Initiating structure, behavior of
supervisors, 545
Injury, disabling, defined, 755 *n.*
Injury frequency, 757-758
Injury severity, 757-758
Institute for Social Research, 35,
535-536, 560
Interaction analysis, 474-475
International Business Machines
Company, 73
International Harvester Company, 634
Interview, selection, 239, 271-282
defined, 272
objectives of, 272
pitfalls in, 281-282
psychological foundations for, 274-
276
research findings, 273-274
skills of interviewer, 276-277
types of, 277-278
Interviewing, nondirective, counseling,
545-549

Job analysis (job organization and
information)
administration of program, 204-206
defined, 185-186
job description, 187, 202-204
job specification, 187, 202-204
obtaining job information, 192-202
uses for, 187-189
Job descriptions, 187, 202-204
"as is or as ought," 203-204
detailed vs. general, 202-203
samples of, 200-201, 205
Job enlargement, 465-466
Job enrichment, 465-466
Job evaluation
defined, 662
elements of, 663
factor comparison system, 664,
673-675
grade description, 665-667
history of, 662-663
point system, 664, 667-672
ranking system, 664-665
Job rotation, 418-419, 466
Job specifications, 187, 198-204
sample of, 201
Judicial body, need for, 626-628

Junior Boards of Executives, 567-573.
See also Multiple management

Kaiser-United Steelworkers'
Long-Range Sharing Plan
employment guarantee, 802-803
incentive feature, 721-724
Key job, and factor comparison
system, 673-675

Labor force
in America, 15-21
composition, changing, 18-20
defined, 16
rising status, 16-18
Labor-Management Cooperation.
See Union-management
cooperation; Scanlon Plan
Labor-management relations *See*
Collective bargaining
Labor market, 213-215, 686
Labor relations, harmonious, 109-111
Labor relations stability, 107-111
Labor supply
to company, 215-216
sources of labor, 226-231
Landrum-Griffin Act (Labor-
Management Reporting and
Disclosure Act of 1959), 124-
127, 574
Layoff and recall, 360-365
of organized employees, 361-365
and seniority, 362-365
of unorganized employees, 361
Leaders, informal, elected, and
appointed, 509-511
Leadership
and authority, 511-515
charismatic, 505
definition, 504
foundations of, 506-509
informal, 484-485
power and, 514-515, 519
situational factors in, 515-522
style, 515-517
traits and situation, 506-509
Learning
defined, 380
principles of, 380-386
Least-squares technique, 677-678
Lecture, as training method, 386,
388-389
Lie detector in employment, 224-226

Life insurance, group, 794-795
Lockheed Aircraft Corporation and
    employment of the
    disadvantaged, 305-306
Long-range sharing plan. *See*
    Kaiser-United Steelworkers'
    Long-Range Sharing Plan

Management
    defined, 5
    functions, 5-6
    levels of, 155-159
    by objectives, 54
    as a profession, 409-410
    responsibilities in recruitment and
      selection, 242-243
    scientific, 24-25
Management development
    defined, 405-406
    evolution of, 408-411
    formal courses, 422-433
    methods of, 416-433
    and personnel management, 32-33
    planning program, 412-416
Management games, 427-429
Management rights, 135-136
Manager, knowledge and skills of,
    407-408
Managerial grid, 432-433
Managing people
    modern philosophy, 51-55
    traditional philosophy, 48-51
    traditional vs. modern, 55
Manpower planning, 73, 211-216
Manpower programs, Federal, 294-
    299, 394
Measured daywork, 701-702
Medical examination, 239-241, 779
Mental health
    defined, 780
    in industry, 780-782
Methods-Time Measurement, 698
Money as motivator, 467-468
Morale
    defined, 460-461
    and participation, 563
    and productivity, 460-462
Motivation, 445-453, 455-460
    achievement motivation, 458-460
    applying motivational concepts,
      462-469
    classification of needs, 446-448
    and competition, 468-469

defined, 445
Herzberg's theory, 455-458
human adjustment, 450-453
level of aspiration, 449-450
Maslow's hierarchy, 448
money as motivator, 467-468
Motivation-hygiene theory
    (Herzberg's), 455-458
Multiple management, 421-422. *See*
    also Junior boards of executives

National Electrical Manufacturers
    Association, 667
National Industrial Conference Board,
    77, 726, 802
National Planning Association, 110
National Safety Council, 28, 757, 758
National War Labor Board, 806
Needs of people. *See* Motivation
Networks of communication, 582,
    588-589
Norris-La Guardia Anti-Injunction
    Act, 118
Nunn-Bush Shoe Company,
    guaranteed employment plan,
    802-803

Objectives, business enterprise, 42-44
    of corporation, 44-45
Occupational health, 779-780
Ombudsman, for grievance handling,
    640-641
Open door policy, 639-640
Organization
    authority and influence, 159-161
    bureaucracy, 173-180
    decentralization, 163-166
    defined, 148
    delegation, 161-163
    grouping activities, 151-159
      by kind, 151-154
      by level, 155-159
    line and staff, 166-172
    span of supervision, 172-173
Organization for wage and salary
    administration, 661-662
Organization, objectives, 42-45
Organization planning, as personnel
    function, 72-73
Organizational behavior and human
    relations, 33-36
Orientation training, 394-397

Participation
    conditions for effective, 564-567
    defined, 553
    as motivator, 467
    pseudo, 555-556
    research into, 559-563
    types of, 567-578
Paternalism, 51
Pay. *See* Wage or wages; Wage and
        salary administration
Penalties, progressive, in discipline,
        613
Pensions, 796-799
Performance appraisal. *See* Appraisal,
        performance
Personnel and industrial relations
    functions, 69-74
        benefits and services, 72
        discipline and discharge, 71
        employment, 69
        health and safety, 70-71
        labor relations, 71-72
        manpower planning, 73
        organization planning, 72-73
        personnel research, 73-74
        training and development, 70
        transfer, promotion, layoff, 69-70
        wage and salary administration, 70
    terminology, 63-64
Personnel counseling, for handling
        grievances, 639
Personnel department
    organization, 74-77
    staff role, 66-68
Personnel-industrial relations as a
        career, 814-818
    job opportunities, 816
    position levels, 815-816
    status and professionalism, 816-818
Personnel management, evolution of
        theory and practice, 21-36
Personnel management: responsibilities
        of first-line supervisor, 65-66
Personnel management, university
        education programs, 64, 814-
        815, 819-820
Personnel policies, 55-59
Personnel practices, accomplishments
        over years, 818-819
Personnel research, as personnel
        function, 73-74
Piecework, 702-704
Pillsbury Flour Mills, 725

Point plan of job evaluation, Allis-
        Chalmers Manufacturing
        Company, 668-671
Policies, personnel, 55-59
    communicating, 58-59
    formulating, 57-58
    reasons for, 56-57
    in writing, 57
Power, and authority, 511-515
    and leadership, 514-515
    and supervision, 540-542
Procter and Gamble Company,
        guaranteed employment plan,
        802-803
Productivity and group relations,
        488-490
Productivity, and morale, 460-462
Productivity and wages, 658
Professional employee in industry, 825
Professionals, compensation for, 745-
        750
Profit sharing, 724-731
    American Motors-U.A.W. Plan,
        728-729
    comparison with Scanlon Plan,
        730-731
        with Kaiser-United Steelworkers
        Plan, 730-731
    defined, 725-726
    union attitudes, 729
Programmed instruction, 392
Promotions, 345-357
    assessment centers, 350-352
    of management and professional
        personnel, 348-352
    of organized employees, 353-355
Proneness, accident, 762-764
Psychology, industrial, 27
Public employee collective bargaining,
        824

Recruitment and selection
    auditing the program, 243-245
    labor market considerations, 213-
        216
    policy issues, 216-226
        credentials barriers, 222-224
        fair employment practices, 218-
        222
        fill vacancies from within, 217-
        218
        lie detector, 224-226

selection process, 232-243
   application blank, 236-238
   background investigation, 241-242
   medical examination, 239-241
  sources of labor, 226-231
Red-circle rate, 681
Restriction of output, 489-490, 708-709
Restriction of output and wage incentives, 708-709
Role playing, as training method, 386, 391-392
Rules and penalties, 615-618

Safety
  occupational, 756-761
   injury rates, 757-760
  program, establishing a, 766-775
   education and training, 771-772
   engineering for safety, 769-770.
    See also Accidents
Safety movement, beginnings of, 28
Salary maturity curves for professional compensation, 748-749
Salesmen, compensation for, 734-736
Scanlon Plan
  as alternative to direct wage incentives, 711, 712
  compared with Kaiser-United Steelworkers Plan, 730-731
   with profit sharing, 730-731
  as incentive based upon cooperation, 719-721
  as union-management cooperation, 575-576
Scientific management, 24-25, 694, 700
Selection procedure (hiring), 235-236
Selection process (hiring), 232-243
Self-concept and personality, 442-443
Seniority in layoffs, 362-365
Sensitivity training, 429-432
Separation pay, 802
Severity, 707
  injury, 757-758
Sherman Act and unions, 117-118
Social and recreational programs, 804-805
Social Security Act
  and growth of benefits and services, 788
  and unemployment compensation, 800
Sociometry, 474
Staff
  "assistant-to," 167-169
  general, 167, 169
  relations with line, 169-172
  specialized and service, 167-168
Standard hour plan, 704-705
Status, 496-499
  criteria, 497-498
  defined, 496
  significance of, 498-499
  symbols, 498
Stock options, for executives, 742-744
Stock plans, restricted plans for executives, 744
Suggestion plan compared with Scanlon plan, 721
Suggestion plans, 576-578, 596, 711
Supervision
  duties of, 528-530
  effective, 535-544
   employee centered, 537-538
   general, 536-537
  problems of foreman, 530-535
  transmittal of style, 544-545
Supervisor and the group, 494-496
Supplemental Unemployment Benefits, 800-802

Taft-Hartley Act (Labor-Management Relations Act)
  definition of supervisor, 527
  and grievance handling, 631
  Landrum-Griffin amendments to, 126-127
  provisions of, 120-123
  and scope of bargaining, 788
Tax saving plans of executive compensation, 742-745
Tennessee Valley Authority and union-management cooperation, 574-575
Tests and testing, selection, 238-239, 248-271
  developing program, 256-261
  and equal employment opportunity, 270-271
  guides to testing, 250-252
  personality tests, 267-270
  reliability, 252-253

Tests and testing *(Cont.)*
  types of tests, 261 - 270
  validity, 253 - 255
Texas Instruments Company, 73 - 74
Time-span of discretion, wage plan,
     675 - 676
Time study, 696 - 697
Training
  benefits of, 376 - 377
  defined, 375
  discovery of needs, 379 - 380
  evaluation of, 400 - 401
  learning process, 380 - 386
  methods, 386 - 393
  and personnel management, 31 - 32
  programs, 393 - 400
     adult basic education, 397
     apprentice, 398 - 400
     orientation, 394 - 397
Training and development, as
     personnel function, 70
Transfers, 358 - 360

Understudies, 417 - 418
Unemployment insurance, 800
Union growth in public sector, 90 - 91
Union-management cooperation,
     574 - 576
Union-management relations,
     accomplishments over years,
     820
Union-management relations,
     problems, 824
Unions
  AFL - CIO, 97 - 101
  impact on management, 105 - 107
  intermediate units, 95 - 96
  local, 94 - 95
  management reactions, 28 - 30
  membership and growth, 86 - 93
  motivation to join, 82 - 85
  motivation to reject, 85 - 86
  national and international, 96 - 97
     membership of, 92 - 93
  objectives and behavior, 101 - 105
  organization, 93 - 101
Union security, 134 - 135
  union shop, 134
United Automobile Workers Union,
     627, 634
United States Steel Corporation, 637
University of Iowa, State, experiments
     in leadership, 516 - 517, 559

University programs, as method of
     management development,
     425 - 427

Vacation practices in United States,
     805 - 806

Wage and salary administration
  defined, 650 - 651
  establishing pay structure, 677 - 683
  job evaluation systems, 664 - 676
  organization for, 661 - 662
  principles of, 661
  rationale of compensation, 652 - 655
  time-span of discretion, 675 - 676
  union considerations, 684 - 686
  wage criteria, 656 - 659
  wage surveys, 686 - 688
Wage and salary determination, in
     evolution of personnel
     management, 31
Wage incentives
  or daywork, 692 - 694
  essential requirements of, 699 - 701
  historical development, 694 - 695
  and human relations, 706 - 712
  types of plans, 701 - 706
  union attitudes toward, 712 - 713
  and work measurement, 695 - 699
Wage incentives, and Kaiser plan, 724
Wage or wages
  and collective bargaining, 136 - 137
  criteria, 656 - 659
  labor costs and, 650
  policy and principles, 660 - 661
  surveys, 686 - 688
  viewpoints of, 649 - 650
Wagner Act (National Labor Relations
     Act)
  provisions of, 118 - 120
  and scope of bargaining, 788
  and wage bargaining, 685
Welfare movement, 25 - 26
Westinghouse Electric Company, 576
Work and leisure, 806 - 807, 825 - 826
Work measurement methods, 695 -
     699
Work organization, defined, 4 - 5
Workmen's Compensation, 777 - 779

Yale and Towne Manufacturing
     Company, 576